MW01198894

# PORT ECONOMICS, MANAGEMENT AND POLICY

*Port Economics, Management and Policy* provides a comprehensive analysis of the contemporary port industry, showing how ports are organized to serve the global economy and support regional and local development.

Structured in eight sections plus an introduction and epilog, this textbook examines a wide range of seaport topics, covering maritime shipping and international trade, port terminals, port governance, port competition, port policy and much more.

Key features of the book include:

- Multidisciplinary perspective, drawing on economics, geography, management science and engineering
- Multisector analysis including containers, bulk, break-bulk and the cruise industry
- Focus on the latest industry trends, such as supply chain management, automation, digitalization and sustainability

Benefitting from the authors' extensive involvement in shaping the port sector across five continents, this text provides students and scholars with a valuable resource on ports and maritime transport systems. Practitioners and policymakers can also use this as an essential guide towards better port management and governance.

**Theo Notteboom** is Chair Professor at the Maritime Institute of Ghent University, a part-time Professor at Antwerp Maritime Academy and the University of Antwerp, and Visiting Research Professor at Shanghai Maritime University.

**Athanasios Pallis** is Professor in Management of Ports and Shipping at the Department of Port Management and Shipping, National and Kapodistrian University of Athens and is President of the International Association of Maritime Economists (IAME).

**Jean-Paul Rodrigue** is Professor of Geography in the Department of Global Studies and Geography, Hofstra University, New York.

# PORT ECONOMICS, MANAGEMENT AND POLICY

Theo Notteboom,

Athanasios Pallis and

Jean-Paul Rodrigue

Routledge
Taylor & Francis Group

LONDON AND NEW YORK

Cover image: Long Beach Container Terminal (LBCT), Port of Long Beach, Los Angeles, California. Photograph © Jean-Paul Rodrigue

First published 2022
by Routledge
4 Park Square, Milton Park, Abingdon, Oxon OX14 4RN

and by Routledge
605 Third Avenue, New York, NY 10158

*Routledge is an imprint of the Taylor & Francis Group, an informa business*

© 2022 Theo Notteboom, Athanasios Pallis and Jean-Paul Rodrigue

The right of Theo Notteboom, Athanasios Pallis and Jean-Paul Rodrigue to be identified as authors of this work has been asserted in accordance with sections 77 and 78 of the Copyright, Designs and Patents Act 1988.

All rights reserved. No part of this book may be reprinted or reproduced or utilised in any form or by any electronic, mechanical, or other means, now known or hereafter invented, including photocopying and recording, or in any information storage or retrieval system, without permission in writing from the publishers.

*Trademark notice*: Product or corporate names may be trademarks or registered trademarks, and are used only for identification and explanation without intent to infringe.

*British Library Cataloguing-in-Publication Data*
A catalogue record for this book is available from the British Library

*Library of Congress Cataloging-in-Publication Data*
A catalog record has been requested for this book

ISBN: 978-0-367-33156-6 (hbk)
ISBN: 978-0-367-33155-9 (pbk)
ISBN: 978-0-429-31818-4 (ebk)

DOI: 10.4324/9780429318184

Typeset in Palatino
by codeMantra

Visit the companion website: https://porteconomicsmanagement.org/

# CONTENTS

# DETAILED TABLE OF CONTENTS

**Epilog**

# PREFACE

*Port Economics, Management and Policy* analyzes the contemporary port industry and how ports are organized to serve the global economy and regional and local development needs.

The economic importance of the port industry would lead to the assumption that an abundance of books already examines the port industry. However, this number is limited and usually consists of compilations or endeavors discussing a limited number of issues.

Having collaborated in port research for more than two decades, we decided to fill the gap by presenting a book that would navigate the reader across the dimensions of port economics, management, and policy. Over these two decades, we investigated ports, blending academic research with practical experience. We did so with a global reach, working with scholars, port authorities, terminal operators, international and regional port associations, and international organizations. We embarked on this project affiliated with Universities on three different continents: the Americas, Asia, and Europe. The insights gained throughout this exciting journey of knowledge are worth sharing.

Globalization, containerization, and technological advancements continue to transform seaports. Throughout centuries ports have been the critical infrastructure that allowed civilizations to advance themselves. In the twenty-first century, this is a multifaceted industry serving the global economy via its integration to supply chains. Specialized terminals, port authorities with a different but equally important role, and the involvement of private actors have evolved in the midst of the core pillars of the modern port industry. Thus, investigating economics, management, and policies related to contemporary ports have captured the interest of an expanding community of scholars. The study of ports demands a multifaceted approach covering macro, meso, and micro levels, and including themes such as the features of world ports, terminals, port markets, and related distribution networks; the economic, logistics, technological, and environmental factors affecting port development and strategy; port governance strategies; port policies; and port competition and performance. All these are equally important for stakeholders who strive to identify ways to secure competitive port development in an economically, environmentally, and socially sustainable manner.

*Port Economics, Management and Policy* uses a conceptual background supported by extensive fieldwork and empirical observations, such as analyzing flows, ports, and the strategies and policies articulating their dynamics.

The port industry is comprehensively investigated in this unique compilation with:

- **Multidisciplinary perspective** on the port industry relying on economics, geography, management science, and engineering.
- **Abundance of graphic elements** such as maps, figures, photos, and tables.
- **Focus on the latest trends** impacting the industry, such as supply chain management, automation, digitalization, and sustainability.
- **Multisector analysis** including containers, bulk, break-bulk, and the cruise industry.

\*\*\*

The **Introduction** sets out the considerations that underlay the writing of this book. *Port Economics, Management and Policy* is a multifaceted approach to seaports, with the economic, social, and environmental value of seaports providing the foundations for defining modern ports and analyzing them.

**Part I** analyzes the aspects of modern maritime shipping that shape contemporary seaports. The dynamics of maritime shipping and international trade, and those of two growing shipping markets, namely containers and cruises, are investigated. This is followed by the analysis of port-related distribution networks and the importance of port hinterlands, the development of hinterland corridors, and the regionalization of port activities. The crucial role of interoceanic passages for maritime trade networks is also underlined.

Ports in the twenty-first century are facing a series of new dynamics, which are investigated in **Part II**. They are part of a geography with their location and operation subject to economic and technological changes. Port hinterlands have particularly been an emerging landscape for port-related activities, leading to their regionalization, the setting of corridors, and logistical platforms such as dry ports. The digital transformation of the industry and green supply chain management are also trends that have significantly impacted ports in recent years.

**Part III** focuses on port terminals. Terminals and terminal operators maintain a complex portfolio that is usually acquired through concessions and land leases. Forms of terminal funding and the financialization of terminal operations are also a fundamental part of terminal development. The analysis of terminal design and equipment looks at containers, bulk and break-bulk, and cruise port terminals. Attention then turns to dock labor and the ongoing automation of port terminals, particularly container terminals. The concluding part provides insights on port terminal construction.

Port governance is the theme of **Part IV**. Starting with an analysis of the links between governance and performance, this section presents reforms and models that shape global ports. Attention then shifts to port authorities, highlighting how their changing role takes place with the reinforcement of their centrality in contemporary port management. Their evolving role is evident through trends such as the coordination of actors along supply chains, port cooperation, port clusters, and green port management. Port management, governance, and leadership have evolved to reflect a new reality.

Part IV concludes with an invited contribution from Dr. Geraldine Knatz, who has served as CEO of one of the world's biggest ports, the Port of Los Angeles in the United States, providing an insightful contribution to port management, governance, and leadership.

**Part V** focuses on ports evolving within a complex competitive environment with various forms of port competition, such as inter-port and intra-port completion. Two parameters are crucial for competition, marketing and pricing. While marketing underlines the relationships that a port establishes with its customers, pricing remains a determining factor. Conditions for enhancing port competition are of strategic importance, including the potential of lowering entry barriers in port operations.

**Part VI** underlines that since ports are in a competitive environment, their performance is subject to careful consideration and monitored through a series of indicators. Port performance is composed of efficiency, performing tasks to minimize their costs and externalities, and effectiveness, performing tasks that meet the expectations of users. Performance tends to be an operational criterion, while effectiveness is a market criterion. Ports can be subject to disruptions impairing their operations, testing their resilience to maintain operations.

**Part VII** analyzes port policies and development. Ports are political and economic tools. A wide array of principles and themes for national and international port and port-related policies exist, including international initiatives, such as emissions control, port security, and port labor, and there is also the controversial role of geopolitics in port development. The role of ports in economic development and strategic port planning is a relevant theme. The relationships between ports and their localities remain a challenge involving various facets of port–city interactions. To mitigate the political climate, associations are formed at different levels and with different priorities to represent port interests.

**Part VIII** focuses on ports, like transportation, serving a derived demand that can be segmented into specific markets. The most salient markets include cruise ports and terminals, the break-bulk market, ports as complexes supplying and distributing energy, the provision and management of containers, and how cold chain technology has allowed ports to play an active role within these supply chains, particularly with refrigerated containers (reefers).

The **Epilog** of this book discusses our perspectives on the emerging issues that will shape the economics, management, and policies of ports.

We hope that this book will support the expanding community of scholars involved in the study of this maturing research field to identify foundations of knowledge and stimuli for future research. Students will gain an all-inclusive approach to the port sector and its dynamics. Port professionals and stakeholders along the maritime supply chains will gain further insights on the dynamic port environment in which they want to expand their presence and competitiveness.

* * *

Conducting research forms a big part of our academic life. We consider this book as a milestone in our endeavors to share meaningful research with port enthusiasts from around the world. These endeavors were shaped by countless interactions with multiple port professionals, fellow scholars, and students. All three of us would like to thank them for enriching our perspectives of port economics, management, and policy. Special thanks go to our fellows in the Port Economics initiative and all those who worked with us in joint research efforts. We also extend special thanks to our colleagues at the International Association of Maritime Economists (IAME) and the Port Performance Research Network (PPRN). Theo Notteboom would particularly like to thank his current and former colleagues at the maritime and port-related centers of the University of Antwerp, Ghent University, Dalian Maritime University, and Shanghai Maritime University, many of whom have become friends. Special thanks to Emeritus Professor Willy Winkelmans from the University of Antwerp, who not only introduced him to the world of ports, but also opened many windows of opportunities to grow as a person and port economist. Thanos Pallis would like to thank his colleagues at the University of the Aegean for providing the environment for developing research in shipping and ports.

Special gratitude goes to Costas Chlomoudis, George Vaggelas, Aimilia Papachristou, and Evie Kladaki, prominent members of the Greek port studies cluster, who have been long-term partners in many good and challenging moments of research, and great friends in life. He also extends special thanks to Thomas Vitsounis, Spiros Tsiotsis, and Stefania Kollia, for the opportunity to supervise their doctoral research that has expanded his conceptual horizons. He would also like to thank Mary Brooks and Gordon Wilmsmeier for hosting intellectually stimulating sabbaticals that expanded horizons and provided opportunities for most productive research collaborations. Jean-Paul Rodrigue would like to thank his Port Economics colleagues, many of whom became friends over the years. Gratitude to Claude Comtois and Brian Slack for their introduction to the world of transportation many decades ago.

This book is dedicated to our families. The writing of this book is an idea that was conceived during a dinner at the Chart House in New York, United States. Since then, the 'ChartHouse team' embarked on a number of research trips, and finally made the long and passionate journey to conclude this book during pandemic times. Hui, Jayden, Luca, Valia, Gordana, and Nikola supported us on all of these hard-working days and nights. This book is dedicated to them.

Theo Notteboom, Thanos Pallis, Jean-Paul Rodrigue
Antwerp–Athens–New York, January 2022

# INTRODUCTION: A MULTIFACETED APPROACH TO SEAPORTS

*A seaport is a node in global supply chains with a strong maritime character and a functional and spatial clustering of port-related activities.*

## 1 A COMPREHENSIVE PORT DEFINITION

The seaport has a long history going back to the early days of human endeavors. As soon as civilizations emerged across the world, trade networks supported by ports emerged as well. Although maritime transport technology has evolved substantially, the role and function of ports remain relatively similar. Conventionally, a port is defined as a transit area, a gateway through which goods and people move from and to the sea. It is a place of contact between the land and maritime space, a node where ocean and inland transport systems interact, and a place of convergence for different transportation modes. Since maritime and inland transportation modes have different capacities, the port assumes the role of a point of **load break** where cargo is consolidated or deconsolidated.

Even if the term port appears generic, it expresses a substantial diversity of sizes and functions. Ports also have a geographical diversity in terms of the sites being used for port activities, which can range from rivers, bays, to offshore locations. They are complex and multifaceted and can be approached primarily from a supply chain perspective, which leads to the following definition:

> *A seaport is a logistic and industrial node in global supply chains with a strong maritime character and a functional and spatial clustering of activities directly or indirectly linked to transportation, transformation, and information processes within global supply chains.*

A modern seaport is not regarded solely as a load breakpoint in various supply chains but should be considered a **value-adding transit point**. As nodes within transportation and logistics networks, ports have a location whose relative importance can fluctuate given economic, technical, and political changes. This location tries to capitalize on the advantages of a port site characterized by fundamental physical features influencing the nautical profile, such as water depth, access channels, and the available land.

The following geographical elements help define a seaport:

- **Location**. The relative position of the port in relation to other ports serviced through shipping networks and through its hinterland.
- **Site**. The physical characteristics of the port, such as its nautical profile (depth, access channel) and the land available for port activities, particularly for terminals.

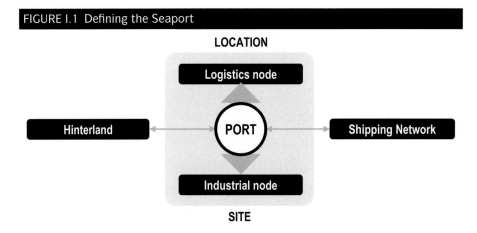

FIGURE I.1 Defining the Seaport

The following functional elements help define a seaport (Figure I.1):

- **Logistics node**. The added value performed by the port's transportation function, including handling, consolidation, and deconsolidation.
- **Industrial node**. Activities depending on the port as a platform to supply inputs such as raw materials and distribute outputs such as parts and finished goods.

## 2 TYPOLOGIES OF SEAPORTS

An approach to understanding the diversity of ports is their classification into typologies to analyze their specific role and functions. Conventionally, ports can be categorized based on a large number of dimensions, such as:

- **Scale**. Refers to an assessment of port size in terms of its area, annual cargo throughput, the size of its hinterland, the number of shipping services it is connected to, or the number of customers. The scale of a port is commonly associated with its economic and commercial importance in the market it serves (Figure I.2).
- **Geographical attributes**. Refers to the main characteristics of the port site and situation. Coastal and inland geography conditions create variety in the locational setting of port sites such as in a bay, along a coastline, on a river, or in an estuary. Many sites have natural advantages, while for others, the site needs to be improved with dredging and landfills. Although a port site is fixed in space, its situation is relative to the main shipping lanes and hinterland, or its proximity to and interactions with cities or urban conurbations.
- **Governance and institutional settings**. Refers to the terms of land ownership and the roles of institutional arrangements between the public and private sectors. Many ports are publicly owned but have terminals operated by private organizations.
- **Port functions**. Refers to the range of services offered by the port such as cargo handling, logistics, and distribution, industry, and maritime services. They are subject to competitive pressures since the services offered by a port can be offered by another port.

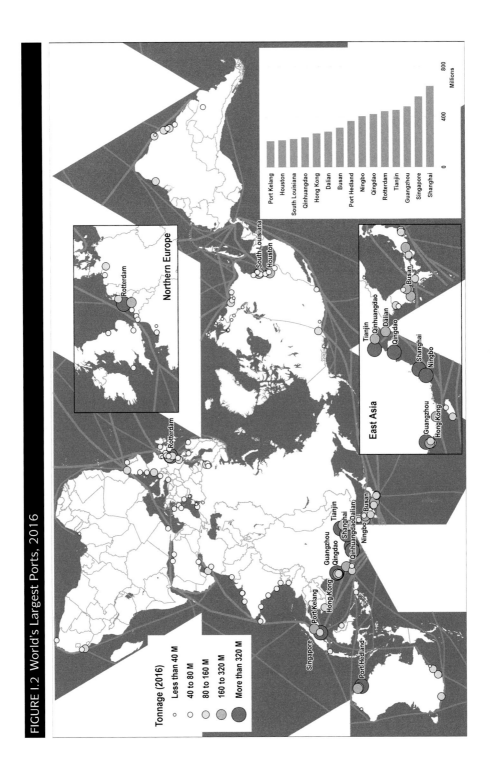

FIGURE I.2 World's Largest Ports, 2016

- **Specialization**. Refers to the cargo handled, such as containers, conventional general cargo, liquid bulk, dry bulk, or roll-on/roll-off cargo. Some ports are specialized in handling passenger traffic, namely cruise ships and ferries. Another specialization concerns port-centric industries such as steel plants, energy plants, automotive, or chemical industries. Further, logistics activities are an important contributor to port specialization.

Through generations of port development, **port functions have changed and expanded**, responding to technical, economic, and social developments. From the traffic being generated, functions such as trade, distribution, and industry have emerged in seaports, broadening and deepening their functions. In recent decades, the main driving forces include containerization, diversification of cargo types and equipment, intermodal transport, and information technologies. Port functions are extended to trade, logistics, and production centers with an extensive portfolio of operations, including production, trade, and service industries. Some seaports have grown to become industrial complexes comprising a large number of industrial activities.

Successive stages in port development, in part coordinated by different economic opportunities, have favored the establishment of a hierarchy of ports, ranging from small ports servicing a niche market to large gateways servicing a vast area composed of an extensive range of economic activities. Like most hierarchies, there are a small number of very large ports accounting for a significant share of the total traffic and many small ports that account for limited traffic. For instance, in 2019, the 20 largest container ports accounted for 44% of the total traffic, reflecting a well-established hierarchy (Figure I.3). This does not imply that small ports are of limited importance for the economies they serve. Small islands and nation-states have a high dependence on their ports to access global markets.

From a supply chain perspective, seaports are increasingly functioning not as individual places that handle ships but as turntables within global supply chains and global transportation networks. The contemporary port (labeled fourth-generation port) is characterized as a platform commanding freight flows and requiring knowledge-intensive coordination activities. A seaport is not self-contained as port activities contribute to the industrial and logistics development in the port areas and its hinterland. Thus, ports act as **service centers and logistics platforms** for international trade and transport.

In recent decades ports have been subject to a wave of reforms that reflects the increasing business and market-oriented approach to port management. From governance and institutional perspectives, many ports have become independent commercial organizations aiming at profitability, cost recovery, and customer service.

## 3 STAGES IN PORT DEVELOPMENT

The widely cited port-type generations of United Nations Conference on Trade and Development (UNCTAD) and later port generation models look at port roles and functions, but also at institutional structuring and operational and management practices. In 1994, UNCTAD coined the term

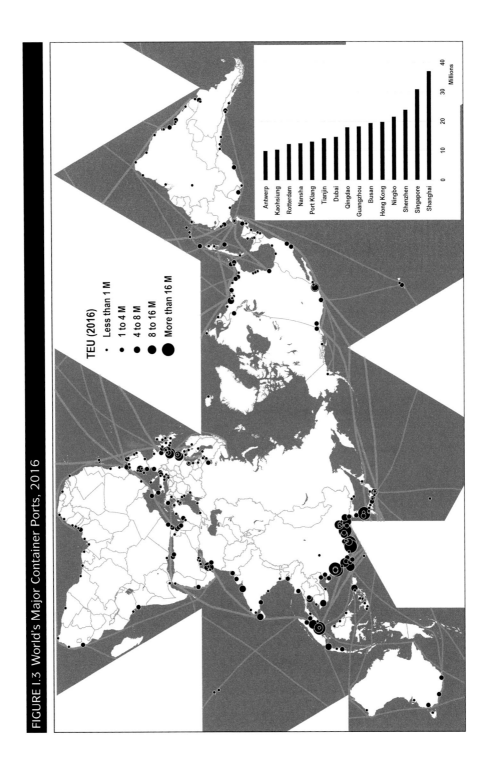

FIGURE I.3 World's Major Container Ports, 2016

'**third-generation port**', to describe a port which has functions dealing with cargo handling plus other value-added services such as warehousing, packaging, and distribution, providing additional employment and revenue to the port community. In 1999, UNCTAD defined port-type generations from the first to the fourth-generation port based on interfaces of ship and shore with the operation of cargo types, a higher dependency on capital rather than labor, the development of containerization and logistics, and changes in port operators and administration with vertical and horizontal integration strategies (Figure I.4).

Therefore, ports develop both functionally, in terms of the cargo they handle, and spatially, in terms of the extent of their infrastructure and position in shipping networks. Four major generations (or stages) can be identified, each corresponding to a specific era in the commercial geography of ports. Three main typological factors can articulate the temporal sequence of port development:

- **External environment**. A series of external political, economic, and technological developments impact the role and function of ports. The most recent driving forces concern globalization, sustainability, and digitalization.
- **Spatial organization**. The scale and scope of port activity have substantially expanded with the setting of port networks.
- **Organization and strategy**. Port authorities have become complex entities managing the port network communities with the goal of developing integrated transportation and logistics services for their hinterland.

Some scholars have proposed a '**fifth-generation port**' (5GP) with the introduction of a 'port ladder' towards customer-centric community-focused ports. The 5GP involves customer-centric community ports that increasingly look at market opportunities through the eyes of their customers and adapt to meet the ever-higher expectations of their host communities.

## 4 PORT DIMENSIONS

Four main dimensions help define the role and function of a port (Figure I.5):

- **Location**. A port is a location that has convenient physical characteristics (such as a protected bay) and thus supports a more effective interface between the maritime and land domains than other locations. Although the location of a port does not change, the site can be improved through dredging and land reclamation, which requires substantial capital investments. This allows the port to expand its scale in terms of its surface and the amount of traffic it can handle. The situation of a port can also change as it is dependent on large zones of production and consumption.
- **Operations**. A port has operational characteristics in terms of the type of traffic it can handle and related volumes. This is contingent upon the infrastructure (berths) and the superstructure (cranes and yard equipment) linking the port foreland (the ports it is connected to) and the port hinterland (inland market area). With capital investments and

**FIGURE I.4 Functional and Spatial Development of a Seaport**

| | First Generation (Before 1960s) | Second Generation (1960s to 1980s) | Third Generation (1980s to 2000s) | Fourth Generation (Since 2000s) |
|---|---|---|---|---|
| **External Environment** | | | | |
| Development factors | Steamships; Rise of nations; Rise of trade | Petrochemistry; Trucks and pipelines; Structural prosperity; Industrialization | Multinational corporations; Containerization; Environmentalism; Globalization. | Global economy; Information systems; Sustainability; Digitalization |
| Port functions | Transshipment (1); Storage (2); Trade (3) | (1) to (3) + Industry (4) | (1) to (4) + Distribution (5) | (1) to (5) + Logistics (6) |
| Nature of production | Cargo flow; Simple services; Low added-value. | Cargo flow; Cargo transformation; Combined services; Improved value-added | Cargo/information flow; Cargo distribution; Multiple service package; High value-added | Cargo/information flow; Cargo/information distribution; Multiple service package; High value-added; Chain management |
| Type of cargo | General cargo and bulk | General cargo, bulk and liquid bulk | Bulk and unitized/containerized cargo | General/containerized cargo; information |
| **Spatial Organization** | | | | |
| Port spatial scale | Port city | Port area | Port region | Port network |
| Port spatial expansion | Quay and waterfront area | Enlarged port area | Terminals and inland corridors | Network-related functional expansion |
| Location factors | Labor and market access | Access to raw materials; Access to sales market; Availability of capital | Availability of transshipment facilities; Access to sales market; Space; Flexibility; and labor costs | Availability of transshipment facilities; Access to sales market; Space; Flexibility; and labor costs |
| **Strategy** | | | | |
| Organization | Independent activities within port; Informal relationship between port and port users | Close port / users relationship; Loose port / activities relationship; Causal port / city relationship | Port community; Port / transport chain integration; Close relation between port and municipality; Enlarged port organization | Port network community; Close relation between port network and public authorities on different levels |
| Role of port authority | Nautical services (1) | 1 + land and infrastructure development (2) | (1), (2) + Port marketing (3) | (1) to (3) + Network management (4) |
| Port strategy | Port as changing point of transport | Transport, industrial and commercial center | Integrated transport and logistic center | Integrated transport, logistic and information complex and network |

Source: Adapted from Van Klink (2003).

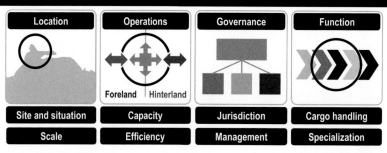

FIGURE I.5 Port Dimensions

management, the operational efficiency of a port can be improved with changes to land, equipment, and management.

- **Governance**. A port is a well-defined administrative unit that involves land ownership and a jurisdiction (what a port can legally do). The port authority is a common administrative framework for a port, and in many cases, terminal management and operations are leased to private companies. Port authorities usually have the right to spearhead port development projects and secure funding.
- **Function**. A port adds value to transport and supply chains through its cargo handling. Historically, heavy industrial activities such as steel mills and petrochemical plants had a propensity to locate within or nearby ports. This process is still going on and being complemented by a large array of freight distribution activities. There is a diversity of port functions associated with specialization forms, such as ports involved in minerals, energy, and containers. Large ports tend to be polyfunctional, while smaller ports tend to be monofunctional.

Port sites have been the subject of geographical considerations, with a preference for sites combining a good maritime profile with inland accessibility. There is a vast array of port sites linked to specific nautical profiles, which are articulated around seaports and mainland ports (Figure I.6):

- **Seaports**. These ports have direct access to the sea and try to take advantage of a local geographical feature. This can involve (A) bays or direct coastline, and (B) natural harbors, or protected locations. These sites are often associated with a lateral expansion of the port facilities, often towards locations with a deeper nautical profile.
- **Mainland ports**. These ports are linked to a major river, which often serves a vast hinterland. There are ports in (C) an estuary, (D) a delta, and (E) along a river, often at the furthest point of inland navigation. These sites are associated with an upstream expansion of port facilities.

The most common sites are those in bays or by the coastline (50%), followed by natural harbors (20%). This underlines the importance of maritime accessibility for the world's largest ports. The remaining 30% involve ports located along river systems.

FIGURE I.6 Port Sites

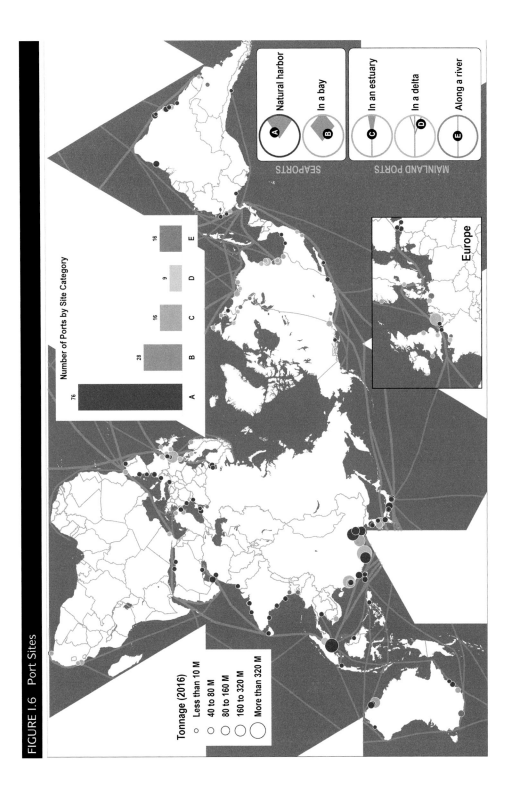

FIGURE I.7 Global Cruise Port Activity, 2012

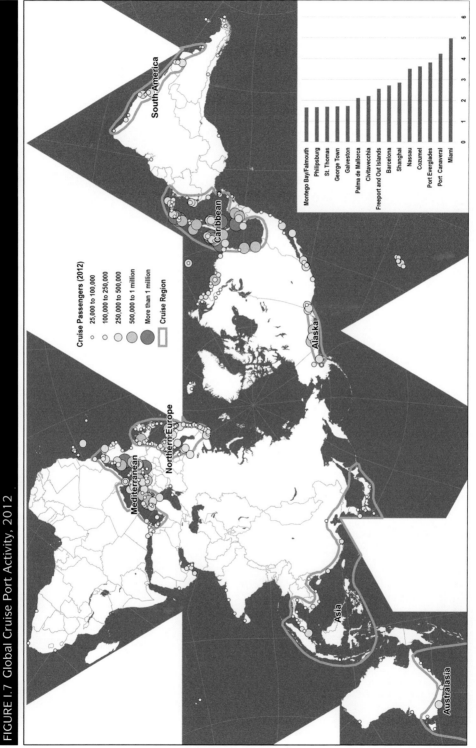

Source: Data adapted from Cruise Market Watch (www.cruisemarketwatch.com). Cruise port visits based upon the published itineraries of about 90% of the global cruise shipping capacity.

Container ports are reflective of the world's **commercial geography**, particularly since they predominantly handle finished and intermediate goods. Commodities are becoming more prevalent but remain a niche market. Prior to the 1990s, the world's most important ports were North American (e.g. New York) and Western European (e.g. Rotterdam). Globalization, supported by containerization, completely changed the world's commercial geography with the emergence of new port locations reflecting changes in the global geography of production, distribution, and consumption. This geography indicates a high level of traffic concentration around large port facilities, notably Pacific Asian ports along the Tokyo-Singapore corridor. As export-oriented economic development strategies took shape, the number of containers handled in Pacific Asian ports, notably Chinese ports, surged.

The comparative size of ports requires caution as several ports can be considered more as **statistical agglomerations** than functional entities. For instance, the port of Shenzhen in the Pearl River Delta is composed of several large port facilities (e.g. Yantian, Chiwan, Shekou) that act as distinct entities within their operations and even service different hinterlands. The same observation applies to Guangzhou and Shanghai that are multiport (and multi-terminal) entities.

The **global cruise port system** is characterized by a high level of regional concentration as well as a clustering of port visits (Figure I.7). The observed destination patterns clearly underline the prominence of port visits around the Caribbean and the Mediterranean, in line with the operational characteristics of seven day cruises calling at three to five ports. Other clusters of significant activity concern the US Northeast and Atlantic Canada, Alaska, Hawaii, Hanseatic ports, and the coast of Norway. In the 2010s, Asia has been the most significant growth market for the industry. New cruising clusters are emerging to serve a latent demand from a growing middle and upper class in Asia, the Middle East, and South America. With a number of cruise vessels deployed in the Australian market offering their services in the region, cruise ports are developing in all parts of the world.

## 5 PORT SYSTEMS: BEYOND INDIVIDUAL SEAPORTS

Seaports are part of a system with specific spatial and functional characteristics, supporting global logistics and transport networks. They interact with other nodes such as overseas and neighboring seaports, intermodal terminals, and inland logistics platforms. Seaports are subject to three types of functional interdependences with other nodes (Figure I.8):

- **Chain networks**. Ports are nodes, part of a sequence of flows where the output of one node in the network is the input for another. An example is a relation between container ports and inland load centers. Rotterdam services of a chain of inland terminals along with the Rhine river, a role similarly assumed by Shanghai for inland terminals along the Yangtze River. Chain networks also apply for trans-ocean relations, including deep sea liner services such as the Rotterdam–Singapore chain supporting the Europe–Far East trade.

FIGURE I.8 Functional Interdependencies of a Seaport

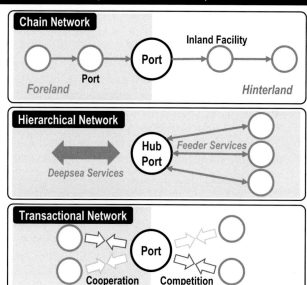

- **Hierarchical networks**. Ports are nodes, part of different connectivity levels, implying that some locations can be reached indirectly as opposed to directly. An example is the hub-feeder port relation in container shipping linking the South Korean container port Busan to smaller feeder ports in Northeast Asia.
- **Transactional networks**. Ports are nodes in a system of commercial relations where they can be competitive or complementary. They use advantages such as location, cost, and productivity to attract or retain shipping services and traffic.

## 6  INTERDEPENDENCIES WITH OTHER NODES

Ports rarely operate in isolation from other ports but are part of complex networks of interactions. A **port system** can be defined as a system of two or more ports located in proximity within a given area. They can relate to a complete coastline such as the West coast of North America. The port range is one of the largest consistent port systems.

*A **port range** can be defined as a group of ports situated along the same seashore and potentially sharing access to a hinterland.*

There are many maritime ranges worldwide, each with its inherent geographical, economic, and functional characteristics. The Hamburg–Le Havre range in Europe is a typical example, which can be expanded to include the Gdansk–Le Havre range. An acute intra-range competition can be observed at the multiport gateway level.

*A **multiport gateway region** refers to a group of ports in proximity competing for the same port calls and hinterland. It has a smaller geographical scale than a container port range. The locational relationship* *to nearby identical traffic hinterlands is one of the criteria for grouping adjacent container ports into the same multiport gateway region. The port-calling patterns in the maritime service networks and hinterland connectivity profile can also help group ports to a multiport gateway region.*

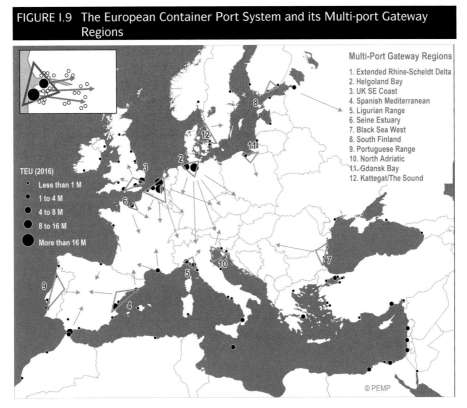

FIGURE I.9   The European Container Port System and its Multi-port Gateway Regions

Source: Rodrigue and Notteboom (2010).

Typical examples include the Rhine–Scheldt Delta (Belgium and the Netherlands) and the Yangtze River Delta and Pearl River Delta in China. A port range can be home to several multiport gateway regions (Figure I.9). For example, the Gdansk–Le Havre range includes the multiport gateway regions of the Gdansk Bay in Poland, North-Germany, the Rhine–Scheldt Delta, and the Seine Estuary in France.

**Inland nodes and feeder ports** are also considered as part of the port system. They are competing to attract economic activities associated with seaports, which leads to functional changes in the port system. These nodes can also co-operate and coordinate their development by bundling transport flows and offering land for development. This gives economic activities such as manufacturing and logistics a range of locational options for nodes that are the most suitable to their operational and market access needs.

## 7 PORTS AS ECONOMIC CATALYSTS

The core value of ports is economic since they support trade flows and the ecosystem of related activities. As they can represent a substantial economic investment, ports are expected to provide enough value to justify these investments. From an economic and public policy perspective, ports are viewed as economic catalysts for the regions they serve. Two distinct approaches can be followed when evaluating the strategic and economic significance of ports (Figure I.10). The first is to measure the economic significance of ports via distinct parameters. There exists a large range of potential indicators. Some are expressed in absolute figures, while others are expressed in relative terms. A non-exhaustive list includes:

- **Gross value-added**, which provides an insight into the contribution of port activity to the GDP (Gross Domestic Product) or GRP (Gross Regional Product) in a given time period (often annually). This added-value can be complex to evaluate since ports directly impact those activities directly connected to them and without which the port could not effectively function. There is also a range of indirect impacts on the whole ecosystem of economic activities that may interact with the activities directly related to the port. As international trade grew, the indirect impacts of ports on national or regional economies became even more important.
- **Employment**, which is mainly expressed in full-time equivalents (FTEs) and provides an insight into how port activities contribute to employment creation. In most cases, a snapshot is taken once a year to provide the total employment or port activities. Similar to added-value, there is a whole range of employment that is indirectly related to port activities.
- **Trade volumes and values**, which provide an insight into the importance of ports for international trade. Traffic direction can also be considered since several ports are dominantly export platforms while others are focused on imports. In these cases, the same volume and trade composition can support different economic structures.
- **Fiscal revenue**, which indicates how port activities contribute to the taxation income within their jurisdictions, ranging from national to municipal governments. This is particularly relevant to justify the public expenses supporting port activities, particularly infrastructure.

FIGURE I.10 The Economic Significance of Ports

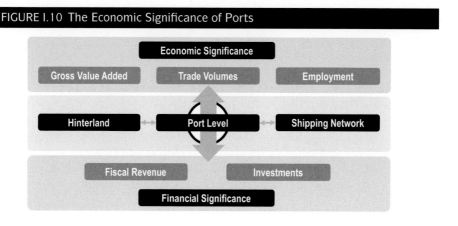

- **Investments** by the public and private sector in port activities over a given period. Port superstructure and infrastructure are capital intensive and require constant maintenance.

The second approach is of a more qualitative nature and tries to evaluate the significance and value of seaports for the economic development and performance of their market. These strategic aspects are difficult to quantify but deserve attention.

## 7.1 Ports as generators of added value and employment

The first approach asserts that ports contribute to the **generation of socio-economic benefits and wealth**, particularly direct and indirect added-value and employment. The external spill-over effects of ports can be substantial. Simultaneously, the economic effects of seaport activities are no longer limited to the local environment. They are increasingly spread over a much wider geographical area and among a large number of international players. In other words, the economic benefits of port activities are expanding from the local port system towards a much larger economic system. The geographical dispersion of economic effects is apparent when a port does not develop local added value activities linked to transit cargo or establish a strong local industrial and logistics cluster. In that case, cargo flows are transiting the port, thereby generating employment and value-added effects for the local community, mainly in cargo handling, ship services, and inland transport operations.

The changing distribution of benefits is also illustrated by the **development of logistics zones** in the vicinity of seaports or inland locations along the main corridors towards the hinterland. This trend has been supported by growing containerization and intermodal transport systems. In many cases, these logistics sites and zones generate considerable economic benefits by providing low-end, high-end value-added logistics services (VALS) to the cargo and only using ports as a transit point. However, it is unlikely that these sites and zones would have developed if it were not for seaports.

Policymakers and public authorities typically approach the macro-economic impacts of ports from a **national or regional competitiveness perspective**. Most available reports and figures on the economic impact of seaports portray the national or regional economic effects. Ports impact the wider economic space and international trade, with logistics receiving less attention. While leakages of port-related benefits to regions in the more distant hinterland can be substantial, policymakers focus on maximizing the port's input payback for the local or regional communities under their jurisdiction. The main port development objective is to provide infrastructures for the local, regional, or national interest at the lowest combined cost to the port and its users.

From a macro-economic perspective, seaports typically are important **generators of employment**. The employment effects of a port activity usually extend beyond the initial round of employment generated by that activity. The extent of the employment effects of ports is affected by the boundaries of the economy that is being analyzed. The increasingly international nature of port and shipping activities and the characteristics of global supply chains make the employment effects of port activities typically extend beyond the local level to a regional or even supranational level. For instance, shipping lines are operating on a global scale with related employment effects such as for ship crews. On a local scale, they might generate employment via their liner shipping agencies in the ports of call.

Employment related to ship management, container fleet management, and investment and commercial strategies is usually concentrated in global or regional headquarters. The same applies to global container terminal operators such as PSA (headquartered in Singapore), Hutchison Ports (Hong Kong), DP World (Dubai), or APM Terminals (The Hague). While these companies generate many operational jobs at the local port level, they keep some activities centralized in global or regional headquarters, such as equipment purchases and research and development. Terminal operators might purchase terminal equipment from foreign suppliers such as Kalmar, Konecranes, or Shanghai-based ZPMC. For a particular port activity, the flow-on employment effects to the national or international economy will generally be larger than the flow-on effects to the regional economy.

## 7.2 The strategic value of ports

By providing cost-efficient, reliable, and frequent connections to overseas and inland markets, seaports play an essential role in **facilitating trade** and **increasing the competitiveness** of a nation or region. This strategic value manifests itself in different ways:

- First, the **proximity of efficient seaports** can be an important factor in the location decisions of firms.
- Second, the **availability of a competitive seaport system** can reduce reliance on foreign ports for trade and can reduce the total logistics costs for firms located in the region.
- Third, **seaports can substantially contribute to the international competitiveness of firms** in a region or country, mainly through existing innovation and advanced business networks and management.

**Good infrastructure** and **high accessibility or connectivity** are increasingly becoming basic requirements for competitiveness. For high-income economies, innovation and advanced production factors become essential to remain competitive. This also alters the strategic role of seaports. Instead of just ensuring connectivity to overseas and inland markets, seaports also play a role as innovation centers. A port is no longer a quayside area where cargo is simply shifted from land to sea. It becomes a vital link in global supply chains and international transport networks. By striving for competitiveness and efficiency improvements, seaports can become drivers of innovation. This sense of innovation is strengthened by port cluster management that enhances knowledge exchanges among organizations within and outside the cluster. Through clustering, a knowledge spill-over is created, increasing innovation and added value.

Ports can be sources for **innovation, productivity enhancements**, and **strategic cooperation** through the presence of large multinational firms, leading firms, and clusters of related and supporting industries. Ports can also enhance specialization, innovation, and productivity improvements through cooperation with ports and other logistics hubs in the region. Finally, ports can help support the diffusion of competencies and the further gathering of knowledge in port management and logistics. Next to pure economic arguments, these more strategic aspects should be considered when evaluating port development plans.

The importance of a port to a regional, national, or supranational economy is greater than is shown by measures of direct and indirect value-added and employment. For example, a 2015 study estimated the strategic value of the seaport system in Belgium at €45 billion, or 60% more than reported in the annual port economic impact studies of the National Bank of Belgium.

## 8 FROM CARGO HANDLING TO NODES IN GLOBAL SUPPLY CHAINS

Next to the macro-economic perspective, seaports can also be analyzed using a microeconomic approach. Port operations are usually oriented towards the two traditional components of ships and cargo (Figure I.11).

- **Services to ships** include those performed at the sea or waterways side (dredging, pilotage, mooring/unmooring) and the ship/shore interface (berthing, repair and maintenance, supply, and bunkering).
- **Services to cargo** can be divided into those performed at the ship/shore interface (stowing, loading, discharging) and those entirely performed in landside areas such as consolidation, storage, and distribution.

Key in the micro-perspective approach are the concepts of **efficiency, performance**, and **sustainability** at the operational level (i.e. a company or a terminal). This approach to ports advocates that corporations and their terminals are the relevant units of analysis when analyzing or assessing port competition, not seaports.

While the transit, transport, and handling of cargo is the rationale for ports, seaport functions have become diverse in scope and nature and evolve over time. The complexity of seaports goes beyond the loading and discharging of vessels along the quay. Fundamental processes of economic and technological change have broadened and deepened the functions of seaports. Seaports added new functions to their traditional role of transshipping and storing goods. After the Second World War, the industrial function grew rapidly. Some seaports have grown out to become **industrial complexes** comprising a large number of related industrial activities, the so-called maritime industrial development areas (MIDA).

In more recent years, the **logistical function of seaports** received attention. The increasing importance of integrating ports and terminals in value-driven supply chains has increased the focus on creating added value linked

FIGURE I.11 Transport and Cargo Handling Functions of a Port

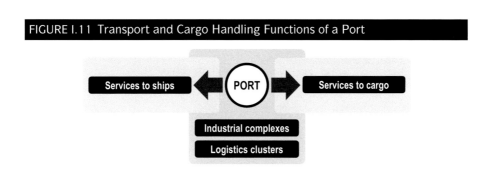

to cargo passing through the port. The gateway position of major seaports offers opportunities to enhance value-added logistics services (VALS) by integrating the production and distribution chain. By offering VALS, ports aim to attract a large portion of the value-added creation within product chains. Modern seaports have evolved from pure cargo handling centers to a function in a logistics system.

The competitiveness of ports can be better understood by following a supply chain approach. Ports compete not as individual places that handle ships but as crucial links within global supply chains. Port and route selection criteria are related to the entire network in which the port is just one node. The selected ports are those that will help to minimize the sum of sea, port, and inland costs, including inventory and quality considerations of shippers. Port choice becomes more a function of the overall network cost and performance. A well-coordinated logistics and distribution function of seaports with the cooperation of various service providers facilitates the integration of ports in advanced logistical and distributional networks through a new range of high-quality value-adding services.

## 9 PORTS AS CLUSTERS OF ECONOMIC ACTIVITY

At the intermediate level, ports are often approached as **clusters of companies and economic activities** (Figure I.12). Ports typically consist of geographically concentrated and mutually related business units centered around transport, trade, and industrial production. Port clusters exhibit strong scale and scope advantages linked to physical cargo flows. The concentration of activities opens more opportunities to the bundling of cargo flows via intermodal transport (shortsea, barge, or rail) and to achieve higher connectivity to the rest of the world via frequent transport services. Port clusters can be home to a wide range of activities.

While industrial activities in ports are often associated with negative effects in terms of emissions and noise pollution, port clusters can exert strong environmental advantages. For example, **'ecologies of scale'** are achieved in the petrochemical industry through which companies utilize waste material or by-products such as heat. It would be far more difficult to achieve this if the concerned plants would be spatially scattered. Ecologies of scale advantages are increasingly being acknowledged in environmental policy. Successful port clusters might also face some challenges, mainly in terms of accessibility (congestion) and higher land costs.

FIGURE I.12  Ports as Clusters of Economic Activity

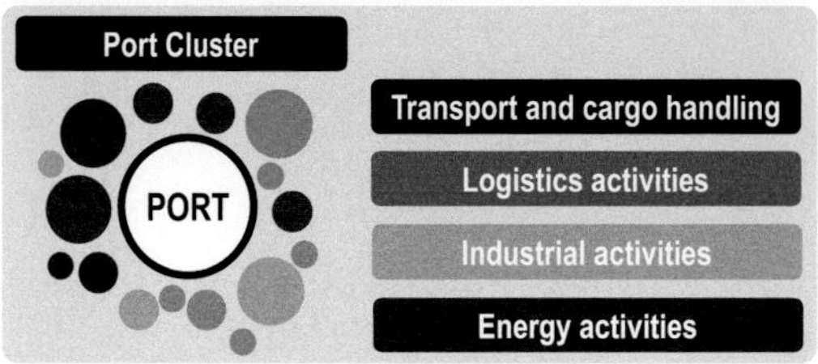

Seaports interact with other nodes such as overseas and neighboring seaports, intermodal terminals, and inland logistics platforms. They rarely operate in isolation from other ports.

## 10 THE PUBLIC IMAGE OF PORTS

The general public often considers port areas as desolate, dangerous, dirty, and unattractive, characterized by buildings with low aesthetics and large machinery emitting noise and air pollutants. People might feel **disconnected** from ports, particularly in those areas where the port has moved away from the city. In short, ports cannot take broad public support for granted. This aspect of port competitiveness will undoubtedly become more important in the future as resources such as land are becoming increasingly scarce and as broader social and environmental functions are challenging the economic function of seaports.

As such, port managers and government bodies nowadays are trying to make sure that new port developments are socially broadly based. **Conflicts of interest among different stakeholders** may overshadow the community of interests. Major socio-economic confrontations related to port development and operations can occur when community groups perceive a clear imbalance between the benefits and costs for the local community of having larger ports. Public support for ports becomes particularly bleak when a large part of the population is unaware of how the port is organized and operated and to what extent the port contributes to the local economy. The concerns solely focus on potential negative effects for the local community, such as road congestion, intrusions on the landscape, noise and air pollution, and the use of scarce land. The potential erosion of public support for seaports is a real concern to port managers.

Next to pure economic effects, ports increasingly need to be guided by **social and environmental considerations**. Public policymakers and port managing bodies are challenged to design effective port-related policies in urban planning and expansion, safety, security, and sustainability. The economic value of a port now tends to be taken as a given by some stakeholders, so the argument concentrates on environmental issues and social issues.

Ports must demonstrate a high level of environmental value to ensure community support. However, environmental aspects also play an increasing role in attracting trading partners and potential investors. A port with a strong environmental record and a high level of community support is likely to be favored. From an environmental perspective, port planning and management should ensure sustainable development. The environmental sustainability of port projects and activities has become as important as economic and financial viability.

Measuring the **social value of ports** is an extremely difficult exercise. Many ports directly support a wide variety of community events and projects through sponsorship in an effort to attract community support. However, it is the indirect social contributions that most benefit local communities. For example, ports might invest in training and education programs. Such forms of social commitment are an important part of the success of ports, linking commercial responsibility to social acceptability and accountability.

Ports are challenged to improve their public image, which can be done by combining several approaches:

- **External communications policies and public events and festivities** in and around port areas – such as Port Days.
- Convince the general public of the **importance of ports** by presenting figures on employment effects and added value.
- Adopt a **green port management strategy** that focuses on mitigating externalities such as energy consumption, the emissions of pollutants, and waste disposal.
- **Stakeholder relations management**, such as the development of good relations with all parties concerned, particularly with respect to port expansion plans or redevelopment/regeneration plans focusing on older port areas (i.e. waterfront redevelopment).

Reinforcing the public image of ports is also a matter of attracting a new generation to work in the port. Ports have to offer attractive careers by offering good working conditions and the potential for career advancement, and by stimulating a sense of pride about the port.

## 11 THE PORT–CITY INTERFACE

The port–city interface is a core theme in discussing the public image of ports and the balance between economic, social, and environmental aspects. Ports and cities worldwide have developed extensive initiatives to (re)establish mutual links. The redevelopment of older abandoned port areas, also called waterfront redevelopment, is one of the focus areas.

A waterfront redevelopment program that respects the maritime heritage of the port and re-establishes the link between the city and the port can revive the public acceptance of ports. It can also bring new jobs to derelict port areas. In many ports, public and private investments have been channeled to revitalize older port areas encompassing housing, hotels, maritime heritage projects, sports, recreation, tourism, and local commerce. Residential, recreational, commercial, retail, service, and tourist facilities are mixed to create **multifunctional areas** with a broad range of employment opportunities.

At first glance, redeveloped docklands all over the world look very much the same. However, the objectives, approach, and focus of waterfront projects can differ considerably. For example, in the pioneering London Docklands scheme, the focus was on the provision of office accommodation. In Barcelona (Spain), the waterfront conversion project contributed to an unprecedented investment, tourism, employment, and population boom with a clear emphasis on the creation of leisure and shopping facilities and the rearrangement of traffic flows. Similar redevelopment initiatives have been taken in other port cities as well, turning port areas into very attractive places for living, working, and recreation.

Many waterfront projects bring in a **clear cultural component** through museums (e.g. the Guggenheim Museum in Bilbao, 'Museum aan de Stroom' in Antwerp), opera houses, and concert halls (e.g. Elbphilharmonie in Hamburg), and conference centers (e.g. Dalian International Conference Center in Dalian, China). The link with the maritime heritage is often enhanced by the establishment of port museums. The new urban waterfront also provides many **service jobs** linked to bars, restaurants, convenience stores, and jobs linked to the usual range of services expected by the new residents of the waterfront. Hotels have become a prominent feature of urban waterfronts all over the world. These hotels are usually accompanied by a cluster of restaurants that look out over the water and often specialize in seafood. Increased visitor expenditure through multipliers can create **new investment and employment opportunities**. Waterfronts are also **recreation areas** with facilities for yachting harbors and marinas, watersport areas, and theme parks. Many ports provide jobs to people working in marinas, sailing schools, yacht and boat repair and maintenance yards, and similar waterfront operations.

A number of ports have become turntables in the **cruise industry**, with most cruise terminals located close to the city center. Cruise vessels near the city generally reinforce the maritime link between cities and ports and are visible signs of the touristic attractiveness of the city. Expenditure by passengers from visiting cruise ships may have a significant impact on the regional economy. This is most likely to occur where the port has relatively frequent visits by cruise ships, or the region is small. Cruise passengers may also spend time in the metropolitan area before or after their voyages, generating additional economic impacts through their visitor expenditures. Cruise vessels calling at a port also generate jobs at the level of pilotage, tugs, provisions, fuel, crew shore leave, passenger services, inspections, immigration, hotels, restaurants, local attractions, and other visitor activities in the port area. Further employment is provided by inland transportation involving cruise passengers, including by air, private car, bus, transit, and taxi. Some ports (e.g. Rotterdam, Amsterdam, and Antwerp in Europe, or Chongqing, Yichang and Shanghai in China) are regular ports of call for river cruises on major rivers (respectively the Rhine and Yangtze).

## 12 THE GREENING OF PORTS

From an environmental perspective, port planning and management should ensure sustainable development. The environmental sustainability of port projects and operations has become as important as economic and financial viability. As such, ports, as clusters of economic actors and activities, have adopted an environmental role and function and thus contribute to the greening of supply chains.

Ports, as nodes in extensive global transport networks, and intersections of large bundles of supply chains covering a multitude of commodities and cargo types, create environmental impacts through their various functions. Terminal activities are one source of the environmental impact of seaports which can be summarized in several categories, namely:

- Pollution related to **port construction and maintenance**.
- **Air emissions** of ships at berth and terminal handling equipment (such as cranes and yard equipment).
- **Noise** associated with cargo handling operations.
- The environmental effects and potential **congestion** associated with landside operations of barges, rail, and trucks.

Environmental impacts occur at **all stages of a terminal's life cycle**, such as port planning, terminal construction, terminal operation, terminal expansion, or terminal closure/termination. Regarding landside operations connecting to inland transport, environmental impacts caused by intermodal connections and congestion lead to adverse effects such as air pollution. Depending on modal choices and the associated cost and transit time requirements from shippers, such environmental effects vary. Other port functions also generate environmental impacts, such as industrial and semi-industrial activities in ports and warehousing and distribution activities.

Port-related pollution damages the ecological balance of nature and the urban environment. It causes an adverse effect on global climate change, further increasing the risk associated with port operations. The development of a low-carbon economy is considered to be a fundamental way to solve environmental problems.

The greening of ports is attracting growing attention. In business practice, it is mirrored in the many green initiatives of individual ports and the coordinated actions of the wider port community. The emergence of the **green port** concept is closely associated with the growing environmental awareness of seaport actors. The concept of green port (or low-carbon port) was officially proposed at the United Nations Climate Change conference in 2009. Based on an organic combination of port development, utilization of resources, and environmental protection, the green port concept refers to a development characterized by a healthy ecological environment, reasonable utilization of resources, low energy consumption, and low pollution. The green port concept or sustainable and climate-friendly development of the port's infrastructure in a broader sense entails responsible behavior of all stakeholders involved in port management and operations.

# PART I

# Ports and maritime shipping

## Chapter 1.1 Maritime shipping and international trade

*Seaports are affected by a wide range of economic, technological, and geopolitical developments. Shifts in global production and international trade are affecting port activity levels and operations. The demand for port traffic is derived from world trade.*

### 1 MARITIME SHIPPING AS A DRIVER OF GLOBALIZATION

Global **economic integration** is a key factor behind the rising significance of international trade. Historically, trade was prevalent but set up under constraining conditions in terms of the technical means to support it. Trading over long distances remained slow and expensive, limiting its scale and scope. By the early twentieth century, transport technologies such as the steamship became ubiquitous and efficient enough to support a complex international trade system. Particularly, the steamship enabled economies of scale that could not be achieved beforehand. However, it was not until the mid-twentieth century that the global regulatory regime became open enough to allow an expanded form of globalization.

Global trade is impossible without transportation, making efficient transport a key trade facilitator. By definition, almost all the cargo carried by maritime shipping is considered to be international trade. Transport costs (both freights costs and time costs) constitute a key component of **total trade costs**. These trade costs also include other costs incurred in getting goods to final users, other than the marginal cost of producing the good itself, such as policy barriers, information costs, legal and regulatory costs. Lower trade costs contribute to trade growth as it has been underlined that, for developing economies, a 10% reduction in transportation costs was associated with a 20% growth in international trade.

DOI 10.4324/9780429318184-1

Since the end of World War II, ongoing trade liberalism under the banner 'World Peace through World Trade', has led to gradual removal of political, regulatory, and cultural obstacles to trade. Integration processes took place both at the regional level and at the global level. The collapse of the Soviet Union and the opening up of China in the 1990s represented landmark events that incited the entry of close to two billion consumers as well as the related resources into the global economy. Regional trading blocs have been formed with differing levels of trade liberalization, such as NAFTA in North America, the EU Single Market in Europe, ASEAN in Southeast Asia, Mercosur in South America, and ECOWAS in West-Africa. An important share of international trade occurs **within economic blocs**, especially the European Union and NAFTA, which rely more on land transport modes such as road and rail. The European Union and NAFTA are considered the world's most integrated trade agreements, with 62.3% and 51.2% of their respective trade concerning member nations. For ASEAN, 75.5% of its trade concerns nations outside the agreement, implying a greater relative share of maritime shipping.

The **globalization of production** is a driver for the **globalization of trade** as they are interrelated. The **scale**, **volume,** and **efficiency** of international trade have continued to improve. The liberalization of global trade is supported by the continuing evolution of the World Trade Organization (WTO) and initiatives by organizations such as the United Nations Conference on Trade and Development (UNCTAD), or the World Bank. After World War II, a number of international corporations sought the support of intergovernmental organizations such as the United Nations for regulatory frameworks that enabled the pursuit of international operations. In such an environment, multinational corporations assumed growing importance as investors and traders. As a result, it might be argued that the slogan 'World Peace through World Trade' slowly shifted to 'World Peace for World Trade'. At present, inter-governmental organizations still play an essential role in shaping the rules of the game in international competition and global trade.

## 2 ONGOING GROWTH OF INTERNATIONAL TRADE

World trade has experienced a significant increase since the 1950s and represents a growing share of global economic output. In 2007, international trade surpassed 50% of the global Gross Domestic Product (GDP) for the first time, a share that was conventionally in the 20% to 25% range in the first half of the twentieth century. In the nineteenth century, this share was around 10%. Several factors explained this growth:

- **Income growth** linked with additional consumption of goods and services, some of which are traded.
- **Falling transport costs** allowing more options and opportunities to trade.

- **Trade liberalization** and the associated tariff rate reductions, easing trade transactions.
- **Economic convergence** of countries around trade agreements and common commercial policies.
- **Increase of intermediate goods trade** in the context of global production chains, outsourcing, and offshoring.

Between 1958 and 1988, income growth explained 67% of the real growth of world trade, while tariff reductions accounted for about 26% and transport-cost reductions roughly 8%. However, developed and developing economies might face different economic characteristics, and those play a different role in the growth of international trade. Low-income economies tend to have a high reliance on the trade of resources and low added-value goods; intermediate income economies are oriented around manufacturing; and high-income economies tend to be net importers of products and services.

The ongoing growth of international trade also impacted firms, many of which expanded to become multinational corporations. The benefits that multinational corporations derive from trade are varied:

- **Competition**. Seeking new resources, markets, and processes in international markets increases the competitiveness of corporations.
- **Economies of scale**. International markets allow firms to produce larger quantities of goods, which enable lower unit costs.
- **Innovation**. International markets incite the development of new products or the adaptation of existing products to different market characteristics.

As international trade depends on the provision of distribution and transactional services, the demand for these services has increased substantially, leading to the growth of carriers, cargo owners, terminal operators, third-party logistics service providers (3PL), freight forwarders, and insurers. International transportation and transaction service providers represent a complex ecosystem aiming at supporting international trade and extracting added value. The providers of transportation services, like manufacturing firms, have become large multinational corporations due to the extensive markets they cover.

International trade requires several types of services assumed by a number of actors (Figure 1.1):

- **Distribution services** are related to the function of transportation and warehousing, which are physical operations performed on trade goods. A carrier, such as a truck or a maritime shipping company, and a terminal operator provide transportation services while a cargo owner can have own account transportation and warehousing.
- **Transaction services** include activities for managing international trade. Procurement involves finding suppliers, setting up contracts, and ensuring continuity in the supply. Customs comprise the regulatory compliance so that traded goods meet national standards and duties are paid. Freight forwarders regularly assume this function on behalf

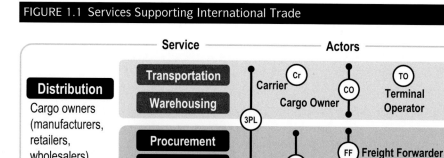

FIGURE 1.1 Services Supporting International Trade

of their customers. Finance provides capital to invest in trade activities, such as the purchasing (leasing) of equipment and the construction of facilities, an activity performed by investment banks. Cargo also needs to be insured against common risks (delays, theft, damage), a function assumed by insurance companies, some also involved in finance. Since many trade transactions are settled through currency exchange drawn from corporate deposits, commercial banks are major actors in settling transactions and letters of credit.

In recent years, actors known as third-party logistics providers (3PLs) have offered a wider range of trade services to their customers by controlling crucial transportation and transaction services. Several 3PLs are carriers that have decided for strategic purposes to expand their range of services to provide added value by combining the physical assets they control (ships, vehicles, warehouses) with procurement and customs services. Fourth-party logistics providers (4PLs) have also emerged, mainly focusing on non-physical asset trade services.

The nature of what is being traded, and the main traders involved, influence the transportation modes used for international transportation (Figure 1.2). Maritime transportation dominates, handling about 80% of the volume and 70% of the value of international trade.

Many of the world's most traded goods require specialized maritime transport conveyances. Cars are the most traded goods in terms of value, implying the deployment of a car carrier fleet. The second most traded commodity is refined petroleum, which is carried in tankers. A wide range of commodities is carried in containers, such as vehicle parts.

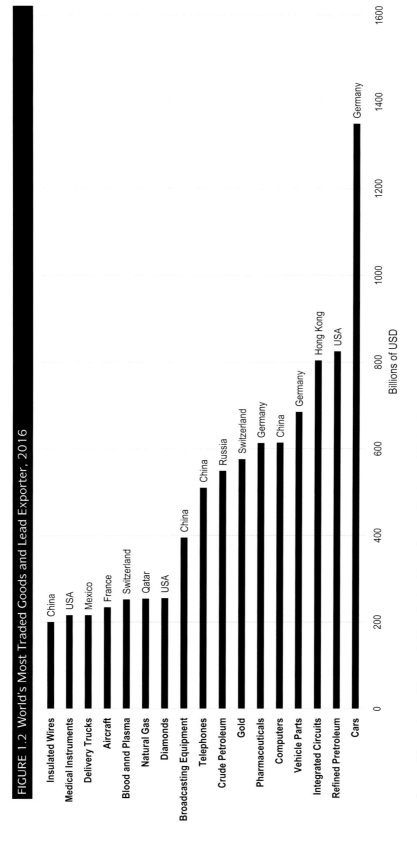

FIGURE 1.2 World's Most Traded Goods and Lead Exporter, 2016

Source: Observatory of Economic Complexity, Massachusetts Institute of Technology.

## 3 THE CONTAINERIZATION OF TRADE

### 3.1 The emergence of the container

The container and the associated maritime and inland transport systems have proved to be instrumental to the consecutive waves of globalization and global trade growth since the 1970s. The launching of the first containership by Malcolm McLean in 1956, the Ideal X, marked the beginning of containerization. The first transatlantic container service between the US East Coast and Northern Europe in 1966 marked the start of long-distance containerized trade. The first specialized cellular containerships were delivered in 1968, and containerization expanded over maritime and inland freight transport systems. Container shipping developed rapidly due to the adoption of **standard container sizes** in the late 1960s. The cost savings resulting from faster vessel turnaround times in ports, the reduction in the level of damages and associated insurance fees, and the integration with inland transport modes such as trucks, barges, and trains became acknowledged as clear containerization advantages.

The container offered a standard around which physical distribution systems could operate. Hence, emerging container shipping networks allowed changes in the economic and transport geography as they significantly reduced maritime costs between production and consumption centers across the world. Container shipping also became an **essential driver in reshaping global supply chains** allowing sourcing strategies of multinational enterprises and developing global production networks. New supply chain practices increased the requirements on container shipping in terms of frequency, schedule reliability/integrity, global coverage of services, rate setting, and environmental performance. The outcome has been an ongoing growth of the global container throughput (Figure 1.3).

The large-scale adoption of the container combined with the globalization process drove the global container port throughput from 36 million TEU (Twenty Foot Equivalent Unit) in 1980 to 237 million TEU in 2000, 545 million TEU in 2010, and more than 740 million TEU in 2017. Global container throughput reached approximately 802 million TEU in 2019, increasing by

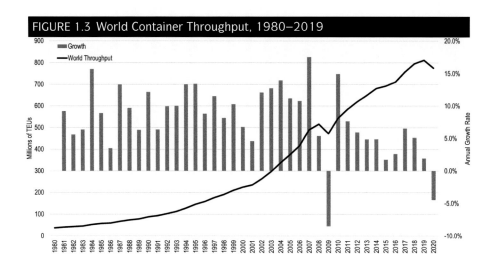

FIGURE 1.3 World Container Throughput, 1980–2019

2.3% compared to 2018, including full and empty containers. Container traffic, the absolute number of loaded containers being carried by sea (excluding empties), has grown from 28.7 million TEU in 1990 to 152 million TEU in 2018. The ratio of containerized trade over container port throughput shows that a container on average is loaded or discharged multiple times between the first port of loading and the last port of discharge.

The container has evolved from a transport unit to a supply or commodity chain unit. Containerization is inherently linked to the **transport of load units** (containers) across several transportation modes. It is more than a box as it acts as a vector for production and distribution. Containerization has led to various changes in the geography of transport, trade, and distribution, particularly in how production and physical distribution interact. The container can be considered revolutionary, as new practices have taken place after its introduction. It has become a ubiquitous transport product servicing mobility requirements at almost all stages of supply and commodity chains and is able to be carried virtually everywhere there are transport infrastructures.

## 3.2 Containerized trade networks

Before containerization, many goods subject to trade had to be handled manually. Emerging worldwide container shipping networks allowed changes in the economic and transport geography as they significantly shortened the maritime cost distances between production and consumption centers around the world. Container shipping also became an essential driver in reshaping global supply chain practices, allowing global sourcing strategies of multinational enterprises, pull logistics solutions, and the development of global production networks.

Containerization has been the most dynamic physical component of globalization, far exceeding the growth of the value of exports and the GDP (Figure 1.4). As globalization developed, each new individual, GDP, or export

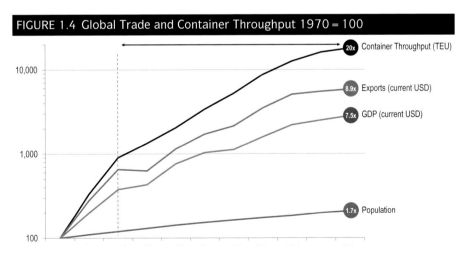

FIGURE 1.4  Global Trade and Container Throughput 1970 = 100

Sources: Population and GDP from World Bank, World Development Indicators. Exports from World Trade Organization. Container port throughput compiled from Containerization International.

unit was associated with a higher level of container flows. While up to 1980, the growth of container port throughput was on a par with the growth of the value of exports, a divergence is noted afterward with container flows growing faster than trade flows. Containerization entered the acceleration phase of its diffusion cycle as the fundamental support of export-oriented strategies pursued by Asian economies.

The composition of international trade goods carried in containers is impressive in its diversity. The 20 most important SITC (Standard International Trade Classification) categories accounted for 65% of the global containerized trade, underlining that the container has been used to carry any possible good that could be fitted in. However, many of the most significant categories of containerized trade are the outcome of comparative advantage factors, namely labor, that can be temporary and subject to change. If these advantages were to shift because of technological changes (e.g. automation), then a notable share of the containerized trade could be impacted.

About one out of every ten containers handled worldwide is handled in ports of the **Yangtze River Delta**. In East Asia, export-oriented industrialization policies undertaken by Hong Kong, Taiwan, and South Korea sustained the strong growth in container throughput handled by these economies from the 1980s. China developed similar strategies in the late 1980s, resulting in elevated growth first in the Pearl River Delta and then in the Yangtze Delta port system and the Bohai Bay region. In the past ten years, Shanghai, Guangzhou, Shenzhen, Qingdao, and Ningbo joined Hong Kong, Busan, and Singapore as the world's busiest container ports. The Rhine-Scheldt Delta (Belgium/the Netherlands) was the world's number one container handing region in the world till the mid-1990s when south China took the lead. While the dynamics of containerization and container flows are well known, much less is known about what is being carried by containers, particularly as it concerns commodities.

Several growth factors are at play to explain the substantial growth of containerization and, more interestingly, how the contribution of these factors varies in time. While additional traffic resulting from organic economic growth is the most salient factor, imbalanced trade flows (empty containers) and the configuration of shipping networks relying on transshipment hubs (double counting) have also contributed to additional containerized flows and port handlings. As economies of scale are applied to maritime shipping, transshipment becomes more salient. The number of containers being transshipped increased from around 11% of all cargo handled by container ports in 1980 to about 30% in 2015, which is also a notable factor in the growth of containerized traffic.

### 3.3 Containerized growth dynamics

The conventional growth dynamics of containerization have mainly relied on an array of drivers, which include (Figure 1.5):

- **Derived growth**. Often labeled as organic growth, derived growth is an economic development outcome with greater quantities of containerized cargoes being traded. Globalization also implies a growth of the average distance over which containerized freight is being carried. In both cases,

## FIGURE 1.5  Containerization Growth Factors

| FACTOR | Volume Growth | Volume Decline |
|---|---|---|
| **Derived** | • Economic and income growth<br>• Outsourcing and offshoring<br>• Complex supply chains | • Economic recessions<br>• Trade protectionism<br>• Automation |
| **Substitution** | • Capture of bulk and break-bulk markets<br>• New niches (commodities and cold chain) | • Peak substitution<br>• Composition of container fleet |
| **Incidental** | • Trade imbalances<br>• Repositioning of empty containers | • Trade protectionism<br>• Automation |
| **Induced** | • Transshipment (hubbing, relay and intersection) | • Changes in shipping networks (more direct services) |

greater containerized capacities are required, average voyage days per vessel increase, and the number of vessel roundtrips per year decreases. The dynamics based on derived demand may have reached maturity in containerization potential as many global supply chains are now fully containerized.

- **Substitution-based growth**. Initially, substitution was the main factor behind containerization with the gradual capture of the breakbulk cargo market. This process has been particularly visible in many ports, as illustrated by rising containerization degrees (the ratio between containerized throughput of the port and the total general cargo volumes). Since almost all break-bulk cargo that could be containerized has been containerized, this substitution process is essentially near completion in developed economies. It is also rising rapidly in emerging economies and developing countries. This leaves the possible further containerization of niche markets, namely commodities and temperature-sensitive cargo.

- **Incidental growth**. Production and trade imbalances in the global economy are reflected in physical flows and transport rates and lead to specific container repositioning strategies. Containerized flows are rarely balanced, implying that empty containers must be repositioned to locations where export cargo is available.

- **Induced growth**. The growth of deep-sea services and the use of larger containerships has led to the setting up of intermediary hubs connecting different systems of circulation via transshipment. Intermediary hubs emerge in locations offering clear advantages over direct port calls at mainland ports. The setting up of intermediate hubs occurs around specific regions ideally suited for maritime hub-and-spoke distribution patterns. Transshipment has proven to be a major driver for global container port throughput, with substantially higher growth rates than observed for gateway traffic. The worldwide transshipment incidence has steadily increased from around 18% in 1990 to around 35% in 2018.

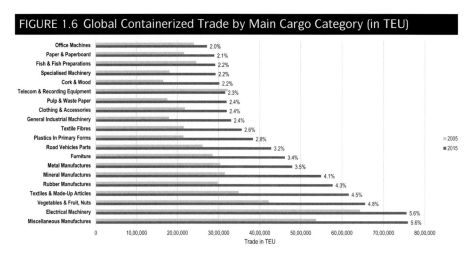

FIGURE 1.6 Global Containerized Trade by Main Cargo Category (in TEU)

Source: MDS Transmodal, World Cargo Database. Note: Groups are at the SITC 2 digits level.

It is estimated that in 2015, 135.5 million TEU of trade was carried in containers, compared to 88.5 million TEU in 2005 (Figure 1.6). The composition of global containerized trade shows an extensive diversity of the goods being carried, with no particular category (SITC two digit level) dominating. The four most important categories accounted for 20.6% of the containerized trade volumes in 2015:

- Miscellaneous manufactures (SITC 89) include articles made of plastics (e.g. bags), toys, sporting goods, or office supplies. The manufacturing of these goods has been highly impacted by outsourcing and offshoring since it requires significant labor input.
- Electrical machinery (SITC 77) includes machines powered by electricity, such as electric cables, appliances, batteries, and integrated circuits. The production of these goods has also been substantially internationalized, particularly for electronics.
- Vegetables and fruits (SITC 05) compose an important segment of transportation by refrigerated containers. This sector has been the object of notable growth with more reliable cold chain logistics.
- Textiles and made-up articles (SITC 65) include yarn, woven fiber, blankets, linen, curtains, and carpets. The textile industry has been the object of internationalization for several decades.

## 4 THE SHIFT IN GLOBAL TRADE PATTERNS

The recent decades have seen important changes in international trade flows. Prior to the 1970s, global trade flows were dominated by three major poles, North America, Western Europe, and the developing economies of East Asia (Japan, South Korea, and Taiwan). A trade dichotomy was observed between developed and developing economies as raw materials were mainly flowing north and finished goods were flowing south. This situation can mainly be explained by differences in development levels, better economies of scale in developed economies, and unequal trade relations set up during the colonial era.

From the 1970s, this situation changed as economic development took place across a range of nations in Latin America (Mexico), Southeast Asia (Malaysia, Thailand, Indonesia), and East Asia (China, South Korea, Taiwan) (Figure 1.7). Many manufacturing activities that had emerged in developed economies were relocated to lower input cost locations, because of cheaper labor. Emerging multinational corporations were actively involved in this process. Such a structural shift is well illustrated by the variation in the share of developing economies in seaborne trade, which used to be highly imbalanced with much more cargo being loaded than unloaded. Economic development resulted in a growing share of developing economies as a destination for cargo. Consequently, global trade is now characterized by significant flows of cargoes (raw materials, intermediate and finished goods) from developed to developing economies.

A growing share of international trade occurs within regions (and particularly economic blocs) even if long-distance trade has increased in absolute numbers. Trade predominantly takes place within Europe, North America, and East Asia, commonly referred to as the triad. Still, a shift in trade relations between the northern and southern hemispheres, particularly between

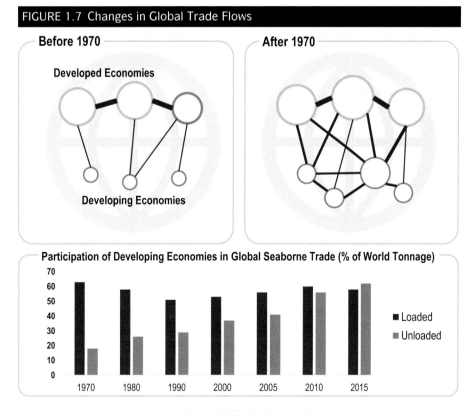

**FIGURE 1.7  Changes in Global Trade Flows**

Source: Seaborne trade data adapted from UNCTAD, Review of Maritime Transport.

developed and developing economies, has occurred. The structure of global trade has become much more complex in its relations and diversified in what is being traded. The pattern of trade relations is mainly explained by the following factors:

- **Geographical proximity**. The intensity of trade relations is commonly a function of proximity unless notable advantages can be found further away. The European Union has significant trading linkages with adjacent areas in Eastern Europe, North Africa, and the Middle East. North America also maintains important trade linkages with Latin America, notably Mexico, as part of the USMCA (United States–Mexico–Canada Agreement). Shorter distances have an important impact on the modes used for trade, with maritime shipping less suitable outside short sea shipping. Still, a key advantage of maritime shipping is that it substantially attenuates the negative effects of long distances on trade, as the development of containerized shipping underlines.
- **Resources availability**. The scarcity and availability of resources have shaped maritime networks for close to two centuries and remain the main component, ton-wise, of maritime shipping. Energy, mineral, and agricultural trades have distinct shipping networks and specialized port facilities designed to handle bulk cargoes such as petroleum, natural gas, coal, grains, alumina, and iron ore.
- **History and culture**. The trade networks established during the colonial era have endured in relations such as those between Europe and Africa or between the United States and Latin America. China has commercial historical ties with Central Asia and Southeast Asia which have been recreated and expanded in recent decades. Irrespective of the political context, trade networks tend to endure because of the reciprocal systems of supply and demand on which they depend.

Another characteristic of the contemporary commercial setting concerns **imbalances in trade flows**. For instance, China exports more than it imports with partners such as the United States and the European Union. Trade imbalances directly reflect imbalances in shipping flows. For bulk trade such as energy and minerals, it is common that a return trip will be empty. For containerized trade, the load factors of return trips are lower, and the share of empty containers higher. The imbalanced trade structure is also reflected in the composition of container imports and exports that differs substantially. Further, trade imbalances imply the repositioning of empty containers that accounts for about 20% of global container moves.

Geographical and economic shifts in international trade are directly observable in the evolution of the level of trade intensity by ocean, as the Trans-Pacific trade has grown faster than the Trans-Atlantic trade. The most significant trade flows are between Asia and North America (especially the United States), between Europe and North America, and between Europe and Asia. The associated maritime routes are the most commercially used with sizeable trade going through chokepoints such as the Strait of Malacca (30% of global trade transiting), the Suez Canal (15%), the Strait of Gibraltar, and the Panama Canal (5%). These bottlenecks allow connection between the major systems of maritime circulation

where the transatlantic, the transpacific, and the Asia–Europe routes dominate. north-south flows are complementing these east-west routes, many of
which interact at major transshipment hubs around Singapore, Dubai, and
the Caribbean (Panama, Cartagena, Kingston). The evolution of international trade shapes the structure of maritime shipping networks and port
development as shipping lines tend to organize their services to connect
the dominant trade flows directly, and the less dominant trade flows indirectly through transshipments.

## Box 1.1  World seaborne trade by cargo type, 1970–2018

*Weight-wise, raw materials dominate maritime trade as they are ponderous and
carried over long distances (Figure 1.8). Oil, iron ore, coal, and grain accounted
for 28% of the ton-miles carried by maritime shipping, while other dry cargoes,
which include containers, accounted for 40%. Oil is the most significant commodity, with 25% of ton-miles in 2018, but this share is significantly lower than
in 1970 when it accounted for 60% of global ton-miles.*

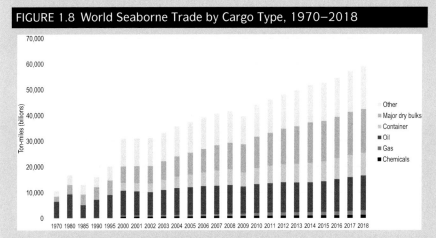

FIGURE 1.8 World Seaborne Trade by Cargo Type, 1970–2018

Source: UNCTAD Review of Maritime Transport, various years.

*Since the 1980s, a significant rebalancing of the intensity of trade by ocean
has taken place, particularly over containerized trade (Figure 1.9). As the international trade taking place over the Pacific Ocean increased, the Atlantic Ocean
experienced a relative decline of its share. While the Atlantic accounted for 46%
of global trade activity in 1980, this share decreased by more than half to 21%
in 2010. The share of the Indian Ocean doubled to 10%, but this figure does
not account for the substantial traffic transiting along the Asia/Mediterranean/
European trade route.*

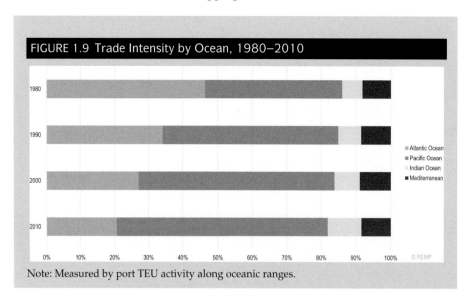

FIGURE 1.9 Trade Intensity by Ocean, 1980–2010

Note: Measured by port TEU activity along oceanic ranges.

## Box 1.2 American foreign trade by maritime containers

*American containerized trade is characterized by an asymmetry between the nature of its imports and exports (Figure 1.10). North American retailers account for a substantial share of containerized imports, mostly involving finished consumption goods bound to major inland freight distribution centers. The largest importers, such as Wal-Mart, Home Depot, Target, Costco, Ikea, and Lowe's, are all mass (Big Box) retailers relying on high volume and low margin goods, which are predominantly produced in China. It is worth mentioning that about 60% of all Chinese trade surplus with the United States is the outcome of American-owned firms operating in China and importing their output to the United States.*

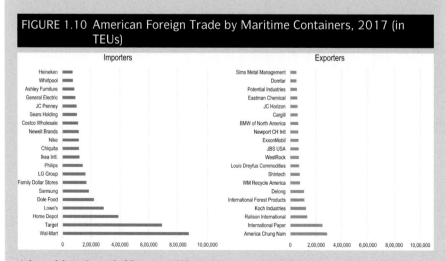

FIGURE 1.10 American Foreign Trade by Maritime Containers, 2017 (in TEUs)

Adapted from *Journal of Commerce*, US top 100 importers and exporters. Data from PIERS.

> *Exporters show a completely different profile. A major category of containerized export concerns recycles with exporters such as America Chung Nam, Ralison International, WM Recycle America, or Potential Industries. Other major exporters include diversified resource-based (Koch Industries) forest and paper products (e.g. International Paper, International Forest Products), agribusiness (e.g. Cargill, Archer Daniels Midland), or chemicals (e.g. Shintech, Dow, DuPont). Yet, a significant containerized trade imbalance remains.*
>
> *The trade asymmetry being depicted is reflected in the relative value of imports and exports. While the average value of American imports is about $4.75 per kilogram, the value of exports stands at $2.50 per kilogram. This has also had significant impacts on North American logistics. The import-driven segment involves a series of stages to reach a multitude of outlets with a freight density correlated with population density. Since the retail trade is essentially unidirectional, many retail goods are transloaded at gateways into domestic containers while the maritime (ISO) containers are re-exported empty. The export-driven segment relies on the massification of shipments at major gateways and inland ports.*

## 5 INTERNATIONAL TRADE AND MARITIME SHIPPING SERVICES

International trade relies volume-wise for about 80% on maritime transportation, which involves several markets such as dry bulk, roll-on/roll-off, general cargo, and containers.

### 5.1 Maritime services in dry bulk shipping

The maritime transport of **major bulks** such as iron ore and coal typically relies on end-to-end services between a port of loading (connected by rail to mines) and a port of discharge. Economies of scale in vessel size are significant in dry bulk shipping, so operators will try to maximize vessel size on the end-to-end tramp service. The nautical accessibility in the port of loading and port of discharge, the charter price level, and the availability of vessel types play a decisive role in vessel size choice. Inland transport costs per ton-kilometer are typically 20 to 30 percent higher than sea transport costs per ton-kilometer.

Consequently, market players make a trade-off between, on the one hand, the minimization of inland transport costs by routing the bulk flows via the ports that are closest to the final destination and, on the other hand, maximizing the scale economies in vessel size by calling at the ports that offer the best nautical accessibility. This exercise in some cases leads to multiple calls whereby a large Capesize vessel will first call at a deepwater port to discharge part of the cargo and then proceed to the second port of call with a less favorable nautical access to discharge the remainder (e.g. a call sequence starting in Dunkirk and ending in Antwerp). Another practice consists of lightening deepsea vessels on stream, whereby floating cranes discharge part of the load to barges given decreasing vessel draft (e.g. lightening operations on River Scheldt to access the Canal Ghent-Terneuzen).

The vessels deployed in the **minor bulk segments** (grain, fertilizers, minerals) are generally much smaller, so that vessel operators have a much wider range of potential ports of call at their disposal. The eventual call patterns will be determined by factors such as proximity to the market, the specificities of the distribution network (centralized or decentralized), the number of cargo batches on the vessel, and the need for dedicated terminal facilities (e.g. grain silos).

## 5.2 Maritime services in the roll-on/roll-off (RoRo) market

The operational characteristics of maritime services in the RoRo segment depend on the submarkets considered:

- Intra-regional **RoRo and ropax services** are typical of the end-to-end type with a port of call at either side of the route. The shipping services follow a fixed schedule with medium to high frequencies (sometimes several times a day). The ferry capacities tend to vary greatly with the cargo density on the route and the one-way distance. For example, in Europe, large units are deployed on the English Channel and parts of the Baltic (e.g. 120 trucks per voyage on the Dover-Calais link and several hundreds of passengers between Travemünde and Finland). In contrast, vessel capacities on services in smaller markets (e.g. the Irish isles) tend to be much smaller. Trucks using ferry services can have a long pre- and end haul by road (for instance, a truck driving from Dortmund to Zeebrugge to catch a ferry to Hull and onward by road to the final destination, Manchester).
- The market for **unaccompanied RoRo transport** is based on end-to-end services with dedicated RoRo freight vessels, which often have reserve space for containers.
- The **deepsea and shortsea car carrying trade** is another submarket in the RoRo market. On intercontinental routes, the operators deploy Pure Car and Truck Carriers (PCTC) with capacities of up to 8,000 CEU (car equivalent unit), resulting in significant cost savings on the sea leg (economies of scale). The number of ports of call is kept to a strict minimum as shipping lines aim for a short port time and they face a shortfall in the number of ports that have the infrastructure to accommodate large quantities of new cars. As a result, a significant part of the market is concentrated in large car handling ports. The port of Zeebrugge in Belgium is a good example, with 2.96 million units handled in 2019. The position of the main ports is strongly entwined with their proximity to the main buyer markets and the spatial concentration of car assembly plants. A number of large car ports have successfully combined deepsea services with intra-regional shortsea services. The resulting hub-and-spoke network configuration is combined with growing local clusters of automotive logistics companies. While road haulage is by far the dominant mode of inland transport to/from car terminals, rail and barge play an ever more important role in securing inland access for the larger car ports, particularly in Belgium, the Netherlands, and the Rhine and Yangtze river basins.

## 5.3 Maritime services in the general cargo market

The diversity in maritime service configurations is probably highest in the market of **conventional general cargo**. In contrast to the bulk cargo market, where parcel sizes are usually big enough to fill an entire ship, the general cargo market deals with the shipment of consignments smaller than a ship or hold size. Given the enormous variety of different cargoes involved, there are several ways in which breakbulk cargoes can be shipped. The most common is the conventional liner-type concept of weekly fixed-day services, characterizing the liner shipping industry, which is something the deepsea trade of conventional cargo has never really been able to achieve. Instead, the following service/schedule options can be distinguished in the case of breakbulk shipping (the typology is based on Dynamar):

- Services of a specific frequency operated with dedicated ships.
- Services offering sailings within a certain period, deploying trip charters.
- Services operated on inducement but still within a more or less defined trade lane.
- A mixture of two or three of the above options.
- 'Parcelling', such as tramping, whereby a vessel is chartered (usually on a trip-out basis) once a specific cargo volume is available.

The conventional general cargo market includes many specialized ships designed to carry specific cargo loads. For example, heavy-lift vessels do not operate on fixed routes, but they are attracted to those areas where large investments in the oil and gas industry are being made. Conventional reefer ships mainly carry high-value foodstuffs that require refrigeration and atmosphere control on an end-to-end service (e.g. bananas from a port of loading in Latin America to a specialized terminal in Europe). Examples of reefer cargoes include fresh and frozen fruit (e.g. bananas, deciduous and other citrus fruits), vegetables, fish, meat, poultry, and dairy products. Reefer shipping is a prime example of a one-way (and for some products seasonal) business with cargoes mainly exported from the southern hemisphere to the rest of the world. The reefer shipping sector is increasingly being put under pressure from container shipping.

## 5.4 Maritime services in container shipping

The most advanced structures in maritime services are found in **container shipping**. Shipping lines design the networks they find it convenient to offer, but at the same time they are bound to provide the services their customers want in terms of frequency, direct accessibility, and transit times. In the last two decades, increased cargo availability has made carriers and alliances reshape their liner shipping networks by introducing new types of liner services on the main east-west trade lanes.

Observing recent developments in liner shipping, productivity has been improved by using larger ships and devising **new operational patterns and co-operation between shipping lines**. Since the 1990s, a great deal of attention has been devoted to larger, more fuel-economical vessels, and this indeed has produced a substantial reduction in the cost per TEU of capacity provided. Alliances and consolidation have created multi-string networks on the major trade routes, and both shippers and liners have adapted. The networks are based on traffic circulation through a network of specific hubs. A more detailed analysis of the container shipping market is provided later in this book.

# Chapter 1.2  Ports and maritime supply chains

*Seaports are functioning as platforms within global supply chains and global production networks. These supply chains are highly dynamic as they react to changes in global trade patterns, consumer preferences, and advances in supply chain management and information technology.*

## 1 GROWING COMPLEXITY IN SUPPLY CHAIN MANAGEMENT

*Supply Chain Management (SCM) is the coordination and management of a complex network of activities delivering a finished product to end-users or customers. The process includes sourcing raw materials and parts, manufacturing and assembling products, storage, order entry and tracking, distribution through the various channels, and finally delivery to the customer.*

Ports are a nexus in supply chains as they support the interaction between global supply chains and regional production and consumption markets (Figure 1.11). Global supply chains have become complex, pressuring the logistics industry to simultaneously improve their costs, performance, and resilience to disruptions. Logistics services that still offer value may experience a debasement and become basic services, only generating a small margin. This is especially the case for physical added value.

Within supply chains, corporations interact with external suppliers, internal departments, external distributors, and customers. The successful management of a supply chain is influenced by customer expectations, globalization, technological innovations, government regulation, competition, and sustainability concerns.

FIGURE 1.11 The Port as a Nexus in Global Supply Chains

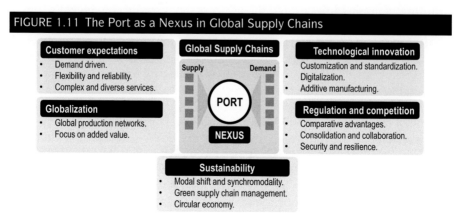

## 1.1 Customer expectations

**SCM models evolve continuously** due to influences and factors such as globalization and expansion into new markets, mass customization in response to product and market segmentation, lean manufacturing practices, and associated shifts in costs. Service expectations of customers are moving towards a push for higher flexibility, reliability, and precision. In many industries, product innovation has become a significant competitive factor. This has led companies to compete to be the first to launch new products and technologies. As a result, average product life cycles and supply chain cycles such as lead time have decreased.

The number of products to be shipped and the shipment frequency increase, whereas batch sizes are becoming smaller. There is a growing demand from the customer for make-to-order or customized products, delivered at maximum speed, with high delivery reliability, at the lowest possible cost. While costs remain an important factor in customer satisfaction, factors related to reliability are becoming central. The focus is on supply chain excellence and efficient customer service.

A **growing skills shortage** is a distinct possibility in the logistics industry as the labor force is challenged to provide an increasing array of complex and diverse services. Logistics companies are trying to recruit sufficient talent to maintain the labor force and provide ongoing training to improve their productivity. Considering the digitalization of all parts of society, including logistics, the requirement for new skill sets will further intensify this shortage. Besides, the targeted labor force might be attracted by other, more high-profile sectors. The port and logistics sectors have difficulties competing for talent.

## 1.2 Globalization

One of the main basic driving forces of change in the port industry emerges from globalization and the structural shift from **supply-driven to demand-driven economies**. The supply-driven economy was based on economies of scale in production, standardization, and mass consumption of standard products. This approach was scrutinized as productivity increases linked to economies of scale met their structural boundaries and as a growing individualism began to have an impact on consumption patterns. The outcome was a shift to a more demand-driven economic system, combined with global production networks on the supply side of the markets.

**Multinational enterprises** (MNE) are the key drivers of globalization. A shift has taken place from capital-intensive activities – such as ownership and management of a large number of manufacturing sites, distribution centers, and sales outlets – towards another type of activity, which is far less capital intensive and focuses more on developing a strong brand. Branding forms a key concept in the new business model of MNEs. This involves a strong focus on customers and product innovation, whereas production is outsourced to a network of suppliers. MNEs increasingly develop long-term relationships with a limited number of logistics suppliers based on co-makership. As such, a large number of MNEs have adopted flexible multi-firm organization structures on a global scale.

Many of the world's largest MNEs manage extensive **networks of globally dispersed inputs**. Global sourcing, as such, is a major driver of world trade. However, at the customer end of the value chain, very few of the world's largest multinational enterprises operate globally, in the sense of having a broad and deep penetration in foreign markets across the world. Instead, they are regionally based on breadth and depth of market coverage, with most of their sales situated within their home leg of the 'triad', namely in North America, the European Union, or Asia. The broad geographic distribution of sourcing and production (back end) versus less broad geographic distribution of sales (customer end) is reflected in trade patterns, supply chain management needs, and shipping requirements.

## 1.3 Technological innovation

The streamlining of supply chains through customization and standardization using advances in data analytics and visibility leads to concepts such as 'plug-and-play supply chains'. These are finely-tuned, agile supply chains consisting of core standardized, easily replicable solutions, augmented by standardized, proven processes tailored to unique segment or market needs. These supply chains need to be supported by **digitalization** involving intelligent, data-driven decision support systems around customers, markets, and profitability.

The focus will be on more **local and sustainable supply networks** in which clean forms of transport will meet shippers' expectations regarding cost and efficiency performance indicators. Goods will have to be transported in economically, with limited environmental impacts, and in a sustainable manner. To this extent, shippers will expect an orchestration function from service providers in which operational excellence is supported by obtaining a greater convergence between physical and data processes.

**Postponed and additive manufacturing** (3D printing) will challenge existing business models. This trend will affect transport and logistics demands. More manufacturing is likely to be regional, be it in local factories, independent manufacturing farms, or even with a new role for logistics service providers that will offer production services and integrate them with their transport, storage, and distribution services.

## 1.4 Regulation and competition

**Changing comparative advantages in economies** like China, where costs and inflation keep rising, and with their 'China plus one' scenario in which China will transition from an export producing towards a consumption-driven economy, have a major impact on the complexity and challenges of current supply chains. Combined with manufacturing risks, such as time to market or responsiveness, import duties, the availability of skilled labor force, synergies with ecosystems, the cost of energy, and automation, this means that more sub-assembly and manufacturing will relocate to other regions.

More horizontal collaboration between transport companies and logistics service providers will be needed to deal with the need for shorter, more sustainable, and cost-efficient supply chains. This will entail its own complexities, mainly where it concerns mutual trust concerning data-sharing protocols and protection of one's competitiveness.

**Consolidation in the logistics sector** will result in a smaller number of companies that will empower the supply chain to support increasingly efficient ICT systems. The data component will leverage performant and pro-active service providers to transform into companies with a new outlook on logistics services. Next to an increasing number of traditional activities being outsourced, such as transport, warehousing, and various types of value-added services, the presence of collaboration platforms will capacitate certain service providers to develop new types of logistics services.

The **security of supply** is becoming increasingly important. Supply chain resilience is a crucial element in dealing with the risk of supply chain disruptions due to factors such as local political instability, natural disasters, health crises and acts of terrorism. Supply chains increasingly have redundancy built-in and are designed for resilience, with visibility and data sharing between supply chain stakeholders a key strategy.

## 1.5 Sustainability

The systematic use of greener alternatives for logistics needs to be developed as environmental pressures from society increase, including through more stringent regulations and consumer behavior changes. This impacts the way ports operate and how they are linked, which is associated with a re-engineering of supply chains in favor of modal shift and synchromodality. This results in the development of sustainable hubs and corridors along which new supply chain networks need to be developed. Corporations are adapting their business models to include sustainability criteria in their procurement and operations, which impacts the related supply chains through the setting up of Green supply chain management strategies.

> *Green Supply Chain Management (GSCM) is a business model that integrates environmental concerns into the inter-organizational practices of SCM.*

GSCM has gained increased attention within the industry as there is a growing need for integrating environmentally sustainable choices into SCM practices. The growing importance of GSCM goes hand in hand with environmental issues such as climate change, the scarcity of some new-renewable material resources, waste disposal, and increasing pollution levels in developing economies. Adding the 'green' component to supply chain management involves addressing its influence and relationships to the natural environment.

The main idea behind GSCM is to strive for a reduction in environmental impacts by focusing on a series of supply chain strategies known as the 5Rs; Reduce, Reuse, Recycle, Remanufacture, and Reverse logistics. The fields of action in GSCM include product design, process design and engineering, procurement and purchasing, production, energy use and mix, and logistics (distribution and transportation).

An important part of the success of the **circular economy** hinges on the way logistics will enable the transparency needed to set up efficient and integrated fully circular supply chain networks. Next to the physical aspect of integrating supply chain flows to maximize circular economy opportunities, end-to-end integration of supply chain processes will be crucial. Thus, the circular economy offers new opportunities for shipping and logistics service providers and challenges them to collaborate with the industry stakeholders.

## 2 IMPROVING COMPETITIVENESS

### 2.1 Operating margins and cost control

The developments in supply chain management are taking place in a logistics market usually characterized by low margins. It can be characterized as a buyers' market, giving shippers and cargo owners an advantage over the sellers of logistical services in price negotiations. The logistics tendering practices of (large) shippers add to the **pressure on operating margins**. The buyer's market stems from the law of supply and demand, where downward pressure on prices is associated with supply increases amid a constant demand. The competition in the marketplace exists between sellers (i.e. the logistics service providers), who often must engage in a price war to entice buyers (i.e. shippers) to use their services. The resulting low margins force market players such as logistics service providers, terminal operators, shipping lines, and land transport operators to focus on cost control without yielding efficient performance and timely delivery (Figure 1.12).

Although logistics costs differ between corporations, they generally include transportation, labor, storage/inventory, and administrative costs. Logistics costs largely depend on the nature of the goods. The possibility to achieve a lower cost base can be negatively affected by a broad range of factors such as the volatility of resource and fuel costs and delays caused by complex regulations governing international trade, weather circumstances, or technical problems. In general terms, cost control entails specific actions over a variety of operational fields:

- **Optimized use of resources**. The under-use of key assets, such as conveyances (ships, vehicles) or warehousing facilities, directly affects the cost base and operating margins. By optimizing assets, utilization market players can improve their business efficiency. Efficient asset management also includes a focus on preventative maintenance.
- An increase in **fleet size and service network size** to benefit from economies of scale and scope (see container shipping market).
- **Consolidated shipments and cargo bundling** to reduce the cost per unit transported.
- Using a **single integrated platform**, accessible to involved parties to avoid time-consuming and inefficient duplication of activities and processes across operations.

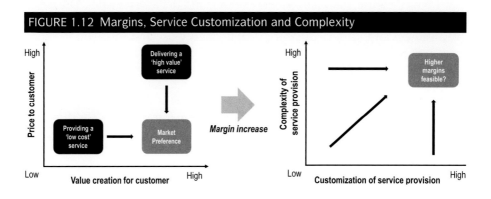

FIGURE 1.12 Margins, Service Customization and Complexity

- **Optimize outsourcing vs. vertical integration**. In some cases, market players can save costs by outsourcing a portion of their supply chain operations. In other cases, extending the reach of activities through a vertical integration process can bring higher margins. Logistics service providers might use outsourcing to lower their cost base. They manage what they can control best to keep costs down and look for low-cost outsourcing for the remaining. This outsourcing strategy is not without risk as a corporation might outsource activities which it failed to recognize as value-enhancing.
- **Improvement in supply chain visibility** can result in more efficient planning and lower operating costs by better managing mobile and fixed logistics assets. Although there is no way to predict or prevent disruptions in the logistics process, proper supply chain visibility provides insight into such issues. Using real-time dashboards that refresh data automatically provides supply chain managers and financial executives with the most current and relevant information.
- **Labor inputs for logistics operations**. Labor Management Software systems combined with specific labor-related Key Performance Indicators (KPIs) and incentive-based human resources practices help corporations efficiently manage and motivate personnel.
- For some corporations, logistics costs can be reduced by **automation of assets** such as vehicles, warehouse management systems, and yard operations. Regulating, automating, and optimizing manual processes offers opportunities to reduce staff requirements, centralize operations to lower-cost areas, and create a more proactive approach to ensuring customer satisfaction.
- **Collaboration and partnership with suppliers** can help reduce costs by allowing partners to focus on their respective comparative advantages over processes and markets. Suppliers can sometimes absorb direct logistics costs.

## 2.2 Cost leadership and differentiation strategies

At a more strategic level, logistics companies are challenged to design **business models** that ensure their competitiveness and growth. In an efficiency-oriented market environment, customers may choose to purchase from one company rather than another because the service price is lower than competitors, or the customer perceives the service to provide better-added value or benefits. However, these are broad generalizations as efficiency-oriented companies in the logistics, port, and maritime industries aim at achieving competitive advantage by either cost leadership or differentiation. **Cost leadership** implies that market players try to achieve a competitive advantage by becoming low-cost logistics services providers. A **differentiation strategy** tries to provide specific services in market niches distinct from those provided by competitors, offering greater value to the client (Figure 1.13).

A corporation aiming to achieve competitive advantage by reducing prices is likely to be followed by competitors, with the risk of lower margins across the industry and an inability to reinvest to develop services for the long term. Therefore, a low cost or cost leadership strategy requires:

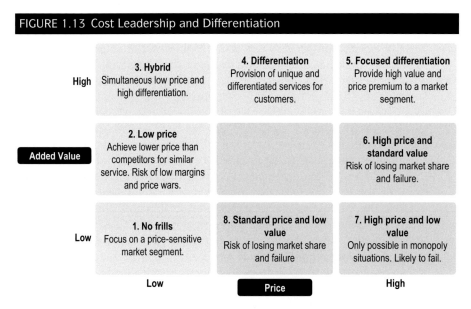

FIGURE 1.13 Cost Leadership and Differentiation

Source: Adapted from Notteboom (2004).

1. A **low-cost base** that competitors cannot match.
2. A **market segment** in which low price is important. Sustaining a low price advantage is challenging, and cost leadership is very difficult to achieve.

Cost advantages typically emanate from specific competencies driving down costs throughout the value chain, such as economies of scale and scope, market power, buying power, and gaining from operational experience (curve effects). It may be possible to substantially reduce operational costs by outsourcing provision or by a careful examination of missing capabilities and competencies in parts of the value chain. A large part of the logistics industry traditionally thrived on low-cost strategies. Conventional transport operators function as the last segments in outsourcing, delivering basic services (i.e. trucking) with little room for service differentiation. Margins are low and fierce competition, combined with the high customer bargaining power, prevents these operators from increasing their revenue base.

**Differentiation strategies** aim to achieve a higher market share than competitors (which yields cost benefits) by offering better products or services at the same price or enhanced margins by pricing slightly higher. Differentiation comes in many forms:

1. **Uniqueness or improvements in services** through R&D or building on the innovative capabilities of the company.
2. **Marketing-based approaches** to underline value to the customer of services.
3. **Competency-based approaches** in which the company tries to build differentiation based on its competencies that are difficult for competitors to imitate.

If the aim is sustainable differentiation, there is little point striving to be different if others can imitate quickly. The most important resources and capabilities for a company are durable, difficult to identify and understand, imperfectly transferable, and not easy to replicate. Resources for which a corporation possesses clear ownership and control (e.g. patents) are among the most valuable differentiation factors.

Companies in the logistics industry can build sustainable **competitive advantage** by leveraging their core competencies. The prime resources of the company consist of physical assets such as equipment and locations, human resources such as the workforce, management team, experience and training, and organizational resources associated with the corporate culture. These need to be transformed into capabilities, often through the diffusion of corporate knowledge across offices. In time, new core competencies emerge, representing the fundamental strengths of the corporation.

While following a **differentiation strategy**, high margins might be achieved by offering tailor-made and highly complex services. However, this requires the corporation to understand what is valued by customers and to have a better sense and response to customer needs. As customer needs change, a corporation following a differentiation strategy may have to review these strategies continuously. A clear sign of an effective differentiation strategy is the continuity of good profit margins and the difficulty competitors have in keeping up.

A logistics company following a differentiation strategy might create an environment in which the actual or perceived cost for a buyer of changing the source of supply of a service is high. In these circumstances, the customer might depend on the supplier for particular services, or the benefits of switching to another supplier might not be worth the cost or risk. A port or maritime shipping company that offers unique and integrated tailor-made services to its customers has more chances of limiting the footloose behavior of that customer and, as such, increases customer loyalty. If a company succeeds in becoming an industry standard, other businesses typically have to conform to that standard to remain competitive.

In following a differentiation strategy, corporations have to choose between a broad differentiation strategy across a **specific market or a focused strategy**. New ventures often start in a very focused market. Maintaining a highly focused strategy might not be feasible in the long run, as customers might not be willing to pay a higher price. Therefore, corporations might opt at a specific moment to lower the price while maintaining differentiating features (i.e. a move towards a 'normal' differentiation strategy).

## 3 THE ROLE OF THIRD-PARTY LOGISTICS SERVICES

Innovative corporations are taking a broader view of the business segments they seek to control and manage. As the ambition of global corporations often exceeds their capability and resources, outsourcing of logistics functions can be an important strategic option. **Outsourcing** enables a producer to transform fixed costs into variable costs, freeing internal resources for investments in core activities. Four basic forms of outsourcing can be distinguished concerning supply chain management:

- The **outsourcing of the production of components**. Large production units are replaced by a network of suppliers organized on a global or local scale (global sourcing and local sourcing). Global corporations increasingly develop long-term relationships with a limited number of suppliers based on mutual trust (co-makership).
- The outsourcing of **value-added logistics** (VAL). VAL implies that the production and distribution parts of a supply chain become truly integrated into one. For example, production companies in the high-tech industry increasingly outsource logistics manipulations to their products towards the distribution centers located near the consumer markets. As such, a large part of the value creation in the supply chain is transferred to logistics service providers. VAL might even include secondary manufacturing activities like systems assembly, testing, and software installation.
- The **outsourcing of transportation, warehousing, and distribution**. Third-party transportation is already widespread, but warehousing and distribution activities have also become key outsourcing businesses. The observed outsourcing trend encourages logistics service providers to engage in supply chain management.
- The **re-engineering of supply chain processes** (including customer order management, procurement, production planning, and distribution) to enhance performance typically results in collaborative networks with logistics partners.

Increasing customer demands drive the **3PL (Third Party Logistics) service industry** forward.

> *A **3PL** is an asset-based company that offers logistics and supply chain management services to its customers (manufacturers and retailers). It commonly owns assets such as distribution centers and transport modes.*

The need for a wider array of global services and integrated services and capabilities (design, build and operate) triggered a shift from transportation-based 3PLs to warehousing and distribution providers. At the same time, this trend opened the market to innovative forms of non-asset-based logistics service providers, leading to the development of **4PL (Fourth Party Logistics)**.

> *A **4PL** is a supply chain integrator that assembles and manages the resources, capabilities, and technology of its organization with complementary service providers to deliver a comprehensive supply chain solution. The competence of 4PLs lies in selecting, linking, and bundling service providers and aligning all concerned stakeholders in the supply chain.*

Whereas a 3PL service provider typically invests in warehouses and transport assets, a 4PL service provider restricts its scope to IT-based supply chain design. Consultants and IT firms help 3PLs and 4PLs expand into new markets and to become full-service logistics providers. Notwithstanding the emergence of non-asset-based 4PLs, the role of 3PLs in logistics markets remains strong. Hence, asset-based full-service providers increasingly develop their own IT control systems. Moreover, many logistics users prefer to keep control of the design of the supply chain in-house instead of being dependent on 4PLs, mainly for the purpose of maintaining their added value (Figure 1.14).

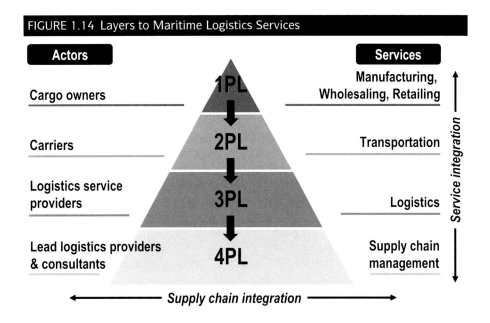

FIGURE 1.14 Layers to Maritime Logistics Services

## 4 FUNCTIONAL INTEGRATION IN THE LOGISTICS INDUSTRY

The logistics industry is subject to integration forms aiming to improve its scale, scope, and market reach. Functional integration involves horizontal consolidation and vertical integration strategies creating a logistics market consisting of a wide variety of service providers ranging from megacarriers to local niche operators (Box 1.3). Not only does the geographic coverage of the players differ (from global to local), but major differences can also be observed in **focus** (generalist versus specialist), the **service offering** (from single service to one-stop-shop), and **asset-orientation** (asset-based versus non-asset-based).

### 4.1 Vertical integration

Globalization and outsourcing open new windows of opportunities for shipping lines, forwarders, terminal operators, and other logistics service providers and transport operators. Manufacturers are looking for global logistics packages rather than just shipping or forwarding. Global logistics is the dominant paradigm where most transport chains have responded by providing new value-added services in an integrated package through a **vertical integration along supply chains**.

The level of vertical integration has increased in the past decades. In a conventional situation, the majority of logistics activities were performed by different entities ranging from maritime shipping lines, shipping and customs agents, freight forwarders, and rail and trucking companies. Regulations often prevented multimodal ownership, leaving the system fragmented. With an increasing level of functional integration, many intermediate steps in the transport chain have been removed. Mergers and acquisitions among companies performing specific functions in the supply chains have permitted the emergence of large logistics operators that control many segments of the supply chain. The term **megacarrier** refers to a highly integrated logistics service provider, such as a 3PL or 4PL. These corporations can, in principle, meet the requirements of many shippers to have a single contact point on a regional or even global level, known as a one-stop-shop.

Technology has also played an important role in this process, namely in IT (control of the process), intermodal integration, and synchromodality (control of the flows). Vertical integration increases competition between corporations with different core businesses. For example, a railway company getting involved in global logistics (e.g. DB Schenker) becomes a competitor of established logistics service providers. A shipping line entering the terminal operator business engages in a competitive relationship with independent terminal operators unless some form of partnership is formed. As such, vertical integration leads to overlaps in the activity portfolio of corporations, particularly when they share the ambition to become 'one-stop shops' in global logistics. While vertical integration serves as a business model in the logistics and transport market, external economic shocks and poor market conditions can swing the pendulum towards de-integration. For example, the financial-economic crisis of 2008–2009 forced several corporations to reassess their vertical integration strategies in order to secure enough liquidity for their core activities. In some cases, this led to divestment and a re-focus on core activities.

## 4.2 Horizontal integration

Mergers and acquisitions (M&A) shape the contemporary business environment, not only between different types of corporations (vertical integration) but also between corporations involved in the same type of activity or core business (**horizontal integration**). Several waves of horizontal integration activity have resulted in a high market consolidation level in the logistics industry. Many of the top 3PL companies were involved in large-scale M&A activities.

M&A activity is not only driven by corporations searching for take-over candidates and the necessity to improve competitiveness and long-term survival. In addition, corporations that have decided to divest aspects of their portfolio are, as a consequence, looking for buyers. The logistics challenges emerging from mergers and acquisitions include the proliferation of customer service policies to multiple, overlapping distribution networks and infrastructure overcapacity.

### Box 1.3 Functional integration of maritime supply chains

*The efficiency of freight distribution is linked with the level of functional integration along supply chains (Figure 1.15). It is dependent not only on physical flows generated by its various functions (manufacturing, physical distribution, after-sales service) but on how well each element is linked with the others. Since transportation is a core component in this process of functional integration and*

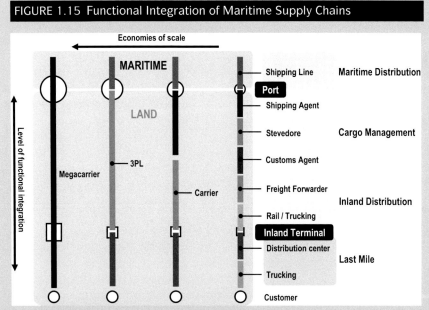

FIGURE 1.15 Functional Integration of Maritime Supply Chains

Source: Rodrigue (2006).

*economies of scale in distribution, the emergence of 'megacarriers' involved in numerous segments of the transport chain can be seen as a logical process.*

*In a push logistics context, freight distribution was highly fragmented and was assumed by different entities ranging from maritime shipping lines, shipping and customs agents, freight forwarders, and rail and trucking companies Moving freight from one part of the supply chain to the other involved additional costs and delays, either administrative or physical (namely intermodal) in nature.*

*Mergers and acquisitions have permitted the emergence of large logistics operators that control many segments of the supply chain, a process supported by the development of economies of scale in distribution. Carriers can offer comprehensive services, including cargo handling and information processing. Technology also plays a significant role in this process, with information technologies enabling better control of the process and intermodal integration enabling better control of the flows. Another significant outcome has been that maritime and land distribution systems have become closely integrated, with some transport companies involved in both.*

*The control of the supply chain through functional integration challenges derived demand as the concerned actors (3PLs and megacarriers) can anticipate and regulate freight flows. These integrators behave in a manner reflecting that they are not responding to a derived demand, but with a view to controlling their respective supply chains and answering the needs of their customers, if not actually shaping them, or at least the time sequence at which they are serviced.*

## 4.3 E-fulfilment and e-commerce

The rise of 4PLs and related online players triggered a whole range of e-market business models with proper functionalities, often with mixed success. Acquiring critical mass seems to be the main obstacle. The e-business environment creates **new distribution requirements** in terms of e-fulfillment. The growth of e-fulfillment and e-commerce affected B2B (business-to-business) activity and boosted the online transactions at the levels of B2C (business-to-consumer), C2B (consumer-to-business), and C2C (customer-to-customer). E-commerce increasingly shapes how people shop for goods. It has become an important tool for small and large businesses worldwide, not only to sell to customers but also to engage them with efficient delivery services. Information system quality, service quality, and users' satisfaction are key in this respect. E-commerce offers more opportunities to reach out to customers worldwide and cut down unnecessary intermediate links, reducing the cost price. The vast amount of customer-related data allows e-commerce firms to achieve a high degree of personal customization and targeted marketing. Data integrity and (cyber)security are pressing issues for the e-commerce market.

The growth of e-fulfillment and e-commerce activity has considerable implications for supply chain management practices. Online markets and retailers have new strategies and distribution channels to fill orders and deliver products using specific distribution centers and networks that differ from traditional distribution channels and systems. Small companies usually control their logistic operation because they do not have the ability to hire a third party. Most large corporations hire a fulfillment service that takes care of their logistic requirements. However, in recent years large e-commerce firms, such as Amazon and Alibaba, have developed a keen interest in controlling e-commerce logistics. The volume they command is starting to have notable impacts on port-centric logistics systems.

## 5 INFORMATION TECHNOLOGIES AND DIGITAL TRANSFORMATION

Outsourcing logistics activities in a wide variety of economic sectors has led to a surge in 3PL and the creation of very large logistics groups. Supply chains need to be supported by a wide range of advanced communication tools and robust, reliable, and cost-effective transportation networks to be set up and operated by IT-supported logistics service providers. Competition between logistics service providers is no longer focused only on services to the cargo flows. Advanced services in the management of information flows are key to gaining a competitive advantage. These advanced services are increasingly aimed at offering supply chain visibility to customers in terms of reliability through advanced tracking and tracing, environmental impact measurement (e.g. carbon footprint calculator), security risks, and related event management. In particular, modern IT systems are geared towards improving channel visibility in three core areas:

- **Improved product flow visibility** is achieved through real-time information presented based on user needs with the ability to re-plan and re-direct product flows.

- **Event management** forecasts events, has real-time information on actual events, and generates proactive notifications of failures.
- **Performance management** is supported by quantitative carrier and asset performance data, performance accountability, and continuous performance improvement opportunities.

Supply chains are evolving towards an **open global logistic system** founded on physical, digital, and operational interconnectivity through encapsulation, interfaces, and protocol design. It aims to move, store, realize, supply, and use physical objects throughout the world in an economically, environmentally, socially efficient, and sustainable manner. It will require the **standardization** of internationally recognized consignment codes to communicate throughout the physical reality of the chain. The various transport systems and IT platforms are beginning to integrate horizontally and vertically to become an open IT infrastructure for the logistics sector. In other words, the globally independently developed logistics networks will have to be connected, enabling shippers to have an overall view.

Intermediary forwarding agents are the most at risk from new technology providers or business models unless they adapt, such as in offering supply chain visibility. Differentiation and cost optimization can be achieved through **improved online customer experience and automation**. Major freight forwarders and third-party logistics providers thus have the responsibility to develop innovative new booking and logistics platforms in order to mitigate potential threats coming from within or outside the logistics sector. New technology-driven companies, particularly those within the e-commerce space, are likely to enter or have already entered the transport and logistics arena, giving them a competitive edge or a chance to see a competitive opportunity to bring new models to the market.

Forwarders are challenged to opt for **collaborative technology-driven networks**, and freight forwarders need to recruit new talent outside of the logistics sector, including from IT-driven potential disruptors. Integrating new business approaches and models in the relatively conservative freight forwarding businesses requires new perspectives.

The small and mid-size shipper, spot shipment, and LCL (less than container load) segment will move online extensively through web-based forwarding services (from instant quote and booking, up to payment) as well as **online sales platforms** that dynamically push public and customer-specific rates. These platforms may only target and penetrate specific markets where a certain degree of automation can be achieved. Customer profiling and market segmentation will be at the core of the business model of these online sales channels. Large shippers will have access to more procurement options, benchmarking, and insight capabilities. Large exporters and importers will continue to tender their sea-freight (port-to-port or port-to-rail ramp) and land transport directly with their core carriers and with their forwarders for some part of their volumes. This practice will be available to many at a lower transactional cost with more flexibility using tailored e-tools. **E-forwarding and spot procurement** will complement traditional contract-based procurement channels.

# Chapter 1.3 Ports and container shipping

*Maritime services vary with the commodities carried. In liner shipping, individual maritime services are combined to form extensive shipping networks in which seaports play a pivotal role as high connectivity hubs.*

## 1 AN ASSET-BASED INDUSTRY

The container shipping industry consists of **shipping companies** transporting containerized goods overseas via regular liner services as their core activity. Container liner services are focused explicitly on transporting a limited range of standardized load units, mainly the 20-foot dry cargo container or TEU of 20 feet long and the 40-foot dry cargo container or FEU (40' long). High-cube containers are similar in structure to standard containers but taller. In contrast to standard containers, which have a maximum height of 8'6", high-cube containers are 9'6" tall. For the most part, high-cube containers are 40 feet long but are sometimes made as 45-foot containers. Occasionally, slightly diverging container units are also loaded on container vessels, such as tank containers, open-top containers, and flat rack containers. The diversity in unit loads in the container shipping industry is low due to uniformity when stacking containers below and on the deck of specialized container vessels (cellular containerships where each cell is designed to store a container).

> *Stopford defines a liner service is a fleet of ships, with common ownership or management, which provide a fixed service, at regular intervals, between designated ports and offer transport to any goods in the hinterland served by those ports and ready for transit by their sailing dates.*

Container shipping is a **highly capital-intensive industry** where some assets are owned, others are leased, and where there exists a wide variability in cost bases. Asset management is a key component of the operational and commercial success of container shipping lines since they are primarily asset-based. Common asset management decisions for shipping lines include equipment management to reduce downtime and operating costs, increase the useful service life and the residual value of vessels, increase equipment safety, reduce potential liabilities, and reduce costs through better capacity management.

Container shipping lines are particularly challenged to develop an effective **asset management program** for the fleet they own or operate (Figure 1.16):

- **Vessel lifecycle management** includes the procurement, acquisition, deployment, and disposal of container vessels.
- **Fleet capacity management** is complex given the inflexible nature of vessel capacity in the short run due to fixed timetables, the seasonality effects in the shipping business, and cargo imbalances on trade routes.

Shipping lines seek gains in market share with capacity usually added as additional loops (in large segments) to existing services, which incurs high fixed costs. For example, 10–11 ships are needed to operate one regular liner service on the Europe–Far East trade. Each of the post-Panamax container vessels has

## FIGURE 1.16 Asset Management Domains in Container Shipping

**Lifecycle Management**

- Ship and container assets
- Purchase / ordering
- Deployment
- Performance measurement
- Maintenance
- Disposal (second-hand market, scrapping)

**Cost Management**

- Total cost of ownership and operation
- Ship/box finance
- Depreciation / amortization
- Decision on flag state (ship registry)
- Operational, financial and fiscal accounting
- Location and modalities of ship management

**Contract Management**

- Leases / charter parties (C/P)
- Warranties
- Service-level agreements
- Outsourcing of services

**Risk Management**

- Safety / security (assets, people, IT)
- Regulatory compliance

a typical newbuilding price ranging from USD 100 to 150 million depending on the unit capacity of the ship and the market situation in the shipbuilding industry at the time of the vessel order. On average, container shipping lines charter about half of the vessels from third-party ship owners. Ship chartering is a particularly common practice for mid-size containerships in the range of 1,000 to 3,000 TEU.

Container shipping lines also face large investments in their **container fleets**. For example, a container carrier operating regular service on the Asia–Europe trade with ten vessels of 18,000 TEU needs a container fleet of at least 360,000 TEU to support the service. Container shipping lines and other transport operators typically own 55% to 60% of the total global container equipment assets, while the remainder is leased from specialized companies.

Despite sustained growth brought by containerization, container carriers tend to underperform financially compared to other logistics sectors (Box 1.4). This weaker performance is linked to the combination of **capital-intensive operations and high risks** associated with revenues. The large investments in assets and the fixed nature of the liner service schedules, even if cargo volumes are too low to fill the vessel, lie at the core of the risk profile in the container liner shipping industry. High commercial and operational risks are associated with deploying a fixed fleet capacity within a fixed schedule between a set of ports of call at both ends of a trade route (Figure 1.17).

The deployment of containerships is following three separate trends:

- **Technical**. Following the principle of economies of scale and ongoing demand from international trade, the deployed capacity has doubled between 2006 and 2016. This is particularly reflected in the size of the largest containership.
- **Geographical**. The number of container ports being called to has remained relatively stable, implying that port forelands are well established, if not mature, in the majority of regions.
- **Operational**. In a direct relationship with technical trends, operations trends show a decline of direct connections, weekly calls, and the number of shipping services as well as shipping lines. This is illustrative of the segmentation of services between deepsea services and feeder services.

Unused capacity cannot be stored and represents missed revenue opportunities. Once large and expensive liner services are set up, the pressure is to fill

**FIGURE 1.17  Trends in Containership Deployment, 2006–2020**

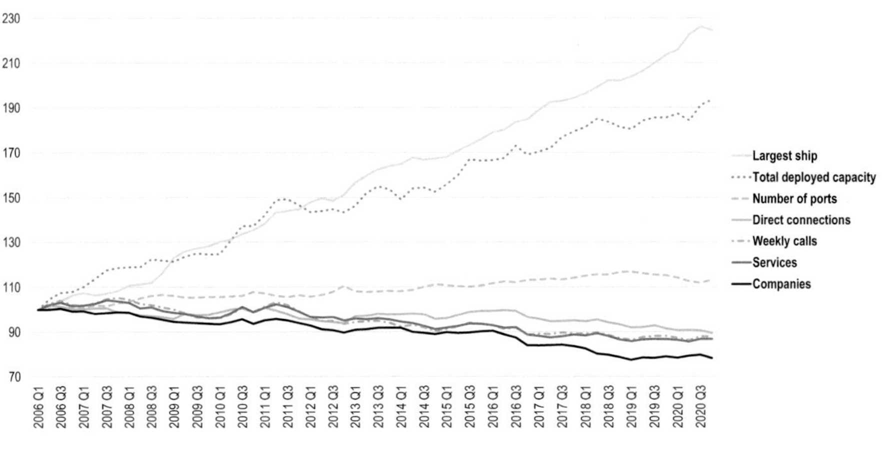

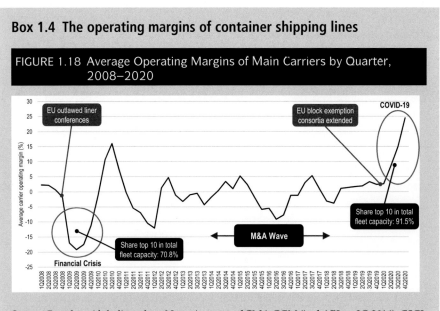

Source: UNCTAD and MDS Transmodal. Note: 2006=100.

the ships with cargo. When there is an oversupply of vessels in the market, the high fixed costs and product perishability give shipping lines incentives to fill vessels at a marginal cost, often leading to downward freight rates in the market and direct operational losses on the trades considered. Since the financial crisis of 2008–2009, the shipping industry has undertaken strategies aiming at increasing operating margins, mainly through alliances and capacity management.

## Box 1.4  The operating margins of container shipping lines

**FIGURE 1.18  Average Operating Margins of Main Carriers by Quarter, 2008–2020**

Source: Based on Alphaliner data. Note: Average of CMA CGM (incl APL to 2Q 2016), CSCL (to 1Q 2016), COSCO (from 3Q 2018), Evergreen, Hanjin (to 3Q 2016), Hapag-Lloyd (incl CSAV to 2014), HMM, Maersk, ONE (from 2Q 2018, formerly K-Line, MOL and NYK), Wan Hai, Yang Ming and Zim.

The **2008–2009 financial crisis** dramatically impacted profitability in the liner shipping market. Various analyses underlined an overall operating loss in 2009 of more than USD 20 billion. The industry average in terms of operating margin fluctuated between -17% and -19% in the first three quarters of 2009. The poor financial situation of many carriers led to an array of bail-out and debt restructuring programs. Many liner companies resorted to raising capital to strengthen balance sheets and seize opportunities or simply to survive.

With the **outlawing of liner conferences** in Europe after October 2008, market-related information about capacity deployment, demand/supply dynamics, and pricing of liner services became scarcer. Therefore, there was **no longer a stabilizing mechanism** in terms of freight rates and joint capacity management. Existing strategic alliances among shipping lines at that time (i.e. New World Alliance, Grand Alliance, and CKYH alliance) were not able to roll out effective capacity management programs to significantly reduce fleet capacity in line with the observed drops in demand. Container shipping entered a period of depressed freight rates partly due to poor capacity management and the lack of any rationalization in the industry. Major M&As only started in 2014, and the bankruptcy of Hanjin took place in 2016.

During the **COVID-19 pandemic**, carriers resorted to effective capacity management. Despite the pandemic, shipping lines and their alliances (i.e. The Alliance, Ocean Alliance, and 2M) maintained network integrity and resorted to **blanked sailings** to deal with declining demand in the first half of 2020. In April/May 2020, carriers were withdrawing up to 20% of their network capacity on the main trade lanes and idling more than 2.7 million TEU of fleet capacity, or more than 11% of the world container fleet. In the late Summer of 2020, shipping lines drastically reduced the number of blank sailings to accommodate the demand growth: the share of idle vessels in total fleet capacity decreased from 11.6% in May 2020 to only 1.8% in October 2020. All major carriers posted positive operating margins in 2020, in contrast to the 2008–2009 financial crisis (Figure 1.18).

In late 2020 and 2021, the **strong demand peak** on the Europe-Far East and trans-Pacific trade routes resulted in vessel capacity shortages and severe box availability issues. The demand/supply imbalance resulted in port congestion, box rollings, ship deviations and a historically low schedule integrity. All these factors combined led to sharp increases in container freight rates and carriers' operating margins.

## 2  FREIGHT RATES AND SURCHARGES

The **revenue base** of container shipping lines consists of **freight rates** collected from the shippers or their representatives for the maritime transport of containerized cargo and is mostly complemented by a set of **surcharges**. All-in ocean freight rates have fluctuated significantly since 2009, as exemplified by the Shanghai Containerized Freight Index and other similar indices such as the World Container Index (WCI) or the China Containerized Freight Index (CCFI). Also, contract container freight rates are influenced by the balance of power between shippers and shipping lines in rate negotiations. Customers generating large cargo volumes tend to have better leverage.

## Box 1.5  Shanghai Containerized Freight Index (SCFI) and other freight rate indices

*Several metrics or freight indices exist that can be used for benchmarking spot rates and trends in the container market, for settling container derivative contracts, and in the context of Index Linked Container Contracts (ILCCs). ILCCs are long term freight contracts that allow the freight rates to fluctuate with market conditions based on agreed mechanisms (such as an upper and or lower limit for the rate, dampeners, time-lagged adjustments, etc.). The mechanism for this fluctuation needs to be based on trusted and independent sources which publish metrics/indices. The Shanghai Containerized Freight Index (SCFI) is such a metric. Another example of a metric on the freight market is the World Container Index (WCI) assessed by Drewry. The WCI provides weekly assessments of container freight rates, daily forward price estimates and a bank of historical price movements.*

*The SCFI moves up and down based on the weekly spot rates of the Shanghai export container transport market based on data compiled from 15 different shipping routes. The SCFI is published for each of these routes, but there is also a comprehensive index covering all routes. The SCFI's spot rate fluctuates not on the basis of real-time rates, but on what carriers intend to charge. The SCFI is one of the metrics or indices exporters and shipping companies can use to trade derivatives against, which in theory would allow them to mitigate the extreme volatility in the freight market. While this was one of the primary goals behind the index's creation, the SCFI failed to create a proper derivatives market, but that hasn't stopped industry analysts from tracking it closely. The much broader China Containerized Freight Index (CCFI) is based on the price of containers leaving from all major ports in China, and is a composite of spot rates and contractual rates. Spot rates can deviate from long-term contract rates. By comparison, roughly 75% of the global market runs on contracted rates, so while the SCFI is useful, it is not necessarily an accurate reflection of the price being paid by the majority of shippers.*

Freight rates can vary greatly depending on the economic characteristics (e.g. cargo availability, imbalances and the competitive situation among shipping lines) and technological characteristics (e.g. maximum allowable vessel size) of the trade route concerned. The existence of large **cargo imbalances** on a number of trade routes has a significant impact on pricing. Trade imbalances also affect shippers in their ability to access equipment. In order to guarantee space, shippers may double book their container loads, leading to missed bookings for shipping lines. Container liner companies can react by imposing surcharges in the form of a 'no show' fee.

**Base freight rates or Freight All Kinds** (FAK) rates are applicable in most trades. These freight rates are lump sum rates for a container on a specific origin-destination pair irrespective of its contents and irrespective of the quantity of cargo stuffed into the box by the shipper. On top of these base freight rates, liner companies charge separately for additional items through various surcharges. Still, some (larger) customers receive all-in prices. The most common surcharges include:

- Fuel surcharges (Bunker Adjustment Factor or BAF, but other terms are also used).
- Surcharges related to the exchange rate risk (Currency Adjustment Factor or CAF).
- Terminal handling charges (THC).
- Port congestion surcharges.
- Piracy surcharge.
- Surcharge for dangerous cargo.
- Various container equipment-related surcharges, such as demurrage charges, detention charges, equipment handover charges, equipment imbalance surcharge, a special equipment additional for open-top container, and heavy lift.

Most carriers have developed a broad array of possible mandatory and optional charges and surcharges. In order to improve transparency and facilitate the ease of doing business, shipping lines have made efforts to simplify surcharge systems, as exemplified by the steps taken by Maersk Line in 2013. Despite these efforts, the list of possible surcharges remains rather long.

> **Fuel surcharges** *aim to pass (part of) the fuel costs on to the customer through variable charges.*

Initially, fuel surcharges or BAFs were a percentage of the base freight rate levied only when the bunker price per ton was above a certain threshold value. In October 2008, after the lifting by the European Commission of the Block Exemption on anti-cartel rules for liner conferences, each shipping line had to set its fuel surcharges based on its own formula. Fuel surcharges tend to fluctuate greatly depending on bunker prices and the pricing strategy of the shipping line. In the second half of 2018, container shipping lines started to adjust fuel surcharges on a trade-by-trade basis ahead of the IMO deadline for introducing low sulfur fuel rules. As of 2020, a global sulfur cap of 0.5% was imposed on ship fuel.

The Currency Adjustment Factor (CAF, also known as the Currency Adjustment Charge or the Currency Surcharge) is usually a percentage of the basic freight rate (e.g. 8%). When the USD started to become more volatile in the 1960s and 1970s, liner conferences came up with tariff surcharges to ensure that they would continue to enjoy a more or less stable income in the currency of their own country. CAF and BAF have been contested by some shippers on the ground that the costs covered by these surcharges belong to the commercial risk of the entrepreneurial shipping line and should thus be included in the freight rate.

> **Terminal Handling Charges** *(THC) are a tariff charged by the shipping line to the shipper and which (should) cover (part or all of) the terminal handling costs, which the shipping line pays to the terminal operator.*

THC vary per shipping line and per country and are a negotiable item for large customers. The party who pays the THC at the port of loading and/or the port of discharge depends on the Incoterms used (Figure 1.19). The Incoterms 2020 have been developed by the International Chamber of Commerce and are the world's essential terms of trade for the sale of goods. They include EXW (Ex Works), FCA (Free Carrier), CPT (Carriage Paid To), CIP (Carriage

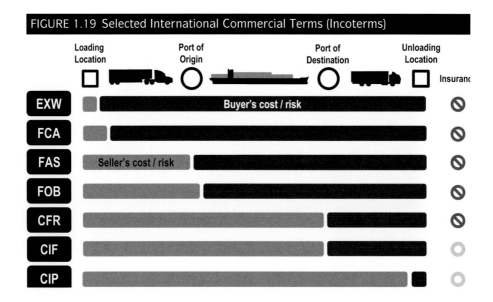

FIGURE 1.19 Selected International Commercial Terms (Incoterms)

and Insurance Paid To), DAP (Delivered at Place), DPU (Delivered at Place Unloaded), DDP (Delivered Duty Paid), FAS (Free Alongside Ship), FOB (Free On Board), CFR (Cost and Freight) and CIF (Cost Insurance and Freight). These terms all have exact meanings for the sale of goods around the world (Figure 1.19).

THC for exports are usually collected by shipping lines while releasing the Bill of Lading after completing export customs clearance procedures. Shipping lines usually collect the import THC at the time of issuing the delivery order to the consignee to take delivery of goods. THC may recover a major share of actual costs in some ports of call. In other ports, the applicable THC are higher than the actual container handling rates charged by the terminal operators, and are thus a revenue-making instrument for the carriers. Shippers might argue that THC are arbitrarily fixed and used as a revenue-making instrument, particularly when base freight rates are low. Carriers typically argue that THC are aimed at cost recovery and are not a profit center.

## 3  SCALE ENLARGEMENT IN VESSEL SIZE

The growing demand for maritime container transport has been met via **vessel upscaling**. The mid-1970s brought the first ships of over 2,000 TEU capacity. The Panamax vessel of 4,000 to 5,000 TEU (maximum dimensions for transit through the old Panama Canal locks) was introduced in the early 1990s. In 1988, APL was the first shipping line to deploy a post-Panamax vessel. In 1996, Maersk Line introduced the 'Regina Maersk' with a nominal vessel capacity of about 7,400 TEU. Consecutive rounds of scale increase led to the introduction of the 'Emma Maersk' in 2006, a containership that can hold more than 15,000 TEU and measures 397 m in length overall, with a beam of 56 m, and a commercial draft of 15.5 m. Since 2010, vessel capacity has been pushed beyond the 20,000 TEU mark (Figure 1.20). The introduction of the Triple E class (about 18,000 TEU) by Maersk Line in 2013 was followed by the even larger vessels

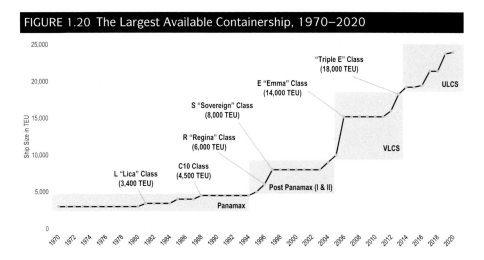

FIGURE 1.20 The Largest Available Containership, 1970–2020

of competing lines, such as COSCO Shipping (ships of up to 21,237 TEU), CMA CGM (up to 20,954 TEU), and OOCL (units of up to 21,413 TEU). The 18,000 TEU threshold was overtaken in 2014 and by 2017, ships above 20,000 TEU were available. The first ULCSs of 23,000 TEUs were delivered in 2019. As of September 2021, the world's largest container vessel was the Ever Ace, with close to 24,000 TEU. The introduction of ever-larger container vessels has resulted in an overall upscaling across the main east-west trade routes, with large vessels cascading to north-south routes.

In the early 2020s, the largest vessels of all operate at the Far East–Europe routes, also calling in ports in the Gulf and the Indian Sub-Continent (ISC) (Figure 1.21). North American ports also serve some of the largest container vessels in operation, with the biggest vessel of all those calling in North America having a 23,756 TEU capacity. A decade ago, in 2010, the maximum vessel size in all these regions of the world stood at less than 15,000 TEU. The biggest vessels do not call in the other regions of the world. The biggest container vessel calling in sub-Saharan Africa stands at 15,000 TEU capacity, in Latin America at a capacity slightly less than that (14,354 TEU) and in Oceania at 11,000 TEU. Yet, since 2010 the scale of the maximum container vessel calling has doubled in these regions of the world as well.

The increase in vessel size is not reflected in the maximum size vessel only. It has been accompanied by a cascading effect in the feeder market as well. As larger vessels call at major hubs, the feeder market is served by vessels that had been previously engaged in main maritime transportation routes, increasing the pressures on medium and small size container ports to adjust as well. Today, calls of post-Panamax size vessels take place in a large cluster of container ports in all the different parts of the world. Ports have to continuously adjust to this upscaling of operations in terms of both infrastructure and operations.

Large vessels come with **operational challenges** mainly related to port calls, terminal operations, and hinterland transport (Figure 1.22). Port and terminal-related factors are the main impediments to scale increases, such as terminal productivity, port congestion, nautical accessibility, berth length, and

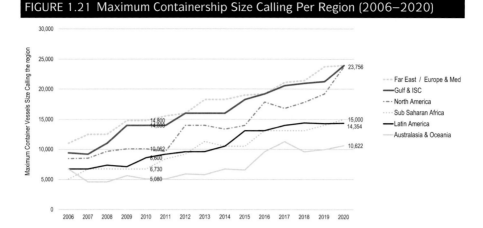

FIGURE 1.21  Maximum Containership Size Calling Per Region (2006–2020)

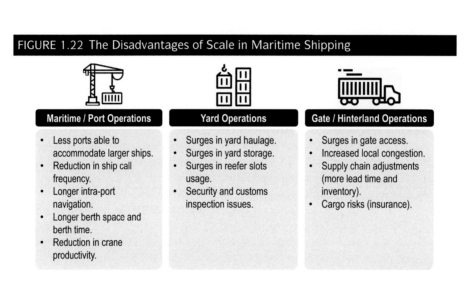

FIGURE 1.22  The Disadvantages of Scale in Maritime Shipping

| Maritime / Port Operations | Yard Operations | Gate / Hinterland Operations |
| --- | --- | --- |
| • Less ports able to accommodate larger ships. <br> • Reduction in ship call frequency. <br> • Longer intra-port navigation. <br> • Longer berth space and berth time. <br> • Reduction in crane productivity. | • Surges in yard haulage. <br> • Surges in yard storage. <br> • Surges in reefer slots usage. <br> • Security and customs inspection issues. | • Surges in gate access. <br> • Increased local congestion. <br> • Supply chain adjustments (more lead time and inventory). <br> • Cargo risks (insurance). |

turning circles. In the past decades, ports, terminals, and entire transport systems have been expanded and upgraded to accommodate increased ship size. Even large upstream seaports such as Antwerp and Hamburg adapted to the new imperatives brought by mega container vessels by expanding their terminal facilities. The revealed adaptive capacity of the port and terminal industry in terms of investments and productivity gains typically did not result in the penalization of larger vessels through port and terminal pricing. Simultaneously, advances in port productivity have resulted in disproportionately lower growth of port turnaround time as a function of vessel size. In other words, port authorities, terminal operators, and other actors in the chain have fully or partially absorbed the potential diseconomies of scale linked to larger vessels, thereby enabling shipping companies to pursue consecutive rounds of scale increases in vessel size.

In recent years, attention has been paid to **emission reductions and energy savings** associated with ship size. Scale increases in vessel size combined with advances in ship technology and slow steaming can decrease annual $CO_2$ emissions of the world containership fleet. Container shipping is increasingly confronted with stronger environmental considerations and stricter regulatory frameworks on ship emissions and energy efficiencies.

The focus of container carriers on larger vessels does not necessarily lead to a more stable market environment. Consecutive rounds of scale enlargements in vessel size have reduced the slot costs in container trades, but carriers have not always reaped the full benefits of economies of scale at sea (Box 1.6). The volatility of business cycles has more than once resulted in unstable cargo demand to shipping lines. Adding post-Panamax capacity can give a **short-term competitive edge** to the early mover, putting pressure on competing lines to upgrade their container fleet to avoid a unit cost disadvantage. A **boomerang effect** can result in overcapacity, impacting the margins of the industry, including the carrier who started the vessel scaling up round. Vessel lay-ups, order cancellations, slow steaming, and service suspensions are the primary tools used by shipping lines in an attempt to absorb overcapacity when it occurs.

---

### Box 1.6  The optimal container ship size

*The economic efficiency of ship size has been researched since the early 1970s. A seminal work by Jansson and Schneerson, published in 1982 pointed out that the optimal ship size represents a trade-off between the positive returns earned at sea (i.e. economies of size during the line-haul operation) and the negative returns accruing while in port (i.e. diseconomies of size during the handling operations in ports). In the late 1990s, numerous scholars demonstrated that port and terminal-related factors indeed have a large impact on the feasibility of deploying bigger vessels. Academic studies of that period seemed to agree that the 8,000 TEU ship was the optimal ship size for the Europe–Far East trade. The economies of size diminished very rapidly beyond the 5,000 TEU scale.*

*More recent research shows that economies of scale at sea do not stop at the 6,000, 8,000 or 10,000 TEU threshold as suggested in studies published 15 to 20 years ago. Economies of scale at sea seem not to have been fully exhausted, while ports, terminals and entire transport systems have been expanded and upgraded to significantly reduce possible diseconomies of scale in ports. In other words, one could argue that the potential diseconomies of scale linked to larger vessels have been fully or partially absorbed by port authorities, terminal operators and other actors in the chain (see righthand side of Figure 1.23), thereby enabling/facilitating shipping companies to pursue consecutive rounds of scale increases in vessel size. The further benefits of lower slot costs diminish as ships get larger, and savings might not even be (fully) realized. The effort necessary to prepare ports and terminals for ships of ever-increasing size is growing disproportionately. Supply chain risks related to bigger containerships could rise.*

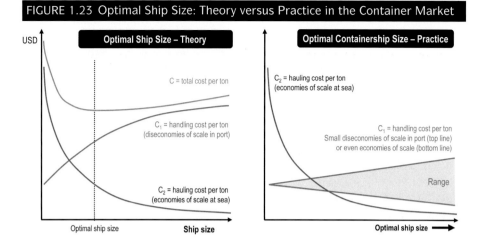

FIGURE 1.23 Optimal Ship Size: Theory versus Practice in the Container Market

## 4 HORIZONTAL INTEGRATION: OPERATIONAL AGREEMENTS AND M&A

Shipping lines view cooperation as one of the most effective ways of coping with a trade environment characterized by intense pricing pressure. Trade agreements such as **liner conferences** were prevalent until the European Commission outlawed this type of cooperation in October 2008 (Box 1.7). At present, the horizontal integration dynamics in the container shipping industry are based on **mergers and acquisitions** (M&A) and operational cooperation in many forms ranging from slot chartering and vessel sharing agreements to strategic alliances.

> *A slot chartering agreement (SCA) is a contract between partners who buy and sell a defined allocation (space, weight) on a vessel in general on a 'used' or 'unused' basis at an agreed price and for a minimum defined time period. In some cases, shipping lines engage in a slot exchange agreement.*
>   *A vessel sharing agreement (VSA) involves a limited number of shipping companies agreeing to operate a liner service along a specified route using a specified number of vessels. The partners do not necessarily each have an equal number of vessels. The capacity that each partner gets may vary from port to port and could depend on the number of vessels operated by the different partners.*

A vessel sharing agreement for one regular liner service is slightly different from that of an alliance. A vessel sharing agreement is usually dedicated to a particular trade route with terms and conditions specific to that route. In contrast, an alliance is more global and could include many different trade routes, usually under the same terms.

The first **strategic alliances** among shipping lines date back to the mid-1990s, which coincided with the introduction of the first vessels above 6,000 TEU on the Europe–Far East trade route (Figure 1.24). In 1997, about 70% of the services on the main east-west trades were supplied by the four main strategic alliances. As of 2020, three alliances were operational in the market:

## FIGURE 1.24 Alliances in Container Shipping, 1996–2020

| Q2 1996 | Q1 1998 | Q4 2001 | Q4 2005 | Q4 2009 | Q1 2012 | Q2 2015 | Q2 2017 | Q2 2020 |
|---|---|---|---|---|---|---|---|---|
| **GLOBAL ALLIANCE** APL, MOL, Nedlloyd, OOCL, MISC | **NEW WORLD ALL.** APL/NOL, MOL, HMM | **NWA** APL/NOL, MOL, HMM | **NWA** APL/NOL, MOL, HMM | **NWA** APL/NOL, MOL, HMM | **G6 ALLIANCE** APL/NOL, MOL, HMM, Hapag-Lloyd, NYK Line, OOCL | **G6 ALLIANCE** APL/NOL, MOL, HMM, Hapag-Lloyd, NYK Line, OOCL | **THE ALLIANCE** Hanjin, MOL, K-Line, NYK Line, Yang Ming, Hapag-Lloyd | **THE ALLIANCE** ONE, Yang Ming, HMM, Hapag-Lloyd |
| **GRAND ALLIANCE** Hapag-Lloyd, NYK Line, NOL, P&OCL | **GRAND ALLIANCE II** Hapag-Lloyd, NYK Line, P&O Nedlloyd, OOCL, MISC | **GRAND ALLIANCE II** Hapag-Lloyd, NYK Line, P&O Nedlloyd, OOCL, MISC | **GRAND ALLIANCE III** Hapag-Lloyd, NYK Line, OOCL, MISC | **GRAND ALLIANCE IV** Hapag-Lloyd, NYK Line, OOCL | **CYKH** Hanjin, K-Line, Yang Ming, COSCO | **CYKHE** Hanjin, K-Line, Yang Ming, COSCO, Evergreen | **OCEAN ALLIANCE** CMA CGM, COSCO, OOCL, Evergreen | **OCEAN ALLIANCE** CMA CGM, COSCO/OOCL, Evergreen |
| | **CYK ALLIANCE** K-Line, Yang Ming, COSCO | **CYKH** Hanjin, K-Line, Yang Ming, COSCO | **CYKH** Hanjin, K-Line, Yang Ming, COSCO | **CYKH** Hanjin, K-Line, Yang Ming, COSCO | **MSC/CMA CGM** MSC, CMA CGM | **2M ALLIANCE** MSC, Maersk Line | **2M ALLIANCE** MSC, Maersk Line | **2M ALLIANCE** MSC, Maersk Line/ Hamburg-Sud |
| | **UNITED ALLIANCE** Hanjin, Cho Yang, USAC | | | | | **OCEAN THREE** CMA CGM, China Shipping, UASC | | |
| **Maersk** Sea-Land | **Maersk** Sea-Land | | | | | | | |

| **Main Carriers Not Part of an Alliance** | | | | | | | | |
|---|---|---|---|---|---|---|---|---|
| | | Maersk SeaLand | Maersk Line | Maersk Line | Maersk Line | | | |
| MSC | MSC | MSC | MSC | MSC | | | | |
| CMA CGM | CMA CGM | CMA CGM | CMA CGM | CMA CGM | | | | |
| Evergreen | Evergreen | Evergreen | Evergreen | Evergreen | Evergreen | | | |

Source: Adapted from Notteboom and Haralambides (2020).

2M, Ocean Alliance, and THE Alliance. This represented an evolution from just five years earlier when four alliances were still active: 2M, Ocean Three, CKYHE, and G6. Alliance partnerships evolved due to mergers and acquisitions and the market exit of liner shipping companies, such as the bankruptcy of South Korean carrier Hanjin in 2016.

Alliances can also be affected by the exit of carriers. For example, Malaysian carrier MISC left the Grand Alliance in the late 2000s, and Hanjin became the first large carrier to go bankrupt due to continued weak market conditions. Initially, many of the largest carriers did not opt for alliance membership. These firms reached a sufficient scale to benefit from the same economies of scale and scope that strategic alliances offer. Four of the top six carriers, which are Maersk Line, MSC, CMA CGM, and Evergreen, are notable examples. In comparison, the remaining two top-six carriers (i.e. COSCO and Hapag-Lloyd) have always opted for alliance membership despite the scale of their activities. Several shipping lines, such as Evergreen, initially did not participate in alliances due to commercial independence and flexibility. However, in more recent years, even the largest shipping companies have resorted to joining alliances as a competitive strategy and to increase margins. The case of Evergreen demonstrates that even outsiders have had to pursue alliance membership.

The main incentives for alliance formation relate to achieving a critical mass in the scale of operation, exploring new markets, enhancing global reach, improving fleet deployment, and spreading risks associated with investments in large container vessels. Strategic alliances provide their members with easy access to more loops or services with relatively low-cost implications and allow them to share terminals to cooperate in many areas at sea and ashore, thereby achieving cost savings in the end. Alliance members engage increasingly in vessel sharing agreements with outside carriers. As such, individual shipping lines show an increased level of pragmatism when setting up partnerships with other carriers on specific trade routes.

> **Box 1.7  Conferences in liner shipping**
>
> *A liner conference is defined by UNCTAD's Convention on a Code of Conduct for Liner Conferences as 'a group of two or more vessel-operating carriers which provides international liner services for the carriage of cargo on a particular route or routes within specified geographical limits and which has an agreement or arrangement, whatever its nature, within the framework of which they operate under uniform or common freight rates and any other agreed conditions concerning the provision of liner services'. Liner conferences are essentially trade agreements between shipping lines, which could legally fix prices and coordinate capacity on their respective trade lanes. Examples of liner conferences that existed until late 2008 include the Far Eastern Freight Conference (FEFC) and Trans-Atlantic Conference Agreement (TACA).*
>
> *In Europe, liner conferences have long benefited from the broad block exemption from the usual ban on restrictive agreements given to traditional maritime liner conferences (EC Regulation no. 4056/86). However, the European Union repealed EC Regulation No. 4056/86 in 2008 through Council Regulation 1419/2006. This ended the anti-trust immunity that liner conferences had long enjoyed and thus made an end to the liner conference era concerning Europe.*

The three alliances (2M, THE Alliance, and Ocean Alliance) play a key role in capacity management on the main east-west routes. Alliances have been under legal scrutiny by the EU recently. In 2009, the EU adopted a Consortia Block Exemption Regulation (Commission Regulation (EC) No 906/2009), allowing shipping companies to operate joint liner shipping services. This regulation was prolonged in 2014 by five years and was due to expire on 25 April 2020. After a lengthy and heated public consultation launched in September 2018, the EU decided in late 2019 to prolong the regulation for another four years till 25 April 2024.

The shipping business has been subject to several waves of mergers and acquisitions (M&A). The number of acquisitions rose from three cases in 1993 to 13 in 1998 before peaking at 18 in 2006. The main M&A events included the merger between P&O Container Line and Nedlloyd in 1997, the merger between CMA and CGM in 1999, and the take-over by Maersk of Sea-Land in 1999 and P&O Nedlloyd in 2005. The economic crisis of late 2008 had an impact on the market structure. There was no major M&A activity in liner shipping between October 2008 and early 2014, but a new wave of acquisitions and mergers appeared inevitable in the medium term. The most recent wave in carrier consolidation started in the mid-2010s.

Shipping lines opt for mergers and acquisitions to obtain a larger size, secure growth, and benefit from scale advantages. Other motives relate to gaining instant access to markets and distribution networks, obtaining access to new technologies, or diversifying the asset base. Acquisitions typically feature some pitfalls associated with the internationalization of the maritime industry: cultural differences, overestimated synergies, and high expenses concerning the integration of departments. Still, acquisitions make sense in liner shipping as the maritime industry is mature because entry barriers are relatively high due to the investment required and the development of the customer base. For example, through a series of major acquisitions, Maersk Line increased its market share substantially and made strategic adjustments to secure its competitive advantage on key trade routes. In contrast to Maersk

Line, MSC reached the number two position in the world ranking of container lines based on organic or internal growth.

The liner shipping industry has witnessed a concentration trend in slot capacity control, mainly as a result of M&A activity. The top 20 carriers controlled 89.7% of the world's container vessel capacity in April 2019. This figure amounted to about 83% in late 2009, 56% in 1990, and only 26% in 1980. The consolidation trend has raised concerns about an overly concentrated market and potential oligopolistic behavior of the large carriers and alliances between them. Therefore, M&A activity and alliance formation in liner shipping is under scrutiny by competition authorities worldwide. Alliances and carrier consolidation have their full impact on inter-port competition, given the large container volumes and associated bargaining power.

## 5 VERTICAL INTEGRATION: EXTENDING THE SCOPE OF OPERATIONS

In response to low margins in shipping and customer demand for door-to-door and one-stop shopping logistics services, shipping lines may extend the reach of their activities to other parts of the supply chain (Figure 1.25). Over recent decades, the largest container lines have shown a keen interest in developing dedicated terminal capacity to control costs and operational performance, improve profitability, and as a measure to cope with poor vessel schedule integrity. For example, Maersk Line's parent company, AP Moller-Maersk, operates many container terminals through its subsidiary APM Terminals. CMA CGM, MSC, Evergreen, and Cosco are among the shipping lines fully or partly controlling terminal capacity worldwide. Independent global terminal operators such as Hutchison Ports, PSA, and DP World are increasingly hedging risks by setting up dedicated terminal joint ventures in cooperation with shipping lines and strategic alliances. The above developments have given rise to growing complexity in terminal ownership structures and partnership arrangements.

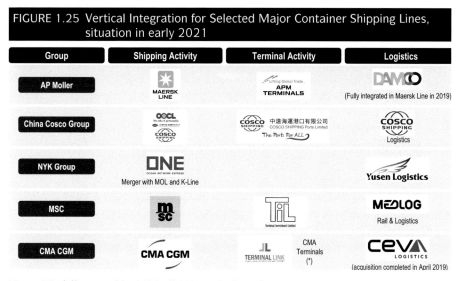

FIGURE 1.25 Vertical Integration for Selected Major Container Shipping Lines, situation in early 2021

Notes: TIL fully owned by MSC till 2013, stake brought to 60% in May 2019. Other shareholders are Global Infrastructure Partners (GIP) and GIC Private Limited, a Singaporean Sovereign Wealth Fund; (*) Terminals controlled by CMA Terminals were transferred to Terminal Link in late 2019.

The scope of extension of several shipping lines goes **beyond terminal operations** to include inland transport and logistics. Many shipping lines are **developing door-to-door services** to get a stronger grip on the routing of inland container flows. Some shipping lines **enhance network integration** through structural or ad hoc co-ordination with independent inland transport operators and logistics service providers. They do not own inland transport equipment. Instead, they use the services of reliable, independent inland carriers on a (long-term) contract base. Other shipping lines combine a strategy of selective investment in key supporting activities (e.g. agency services or distribution centers) with sub-contracting of less critical services. With a few exceptions (e.g. CEVA Logistics as part of CMA CGM, Medlog as part of MSC, and Damco, now fully integrated with Maersk Line), the management of pure logistics services is done by subsidiaries that share the same mother company as the shipping line but operate independently of liner shipping operations. Another group of shipping lines is increasingly active in the management of hinterland flows. The focus is now on the efficient synchronization of inland distribution capacities with port capacities.

Shipping lines face important challenges to improve inland logistics further. Competition with the logistics service provider and freight forwarding options remains fierce since they have a broader and more established market base on which to offer their services. The logistics requirements of customers (e.g. late bookings, peaks in equipment demand) typically lead to peak activity levels and high inland logistics costs. Given the mounting challenges in inland logistics, shipping lines that succeed in achieving better management of inland logistics can secure an important cost advantage compared to rivals.

Many shipping lines are also heavily focusing on digital transformation. Through investments and initiatives in digital infrastructure and services, shipping lines are aiming for the creation of value-adding activities in the following areas:

- The **optimization of operations** by using data for the real-time network leads to bunker fuel cost savings. Other forms of operational optimization include automated vessel stowage planning, the planning of container repairs, the repositioning of empty containers, and the predictive maintenance of vessels, containers, and other shipping assets.
- The development of advanced **commercial decision-making instruments** by using data to target customers and optimize the cargo mix within restrictions (e.g. dangerous goods), generate transparency in the supply chains of the customers, and develop intelligent pricing engines.
- The development of new services that can **generate new revenue streams**. Examples include consultancy and advisory services related to logistics chains, the aggregation and selling of trade data, or the commercialization of weather data collected by vessels navigating the open seas.

Shipping lines are setting up cooperation schemes to support digital transformation. For example, Maersk, MSC, Hapag-Lloyd, and ONE launched a digital container platform in 2019. This **Digital Container Shipping Association** (DCSA), whose members are currently responsible for 70% of global container trade, has been established to set standards for the digitalization of container shipping to overcome the lack of a common foundation for technical interfaces and data. The neutral and non-profit association is open to all ocean carriers who wish to join. DSCA interacts with other associations and organizations such as the United Nations (i.e. Rules for Electronic Data Interchange for Administration, Commerce and Transport or UN/EDIFACT), the International Organization for Standardization (ISO), the Blockchain in Transport Alliance (BITA), and OpenShipping.org, which offers an open-source standard for global shipping. In late 2020, DSCA published its new data and process standards for the creation and use of **electronic bills of lading** (eBL). This is the first step in a multi-year eDocumentation initiative to deliver standards to enable the digitalization of end-to-end container shipping documentation.

## 6  CONTAINER SERVICES AND NETWORKS

### 6.1  Container service network patterns

When designing their networks, shipping lines implicitly have to make a **trade-off between the customers' requirements and operational cost considerations**. Higher demand for service segmentation adds to the growing complexity of the networks. Shippers demand direct services between their preferred ports of loading and discharge. The demand side thus exerts strong pressure on the service schedules, port rotations, and feeder connections. However, shipping lines have to design their liner services and networks to optimize ship utilization and benefit from scale economies in vessel size. Their objective is to optimize their shipping networks by rationalizing the coverage of ports, shipping routes, and transit time according to direct routes and strategic passages.

Shipping lines may direct flows along paths optimal for the system, with the lowest cost for the entire network being achieved by indirect routing via hubs and the amalgamation of flows. However, the more efficient the network from the carrier's point of view, the less convenient that network could be for the shippers' needs. **Bundling** is one of the key drivers of container service network dynamics and can occur at two levels:

1. Bundling within an individual liner service.
2. Bundling by combining two or more liner services.

The objective of **bundling within an individual liner service** is to collect container cargo by calling at various ports along the route instead of focusing on an end-to-end service. Such a line bundling service is conceived as a set of x roundtrips of y vessels, each with a similar calling pattern in terms of the order of port calls and time intervals (i.e. frequency) between two consecutive port calls. By overlaying these x roundtrips, shipping lines can offer the desired calling frequency in each of the ports of call of the loop. Line bundling operations can be **symmetrical** (i.e. same ports of call for both sailing directions) or **asymmetrical** (i.e. different ports of call on the way back). Most liner services are line bundling itineraries connecting two and five ports of call scheduled in each of the main markets. The trade between Europe and the Far East provides a good example. Most mainline operators and alliances running services from the Far East to North Europe stick to line bundling itineraries with direct calls scheduled in each of the main markets.

Notwithstanding diversity in calling patterns on the observed routes, carriers select up to five regional ports of call per loop. Shipping lines have significantly increased **average vessel sizes deployed** on routes. In October 2019,

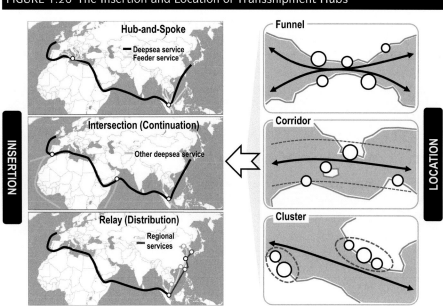

FIGURE 1.26  The Insertion and Location of Transshipment Hubs

the average container vessel on the Asia–North Europe trade had a capacity of 16,100 TEU compared to 11,711 TEU in 2015, 9,444 TEU in 2012, 6,164 TEU in 2006, and 4,250 TEU in 2002. These scale increases in vessel size have put downward pressure on the average number of European port calls per loop on the Far East–North Europe trade: 4.9 ports of call in 1989, 3.84 in 1998, 3.77 in October 2000, 3.68 in February 2006, 3.35 in December 2009 and 3.48 in April 2012. However, in recent years, the number of port calls has slightly increased, mainly driven by the carriers' focus on increasing vessel utilization. As a result, the average number of European port calls per loop on the Far East–North Europe trade reached 4.52 in July 2015, 4.59 in April 2017, and 4.11 in June 2019.

Two extreme forms of line bundling are **round-the-world services** and **pendulum services**. The first round-the-world routes were introduced in 1984 by the Taiwanese maritime shipping company Evergreen. This route took about 69 days and was serviced by about ten containership of 4,000 TEUs in each direction (Westbound and Eastbound). However, by early 2002 this service was replaced by two pendulum services (North Europe, North and Central America, and East Asia; North Europe, Asia, and the Pacific North West) offering higher service frequencies.

The second possibility is **bundling container cargo by combining two or more liner services**. The three main cargo bundling options include a **hub-and-spoke** network (hub/feeder), **interlining/intersection**, and **relay** (Figure 1.26). The establishment of global networks has given rise to hub port development at the crossing points of trade lanes. Intermediate hubs have emerged since the mid-1990s within many global port systems: Free-port (Bahamas), Salalah (Oman), Tanjung Pelepas (Malaysia), Gioia Tauro,

Algeciras, Taranto, Cagliari, Damietta, Tanger Med, and Malta in the Mediterranean, to name but a few. Hubs have a range of common characteristics in terms of nautical accessibility, proximity to main shipping lanes, and ownership, in whole or in part, by carriers or multinational terminal operators.

Most intermediate hubs are located along the global beltway or equatorial round-the-world route (i.e. the Caribbean, Southeast and East Asia, the Middle East, and the Mediterranean) (Box 1.8). These nodes multiply shipping options and improve connectivity within the network through their pivotal role in regional hub-and-spoke networks and cargo relay and interlining operations between the carriers' east-west services and other inter and intra-regional services. Container ports in Northern Europe, North America, and mainland China mainly act as gateways to the respective hinterlands and do not account for significant transshipment volumes.

Two developments undermine the **position of pure transshipment/interlining hubs**. First, the insertion of hubs often represents a temporary phase in connecting a region to global shipping networks. Hub-and-spoke networks allow considerable economies of scale of equipment. Still, the cost-efficiency of larger ships might not be sufficient to offset the extra feeder costs and container lift charges involved. Once traffic volumes for the gateway ports are sufficient, hubs are bypassed and become redundant. Second, transshipment cargo can easily be moved to new hub terminals that emerge along the long-distance shipping lanes, implying a volatile market condition for transshipment hubs. Seaports that can combine a transshipment function with gateway cargo having a less vulnerable and thus more sustainable position in shipping networks.

In channeling gateway and transshipment flows through their shipping networks, container carriers aim to control key terminals in the network. Decisions on the desired port hierarchy are guided by strategic, commercial, and operational considerations. Shipping lines rarely opt for the same port hierarchy because a terminal can be a regional hub for one shipping line and a secondary feeder port for another operator.

The liner service configurations are often combined to form **complex multi-layer networks**. The advantages of complex bundling are higher load factors and the use of larger vessels in terms of TEU capacity, higher service frequencies, and more destinations served. Container service operators must make a trade-off between frequency and volume on the trunk lines. Smaller vessels allow meeting the shippers' demand for high frequencies and lower transit times, while larger units allow operators to benefit from vessel scale economies. The main disadvantages of complex bundling networks are the need for extra container handling at intermediate terminals and longer transport times and distances. Both elements incur additional costs and could counterbalance the cost advantages linked to higher load factors or the use of larger unit capacities. Some containers in such a system undergo as many as four transshipments before reaching the final discharge port. The global container shipping grid allows shipping lines to cope with the changes in trade flows as it combines a large number of potential routes in a network.

Existing liner shipping networks feature substantial diversity in the types of liner services and great complexity in the way end-to-end services, line bundling services, and transshipment (including relay and interlining) operations are connected to form extensive shipping networks. Profound differences exist in service network design among shipping lines. Some carriers have clearly opted for truly global coverage. Others are somewhat stuck in a triad-based service network, forcing them to develop a strong focus on cost bases. A large number of individual carriers remain regionally based. Asian carriers such as the Japanese carrier ONE (Ocean Network Express) and the South Korean carrier HMM mainly focus on intra-Asian trade, transpacific trade, and the Europe–Far East route. This is partly because of their huge dependence on export flows generated by the respective Asian home bases. Evergreen and Cosco Shipping are among the exceptions frequenting secondary routes such as Africa and South America. Alliance structures (cf. THE Alliance, Ocean Alliance, and 2M) provide members with access to more loops or services with relatively low-cost implications and allow them to share terminals.

## Box 1.8  Main intermediate hubs and markets

*With the growth of long-distance containerized trade, intermediate hubs grew in importance in connecting different systems of maritime circulation. They tend to be located along the main circum-equatorial maritime route through Panama, the Strait of Malacca, Suez, and Gibraltar (Figure 1.27). Intermediate hubs usually have a low maritime deviation, and many provide connectivity between north-south and east-west shipping lanes. Transshipment incidence is the share of the total port throughput that is 'ship to ship', implying that the final destination of the container is another port. The higher it is, the more a port can be considered as a transshipment hub. For ports with low transshipment incidence (less than 25%), transshipment is an incidental activity, while ports having a transshipment incidence above 75% can be considered 'pure' transshipment hubs.*

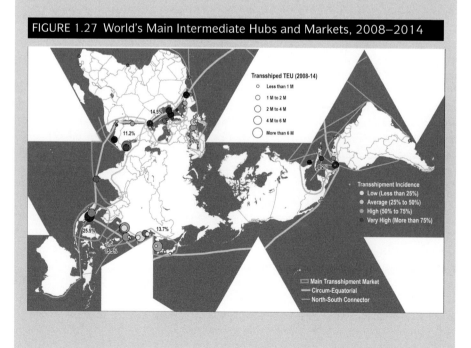

FIGURE 1.27 World's Main Intermediate Hubs and Markets, 2008–2014

*Transshipment emerged in the 1970s as trade with Asia increased, but volumes were insufficient to justify direct connections to many ports. Ports such as Singapore, Busan, Tokyo, and Kaohsiung emerged as the first transshipment hubs. This eventually led to the setting up of pure transshipment hubs at key locations along major shipping routes, such as Colombo, Salalah, Gioia Tauro, Algeciras, and Kingston. The emergence of major intermediate hubs favored a concentration of large vessels along long-distance high capacity routes while smaller ports could be serviced with lower capacity ships. Economies of scale over long distances are thus reinforced, permitting liner services that would otherwise be economically unfeasible. However, there is a limit to the hub-and-spoke network configuration and consequently also to the size of the vessels being deployed on the trunk routes.*

*Seven major transshipment markets account for the bulk of transshipment activity. They are referred to as markets since transshipment is an activity that is not tied to a specific port, unlike gateway traffic linked with a hinterland and inland freight distribution. Therefore, transshipment hubs compete for traffic related to a region/market. Geography plays an important role in the setting up of a transshipment market, which is often at the crossroads of north/south shipping routes and where there is a bottleneck.*

*The world's most important intermediate hub is Singapore, where 85% of the traffic is transshipment. Major Asia–Europe shipping lanes are constrained to pass through the Strait of Malacca, which led to the setting up of an adjacent transshipment hub competing with Singapore; Tanjung Pelepas.*

*There can also be a shift in transshipment dynamics due to the changing commercial environment. For instance, transshipment incidence levels in the Japanese ports of Tokyo and Yokohama used to be in the 20% range but have declined to less than 10% as Japan was losing its role as a manufacturing center, with many transshipment activities shifting to Korea or China.*

*The Mediterranean has only two points of entry (Suez and Gibraltar), both of which have significant transshipment activity and ports that are at the center of the basin (e.g. Marsaxlokk and Gioia Tauro).*

*Although the Caribbean has a large exposure on the Atlantic side, it has one outlet for the Pacific; the Panama Canal, which has significant transshipment activities on the Atlantic and Pacific coasts. The Caribbean generates limited cargo demand, but neighboring regions are a substantial generator of traffic, some of which is being transshipped in the region (East and Gulf coast of the United States, Central America, and northern South America).*

*The North Sea and the Baltic are another transshipment market, but of lower incidence since the Baltic generates lower freight volumes. Since the Baltic is a dead end, it is subject to tail-cutting with its ports serviced by feeder services from northern Europe (e.g. Antwerp, Hamburg).*

## 6.2 The design of container liner services

Before an operator can start with regular container service design, the targeted trade route(s) need to be analyzed. The analysis should include elements related to the supply, demand, and market profile of the trade route. On the **supply side**, key considerations include vessel capacity deployment and utilization, vessel size distribution, the configuration of existing liner services, the existing market structure, and the port call patterns of existing operators. On the **demand side**, container lines focus on the characteristics of the market to be served, the geographical cargo distribution, seasonality, and cargo imbalances. The interaction between demand and supply on the trade route considered for liner services results in seasonal freight rate fluctuations and reflects its earning potential..

The ultimate goal of market analysis is not only to estimate the potential cargo demand for a new liner service but also to estimate the volatility, geographical dispersion, and seasonality of such demand. These factors will eventually affect the earning potential of the new service. Once the market potential for new services has been determined, the service planners need to decide on several inter-related core **design variables** that mainly concern (Box 1.9):

- the liner service type.
- the number and order of port calls in combination with the actual port selection process.
- the vessel speed.
- the frequency.
- the vessel size and fleet mix.
- the array of liner service types and bundling options available to shipping lines (see the previous section).

Limiting the **number of port calls** shortens round voyage time and increases the number of round trips per year, minimizing the number of vessels required for that specific liner service. However, fewer port calls mean poorer access to cargo catchment areas. Adding port calls can generate additional revenue if the additional costs from added calls are offset by revenue growth. The actual selection of ports is a complex issue. Traffic flows through ports are a physical outcome of route and port selection by the relevant actors in the chain. Port choice has increasingly become a function of the overall network cost and performance. Human behavioral aspects might impede carriers from achieving an optimal network configuration. Incorrect or incomplete information results in bounded rationality in carriers' network design, leading to sub-optimal decisions. Shippers sometimes impose bounded rational behavior on shipping lines where the shipper asks to call at a specific port. The selection of the ports of call by a shipping line can also be influenced by market structures and the behavior of market players. For example:

- **Important shippers or logistics service providers** might impose a certain port of call on a shipping line leading to bounded rationality in port choice.
- If a shipping line is part of a strategic alliance, the port choice is subject to **negotiations among the alliance members**. The collective choice can differ from the choice of an individual member.
- A shipping line might possess a **dedicated terminal facility** in a port of a multi-port gateway region and might be urged to send more ships to that facility in view of optimal terminal use.
- Carriers might **stick to a specific port** as they assume that the decision-making efforts and costs linked to changes in the network design will not outweigh the costs associated with the current non-optimal solution.

Next to the number of port calls, the **call order** is of importance. If the port of loading is the last port of call on the maritime line-bundling service and the port of discharge the first port of call, then transit time is minimized. A port regularly acting as the last port of loading or first port of discharge in a liner service schedule in principle has more chance of achieving a higher deepsea call efficiency ratio (i.e. the ratio between the total TEU discharged and loaded in the port and the two-way vessel capacity) compared to rival ports which are in different segments of the loop. In practice, shipping lines' decisions on the number and order of ports of call are influenced by many commercial and operational determinants, including the **cargo generating effect of the port** (i.e. the availability of export cargo), the distribution of container origins and destinations over the hinterland, the berth allocation profile of a port, the nautical access, the time constraints of the round voyages and so on.

The choice of **vessel speed** is mainly affected by the technical specifications of the vessel deployed (i.e. the design speed), bunker fuel prices, environmental considerations (e.g. reduction of $CO_2$ through slow steaming), and the capacity situation in the market (i.e. slow steaming can absorb some of the vessel overcapacity in the market). Since 2008, slow steaming and super slow steaming have gradually become common in the container shipping market.

The **number and order of port calls**, the total two-way **sailing distance**, and the vessel speed are the main determinants of the total vessel roundtrip time. The theoretical roundtrip time will not always be achieved in practice due to delays along the route and in ports giving rise to schedule reliability problems. Low **schedule integrity** can have many causes ranging from weather conditions, delays in port access (pilotage, towage, locks, tides) to port terminal congestion, or even security considerations. To cope with the chance of delays, a shipping line can insert time buffers in the liner service, which reduce schedule unreliability but increase the vessel roundtrip time.

When it comes to **service frequency**, carriers typically aim for a weekly service. The service frequency and the total vessel roundtrip time determine the number of vessels required for the liner service. Carriers have to secure enough vessels to guarantee the desired frequency. Given the number of vessels needed and the anticipated cargo volume for the liner service, the shipping line can then decide on the optimal vessel size and fleet mix. As vessel size economies are more significant over longer distances, the biggest vessels are typically deployed on long and cargo-intensive routes.

Decisions on all of the above key design variables will lead to a specific **slot capacity** offered by the new liner service. It should be in line with the actual demand to maximize average vessel utilization (given expected traffic imbalances, cargo dispersion patterns, and cargo seasonality and volatility).

### Box 1.9 Port and terminal selection by container shipping lines

*Port selection is a complex process subject to several criteria (Figure 1.28). The direct impact of shippers and other cargo interests on terminal operations depends on the commodity and terminal activity type. There are typically no contractual arrangements between terminal operators and shippers in the container business or their representatives, such as freight forwarders. The market demand is exerted indirectly via the shipping lines that have contractual arrangements with the terminal operators.*

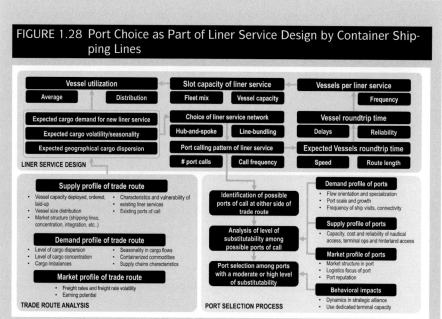

FIGURE 1.28 Port Choice as Part of Liner Service Design by Container Shipping Lines

Source: Adapted from Notteboom, Parola, Satta and Pallis (2017).

*The port choice criteria used by shipping lines include four distinctive groups of selection factors relevant to shipping lines. These factors are related to the* demand profile *of the port or terminal, the* supply profile, *the* market profile, *and* carrier dynamics *linked to carrier operations and cooperation. The above figure conceptualizes the port selection process by container lines, combining these four groups of selection factors. The shaded areas refer to decision variables in liner service design. They include the choice of the liner service type (e.g. direct service vs. transshipment), the number and order of port calls, vessel speed, service frequency, and vessel size and fleet mix.*

*Terminal ownership of shipping lines (or their affiliated companies) and the strategic alliance dynamics among shipping lines belong to the fourth category of port selection factors. Thus, strategic considerations at the company level play a role in port and terminal selection. These strategic considerations include alliance developments and the location of the container terminals of the carrier or alliance. Other strategic factors include the fit of the port in the trade (or string), the location of key customers, present contracts with independent terminal operators, and the location of decision-makers (head office vs. more regional offices). Port choice can be subject to negotiations among the alliance members and can deviate from the choice of one particular member.*

# 7  THE CONNECTIVITY OF CONTAINER PORTS IN MARITIME NETWORKS

The liner service networks of shipping lines revolve around a set of strategic hubs. Each hub has high connectivity (in terms of frequency and range of ports served) to secondary ports in the network and major inland markets. A few important points need to be made in this respect:

- Container shipping lines have been very active in securing **dedicated terminal capacity** in the strategic locations within their liner service networks. A substantial number of container terminals worldwide feature a shipping line among their shareholders, mostly through their terminal sister companies. Examples include CMA CGM's Terminal Link (51% shareholding), the Cosco group's Cosco Shipping Ports (100%), MSC's TIL (60%), and APM Terminals of the AP Moller group (100%).
- Shipping lines do not necessarily opt for the same hubs but have **similar transshipment areas** (e.g. Southeast Asia, the Middle East, or the Caribbean).
- There is an upper limit to the concentration of flows in only a few hubs. For instance, Maersk Line did not opt for one European turntable, but several major hubs. The optimal number of hub ports in the network depends on various factors, including the cost trade-off between the hub-feeder option versus the direct call option. Also, shipping lines can have commercial reasons for not bundling all their cargo in one port, such as diversification and resilience strategies.

The **maritime connectivity** of a container port can be measured in different ways:

- UNCTAD publishes the **Liner Shipping Connectivity Index** (LSCI) for countries and individual ports as an aggregation of five statistics: number of liner services calling, number of liner companies providing those services, number of ships in those services, combined container capacity of those ships (in TEUs), and capacity of the largest ship calling.
- The measurement of the **centrality** of ports in the network. The centrality of ports in the network can be approached at the local and global levels. **Degree centrality** is a local level measure counting for each port the number of connections to other ports. **Betweenness centrality** is a global level measure summing for each port the number of its positions on the shortest possible paths within the entire network. Degree centrality is a measure of connectivity, while betweenness centrality can be regarded as a measure of accessibility. Hub ports typically have a high degree of centrality and a high betweenness centrality due to their role as inter-regional pivots in the global network.

Empirical work on the centrality of ports in the global container shipping network shows that the Asia-Pacific network is centered on the Singapore–Busan axis and Europe–Atlantic with the Le Havre–Hamburg range (Box 1.10). Due to their lack of hub and feeder activities, large North American and Japanese ports are poorly represented despite their traffic volume. Singapore is the most central port of the global system, mainly associated with its position in the Strait of Malacca. The very high centrality of the Suez and Panama canals underlines the strong vulnerability of the global network. In East Asia and the Mediterranean, an increasing number of ports have high connectivity (for example, Port Klang, Xiamen, Shenzhen in Asia; Marsaxlokk, Piraeus, and Tanger Med in the Mediterranean).

**Box 1.10  The connectivity of the emerging global maritime transport system**

*A global maritime freight transport system has been established since the late nineteenth century and has expanded with containerization. It includes east-west and north-south routes and locations enabling interconnectivity between these systems of circulation (Figure 1.29).*

**FIGURE 1.29  The Emerging Global Maritime Transport System**

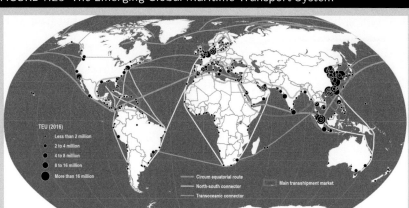

*Circum-equatorial route. With the expansion of the Panama Canal, a relative parity exists for the first time between the Panama and Suez canals. In such a setting, maritime shipping companies may elect to establish circum-equatorial routes in both directions using high capacity (8,000 to 14,000 TEU) containerships. This high-frequency 'conveyor belt' could support a significant share of global east-west freight movements in a cost-effective way. This does not imply a homogeneous service as several different configurations of ports of call are possible along this route, particularly if a 300 nautical mile deviation is considered. This enables different circum-equatorial network configurations.*

*North–south connectors. These connectors reflect existing commercial relations, namely for raw materials (oil, minerals, agricultural goods), such as South America/North America, Africa/Europe, or Australia/Asia. For container shipping they are mostly based on the rationale that there is not enough volume to support transoceanic services, so cargo is collected/delivered along a latitudinal sequence of ports. This conventional network will be expanded with transshipment opportunities with the circum-equatorial route.*

*Transoceanic connectors. These connect a series of ports along ranges of large oceanic masses. The three main transoceanic connectors are transpacific, Asia–Europe (through the Indian Ocean), and transatlantic. The industrialization of Asia (China in particular) has made Asia–Europe and the transpacific connectors particularly important. The emergence of a new connector in the southern hemisphere between the east coast of South America, the Cape of Good Hope, and Southeast Asia is also observed.*

*     **Transshipment markets**. They connect regional port systems to trans-oceanic and circum-equatorial routes, mainly through hub-and-spoke services. The intersection and relay functions between long-distance shipping services performed by those markets are also significant. The most important markets are Southeast Asia, the Mediterranean, and the Caribbean. They are referred to as markets because the transshipment function can be substituted for another port. Therefore, ports in a transshipment market are vying to attract port calls as this type of traffic is difficult to anchor. The development of circum-equatorial routes is thus likely to expand the opportunities for transshipment.*

*     **Polar routes**. Consider using circum-polar routes as shortcuts to link East Asia, Western Europe, and North America (both east and west coasts). Even if the distance advantages of these polar routes appear significant, they are subject to the uncertainties of climate change and niche market opportunities.*

# Chapter 1.4 Ports and distribution networks

*Ports are nodes within distribution networks that include warehouses and fulfillment centers and provide the management of freight flows.*

## 1 PORTS AS LOCATIONS FOR DISTRIBUTION CENTERS

The dynamics in distribution networks are affected by the **large-scale development of inland ports**. The functions of inland logistics centers are wide-ranging, from simple cargo consolidation to advanced logistics services. Many inland locations with multimodal access have become broader logistics zones and have assumed a significant number of traditional cargo handling functions and services. They have also attracted many related services, among other distribution centers, shipping agents, trucking companies, forwarders, container repair facilities, and packing firms. Quite a few of these logistics zones are competing with seaports for the location of warehousing and distribution facilities. Shortage of industrial premises, high land prices, congestion problems, the inland location of markets, and severe environmental restrictions are some of the well-known arguments for companies not to locate in a seaport.

     Notwithstanding the rise of inland ports and inland logistics platforms in many parts of the world, seaports typically remain key constituents of many supply chains. Several ports have actively stimulated logistics polarization in port areas by enhancing flexible labor conditions, smooth customs formalities (combined with freeport status), and powerful information systems. Logistics activities can take place at the terminal, in a logistics park where several logistics activities are concentrated, or, in the case of industrial subcontracting, on the site of an industrial company. While there is a clear tendency in the container sector to move away from the terminal, an expansion of logistics on the terminals can be witnessed in other cargo categories. As such, a mix of pure stevedoring and logistics activities occurs.

An array of port-centric logistics activities are performed at terminals, mainly around two tiers. The **first tier** covers the activities directly related to the cargo, while the **second tier** concerns freight distribution. Concerning the second tier, many seaports have created logistics parks inside the port area or in the immediate vicinity of the port. Three basic types of port-centric logistics parks in seaport areas can be distinguished:

- **Traditional seaport-based logistics park**. This type of logistics park is associated with the pre-container area in seaports. It is mainly associated with manufacturing and heavy industry having a high material input carried by maritime transportation. Others were created to convey the benefits of free trade zones outside specified custom regulations.
- **Container-oriented logistics parks**. This is the dominant type with a number of large warehouses in proximity to or co-located with the container terminal locations and intermodal terminal facilities.
- **Specialized seaport-based logistics parks**. These cover a variety of functions, often closely related to the characteristics of the seaport. The park may focus on the storage of liquid bulk (chemicals), on trade in which a combination of warehousing and office space is offered to several import-export companies, or on high-value office-related employment such as fourth-party logistics service providers, logistics software firms, and financial service providers.

Logistics parks also have a functional orientation depending on the general directions of the flows, with export, intermediate, and import focuses. A non-exhaustive list of logistics activities that typically opt for a location in a port includes:

- Logistics activities involving **large volumes of bulk cargoes**, suitable for inland navigation and rail.
- Logistics activities directly related to companies that have **a production site in the port area**.
- Logistics activities related to cargo needing **flexible storage** to create a buffer (products subject to seasonality or irregular supply).
- Logistics activities with a **high dependency on short sea shipping**.

Moreover, ports are competitive areas for distribution centers in a multiple import structure and as consolidation centers for export cargo. The decision to locate a distribution center inside a port implies advantages and disadvantages that include:

- Good **integration and cooperation** between terminal operations and distribution center activities.
- A possibility to **re-export from the port to other markets**.
- A reduction in local traffic congestion and pollution when operating distribution activities are inside the port area.
- Port real estate tends to be more expensive than the surrounding areas. The market price of port real estate is often higher, particularly because

it is scarcer and located in high accessibility and connectivity areas. Port managers want to avoid facing opportunity costs linked to the sub-optimal use of prime locations in the port area. Still, port managers cannot price the port real estate too high as they have to consider the competitive setting in attracting logistics operations.

- Port real estate tends to be priced differently. Very often, the logistics service provider cannot buy the land as most ports are landlords whereby the port authority gives the port real estate as a concession to the private port or warehouse operator for a specific term.
- Manufacturers have **less flexibility** because of the constraint to call the port where the distribution center is located, giving fewer routing options. A distribution center located at an intermediate location can have more options and benefit from inter-port competition.
- Logistics service providers might decide not to locate a distribution center in a port partly because of the complexity of the dock labor system. This can involve a lack of experience with the existing social dialog patterns in that port, such as labor unions.
- In some cases, the port is located far away from the final destination of goods and offers a **locational disadvantage**.

## 2 WAREHOUSING ACTIVITIES IN SUPPLY CHAINS

### 2.1 Warehouses and fulfillment centers

Warehousing involves the administrative and physical actions required to store and distribute goods and materials located at the beginning, middle, and end of the supply chain or near production and industrial facilities. Warehousing facilities act as important nodes in logistics networks and have become key components of informational flow management. The terms **warehouse** and **fulfillment center** are often used interchangeably but can have very different connotations (Figure 1.30). Both are large buildings that hold inventory. However, the use of cases and services provided are often quite different.

> *A warehouse is a facility designed to store goods for longer periods of time. Goods stored in a warehouse have usually not yet been sold and are held in inventory until a buyer is found. A warehouse is driven by the supply of manufacturers and wholesalers.*

There are warehousing providers geared toward businesses that primarily do wholesale or B2B orders in large quantities. Some major retailers will have their own warehouse(s) to store excess inventory, while others rent warehousing space in conjunction with other businesses.

> *A distribution center (or fulfillment center) is a facility that performs consolidation, warehousing, packaging, decomposition, and other functions linked with handling freight. Orders are received, processed, and filled. Their main purpose is to provide value-added services to freight, which is stored for relatively short time periods (days or weeks). Goods stored in a distribution center have usually been sold and are in transit to their destination. They can also perform light manufacturing activities such as assembly and labeling. A distribution center tends to focus on the demands of customers.*

## FIGURE 1.30 Warehouses and Distribution Centers

**Warehouse**    Storage

- Supply-driven (storage).
- Buffer related function (inventory holding).
- Inventory stored for weeks or months.
- Cargo ownership usually by supplier / producer.
- Consolidation of cargo.
- Limited added value outside storage.
- Coping with unforeseen demand.

**Distribution Center**    Throughput

- Demand-driven (throughput).
- Fulfilling orders (processing and fulfillment).
- Inventory stored for days or weeks.
- Cargo ownership usually by distributor / customer.
- Consolidating, deconsolidating, sorting a cargo load or changing the load unit.
- Assembly, packaging and light manufacturing.
- Coping with stable and predictable demand.

Thus, a fulfillment center is focused on getting orders to customers in a timely fashion and can relieve companies of managing this process when a 3PL is used. Orders are increasingly processed through online platforms linking demand with available inventory, which is stored strategically in preparation for fulfilling customer orders. Once an order has been placed, inventory is picked (i.e. order picking process), and boxes are packed, then labeled and, if needed, consolidated for shipment. Fulfillment centers can process both B2B orders, typically a high volume of goods sent to a large customer such as a retailer, and B2C orders. Fulfillment companies work with cut-off times for orders to be placed. For example, customer orders placed by noon local time will be processed in the fulfillment center and shipped out the same day.

In contrast to a warehouse, fulfillment centers turn inventory over quickly. The challenge is to make sure there is enough inventory on hand before shipment. Unlike warehouses that are more static or inactive, fulfillment centers thus have continuous movement in a more complex operational setting. Typical fulfillment services include receiving inventory, order picking, kitting and packing items, labeling shipments, and managing returns. The equipment used in distribution centers and (rapid) fulfillment centers includes forklifts, (automated) stacking cranes, shelves, cargo consolidation and deconsolidation infrastructure (such as conveyor belt systems), a cargo management system, scanning devices (barcodes, QR-scanner, or a system of radio frequency identification tags - RFID) and loading bays for trucks (and occasionally also rail). Contemporary fulfillment companies depend highly on technology for delivering fulfillment services. Every step of the fulfillment process is automatically documented in real-time.

Like most segments of the supply chain, warehousing has gone through several **evolutionary stages**. Initially, warehouses were used in proximity to manufacturing facilities as a primary means to store materials needed to produce finished goods waiting to be transported to the customer. Since most production facilities were located close to ports and major access points, the need for inland or part-way warehouses was somewhat limited. Except for the production and sales storage areas, where buffer and cargo bundling activities surrounding ports and major transport nodes took place, little or no warehousing activity was present. This changed with the onset of globalization, containerization, and the emergence of more complex and global supply chains. Warehousing slowly evolved from a purely industrial derived activity to a more defined and specialized industry. It is still part of the production process and takes a more prominent role in the logistics and transport industry by offering rapid fulfillment and added value activities.

Activities linked to warehousing are limited to the basic storage of goods within a covered storage space and the activities like receipt, identification, verification (customs), and retrieval. The term warehousing is, therefore, a universal connotation. Still, the types of specific warehousing facilities differ greatly depending on the stage within the supply chain (distance to consumer) and the level of specialization of the product. As a rule of thumb, the closer warehousing is to the consumer and the more specialized the product, the more complex are the required storage facilities and related activities.

## 2.2 Main trends in the warehousing sector

The **main economic and logistics trends** impacting the warehousing sector are roughly the same as the trends impacting the logistics industry. Globalization, just-in-time supply chains, mass customization, and increased sustainability all play their role. The resulting landscape is increasingly complex in its geography, the supply chains involved, the distribution networks, and its technologies. Continuous innovation and efficiency improvements are key to keeping a competitive edge in this rapidly evolving market. The warehousing sector has been subjected to several specific trends:

- **Lean warehousing**. The lean principles were originally created in the automotive industry in order to reduce waste in terms of time and inventory. The strategy is also used in the logistics and warehousing sector, resulting in cost reduction, customer satisfaction, and production efficiency. The lean warehousing philosophy aims to reduce activities that do not generate added value for the customer. By reducing various types of waste in the process, such as too much inventory, or too many movements (no optimized workspace distribution), the lean principles impact the core of the warehousing.
- **Green and sustainable warehouses**. The warehousing sector is undergoing a green wave and an improved sustainable footprint by specializing and optimizing the warehouse and transporting goods in an environment-friendly fashion. Several principles enable large-scale environmental impact reductions, such as the use of sustainable construction materials, energy efficiency, and the use of electric equipment (Box 1.11).
- **Collaborative warehousing**. A group of warehouse managers can share warehousing space according to their respective availability and locations. The underlying operating model requires high levels of trust and data sharing using advanced IT management systems.

- **TMS and WMS alignment**. A TMS (Transportation Management System) is software used to plan freight operations with a given allocation of supply and demand, such as finding carriers and rates, the routing, and related transactions (bill of lading, receivables). A Warehouse Management System (WMS) is software used to manage all warehousing operations, from inventory to shipping and receiving. Advanced capabilities like directed put away, cycle counting, and master schedules allow users to track and control everything happening in a warehouse using real-time information, which is constantly at their disposal. WMS and TMS integration may lead to optimized operation solutions by creating better planning, accurate delivery times, and faster processes while increasing visibility throughout the supply chain. The main benefits linked to such integration include improved visibility (transparent supply chain), operational synchronization (shelf distribution and truck distribution alignment), pick efficiency improvements (batch sizes linked to transport mode), and improved customer service.
- **Labor management software** gives the ability to track the productivity of warehouse employees. For example, it allows comparing the time it takes an employee to finish a task to a pre-defined standard. The data collected helps avoid bottlenecks in the order fulfillment process before they occur, thereby indirectly improving lead times. This technology also allows for easier decision-making and increased labor productivity and accuracy.
- **Voice-enabled technology** complements classic input options for warehousing activities. The devices allow employees to interact with software applications through microphones and headphones. This creates a hands-free work environment and facilitates their jobs to a great extent. The picking process is made easier since users are now directed to pick designated items for an order. Information on location, quantity, and other useful items are given directly through the headphones.

---

### Box 1.11  Green and sustainable warehouses

*Warehouse managers are investing to make warehousing operations greener and more sustainable (Figure 1.31). This includes actions in the following areas:*

*__Construction materials__. The use of sustainable construction materials contributes to a lowering of the ecological footprint of warehouses. Using non-toxic paints and high-value insulation and installing skylights or natural light access points leads to a more efficient building.*

*__Energy efficiency__. Solar panels and stormwater management systems improve energy efficiency and self-sufficiency. Other improvements include the use of light-colored materials and natural native landscaping. High-efficiency climate control systems can help to manage building temperature and airflow for reduced heating and cooling expenditure. The use of solar panels is once again a major impact factor here.*

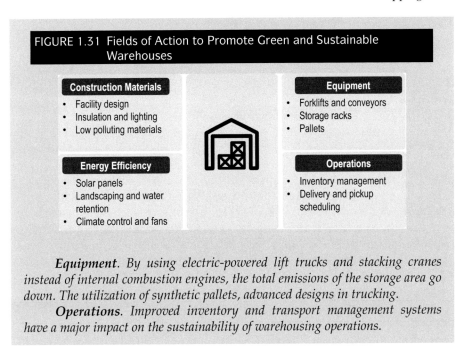

FIGURE 1.31  Fields of Action to Promote Green and Sustainable Warehouses

**Construction Materials**
- Facility design
- Insulation and lighting
- Low polluting materials

**Energy Efficiency**
- Solar panels
- Landscaping and water retention
- Climate control and fans

**Equipment**
- Forklifts and conveyors
- Storage racks
- Pallets

**Operations**
- Inventory management
- Delivery and pickup scheduling

*Equipment*. By using electric-powered lift trucks and stacking cranes instead of internal combustion engines, the total emissions of the storage area go down. The utilization of synthetic pallets, advanced designs in trucking.

*Operations*. Improved inventory and transport management systems have a major impact on the sustainability of warehousing operations.

## 3 REGIONAL DISTRIBUTION NETWORKS

Many warehousing facilities have evolved or have been specifically designed to act as distribution centers as part of an extensive regional distribution network. The decoupling of orders and delivery encourages the reconfiguration of distribution networks. The trend towards the decoupling of orders and deliveries is reinforced by the rise of digital ordering platforms and the associated rise of e-fulfillment and e-commerce. Therefore, distribution networks have to adapt to new requirements. When it comes to the regional distribution of goods, corporations are challenged to find optimal solutions at various levels (Figure 1.32).

FIGURE 1.32  Key Decision Levels in the Development of a Regional Distribution Network

Location of VALS — **Level 3**

Location of DC — **Level 2**

Choice of Distribution System — **Level 1**

**Regional Distribution Network**

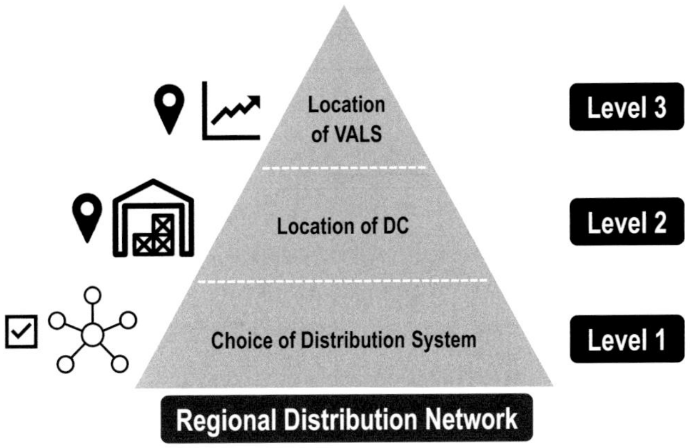

1. The choice of the distribution system.
2. The location of distribution centers.
3. The location of value-added logistics services (VALS).

## 3.1 Choice of distribution system

A general distribution structure does not exist as corporations have a multiplicity of options (Figure 1.33). They can opt for direct delivery without going through a distribution center, distribution through the main distribution center (MDC), distribution through a group of national distribution centers (NDCs) or regional distribution centers (RDCs), or a tiered structure in which one or a few MDCs and several NDCs and RDCs are combined to form a distribution network. These decisions are based on the characteristics of the respective supply chains, the type of products, and the demand level.

Multiple determinants exist when choosing between a **centralized distribution center** in comparison with **several decentralized distribution centers**. On the one hand, the number of distribution centers serving regional markets is growing, favoring inland locations close to markets. On the other hand, the number of centers serving global markets is also growing, favoring locations close to large international seaports or airports. The choice between the various distribution channels depends on the type of product (consumer goods, semi-finished products, and foodstuffs) and the frequency of deliveries. For example, in the fresh food industry, main distribution centers are unusual because perishability dictates a local distribution structure. In the pharmaceutical industry, main distribution centers are common. Regional or local distribution centers are still not present because the pharmaceutical products are often manufactured in one central plant and delivery times are not critical (hospitals often have their own inventories). However, in the high-tech spare parts industry, all of the distribution center functions can be present because spare parts need to be delivered within a few hours. High-tech spare parts are usually costly, which encourages the use of centralized distribution structures).

FIGURE 1.33 Distribution Network Configurations for Containerized Import Cargo.

| Gateway-based | Tiered-based | Regional DC | Local DC |
|---|---|---|---|
| • Selected mass market goods (economies of scale in distribution).<br>• Selected specialized goods (economies of scale in warehousing).<br>• Little transformations.<br>• Transloading. | • Mix of retail goods coming through a few gateways.<br>• Some customization.<br>• Large suppliers and large retailers (Big Box and e-commerce).<br>• Transloading, postponement and cross-docking. | • Complex set of goods coming from numerous suppliers (e.g. automotive parts).<br>• Regional variation of the nature and extent of demand.<br>• Deconsolidation. | • Time sensitive bulky cargo (e.g. perishables).<br>• Low lead times.<br>• City logistics (delivery stations). |

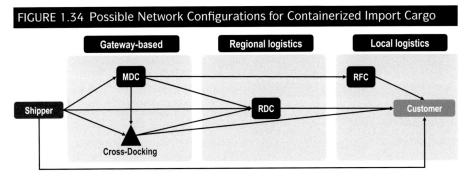

FIGURE 1.34 Possible Network Configurations for Containerized Import Cargo

*MDC: Main distribution center. RDC: Regional distribution center. RFC: Rapid fulfilment center.*

Corporations often opt for a hybrid distribution structure of centralized and local distribution facilities (Figure 1.34). For instance, they use an MDC for medium- and slow-moving products and RDCs for fast-moving products. These RDCs typically function as fulfillment centers rather than holding inventories. The conventional or multi-country distribution structures are being replaced by merge-in-transit, cross-docking, or other fluid logistics structures. The cross-docking principle means that the products are almost immediately transferred from the discharge area to the load area with no or limited storage.

Cost-service trade-offs also have an impact on the choice between a centralized or decentralized distribution network configuration. On the one hand, the centralization of inventories offers an opportunity to reduce costs. On the other hand, storing products close to the final consumers could increase customer responsiveness.

### 3.2 Location selection for distribution centers

A second key decision level in developing a regional distribution network concerns **decisions on the locations of the distribution centers** once the distribution system has been chosen. When referring to distribution centers, the terms warehouse and fulfillment center are often used interchangeably but can have very different connotations.

Distribution center location analysis has received considerable attention. The optimal distribution location decisions involve careful attention to inherent trade-offs between **facility costs**, **inventory costs**, **transportation costs**, and **customer responsiveness**. Also, they are influenced by the inventory stocking policy of the corporation. The variables that affect site selection are numerous and quite diverse and can be quantitative or qualitative. Of particular relevance are centrality, accessibility, market size, firm's reputation and experience, land and its attributes, labor (costs, quality, productivity), capital (investment climate, bank environment), government policy and planning (subsidies, taxes), and personal factors and amenities.

Conventional location selection criteria have emphasized cost-related variables such as economies of scale and transportation costs (Figure 1.35). They include major factors that may strongly influence international

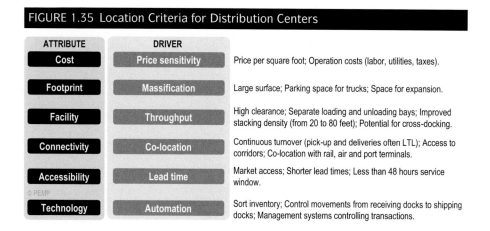

FIGURE 1.35 Location Criteria for Distribution Centers

| ATTRIBUTE | DRIVER | |
|---|---|---|
| Cost | Price sensitivity | Price per square foot; Operation costs (labor, utilities, taxes). |
| Footprint | Massification | Large surface; Parking space for trucks; Space for expansion. |
| Facility | Throughput | High clearance; Separate loading and unloading bays; Improved stacking density (from 20 to 80 feet); Potential for cross-docking. |
| Connectivity | Co-location | Continuous turnover (pick-up and deliveries often LTL); Access to corridors; Co-location with rail, air and port terminals. |
| Accessibility | Lead time | Market access; Shorter lead times; Less than 48 hours service window. |
| Technology | Automation | Sort inventory; Control movements from receiving docks to shipping docks; Management systems controlling transactions. |

location decisions, such as the costs of the factors of production (land, labor), infrastructure, labor characteristics, political factors, and economic factors. Nowadays, however, **non-cost-based variables**, such as infrastructure support, local labor market characteristics, and institutional factors, also play an important role when selecting the location of distribution centers.

### 3.3 Value-added logistics services

The third key decision level in developing a regional distribution network refers to deciding where to add value to products. Many products need to be made country or customer-specific (labeling, kitting, adding manuals in local languages) before they can be delivered to the customer. Historically these country or customer-specific activities were mostly done in the factory, leading to high inventory levels. Due to the increasing variety of products and shorter product life cycles, many companies have chosen to move their country and customer-specific kitting or assembly operations as close to the customer as possible. This implies that the traditional storage and distribution functions of many distribution centers are supplemented by light manufacturing activities such as customizing and localizing products, adding components or manuals, product testing, quality control, or even final assembly.

> *Value-added logistics services* (VALS). *Activities integrating the production and distribution segments of a supply chain. They range from low-end activities that add little value to the goods, mostly transport and storage, to high-end activities such as postponed manufacturing, including systems assembly, testing, and software installation.*

VALS connect production and transport chains in areas where international inflows and outflows of goods can be linked to regional flows. Logistics platforms incorporate additional functions such as back-office activities like managing goods and information flows, inventory management, tracking and tracing of goods, and fulfilling customs documentation and other formalities. While setting up their logistics platforms, logistics service providers favor locations that combine a central location, such as proximity to the consumers' market, with an intermodal gateway function. Seaports and sites along hinterland corridors typically meet these requirements.

VALS are a prime source for revenue generation and value-added in distribution/fulfillment centers and warehousing facilities. A key issue for logistics service providers is to decide on where to perform these value-added logistics services. These activities can be performed at the source in the country of export (e.g. in a Chinese warehouse), an intermediate location (e.g. a distribution center near a major port), or somewhere close to the consumer markets (e.g. close to an inland logistics platform). Even if VALS often take place in distribution centers and warehouses, the factors influencing the location decision for distribution centers are not necessarily identical to the determinants that guide the location of VALS. A complex interaction between selection factors determines where to perform value-added logistics activities at the level of the choice of the distribution system, the location of distribution centers, and the logistical characteristics of the product concerned (Box 1.12).

When considering VALS, the most relevant logistics characteristics of products include:

- **Distribution focus measurements**. For most labor-intensive activities, lower costs may outweigh the associated higher costs of transport and the longer lead times. As a result, these activities are performed in a warehouse at the source or at a centralized distribution center. In contrast, service-oriented activities that imply quick responses typically operate near the final market within several decentralized distribution centers. The higher the service requirement, the closer to the final market the VALS are positioned, and the more relevant are decentralized distribution centers.
- **Intensity of distribution and economies of scale**. The delivery frequency is expected to increase as manufacturers and retailers seek to achieve even greater economies linked with low levels of inventory as well as time-based distribution. This is the paradox of pressures toward economies of scale and high-frequency delivery. While centralized distribution systems are sensitive to large economies of scale and low delivery frequency, lower economies of scale and a high delivery frequency push logistics services in the opposite direction.
- **Replenishment lead time and demand uncertainty**. Replenishment lead time is the time that elapses once an order has been placed until it is physically on the shelf and available for consumption. Generally, the longer the replenishment lead time, the more safety stock needs to be kept, and the more relevant is keeping the inventory in a centralized distribution center structure. The demand variability of the product is also a major element affecting logistics decisions. Stable and predictable demand would lead to a location closer to low-cost sites and centralized distribution. Unstable and unpredictable demand requires a quicker response and a higher service level, resulting in locations closer to the final market and the decentralization of distribution.
- **Ratio of transportation costs over total costs**. A high ratio of transportation costs as part of total costs implies longer transport distances

within supply chains and energy costs. The share of transportation costs in total costs is determined by factors such as the future balance between global sourcing strategies and more local sourcing and the continued attractiveness of low-cost countries in global supply chains. In other words, a high share of transportation costs in total costs might motivate logistics service providers to move their activities closer to the customers.

- **Product life cycle**. Longer life cycles are typical for standard products, such as canned soup, which have relatively stable customer demand, lower market requirements, and a lower profit margin. This kind of product is more appropriate to operate at a centralized low-cost site. VALS on products with a shorter life cycle would be better performed closer to the final markets.
- **Market response flexibility**. If the products are needed to respond quickly to any changes in the market, it would be better to position the VALS near the customer base.
- **Product profit margin**. A low-profit margin product will have to reduce costs and be better served via a more centralized distribution concept. High-profit margin products generally demand a closer link with the customers to increase the service level.
- **Country-specific products or packaging requirements**. For example, if packaging requirements result in product volume increasing significantly, it would be better to perform this activity close to the final market to reduce shipping volume and transportation costs. However, power supply customization can easily be implemented in product manufacturing to meet regional standards.

When deciding where to operate VALS, distribution systems are first selected, followed by a specific location for the distribution center(s), and then the kind of VALS to be performed at each of the distribution centers. However, VALS can also have a significant impact on choices regarding the **structure of distribution systems** and the **location of distribution centers**. This is due to differences in logistics characteristics and requirements for each product category. The mix of structural logistics factors related to products will have a significant impact on determining which distribution network structure will be adopted, and where to locate distribution centers, as well as where to operate VALS.

It is also important to notice that once a VALS location has been selected, the situation does not remain unchanged. At any moment, the factors behind the selection of a specific VALS location may change, requiring an adjustment. This can take from a few weeks to a few months, depending on the scale of the inventory and the availability of new facilities on the leasing market. Relocating a distribution center takes much longer. Once a distribution center has been set up, the logistics service provider typically operates the facility for at least five to ten years, mainly because of the sunk costs. A complete change in the choice of the distribution system will be even more complex and time-consuming. By redistributing the location of VALS within existing nodes, a short-term impact on the quality and service attributes within the distribution network can be experienced without having to change the distribution structure or facility location.

**Box 1.12  Case study of the Nike European Logistics Campus in Belgium**

*Level 1: Choice of distribution system*. *Before the creation of the European internal market in 1993, Nike – just like many other international companies – had national DCs to serve different European countries. In 1994, Nike built one EDC of operations and logistics to serve all European countries at Laakdal in Belgium. The Nike European Logistics Campus (ELC) coordinates all the logistical activities between 700 factories (mainly in Asia) and 25,000 customers. All the Nike shoes, clothing, and accessories found in stores in Europe, the Middle East, and Africa (the so-called EMEA region) pass either virtually or physically through the facility in Laakdal. While Nike operates the ELC in Laakdal, distribution centers of large customers (such as Footlocker and Decathlon) are acting as some sort of 'external' RDCs which mainly involves cross-docking. By changing from 32 decentralized DCs prior to 1994 to 1 EDC, Nike realized big savings on inventory costs and close-outs after each season. The savings on warehousing and transportation costs were more limited. While deciding whether to build one centralized distribution center, Nike took into account a trade-off between the product life cycle and demand variability. With a short product life cycle and high demand variability, it is better to have one centralized distribution center. If the product life cycle is long and demand is stable, the company can decentralize its products at low risk. The main logistics characteristics of Nike apparel and footwear are a short product life cycle (typically three months due to seasonality), unpredictable customer demand, a high product profit margin, and a distribution focus on service. The strong seasonality and high demand variability were strong incentives for Nike to build one centralized distribution center at Laakdal.*

*Level 2: Location of DC*. *The Laakdal facility is located along the Albert Canal about 45 km east of the port of Antwerp and adjacent to a large inland container terminal. In the early 2010s, the facility underwent a major expansion with the realization of a new building for storing and handling equipment. The decision of Nike to set up the ELC in Laakdal in 1994 and to further expand the facility was mainly based on its central location and good infrastructure. Some 96% of Nike's inbound flow is over water via regular container barge services coming from the ports of Antwerp, Rotterdam and Zeebrugge. The ELC is very close to highway E313 which connects Antwerp to Germany. The cargo airports of Brussels and Liège are within a 100 km distance. In March 2007, Nike welcomed its first inbound container delivery via rail. Other important location factors relate to co-operation with local authorities, the availability of an educated work force and the integration process within Nike Belgium.*

*Level 3: Location of VALS*. *Products of Nike can be delivered to their European customers via three different supply chain models: directly from the factory to the customer (one container/one customer); from factory to the customer via a deconsolidation center (one container/multiple customers); from factory to the customer via the ELC in Laakdal. The main VALS activities in the Laakdal ELC are related to quality control, cross-docking, product labelling, shoebox labelling, the application of security tags, outer carton labelling, palletizing, final packaging, and order picking for parts of the Nike store online orders.*

# Chapter 1.5  Ports and cruise shipping

*The global cruise industry offers a combination of local destinations accessible through the cruise port and onboard amenities offered by the cruise ship.*

## 1 EVOLUTION OF CRUISE SHIPPING

Cruise shipping was first established to transport pleasure-seeking upper-class travelers on seagoing vessels, offering one or more ports of call in the United States and the Caribbean. From the mid-nineteenth century, **liner services** supported long-distance passenger transportation between continents, particularly between Europe and North America. The need to accommodate a large number of passengers of different socioeconomic statuses for at least a week led to the emergence of specific ship designs, radically different from cargo ships, where speed and comfort (at least for the elite) were paramount.

The rapid growth of the cruise industry can be traced to the demise of the ocean liner in the 1960s as it was replaced by fast jet services with which it could not compete. The last liners became the first cruise ships, following the complete demise of liner passenger services as it was realized that long-distance travel was to be assumed by air transport. The availability of a fleet of liners, whose utility was no longer commercially justifiable, led to their reconversion to form fleets of cruise ships. For example, one of the last purposely designed liners, the SS France, served as a cruise ship (SS Norway) between 1980 and 2003. However, liners were not particularly suitable for the requirements of the emerging cruise industry. Since they were designed to operate on the North Atlantic throughout the year for scheduled passenger services, their outdoor amenities, such as boardwalks and swimming pools, were limited. Additionally, they were built for speed (which was their trademark) with the related high levels of fuel consumption.

The beginning of the modern cruise industry was also to a certain extent invented in Greece by the pioneer Epirotiki Lines and an aggressive expansion strategy that identified the demand limits of the East Mediterranean market and planned itineraries on the other side of the Atlantic. The founding of Norwegian Cruise Line (1966), Royal Caribbean International (1968), and Carnival Cruise Lines (1972), which have remained the largest cruise lines, and the presence of a major passenger source market, led rapidly to a focus on the United States and the Caribbean that provided the basis for the remarkable growth and expansion of the idea of cruising. While less celebrated, during the same period, refurbished liners were offering cruises in Eastern Europe just as such cruises were offered in the Black Sea and the Baltic Sea during the Soviet era.

In the twenty-first century, following an uninterrupted growth and modernization, cruise shipping offers itineraries in a global network of local destinations accessible through the cruise port, with the features of cruise ports and associated transportation and tourist services being as

## FIGURE 1.36 Global Cruise Passengers Carried and Growth Rates, 1990–2020

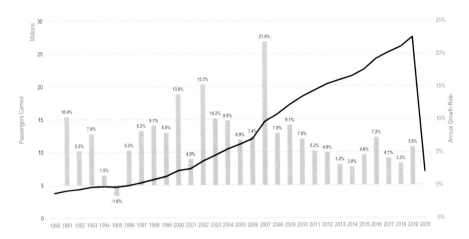

Note: Growth rate not depicted for 2020 (−74.2%).
Source: Adapted from Cruise Market Watch (2020).

important as the onboard amenities. The cruise industry is a mixture of maritime transport, travel, and tourism services, facilitating the leisure activity of passengers paying for an itinerary and, potentially, other services on board.

> *A cruise includes at least one night on board on a seagoing vessel having a capacity of at least 100 passengers. Transportation (the cruise ship) is the core element of the experience instead of a simple conveyance.*

Since the late 1970s, cruise shipping has experienced unprecedented growth. The global growth rate of the cruise industry has been enduring despite economic cycles of growth and recession (Figure 1.36). In the 1990s and the 2000s, the size of the global cruise markets doubled about every ten years, which represents an annual growth rate of about 7%. In 2000, 7.2 million people took a cruise. Only 3.8 million people had done so in 1990. In 2004, this number exceeded the 10 million threshold. Fifteen years later, in 2019, almost 30 million single persons cruised worldwide on one of the 400 cruise vessels, generating more than 150 million passenger movements in world cruise ports.

The globalization of a cruise industry that calls in at a growing number of ports around the globe appeared to be unstoppable, with the COVID-19 pandemic the first major setback in almost a half-century. Cruise growth was halted for the first time by the pandemic, a sanitary crisis resulting in restrictions on social/human contacts for reasons that were not purely economic. Before that, cruise growth had recorded a remarkable **resilience** in the face of economic, social, political, or any other crises that regularly challenge both the shipping and tourism sectors. While the global financial crisis of 2008–2009 had a major impact on ocean-going cargo shipping, cruise shipping and ports continued to experience steadily rising passenger numbers. Stagnation did not occur even when, in 2012, the Costa Concordia grounding generated negative public relations or through minor incidents on cruise ships operated by leading firms. Environmental and social challenges (i.e. emissions) were seemingly unable to undermine the operating context and growth prospects. However, after the financial crisis of 2008–2009, growth rates were relatively lower than in the 1990s and first half of the 2000s.

At the beginning of 2021, the cruise fleet numbered 412 vessels with an annual capacity of 32.3 million passengers and an estimated sales revenue, based on the average revenue generated by each passenger for the major cruise companies over 2019, standing at approximately 1,675 US dollars per cruise passenger. The worldwide market share taken by the North American market was 53%, and that of the European market was 32.4%. Asia was the third biggest market with a 14.7% share.

Subsequently, the COVID-19 pandemic triggered unprecedented global health and economic crisis with **structural consequences** for the cruise industry. In early 2020 COVID-19 outbreaks associated with three cruise ship voyages generated more than 800 confirmed cases among passengers and crew. The whole industry voluntarily suspended operations worldwide, with the timing and return conditions remaining questionable. Later in 2020, a second wave of the pandemic resulted in a further postponement of cruise calls in most world ports, including the regions that have seen a restart of cruising, suggesting that 2020 was the most disastrous year in the history of cruise shipping, with the number of passengers dropping from 27.5 million in 2019 to just above 7 million. This represents a 75% drop in traffic. As the post-COVID-19 new normal continues to evolve, making a precise assessment of the longer-term implications is challenging.

Traditionally, cruise statistics have counted the number of onboard guests, measuring the size of the market by the number of persons who decide to take a cruise each year (Box 1.13). This can be misleading, as it underestimates both the size of operations and the importance of the market for the port industry and the respective destinations. Each passenger embarking on a cruise visits between 4.6 and 5.2 cruise ports. As a result, the total number of cruise passenger movements hosted is remarkably higher than that of single passengers. Driven by industry trends, a ship with a capacity of 4,000 passengers on annualized 50 weeks deployment in a standard seven-day itinerary of six ports (one homeport, five transit ports) in the West Mediterranean market, and excluding any effect of inter-porting, generates 1.4 million passenger movements per year. In total, the 27.5 million cruisers of 2019 generated more than 150 million passenger movements in cruise ports around the world. Thus, **cruise passenger movements** stand as a unit that most matters for the ports and is increasingly used in related industry reports.

## Box 1.13 Cruise passengers' visits in mediterranean cruise ports

FIGURE 1.37 Cruise Passengers' Visits in Mediterranean Cruise Ports

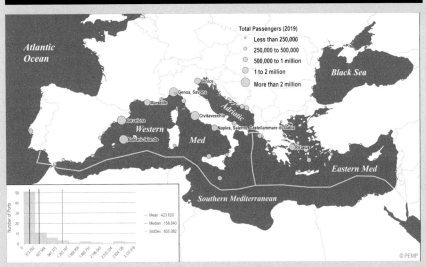

Source: MedCruise (2020).

*The Mediterranean is the world's second-largest cruise shipping market, representing over 16% of the annual cruise capacity. It can be broken down into distinctive multi-port regions, the Western Med, the Eastern Med, and the Adriatic. The Western Med represents the main market, but congestion is encouraging the consideration of new itineraries in the Eastern Med and the Black Sea. The proximity of the Mediterranean to Europe provides the advantage of a large pool of customers with discretionary spending potential. It is a perennial cruise market with a summer peak season (several itineraries are not serviced in the winter) (Figure 1.37).*

*The Mediterranean offers at the same time seaside resort destinations (e.g. Palma de Mallorca, Mykonos) as well as world-class cultural amenities as several cities are museums by themselves (e.g. Venice). The Eastern Med lacks airport capacity and connectivity, with limited cruise terminals, except for the Greek Islands, which are predominantly serviced from Piraeus with smaller ships.*

*Typical seven day itineraries are structured as small loops of four to five ports of call, each covering a specific sub-region such as the Adriatic or the Spanish coast. Since the distances between ports of call are relatively short, this leaves additional time for shore excursions at each port of call, offering a wide array of cultural amenities. Fourteen day itineraries are also being offered to cover large parts of the European side of the Mediterranean.*

*Many of the itineraries are focused on historical sites and exceptional scenery. The most popular countries for cruise ports of call in Europe are Spain, Italy, and Greece. Strong growth in Mediterranean cruises in recent years has resulted in some ports getting very crowded. This is particularly felt in top cruise tourist destinations such as Santorini in Greece, Venice in Italy, and Dubrovnik in*

*Croatia. Hub ports such as Civitavecchia and Barcelona are challenged to cope with the strong growth.*

*Eight ports serve more than 1 million cruise passenger movements per year, with the biggest of all, Barcelona, serving more than 3 million passengers and two more (Civitavecchia (Rome) and Balearic islands), hosting over 2 million passengers. The cruise period is marked by substantial seasonality.*

## 2 GROWTH DRIVERS

Six trends shape the modern cruise market as drivers of growth:

- **Expansion and capturing of cruise lines revenue streams** via regular fleet renewal and the offering of expanded onboard amenities as well as shore-based excursions (shorex). The cruise ship has become an essential part of the cruise experience since it also represents a destination in itself.
- **Upscale of cruise ship size**. The principle of economies of scale and the development of a broader customer base has generated the deployment of larger cruise ships. While in the 1990s, cruise ships rarely exceeded 2,000 passengers, by the 2010s, ships of 6,000 passengers were being deployed. Also, larger ships are able to support a wider range of amenities.
- **Market segmentation** with different types of vessels, associated with different amenities offered onboard and ashore, with the variety of types of cruises offered, targeting different (social and age) groups of potential cruisers.
- **Globalization of deployment patterns**, along with sophisticated itinerary planning through the deployment of cruise shipping vessels in multiple world markets. First, cruise lines offer itineraries where the whole is essentially greater than the sum of its parts. Specific regional and cultural experiences are being offered through a combination of sailing time and choice of ports of call. Second, they adapt to seasonal and fundamental changes in demand by repositioning their ships (seasonal) and changing the configuration of their port calls (fundamental). A core strategy of some cruise lines is not to offer fixed itineraries per season but regularly move their cruise vessels from one region to another for certain periods of a calendar year.
- **Internationalization of passenger source markets**, with cruise shipping developing strategies leading to an expansion of the sources of their guests. This is also linked with the expansion of the population groups attracted by modern cruises.
- **Concentration**. The industry has a high level of ownership and market concentration, with each conglomerate operating a number of different brands in order to expand the targeted passenger groups. Carnival and Royal Caribbean, the two leading cruise conglomerations, account for 73% of the market.

These six trends underline a unique foundation of the cruise industry. The **supply push strategy** of cruise operators aims to create demand simply by providing new capacity (ships) and finding customers, called guests, to fill them through itinerary planning, marketing, and discounting strategies. The possibility of cruise ship operators successfully following a supply push strategy makes the cruise industry quite different from other shipping markets, such as container shipping. This is counter to the tourism sector in general, which is highly demand-derived and sensitive to the general economic context. Hence, in most shipping markets, the shipping activity is a clear derived trade activity, and demand is rather inelastic price-wise. Demand in the cruise business is created through pricing, branding, and marketing. Cruise operators are challenged to develop competitive cruise packages that involve a high-quality stay onboard, an array of shore-based activities offering access to a variety of cultures and sites, and easy transfers from the vessel. Most cruise lines have a logistics office responsible for supplying ships, particularly food, which is a core amenity. Variation in preferences is observed depending on the itinerary, and the composition of passengers, including factors such as origin and age.

## 3 UPGRADED VESSELS AND ONBOARD AMENITIES

The construction of cruise ships tends to occur in cycles where several ships are ordered and enter the market within a short time frame (Box 1.14). Since the cruise industry is a relatively small segment of the tourism sector, it has so far been very successful at finding customers to fill a greater number of ever larger ships. The cruise product has become diversified to attract new customers and respond to the preferences of a wide array of customer groups. With a view to fulfilling the expectations of its guests, the cruise industry has innovated through the development of new destinations, unique ship designs, new and diverse onboard amenities, facilities, and services, plus wide-ranging shoreside activities. Most cruise ship operators work around specific cruise themes, and voyage lengths can vary to meet the changing vacation patterns of customers, thus contributing to cruise market concentration.

### Box 1.14  Ocean-going cruise vessels newbuilds in European yards

*Although conventional merchant shipbuilding has been in decline in Europe since the late 1970s in the face of lower-cost competition from the Far East, the European industry has been more successful in retaining market share in a number of specialist sectors. The most important is cruise ship construction, in which the European industry has been the world leader for nearly 50 years.*

*The yards in Italy, Germany, France, and Finland are the most important suppliers to the market and account for most ships due for delivery. Germany and Italy are the current leaders with 70% of the order book between them. Europe offers an abundance of specialist skills and sophisticated technology in navigation and outfitting, which support European cruise ship construction and assist the yards in maintaining a competitive edge. The outstanding reputation of European yards has meant that US cruise lines have continued to order ships in Europe. Most of the oceanic cruise ships constructed in the second half of the 2010s were built in European yards (Figure 1.38).*

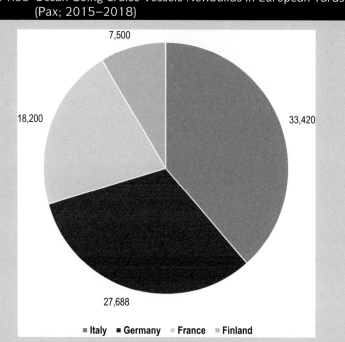

FIGURE 1.38 Ocean-Going Cruise Vessels Newbuilds in European Yards (Pax; 2015–2018)

*Although other non-European yards have the capacity and technology to build cruise ships, they may not have project management capability, aptitude or the desired balance of labor and skills required to deliver a cost-effective result within a required budget in the contracted delivery time. However, Far Eastern yards have been studying the market diligently, and prospective orders have been reported for yards in China. Japan had orders for few ships, but its market participation was sporadic; ships were previously delivered in 1998 and 2004.*

*The majority of cruise ships serving the European market are dry-docked in Europe, together with several North American ships summering in the region. European yards also undertake major conversions such as replacing main engines and inserting a mid-body to lengthen the ship.*

The new, more innovative cruise ships make the companies even more profitable as passengers are usually willing to pay more for cruising onboard the newest vessel, which tends to offer more spending opportunities onboard while being more efficient to operate. Innovative cruise ships enable major improvement of services. For instance, they allow easy-to-use systems that expand guest choices and simplify schedules, as well as advanced technology that speeds up processes (i.e. boarding, luggage tracking, etc.) and improves experiences. The average ship of the late twentieth century period had eight guest decks, while modern vessels of 13, 14, or even 18 guest decks provide opportunities to have cabins with more room and private verandas. Ships also changed their sailing technology by adding stabilizers, which are underwater wings attached to the hull, reducing effects of the motion of the ocean.

The market drivers of the cruise industry are similar to those that fostered the growth of tourism after World War II, particularly the rising affluence of the global population and the growing popularity of exotic and resort destinations. The general aging of the population is also a factor in favor of cruise shipping, as the primary market remains older adults, albeit cruise guests are getting significantly younger. While, in 1995, the average age of a cruiser was about 65 years, this figure dropped to 45 years by 2006.

What is novel with cruising is that the ship represents in itself a **destination**, essentially acting as a floating hotel (or a theme park) with all the related facilities (bars, restaurants, theaters, casinos, swimming pools). This has permitted cruise lines to develop a captive market within their ships as well as for shore-based activities, particularly for excursions or facilities entirely owned by subsidiaries of the cruise line (Box 1.15).

Some cruise operators go a long way in developing **new entertainment concepts** onboard their vessels, including surf pools, planetariums, on-deck LED movie screens, golf simulators, water parks, demonstration kitchens, multi-room villas with private pools, and in-suite Jacuzzis, ice-skating rinks, rock-climbing walls, and bungee trampolines. All these lead to increased economic returns via strong performance in both onboard and onshore revenues. Onboard services account for between 20% and 30% of the total cruise line revenues. The average customer spends about $1,700 for their cruise, including ship and off-ship expenses for goods and services. The majority of these expenses are captured within the cruise ship as passengers spend on average $100 per port of call.

### Box 1.15  Revenue and expenses per average cruiser

*While in 2018, the average revenue was about $1,791 per cruiser, the associated expenses were $1,562, implying a profit margin in the range of 12–13%. At the beginning of the decade, these percentages stood at 77% ($1.663) and 23% ($1.485) respectively, a clear indication that the upgrade of tvhe amenities onboard provides higher yields to cruise lines. The breakdown of revenues and expenses has the following characteristics:*

*Revenue. The base fare paid by the average cruiser accounts for 72% of the revenue, implying that cruise lines are able to generate an additional 28% revenue tranche with onboard services, such as gambling, excursions, drinks, and personal services. Additionally, cruisers are spending on goods and services at ports of call, which are not accounted for here.*

*Expenses. The main expenses related to the ship operations, which include port fees and taxes (often levied per cruiser), ship maintenance, fuel (12%), payroll (13%), food & beverages, and the provision of onboard services. A standard cruise package includes food services as well as onboard services such as shows. Since the booking of ships is a marketing-intensive activity involving advertisement, agent commissions account for a notable share of expenses (15%). Cruise ships are capital intensive (a ship carrying 3,500 passengers costs more than $800 million), with approximately 15% of the expenses related to servicing the debt contracted for their purchase (Figure 1.39).*

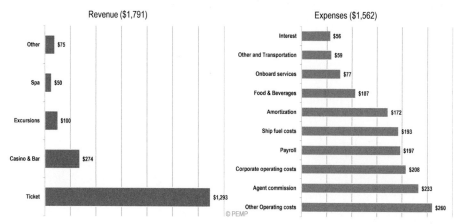

FIGURE 1.39 Average Cruise Revenue and Expense Breakdown Per Passenger

Sources: Carnival Corporation & Plc., Royal Caribbean Cruises, Norwegian Cruise Lines, Thomson/First Call, Cruise Lines International Association (CLIA), Florida Caribbean Cruise Association (FCCA), DVB Bank, Cruise Pulse; www.cruisemarketwatch.com. Note: Excursions only cover those organized by the cruise line.

## 4 SCALE AND MARKET

All leading cruise conglomerates such as Carnival, Royal Caribbean Cruises Lines (RCCL), MSC Cruises, and Norwegian Cruise Line (NCL), have invested in the ordering and operation of **bigger capacity cruise ships**. The pursuit of economies of scale in cruising has been very successful, earning record profits for the cruise lines. The first dedicated cruise ships appeared in the 1970s and could carry about 1,000 passengers. By the 1980s, economies of scale were further expanded with cruise ships that could carry more than 2,000 passengers. Today, the capacity of each of the 50 largest vessels in operation exceeds 3,000 passengers, with the largest (the Royal Caribbean Oasis Class vessels) having a capacity of just over 6,600 passengers and 228,000 Gross Tons (GT). By the mid-2000s, the average ship size exceeded 82,000 GT with a capacity of 2,000 passengers. The average dimensions of a cruise ship are 200 meters in length and 26 meters in width. The standard deviation of ship dimensions is large, and average numbers need to be treated with caution. Nevertheless, these dimensions have little to do with the situation observed in the early 2000s, when cruise ships with a capacity above 2,000 passengers were rare. As the capital, operating, and voyage costs associated with the construction and operation of the largest cruise vessels suggest, the potential to further upscale cruise vessel size is not evident (Box 1.16).

## Box 1.16 Economies of scale in cruise shipping

FIGURE 1.40 Costs of Super- and Mega-Size Cruise Vessels (> 120,000 GT)

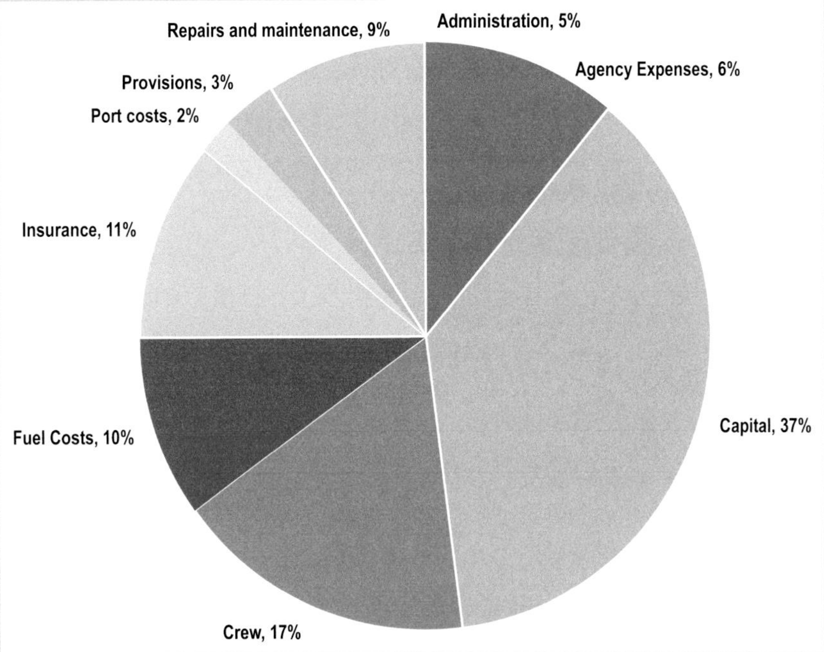

Source: Chaos, Pallis, Marchán, Roca and Conejo (2020).

*Recent research on the capital, operating, and voyage costs associated with the construction and operations of the cruise fleet suggests that further upscaling of cruise vessels' size should not go unchallenged. This is because a further increase in cruise ship size is not necessarily associated with diminishing costs per passenger (guest) (Figure 1.40).*

*Capital costs are the costs of building the cruise ship plus any related interest. Operating costs are the expenses related to the daily operation of the vessel, including crew costs, maintenance and repairs, insurance, and administration costs. Voyage costs are the costs for commercial use of the ship (i.e. fuel costs, provisions, port costs, canal dues, agency expenses, and others).*

*The study of these costs for the world cruise fleet concluded that capital costs are the highest cost component (28%–38%) for a cruise vessel. The second highest cost component is staffing (16%–26%), due to the large number of auxiliary personnel required. Insurance costs represent 10%–11% of the total costs. This percentage is higher than the respective 5% that is observed in other types of seagoing vessels. Yet, it is justified by the substantially higher construction costs of the newly built cruise vessels. In contrast to different types of passenger ships or cargo vessels, operating costs (between 41% and 50%) are higher than voyage costs (between 21% and 22%).*

*Based on these results, a model detailing the unit costs per passenger and per year (€/pax·year) for different size cruise vessels, under the assumptions of full occupancy and a low operating time of 60 days (which is the case for approximately 60% of such vessels) estimates a decline in the average voyage, operating, and capital costs, in mid-sized (20,000–60,000 GT) and big (60,000–120,000 GT) cruise vessels compared to small cruises (under 20,000 GT) at over 30%. From this size upwards (i.e. in the case of super (120,000–200,000 GT) or mega-size (over 120,000 GT) cruise vessels), the average costs remain stable. The explanation lies in the significant weight of capital costs in relation to the other costs.*

*When the cruise vessels are utilized for more prolonged operating time, increasing to 120 days per annum, the voyage costs are altered, and economies of scale are realized since average total costs decrease as the size of the ship increases. However, the presence of scale economies is limited to a certain size (60,000–120,000 GT). From this size upwards, average total costs (per passenger) were found to increase again. It is important to highlight that larger cruise ships are more sensitive to passenger occupancy than smaller ones due to their high capital and operating costs. Although the number of passengers increases significantly with ship size, the capital cost of the biggest vessels (construction and financing cost) is such that the average capital cost per passenger increases instead of decreasing.*

Each cruise line classifies its vessels in classes of cruise ships of similar size and similar experiences offered to guests (Figure 1.41). All cruise ships in a particular class share a handful of amenities and stylings, and a reasonably similar experience. Still, newer ships within a class will likely have newer amenities and technologies. The construction of higher capacity cruise ships is the outcome of three drivers:

- The link between vessel size increases with the **creation of new passenger demand**, as bigger vessels enable the addition of a variety of onboard activities and services and expand the targeted social and age groups.
- **Revenue capture** by both additional ticket purchases and the expansion and variation of the services and activities offered on vessels.
- **Economies of scale**, such as lowering average total costs by spreading fixed costs over several additional passengers.

**FIGURE 1.41 Classification of Cruise Ships by Cruise Lines**

| Carnival Cruise Lines | | Royal Caribbean INTERNATIONAL | | Princess Cruises | |
|---|---|---|---|---|---|
| Ship class | Tonnage (GT) | Ship class | Tonnage (GT) | Ship class | Tonnage (GT) |
| Fantasy class | 70.367 – 70.538 | Sovereign class | 69,130 – 82.910 | Explorer class | 30,277 |
| Spirit class | 85,492 – 85,920 | Vision class | 73,937 – 82,910 | Sun class | 77,441 – 77,499 |
| Triumph class | 101,353 – 101,509 | Radiance class | 90,090 | Coral class | 91,627 |
| Conquest class | 100.239 – 110,320 | Voyager class | 137,276 | Grand class | 107,517 – 108,977 |
| Splendor class | 113,323 | Freedom class | 154,407 | Super Grand class | 112,894 – 113,561 |
| Dream class | 182,048 – 128,261 | Quantum class | 168,666 | Diamond class | 115,875 |
| | | Oasis class | 224,746– 227,000 | Royal Class | 142,714 |

In an attempt at further market penetration, cruise lines or specific brands of the larger conglomerates are present in several market segments, with two aims. The first is to expand the social and age groups of potential cruisers. The second is to generate repeat cruisers by providing incentives to past guests to return for a new experience, cruising on another type of vessel or with another itinerary.

There are four cruise market segments (Figure 1.42):

- **Contemporary cruises** are popular amenity-packed cruises for people looking for many activities and great value. These mainstream cruises rival land-based vacations by offering a comprehensive and amenity-filled package, including accommodations, meals, and entertainment, in a casual environment, with newer (or extensively renovated) ships offering modern design and comforts. The biggest market segment (with a market share of approximately 74%), featuring the largest cruise vessels, has an average cruise length of seven days or shorter, and appeals to all age and income cruisers. It also includes budget cruises with older vessels, which is a cruise market segment active in Europe and North America.
- **Premium cruises** are more upscale cruises offering many amenities, with an increased focus on refined service and more space. Priced inclusive of accommodations, meals, and entertainment, the value of premium cruising exceeds or rivals the best packages offered by upscale hotels and resorts. The second biggest cruise market (with a share of approximately 20%), attracts more experienced cruisers.
- **Luxury cruises** are defined by the highest quality and personalized service offered on luxury cruise ships and ashore to exotic as well as more exclusive ports. Expensive compared to the rest of the industry, luxury lines deliver value by offering more inclusive pricing than other cruise lines and opportunities to travel to exotic and less common destinations on medium-sized or small, spacious vessels. Its market share stands at approximately 2%–4% of the cruise market.

### FIGURE 1.42  Segmentation of Cruise Shipping

| | Contemporary Cruise Lines | Premium Cruise Lines | Luxury Cruise Lines | Speciality Cruise Lines |
|---|---|---|---|---|
| Keyword | Quantity | Quality | Exclusivity | Adventure |
| Ships | Large ships | Medium-sized Ships | Small Ships | Very Small ships |
| Typical Capacity | 2,000 –5,600 Pax | 1500 – 2,500 Pax | 100-800 Pax | 100-300 Pax |
| Cabins | Small cabins | Large cabins | Huge cabins or all suites | Mixed cabin accommodations |
| Orientation | Family friendly | Family friendly, but more adult-oriented | Not family-friendly | Not suitable for most families |
| Length of itineraries | 3-7+ night | 7-14 night itineraries | 10+ night | 3-20 night |
| Quality of Services | 3-4 star service | 4-5 star service | 5-6 star service | 3-5 star service |
| Price point | $-$$$ | $$-$$$ | $$$$$ | $$$$-$$$$$ |
| Cruise Lines (examples) | Carnival Cruise Line; Costa Cruise Line; Disney; MSC; Norwegian Cruise Line; Royal Caribbean Internt | Azamara Cruise Line; Celebrity Cruises; Holland America; Oceania Cruises; Princess Cruises | Crystal Cruises; Cunard Line; Regent Seven Seas Cruises; Seabourn; Sea Dream; Silversea Cruises | Cruise West; Delta Queen Steamboat; Discovery World Cruises; Hurtigruten; Peter Deilmann; Star Clippers; Viking ; Windstar |

• **Specialty cruises** focus on a destination niche or a unique cruising style, including expedition-style cruises, sailing ships, and a growing number of river cruises. They offer long itineraries and visit some of the world's most remote and unspoiled places (such as Antarctica and the Arctic) to offer a unique experience that guests find educational and adventurous. Their market share is approximately 3%.

## 5 GLOBALIZATION OF DEPLOYMENT PATTERNS

The deployment of cruise vessels per cruise region reflects a combination of the existing demand and the willingness of cruise lines to develop new markets. Differences among the markets and regions exist, the most obvious being the variance in profitability. Each market also has its own characteristics. As such, the cruise industry must address multiple considerations related to onboard amenities, itineraries, ports of call, and shore excursions.

The Caribbean has been the dominant deployment market of the cruise industry since its inception, but the Mediterranean cruise market has grown substantially in recent years (Figure 1.43). The Caribbean and the Mediterranean are complementary markets because the Caribbean is predominantly serviced during the winter while the Mediterranean experiences a summer peak season. An important factor behind the popularity of both the Caribbean and Mediterranean is that the distances between port calls are relatively short and they involve a wide variety of cultural experiences. Both markets offer a variety of cultures in proximity. Furthermore, strong niche markets have developed, focusing on history (Hanseatic cities in northern Europe) or natural amenities (Alaska). Asia is the rising cruise market of the twentieth century, with China standing at the epicenter of the growth. In the early 2020s, cruise shipping has started exploring the potential of Middle East destinations.

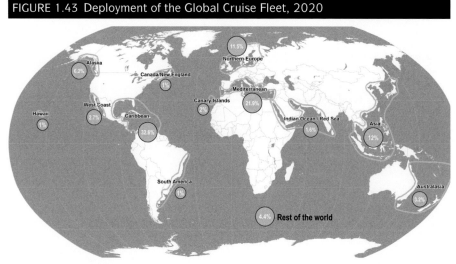

FIGURE 1.43 Deployment of the Global Cruise Fleet, 2020

Source: Adapted from Cruise Lines Industry Association (CLIA) (2019). Note: The boundaries of cruise regions focus on the main areas of activity.

In 2019, the Caribbean, including the Bahamas, hosted over 38% of the global cruise capacity, with Alaska the second largest. The West Coast (Mexico), Bermuda, Canada–New England, and the Panama Canal were comparatively smaller markets. An additional element contributing to the growth of cruising in the region is the new destinations in the form of private islands or private parts of islands, leased and developed by cruise lines. Cuba and the further opening of the island economy to American and international cruisers and entrepreneurs is the final milestone in the globalization process. While cruises to Cuba have been popular among international travelers for decades, Americans have missed out. Regulatory changes mean more cruise lines are willing to offer visits to Cuba. The demand for cruising to the island is now coupled with the decisions of European cruise lines (i.e. MSC and Celectyal) to deploy vessels in Cuba and of US-based cruise lines (i.e. RCCL and Norwegian Cruise Line) to include Cuba in their itineraries.

Two distinctive markets exist in Europe, as vessels are deployed either in the Mediterranean and its adjoining seas or in the North European market. The Mediterranean and its adjoining seas stand as the bigger region of the two, hosting 16% of the deployed cruise fleet. Within the on-going globalization of the cruise industry, this is the region of the world that has grown fastest of all during the first 15 years of the twenty-first century, emerging as the second most popular cruise destination worldwide. Yet, this is also the region where growth trends in several countries evaporated in recent years, affected by geopolitical turmoil and tensions. The North European market ranks as the third biggest cruise market globally, hosting approximately 11% of the globally deployed cruise vessel capacity.

The Asian market, in particular China, has experienced the most growth in recent years. In the 2010s, the number of ships deployed in Asia grew, operating days expanded, and passenger capacity almost tripled, reaching a double-digit share for the first time in 2019 (10%). Increased capacity deployment, combined with the opening of sales offices by many cruise lines in China, Hong Kong, Korea, Singapore, and Taiwan, resulted in a growth of cruise passengers from 1.3 million in 2012 to almost 4 million in 2019. Beyond China, the destinations with the most significant growth in total port calls were Japan and Thailand with port calls also growing in Hong Kong, Taiwan, and the Philippines. The increase is mainly based on the number of Chinese cruise passengers, which surpasses all other Asian markets combined. Asia has quickly progressed to becoming a region that almost equals the Med in passenger capacity deployment.

The type of vessels deployed and the length of the offered cruise hint at the peculiarities of the Asian cruise market. Large and mega-ships offering cruises in Asia are seasonally operated. Middle-size and small-size ships are most common, as short cruises dominate. The peculiarities result from the geographical features and the cultural differences of this market compared to others that have developed in recent times. First, the very short, or short, distances between calling ports and destinations available in the Caribbean, the Mediterranean, and the rest of the European market are not present. To combine destinations of interest or broader geographical parts, distances have to be longer and a full day, or more, at sea might be an essential itinerary feature. Also, shorter vacations are most common, as people have limited vacation entitlement. As for the cultural dimension, cruises in Asia tend to offer different onboard amenities. For example, casinos and more extended luxury shopping are high in the agendas of people taking a cruise in the region. However, they might not be prioritized by those opting for a cruise in other parts of the world.

Long-term, **China** remains a bullish market. However, this is not an unchallenged process. The expansion requires port infrastructure development, which is associated with several financial and non-financial tests. The former have met with success as state and private investors in several destinations in China (i.e. Shanghai), Hong-Kong, and not least the broader region (Singapore, Busan, etc.), have developed modern terminals serving the needs of cruise lines. Issues such as terminal locations and development choices have been subject to social and political controversies in the absence of relevant culture.

In contrast, some of the newly built cruise terminals are remarkably large in size and capacity, raising concerns that they stand as prestige investments with rather limited potential utilization. Supply concerns, a lack of destinations to sail short cruises to, price wars, and geopolitical tensions, such as issues involving North Korea and Taiwan, are undermining growth potential. That said, Singapore, Taiwan, Malaysia, and the Philippines, are where more cruise capacity has been deployed, counterbalancing any downtrends.

Other regions of the world continue to provide smaller yet important markets for cruise shipping. The overall changes in these smaller markets are in response to market capacity and geopolitical events. South America, meaning mainly Brazil, has been a smaller market, which is recovering from stagnation, yet is hampered by poor infrastructure and high port costs. The Australian market has been active since the earlier days of modern cruising and hosts more than 1 million cruise passengers in a country with a total population of 24 million. This has already given Australia the highest market penetration in the world. Africa is slowly coming into the picture, with cruise lines exploring options in several parts of the continent and ports and destinations expressing an interest in developing effective strategies to accommodate cruise calls.

The cruise industry is also expanding to provide more options for passengers, particularly for niche markets commanding higher prices. The Caribbean and the Mediterranean remain competitive mass markets. Cruises are set up for the Antarctic, the Canadian Arctic, and the South Pacific. In some cases, destinations may have more impacts than itineraries, inciting cruise lines to offer longer shore stay options where the cruise ship can become a temporary hotel near central areas, particularly when there is a major event, such as the Rio Carnival, the Monaco Grand Prix, or the British Open. Cruise ships can also be used for the evacuation of stranded people after natural disasters. For instance, in 2017, cruise ships were used after a major hurricane struck Puerto Rico to evacuate people from the island and nearby islands. For short trips of less than 24 hours, a cruise ship can carry two to five times its design capacity.

Beyond the presence of a port capable of hosting a cruise call efficiently and effectively, factors affecting deployment patterns include:

- The geographical distribution of passenger source markets.
- The need to match brands and ships to source market demographics.
- The links with airlift and landside transportation to/from the potential homeports.
- The opportunity to balance marquee destinations with lesser-known gems or develop new routes and generate itineraries for new markets.
- The potential for shore expedition revenues compared to onboard spending.
- Fuel sourcing.
- Availability and cost considerations.

All these are examined by cruise lines in parallel with cruise time, speed and distance in order to decide where and how to deploy cruise ships.

## 6  INTERNATIONALIZATION OF SOURCE MARKETS

With the cruise industry offering amenities that more people are interested in experiencing, a major expansion and internationalization of passenger source markets is in progress (Figure 1.45), adding to the growth potential of

**FIGURE 1.44** Average Cruise Passenger Age Group

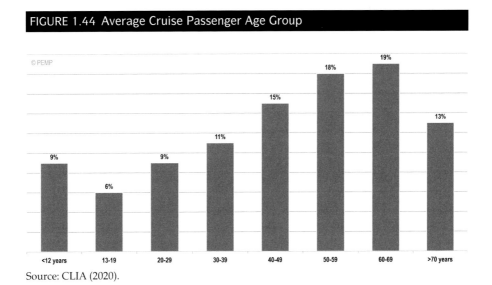

Source: CLIA (2020).

the industry. Its highest market penetration level is in North America, with about 3% of the population taking a cruise each year. This includes people who may take more than one cruise in a year. North America continues to be the primary source market in size as it continues to experience growth, with more than half of the total cruise passengers per year coming from this region. Growth has slowed in recent years, but the low cruise penetration levels in many local markets underline opportunities for expanding cruises in the region. Other markets are also emerging. Between 2000 and 2015, the number of European taking a cruise doubled, providing incentives for cruise lines to build more itineraries throughout the region, particularly in the Mediterranean Sea. Almost one out of four European cruisers live in the UK and Ireland.

Cruise lines are expanding their **target population**, attracting young adults and families with children. While this used to be a '65 years and above' type of market, in 2018, the average age of cruisers was 46.7 years. Just 13% were over 70 years old, and the over 65 group accounted for 32% of all cruisers that year (Figure 1.44). The demographic profile of the average cruiser has rapidly changed.

Countries with a maritime tradition tend to have a higher share of the population taking cruises. Penetration levels in Asia remain low (0.1% to 0.2%) as a cruise is generally not perceived as an accepted form of vacationing, but the situation is changing rapidly. Since the mid-2010s, the passenger source markets for cruise tourism have experienced another transformation (Figure 1.45). The absolute volume of cruise travelers sourced from Asia quadrupled to over 3 million passengers, corresponding to about 15% of the global passenger volume. China accounts for two-thirds of the regional passengers, with other leading source markets including Taiwan, Japan, and Singapore. India and Hong Kong are the other two markets with over 100,000 passengers per year. Demand for cruises outside conventional source markets has grown remarkably, yet the aggregate of cruise passengers in these regions remains small.

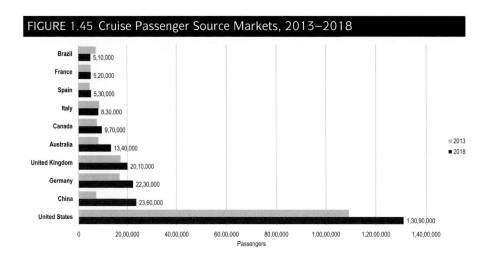

FIGURE 1.45  Cruise Passenger Source Markets, 2013–2018

# 7 MARKET CONCENTRATION AND MULTI-BRAND STRATEGIES

The cruise industry has a very **high level of ownership concentration** as the four largest cruise shipping companies account for 83% of the market (Carnival Lines, Royal Caribbean, MSC Cruises, and Norwegian Cruise Line). High levels of **horizontal integration** are also observable since most cruise companies have acquired parent companies but kept their individual names for product differentiation. Carnival Corporation, with its ten different brands, controls 39% of the global cruise market. In comparison, Royal Caribbean accounts for 24% of the global market serviced under six different brands, such as Celebrity Cruises which caters to higher-end customers. Azamara Club Cruises has smaller ships servicing more exotic destinations with shore stay options. The MSC-owned vessels represent an 8% market share, while Norwegian Cruise Line (NCL) Holdings is the owner of three different brands representing 9.4% of the market. Approximately 35 additional cruise lines are currently in operation (Figure 1.46). The entry of Virgin Cruises, which promised to offer an entirely new product, may further increase differentiation. A continuous consolidation is observable, with the acquisition of Silversea by Royal Caribbean being the latest chapter of this trend.

The four largest players are active in every cruising area, aiming at capturing market shares. The top two corporations consolidate different brands seeking to cover a variety of market segments. Beyond different and potentially more effective corporate entities, this allows for differentiated services to be offered and the marketing of each brand as unique, attracting a larger share of the demand. At the same time, cruise lines act as pioneers. Carnival Corporation was the first cruise company ever to order a cruise ship built in China, dedicated to the Chinese market. Carnival was also the first company to deploy a cruise ship in Asia, aiming to exploit the potentials of the Asian market, especially the Chinese market. Like its cargo shipping counterparts,

FIGURE 1.46 Market Share of Main Cruise Lines, 2020

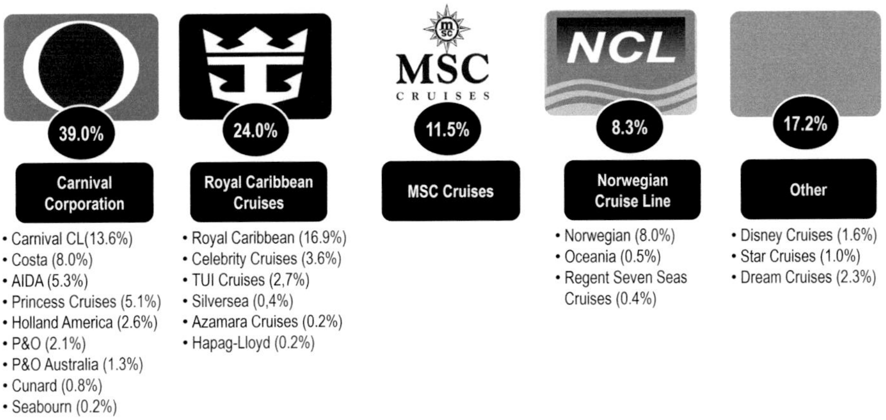

| Carnival Corporation 39.0% | Royal Caribbean Cruises 24.0% | MSC Cruises 11.5% | Norwegian Cruise Line 8.3% | Other 17.2% |
|---|---|---|---|---|
| • Carnival CL(13.6%) <br> • Costa (8.0%) <br> • AIDA (5.3%) <br> • Princess Cruises (5.1%) <br> • Holland America (2.6%) <br> • P&O (2.1%) <br> • P&O Australia (1.3%) <br> • Cunard (0.8%) <br> • Seabourn (0.2%) | • Royal Caribbean (16.9%) <br> • Celebrity Cruises (3.6%) <br> • TUI Cruises (2,7%) <br> • Silversea (0,4%) <br> • Azamara Cruises (0.2%) <br> • Hapag-Lloyd (0.2%) | | • Norwegian (8.0%) <br> • Oceania (0.5%) <br> • Regent Seven Seas Cruises (0.4%) | • Disney Cruises (1.6%) <br> • Star Cruises (1.0%) <br> • Dream Cruises (2.3%) |

Source: Cruise Industry News (2021).

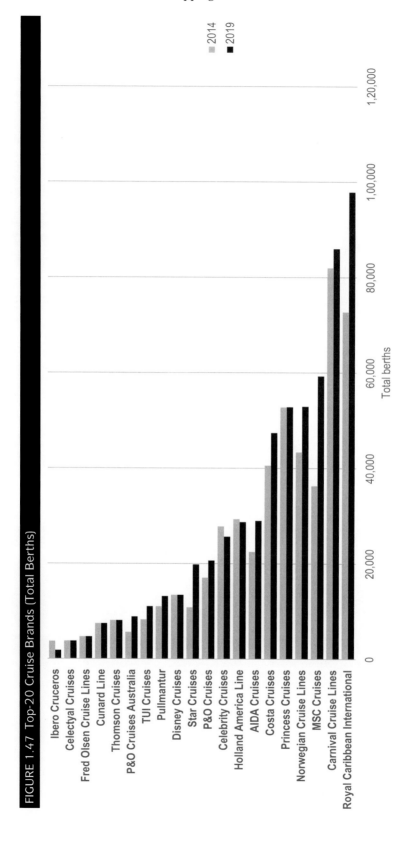

FIGURE 1.47 Top-20 Cruise Brands (Total Berths)

the cruise industry relies on a flag of convenience to gain financial advantages but mostly to secure more lax labor regulations since it is an industry relying extensively on labor. For instance, Carnival Cruises and Princess Cruises have all their ships registered in foreign countries (Panama, Bahamas, and Bermuda). Both Carnival and Royal Caribbean have endorsed a multi-brand strategy. Each of them operates a number of brands, each associated with a specific image, the type of vessels it operates, and the amenities and types of cruise itineraries.

The largest cruise lines, which are also publicly traded (Carnival, Royal Caribbean, and NCL), have achieved solid earnings for many years. Carnival and Royal Caribbean have posted net earnings every single year since the companies went public in 1987 and 1993 respectively. NCL went public in 2008 and has posted net earnings since 2009. MSC, which is privately held, has released financial reports to its bondholders showing earnings in the range of publicly traded companies. Also publicly traded is the Asian-controlled Genting, which has also largely been profitable. The cruise line has three brands, Star Cruises, Dream Cruises that mainly operate in Asia-Pacific, and Crystal Cruises that operate in the luxury market. It has recently emerged as the fifth player with a significant share of the world cruise fleet (3.6% in 2020).

In the 2010s, the top-20 cruise brands, measured in terms of the total berth capacity, have continued to upgrade their fleets. The number of berths relates to the number of people who can sleep on board. A comparison of the evolving berth capacities since 2014 underlines the fact that the largest cruise brands continue to expand faster than the smaller lines. Thus, the market concentration in the supply of cruises will endure and may increase in the future (Figure 1.47).

Simultaneously, and despite the high levels of market concentration, **new entrants** are expected. The expected startups, including Virgin Voyages, Ritz Carlton, Scenic, Swan Hellenic, and Tradewind Voyages, target the premium, luxury, and expedition markets rather than the contemporary segment, with some of them (i.e. Virgin) advocating new cruise practices and packages. The search for new practices is also present in incumbents such as Royal Caribbean and Norwegian, who continue to add novel onboard amenities to expand the appeal of their cruises.

# Chapter 1.6  Interoceanic passages

*Maritime transportation evolves over a global maritime space with its own constraints, such as the profile of continental masses and the detours and passages it creates.*

## 1 GLOBAL MARITIME ROUTES AND CHOKEPOINTS

Maritime routes are corridors of a few kilometers in width connecting economic regions and overcoming land transport discontinuities. They are part of a continuum. Transoceanic maritime corridors are a function of obligatory points of passage, which are almost all strategic places, physical constraints such as coasts, winds, marine currents, depth, reefs, or ice, and political boundaries where sovereignty may impede circulation. When possible, interoceanic canals are built to improve the connectivity of shipping networks.

International maritime shipping routes are forced to pass through specific locations corresponding to passages, capes, and straits (Figure 1.48). These routes are generally located between major markets such as Western Europe, North America, and East Asia, where an active commercial trade system is in place. The importance of these large markets is structuring the exchanges of semi-finished and finished goods. Also, major routes involve flows of raw materials, namely minerals, grains, food products, and petroleum. The location of strategic oil and mineral resources shapes maritime routes for bulks since they represent the most transported commodities.

The most important strategic maritime passages are known as chokepoints (or bottlenecks) due to:

- **Capacity constraints**. Chokepoints tend to be shallow and narrow, impairing navigation and imposing capacity limits on ships. For interoceanic canals such as Panama and Suez, the capacity must in effect be managed with appointment and pricing systems.
- **Potential for disruptions or closure**. Disruption of trade flows through any of these routes could have a significant impact on the world economy. Many chokepoints are next to politically unstable countries, increasing the risk of compromising their access and use, such as through piracy. Closures are a rare instance that have only taken place in war situations as one proponent prevented another from accessing and using the chokepoint (e.g. Gibraltar and Suez during World War II). Closure of a maritime chokepoint in the current global economy, even if temporary, would have important economic consequences with the disruption of trade flows and even the interruption of some supply chains (e.g. oil).

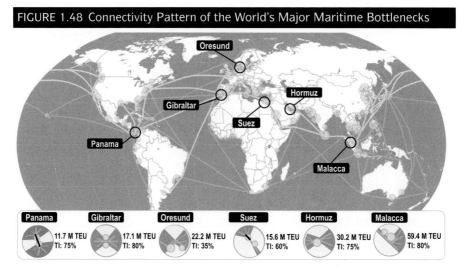

FIGURE 1.48 Connectivity Pattern of the World's Major Maritime Bottlenecks

Source: TEU figures are for 2015 and relate to the total container traffic of selected nearby ports interacting with the bottleneck. TI refers to transshipment incidence; the share of all the containers handled by the port system that are transshipped.

These potential risks and impacts are commonly used to justify using military naval assets to protect sea lanes, even if such benefits are difficult to demonstrate.

Bottlenecks of global maritime shipping have been for decades the object of **geostrategic considerations** as obligatory points of passage for global trade. The connectivity they provide is related to reducing maritime shipping distances for international trade and the convergence of shipping services. The setting up of transshipment hubs, which is another form of connectivity, has been particularly active around major maritime bottlenecks. This usually involves feeder services towards smaller ports, relays connecting deep-sea services towards different maritime ranges, or interlining supporting different port of call configurations along a similar maritime range.

- **Panama**. The connectivity of the Panama Canal system involves three dimensions, the first being the connectivity offered by the Canal itself, which was expanded in 2016 with a new set of locks. In addition, on each of the maritime facades of the Canal (Pacific and Caribbean), transshipment activities have emerged, each supporting feeder services as well as offering relays along deep-sea services. This is particularly the case for the Caribbean, with a large share of transshipment being handled by Panama.
- **Gibraltar**. The connectivity of Gibraltar is the outcome of its role as a bottleneck between the Mediterranean Sea and the North Atlantic, linking Europe/Asia routes and being at the intersection of West Africa/ Europe routes as well. It thus represents a convenient location for relay forms of transshipment and is subject to competition between the main transshipment hubs on its northern (Algeciras) and southern (Tanger Med) facades.
- **Oresund**. The importance of Oresund is derived from the level of economic activity in the Baltic, which is a maritime dead-end and does not have ports generating enough volume to justify a variety of direct deep-sea services. Therefore, the Baltic is mostly covered by feeder services from Northern Range ports, notably Hamburg and Gdansk.
- **Suez**. The growth of Europe/Asia trade routes has been supported by the connectivity offered by the Suez Canal. Transshipment has been particularly active on the Mediterranean facade since deep-sea services can be connected with feeder services towards Southern and Eastern European markets.
- **Hormuz**. Like the Baltic, the Persian Gulf is a dead-end that does not generate enough container volumes to support a wide array of direct services. Large infrastructure investments have enabled Dubai to become a major transshipment hub, acting as a connector along the Asia/Europe routes as well as providing feeder services to East Africa and South Asia.
- **Malacca**. The Strait of Malacca is the world's most important bottleneck. It is the main passage between the Pacific and Indian oceans, combining deep sea relay services and feeder services through Southeast Asia. The port of Singapore is the world's most important transshipment hub, with competing hubs such as Tanjung Pelepas in proximity.

Changes in the technical and operational characteristics of interoceanic canals and passages can substantially impact global trade patterns. The Panama Canal, the Suez Canal, the Strait of Malacca, and the Strait of Hormuz account for the world's four most important interoceanic passages. This is partly because of the chokepoints they create for global freight circulation and in part because of the economic activities and resources they grant more efficient access to. Their continuous availability for global maritime trade is challenging because the global trade system relies on their use. However, they have shaped global trade with the ongoing setting up of rings of circulation comprised of maritime and land corridors, notably in the northern hemisphere (Figure 1.49). The setting up of a global 'containerized highway' involving continuity between inland and maritime transport systems is expected as containerization continues to spread. For the northern hemisphere, where the bulk of economic activity occurs, this would involve three major rings or circulations; the equatorial ring, the middle ring, and the speculative Arctic ring.

The shortest path to circumnavigate the world is the so-called **circum-equatorial route** using the Panama Canal, the Strait of Gibraltar, the Suez Canal, and the Strait of Malacca. Two of these shortcuts are artificial, implying that significant additional detours were imposed before their construction through the Cape of Good Hope (southern Africa) and the Strait of Magellan (southern America). In the age of globalization, this simple pattern remains

FIGURE 1.49 Circum-Hemispheric Rings of Circulation

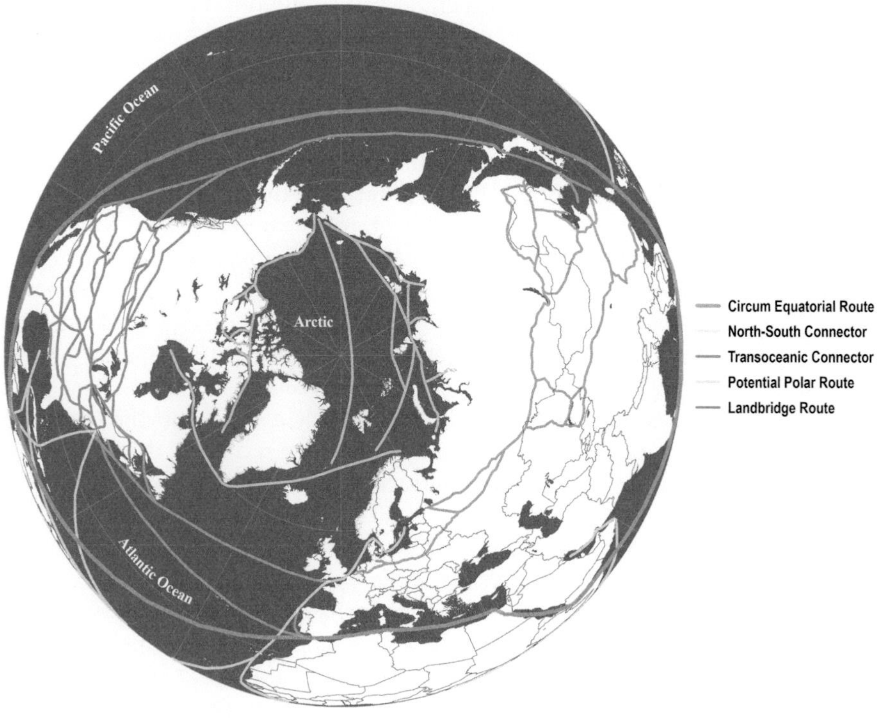

Source: Notteboom and Rodrigue (2009).

a fundamental element shaping global maritime routes that are mostly composed of longitudinal and latitudinal connectors.

The circum-equatorial route can be perceived as a conveyor belt where high capacity and high-frequency containerships are assigned and can interface with the middle ring at specific high throughput transshipment hubs. The widening of the Panama Canal will improve the operational efficiency of the system, placing it close to parity with the capacity of the Suez Canal. Under such circumstances, the setting up of true bi-directional and high-frequency round-the-world services could finally take place.

The most important ring of circulation, the **middle ring**, comprises two large continental rail land bridges linked by transatlantic and transpacific connectors. The North American landbridge, is fully operational, while the other, the Eurasian landbridge, is still a concept. The middle ring requires a full-fledged maritime/land interface with major gateways and corridors. The **Arctic ring** is problematic as a full ring of circulation, but specific maritime bridges could be established (e.g. Narvik-Churchill), which would complement the middle ring.

In addition to the interoceanic canals, 'dry canals' have also been constructed or are under consideration. They are called dry canals because they replicate the role of regular canals, implying that they are relatively short overland corridors of rail, road, and pipeline infrastructures connecting two ports where cargo is transshipped. Several dry canals started as portage routes and were either discontinued as they lost their capability to compete or, in contrast, complemented by a canal, such as the Panama Canal, which has road, rail, and pipeline complementarity to the Canal's traffic. The main disadvantage of dry canals is the load break at both ends, which adds costs and delays, as well as limited economies of scale on the overland route. Still, they represent routing options that can stimulate national imports and exports and the development of logistical activities. Such an imprint on regional development is much less evident in passages since they are simply transit points.

## 2 THE SUEZ CANAL

The Suez Canal is an artificial waterway of about 190 km in length running across the Isthmus of Suez in northeastern Egypt, connecting the Mediterranean Sea with the Gulf of Suez, an arm of the Red Sea. The Suez Canal has no locks because the Mediterranean Sea and the Gulf of Suez have roughly the same water level, making Suez the world's longest canal without locks. It acts as a shortcut for ships between European and American ports and ports located in southern Asia, eastern Africa, and Oceania. Because of obvious geographical considerations, the maritime route from Europe to the Indian and Pacific oceans must round the Cape of Good Hope at the southernmost point of the African continent.

The Suez Canal was constructed between 1859 and 1869 by French and Egyptian interests, spearheaded by Ferdinand de Lesseps, with a cost of about 100 million dollars. The opening of the Suez Canal in 1869 brought forward a new era of European influence in Pacific Asia. The journey from Asia to Europe was considerably shortened with a saving of 6,500 km from the circum-African route. In 1874, Great Britain bought the shares of the Suez Canal Company and became its sole owner. According to the Convention of Constantinople signed in 1888, the Canal was to be open to vessels of all nations in time of peace or war. However, Great Britain claimed the need to control the area to maintain its maritime power and colonial interests (namely, South Asia). In 1936, it acquired the right to maintain defense forces along the Suez Canal, which became of strategic importance during World War II in upholding Asia–Europe supply routes for the Allies.

The second half of the twentieth century saw renewed geopolitical instability in the region with the end of colonialism and the emergence of Middle Eastern nationalism. In 1954, Egypt and Great Britain signed an agreement that superseded the 1936 treaty and provided for the gradual withdrawal of all British troops from the zone. All the British troops were gone by June 1956 as Egypt nationalized the Canal. This triggered issues with Israel, as Israeli ships were not permitted to cross the Canal. This threat was also extended to France and Britain, the former owners of the Canal, because they refused to help finance the Aswan High Dam project, as initially promised. Israel, France, and Britain thus invaded Egypt in 1956. Egypt responded by sinking ships in the Canal, effectively closing it between 1956 and 1957. An agreement about the usage of the Canal was then reached.

With additional deepening and widening projects, the depth of the Canal reached 22.5 meters in 2001 and 23.5 meters in 2008. In 2014, a new expansion project that increased the capacity to about 100 transits per day took place. The New Suez Canal was inaugurated in August 2015 at the cost of over 8 billion dollars and the depth was expanded to 24 meters (78 feet). This expansion included a new 35 km section enabling the Canal to transit ships in both directions at once. The expanded Suez Canal has draft limitations similar to those of the Strait of Malacca, which helps improve the continuity of maritime shipping on Asia–Europe trades. The Canal has the capacity to accommodate up to 25,000 ships per year (about 78 per day) but handled about 17,500 in 2017, on average 55 ships per day, which roughly accounts for 15% of the global maritime trade. A rail line also runs parallel to the Canal.

Before its expansion in 2015, the Canal could only handle unidirectional traffic, with **crossings organized into convoys** of about ten to 15 ships. Three convoys per day, two southbound and one northbound, were organized, with a transit time of about 17 hours. After the 2015 expansion, two simultaneous convoys per day were organized since a longer section of the Canal became bi-directional. Missing a convoy can incur supplementary delays to the point that, on occasion, maritime shipping companies (particularly for containers) would skip a port call to ensure on-time arrival at the Suez Canal to be part of a daily convoy. The growing ship size transiting the canal can involve risks, such as the grounding of a 20,000 TEU containership in 2021, which blocked the canal for six days.

The transit rates are established by the Suez Canal Authority (SCA) and are computed to keep the canal transit fees attractive to shippers. In the fiscal year 2014, Egypt earned USD 5.3 billion in canal fees, making it the country's third-largest revenue generator after tourism and remittances from expatriate workers. Container ships account for just under half of the Canal's traffic and a slightly higher percentage of its net tonnage and revenues. The average canal transit fee (at 90% vessel utilization) amounts to 102 USD per TEU for a vessel of 1,000 TEU, down to 56 USD per TEU for the largest container vessels. The Far East–Europe trade constitutes about 75% of the traffic handled by Suez. In

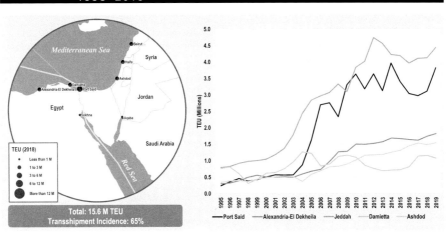

FIGURE 1.50 Container Traffic Handled at the Main Ports Around the Suez Canal, 1995–2019

recent years, services to the North American East Coast from Asia and transiting through the Suez Canal have increased to account for more than 15% of the traffic it handles. The canal area has also become a major transshipment cluster (Figure 1.50).

## 3 THE PANAMA CANAL

The Panama Canal's 82 kilometers join the Atlantic and Pacific oceans across the Isthmus of Panama, running from Cristobal on Limon Bay, an arm of the Caribbean Sea, to Balboa, on the Gulf of Panama. Since its expansion in 2016, it involves two locks systems that can both be used at the same time. The **old locks**, completed in 1914, can handle ships with a draft of 12.2 meters (40 feet), a width of 32 meters (106 feet), and a length of 294 meters (965 feet). The expanded locks, completed in 2016, can handle ships with a draft of 15.2 meters (50 feet), a width of 49 meters (160 feet), and a length of 366 meters (1,200 feet).

The construction of the Panama Canal and subsequent expansion rank among the greatest engineering works of the twentieth century as the canal replaces a long detour around South America, thus improving global trade connectivity. The Panama Canal is of particular strategic importance to the United States as it enables quicker linkage between the East and the West coasts, saving about 13,000 km (from 21,000 km to 8,000 km) on a maritime journey.

The Panama Canal is composed of three main elements, the Gatun Locks (operational in 1914) and Agua Clara Locks (operational in 2016), giving access to the Atlantic Ocean, the Culebra Cut (Gaillard) crossing the continental divide, and the Miraflores and Pedro Miguel Locks (1914) and Cocoli Locks (also part of the 2016 expansion) accessing the Pacific Ocean (Figure 1.51). The canal handles about 5% of the global seaborne trade and about 12% of the American international seaborne trade. Besides, close to 70% of the Panama Canal traffic either originates or is bound to the United States.

FIGURE 1.51 Main Components of the Panama Canal

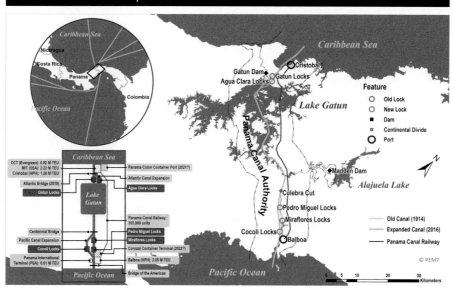

The Panama Canal was constructed between 1904 and 1914 by American engineers at the cost of $387 million (including the $10 million compensation to Panama and $40 million to purchase the previous project from the French Canal Company). In 1906, President Theodore Roosevelt, mainly credited for the achievement, placed the construction of the canal under the authority of the U.S. Army Corps of Engineers. The Soo Locks linking Lake Huron to Lake Superior, which at the time were the most heavily used in the world, became the engineering template for Panama's locks. The construction of Gatun Dam enabled the creation of an artificial lake (Lake Gatun), which reduced the need for excavation (higher water levels) as well as providing a large reservoir of water to supply the locks. A total of 70,000 people worked on the project, and about 5,600 died in the process, mainly because of tropical diseases. The work was completed in 1914 and involved excavating 143 million cubic meters of earth and sanitizing the entire canal area, which was infested with mosquitoes that spread yellow fever and malaria.

Since its completion in 1914, more than 1.14 million vessels have transited the canal, carrying 13.94 billion tons of cargo (as of 2020). It is synonymous with a standard in maritime transport-related to capacity, the **Panamax standard**, which equals 65,000 deadweight tons, a draft of 12 meters, and a capacity of about 4,500 TEUs depending on the load configuration (about 5,200 TEU if most of the containers are empty). About 14,000 ships transit the canal every year, with an average of 35 ships per day. There are two major components in the transit time for the Panama Canal. The canal transit time (CTT) is the average time it takes for a ship to cross the canal from its entry point in Balboa to its exit in Colon (or vice-versa). The time spent in Panama Canals' waters (PCWT) includes the transit time in addition to the time spent waiting for a transit slot to become available. However, the canal has the optimal capacity to handle 50 ships per day. Using the canal requires an average transit time of about 16.5 hours if the passage has been reserved in advance. With no reservations, the transit takes an average of 35 hours due to the additional time spent waiting for a transit slot. Containers, grains, and petroleum account for the dominant share of the cargo transited. The introduction of super-tankers at the beginning of the 1950s forced the reconsideration of its strategic importance as economies of scale in petroleum shipping are limited by the size of the canal.

The Panama Canal Authority undertook a privatization policy that began with concessioning its port terminal facilities. The first private project was Manzanillo International Terminals (MIT), which began operations in 1995. In 1999, Hutchison Port Holdings (HPH) was granted a 25 year concession for the operation of port terminals on both the Atlantic (Port of Cristobal) and Pacific (Port of Balboa) sides of the canal. The rail line between the Atlantic and Pacific sides was reopened in 2002 as a private concession to handle the growing containerized traffic. The Panama Canal Railway Company supports transshipment activities between the Atlantic and the Pacific sides through doublestack services, allowing for repositioning containers between the maritime facades without transiting through the canal. The same rationale applies to oil circulation with the trans-Panama pipeline that resumed its operations in 2003, but the additional capacity this pipeline conveys is only about 1 Mb/d (million barrels per day).

The continuous growth of global trade since the 1990s has placed additional pressures on the Panama Canal to handle a growing number of ships in a timely and predictable manner. This raised concerns that the existing canal could reach capacity by the second decade of the twenty-first century. Because of these capacity limits, many shipping companies changed the configuration of their routes. This became increasingly apparent as a growing share of the global containership fleet reached a size beyond the Panama Canal capacity, coming to be known as 'post-Panamax' containerships. Through economies of scale, they offer significant operational cost advantages that the old canal could not exploit. The increasing usage of those ships along the Pacific Asia/Suez Canal/Mediterranean routes and the development of the North American rail landbridge created substantial competition to the canal as an intermediate location in global maritime shipping. Thus, there is a range of alternatives to the Panama Canal trade routes, with the North American landbridges being the most salient. However, concerns about the reliability of the landbridge connection stimulated the setting up of 'all-water routes' directly linking Pacific Asia and the American East Coast, particularly in light of the booming China–United States trade relation.

A decision to expand the Panama Canal was reached in 2006 by the Panamanian government. The expansion was a 5.4 billion US dollars project that involved building a new set of locks on both the Atlantic and Pacific sides of the canal, which would accommodate ships up to 12,500 TEU depending on their load configuration. The dredging of access channels and the widening of several sections of the existing canal were also required. This allows Aframax and Suezmax vessels to pass through the canal, thus permitting new opportunities for container shipping services such as the re-emergence of round-the-world services. Essentially, a new containership class was created to add to the existing Panamax ship class. It was dubbed **New-Panamax** (or **NeoPanamax**; NPX). The announcement of the expansion also stimulated the upgrade of port and related infrastructures along the North American east coast since larger containerships were expected to call.

The new locks complement the existing lock systems, creating a two-tier service, one for the very large ships and the other for Panamax, or smaller ships. The outcome allows about 12 ships per day in the new lock system to be added to the existing capacity of about 45 ships per day in the existing locks. However, the additional capacity is constrained by the fact that the new locks are unidirectional compared with the existing double locks. The new infrastructures came online in July 2016 after some delays, since the expansion was initially expected to be completed for 2014.

Despite being more than a century old, the Panama Canal remains a critical bottleneck in global trade (Figure 1.52). The Panama Canal expansion took place in an environment of notable commercial changes such as a revision of sourcing strategies and the possibility of building a competing canal in Nicaragua (Box 1.17). Further, the latest generation of containerships (such as the Triple E class) has reached sizes beyond the expanded locks. Within the foreseeable future, the expanded Panama Canal will still handle 95% of the global containership capacity. As a global intermediary location, Panama is shifting from being a point of transit towards being a logistics cluster and a trading platform for the Americas.

**FIGURE 1.52**  Container Traffic Handled at the Main Ports Around the Panama Canal, 1995–2019

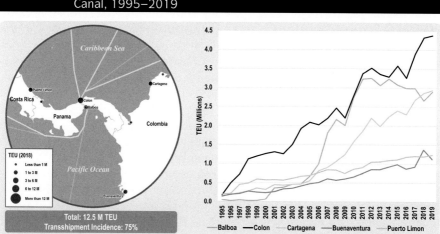

## Box 1.17 The Nicaragua canal project

*Plans for a canal crossing in Nicaragua first emerged in the nineteenth century. In 1899, the American government established an Isthmian Canal Commission to investigate two routes, one via Nicaragua and the other via Panama. The Commission report came out in 1901 and favored the Nicaragua route. However, the US Senate voted for the Panama route, in large part because of a sharp decrease in the asking price for the real estate and assets owned by the French New Panama Canal Company.*

*From the late nineteenth century to the twenty-first century, the Nica-*
*ragua Canal option resurfaced from time to time, with various stakeholders*
*expressing interest in constructing or financing the project. However, these*
*interests never went further than surveys and feasibility studies that traced*
*possible routes.*

*In the twenty-first century, new ambitions emerged to construct such a*
*canal with a view to introducing a direct competitor to the Panama Canal. In*
*2013, the Nicaragua Canal option again came to the fore with the announcement*
*that a 100-year concession had been signed with a Chinese company registered in*
*Hong Kong (HKBD Group). In late 2014, a route was officially retained. How-*
*ever, the chance that the canal will ever be built remains low. First, construc-*
*tion costs would be excessive, with some estimates placing them at more than*
*40 billion dollars, and delays and cost overruns almost always plague megaproj-*
*ects. In comparison, the expansion of the Panama Canal had a price tag of about*
*6 billion dollars. Second, the Nicaragua canal shipping activities would bring*
*serious negative effects to the surrounding tropical rain forest, forest wetlands,*
*natural and biosphere reserves, and other ecological systems. Third, Nicara-*
*gua is perceived to be a highly corrupt country and has no diplomatic relations*
*with China, which is a potentially large risk to Chinese investors. The recent*
*strengthening of economic and diplomatic exchanges between China and Panama*
*undermine plans for the realization of the Nicaragua Canal. Finally, the expan-*
*sion of the Panama Canal in 2016 brought additional capacity but, compared to*
*Nicaragua, it faces fewer pressures to impose high tolls (less capital investment).*
*Compared with Panama, Nicaragua offers limited-time advantages concerning*
*maritime deviation.*

## 4  THE STRAIT OF MALACCA

The Strait of Malacca is one of the **most important strategic passages of the
world** because it supports the bulk of the maritime trade between Europe
and Pacific Asia, which accounts for 50,000 ships per year. About 30% of the
world's trade and 80% of Japan's, South Korea's, and Taiwan's imports of
petroleum transit through the strait, which involved approximately 16 Mbd in
2016. It is the main passage between the Pacific and the Indian oceans, with the
strait of Sunda (Indonesia) being the closest existing alternative. It measures
about 800 km in length, has a width between 50 and 320 km (2.5 km at its narrowest point), and a minimum channel depth of 23 meters (about 70 feet). It
represents the longest strait in the world used for international navigation and
can be transited in about 20 hours.

Historically, the Strait was an important passage point between the Chinese and the Indian worlds and was controlled at different points in time by
Javanese and Malaysian kingdoms. From the fourteenth century, the region
came under the control of Arab merchants who established several fortified
trading towns, Malacca being the most important commercial center in Southeast Asia. Again, control of the trade route shifted as the European expansion
era began in the sixteenth century. In 1511, Malacca fell to the Portuguese,
which marked the beginning of European control over the Strait. In 1867,

England took control of the passage with Singapore as the main harbor and other important centers such as Malacca and Penang forming the Strait Settlements. This control lasted until the Second World War and the independence of Malaysia in 1957. As the transpacific trade increased considerably after the Second World War, so did the importance of the passage. Singapore, located at the southern end of the Strait of Malacca, is one of the world's most important ports and a major oil refining center.

One of the main challenges facing the Strait of Malacca is that it requires some dredging since it is barely deep enough to accommodate ships above 300,000 deadweight tons. The Strait being between Malaysia, Indonesia, and Singapore, an agreement is difficult to reach about how the dredging costs should be shared and how fees for its usage should be levied. Political stability and piracy are also major issues for the safety of maritime circulation, especially on the Indonesian side where the province of Aceh has experienced political instability.

The Strait of Malacca ends up in the South China Sea, another crucial shipping lane and a region subject to contention since oil and natural gas resources are present. The Spratly and Paracel groups of islands are claimed in part by China, Vietnam, Malaysia, Indonesia, Brunei, and the Philippines. The region has proven oil reserves estimated at 7.0 Bb, with oil production accounting for 2.5 Mb/d. With the substantial economic growth in the region, large oil, liquefied natural gas, and other raw materials (iron ore, coal) are transiting towards East Asia. About 25% of the global shipping fleet transits through the region each year, underlining the importance of the South China Sea as an extension of the Malacca chokepoint (Figure 1.53). Still, the potential for disruptions of trade routes in the South China Sea must take into consideration the high level of reliance China has on such routes and its limited interest in seeing them compromised.

Using the Kra Isthmus in Thailand as a shortcut between the Gulf of Thailand (Pacific Ocean) and the Andaman Sea (Indian Ocean) was considered

FIGURE 1.53 Container Traffic Handled at the Main Ports Around the Strait of Malacca, 1995–2019

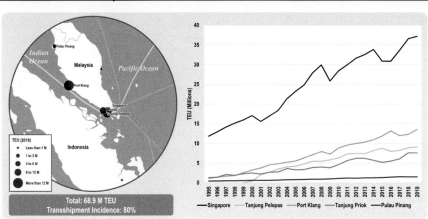

early as the seventeenth century. The Kra Canal project aims at building a 102 km long canal along the narrowest segment of the Kra Isthmus. By avoiding a detour through the Strait of Malacca, the potential canal could reduce shipping distance by 1,200 km, which corresponds to about two to three shipping days in one direction (such figures do not take account of canal transit times). Although the project represents a shortcut, this benefit is relatively marginal, particularly for long-distance shipping routes. The importance of Singapore and Tanjung Pelepas as major transshipment hubs linking Asia/Oceania/Europe trade routes also undermines its viability. Shipping lines using the canal will need to consider the benefits of lower transit times versus the canal tolls. The canal would mainly benefit Thailand, Burma, Cambodia, and Vietnam as they would see more significant shipping time and cost reductions for their maritime trade. China is pursuing this project for commercial and strategic reasons since it will give it an additional alternative to using the Strait of Malacca.

## 5 THE STRAIT OF HORMUZ

The Strait of Hormuz forms a strategic link between the Persian Gulf oil fields, which is a maritime dead-end, the Gulf of Oman, and the Indian Ocean. It has a width between 48 and 80 km, but navigation is limited to two 3 km wide channels, each exclusively used for traffic in one direction (inbound or outbound). Circulation in and out of the Persian Gulf is thus highly constrained, namely because the sizable amount of tanker and containership traffic makes navigation difficult along the narrow channels. Besides, islands essential to control of the strait are contested by Iran and the United Arab Emirates. The strait is deep enough to accommodate all the existing tanker classes.

The security of the strait has often been compromised, and its commercial usage has been contested. Between 1984 and 1987, a 'Tanker War' took place between Iran and Iraq (in the Iran–Iraq War of 1980–1988), where each belligerent began firing on tankers, even neutrals, bound for their respective ports. Shipping in the Persian Gulf dropped by 25%, forcing the intervention of the United States to secure the oil shipping lanes. About 85% of all the petroleum exported from the Persian Gulf transits through the Strait of Hormuz, bound to Asian markets. Its importance for global oil circulation cannot be overstated. For instance, 75% of all Japanese oil imports transit through the strait. Thus, there are very few alternatives to oil exports if the traffic of about 17 million barrels per day going through Hormuz is compromised.

While the Persian Gulf has conventionally been centered on the production and distribution of oil, the growth of container shipping has also expanded its commercial importance. For instance, in 2018 Dubai ranked as the world's tenth largest container port with a traffic of 15 million TEU and it can only be accessed through the Strait of Hormuz (Figure 1.54). It has become a major transshipment hub linking Asian, Middle Eastern, and East African trade routes. Consequently, compromising circulation through the Strait of Hormuz would impair global oil trade as well as commercial trade along Europe/Asia routes.

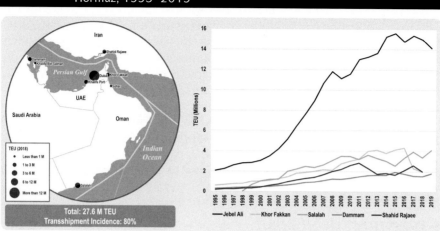

FIGURE 1.54 Container Traffic Handled at the Main Ports Around the Strait of Hormuz, 1995–2019

## 6 OTHER IMPORTANT PASSAGES

The **Strait of Bab el-Mandab** controls access to the Suez Canal, a strategic link between the Indian Ocean and the Red Sea. It has between 48 and 80 km of width, but navigation is limited to two 3 km wide channels for inbound and outbound traffic. The sizable amount of tanker traffic makes navigation difficult along the narrow channels. Closing of this strait would have serious consequences, forcing a detour around the Cape of Good Hope and in the process demanding additional tanker space. Like the Strait of Malacca, Bab el-Mandab is a crucial link in the Europe–Asia trade route.

The **Oresund Strait** is a passage of 115 km between Denmark and Sweden connecting the North Sea and the Baltic, a maritime dead-end. It enables Russia, the Baltic States, Poland, and Germany to access international maritime shipping. The majority of Russian container trade transits through the strait.

The **Strait of Gibraltar** is a peninsula between the Atlantic and the Mediterranean oceans and represents an obligatory passage point between these two oceans. The strait is about 64 km long and varies in width from 13 to 39 km. It has been under British control since its conquest from Spain in 1704 and its formal cession by the treaty of Utrecht (1713). During the Second World War, Gibraltar blocked access to the Atlantic to the Italian and German fleets of the Mediterranean, which represented a major strategic military stronghold. The Strait has become an important transshipment nexus along major Europe/Mediterranean/Asia shipping routes. More recently, the growth of the trade using the Suez Canal to reach the North American East Coast has provided additional transshipment opportunities around the strait.

The **Strait of Bosporus** has a length of 30 km and a width of only 1 km at its narrowest point, linking the Black Sea to the Mediterranean. Its access has been the object of two conflicts, the Crimean War (1854) and the battle of the Dardanelles (Gallipoli, 1915). Turkey fortified the passage after the Convention of Montreux in 1936, which recognized its control of the Bosporus but granted free passage in peacetime to any commercial vessel without inspection. With the Dardanelles passage, Bosporus forms the only link between the Black Sea and the Mediterranean Ocean. In the current context, the Bosporus represents a passage of growing strategic importance, notably after the fall of the Soviet Union. Ukraine has become a major exporter of grains (sunflower, corn, and wheat) and iron ore, relying on the Strait of Bosporus. Further, the Caspian Sea has vast oil reserves, which must transit through the Black Sea and Bosporus to reach external markets, namely around the Mediterranean. Although pipelines offer an alternative, the cost differentials are advantaging the use of maritime transportation.

About 50,000 ships, including 5,500 tankers, are transiting through the passage each year, which is getting close to capacity. Due to its sinuosity, Bosporus is one of the most difficult passages to navigate, particularly for larger ships. Oil transits through the Bosporus have grown substantially in recent years with the exploitation of oil fields around the Caspian Sea, and about 2.4 Mb/d transited through the passage in 2016. The future growth of petroleum circulation through Bosporus is thus highly problematic, notably with the risk of collisions and oil spills at Istanbul. In 2002, the Turkish government forbade the use of the passage by large tankers during the night.

The **Strait of Magellan** separating mainland South America from Tierra del Fuego was crossed in 1520 by the Portuguese explorer, Ferdinand Magellan. It has a length of 530 km and a width of 4 to 24 km. It provides a better-protected passage than the Drake Passage, which is the body of water between South America and Antarctica. It was initially kept secret for more than a century to ensure the supremacy of Portugal and Spain in the Asian trade of spices and silk. With the construction of the Panama Canal in 1916 and, later on, the setting up of the North American transcontinental bridge in the 1980s, this passage lost most of its strategic importance, a marginalization reinforced by limited economic activity at the southern tip of South America.

The **Cape Good Hope** represents the extreme tip of Africa, separating the Atlantic and Indian oceans and it offers no technical limitations of significance to maritime shipping. The early stages of the European maritime expansion in the fifteenth century were oriented towards exploring the west coast of the African continent. After its discovery by the Portuguese in 1488, the cape took the name Good Hope because it offered a maritime passage towards India and Asia, thus the hope of a fortune for those who traversed it. Vasco de Gama got around the cape in 1497 and was the first European to reach India by sea. Afterwards, the Cape of Good Hope became an important point of transit in Europe/Asia trade networks, including a coaling station when steamship technology was developed in the nineteenth century.

The completion of the Suez Canal in 1869 undermined the strategic importance of the Cape Route, particularly following its widening in the 1970s, but the Cape Route remains an important passage. The growth of trade relations between Latin America and East, South, and Southeast Asia has stimulated the growing use of the Cape Route and of South Africa as a transshipment hub. This underlines the fact that the Cape Route is no longer focused on European trade.

# PART II

# Contemporary ports

## Chapter 2.1 The changing geography of seaports

*Ports are embedded in their geography, with their location impacted by technical constraints such as the nautical profile, port users, inland transport networks, and maritime shipping networks.*

## 1 THE GEOGRAPHY OF PORTS

### 1.1 Geographical considerations

Ports serve both ocean and land interests by supporting global trade and the articulation of maritime shipping networks. Maritime shipping networks can be flexible as ship assets can be repositioned, but ports are fixed in space. The geography of the port is derived from its site and situation. While the site relates to the nautical profile and the physical characteristics of the harbor, the situation is derived from the port's centrality to major hinterland markets and its intermediacy to main shipping lanes. On the ocean side, it is beneficial for a port to be located near major maritime networks to allow access to foreland (overseas) areas. On the landside, close proximity to hinterland areas is also beneficial. Three relative states of oceanic and land port location conditions apply (Figure 2.1).

First, when both shipping lane proximity and hinterland location centrality are well met, the port will likely succeed in its mission to serve shippers' needs, given the necessary port infrastructure and effective management. Second, it may be that the foreland and hinterland conditions at each location are not equal, with one being superior to the other. In such cases, one condition may make up for a deficiency in the other. The lack of shipping lane proximity (foreland accessibility) may be offset by high hinterland centrality or access to a valuable resource. Alternatively, nearness to maritime networks may offset

DOI 10.4324/9780429318184-2

FIGURE 2.1 Port Centrality and Intermediacy

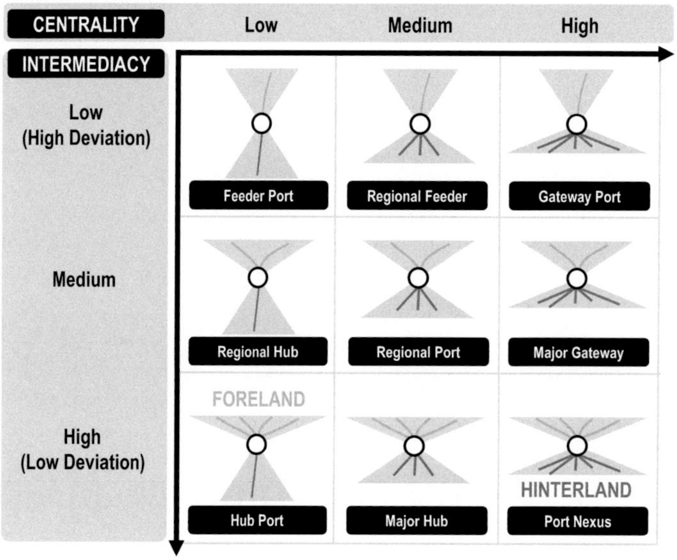

a land location of limited market opportunities. In both cases, ports may be peripheral to shipping lanes and overseas markets or land markets. Finally, in regard to relative location conditions, if ports lack both intermediacy and centrality, they are likely to offer a limited value proposition.

A **port nexus** represents a location characterized by high centrality and intermediacy, representing the best maritime locations in the world. Ports such as Shanghai, Hong Kong, Busan, Tokyo, Los Angeles, New York, and Rotterdam have high maritime connectivity and substantial hinterlands. There are also pure hub ports, such as Panama, Freeport, Colombo, and Gioia Tauro, with high maritime connectivity but poor hinterlands.

The geography of ports takes shape at different scales, ranging from the port and its terminals locally to the global maritime shipping system. Even if maritime shipping networks have a global dimension, ports are deeply regional or local entities. They are the interface between global and regional processes, taking advantage of sites suitable for maritime activities, which is a combination of the foreland (maritime side) and the hinterland (landside). These sites can be modified by adding infrastructures such as piers, docks, basins, and breakwaters, forming a harbor. Therefore, geography is at the core of the added value provided by maritime shipping, and ports are the locations generating this value.

Port sites have been the subject of geographical considerations, with a preference for sites combining a good maritime profile with inland accessibility.

## 1.2 Historical considerations

Throughout history, port cities have continuously had an advantage since maritime transportation allowed long-distance trade, while inland transportation was expensive and of low capacity. The location of port cities reflected the nautical advantages of the site, expanded by hinterland opportunities. Due to the uncertainties of sailing and the vulnerability of ships, a protected harbor was an important factor in port site selection. Ships spent a large amount of time at harbors, implying the need for protection from physical risks like wind and tides as well as security risks such as piracy. Ships carried valuable cargo, and port cities were among the wealthiest. These requirements remained relatively unchanged through the ages, as port sites during the Roman Empire were based on the same considerations as ports operated through the end of the Middle Ages.

Ports along rivers and at the head of a river delta faced an enduring problem of siltation as pre-industrial societies were highly dependent on wood as a source of fuel and construction material. Since rivers were commercial arteries, forested areas around rivers were subject to deforestation, leading to more runoffs and silt carried downstream. Over decades, ports such as Portus (the main port servicing Rome by the second century) could cease to be commercially relevant as their harbor and access channels became clogged by accumulating sediments carried by rivers. Remedial work could be expensive, particularly if economic resources were scarce. Therefore, a port site could be abandoned for a more suitable alternative for security and economic reasons but also owing to specific environmental factors.

Ports through history were strongly associated with **urban development** and were often the key driver of the function and rank of a city within regional and even long-distance shipping networks. Cities gained prominence because of their port and at times lost their prominence because of commercial and technical changes undermining their port. For instance, from the tenth to the fifteenth centuries, city-states such as Venice, Genoa, and Pisa competed to project their respective maritime power over the control of trade routes with Central Asia and the Middle East. Later, the fall of the Byzantine Empire and the search for new maritime trade routes enabled new seaports such as Lisbon and Barcelona to achieve primacy in the seventeenth century.

Up to the industrial revolution, the balance between maritime connectivity and hinterland accessibility did not change much, implying that ports remained the most connected and commercially active locations compared to inland counterparts. The industrial revolution unleashed a series of changes for ports and maritime shipping. On the maritime side, with the introduction of steamships in the nineteenth century, capacity and steering limitations associated with sailships were removed, allowing for a change in network structure, with more direct and quick connections. The decline in cargo costs was linked with a surge in long-distance trade, particularly across the Atlantic.

On the port side, the construction of dedicated facilities led to a specialization of port functions within the port area, such as industrial and energy generation. The transfer of bulk cargo could be undertaken with new systems of cranes and conveyor belts, but break-bulk cargo still needed to be handled manually. This increased the requirement for port labor and the emergence of vast port-based communities adjacent to port sites. The outcome was a significant rebalancing of the global port hierarchy to the advantage of emerging industrial countries such as the UK, the United States, Japan, and Germany. By the early twentieth century, industrial and commercial ports in advanced economies became dominant.

## 2 THE EVOLUTION OF CONTEMPORARY PORTS

Ports are contingent on **geographical constraints**, and changing commercial and technical aspects in maritime shipping are related to changes in the geography of ports. At the regional level, transport terminal development tries to ensure that the supply of infrastructure copes with and even anticipates transportation demand. However, the presence of infrastructures does not necessarily guarantee traffic, as maritime shipping lines can reallocate the sequence of the ports they service as business opportunities change. The growth in port traffic implies the need for more space and better maritime profiles such as depth and pier length. Therefore, as maritime traffic grows, port terminals and activities tend to expand away from their original sites towards locations offering better maritime and land access (Box 2.1).

Port sites are thus the object of a process of **valorization** through capital investments in infrastructures and the convergence of inland and maritime transport networks, as well as the complex management of the concerned supply chains (Figure 2.2). Port development can be perceived within a sequential perspective, where each phase builds upon the previous, from port cities of the nineteenth century to the emerging port logistics network of the twenty-first century. The scale of port activities has increased with the volumes they handle as well as the scope of the activities involved, such as terminal operations, distribution, stakeholder management, and hinterland connectivity.

Since ports are the nexus of maritime and inland transport systems, port hinterlands are strongly shaped by port dynamics, particularly over four interrelated layers ranging from a spatial to a functional perspective:

- The **locational layer** relates to the geographical location of a port concerning the central places in the economic space. It forms a basic element for the intrinsic accessibility of a seaport, which can be a central place or an intermediate location within transport chains. A good intermediate location can imply a location near the main maritime routes such as

FIGURE 2.2 A Multi-Layer Approach to Port Dynamics

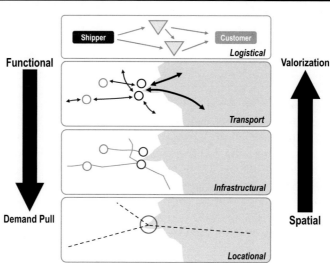

Source: Notteboom and Rodrigue (2009).

offshore hubs (e.g. Singapore or Mediterranean load center ports such as Marsaxlokk and Gioia Tauro) and near production and consumption centers such as gateway ports (e.g. Rotterdam, New York, Santos). For gateway ports, a good location is a necessary condition for attaining high intrinsic accessibility to a vast hinterland, which often builds upon the centrality of the port region. It becomes a sufficient condition when the favorable geographical location is valorized using efficient infrastructures and transport services.

- The **infrastructural layer** involves providing and exploiting basic infrastructure for both links and nodes in the transport system. Containerization and intermodal transportation, and particularly the transshipment infrastructures they rely on, have contributed to a significant accumulation of infrastructures in several ports. This is where the intrinsic accessibility is valorized since a port site has little meaning unless capital investment is provided.
- The **transport layer** involves the operation of transport services on links and corridors between the port and other nodes within the multimodal transport system and the transshipment operations in the nodes of the system. It is a matter of volume and capacity.
- The **logistical layer** involves transport chains and their integration in logistical chains, namely port-centric logistics. This layer is mostly managerial with a decision-making process in terms of the allocation of modes and the booking of transshipment facilities.

In a demand-driven market environment (demand-pull), the infrastructural layer serves the transport and logistical layers. The more fundamental the layer is, the lower the adaptability in facing market changes. For instance, the planning and construction of major port and inland infrastructures (infrastructural level) typically take a decade. The duration of the planning and implementation of shuttle trains on specific railway corridors (transport-level) usually varies between a few months and up to one year. At the logistical level, freight forwarders and multimodal transport operators can respond almost instantly to variations in the market by modifying the commodity chain design, such as routing the goods through the transport system. As adaptable as they may be, they are still dependent on the existing capacity. Still, their decisions often indicate the inefficiencies of the other layers and potential adjustments to be made.

### Box 2.1 The evolution of a port

*Anyport is a model developed by Bird (1963) describing how port infrastructure evolves in time and space. Looking at the evolution of British ports, the five-stage model demonstrates how facilities typically develop. Starting from the initial port site with small lateral quays adjacent to the city center, the setting up of wharves is the product of evolving maritime technologies and improvements in cargo handling. The changing spatial relationships between the port and the urban core are underlined, as docks are built further away from the central business district. In the final stages, increased specialization of cargo handling, growing ship sizes, and ever-increasing demands for space for cargo handling and storage result in port activities being located at sites far removed from the oldest facilities. Port infrastructures are thus constructed over several decades and, in some cases, over several centuries.*

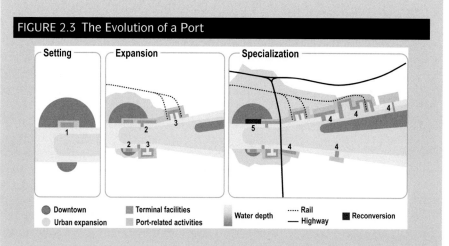

FIGURE 2.3 The Evolution of a Port

*Three major steps can be identified in the port development process identified by Anyport (Figure 2.3):*

*Setting. The initial setting up of a port is strongly dependent on geographical considerations, such as the furthest point of inland navigation by sailships. A standard evolution of a port starts from the original port, commonly a fishing port with trading and shipbuilding activities, which includes several quays (1). Before the industrial revolution, ports remained rather rudimentary in terms of their terminal facilities. Port-related activities were mainly focused on warehousing and wholesaling, located on sites directly adjacent to the port. The port district was a key element of urban centrality with adjacent retailing, wholesaling, and financial activities.*

*Expansion. The industrial revolution triggered several changes that impacted port activities. Quays were expanded, and jetties were constructed to handle the growing amounts of freight and passengers (2). As the size of ships expanded, shipbuilding became an activity that required the construction of docks (3). Further, the integration of rail lines with port terminals granted access to vast hinterlands with a proportionate growth in maritime traffic. Port-related activities also expanded to include industrial activities. This expansion mainly occurred downstream towards deeper draft areas.*

*Specialization. The next phase involved constructing specialized piers to handle freight such as containers, ores, grain, petroleum, and coal (4), which expanded warehousing needs significantly. Larger ships often required dredging or the construction of long jetties granting access to greater depths. This evolution implied, for several ports, a migration of their activities away from their original setting up and an increase in their handling capacities. In turn, original port sites, commonly located adjacent to downtown areas, became obsolete and were abandoned. Numerous reconversion opportunities for port facilities to other uses (waterfront parks, housing, and commercial developments) were created (5).*

*Bird (1971) suggested that Anyport was intended not to display a pattern into which all ports must be forced, but to provide a base to compare port development empirically. The model has been tested in a variety of different conditions (Hoyle, 1967). While local conditions produce differences, there are sufficient*

*similarities to make the Anyport concept a useful description of port morphologi-
cal development. The emergence of new container terminals continues the trend
towards specialization and searching for sites adjacent to deeper water.*

*One of the features that Anyport brings out is the changing relation
between ports and their host cities. The model describes the growing segregation
from the rest of the urban milieu. Several geographers have worked on this aspect,
investigating the redevelopment of harbor land and the involved linkages. One of
these urban linkages is the redevelopment of old port sites for other urban uses,
such as Docklands in London and Harborfront in Baltimore.*

## 2.1 Conventional port sites

Conventionally, port terminals were located close to city cores as many were
the initial rationale for the existence of the city; most of the world's major cities are port cities. The proximity to downtown areas also ensured the availability of large pools of workers to perform the labor-intensive transshipment
activities that characterized port operations. These activities tended to have
low productivity levels as a stevedoring team could handle ten to 15 tons per
day, and a berth could handle 150,000 tons per year. At their peak in the early
1950s, ports such as London and New York each employed more than 50,000
longshoremen.

Over time, changes in ships and handling equipment gave rise to new
site requirements. By the post-World War II period, a growing specialization
of vessels emerged, especially the development of bulk carriers. These ships
were the first to achieve significant economies of scale, and their size grew
very quickly. For example, the world's largest oil tanker in 1947 was only
27,000 dwt, by the mid-1970s it was in excess of 500,000 dwt. Thus, there was
a growing vessel specialization using semi-automated transshipment equipment and an increase in size, which resulted in new site requirements, especially the need for dock space and greater water depths.

## 2.2 Containerization

The introduction of container vessels in the 1960s meant larger cargo volumes
per port call and shorter handling times per ton. Both factors made direct
transshipment no longer feasible since it would require a large number of
trucks, barges, and trains to be in place during the vessel's short port stay. Due
to congestion, capacity, and availability of inland transportation, containerization contributed to a **modal separation** on terminals and the setting up of
a significant buffer in the form of large stocking yards. Each transport mode
received a specific area on the terminal so that operations on vessels, barges,
trucks, and trains could not obstruct one another. This modal separation in
space required setting up a system of indirect transshipment whereby each
transport mode follows its own schedule and operational throughput, implying a modal separation in time.

The containerization of cargo handling changed port storage requirements. Since the container is its own storage unit, port terminals act as temporary storage facilities. Greater vessel capacities have greatly extended the space

demands for port activities. Further, growing ship sizes have implied several new constraints for port sites, such as deeper waterways, larger terminal space, both for ship handling and warehousing, and more efficient inland road and rail access. Containerization had the dramatic impact of lowering labor demand for port operations, further helping to disconnect terminals and labor availability. For instance, the number of longshoremen jobs in the Port of New York and New Jersey declined from 35,000 in the 1960s to about 3,500 in the 1990s.

## 2.3 Mega port facilities

Commercial opportunities and strategic locations within the maritime shipping network allowed for a select group of ports to develop extensive facilities and to become **mega ports**. Many ports, such as Rotterdam and Antwerp, are larger in area than the cities they serve. The expansion of large Chinese ports, such as Shanghai, has required entirely new sites outside central areas (Box 2.2). Modern port infrastructures are often intensive in capital, and several port authorities struggle to keep up with large infrastructure investment requirements.

### Box 2.2  Examples of mega port facilities

*Four recent megaprojects are particularly revealing due to their size and capital requirements:*

*Maasvlakte II (Rotterdam). For decades, the port of Rotterdam, Europe's largest port, has expanded downstream. The growth of container traffic along with a continued expansion of bulk traffic caused the port to consider expansion out in the North Sea. This led to the construction of an entirely new facility on reclaimed land at Maasvlakte in the 1980s. However, subsequent traffic growth in the 1990s resulted in the port authority proposing a new facility further out in the North Sea: Maasvlakte II. The project began construction in 2008, and operations began in 2013, with full completion expected by 2030. Once completed, this terminal facility would likely mark the end of geographical expansion for Rotterdam, outside the reconversion of existing terminal sites into more productive uses.*

*Deurganck dock (Antwerp). Like Rotterdam, the expansion options of the port of Antwerp are limited. With the right bank of the River Scheldt, where the bulk of the port's facilities are located, reaching capacity a new dock complex was built on the left bank. The Deurganck dock opened in 2005 and added about 9 million TEUs to the existing container handling capacity. Two large terminals are located alongside the dock: the Antwerp Gateway terminal operated by DP World and the MPET terminal (MSC and PSA). In 2016, the move of the MPET terminal (formerly known as the MSC Home Terminal) from its old location at the Delwaidedock on the right bank (recently renamed Bevrijdingsdock) to its larger new location at the Deurganck dock presented a huge terminal relocation operation. The port of Antwerp is preparing a further expansion of its container handling capacity with an addition of more than 7 million TEU through smaller extensions of existing facilities and the creation of a new boomerang-shaped dock connected to the Deurganck dock.*

*Yangshan container port (Shanghai). This is a rare case where an entirely new facility has been built from scratch, and this well outside the existing port facilities in the Changjiang delta, at a facility located in Hangzhou Bay,*

*35 km offshore. The first phase opened in 2005 and was built for two purposes. The first was to overcome the physical limitations of the existing port facilities at the Waigaoqiao area at the mouth of the Yangtze river, too shallow to accommodate the latest generation of containerships. The second was to provide additional capacity to meet traffic growth expectations as well as room for new terminal facilities if container growth endures. The fully completed port would have an expected capacity of 15 million TEU. To link the port to the mainland, the world's third longest bridge with a length of 32.5 km was built. In 2017, a fully automated terminal complex opened at Yangshan (phase 4).*

*Tuas container port (Singapore). Singapore is the world's most important transshipment hub, connecting maritime routes between East Asia, Southeast Asia, Oceania, and South Asia. The oldest container terminal facilities of Singapore (Tanjong Pagar, Keppel, and Brani) are located next to the central area. The Tanjong Pagar has been vacant since 2017. In 1993, the construction of the Pasir Panjang 1 project began and was completed in 2009. This was followed by the construction of Pasir Panjang 2. The Tuas port expansion project represents a unique case involving a gradual and complete relocation of Singapore's entire container terminal facilities. Construction began in 2019, and the first terminal went online in 2021. It is expected that the Keppel and Brani facilities will be relocated to Tuas by 2027. By 2040 the remaining Pasir Panjang facilities will be consolidated at the Tuas complex, with the port reaching a capacity of 65 million TEU. The move of port operations to Tuas makes way for the upcoming major city expansion towards the south, also known as the Greater Southern Front development.*

The success of major container ports is jointly the outcome of a shift to containerized shipping in developing economies, the quality of their infrastructure and services, and an efficient interface with inland transport systems. Still, container traffic is subject to fluctuations, mainly related to seasonal variations in demand that vary according to the markets. They remain bound to the economic structure and dynamism of the hinterland they service.

## 2.4 Ports on the periphery

On the opposite side of the spectrum, ports on the periphery are characterized by a limited domestic market and a more remote potential hinterland, for which they may have to compete with other ports. These ports are a specific category that faces a unique competition challenge. It is almost impossible to change a port's location relative to major shipping lanes. Ships are attracted to areas of cargo generation and consumption to serve their derived demand function. How they access those areas depends largely on great circle routes, weather patterns, and maritime chokepoints, such as major straits or canals that limit movement options. Thus, if a port lacks intermediacy, it has little chance to change that condition unless it can generate sufficient cargo to offset extra shipping costs of deviation.

On the other hand, it is not as difficult to overcome a lack of centrality, as long as intermediacy is strong. For this to occur, the land transportation system must be extensive and focused on catering to shipping interests. Otherwise, no amount of advantageous ocean location will overcome the peripheral landside disadvantage. The last situation involving good intermediacy and poor centrality applies to those ports serving interior continental markets with competitive hinterlands.

To improve their competitiveness, peripheral ports need to be more pro-active than centrally located ports near maritime networks or large domestic markets. Proximity to a great circle route and having good facilities and good infrastructure connections are not sufficient. Advantages may be found in a better performing inland transport network, a more customized client approach, a more flexible business environment, and greater reliability that comes from some availability in assets. Competition may differ for these ports depending on whether they compete against a single, large competitor in the region or whether the competitive situation has no single dominant port player.

## 2.5 Automation

Another aspect of port development concerns the automation of port terminal operations. Although container ports are highly mechanized entities, their equipment is conventionally operated manually. Therefore, it is possible to automate one or all three of the main stages of port operations; the portainer (ship to shore moves), the dock to stacking yard movements (lateral moves), and the stacking yard gantry cranes.

A growing number of container terminals are being automated, either fully or partially. A notable advantage of automation is the ability to operate on several work shifts per day. Although a conventional container terminal can add additional work shifts if required, this is easier to implement in automated terminals since fewer workers are involved. A more thorough discussion of terminal automation follows later in this book.

## 3 PORT MIGRATION

As the geography of port traffic can change given shifting commercial trends, the location of port terminals can be subject to migration and relocation. The main difference between terminal migration and **relocation** is that relocation implies closing the old terminal facility once the terminal has migrated to a new site. In contrast, **migration** involves the use of a new terminal site in addition to the existing site. This typically implies a development away from obsolete facilities near the urban core to peripheral locations with ample space and better nautical accessibility for ports within urban areas. These can be downstream on a river, laterally along a coastline, or outward into the sea through land reclamation. If a large share of a port's terminals migrates, then the port itself is said to have migrated, which may stimulate changes in its governance structure as the existing port authority may not have jurisdiction in the locations the facilities have migrated to.

The main drivers of port terminal migration involve (Figure 2.4):

• **Draft limitations**. The push towards economies of scale has been an important driver in maritime shipping, which has led to larger ships with more constraining technical demands in terms of draft and pier length. While a draft of 10 meters was considered suitable for terminal operations in the 1990s, 15 meters is now considered the standard. The existing terminal site may not be suitable, triggering migration to a site with better nautical attributes.

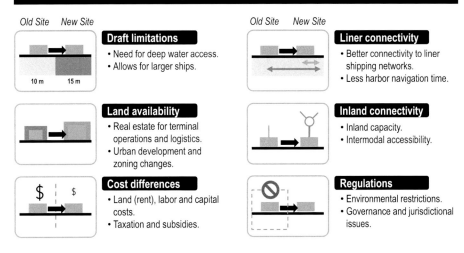

**FIGURE 2.4  Drivers of Port Migration and Relocation**

Source: Compiled from Notteboom (2016).

- **Liner connectivity**. Locations involving lower port turnaround times offer better connectivity to liner shipping networks. If a new terminal location implies less harbor navigation time, it offers better connectivity to maritime shipping networks.
- **Land availability**. Under the indirect transshipment system, the terminal stacking yard functions as a buffer and temporary storage area between deepsea operations and land transport. Consequently, and despite higher turnover levels, the space consumed by container terminals increases substantially. In turn, these space requirements changed the geography of ports and have promoted the migration of terminals to new peripheral sites.
- **Inland connectivity**. The migration to a new terminal facility can result in better access to regional transportation networks such as highways and rail. Peripheral sites usually have less inland congestion, allowing improvement in the capacity and efficiency of hinterland logistics.
- **Cost differences**. The high costs of production factors such as land, labor, and capital at an existing terminal site can encourage migration to peripheral sites where these costs are lower. Since ports are usually near urban core areas, rent pressures are intensive in the face of other competing activities such as commercial and residential uses.
- **Regulations**. An existing terminal site may face increasing environmental regulations and other constraints such as opening hours and circulation bans. These regulations negatively impact terminal operations and could be mitigated by migration to a new site.

Therefore, the port and its geography continue to adapt to technological and economic changes, leading to a variety of location factors and associated port functions such as manufacturing ports, industrial ports, gateway ports, and transshipment ports.

## 4 MARITIME REGIONS

The geography of seaports is concerned about the location of terminals in relation to the technical characteristics of the site, the main users (importers and exporters), inland transport networks (road, rail, barges), and maritime shipping networks. To understand this geography, the maritime range concept allows a look at the largest scale of functional analysis of port systems.

> *A **maritime range** is a bounded region where a set of ports are either in competition, complementary, share a common regulatory regime, or have some basic geographical commonality, such as contiguity, proximity, or being part of an archipelago.*

Maritime ranges can be used as regional units to monitor changes in commercial activity (Figure 2.5). Since oceans are not empty entities (e.g. Hawaii in the Pacific), they can be considered as separate ranges that have oceanic boundaries, such as between the Atlantic (1) and the Indian (3) oceans. However, they are more systems of maritime circulation than functional maritime ranges and account for a marginal share of global port activity. The Arctic (4) is an emerging maritime range with some port activities (e.g. Murmansk, Narvik, Churchill), but limited container traffic. Climate change and the lengthening of the Arctic navigation season have involved additional traffic in the range. The Antarctic is not a maritime range since it has no port activity level and virtually no maritime traffic.

The maritime ranges of the Americas are oriented along the East and the West coasts, with the Caribbean (7) as a subset. Because of North American economic integration (NAFTA), both the West Coast (6) and the East Coast (5) includes the United States and Mexico as a single functional entity. The same rationale applies to the inclusion of Canada in the East and West coast ranges. While for South America, the hinterland boundary is mostly physical (Andean), the North American hinterland boundary is mostly defined by the market areas of rail operators, but the northern boundary with the Arctic range remains ill-defined.

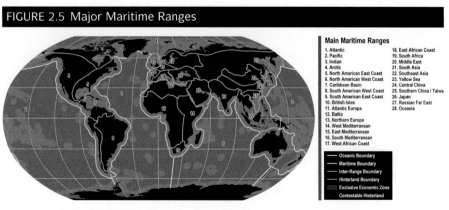

FIGURE 2.5 Major Maritime Ranges

**Main Maritime Ranges**

| | |
|---|---|
| 1. Atlantic | 18. East African Coast |
| 2. Pacific | 19. South Africa |
| 3. Indian | 20. Middle East |
| 4. Arctic | 21. South Asia |
| 5. North American East Coast | 22. Southeast Asia |
| 6. North American West Coast | 23. Yellow Sea |
| 7. Caribbean Basin | 24. Central China |
| 8. South American West Coast | 25. Southern China / Taiwan |
| 9. South American East Coast | 26. Japan |
| 10. British Isles | 27. Russian Far East |
| 11. Atlantic Europe | 28. Oceania |
| 12. Baltic | |
| 13. Northern Europe | |
| 14. West Mediterranean | |
| 15. East Mediterranean | |
| 16. South Mediterranean | |
| 17. West African Coast | |

— Oceanic Boundary
— Maritime Boundary
— Inter-Range Boundary
— Hinterland Boundary
  Exclusive Economic Zone
  Contestable Hinterland

Source: Rodrigue (2020). Note: The boundary of many ranges is based on Exclusive Economic Zones (EEZ). Several EEZs are subject to contention. The boundaries depicted on this map are functional representations and should not be viewed as anything else.

European maritime ranges are organized along two main regions, one linked to the Atlantic (British Isles, Europe Atlantic, and Northern Range) and the other to the Mediterranean (East and West). Due to relatively short hinterland distances, all these ranges compete with one another, with the Northern European range (13) assuming a level of dominance. For the African continent, the Southern Mediterranean range (16) represents a specific market of nonintegrated ports servicing their national markets and with limited competition. A similar observation applies to the West African (17) and East African (18) ranges where ports service poorly connected national markets with the setting up of inland corridors at an early stage. South Africa (20) represents a specific range because of its higher level of economic development and because it is at the interface between two oceans with growing levels of transshipment.

The Middle East (20) and South Asia (21) ranges are impacted by dual functions of accessing regional economies and growing transshipment platforms. Southeast Asia (22) is an archipelago range with a series of ports servicing their respective insular or national markets with the system articulated by a major hub; Singapore. Conventionally, East Asia was considered a single range corresponding to its standard regional definition, including China, the Korean peninsula, and Japan. The substantial level of growth in port activity, particularly in China, has necessitated the fragmentation of East Asia into four maritime ranges. Mainland China is divided into three ranges, each corresponding to the hinterland of its three main river systems. Conventionally, the Korean peninsula was functionally part of the Japan range (26), but the trade reorientation of South Korea towards China supports its inclusion in the Yellow Sea range (23). Japan (26) is a specific range due to its archipelago nature, with its ports oriented at servicing the national economy and supporting cabotage. The Russian Far East range (27) is marginal and does not see significant volumes, but the setting up of the Eurasian landbridge is improving its relevance. Last, Oceania (28) covers the range of Australia and New Zealand, which are active resource and agricultural goods exporters.

# Chapter 2.2 Port hinterlands, regionalization and corridors

*Port hinterlands are strategic market areas interacting and competing. An important strategy has been the setting up of corridors and inland load centers.*

## 1 THE HINTERLAND CONCEPT

The hinterland plays an important role in shaping the supply chain of shippers and logistics service providers. Land scarcity concerns, combined with transport reliability issues, have led seaports and hinterland corridors to take up a more active role in supply chains. Port hinterlands are challenging to delimit as they vary according to the type of commodities, such as for bulk versus containers, seasonality, business cycles, technological changes, changes in transport policy, and the cost structure of inland transportation modes. For example, a large part of the volumes in dry and liquid bulk products is relatively captive to the discharging port region since customers are typically located in the port region or the vicinity of the port, if not directly co-located with a port terminal facility. These include steel plants, power generation plants, oil refineries, and chemical companies. Before containerization, several ports developed expertise in handling specific cargo types, securing the use of gateways according to the cargo base.

> The port **hinterland** is a land area over which a port sells its services and interacts with its users. It is an area over which a port draws most of its business and regroups all the customers directly bounded to the port and the land areas from which it draws and distributes traffic.

The gateway function for major dry and liquid bulks of ports mainly involves one direction for hinterland flows, either incoming or outgoing, a limited number of market players, and a limited number of destinations. However, for containerized cargo, the hinterland profile involves numerous origins and destinations dispersed over a vast hinterland with more competitors, a large number of economic players, and bi-directional hinterland flows. Therefore, the captive nature of container cargo for ports is typically much smaller than for bulk cargo. Moreover, market dynamics make it counterintuitive to have a static concept of port hinterlands being taken for granted and stable in time.

Before containerization, boxes were shipped from the inland production center to the nearest port, and shipping lines designed routes to cover all ports within a coastal range, resulting in captive hinterlands and limited inter-port competition. Containerization has expanded the hinterland reach of ports and has intensified inter-port competition. The expanding hinterland coverage and the associated shift from captive hinterlands to shared or contestable hinterlands has changed the perception of port markets from being monopolistic or oligopolistic to competitive. Thus, port competitiveness is increasingly derived from its hinterland access.

Most ports now act as gateways to often extensive inland networks. These gateways are nodal points where intercontinental transport flows are being transshipped onto continental areas and vice versa. Several factors have facilitated the rise of gateways that vie for contestable hinterlands. First, **containerization** and the deployment of ever-larger container vessels have gone hand in hand with a concentration of vessel calls in a limited number of load centers, especially on the main long-distance routes where economies of scale at sea are most apparent (Figure 2.6). Price fixing systems that ensured the reduction of port calls had no negative price impacts on the customer base. For example, shipping lines put in place **port equalization systems** to compensate inland customers for the longer inland transport distances they might incur when sending or receiving cargo via container load centers.

Terminal operations and hinterland access are influenced by **containership size** since each port call is associated with larger volumes. While the duration of a port call does not change significantly with ship size (less than 24 hours), the volumes that are handled radically change, increasing the terminal and hinterland footprint. Assuming a 35% turnover per port call, a Panamax containership will generate about 1,700 TEU of port traffic per call, combining inbound and outbound flows. Imbalanced traffic creates directional sequences involving larger numbers of repositioned containers, as is the case for most ports.

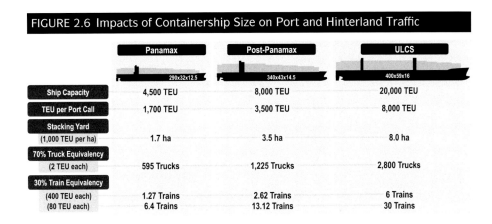

FIGURE 2.6 Impacts of Containership Size on Port and Hinterland Traffic

| | Panamax | Post-Panamax | ULCS |
|---|---|---|---|
| | 290x32x12.5 | 340x43x14.5 | 400x59x16 |
| Ship Capacity | 4,500 TEU | 8,000 TEU | 20,000 TEU |
| TEU per Port Call | 1,700 TEU | 3,500 TEU | 8,000 TEU |
| Stacking Yard (1,000 TEU per ha) | 1.7 ha | 3.5 ha | 8.0 ha |
| 70% Truck Equivalency (2 TEU each) | 595 Trucks | 1,225 Trucks | 2,800 Trucks |
| 30% Train Equivalency (400 TEU each) (80 TEU each) | 1.27 Trains 6.4 Trains | 2.62 Trains 13.12 Trains | 6 Trains 30 Trains |

A typical Panamax containership call requires about 1.7 hectares of yard space, assuming the use of standard rubber-tired gantry cranes, enabling a stacking density of 1,000 TEU per hectare. Larger ports tend to have higher stacking density with equipment such as rail-mounted gantry cranes (1,500–2,000 TEU per hectare), requiring less yard space. Smaller ports have less equipment and lower stacking density levels (500 TEU per hectare or less).

Assuming a 70/30 modal distribution between road and rail, 595 trucks and 1.27 trains (double-stacked 2,000 meters in length; North American standard) would be required to accommodate this volume. Single-stacked trains of 750 meters, common in Europe, can carry about 80 TEU, implying that 6.4 trains are required. Modal distribution varies significantly between ports as North American ports tend to have a higher share of rail services than the global average. Some ports, such as in Northern Europe (Rhine/Scheldt Delta) and China, are also serviced with container barges, which results in variations in the modal composition and the related footprint.

More TEU per port call may be involved for ports assuming a transshipment function but with fewer containers bound to the hinterland. Pure transshipment hubs have almost no hinterland traffic. The impacts of economies of scale are apparent as even if a port was to handle a similar traffic level, the time compression of the volumes requires larger terminal yard space and more hinterland transport assets to be available.

The development of **intermodal corridors** by rail and barge and inland terminals allowed for a deep hinterland penetration via shuttle trains and barges. The rise of intermodalism and associated transport corridors had a significant structuring effect on the hinterland reach of seaports. Not only has intermodalism given incentives for ports to expand their hinterland reach. Hinterlands also became more discontinuous, especially beyond the immediate hinterland of the port (Figure 2.7). Such a process can even lead to the formation of 'islands' in the distant hinterland for which the load center achieves a comparative cost and service advantage vis-à-vis rival seaports. Conventional market perspectives based on distance-decay are ill-fitted to address this new reality. High-volume intermodal corridors typically offer a more favorable relation between transport price, lead time, and distance than the conventional/continuous inland transport coverage.

FIGURE 2.7 Continuous and Discontinuous Port Hinterlands

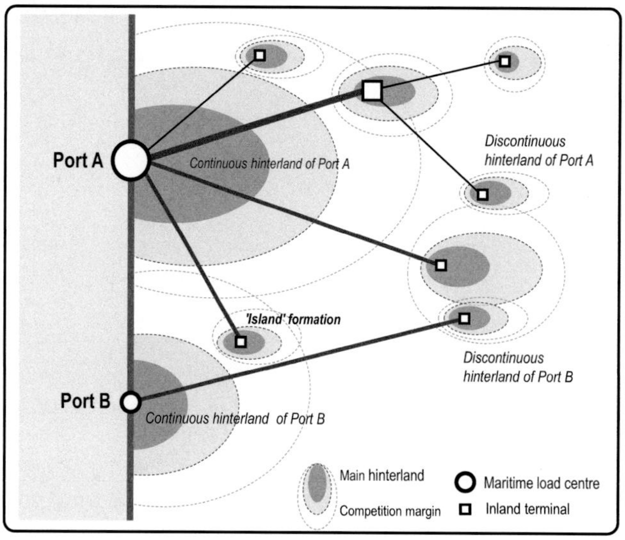

Source: Adapted from Notteboom and Rodrigue (2005).

The **direct hinterland** of a seaport (or another terminal) tends to be continuous. More distant hinterland features tend to be discontinuous in nature since the hinterland density is lower and because of the accessibility effect of transport corridors and inland terminals. The service areas of a container load center by rail and barge form overlapping service areas of individual inland terminals. The size of each of the inland service areas depends on the service frequency and the tariffs of intermodal shuttle services by rail and or barge, and the extent to which the inland terminal acts as a gateway, as well as the efficiency and price of trucking. By developing strong functional links with particular inland terminals, a port might intrude in the natural hinterland of competing ports. 'Islands' in the distant hinterland are created in which the load center achieves a comparative cost and service advantage in relation to rival seaports. This increases competition among ports of the same port system as the competitive margins of hinterlands become increasingly blurred.

The more intermodality serves as a port competition tool, the more ports become dependent on the intermodal carriers offering services along the intermodal corridors. In terms of organizational and operational factors, a highly volatile intermodal market is thus not very conducive to creating a stable and sustainable competitive position for a port vis-à-vis the hinterland segments served through the corridors. The outcome has been a series of port hinterlands serviced by maritime ranges that are a function of economic density, structure, and orientation of transportation networks, which can be contestable.

There is also a directional component to hinterlands. Inbound hinterland traffic in North America and Europe tends to be consumption-based, except when commodities and parts are involved in manufacturing.

In contrast, outbound hinterland traffic is an outcome of extraction or export-oriented manufacturing. The relative importance of forelands and hinterlands varies from a distance and cost perspective. If the distance is considered for an international transport chain, the foreland is usually the most important, while the hinterland is usually where most of the transport costs are realized.

The rise of corridors is a highly relevant development to any policies to generate a modal shift from road haulage to inland navigation, rail, and short-sea shipping. Intermodal solutions based on barges or rail prove competitive on several high-density traffic corridors or in specific niche markets. Still, they cannot serve as a continent-wide alternative for road haulage.

## 2 THE HINTERLAND AS PART OF THE MARITIME/LAND INTERFACE

The **maritime/land interface** concerns the relationships between maritime and inland freight distribution, which are two domains of freight circulation. Maritime shipping is entirely dependent on the performance of inland freight distribution as it ensures continuity in supply chains. While economic activities, such as production and retailing, are built on the concept of interdependency, distribution is a derived outcome of this interdependency. The maritime/land interface is particularly important for the long-distance trade brought by globalization. Thus, the growing distances over which freight is being carried, in addition to a surge in freight volumes, has created multiplying effects on the ability of the maritime/land interface to deal with this new environment. There are four major functional elements that define the maritime/land interface (Figure 2.8):

- **Foreland**. Although conventionally, the foreland is a maritime space with which a port performs commercial relationships, it can be argued that maritime shipping networks are a more valid representation of the concept of the foreland. The network represents the level of service offered by maritime shipping companies in terms of port calls, capacity, and frequency.
- **Port system**. The set up of intermodal infrastructures servicing port operations. The focus is on gateways granting access to large domains on inland freight circulation.
- **Modes**. Each mode has technical constraints and is positioned to service specific inland markets effectively. They are structured as corridors accessing the hinterland and inland hubs acting as intermodal and transmodal centers. Inland modes represent one of the most difficult challenges in terms of reconciling the surge in containerized maritime volume and the capacity of inland transportation to accommodate these flows. There is a growing asymmetry between maritime transport and inland modes.
- **Hinterland**. Although the hinterland is the inland space a port maintains commercial relations with, the emergence of supply chain management has placed the inland port at the core of hinterland transportation. Macro-economic factors linked with economic globalization have become particularly important for explaining the dynamics of hinterlands.

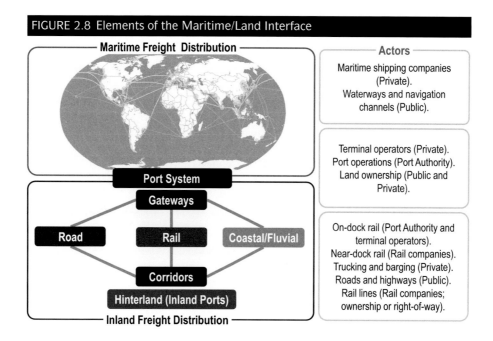

FIGURE 2.8 Elements of the Maritime/Land Interface

The maritime/land interface can also take many transactional forms related to freight and information exchange. There is a trend involving the growing level of integration between maritime transport and inland freight transport systems. Until recently, these systems evolved separately, but the development of intermodal transportation and deregulation provided new opportunities, which significantly impacted maritime and inland logistics. One particular aspect concerns high inland transport costs since they account for between 40% and 80% of container shipping costs, depending on the transport chain. Under such circumstances, there is greater involvement of maritime actors (e.g. port holdings) in inland transport systems.

## 3 THE HINTERLAND FOCUS OF MARKET PLAYERS

Hinterland connections are a key area for competition and coordination among market players involved in the maritime/land interface. Many market players understand that landside operations are key to a successful integration along the supply chain. As a result, competition between ports and across the logistics sector is intensifying. As ports and logistics firms battle to protect and gain market share, the race to find cost savings and efficiency gains becomes even more pronounced.

**Shipping lines** are keen on developing **carrier haulage** volumes, where the sea carrier arranges the hinterland transport of containerized cargo. In the case of **merchant haulage**, the shipper or forwarder manages the inland segment. The deployment of larger vessels, the formation of strategic alliances, and the waves of mergers and acquisitions have resulted in lower costs at sea, shifting the cost burden of shipping lines to the landside. Therefore, several shipping lines extend their scope beyond terminal operations to include inland transport and logistics. To streamline the inland distribution system,

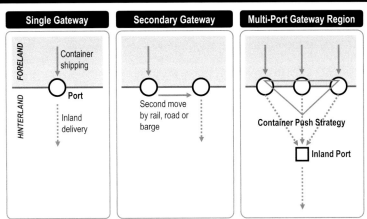

FIGURE 2.9 The Evolving Role of Shipping Lines in the Hinterland

shipping lines and their alliances seek to increase the percentage of carrier haulage. However, in most parts of the world, the inland market is dominated by large shippers or their representatives, such as logistics service providers.

Still, several larger shipping lines such as Maersk Line and MSC are developing hub-concepts in the hinterland of the key ports in their networks. Inland terminals and rail and barge services are combined to push import containers from the ocean terminal to an inland location, from which the final delivery will be initiated at a later stage. This 'push' strategy is initiated by the shipping line prioritized on the required delivery date (Figure 2.9). Export containers are pushed from an inland location to the ocean terminal, initiated by the shipping line, yet prioritized based on available inland transport capacity and the estimated time of arrival (ETA) of the mother vessel.

Carriers are confronted with some important barriers to improve inland logistics further. Landside operations are management intensive and generally involve a high proportion of bought-in services. Moreover, inland movements generate some under-remunerated activities such as repositioning empty units, network control, and tracking. Other barriers relate to volume and equipment-types of imbalances, and unforeseen delays in ports and the inland transport leg, as well as the uncertainty of demand forecasts. Carriers have learned to lessen equipment surpluses and deficits through container cabotage, inter-line equipment interchanges, chassis pools, and master leases. Carriers have very little room to increase the income out of inland logistics. If the carrier haulage tariffs edge above the open market rates, the merchant haulage option might become more attractive. The risk of cost under-recovery on second moves is another challenge in inland logistics. For example, where the line issues a bill of lading (B/L) to port A, but the vessel only calls at port B, it pays the full cost of moving the cargo to port A. Fewer ports of call implies more second moves and more substituted service and, as such, possibly large landside container interchanges between adjacent ports.

**Terminal operators** are also increasing their influence throughout supply chains by engaging in inland transport. They do so mainly by incorporating inland terminals as **extended gates** to seaport terminals and introducing an integrated terminal operator haulage concept (Box 2.3). The advantages of the extended gate system are substantial as customers can have their containers available in proximity to their customer base. Simultaneously, the deep-sea terminal operator faces less pressure on its terminals due to shorter dwell times and can guarantee better planning and utilization of the rail and barge shuttles. However, the success of both extended gates and terminal operator haulage largely depends on the transparency of the goods and information flows. Unfortunately, terminal operators often lack information on the onward inland transport segment for containers discharged at the terminal. Close coordination with shipping lines, forwarders, and shippers is needed to maximize the possibilities for developing integrated bundling concepts to the hinterland.

## Box 2.3 The extended gate concept

*The extended gate concept refers to the strategies by a single terminal operator to improve its hinterland services. Therefore, an extended gate is a specific form of port regionalization where the services offered by a terminal operator go beyond its gate. It involves a horizontal and vertical integration and extension of its services (Figure 2.10).*

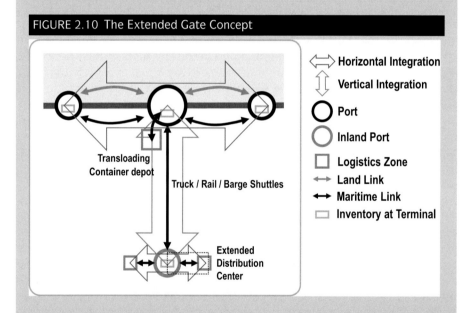

FIGURE 2.10  The Extended Gate Concept

*Horizontal integration. Terminal operators have the option of setting up services to a terminal located in another port, and this either through maritime (feeders) or land (rail shuttles, barge services) connections. Thus, they can deliver containers in a nearby port on behalf of their customers as a service to that port that is only available if a selected port is used. This is particularly the case if a terminal operator has assets in both ports and wishes to improve their utilization level. A new form of port competition takes shape. Extended gates also rely on better management of the inventory that is temporarily stored at the terminal, enabling owners to have the opportunity to pick up or drop cargo (containers) at a moment that better fits their supply chains. Another form of horizontal integration concerns the setting up of extended distribution centers that effectively use the inland port (or the port terminal) as a warehouse, implying that once a container is at the terminal, it can be considered part of the inventory of the warehouse.*

> *Vertical integration.* The integration of a terminal with transloading activities and container depots is a form of vertical integration where a terminal operator offers, or connects to, inland logistical services beyond its gates. However, it is the use of inland ports that represent the most advanced form of vertical integration for an extended gate strategy. By setting up transport services to an inland port facility, a terminal operator can deliver (or pick up) containers at a facility closer to main importers or exporters. The inland port becomes the extended gate of the port terminal. Additional activities, such as customs clearance, can also take place at the inland facility.

## 4  PORT REGIONALIZATION

The focus on hinterland development has transformed the relationships between the port and its surrounding regions and its port system. A port system is defined as a group of ports sharing similar geographic characteristics such as a coastline, or a bay, and to some extent serving overlapping hinterland regions. Since the mid-nineteenth century and up to the diffusion of containerization as a dominant form of freight distribution in the 1980s, the development of a port system evolved from an initial pattern of scattered, poorly connected ports along a coastline to a network consisting of corridors between gateway ports and major hinterland centers (Box 2.4).

Containerization revolutionized maritime shipping and port terminal operations and has supported the substantial growth in international transoceanic trade over recent decades. While, traditionally, most ports had a fairly clear and distinctive hinterland, containerization initiated a trend towards large overlapping or contestable hinterland regions. The competitive landscape became even more complex with large container transshipment facilities set up, in many cases, in locations with a limited or non-existing hinterland. From the late 1980s, the integration of such transshipment hubs led to a new paradigm in port evolution. Transshipment hubs tend to have greater depth in view of accommodating modern containership drafts, placing them at a technical advantage and inciting hub-feeder services and interlining/relay configurations between mainline vessels. As intermediary locations, they offered a compromise between economies of scale in vessels and terminals and the need to maximize connectivity in maritime networks.

The hierarchization and complexification of maritime shipping networks have a correspondence with port hinterlands. The current development phase underlines that ports are going beyond their own facilities to accommodate additional traffic and the complexity of freight distribution, namely by improving hinterland transportation. This has come to be known as **port regionalization**.

> *Port regionalization is the logistical integration between maritime and inland transport systems, particularly through the development of rail and barge corridors between a port and a network of inland load centers.*

Port regionalization addresses two fundamental issues in port development:

- **Local constraints**. Ports, especially large gateways, face a wide array of local constraints that impair their growth and efficiency. The lack of available land for expansion is among the most acute problems, an issue exacerbated by the deepwater requirements for handling larger ships. Increased port traffic may also lead to diseconomies as local road and rail systems are heavily burdened. Environmental constraints and local opposition to port development are also of significance. Port regionalization thus enables to avoid local constraints by partially externalizing them.

• **Supply chain integration**. Global production and consumption have substantially changed distribution, with the emergence of logistics and manufacturing clusters as well as large consumer markets. No single port can efficiently service the distribution requirements of such a complex web of activities. For instance, globally integrated logistics zones have emerged near many load centers, but seeing logistics zones as functionally integrated entities may be misleading as each activity has its own supply chain. Port regionalization allows for developing a distribution network that corresponds more closely to fragmented production and consumption systems.

Regionalization is a process that can take place on both the foreland and the hinterland with the goal of providing continuity between the maritime and inland freight transport systems (Figure 2.11).

The concept of **foreland-based regionalization** refers to integrating intermediate hubs in regional shipping networks, where the maritime foreland of the intermediate hub is functionally acting as a hinterland. For reasons like high deviation, small volumes, and niche hinterland (e.g. agriculture), some ports are not that well-connected to the global long-distance shipping network and show limited opportunities to improve this connectivity. Shipping lines must consider effective network configurations that tend to focus on major gateways and intermediate hubs.

Freight flows on the foreland and hinterland are not taking place with the same momentum, particularly since, on the foreland, economies of scale have

FIGURE 2.11 Foreland and Hinterland-Based Regionalization: From Massification to Atomization

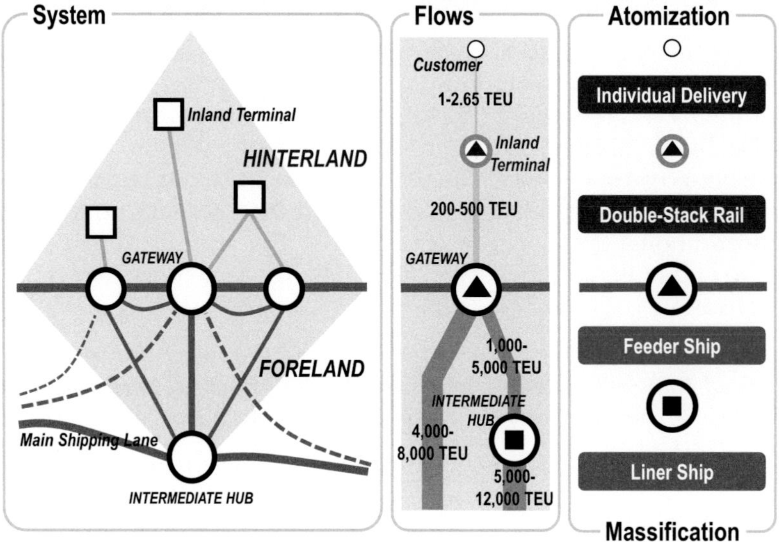

Source: Adapted from Notteboom and Rodrigue (2010).

been more effectively applied than on the hinterland. In light of an increasing massification of containerized freight loads, and while the ultimate goal remains atomization (individual containers delivered to freight owners), the insertion of an intermediate hub can act as a mitigation strategy. The largest containerships can call at intermediate hubs with high capacity and frequency services. Through feedering, ports serviced through the intermediate hub can have smaller feeder ships (e.g. Panamax class) calling at a high frequency.

At a regional level, several small or medium-sized ports may realize that it is in their long-term interests to have a higher level of integration with an intermediate hub, even if it comes at the expense of shorter distance inter-range service calls. Foreland-based regionalization can support export-oriented strategies with better connectivity of more marginal (or early growth stage) ports to global shipping networks and international trade. There are also site constraints, environmental factors, or simple market potentials that may limit the volumes generated by the hinterlands of some ports. On the intermediate hub side, the volatile long-distance transshipment traffic would be complemented by more stable and secure regional traffic. Both the foreland and the hinterland are mutually self-reinforcing, as hinterland stability can anchor the volatility of the transshipment function, particularly in light of footloose operators.

## Box 2.4  The spatial development of a port system

*In its spatial development, a port system would evolve from an initial pattern of scattered, poorly connected ports along the coastline (Phase 1; mid nineteenth century) to the main network consisting of corridors between gateway ports and major hinterland centers (Phase 4; 1980s). Models of port system development did not explain the rise of new hub terminals and did not incorporate inland freight distribution centers and terminals as active nodes in shaping load center development (Figure 2.12).*

### FIGURE 2.12  The Spatial Development of a Port System

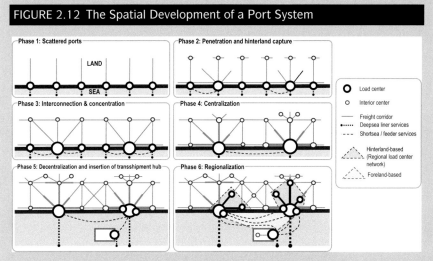

Sources: Notteboom and Rodrigue (2005); Notteboom and Rodrigue (2010).

> *The first extension (Phase 5; late 1980s–early 1990s) encompassed the explicit integration of transshipment hubs. They tend to have greater depth since they were built recently to accommodate modern containership drafts, placing them at a technical advantage. Increasing volumes can lead to an increasing segmentation in liner service networks and a hierarchy in hubs (both 'offshore' and 'mainland').*
>
> *The second extension (Phase 6; from the late 1990s) relates to incorporating inland freight distribution centers and terminals as active nodes in shaping load center development. The port regionalization phase is characterized by strong functional interdependency and even joint development of a specific load center and (selected) multimodal logistics platforms in its hinterland, ultimately leading to the formation of a regional load center network.*

## 5 HINTERLAND ACCESSIBILITY

### 5.1 Definition in a port context

> *Accessibility can be defined as the ease with which activities may be reached from a given location using a particular transportation system. It is a measure of the quality of access from a specific location to several other locations.*

A fundamental distinction can be made between **relative accessibility** and **integral accessibility**. Relative accessibility describes the relation or degree of connection between any two nodes in a transport system, such as a seaport and a central place. In contrast, integral accessibility describes the relation or degree of interconnection between a given node (a seaport) and all other nodes within a spatial network. The former measure is relevant in assessing land access on a specific origin-destination relation via a transport link or corridor. The latter is more appropriate in determining the overall accessibility and connectivity of a seaport.

Another approach to the issue of land accessibility consists of discriminating between the supply characteristics of the transport system and the actual use and levels of satisfaction. On the one hand, hinterland accessibility may be interpreted as the potential to connect to selected markets in the hinterland. This intrinsic accessibility is a function of the supply/capacity of the infrastructure and transport services. It must be borne in mind that the intrinsic land accessibility to seaports is no longer only considered in terms of proximity but more and more in terms of lead time and reliability. Alternatively, it may be held that the proof of access lies in the use of services, not simply in the presence of opportunities. This behavioral dimension could be described as **revealed accessibility** and reflects the demand side, such as the actual traffic flows on specific hinterland corridors. The concept of revealed accessibility is a particularly appropriate criterion for assessing the market's valuation and satisfaction regarding the quality of land access to a seaport.

## 5.2 Stakeholders in hinterland accessibility

Several stakeholders are involved in land access to seaports:

- Through the infrastructure and transport policy, **supranational, national, and regional authorities** significantly impact intrinsic accessibility to seaports. The infrastructural investments in links and partly also in the nodes of a transport system shape the basic access profile of a seaport. Moreover, the transport service operators have to comply with the regulatory specifications issued by governments, such as technical specifications for transport modes and their operational conditions.
- **Shipping companies, road hauliers, inland waterway companies, and rail companies** have a large impact on the second layer (transport-level) as they determine the frequency, reliability, and quality of services on specific origin-destination relations. These services try to match the logistical requirements of their customers.
- By providing physical transshipment and related activities, **stevedoring companies and terminal operators** in seaports and inland terminals contribute to the transition and integration of transport modes and networks.
- The higher the efficiency of **freight forwarders, multimodal transport operators (MTOs), and other logistic organizers** in designing transport chains between origins and destinations, the higher the revealed accessibility for a given intrinsic accessibility. An optimal transport chain design combines quality, reliability, and lead time at the lowest possible costs.
- The role of **port authorities** in enhancing access in the foreland-hinterland continuum can vary from that of a reactive facilitator to a proactive accessibility manager.
- The trade relations of **shippers** and their network formations with other firms (particularly outsourcing) shape their demand for accessibility on the logistical and transport level.

Major freight forwarders, shipping lines, transport operators, terminal operators, integrators, and other logistic service providers are competing for a level of control over door-to-door transport chains. By a vertical and horizontal integration of activities, a large number of these players increasingly affect both the transport level and logistical level of the accessibility profile of an individual seaport or port system in a direct manner.

On the infrastructural level, national and supranational public authorities may be facing severe budget constraints. Any lack of public funds for transport infrastructures puts more pressure on alternative financing via public-private partnerships (PPPs), especially in relation to safeguarding or improving the hinterland access to seaports.

## 5.3 Centrality and hinterland accessibility

The geographical location of a seaport constitutes the foundation for its competitiveness in terms of hinterland accessibility. The **centrality index**, as developed by the Bremer Ausschuss für Wirtschaftsforschung in 1980, is an early example of how to assess the hinterland centrality of a port as a function of port-hinterland distance and population of the main economic regions in the hinterland. The assumption is that the further the nodes are apart, the less interaction there will be because time and cost are presumed to increase with distance (distance-decay hypothesis). Moreover, it is assumed that the larger the size of a place, measured in terms of population or economic output for central places and cargo volumes for gateways, the larger the attraction exerted towards other places (scale hypothesis).

Any definition of the concept of centrality is relative, in that a central location cannot exist other than by reference to other central areas, or a **core area**, which is a cluster of central areas. For Western Europe, this core corresponds to the 'blue banana' (southern England, the Netherlands, Belgium, Luxembourg, the northeast of France, the Rhine axis, southern Germany, and northern Italy). For North America, the most prevalent core is the Eastern Seaboard, a conurbation extending from Boston to Washington. In East Asia, the Pearl River Delta, the Yangtze River Delta, and Tokaido (Tokyo–Osaka) are prevalent core areas. The clusters of container port activity reflect this centrality well.

The distance and scale hypotheses are applied in an imperfect geographical space:

- **Customer valuation and satisfaction of port hinterland** may differ from the basic intrinsic accessibility obtained by scale and location. This is a consequence of the value the customer attaches to the attractiveness of the port in terms of other more qualitative factors.
- The **relation between distance and transport price** is sometimes far from being straightforward and linear. In an optimal system, port hinterlands for a specific commodity are separated by lines of equal costs of carrying cargo to and from the port. However, transport pricing and tariffs can lead to large discrepancies among transport modes for hinterland access to major ports. For example, the container tariff policy of railway companies might include high cross-border interconnection fees, giving rival ports situated in these countries an artificial competitive edge over foreign ports.
- The **transshipment cost** (including the intermediate terminal costs) and its share in the total direct costs related to the inland segment of an intermodal transport chain partly determine the competitiveness of an inland transport mode or intermodal transport solution.
- The **relation between distance and lead time** is sometimes far from straightforward. The lead time on a given origin-destination relation is a function of two factors. First, the travel time on the transport links is affected by vehicle speed and delays/congestion on infrastructural networks and border-crossings. Second, the transit time at the terminals is affected by the terminal productivity and the dwell time of the cargo at the terminal. The dwell time is typically lower for carrier haulage than for merchant haulage.

## 6 TRANSPORT CORRIDORS

### 6.1 Definition and performance

Port regionalization and hinterland transportation tend to be coordinated along corridors, which have become the object of intense modal competition with the growth of movements of freight. Freight corridors are a particularly dominant convergence paradigm of urbanization integrating global, regional, and local transportation and economic processes in the geography of distribution.

> *A corridor is a linear orientation of transport routes and flows, connecting important locations that act as origins, destinations, or points of transshipment.*
>
> *A **freight corridor** is a linear orientation of freight flows supported by an accumulation of transport infrastructures and activities servicing these flows.*

A freight corridor is the main paradigm of hinterland accessibility as it is through a major transportation axis that port terminals gain access to inland distribution systems. Inland corridor formation has allowed seaports to access the formerly captive hinterlands of other ports. Hinterland corridors complement maritime corridors to form the main arteries of world trade. Corridors are created by **economies of scale** (Box 2.5). When compound demand in clusters reaches a critical mass, cargo can be consolidated, allowing other modes of transport and creating (multimodal) corridors. Corridors allow gateways to face less resistance in reaching the natural hinterland of other ports. The outcome has been a wide variety of modal split characteristics of each port hinterland with regional differences, such as between Europe and North America, attributable to hinterland size and market proximity as well as available modal options and massification potential.

The multiplication of hinterland corridors brings about a change in the relationship between gateways and their hinterland. On the one hand, the inland penetration strategy is part of maritime gateways' objective of increasing their cargo base. On the other hand, interior regions recognize that it is in their interest to establish efficient links to as many gateways as possible. This strategy not only prevents these regions from becoming captive to one specific gateway, it also improves the locational attributes of inland economic centers. Hence, linking up to more gateways implies more routing options and flexibility for shippers and logistics service providers. The performance profile of each of the corridors in terms of infrastructure provision (capacity), transport operations (price and quality of the shuttle services), and the associated logistical control is a key competitiveness attribute among various multi-port gateway regions.

**Corridor attractiveness** depends on the corridor's inherent value proposition to stakeholders. Several factors impact corridor competitiveness, including distance from the gateway to market, transit time, logistics performance, political stability, security issues, environmental conditions, and gateway to market costs. A corridor's performance can be analyzed from three perspectives:

- The corridor's **physical infrastructure**, such as the physical capacity of the links and nodes including the level of utilization of the corridor.
- The **quality of services** provided for the goods moving along the corridor, including time and cost dimensions linked to specific links and nodes.
- The **movements of goods in the corridor** are disaggregated for transport services on the links and the processing services at the nodes of the corridor.

## Box 2.5 A spatial model on logistics sites in the port hinterland

*The development of inland terminals is not sufficient to ensure an efficient port regionalization and inland distribution. Infrastructures servicing freight are required inland, a function assumed by distribution centers where vast quantities of freight are processed. The setting up of this logistical system can take place in four phases (Figure 2.13).*

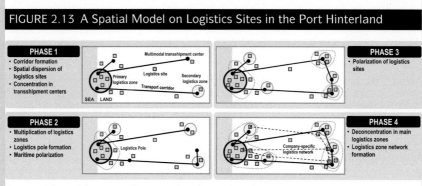

FIGURE 2.13 A Spatial Model on Logistics Sites in the Port Hinterland

Source: Adapted from Notteboom and Rodrigue (2005).

*Corridor development enhances the clustering of logistics sites both at its nodes and along the main axis (**phase 1**). Logistics poles exert a location pull on logistics sites by combining an intermodal orientation with cluster advantages underlined by conventional location theories (growth pole theory). Logistics companies are attracted by the same location factors, such as market proximity and the availability of intermodal transport and support facilities (**phase 2**). The geographical agglomeration of logistics companies creates economies of scale and scope, making a location more attractive and further promoting the agglomeration of related activities (**phase 3**). Geographical differences in labor and land costs, the availability of land, the level of congestion, the location relative to markets, labor productivity, and government policy are among the many factors determining agglomeration within logistics sites.*

*__Phase 4__ in the model introduces the regionalization of port activity and a regional load center network formation. A logistics pole performs well if an efficient regional load center network is in place to support cargo linkages in and between logistics zones. In the regionalization phase, the interaction between seaports and inland ports and terminals leads to developing a large logistics pole consisting of several logistics zones. Scale effects ensure high productivity from intermodalism, and the synchronization of goods flows with the logistics of shippers. Seaports are the central nodes driving the dynamics in a large logistics pole, but they simultaneously rely on inland ports to remain competitive.*

*The process is dynamic as the imbalanced development of inland terminals and corridors may move bottlenecks from the load center ports to corridors and inland centers. Given this constraint, logistics service providers might consider relocating their logistics sites from saturated areas to new locations. Spatial relocation patterns may change the relative importance and internal spatial configuration of logistics poles.*

## 6.2 Rail corridors

Corridors can offer cost and time competitive options to the continuity of maritime distribution. In particular, long-distance rail corridors or **landbridges** can compete with maritime trade routes. This competition and complementarity take shape differently depending on the regional setting. **Eurasian landbridges**, a set of railway lines connecting East Asia, Central Asia, Russia, and Europe, are becoming more commercially viable (Box 2.6). While several segments of the Eurasian landbridge were set up in the late nineteenth century, it was only in the early 2000s that significant landbridge traffic emerged. It was further reinforced by China's Belt and Road Initiative (BRI), seeking to develop long-distance commercial corridors between China, Central Asia, and Europe. The Eurasian landbridge is developing a niche for time-sensitive cargo, offering a complimentary option to maritime shipping.

In North America, longitudinal long-distance rail corridors, often taking the form of landbridges between coastal gateway ports, are servicing a continental hinterland articulated by major transportation and industrial hubs such as Chicago and Kansas City. Double-stack trains have unit capacities of up to 400 TEU and a total length of well above 2 km, enabling a large-scale inland rail freight distribution that is unique in the world, not only because of its size but also because of the direct link between two different coastlines. The major hinterlands in North America have changed with the decline of the industrial belt and the industrialization of the 'sunbelt', both of which have long-term impact on inland freight flows. The setting up of NAFTA in the 1990s stimulated the setting up of new gateways and corridors servicing the American market, namely through Canada (particularly Vancouver and Montreal) and Mexico, and a reorientation of traffic flows. One of the key advantages of North American rail is the almost exclusive freight orientation of the network, allowing the planning and operation of rail freight services without impediments from passenger services.

In Western Europe, the hinterland is not only intense along the coastline but also in the interior, notably along the Rhine river system and its tributary rivers (Main and Neckar), in Bavaria in the South of Germany, in the economics centers around Milan in Northern Italy and Madrid in central Spain and in major markets in Paris, the Liverpool–Manchester–Leeds belt in the UK and the belt reaching from Austria to the growing production clusters in Hungary, the Czech Republic, and southern Poland. Moreover, many European economic centers are somewhat remote from the main shipping lanes, as is the case for the Baltic countries. Therefore, European gateways are not the only major markets but are often intermediary locations, even if many are important industrial centers. The hinterland is accessed from coastal gateways such as Rotterdam, Antwerp, Hamburg, Bremerhaven, Le Havre, Barcelona, Marseille, and Felixstowe by medium-distance corridors involving a variety of combinations of road, barge (where available), and rail services.

The development of the rail corridors in Europe is enhanced by EU policy on creating a Trans-European Transport Network (TEN-T) and initiatives of rail operators, megacarriers, and other market players to extend their European transport networks. Major contestable hinterlands are increasingly being serviced not only by the ports of one region but by several gateway regions. The performance profile of each of the corridors in terms of infrastructure provision (capacity), transport operations (price and quality of the shuttle services), and the associated logistical control (management in a supply chain context) is a key attribute for port competition in Europe. With a few exceptions (such as the Betuweroute in the Netherlands), most long-distance and short-distance rail corridors in Europe have a mixed use by freight and passenger trains. RailNetEurope (RNE), which groups the rail infrastructure managers in Europe, has developed corridor management along a set of European rail freight corridors (RFCS) to plan international train paths and shape corridor infrastructure capacity to market requirements. Therefore, the focus has been on stretching existing capacity on the corridors through advanced traffic management systems and implementing effective cargo bundling and cargo coordination systems. While measures to optimize the use of existing capacity are effective, there are limits to capacity management, implying that new rail infrastructure might need to be developed to service the hinterland.

## Box 2.6  The Eurasian landbridges

*The Eurasian landbridges are a set of railway lines connecting Asia to Europe. The main arteries of the **Northern Corridor** are the Trans-Siberian Railway, the Trans-Manchurian Railway, the Trans-Mongolian Railway, and the Baikal Amur Mainline (BAM; opened in 1991). The Trans-Siberian Railway offers a transit time ranging from 12 to 18 days along a 10,000 km route. According to Russian railways, the Trans-Siberian Railway capacity will amount to 180 million tons in 2023 (1.5 times more than in 2018) (Figure 2.14).*

*Rail connections using the **Central Corridor** between China and Europe (via Kazakhstan and Russia) have seen strong development. Since 2013, Kazakhstan*

FIGURE 2.14  The Eurasian Landbridges

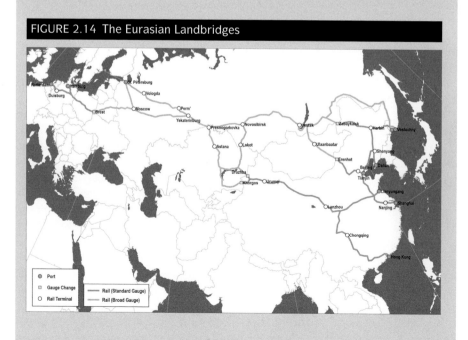

*has become a key transit area with two important border crossings with China: the Alashankou/Dostyk crossing and the Khorgos/Altynkol crossing. At Khorgos Gateway, rail cargo is transferred between trains as the rail gauge in Kazakhstan, Russia, and other former Soviet states is wider than the Chinese and European rail gauge. The dry port Khorgos Gateway also includes a special economic zone. The same type of transit operations take place in a number of terminals at the Belarusian-Polish border, with the Brest (BY)/Małaszewicze (PL) border crossing and Bruzgi (BY)/Kuźnica (PL) crossing being the most important nodes.*

*Dozens of new regular rail services have been introduced since 2013. In 2019, 8,225 trains traveled between China and Europe compared to only 80 trains in 2013. The container volume reached 725,000 TEU in 2019. About 88% of the freight traffic on the Central Corridor is westbound. The container traffic is more balanced: only 5% more trains went from China to Europe than in the opposite direction in 2018. At present, container trains run between 50 cities in China and 40 cities in Europe. Among the main destinations in Europe are Duisburg, Hamburg, and Nuremberg in Germany and Łódź and Małaszewicze in Poland. Duisburg, Europe's largest inland port, has become the most important rail hub for freight trains running between China and Europe, with intra-European connections to many other inland ports and seaports.*

## 6.3 Inland waterways as hinterland corridors

Corridors are also found in the inland waterway infrastructure network. This network is still deeply influenced by geographical considerations concerning the orientation of the waterways in relation to the orientation of commercial flows. Modifying and improving waterways is capital intensive and is undertaken when clear scale advantages are realized. In Europe, the main axes include:

- The Rhine and its tributary rivers (Main, Neckar, Mosel).
- The river system in the Benelux countries and northern France, including main canals such as the Albert Canal between Antwerp and Liège.
- The Rhône-Saône basin.
- The Northern network around the Elbe and Weser and associated canals.
- The Rhine-Main-Danube linking the Alpine Region to the Black Sea.

The Seine-Nord project is among the most significant infrastructure projects with potential structural effects on port competition and cargo routing in the Benelux countries and Northern France. In eastern Europe, ships can reach the Danube from the Rhine, opening up the larger industrial areas in Austria, the Czech Republic, Hungary, Croatia, Serbia, Romania, and Bulgaria. Via the Elbe and the Oder, the industrial areas in Austria, Germany, Poland, and the Czech Republic are within reach. Other countries in Europe that boast inland shipping are Italy, Finland, Sweden, Russia, and Ukraine. However, these pertain to isolated national waterway networks, which (if they are not maritime) have no connection with the European network.

In North America, several large river systems are present, but their latitudinal orientation does not match the general longitudinal orientation of commercial flows. Yet, waterway corridors have played an important role in North America's commercial development, particularly:

- The **St. Lawrence/Great Lakes system** connecting the Atlantic deep inside the North American hinterland. However, limited container flows are taking place, and access to the Great Lakes is constrained by locks, particularly the Welland Canal. Most of the system is impacted by winter seasonality and forced to close between December and March. This impediment undermines the competitiveness of this hinterland option as alternatives must be found during winter.
- The **Mississippi/Missouri system** connecting the Great Lakes and the American Midwest to the Gulf of Mexico. It is mainly used for the ferrying of agricultural resources, with most of the traffic downstream bound.

Attempts have been made in recent years to improve the competitiveness of inland waterways, namely with the designation of 'marine highways' in a manner mimicking the Interstate Highway system.

The **Yangtze River** is the longest and busiest river in China, dominating its inland waterway sector, being the only river that connects the eastern, central, and western parts of the country (Figure 2.15). It thus plays an essential role in supporting commercial activities in the central and western provinces of China. The total length of the Yangtze River is about 6,300 km, of which about 2,800 km is navigable for cargo vessels. It handles over two billion tons of freight annually, making it the world's most important river in cargo volume. Since the turn of the century, when port decentralization started and China joined the WTO, freight volumes on the river have increased significantly. For container transport, the Yangtze River witnessed a development pattern initiated downstream and which is moving upstream. Containerization first occurred at the lower reach in the early 1990s. Manufacturing started along the Yangtze River Delta as this was the first region to be opened to foreign trade due to its high connectivity. The lower reach of the Yangtze River consistently accounted for the majority of the river's total container traffic. However, its share decreased from 91% in 1996 to 67% in 2016 as economic development shifted upstream.

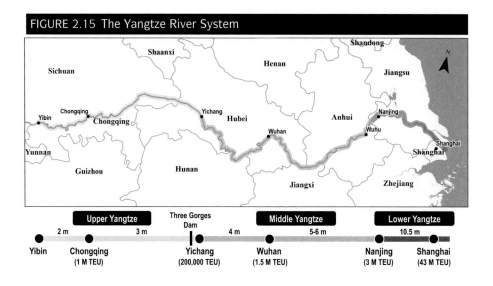

FIGURE 2.15 The Yangtze River System

# 7 CARGO BUNDLING IN HINTERLAND TRANSPORT

## 7.1 Cargo bundling options

Bundling is one of the key driving forces of inland container service network dynamics. The bundling of cargo typically involves several layers starting with the consolidation of parcels onto a pallet up to the bundling of a large number of containers onto a corridor connecting the port to the hinterland. This section focuses on the upper level of bundling activities involving a large number of boxes grouped as one batch on a train or inland barge. Three types of bundling networks can be used as an alternative to direct point-to-point inland services (Figure 2.16). These bundling networks all rely on en route bundling in transfer/intermediate terminals. In rail transport and inland shipping, these types are often combined to form multi-layered networks.

The advantages of cargo bundling are higher load factors, the use of larger transport units in terms of TEU capacity, higher frequencies, and more destinations served. The main disadvantages of complex bundling networks are the need for extra container handling at intermediate terminals resulting in higher transit times and an increased risk of damage, longer transport distances, and a higher dependency on service quality. These elements incur additional costs that could counterbalance the cost advantages linked to higher load factors or larger unit capacities. Longer transport distances combined with time lost at intermediate terminals usually result in a longer transport time than direct services. The attractiveness of direct services with a low frequency largely depends on the ability of the operator to coordinate departure and arrival times with deepsea operations and the normal working hours of firms. There are also some time constraints related to the infrastructure, such as train slots availability for freight trains or lock operating schedules on canals.

Complex bundling networks strongly rely on the speed and cost-effectiveness of the transfers at intermediate terminals. Appropriate handling

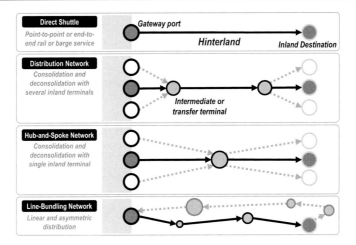

**FIGURE 2.16** Cargo Bundling Options in Hinterland Transportation

Source: Adapted from Notteboom and Rodrigue (2005).

equipment needs to be in place, which is financially justified where there is sufficient traffic. In rail, container transfers between trains offer possibilities as an alternative to shunting container wagons. LoLo (Lift-on/Lift-off) rail hub terminals (also known as thruports) can even outperform marshaling yards in terms of efficiency and speed.

If an operator opts for a line bundling network, a decision must be taken concerning the **number of intermediate stops**. Limiting the number of stops at intermediate terminals shortens round trip times. It increases the number of round trips per year, thereby maximizing revenue and minimizing the equipment required for that specific service. This is a combined result of several effects:

- Lower total (inland) port time and inland port charges on the round voyage.
- A smaller number of units needed to run a service.
- A smaller total round trip length as possible diversion distances to intermediate terminals are avoided.

More intermediate stops can lead to **lower pre- and end-haul costs** by truck. These costs are typically very high in intermodal transport. Moreover, it might be possible to realize a higher utilization rate for the transport equipment by having more calls per roundtrip. Hence, the vicinity of an inland terminal could encourage shippers to opt for intermodal transport. For container transport by barge, the addition of an extra intermediate terminal in a roundtrip might generate additional costs for more complex vessel stowage and restows. In rail transport, the inclusion of an additional intermediate terminal leads to more complex shunting of wagon groups or container Lo-Lo operations.

## 7.2 Cargo bundling in seaport areas

Large seaports with several container terminals often face the challenge of bundling cargo from different terminals on the same train or barge. Two alternative systems exist (Figure 2.17):

- The vehicle (i.e. barge or combination train) **sequentially calls at various deepsea container terminals** in order to fill the available capacity.
- All containers bound for a specific inland service are brought to one (or more) **dedicated rail or barge terminal** in the port area through a network of intra-port services by truck, barge, or rail.

In the first option, barges and trains consume additional time while collecting hinterland cargo. For example, in the ports of Rotterdam and Antwerp, some inland barges might spend more than 48 hours in the port area collecting containers from different deepsea terminals. The use of a central loading/discharging point in the port area dramatically reduces the port time for barges and train combinations. Still, it incurs extra costs related to the operation of inter-terminal container transfers and extra container handlings. The desired configuration depends on the spatial layout of the port area, particularly inter-terminal distances, operational characteristics of terminals, berths, transport equipment, and the decision on who will have to bear the costs of the inter-terminal transfers, mostly the shipping line or the terminal operator.

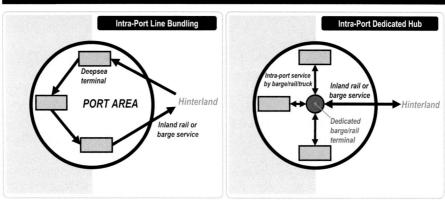

**FIGURE 2.17** Cargo Bundling in Ports with Multiple Deepsea Container Terminals

Source: Adapted from Notteboom (2008).

## 7.3 Specific considerations related to cargo bundling

Cargo bundling typically requires coordination among different supply chain actors supported by digital solutions to increase visibility and transparency of cargo bundling opportunities and overall performance metrics. There might also be tensions between the expectations and objectives of different market actors:

- **Operators** typically aim for cost minimization of their intermodal network operations. As such, transport operators are tempted to design only the bundling networks, they find it convenient to offer. Still, at the same time, they have to provide the services their customers want in terms of frequency, direct accessibility, and connectivity. Moreover, operators have to offer regular schedules with service characteristics, as any change may conflict with existing terminal operations.
- **Customer preferences** are driven by the minimization of generalized costs. These costs include all the costs of freight movements, loading and unloading and transfer, handling operations at groupage points, capital costs of the goods and depreciation during transport, costs related to damages, and inventory costs to the consignee. Shippers also show a keen interest in the qualitative performance of the whole transport chain in terms of reliability, availability, and compatibility. Hence, inefficiencies at this level will generate indirect logistics costs, such as production delays caused by late deliveries. Transport operators have to take account of the wider logistics perspective of the shippers.

Cargo availability has a significant impact on choices made in inland transport services. A port that only serves a dense local economic cluster will have fewer difficulties developing a regular inland service than a port handling containers for a large number of final destinations dispersed over a vast hinterland. A port with a large local cargo base will sooner or later be tempted to increase the inland penetration of its intermodal hinterland network to increase its capture area. From that moment on, the existing dense network of direct shuttles to nearby destinations might complement indirect inland services to more distant destinations built around one or more inland hubs. Extensive cargo concentration on a few trunk lines opens possibilities for economies of scale in inland shuttles through the deployment of longer trains or larger inland barges with higher frequencies.

Finally, the choice of an optimal service configuration also depends on network characteristics. **River systems** typically have a treelike structure with limited or no lateral connections between the different branches. Vessel capacity that can be deployed is restricted and not homogeneous due to varying draft limitations and other physical conditions in various parts of the river system. Rail networks usually have some lateral connections and offer a more homogenous profile in terms of train configurations. These differences between river systems and rail networks imply that the collection-distribution and hub-and-spoke network solutions are mainly found in rail container transport. In contrast, inland container barge services such as on the Yangtze River and the Rhine river heavily rely on line-bundling solutions, calling at several inland terminals per navigation area, such as the upper, middle, or lower sections of the river system.

# Chapter 2.3  Dry ports

*A dry port is a rail or a barge terminal linked to a maritime terminal with regular inland transport services. They are also called inland ports.*

## 1 A NEW ROLE FOR INLAND TERMINALS

Transport development is gradually **shifting inland** after a phase focused on developing port terminals and maritime shipping networks. The complexity of modern freight distribution, the increased focus on intermodal and co-modal transport solutions, and capacity issues appear to be the main drivers behind a renewed focus on hinterland logistics. While trucking tends to be sufficient in the initial phase of the development of inland freight distribution systems, at some level of activity, diminishing returns caused, for example, by congestion, energy consumption, and empty movements become strong incentives to consider the setting up of inland terminals as the next step in regional freight planning (Figure 2.18). The massification of flows in networks, through a concentration of cargo in a limited set of ports of call and associated corridors to the hinterland, has created the right conditions for nodes to appear along and at the end of these trunk lines. Therefore, bimodal and trimodal inland terminals have become an intrinsic part of the transport system, particularly in gateway regions having a high reliance on trade.

A rail-based dry port (or inland port) has three basic requirements to fulfill a relevant commercial role; an intermodal terminal, logistics activities, and a corridor to a gateway. Economies of scale (massification of flows) and economies of agglomeration provide multiplying effects. Particularly, a high capacity and frequently serviced intermodal corridor coupled with an efficient rail terminal helps reduce transportation costs while maintaining reliable

**FIGURE 2.18  Basic Requirements for Dry Ports**

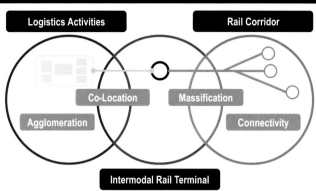

services and therefore benefit the dry port's customers, which are mostly logistics activities (distribution centers). The principle of co-location provides additional value to an inland port, particularly by minimizing drayage. It involves setting up a real estate base that can be sold or leased to freight distribution activities.

The evolution of inland freight distribution can be seen as a cycle in the ongoing developments of containerization and intermodal transportation. The geographical characteristics linked with modal availability, capacity, and reliability of regional inland access have an important role to play in shaping this development. As maritime shipping networks and port terminals become better integrated, the focus shifted on inland transportation and the inland terminal as a fundamental component of this strategy. Thus, after a phase that relied on the development of port terminals and maritime shipping networks, the integration of maritime and inland freight distribution systems has favored the setting up of inland ports.

An inland port has a level of integration with the maritime terminal and supports more efficient access to the inland market for inbound and outbound traffic. This implies an array of related logistical activities linked with the terminal, such as distribution centers, depots for containers and chassis, warehouses, and logistical service providers.

Since the inland terminal is an extension of some port activities inland, the term '**dry port**' has gained acceptance and tends to be the most commonly used term. The term is subject to debate since many inland terminals are, in fact, 'wet' given their direct access to inland waterway systems. Moreover, the inland location can effectively be a port if a barge service is concerned. Still, it fundamentally cannot be considered a port if it involves a rail terminal or, more simply, truck depots. Thus, there seems to be no consensus on the terminology resulting in a wide range of terms, including dry ports, inland terminals, inland ports, inland hubs, inland logistics centers, and inland freight villages. The reason for this lies in the multiple shapes, functions, and network positions these nodes can have. A similar issue applies to the inclusion of airport terminals, mainly their freight activities, as an element of an inland node. A whole array of transport terminal infrastructures is often presented as a dry port. Therefore, the concept of an inland port is polymorphic, implying that it can have different meanings depending on its location, connectivity, role, function, or even the marketing objectives of its promoters. Regardless of the terminology used, three fundamental characteristics are related to an inland node:

- An **intermodal terminal**, either rail or barge, that has been built or expanded.
- A **connection with a port terminal** through rail, barge, or truck services, often through a high capacity corridor.
- An array of **logistical activities** supporting and organizing the freight transited, often co-located with the intermodal terminal (Box 2.7).

The functional specialization of inland terminals has been linked with the **cluster formation** of logistical activities. Inland terminals, in many cases, have witnessed a clustering of logistics sites in the vicinity, leading to a process of logistics polarization and the creation of logistic zones. They have become excellent locations for consolidating a range of ancillary activities and logistics companies. In recent years, the dynamics in logistics networks have created the right conditions for the large-scale development of such logistics zones.

### Box 2.7  Main co-location advantages for dry ports

*Most of the dry ports initially developed were intermodal facilities acting as nodes of convergence for regional freight distribution, enabling a modal shift away from road and freight diversion and away from congested areas. These two key paradigms have been expanded with a more comprehensive approach leaning on the principle of co-location. As a dry port project becomes increasingly capital intensive and prone to risk because of its size, required equipment, and infrastructure, the need for a higher value proposition is now based on the principle of co-locations, many of which are public-private partnerships. The most common actors in a typical co-located dry port project involve a railway operator, a commercial real estate developer, or a local public development office (Figure 2.19).*

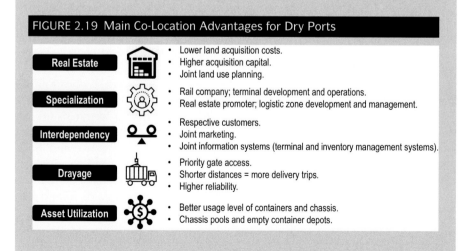

FIGURE 2.19  Main Co-Location Advantages for Dry Ports

**Real Estate**
- Lower land acquisition costs.
- Higher acquisition capital.
- Joint land use planning.

**Specialization**
- Rail company; terminal development and operations.
- Real estate promoter; logistic zone development and management.

**Interdependency**
- Respective customers.
- Joint marketing.
- Joint information systems (terminal and inventory management systems).

**Drayage**
- Priority gate access.
- Shorter distances = more delivery trips.
- Higher reliability.

**Asset Utilization**
- Better usage level of containers and chassis.
- Chassis pools and empty container depots.

*Therefore, co-location expands the market opportunities of the intermodal terminal through a set of value propositions:*

*Real estate*. Logistic zone projects occupy a large amount of space to accommodate existing and anticipated freight distribution activities. Most co-located projects occupy at least 250 acres, and several projects are well above 1,000 acres. Larger projects tend to have lower land acquisition costs. Also, since co-located projects involve at least two large players, a commercial real estate developer, and a railway company, they can tap into capital pools with better conditions than a smaller actor (e.g. interest rates). For instance, CenterPoint Properties is owned by the pension fund CalPERS (California public employees' retirement fund), enabling access to long-term capital pools. Another important aspect is that a co-located logistic project enables the joint planning of facilities.

*Specialization*. A co-location project enables both actors involved to focus on their core competencies, creating multiplying factors. For instance, the rail company can focus on terminal development and operations while the real estate promoter can develop and manage the freight distribution facilities.

*Interdependency*. The terminal operator and freight distribution activities are their respective customers, implying that both partners have vested interests in the efficiency of their operations. The possibility of joint marketing where the logistic zone is promoted as a single intermodal package is also common since the terminal is sold as a value proposition to potential customers.

*Drayage*. A co-location project offers notable operational advantages for drayage, not just because of proximity but because trucks can have priority access through the terminal's gates. Drivers can perform more deliveries per day, and the reliability of these deliveries improves.

*Asset utilization*. Intermodal transportation assets are capital intensive, and there are pressures to increase their utilization level to achieve better returns on investments. Containers and chassis tend to be the assets that are the most prone to such strategies, namely through the setting up of chassis pools and empty container depots.

*Information technologies*. A co-location project offers the possibility to jointly plan information systems for terminal operations and the related supply chains, creating a community system where users can have access to real-time information about the status of their shipments. Both terminal operations and their related supply chains benefit.

One drawback is that co-located logistics activities depend on the performance of the terminal and the level of service offered by the rail operator. If the rail operator has other priorities within its network, then the efficiency of the co-located logistic zone is compromised.

## 2  DRIVING FORCES

Each inland port remains the outcome of transport geography pertaining to modal availability and efficiency, market function, intensity, and the regulatory framework and governance. Their emergence underlines some deficiencies in conventional inland freight distribution that needed to be mitigated. This mitigation includes (Figure 2.20):

- **Input costs**. Land and labor costs are among the highest logistics costs. Many deep-sea terminal facilities have limited land available for expansion, implying higher land costs, while inland locations tend to have

**FIGURE 2.20 Main Driving Forces behind the Setting of Inland Terminals**

**Input Costs**
*Lower logistics costs*

- Land and labor costs as significant logistics costs.
- Intensification of activities at the main terminal and the search of lower value locations supporting less intensive freight activities.

**Capacity and Congestion**
*Expand capabilities*

- Increases the intermodal capacity of inland freight distribution.
- Diminishing returns such as congestion, energy and empty movements.

**Hinterland Access**
*Expand reach*

- Lower distribution costs and improved capacity.
- Allow ports to compete and to extend their cargo base.
- A commercial and trade development tool.

**Supply Chain Management**
*Economies of agglomeration*

- Integrated within supply chain management practices.
- Freight distribution centers, custom clearance, container depots and logistical capabilities.

**Policy and Regulation**
*Improved compliance*

- Economic development strategies, land use policy, and financial incentives by port authorities and economic development agencies.
- Policies related to foreign trade zones and customs procedures.
- Cargo safety and security procedures.

land available. Many port areas are also facing higher labor costs since they are located within large metropolitan areas. High input costs favor intensifying activities at the main terminal and the search for lower value locations supporting less intensive freight activities.

- **Capacity and congestion**. Capacity issues appear to be the main driver of inland port development since a system of inland terminals increases the intermodal capacity of inland freight distribution. While trucking tends to be sufficient in the initial phase of the development of inland freight distribution systems, at some level of activity, diminishing returns such as congestion, energy, and empty movements become strong incentives to consider the setting up of inland terminals as the next step in regional freight planning.

- **Hinterland market**. Inland ports confer a higher level of accessibility through long-distance transport corridors because of lower distribution costs and improved capacity. These high-capacity inland transport corridors allow ports to penetrate the local hinterland of competing ports and extend their cargo base. In such a setting, the inland port becomes a commercial and trade development tool that jointly increases imports, exports, and intermodal terminal use. It is thus better placed to support regional and international trade patterns.

- **Supply chain management**. An inland port is a location actively integrated within supply chain management practices, particularly because of containerization. It reflects the level of vertical integration between the port and hinterland actors such as transport companies and supply chain managers. This takes many forms, such as the agglomeration of freight distribution centers, custom clearance, container depots, and logistical capabilities. The inland terminal can also become a buffer in supply chains, acting as a temporary warehousing facility.

- **Policy and regulations**. Economic development strategies, land use policy, and financial incentives by port authorities and economic development agencies can lead to the development of inland ports. This can be supported by policies related to foreign trade zones and customs proce-dures, enabling a transfer of functions that were previously taking place at the port (customs port of entry) to an inland location. This is com-monly a significant hurdle since many national trade regulations only enable containers to be cleared for imports or exports at a port. A similar trend applies to cargo safety and security procedures, where the inland port becomes a component of a chain of cargo integrity.

The geographical characteristics linked with modal availability and the capac-ity of regional inland access have an important role in shaping the emergence and development of inland ports. Each inland market has its own potential requiring different transport services. Thus, there is no single strategy for an inland port in terms of modal preferences as the regional effect remains funda-mental. In developed countries, namely in North America and Europe, which tend to be at the receiving end of many containerized supply chains, several inland ports have been developed to focus on inbound logistics.

The setting up of global supply chains and the strategy of Pacific Asian countries around the export-oriented paradigm have been powerful forces shaping contemporary freight distribution. Indirectly, this has forced players in the freight transport industry to examine supply chains as a whole and to identify legs where capacity and reliability were an issue. Once maritime ship-ping networks and port terminal activities became better integrated, mainly through the symbiotic relationship between maritime shipping and port oper-ations, inland transportation became a visible issue to be addressed with the inland terminal, a fundamental component of this strategy. This initially took place in advanced economies such as in North America and Europe. The focus has also shifted to considering inland terminals for the early stages of global supply chains (outbound logistics), namely in countries having a marked export-oriented function.

Inland terminals have evolved from simple intermodal locations to their incorporation within logistic zones. Rail terminals, in particular, have histori-cally been locations from which specific market coverage was achieved. Con-tainerization has impacted this coverage through the selection of terminals that serviced a wider market area. This spatial change also came with a func-tional change as intermodal terminals began to experience a specialization of roles based on their geographical location and their function within supply chains.

## 3 FUNCTIONS WITHIN TRANSPORT CHAINS

A functional and added value hierarchy has emerged for inland terminals. They try to replicate several services performed at a port terminal, namely customs clearance, container storage, cargo consolidation, and deconsolida-tion. In many instances, freight transport terminals fit within a hierarchy with a functionally integrated inland transport system of gateways and their cor-ridors, where they serve three major functions (Figure 2.21):

- **Satellite terminals**. They tend to be close to a port facility, but mainly at the periphery of its metropolitan area (often less than 100 km away) since they mainly assume a service function to the seaport facilities. They accommodate additional traffic and service functions that have become

**FIGURE 2.21  Functions of Inland Terminals**

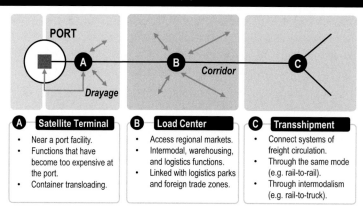

too expensive at the port, such as warehousing and empty container depots, or are less bound to a location near a deep-sea quay. Several satellite terminals only have a transport function transshipping cargo between rail/barges and trucks. Satellite terminals can also serve as load centers for local or regional markets, particularly if the economic density is high. They form a multi-terminal cluster with the main port connected through regular rail or barge shuttle services. For gateways having a dominance in imports, a satellite terminal can serve a significant transloading function where the contents of maritime containers are transloaded into domestic containers or truckloads. As the footprint of container terminals is facing pressure due to increases in traffic and ship sizes, satellite terminals can provide additional terminal footprint at a connected off-port site.

- **Freight distribution clusters** (load centers). This is a major intermodal facility – load center – granting access to well-defined regional markets that include production and consumption functions. It commonly corresponds to a metropolitan area where a variety of terminals serve simultaneously intermodal, warehousing, distribution, and logistics functions. These tend to take place in logistics parks and free trade zones (or foreign trade zones). The inland terminal is thus the point of collection or distribution of a regional market. The more extensive and diversified the market, the more important the load center is. If the load center has a good intermediary location, such as being along a major rail corridor, freight distribution activities serving an extended market will be present.
- **Transshipment facilities**. These link large freight circulation systems either through the same mode (e.g. rail-to-rail) or through intermodalism (rail-to-truck, or even rail-to-barge). In the latter case, the inland terminal assumes the role of a load center. The origin or the destination of the freight handled is outside the terminal's market area, with a function similar to that of transshipment hubs in maritime shipping networks. Such transshipment terminals are often found near country borders, combining administrative processes linked to cross-border

traffic to value-added logistics activities. Although this function remains marginal in most parts of the world, ongoing developments in inland freight distribution, where the scale and scope of intermodal services increase, indicate that transshipment services are bound to become more prominent.

These functions are not exclusive, implying that inland terminals can serve several functions at once. Therefore, there is no single model for an inland port. For inbound or outbound freight flows, the inland terminal is the first tier of a functional hierarchy that defines its fundamental (activities it directly services) and extended (activities it indirectly services) hinterlands. Similar to logistics clusters, dry ports offer unique added value opportunities as inland locations handling cargo. Considering the potential mix of the functions of inland ports, five major criteria ensure that they fulfill their role as an interface between global and regional freight distribution systems efficiently:

- **Site and situation**. Like any transport facility of significance, an inland port requires an appropriate site with good access to rail or barge terminals as well as available land for development. Access to an area of significant economic density, such as one with a large population base, is important since it will be linked to the traffic level handled by the inland port. Transportation remains the highest logistics cost, underlining the importance of an accessible location. Several inland ports also have an airport in proximity, which can help support a variety of freight activities.

- **Massification**. The hinterland massification opportunities (Box 2.8) offered by inland ports are associated with lower transport costs and better accessibility. Massification takes place over two interdependent dimensions. The first concern the massification of flows between the port terminal and the inland port through a high capacity corridor. Intermodal rail and barge services represent the dominant means over which this process is achieved. The second relates to the consolidation and deconsolidation of cargo flows, depending on whether inbound or outbound logistics are involved.

- **Reconciling cargo flows**. Since most long-distance (and some domestic) trade is supported by containerization, there are numerous instances where a regional market imports more than it exports (or vice-versa). Under such circumstances, an inland port must provide the physical and logistical capabilities to ensure that empty containers are repositioned efficiently to other markets if local cargo cannot be found. This can take the form of empty container depots and arrangements with freight forwarders to have slots available for repositioning. Whether there are imbalances in container flows or not, an inland port must ensure that the inbound and outbound flows are reconciled as quickly as possible. A common method involves a cargo rotation from import activities where containers are emptied to export activities where containers are filled with goods. For container owners, whether they are maritime shipping or leasing companies, a rapid turnover of their assets is fundamental and will secure a continuous usage of the inland port. Effective repositioning and cargo rotation strategies ensure higher revenue for both the container owners and the inland port operators.

- **Trade and transactional facilitation**. An inland port can also be a fundamental structure promoting both the import and export sectors of a region, particularly for smaller businesses unable to achieve economies of scale independently. Through these, new market opportunities become possible as both imports and exports are cheaper. The setting up of a Foreign Trade Zone (FTZ) is also an option to be considered as a trade facilitation strategy. The functional pairing of inland ports is a transactional strategy where an inland port is an activity seeking agreements with other inland ports so that reciprocal supply chains are established or reinforced.

- **Governance**. The way an inland port is owned and operated indicates its potential to identify new market opportunities and invest accordingly (Box 2.9). In many cases, the commitment of a large private investor such as a terminal operator or a real estate developer can be perceived as a risk mitigation strategy and provide expertise in developing facilities and related activities. Sections of an inland port can be shared facilities (e.g. distribution centers) so that smaller players can get involved by renting space and equipment. This also applies to the appropriate strategies related to each stage in the life cycle of an inland terminal, from its construction to its maturity where its potential has essentially been realized.

The enduring challenges in inland port development remain the provision of infrastructures and the ability to attract in a timely fashion sufficient cargo volumes to justify returns on investments.

---

### Box 2.8 The massification of transportation in inland systems

*The growth of hinterland traffic, if only supported by drayage (truck) operations, leads to increasing diseconomies such as congestion and capacity limitations. With this, the level of disorder in the inland transport system involves higher transport costs and unreliability in freight distribution. Therefore, the formation of an inland load center network aims at coping with these diseconomies through a massification of several inland flows. It involves a series of inland terminals (IT) linked to the port facilities by high-capacity rail or barge (when feasible) corridors. A supporting land use structure needs to be established, mostly concerning the clustering of logistics activities (e.g. distribution centers) and often in co-location with the terminal facilities. For instance, port-centric logistics zones support freight distribution activities related to maritime shipping and have a dominant international trade orientation. Port authorities tend to be proactive for this type of development since it supports and provides added value to port activities. An inland port is an intermodal terminal (commonly rail) built or updated concomitantly with the development of adjacent (co-located) logistical and service activities. Although in proximity (not co-located) to the terminal facility, an intermodal industrial park is a similar structure (Figure 2.22).*

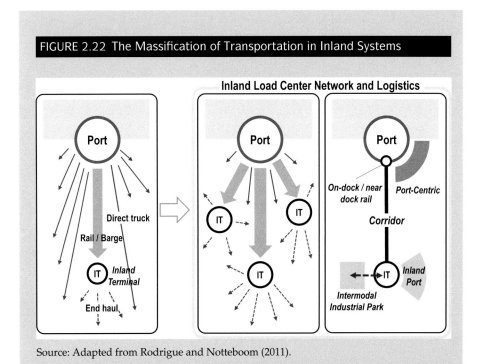

**FIGURE 2.22** The Massification of Transportation in Inland Systems

Source: Adapted from Rodrigue and Notteboom (2011).

### Box 2.9  Main governance models for inland ports and logistic zones

*Inland ports and their associated logistic zones have a wider range of options than ports in terms of their governance models, in which the landlord model prevails. The ownership and the management of an inland port can be public, private, or a combination of both (Figure 2.23):*

*    **Single ownership**. The logistics or inland port project is spearheaded by a single public or private actor. Although this governance model provides a clear purpose for the project, it is also potentially of high risk since only one actor is involved.*

*    **Public–private partnership**. A model where both the public and private sectors share the development of a logistics zone or inland port through the setting up of an entity, commonly with a public charter. Usually, the public sector is responsible for developing infrastructures, while the private sector usually develops real estate.*

*    **Landlord model**. A form of PPP with the public sector owning the real estate and developing the basic infrastructure. However, concessions are offered where private actors develop their own projects, namely warehouses and distribution centers.*

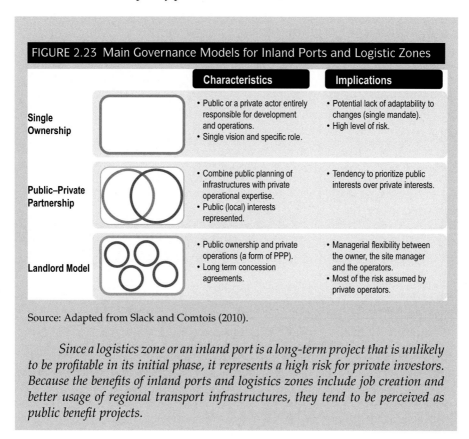

FIGURE 2.23 Main Governance Models for Inland Ports and Logistic Zones

| | | Characteristics | Implications |
|---|---|---|---|
| Single Ownership | | • Public or a private actor entirely responsible for development and operations.<br>• Single vision and specific role. | • Potential lack of adaptability to changes (single mandate).<br>• High level of risk. |
| Public–Private Partnership | | • Combine public planning of infrastructures with private operational expertise.<br>• Public (local) interests represented. | • Tendency to prioritize public interests over private interests. |
| Landlord Model | | • Public ownership and private operations (a form of PPP).<br>• Long term concession agreements. | • Managerial flexibility between the owner, the site manager and the operators.<br>• Most of the risk assumed by private operators. |

Source: Adapted from Slack and Comtois (2010).

*Since a logistics zone or an inland port is a long-term project that is unlikely to be profitable in its initial phase, it represents a high risk for private investors. Because the benefits of inland ports and logistics zones include job creation and better usage of regional transport infrastructures, they tend to be perceived as public benefit projects.*

## 4 THE REGIONAL IMPACTS OF INLAND PORTS

Regional issues, namely how inland ports **interact with their regional markets**, remain fundamental as they define their modal characteristics, regulatory framework, and commercial opportunities. Depending on the geographical setting and the structure, governance, and ownership of inland transport systems, inland terminals have different development and integration levels with port terminals. They are part of a port regionalization strategy supporting a more extensive hinterland.

### 4.1 Europe

In Western Europe, the setting up of inland terminals is the most advanced with close integration of port terminals with rail shuttles and barge services. Rail-based dry ports are found throughout Europe, often linked to the development of logistics zones. Depending on the European country considered, these logistics zones are known under different names, such as 'platformes logistiques' in France, the 'Güterverkehrszentren (GVZ)' in Germany, 'Interporti' in Italy, 'Freight Villages' in the UK, 'Transport Centres' in Denmark, and 'Zonas de Actividades Logisticas (ZAL)' in Spain. The rail liberalization process in Europe supports the development of real pan-European rail services on a one-stop-shop basis. Through Europe, new entrants are emerging while some large former national railway companies have joined forces. Rail terminals in Europe are mostly built and operated by large railway ventures.

The largest rail facilities have bundles of up to ten rail tracks with lengths of a maximum of 800 meters per track. Rail hubs are typically equipped to allow simultaneous batch exchanges (direct transshipment) through the use of rail-mounted gantry cranes that stretch over the rail bundles.

In northwest Europe, barge transport is taking a more prominent role in dealing with gateway traffic. Barge container transport has its origins in transport between Antwerp, Rotterdam, and the Rhine basin. Recent years have seen development along the north–south axis between the Benelux countries and northern France. Antwerp and Rotterdam handled about 6 million TEU of inland barge traffic in 2020, about 92% of total European container traffic on that mode. Promising barging developments are also found on the Seine between Le Havre and the Paris region, in the Rhône/Seine basin between Marseille, Lyon, and Dijon, on the Elbe and the Weser in Northern Germany and the Danube River out of the port of Constantza. Barge services have also been initiated on the Po River connecting the Port of Venice with Mantua and Cremona near Milan.

European integration processes have permitted the setting up of more natural (commercially based) hinterlands that did not exist before. Since a good share of the European market is inland, growth in international trade required intermediary locations inland to help accommodate larger flows between ports and their hinterlands (Box 2.10).

## Box 2.10  Inland ports and logistics zones around the Rhine/Scheldt delta

*A large concentration of inland terminals can be found around the Rhine/Scheldt delta, which is Europe's most important gateway region with a total container throughput of 28.6 million TEU in 2020, and where the function of satellite terminals is prominent. Almost every European port has an inland terminal strategy as a way to secure hinterland traffic (Figure 2.24).*

FIGURE 2.24  Inland Ports and Logistics Zones Around the Rhine/Scheldt Delta

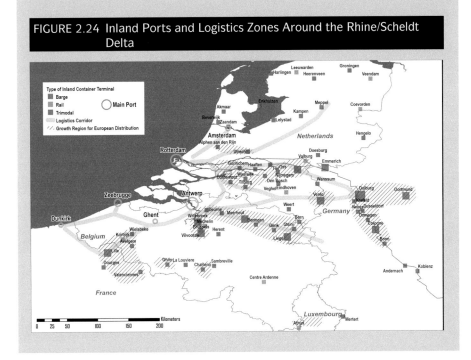

> *The logistics zones in the Netherlands are mainly located in ports or around new or existing barge or rail terminals in the hinterland. Dordrecht and Moerdijk are important overflow locations for the port of Rotterdam. There are now large concentrations of logistics sites in and around the inner port of Liege, along the Geel–Hasselt–Genk axis and the Antwerp–Brussels axis, and in the Kortrijk/Lille border region. The existing geographical concentration of logistics sites has stimulated the development of inland terminals in these areas. Seaports are the central nodes driving the dynamics of large logistics clusters. However, at the same time, these seaports rely heavily on inland ports to preserve their attractiveness.*

## 4.2 North America

There have been large inland terminals in North America since the development of the transcontinental railway system in the late nineteenth century. Their setting up was a natural process in which inland terminals corresponded to large inland market areas, commonly around metropolitan areas commanding a regional manufacturing base and distribution system. Although exports were significant, particularly for agricultural goods, this system of inland terminals mostly supported domestic freight distribution. With globalization and intermodalism, two main categories of inland terminals have emerged in North America.

The first is related to ocean trade. Inland terminals are an extension of a maritime terminal located in one of the three major ranges (Atlantic, Gulf, and Pacific) either as satellite terminals or, more commonly, as inland load centers (e.g. Chicago or Mexico). The second category concerns inland terminals mainly connected to **transborder trade** that can act as custom pre-clearance centers. Kansas City can be considered the most advanced inland port initiative in North America. It combines intermodal rail facilities from four different rail operators, foreign trade zones, and logistics parks at various locations throughout the metropolitan area. Like Chicago, the city can essentially be perceived as a terminal.

Several recent logistic zones projects in North America capitalize on the planning and setting up of a new intermodal rail terminal done at the same time as a logistics zone project. This co-location partnership fundamentally acts as a filter for the commercial potential of the project as both actors must make the decision to go ahead with their respective capital investment in terminal facilities and commercial real estate. Compared to Europe, North American dry ports tend to be larger and cover a much more substantial market area (Box 2.11).

### Box 2.11 Major inland terminal clusters in North America

*The principle of co-location is fundamental to the operational efficiency of an inland port, particularly in North America. There is a distributional hierarchy that is a function of accessibility and connectivity, where locations in the Midwest rank high as distribution hubs. The location of rail terminals is particularly preponderant around distribution hubs, underlining their role as inland load centers (Figure 2.25).*

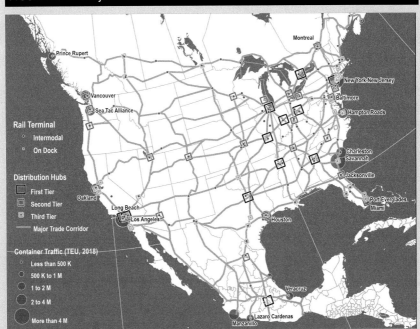

FIGURE 2.25  Major Inland Terminal Clusters in North America

*Several inland port projects in North America are capitalizing on this advantage. The planning and setting up of a new intermodal rail terminal are done at the same time as a logistics zone project. This partnership fundamentally acts as a filter for the commercial potential of the project as both actors must decide to go ahead with their respective capital investment in terminal facilities and commercial real estate. Co-located logistics zone projects tend to be significantly larger than conventional logistics zones solely serviced by road. The convergence between the need for rail companies to develop large terminals to accommodate economies of scale and the capital intensiveness of these investments has stimulated partnerships with large commercial real estate developers who have the capital and expertise to develop large logistics zones.*

*CenterPoint Properties, which was acquired in 2006 by a branch of CalP-ERS (California public employees' retirement fund), is a salient example of a commercial developer actively involved with several rail operators in developing and managing logistics zones. While in most cases, CenterPoint will bring forward a project after a terminal development project has been announced. The trend is shifting towards simultaneous planning of the intermodal rail terminal and the logistics zone. In one case (Crete, Illinois), CenterPoint decided to develop a logistics zone beforehand, and the rail operator CSX latched on afterward with its National Gateway Program.*

## 4.3 East and Southeast Asia

For Asia, inland terminals are in their infancy. Geographical characteristics, namely coastal population concentrations and export-oriented development strategies, have not been helpful to the setting up of inland terminals. Several container depots have appeared inland to improve the availability of export containers within manufacturing clusters (e.g. South Korea, Thailand, India), but containers are mainly carried by truck. It is China that has the largest potential for the emergence of a network of inland terminals, with three main types emerging:

- The first are **satellite facilities** in the vicinity of port terminals. They assume the conventional role of accommodating activities decongesting port operations, such as container depots, as well as performing customs clearance.
- The second type concerns **inland facilities** located in major metropolitan areas to provide better connectivity to port terminals along the coast as well as to support the logistics of a growing internal consumption market. Significant dry port development is taking place on the Yangtze River up to the upper stretches near Chongqing, some 2,400 km upstream from Shanghai. Intermodal rail development faces the prominence of the existing rail network on passengers and dry bulk commodities. As the Chinese economy moves towards a more extensive internal market, intermodal rail and barge traffic is increasing, so is the usage of inland ports.
- The third type is **border facilities** that fulfil the function of custom clearance, consolidation, and deconsolidation of cargo, as well as emerging trans-modal functions of linking different systems or circulation. The setting up of Asia–Europe rail connections along the Eurasian landbridge may promote this function.

Another system of inland terminals is likely to emerge in Southeast Asia, particularly along the Mekong. In light of the North American and European experiences, the question remains of how Pacific Asia can develop its inland port strategy and regionalism. The unique geographical characteristics of the region are likely to rely much on the satellite terminal concept and inland load centers in relative proximity. For this context, the European example is more appropriate. However, the setting up of long-distance intermodal rail corridors within China and through Central Asia favors developing the inland load center system common in North America.

## 5 FUTURE PROSPECTS

The setting up of dry ports has been a dominant paradigm in hinterland transportation development. The growth of maritime shipping and its economies of scale have placed pressures on the inland segment of freight distribution. The prospects for inland ports remain positive, with large continental markets like North America and Europe relying on a network of satellite terminals and load centers as a fundamental structure to support the massification of hinterland freight movements. This has entailed the emergence of extended gates and extended forms of supply chain management in which inland terminals play an active role.

As congestion increases, inland terminals will be even more important in maintaining efficient supply chains. It can also be expected that resources will play a greater role within containerized trade, with inland terminals acting as platforms to export containerized resources. Dry ports play an increasing role as a repositioning strategy for empty containers to improve this repositioning efficiency by providing better cargo rotation opportunities or acting as platforms that can help promote containerized exports. Inland ports are taking part in the ongoing intermodal integration between ports and their hinterland through long-distance rail and barge corridors. They are becoming more important elements within supply chains, particularly through their role as a buffer where containerized consignments can be cheaply stored, waiting to be forwarded to their final destinations.

Like other transport infrastructures, there is a potential for overinvestment, duplication, and redundancy since many inland locations would like to claim a stake in global value chains. This appears to be the case in Western Europe. An abundance of inland terminals, particularly within the Rhine/Scheldt delta, underlines the overly competitive environment and the waste of resources. In North America, because of a different ownership and governance structure, the setting up of an inland port, at least the intermodal terminal component, is mostly in the hands of rail operators. Each decision thus takes place with much more consideration being given to market potential as well as the overall impact on their network structure. The decision of a rail company to build a new terminal or expand existing facilities commonly marks the moment where regional stakeholders, from real estate developers to logistics service providers, readjust their strategies. Further, local governments may devise inland port development with the expectation to create multiplying effects in the regional economy. Therefore, inland ports should develop in alignment with the market and stakeholders they are servicing. Misalignment may result in missed opportunities and wasteful investments.

The development of dry ports worldwide has underlined an emerging functional relation of port terminals and their hinterland. In the case of China, such initiatives can be far-reaching since the goal is to promote trade and economic integration across central Asia, all the way to Europe. Dry ports assume various functions with co-location with logistical zones, a dominant development paradigm based on their regional setting. While the interest in dry ports has increased, each dry port is confronted with a unique regional, economic, and regulatory setting that defines its functions and its relations with seaports. Best practices can only be applied successfully if the relative uniqueness of each dry port setting is considered.

# Chapter 2.4  Digital transformation

*Digital transformation is the integration of information technologies into business processes, changing how they operate and deliver value to their customers.*

## 1 THE DIGITAL TRANSFORMATION OF PORTS

Like several sectors of the economy, the port and maritime industry have been impacted by digital transformation. Technology is used to improve, at times

**FIGURE 2.26 Digital Transformation and Expected Implications**

| | | |
|---|---|---|
| ⊯ | **Demand Responsive** | • Focus on customer and market demands to align production and distribution. |
| ① | **First Mover** | • Importance of speed when bringing a new product to the market. |
| ⚛ | **Cooperation** | • Focus on co-operation and partnerships (intra and inter organization).<br>• Downstream / upstream the supply chain, competitors and start-ups. |
| ⬡ | **Organizational Change** | • New governance and business models with flexible partnerships.<br>• New revenue models and pricing systems. |
| ∝ | **Continuous Change** | • Continuous adaptation in organizational and managerial processes. |
| ⇒‖⇐ | **Agility & Resilience** | • Resilient and flexible infrastructure and assets.<br>• Asset light approach to avoid sunk costs. |
| ⚙ | **Competencies** | • Build organizational digital competencies. |
| ⚏ | **Digital Focus** | • Incorporate digital thinking in all layers of the organization.<br>• Corporate function of Chief Digital Officer or Chief Information Officer. |

Source: Adapted from Van Peteghem (2016).

substantially, the performance or reach of organizations, including their management, operations, and assets. Information technologies, combined with leadership, can turn technology into transformations. Digital transformation implies a cultural change that requires organizations to challenge the status quo and incorporate technology continually (Figure 2.26). Still, digital transformation has been an ongoing process since the 1990s with the massive diffusion of personal computers in organizations, a process expanded by networking in the early 2000s. By 2010, a critical mass of storage and processing capabilities embedded in ubiquitous and large-scale information networks allowed new forms of digital transformation to occur.

Digital transformation challenges organizations to adopt a set of key notions that have an impact on their **governance** and **organization**, including which strategies and business models should be implemented. These generic corporate challenges can also be found in the logistics industry, shipping, and ports. For example, port and logistics companies take on a customer-centric approach by adjusting objectives to include KPIs and metrics that measure customer satisfaction and, if necessary, by overhauling the business processes that are seen as less efficient. Service reliability in a digital era does not only imply that a company can deliver a service, but that it should also do so efficiently, conveniently, and consistently, a concept associated with the ease of doing business.

Another key to competitiveness relates to **cooperation** between supply chain partners and digital and integrated data solutions. Horizontal collaboration between transport companies and logistics service providers deals with the need for shorter, convenient, more sustainable, and cost-efficient supply chains. This entails additional complexities, mainly where it concerns mutual trust concerning data-sharing protocols and protecting respective competitiveness. Thus, cooperation is typically associated with new governance models to build trust among the parties involved and achieve a fair distribution of costs, efforts, revenues, and returns. However, there are several concerns to be addressed when developing cooperation initiatives and introducing performance measurement tools and systems across supply chains:

- **Lack of trust**. Organizations are reluctant to share their internal data. Trust in data sharing, acquisition, and monitoring needs to be built as most of the data can be perceived as market sensitive.
- **Lack of understanding**. Many managers focus on internal systems, so moving to an inter-organizational scale often demands the development of a deeper understanding of what matters when co-operating with other parties in the chain.
- **Lack of control**. Managers and organizations are often focused on initiatives and measures they can fully control. Inter-organizational measures are challenging to manage and thus to control.
- **Different goals and objectives**. The cooperation between organizations might lead to a confrontation between different goals and differing views on achieving these goals.
- **Information systems**. Information systems often have to be adapted to include non-traditional information relating to (green) supply chain performance. Also, information exchanges between organizations might be complicated by a lack of standards (in terms of units to use, structure, format) and harmonized protocols and procedures.
- **Difficulty in linking to customer value**. Not all organizations see the corporate and stakeholder value of co-operating with other organizations. They may have difficulties identifying and measuring possible value.
- **Deciding where to begin**. Organizations might face challenges when starting to develop supply chain-wide practices and related performance measurements.

Service providers in logistics, shipping, and ports improve supply chains with the support of IT systems that are increasingly performant. The data component leverages performant and pro-active service providers to transform into organizations with a new outlook on logistics services. Next to an increasing number of traditional activities being outsourced, such as transport, warehousing, and various types of value-added services, the presence of collaborative platforms enables service providers to develop new types of logistics services.

Further, logistics, shipping, and port companies are rethinking their hiring strategies as the nature of jobs transforms with technology. Service providers invest in **self-service systems** to internally replace operational staff and improve the ease of doing business for customers. For example, advances have been made in cargo booking systems, cargo tracking systems, and invoicing, which have become paperless and available online. The ultimate objective behind these digital systems is to have staff perform only the tasks that the systems cannot do, such as exceptions. This implies staff moves towards new managerial, commercial, and programming roles as basic logistics tasks are automated.

**Data integrity and privacy** challenges and risks have soared with the rise of digitalization and technology. The logistics, shipping, and port industry is challenged to safeguard the data being communicated across players. In the past few years, several market players have been confronted with large-scale cyber-attacks. For example, in 2017, a ransomware cyber-attack infected Maersk Line and its terminal sister company, APM Terminals. In the same year, the 'WannaCry' ransomware attack caused gridlock at FedEx. Such incidents with wide ramifications on supply chains have mobilized market players to increase cybersecurity efforts. Failure to protect data hampers the digital revolution as this represents a risk not only for the end customers but also for the suppliers.

## 2 DISRUPTIVE ICT INNOVATIONS FOR PORTS

### 2.1 Automation and innovation

The port and logistics sector is implementing **technology and digital transformation strategies** to a certain extent. Some innovations are particularly relevant and will affect almost all aspects of the transportation process. There are four categories of automation (Figure 2.27):

- **Robotics** encompasses the use of robotics in container handling equipment, such as automated mooring systems and automated ship-to-shore cranes. With automated ship-to-shore cranes, over 90% of the work duties are performed autonomously with the final movement of the spread guided by an operator from a remote control room. Most container ports that have employed a significant form of robotics-based automation within the terminal have similarly incorporated automation into process-based and decision-based elements of the terminal operations.
- **Process automation** involves the use of technology to automate processes external to cargo handling. These include gate processes in which a combination of hardware and software is used to minimize human involvement through appointment systems, vehicle and container identification detection, radiation scanning, driver identification, and routing within the terminal. It typically involves gate systems in which optical character recognition (OCR) and radio frequency identification (RFID) automate the inspection, clearance, and tracking of people and equipment moving into, out of, and within a terminal, with supervision and exceptions handled from a control room.
- **Decision-making automation** involves using technology to guide and optimize decisions related to stowage and yard planning, container positioning, and vehicle and equipment scheduling. It involves intelligent

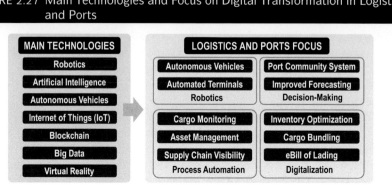

FIGURE 2.27 Main Technologies and Focus on Digital Transformation in Logistics and Ports

terminal operating systems (TOS) technology to optimize planning, monitoring asset utilization, and administrative tasks.

- **Digitalization** involves applying digital technologies to commercial operations, planning, and support functions, with a particular emphasis on data aggregation and analytics, and network optimization.

Technologies such as the Internet of Things (IoT), Big Data, and Artificial Intelligence (AI) and their predictive capabilities have all, in one way or another, allowed for smarter and more efficient supply chains. Smart warehousing, real-time tracking, and supply chain visibility, including transportation assets, have become widespread in the industry. Blockchain is adding a new layer of transparency and credence between supply chain players.

## 2.2 Automation and robotics

Automation can be implemented at the level of processes, infrastructure, and mobile assets. **Process automation** can play a key role in the transformation of logistics service providers. For example, technological advances make it increasingly possible to dynamically integrate pricing, schedules, bookings, shipment visibility with customers, carriers, and marketplaces in real-time. Rate automation and shipment visibility technology facilitate online sales. This can create new opportunities for service providers, as these decision tools enable deeper integration with carriers, which will further facilitate shipment and asset allocation optimization.

**Asset and infrastructure automation** and the use of robots are not new to the logistics industry. For example, automated stacking systems in warehouses have been in place since the early 1990s. The world's first container terminal using automated stacking cranes and automated guided vehicles (AGV) became operational in Rotterdam in 1990. Driven by cost control (such as labor and land) and efficiency, automation in warehouses and terminals has firmly progressed in recent years. The extent of automation ranges from remotely controlled operations under safe and efficient conditions to fully autonomous operations with limited oversight.

Since the 2010s, automation has started to move beyond the warehouse and terminal. When opting for automation in terminals or warehouses, market actors can fully control the working conditions for **automated vehicles or equipment**. Enclosed entities offer a controlled environment for automation less subject to random disruptions. However, outside these controlled environments, automated vehicles are subject to many influencing factors that cannot be controlled, such as the weather, traffic conditions, and topological conditions (turn priorities, one-ways). Moreover, using automated vehicles in the public domain (sea, land, and air) requires legislative and regulatory actions. A broad range of autonomous or remotely-controlled vehicles is being developed from small last-mile solutions (e.g. drones) to full-sized autonomous sea-going vessels. The development and implementation of these robots will entail its own threats and opportunities that may lead to setbacks, unintended consequences, and new market opportunities.

The development of **driverless trucks** is in full swing. Because autonomous trucks will still be required to carry drivers (to handle exceptional conditions) for the foreseeable future, advanced levels of autonomous driving are still some way away. The immediate impact on logistics and port operations will most likely consist of increased efficiency because of assisted maneuvering, improved planning, and synchronized timing, allowing for increased terminal and truck operator efficiency. In a similar vein, **drones** are already being used for security surveillance and inventory checks in warehouses and some ports (such as Abu Dhabi's Khalifa Port). They could also have a role in monitoring other logistics operations and detecting problems requiring maintenance. The main barriers to using drones are regulatory, but that may be only a short-term obstacle.

The first serious initiative for a **crewless ship** was unveiled in 2014 by Rolls Royce. The main challenges for having crewless ships are regulatory, considering international maritime conventions have clear specifications on minimum crew requirements. Another challenge is safety concerns, especially weather, obstacles, and in-trip repair requirements. This includes the uncertainty about how such autonomous or remotely operated ships would cope with unforeseen or irregular events. The main advantages include a reduction in fuel consumption, and therefore emissions. Even though safety is currently considered a concern, overcoming the challenges effectively would mean that maritime safety could be improved, as most shipping accidents result from human error, often related to fatigue. The debate focuses mainly on the **projected costs**. One concerns reduced operational costs where the absence of a crew can be seen as a liability in case of the need for repairs or problem-solving, resulting in higher operating costs. Another concern is reduced construction costs because crewless ships do not require crew facilities such as cabins and galleys.

## 2.3 The Internet of Things (IoT) and big data analytics

The IoT refers to a wide and increasingly large range of physical objects ('things') connected to a network and able to send and receive data. This effectively means all such items can be tracked and that any activity such an item is engaged in, or any circumstances it is exposed to, can be monitored and measured. The IoT is a development that is rapidly taking place across all industries and throughout society. Such a network of communicating units opens up a large array of possibilities for logistics. These sensor-driven items will allow all assets, including autonomous and robotized vehicles and equipment, port equipment, and infrastructure as well as the goods themselves to become connected. This will result in massive amounts of data being produced and made available for analysis. This offers a large array of possibilities for logistics and port operators and stakeholders to optimize and automate processes and gather an ever more precise and real-time insight into their operations.

To effectively and successfully implement applications built on the IoT, robust communications systems need to be in place. Ports, with containers and equipment interfering with signals, and warehouses with attenuated and scattered signals, are notoriously difficult environments. Even though many ports and warehouses have network infrastructure available, it is often not suited to IoT requirements of high bandwidth and secure protocols. The possibilities are vast, and the evolution of IoT and the use of big data create prospects for logistics to become a data-centric industry where information takes precedence in the value proposition of logistics services over the actual ability to move cargo.

## 2.4 Simulation and virtual reality

**Big data applications** allow logistics service providers and port operators to fully exploit the advantages of simulation software. Operations can be modeled to analyze operational flows, pinpoint possible barriers, define enhancements, and simulate and assess a variety of design and throughput scenarios. This can be done for existing or newly planned facilities and networks. An additional benefit is that such simulation software can also be used to train staff in a realistic environment and allows for the simulation of all sorts of events to be problem solved.

Virtual reality (VR), defined as the expansion of physical reality by adding layers of computer-generated information to the real environment, will further support such simulations. In a logistics environment, one can envisage enhanced feeds from infrastructure, equipment, automated vehicles, and various drones. It is to be envisaged that VR will have a wide field of applications ranging from operational support of how to execute specific processes to active safety or security interventions. VR allows filtering of complex visual environments and highlights important elements such as an individual vehicle or container.

## 3 PORT COMMUNITY SYSTEMS AND BLOCKCHAINS

Automation relies on complex information systems supporting transactions and operations related to ports and maritime shipping. This strategy is often referred to as digitalization, for which port community systems and blockchains are salient examples.

> *Port Community Systems (PCS) are an information entity that makes available logistical information to the actors involved in port-related freight distribution, including freight forwarders that act as intermediaries for importers (consignees) or exporters (consignors), terminal operators that are the interface between the port foreland and hinterland, customs, ocean carriers, inland carriers and the port authority itself.*
>
> > *Blockchains are distributed electronic ledgers shared across a network of servers that record transactions in cryptographic units that are called blocks in a permanent and verifiable manner. They are often referred to as digital ledger technologies (DLT).*

The digital transformation of terminals is integrated into emerging blockchains and other information systems that effectively link together a wide variety of port and intermodal stakeholders such as customs, freight forwarders, and carriers. The purpose of digitalization is not necessarily to create new information systems to manage freight activities but to effectively link existing databases and management systems through a portal, particularly through the conversion of different formats and the adoption of standards.

While blockchains focus on **transactions and asset tracking**, PCS focus on **stakeholder interactions**. Portals are particularly suitable as an interface as web access is close to ubiquitous and supported by portable devices such as smartphones. The outcome is an improvement in transactional efficiency along the logistical chain and, correspondingly, the efficiency of the regional freight distribution system. Thus, there are opportunities to improve performance (costs and reliability) that the users can use as marketing strategies. It is important to underline that digitalization can take different forms for each port region due to various physical, modal, jurisdictional, and operational characteristics. Conventionally, the transactional relations between these actors were very complex, with some being unilateral and proprietary.

Digitalization is a process that takes place sequentially. Depending on the current level of information technology usage, some steps may not be required, with the setting up becoming a matter of portal development and data interoperability. Therefore, freight digitalization can be developed over three major phases:

- **Development of key channels**. The first fundamental step in digitalization concerns the setting up of channels with key port users exchanging digital information they need for their operations. This included cargo manifest, customs declaration, vessel call requests, and the reporting of dangerous goods. Carriers are the main drivers in implementing blockchains because they are commonly the key support of the intermodal transport chain, which becomes a channel that can be integrated. Maersk, the world's largest shipping line, has developed a blockchain platform called TradeLens in collaboration with IBM. Its ongoing adoption as an industry standard allows actors along transport chains to track and trade shipments, handle documentation such as bills of lading, and eventually settle transactions through letters of credit.
- **Regional digital freight platforms**. Once key channels have been created, then the setting up of an operational port community system becomes possible, particularly by focusing on maritime shipping and inland freight distribution information channels within an area where a port authority acts as a key driver. Additional actors are brought in, notably freight forwarders and inland transport firms, which creates a freight market. The purpose is to build a continuous information chain within the port region that includes the majority of the steps from the ship access to the port facility to the delivery of a container at an inland freight distribution center. Among the world's major ports, different port community systems have been designed.
- **Global digital freight systems**. Once digitalization has been established and has effectively been adopted by ports and cargo users, the next step tries to establish additional multiplying effects and quality improvements. This implies the further promotion of automation, such as RFID usage, to favor the seamless movement of cargo and a complete digitalization of documents so that all transactions take place in a paperless environment. This also implies the diffusion of best practices with other ports (and inland ports) with their eventual integration in a wider system. This could eventually lead to a comprehensive integration of information flows along supply chains through widely available blockchains, from the factory door to the distribution center of an overseas consignee.

One of the key challenges in digitalization concerns creating a consensus among port users that are traditionally disconnected and often in competition for a market share. Since many ports already have various IT strategies, digitalization does not mean using the same template, as substantial efforts need to be made to adapt to the cultural and operational reality of the locale. The development of web-based applications and wireless networks has made digitalization such as PCS an operational reality. The issue is to assess the extent to which digital transformations generate added value to the port community through improvements in supply chain productivity, efficiency, and reliability. As an asset-based industry, ports remain cautious about adopting technologies, including digital means. On the positive side, once a technology has shown clear outcomes, the potential for its adoption, diffusion, and scalability is high (Boxes 2.12 and 2.13).

## Box 2.12  Port community system

*As a digital freight platform, a port community system can be an ad hoc entity built upon available opportunities and existing stakeholder relationships within a port community (Figure 2.28).*

### FIGURE 2.28 Port Community System

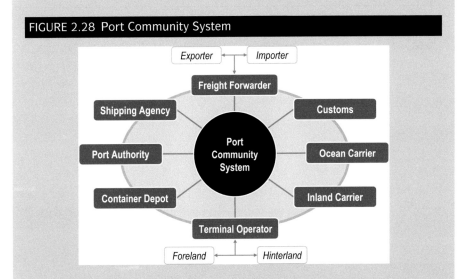

*Vessel call management.* A carrier can issue a berth and anchorage request and receive authorization from the terminal operator. The firms involved in port services, such as pilotage, towage, and mooring, can also receive a service request. Simultaneously, related public authorities are notified, such as the port authority, customs, and the port police.

*Container handling management.* Carriers (such as shipping companies or trucking firms) can interact with respective terminal operators through a standard interface, removing the issue of dealing with different terminal information systems. The cargo manifest is simultaneously provided to the carrier and the terminal operator as well as to regulatory agencies such as customs and the port authority. This enables an automatic cross-referencing with customs, clearing the cargo for import or export much faster.

*Gate management.* This involves electronic management of inbound and outbound movements at the terminal gate, which predominantly concerns freight forwarders, shipping lines, trucking firms, and terminal operators. It is possible to cover all the inland logistical operations, such as transport contracts, release orders, and admittance orders, with a single electronic document. If the e-document is provided in advance, often by 24 hours, then all the processes can be pre-cleared, leaving only the physical movement of pick up or delivery to take place. This improves the throughput of existing gates, often more than doubling their capacity, without new infrastructures except for automatic gate processing equipment.

*Security and control.* This covers strategies to automate the authorized and secure usage of the facilities, including access to cargo. A particular approach leans on the optical character recognition of license plates and container identification numbers. Real-time observation can be cross-checked with bills of lading with discrepancies, which are subject to manual verification. This can also include other scanning devices such as radiation detection or RFID. Again, this results in better usage of existing assets and, at the same time, it improves security procedures.

*Tracking.* All of the above enable, through IT integration, the tracking of container loads throughout the port community, from the moment they have been unloaded from a containership, while they are clearing the terminal gate, or when they have been delivered. This permits a better level of supply chain management and asset utilization within the port community.

## Box 2.13 Blockchains and intermodal transportation

*A simple intermodal chain can involve an exporter, an importer, and the different carriers and terminals acting as intermediaries. Assuming one full dry container load (reefers or hazardous materials trade would generate more transactions and information), for an intermodal transportation chain to occur, a series of operations and related information flows are required. Although blockchain technology has little to do with operations, it substantially changes how the related information flows are stored and shared among the involved parties.*

*For instance, the preparation of an order may require tasks such as packaging and stuffing the consignment into a container. This order generates information flows such as a certificate of origin, a commercial invoice, a packing list, and an insurance certificate as well as the booking of a carrier (or a third-party logistics provider) to move the container consignment to a specified destination. This information can be stored in a blockchain and made available to the carriers and other concerned actors along the intermodal transport chain to use for their own purpose. One particular use is the construction of **blockchain bills of lading** (Figure 2.29).*

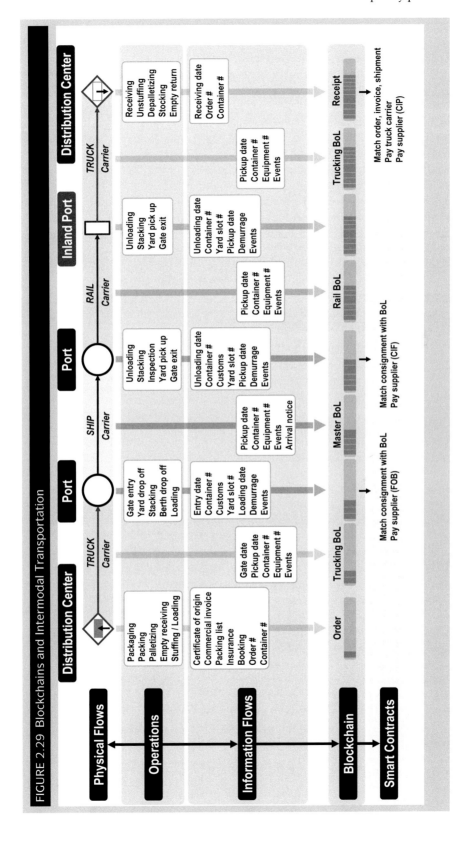

FIGURE 2.29 Blockchains and Intermodal Transportation

*The truck carrier uses the blockchain information to issue its bill of lading, which is appended to the blockchain and comes into force once the container has been picked up. This blockchain is populated with additional blocks as the carrier performs its transportation service, such as the equipment used (truck and chassis), the date the container was picked up, and the container identification number, as well as any notable events during transportation. An event can be passing at a specific location (e.g. a toll), the duration of a stop (for rest), or a change of driver and/or truck. Through the use of sensors, it is possible to automatically input event information in the blockchain, such as location at a given time.*

*At the container port terminal, various operations will continue to populate the blockchain. The time the container crossed the terminal gate (transfer of liability) and its yard storage location, as well as the customs export clearance, are among the most important. A series of events can also be input into the blockchain, such as the equipment used to handle the container or if it was re-stacked (for yard management purposes). Once the container has been brought quayside and loaded into a containership, a smart contract can automatically be executed if the Incoterms involved Free On Board (FOB), which would pay the supplier since the terms of the contract have been met (under this contract, the supplier would also pay the truck carrier and the terminal operator). There is also the possibility of using cryptocurrencies to settle blockchain smart contracts and act as booking deposits in case of no-shows from the shipper or over-booking from the carrier.*

*The shipping line issues a master bill of lading, which is its obligation to carry containers from the stated port of origin to the destination port. A series of events can also be recorded, such as daily location or the use of a transshipment hub involving terminal operations and a change of ship (and even of shipping line). A few days before arrival, the shipping line can issue an arrival notice (with ETA) on the blockchain to the consignee to arrange land transportation.*

*At the port of destination, similar intermodal operations are performed and appended to the blockchain. If the Incoterms are Cost Insurance Freight (CIF), then a smart contract can automatically pay the supplier (including the shipping line, the terminal operator, and the truck carrier). Once the container receives customs clearance (compliance met and duties paid and appended on the blockchain), it is ready to be picked up by the land carrier. In this case, we assume a rail link performed from an on-dock rail facility with its own bill of lading to be appended to the blockchain. The sequence is then repeated for the last mile truck haulage with all the appended information to the blockchain.*

*At the destination, the final operations are performed on the container, such as destuffing and stocking the items in the distribution center. Upon inspection, if the shipment matches the order, then the commercial invoice can be cleared, the blockchain updated and the supplier paid if the Incoterms were Carriage and Insurance Paid (CIP). This marks the end of this blockchain, which now contains the complete transport, intermodal, and transactional sequence of this intermodal chain.*

## 4 DIGITALIZATION IN CRUISE PORTS

Digitalization is a process that is transforming cruise ports as well. While digitalization in the maritime freight sector focuses on operations and integration between stakeholders, digitalization in the cruise industry focuses on improving customer satisfaction. The evolution of the check-in processes is an illustrative example. Guests complete their online check-in at home, which is verified by the cruise line. Passengers can then print their tickets or save them to their smartphones. The identification and ticket authentication occur at the port through check-in agents with scanning devices or self-service check-in kiosks. Cruisers receive their room key and RFID wristbands and proceed to the cruise ship. The industry is considering online visa processing, but differing national regulations impede its development.

Digitalization has multiple impacts on cruise terminal operations. Ports and cruise terminal operators, or any other responsible stakeholders, might redesign the terminal as the process provides them with more flexibility due to a reduced number of check-in desks. A further redesign relates to security arrangements, with potentially more X-ray machines and security lanes required to avoid guest congestion. The technology used at the cruise terminal is also upgraded with the need to use high-speed broadband wi-fi to support a large number of mobile devices.

A further implication is less in-port shopping due to less pre-cruise shopping due to expedited ship access. Combining this with the increased amenities and shopping facilities that cruise ships offer onboard, the presence of shipping malls as a cruise port selection criteria declines. **Ground handlers** that provide services at the cruise terminal are assigned with reduced documentation checks, and pier staff with a greater focus on customer service, guest flow planning, and transfer through manual check-in, which is required for guests who have forgotten documentation. As a mitigation strategy for digital services, a backup plan is required if the system goes down. For example, deployable check-in desks and staff on standby are essential for dealing with any unexpected event.

**Cruise lines** benefits from efficient port operations, safeguarding real-time digital updates for the boarding process, and increase comfort for guests during check-in with less paperwork and reduced shoreside staffing. The **cruise passenger** benefits from a seamless and simpler process, involving fewer documents, fewer queues, or even no queues, and a quicker journey to the cruise ship.

Digitalization leads to a number of additional innovations, such as the presence of holograms throughout the port directing guests to the terminal and the ship. Cruise line apps provide guests with information such as boarding procedures, onboard entertainment, luggage tracking, tour transfers, and last-minute shore excursion offers. Ground Handling Operation support Systems are also upgraded due to digitalization. For instance, smart staffing systems facilitate scheduling, training needs, invoicing, and related operations. Another example is operation report applications, which provide reports generated after an operation which are then shared with all stakeholders with the aim of further improving future services to cruise passengers and shipping.

# Chapter 2.5 Green supply chain management in ports

*Green supply chain management integrates environmental concerns into its organizational and operational practices, with ports as key nodes in environmental strategies.*

## 1 THE GREENING OF SUPPLY CHAINS

Green supply chain management (GSCM) has gained increased attention within the maritime industry as there is a growing need for integrating sound environmental choices into supply chain management (SCM) practices. The growing importance of GSCM goes hand in hand with **environmental concerns** such as the scarcity of some resources, the footprint of human activities on ecosystems, waste disposal, and the emission of pollutants, including carbon emissions. Adding green components to supply chain management involves addressing the influence and relationships of supply chain management with the natural environment.

During the 1960s and 1970s, both economists and environmentalists started to underline the role of industrial activities, their outputs, and implications on the environment. In the 1980s, **industrial ecology** and **life cycle assessment** concepts were conceived to better assess and quantify environmental impacts. The pursuit of **environmental standards** in product development, process design, operations, logistics, regulatory compliance, and waste management was spread over a large number of organizational units within corporations. This led to a multitude of uncoordinated mitigation attempts, which started to change with the SCM revolution of the 1990s as environmental management became more integrated with operations.

Environmental practices for gaining competitive advantage and economic benefits became a formal field of investigation with the formalization of strategies. Investments in greening can be resource-saving, waste eliminating, and productivity improving. Thus, the greening of supply chains does not have to be just a cost center but could constitute a potential source of competitive advantage. These ideas further developed in the early 2000s with a shift from environmentally friendly approaches to integrating green initiatives to achieve good business sense and higher profits. The industry started to show a growing awareness that GSCM could constitute a **business value driver**, not just a cost center.

The main idea behind GSCM is to strive for a reduction in environmental impacts by focusing on a series of strategies throughout the supply chain (Figure 2.30). They include **Reduce, Reuse, Recycle, Remanufacture**, also known as the 4Rs that comprise reverse logistics. GSCM is often linked to **life-cycle assessment** (LCA), a process for assessing and evaluating the environmental, occupational health, and resource-related consequences of a product or service through all the phases of its life cycle. This includes extracting and processing raw materials, production, transportation and distribution, use, remanufacturing, recycling, and final disposal. The scope of LCA involves tracking all the

FIGURE 2.30 Functional Model of an Organizational Green Supply Chain

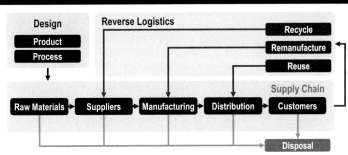

Source: Adapted from Sarkis (2003).

material and energy flows of a product from the extraction of its raw materials to its disposal. The fields of action in GSCM include product design, process design and engineering, procurement and purchasing, production, energy use and mix, and logistics (including distribution and transportation).

## 2 GREEN DESIGN, PROCUREMENT AND MANUFACTURING

### 2.1 Eco-design and green process engineering

Part of the environmental impact of a resource, goods, or even a service is determined in its **design phase** when materials and processes are selected. For example, effective reverse logistics practices largely depend on an eco-design focused on design for disassembly, design for recycling, and design for other reverse logistics practices.

Eco-design, also called **design for environment** (DfE) or **environmentally conscious design** (ECD), helps improve environmental performance by addressing product functionality while simultaneously minimizing life-cycle environmental impacts of the supply chains. One of the key aspects of eco-design is **facilitating reuse, recycling, and recovery** through designs such as easy disassembly of used products. Eco-design also involves other fields for action, such as the design of products for reduced consumption of material or energy, or the design of products to avoid or reduce the use of hazardous goods and their manufacturing process. For example, a company might decide to replace a potentially hazardous material or process with one that appears less harmful, thereby taking into account potential impacts on the depletion of a scarce resource or increased extraction of other environmentally harmful materials.

The roles of eco-design and environmental processes change with the stage in the **product life cycle**. When a new product is introduced, the eco-design of the product is a crucial aspect. In the more mature and declining stages of the product life cycle, more focus will be on improving processes and having an efficient reverse logistics system in place. Eco-design is an important GSCM practice aimed at combining product or service functionality to minimize environmental impacts. Successful eco-design typically requires internal cooperation within the company and external cooperation with other partners throughout the supply chain.

## 2.2 Green procurement and purchasing

Organizations have established global networks of suppliers that take advantage of country-specific characteristics. Key factors for green purchasing include providing design specifications to suppliers that include environmental requirements for purchased items, cooperation with suppliers for their environmental objectives, environmental audits, and internal management and ISO 14001 certification. Companies can encourage or even require their suppliers to develop environmental management systems in compliance with ISO 14001, or their suppliers to be certified with ISO 14001. **Procurement or purchasing decisions** will impact the green supply chain through purchase of materials that are either recyclable or reusable or have already been recycled.

Many large customers, such as multinational enterprises, have exerted pressure on their suppliers for better environmental performance, which results in greater incentives for suppliers to cooperate with customers for environmental objectives. Also, the pressure of the final customer is a primary driver for enterprises to improve their environmental image and practices.

**Green procurement strategies** are typically supported by national or supranational regulations. For example, the European Community Directives on Waste Electrical and Electronic Equipment (WEEE) and Registration, Evaluation and Authorization of Chemicals (REACH) have led many European and non-European suppliers to increase organizational efforts for product recovery. Environmental compliance is increasingly becoming a criterion for accessing a specific market.

## 2.3 Green production and remanufacturing

Green production complements eco-design, green purchasing, and green logistics. Cooperation with suppliers and customers is indispensable for moving towards cleaner and greener production processes. Green production has often been associated with the concept of **industrial ecology**, which views the industrial world as a system that is part of local ecosystems and the global biosphere. In practice, green production mainly focuses on:

- Techniques for **minimum energy and resource consumption** in order to reduce the use of new materials.
- A shift towards a more **sustainable energy input** with fewer environmental and carbon emissions.
- Techniques of **product recovery**, often considered within a circular economy.
- **Waste management** to minimize the environmental footprint of waste disposal.

Product recovery refers to the broad set of activities designed to **reclaim value** from a product at the end of its life cycle in order to reuse products and materials. This can be achieved through recycling, remanufacturing, repair, or refurbishment. Recycling is performed to retrieve the material content of used and non-functioning products and is often driven by regulatory and economic factors. Remanufacturing is recycling-integrated manufacturing that implies a thorough rethinking of traditional production planning and scheduling methods. Industries that apply remanufacturing typically include automobiles, electronics, and tires. The purpose of repair is to return used products to working order. The purpose of refurbishing is to bring used products up to a specified quality standard allowing their sale on second-hand markets. Remanufacturing and the associated recycling activities typically involve disassembly to separate a product into its constituent parts, components, subassemblies, or other groupings.

Cleaner production requires effective **waste management** for products and materials that cannot be reused. The supply chains of non-reusable waste involve waste collection, transportation, incineration, composting, and disposal. The general idea of cleaner production is to prevent pollution at source. Thus, cleaner production initiatives are also focused on preventing waste creation rather than its post-generation management.

## 3 ENERGY AND TRANSPORTATION EFFICIENCY

### 3.1 Energy efficiency in supply chain management

Supply chains require energy to fuel production and logistics processes. The world's energy needs continue to grow, with a 30% rise in global energy demand expected by 2040. Still, higher energy efficiency and the growing use of cleaner energy sources worldwide should help to curb energy-related carbon emissions. The majority of the required energy has conventionally been derived from fossil fuels. However, a shift is taking place with a growing share of renewable energy sources. Changing towards a greener energy mix is a key field of action in GSCM. Efficiency gains from more stringent energy performance standards play an important role in the evolution of energy demand.

The share of electricity in global final energy consumption is approaching 20% and is set to rise further. Electricity is increasingly used in economies focused on lighter industrial sectors, services, and digital technologies. In advanced economies, electricity demand growth is modest, but the investment requirement is massive as electrical generation and distribution infrastructures are upgraded. A common issue with electrification, which has a much lower environmental footprint, is how electricity is generated. The usage of fossil fuels to generate electricity upstream in energy supply chains undermines its environmental benefits downstream.

**Renewable energy** is expected to see the fastest growth, with natural gas expected to have the strongest growth among fossil fuels, with consumption rising by 50% by 2040. Coal use has seen strong growth in recent years, but consumption levels are expected to stabilize and decline, as is already the case in Europe and North America. Growth in oil demand is expected to peak by 2030, and a shift in the balance of energy consumption is taking place between developing and advanced economies. By the mid-2030s developing economies in Asia are expected to consume more oil than Europe and the United States.

International agreements concerning the environmental footprint of climate change have been implemented with mitigated outcomes. For instance, the objectives of the Paris Agreement on climate change, which entered into force in November 2016, are related to transformative changes that take place in the energy sector. Countries are generally on track to achieve, and even exceed in some instances, many of the targets set in their Paris Agreement. While these efforts may be sufficient to slow the projected rise in global energy-related $CO_2$ emissions, they may be insufficient to limit warming below an additional 2°C. Therefore, five-year review mechanisms, built into the Paris Agreement, underline the importance of reviewing pledged commitments. This should include actions such as:

- The acceleration of the deployment of **renewables, nuclear power, and carbon capture and storage**.
- Greater **electrification** and efficiency across all end-uses.
- **Clean energy research** and development effort by governments and companies.

By 2040, about 60% of all new power generation capacity is expected to be derived from **renewables**, with the majority of renewables-based generation being competitive without relying on subsidies. Therefore, it is expected that by the 2030s, global subsidies to renewables will start declining. However, there is a risk that cost reductions for renewables could be insufficient to decarbonize electric power generation systems. Structural changes to the design and operation of the energy grid are needed to ensure adequate incentives for investment and to allow for a higher contribution of wind and solar power.

The rise of **solar power** and **wind power** gives unprecedented importance to the flexible operation of power systems in order to secure enough energy at all times. The cost of battery storage is declining fast, and batteries increasingly compete with gas-fired peaking plants to manage short-run fluctuations in supply and demand. However, conventional power plants remain the primary source of system flexibility, supported by new interconnections, storage, and demand-side response. The European Union aims to create an 'Energy Union' to deal with imbalances in demand and supply between different member states, replicating the existing electric grid exchange systems in North America.

Despite expectations on renewables, fossil fuels such as natural gas and oil will continue to form the backbone of the global energy system for many decades to come. By 2040 oil demand is expected to drop to levels similar to the 1990s, while coal use will move to levels last seen in the mid-1980s. Only gas will see an increase relative to the current consumption level. Based on an increase in oil prices in the long-term, the trend for exploring fossil energy sources will continue to offshore locations, including deeper waters and harsher environments. More complex energy sources such as tar sands or methane hydrates are also being exploited. Energy production on offshore wind farms will significantly increase, and other water-based energy production devices using wave and tidal current energy will also have a broader market. These developments will lead to a massive increase in renewable energy, particularly in Europe. They will also result in a significant increase in the production and transport of cleaner fuels such as LNG, shale gas, and hydrogen.

## 3.2 Green logistics, distribution and transportation

The implementation of GSCM has a large impact on how goods move across supply chains. GSCM implies a green logistics approach to reconcile environmental concerns with transportation, warehousing, and distribution activities. Green logistics ties environmental and economic efficiency into logistics by reducing the impact of the sector on the environment. Logistics service providers are challenged to be eco-conscious, comply with existing environmental regulations, and prepare for upcoming regulations while performing their activities at the lowest possible cost.

Logistics service providers have to focus on supply networks in which clean forms of transport meet shippers' expectations regarding cost and efficiency. Goods are increasingly transported in an economical, environmentally aware, and sustainable manner. To this extent, shippers expect coordination from service providers in which operational excellence is supported by obtaining a greater convergence between physical and data processes. The main fields of actions in green logistics are related to:

- **Eco-friendly packaging**. Packaging characteristics such as size, shape, and materials impact distribution due to their effect on the transport characteristics of the goods. Better packaging, along with rearranged loading patterns, can reduce materials usage, increase space utilization in the warehouse and the transport modes, and reduce the amount of handling required. For instance, having strong and sturdy pallets ensures their long-term use. Systems that encourage and adopt returnable packaging require a strong customer-supplier relationship and an effective reverse logistics channel. Efficiencies in packaging directly affect the environment. In many countries, take-back legislation on the packaging has made packaging operation and planning a critical environmental logistics consideration.
- **Eco-friendly transport mode choice and synchromodality**. Environmental pressure from the customer base, society, and legislation forces companies to use greener alternatives for logistics. Advancing GSCM requires a massive re-engineering of supply chains in favor of a modal shift to environmentally-friendly transport modes and synchromodality. Modal shift and co-modality policies have been implemented to encourage the use of barges, rail, and shortsea shipping. Modal shift and co-modality have been expanded to include the notion of synchromodality, which is defined as 'the optimally flexible and sustainable deployment of different modes of transport in a network under the direction of a logistics service provider so that the customer (shipper or forwarder) is offered an integrated solution for his (inland) transport'. Implementing a synchromodal solution requires the involvement of several actors. Shipping lines, terminal operators, inland terminals, inland transport operators, 3PL companies, shippers, and public authorities all play a role in developing synchromodal solutions. A synchromodal approach assumes that the shipper books without specifying the mode, thereby leaving modal decisions to logistics service providers. This renders the whole transport system more flexible in terms of modal choice. Synchromodal transport is particularly effective for corridors and regions where sufficient volumes are present, allowing for economies of scale supported by modes such as rail and barge.
- **Load and route optimization**. One example of load optimization can be to send a truck only as a full truckload (FTL). Route optimization is about reducing transport costs, time or distance. By choosing the best route, it is possible to save fuel and reduce emissions. Synchromodality allows

for the consolidation of cargo consignments and finds the optimal route, thus achieving additional efficiency benefits.

• **Green distribution networks and distribution hubs**. GSCM encourages logistics service providers to include green considerations in the design and implementation of distribution networks and the location choice and operational modalities of their distribution hubs and warehousing facilities. The type of product mainly influences these choices and the frequency of delivery, but green considerations are increasingly considered when making such decisions. For example, distribution network configurations might involve internalizing the environmental costs of transport and distribution, for example through environmental taxes such as a $CO_2$ tax. The future configuration of distribution systems has an impact on cargo routing patterns.

## 4 DRIVERS OF GSCM AND CORPORATE STRATEGY

### 4.1 Green supply chains and environmental management systems

An **Environmental Management System** (EMS) consists of a collection of internal policies, assessments, plans, and implementation actions affecting the entire organization and its relationships with the environment. In practice, an EMS is a strategic management approach that defines how an organization will address its environmental impacts. An EMS typically includes establishing an environmental policy or plan and performing internal assessments of the organization's environmental impacts. This includes the quantification of environmental impacts, how they change over time, and how to create mitigation strategies, provide resources, train workers, monitor implementation progress, and undertake corrective actions if goals are not met. An EMS can be regarded as a valuable element in improving environmental and business performance. Once an organization implements an EMS, it may elect for its certification to the ISO 14001 standard. Organizations that develop an EMS typically show higher regulatory compliance, enhancing their corporate image and increasing profits.

There are different views on the relations between EMS and GSCM. One of the limitations of an EMS is that it mainly focuses on enhancing the environmental performance of an organization and not on extending this strategy throughout the supply chain. A corporation with an EMS may have little incentive to green its supply chains since it can market itself as being environmentally focused without undertaking additional efforts. However, by developing an EMS, a company develops skills and insights, helping develop more comprehensive GSCM initiatives. Therefore, organizations that adopt an EMS may have a stronger focus on implementing GSCM practices as well.

### 4.2 GSCM and corporate profitability

There is a growing need to integrate sustainability principles into supply chain management. There are pressures to consider environmental issues when pursuing portability within supply chains, which is a demand-pull. Simultaneously, government regulations increasingly **force companies to become more**

**environmentally friendly**, which is a regulatory push. Thus, organizations might initiate several environmental practices due to drivers such as sales to customers, and legislative and stakeholder institutional pressures. Even though GSCM has significant environmental motivations, regulatory, competitive, and economic pressures also play roles in its adoption across industries.

When focusing on the corporate context, there are clear signs that not opting for green supply chains can negatively affect cost base and profitability. A focus on GSCM may help secure revenue growth, achieve cost reductions, develop brand value, and mitigate risks, resulting in increasing revenue by a factor of 20% and reducing carbon emissions by 20%. Furthermore, a focus on the environment has a positive impact on brand value. However, corporations cannot roll out green initiatives as part of GSCM without due consideration.

Logistics and supply chain managers have to **balance efforts** to reduce costs, improve service quality, increase flexibility, and innovate while maintaining environmental performance. When deciding on green initiatives, corporations consider strategic performance requirements, which may not be environmentally based, such as cost, return on investment (ROI), service quality, and flexibility. Green initiatives should not only support green supply chains but also make business sense. Otherwise, the competitive and financial position of the organization may be negatively affected.

**Investment recovery** is often cited as a critical aspect of GSCM, typically at the back end of the supply chain cycle. Financial incentives or penalties are available from public authorities, such as subsidies and tax breaks for green investments or penalties for non-compliance, or by private service providers, such as a commercial bank providing favorable loan conditions for green investments, which are often very important in investment or divestment decisions and to achieve investment recovery.

## 4.3 Incentives for GSCM

**Financial incentives and penalties** are just one way for governments and public entities to support the greening of supply chains. Whatever governments and public entities do in terms of environmental policy development, the business world is very sensitive to coherence and continuity in existing policies, the legal coherence of implemented policies, and the enforcement of policies through inspection and control. As many investment decisions have a medium to long-term amortization, any changes in government policy, such as abolishing subsidy schemes for certain green investments, can have large ramifications on the soundness of the initial corporate decision related to a green initiative. Thus, government policies and regulations typically significantly impact green strategies, investments, and GSCM initiatives pursued by corporations, but should provide legal and investment stability to the affected companies.

There is a growing awareness that GSCM can be an important business value driver and a source of competitive advantage. However, this does not imply that all organizations follow the same approach when dealing with GSCM challenges. Corporate attitudes towards GSCM can range from **reactive monitoring** of the general environment management programs to more proactive practices implemented through the various Rs (Reduce, Reuse, Recycle, Remanufacture, Reverse logistics).

**Internal environmental management** is central to improving corporate environmental performance. A supporting managerial structure is necessary and, often, a key driver for successfully adopting and implementing most innovations, technology, programs, and activities in GSCM. Successful GSCM initiatives often involve several departments (at times several corporations), and such cooperation and communication is essential to successful environmental practices. Sharing responsibility inter-organizationally for various aspects of environmental performance is the key to successful GSCM.

It is not solely individual companies that can opt for cooperation on a bilateral or multilateral basis. Industry and branch organizations often play an essential role in coordinating several organizations to take **joint initiatives** in GSCM. In other cases, private companies, sometimes with different backgrounds, and organizations such as public entities form coalitions to advance the design and implementation of GSCM solutions.

## 5. GSCM AND PORTS

Seaports are **active environments** for multiplying the scale and scope of initiatives to improve green supply chain management. Five fields of action can be distinguished to pursue GSCM objectives; **green shipping**, **green port development and operations**, **green inland logistics**, **circular economy**, and **knowledge exchange and development**. A broad array of market players and public entities have a role to play in each of these fields (Figure 2.31).

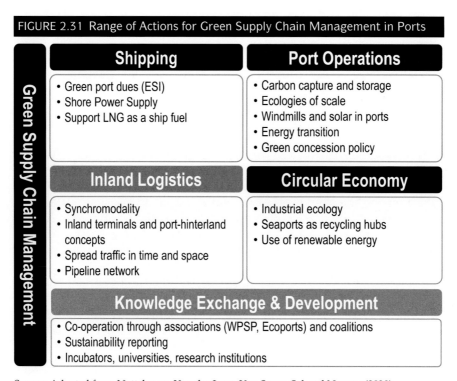

FIGURE 2.31 Range of Actions for Green Supply Chain Management in Ports

**Green Supply Chain Management**

**Shipping**
- Green port dues (ESI)
- Shore Power Supply
- Support LNG as a ship fuel

**Port Operations**
- Carbon capture and storage
- Ecologies of scale
- Windmills and solar in ports
- Energy transition
- Green concession policy

**Inland Logistics**
- Synchromodality
- Inland terminals and port-hinterland concepts
- Spread traffic in time and space
- Pipeline network

**Circular Economy**
- Industrial ecology
- Seaports as recycling hubs
- Use of renewable energy

**Knowledge Exchange & Development**
- Co-operation through associations (WPSP, Ecoports) and coalitions
- Sustainability reporting
- Incubators, universities, research institutions

Source: Adapted from Notteboom, Van der Lugt, Van Saase, Sel and Neyens (2020).

### 5.1 Green shipping

Ships are major contributors to emissions in ports, even when they are idling or berthed. Next to shipowners, ship operators, and supranational organizations such as the International Maritime Organization (IMO), ports play a role in reducing ship emissions. The main fields of actions include:

- **Reduce ship emissions** in ports by decreasing waiting times and the turnaround time of vessels, such as by synchronizing and integrating the nautical chain through optimized vessel traffic management systems.
- Implement **green port dues** and voluntary green shipping schemes to incentivize operators to improve the environmental performance of their ships. The Environmental Ship Index (ESI) initiated by the International Association of Ports and Harbours (IAPH) is a certification scheme that ranks a ship's environmental performance, which is correlated with port dues. Shipping companies can register their ships for this index on a website. Based on the data entered, such as fuel consumption and emissions, each ship has a given score from 0 to 100 (from highly polluting to emission-free). The ports themselves decide what advantages to offer participating ships, but they mostly involve a rebate in port dues. While ports or other public authorities could, in principle, also decide to implement strict regulation on emission criteria for ships entering the port (i.e. dirty ships are not granted access), such access restrictions have only been implemented in a few ports around the world.
- Implement Cold Ironing, Shore Power Supply, or Alternate Marine Power (AMP) whereby seagoing vessels and barges at berth **use shore power** for auxiliary engines instead of bunker fuel (Box 2.14). At present, cold ironing is most widespread in the cruise shipping market and ferry business. There are challenges related to the investment cost (terminal and ship), the division of these costs between different stakeholders, and the break-even cost compared to bunker fuel.
- **Support the transition to LNG** as a ship fuel. In past years, investments in LNG bunkering infrastructure in ports have taken off. Several public port authorities play a proactive role in facilitating LNG as a marine fuel, often in close partnership with industrial actors.

---

### Box 2.14  Cold ironing: on-shore power supply for vessels

*Cold ironing for seagoing vessels and barges implies that a ship at berth uses shore power for the auxiliary engines instead of bunker fuel. This reduces emissions from the ships by a substantial margin, although the reduction in pollution occurs only when the ship is stationary at berth. Power cables are plugged into an electricity supply board at the terminal on one end and to the ship's power supply board on the other. The power is used for lights, refrigerators, air-conditioners, and other equipment on a ship. The power coming from the shore can be from a separate power generation unit or the power plant supplying power to the port city or town.*

*At present, cold ironing is most widespread in the cruise shipping market and ferry business as the pressure on cruise and ferry terminals to reduce emissions is high, particularly when they are located close to (historical) city centers.*

*Due to strict local and state environmental regulations for idling ships, early adopters of cold ironing practices are found along the west coast of North America (i.e. Vancouver, Seattle, Los Angeles, San Diego, San Francisco, and Oakland). Cold ironing for commercial vessels was launched in Los Angeles in 2004 when China Shipping's container ships were plugged into a dedicated port barge floating close to the berth.*

*In Northern Europe, Scandinavian countries, Germany, Belgium, and the Netherlands have already developed cold ironing solutions. Since 2010, vessels berthing for more than two hours have switched to a 0.1% sulfur fuel or use alternative technologies, such as shore-side electricity. The EU approved Directive 2014/94/EU on the deployment of alternative fuel infrastructure in 2014. This directive obliges member states to implement alternative infrastructure networks such as shoreside power technology by December 2025. The EU's TEN-T program has indicated that shore power is an area where funding is available to help with up to 50% of the costs of research and 20% of its implementation costs.*

*Cold ironing technologies are also being implemented in several Asian ports. China has included cold ironing in its twelfth five-year plan and links it to the existing domestic emission control areas.*

*Despite its potential contribution to promoting green shipping, the cold ironing solution faces some major challenges.*

*There are challenges related to the investment cost (terminal and ship), the division of these costs between different stakeholders (shipping line, terminal operator, and port authority), and the break-even cost compared to bunker fuel.*

*There are still some issues with the standardization of on-shore power systems in terms of on-board and terminal equipment and voltages.*

*Shipping lines are not always eager to invest in the retrofitting of ships as long as cold ironing possibilities are limited to only a few ports of call (a 'chicken and egg' problem). Certain ships are not even compatible and suitable for the process of on-shore power. Most new-build ships are pre-equipped.*

*The large-scale application of cold ironing in a port might require extensive capacity upgrading of the local or regional power grid. For example, a large container ship typically requires approximately 1,600 kilowatts (kW) of power. In contrast, at berth, the power requirements can differ substantially (cruise ships need a lot more power), depending on the size of the vessel and the number of refrigerated containers on board.*

*Environmental advantages of cold ironing depend on how clean the shore-based electricity production process is. If shifting the power production from ship to shore increases the load on fossil-fuel power plants and increases the air emissions, then the overall impact on emissions might be marginal.*

## 5.2 Green port development and operations

Green port development is about actions that make the port and its environment greener and more sustainable. Multiple instruments and concepts of green port development and operations exist, including:

- Develop a **green concession and lease policy** by implementing green elements in terminal concession, lease procedures, and contracts. This involves the setting of standards such as for emissions and waste management.
- Maximize the **ecologies of scale and industrial symbiosis** in industrial clusters or ecosystems. Environmental zoning and co-location can help to achieve these effects.
- Develop **green zones and buffers** in the port area, with nature forming a shield between heavy port industry and residential areas. This can also involve the restoration of marine ecosystems.
- Develop **wind and solar parks and wave energy**, combined with port energy management.
- Implement **Carbon Capture and Storage** (CCS) and fume return systems. Carbon can also be used as a base for other products, such as Carbon Capture and Utilization (CCU).
- Support the **production of biofuels** and bio-based chemicals.
- Facilitate the use of **low-emission or zero-emission quay and yard equipment** on terminals, particularly through electrification.
- Reduce **idling of ships and inland transport modes** and waiting times at terminals through information sharing via data platforms.
- Develop **green warehousing and distribution activities** in ports through optimal location choice, optimal distribution system design, sustainable warehouse design (LED lighting and smart cooling and heating systems), energy, and material recycling.

## 5.3 Green inland logistics, modal shift and inland terminals

Inland logistics comprises the transportation of goods from the hinterland to the port or from the port to the hinterland via barge, rail, truck, or pipeline. Port authorities can play a role in the following GSCM areas:

- Stimulate a modal shift and implement multimodal transport solutions through pricing (taxes and incentives), regulation on emission standards, information provision to users, a liberalization of freight markets, and infrastructure investments to make specific transport modes more attractive.
- Optimize the use of each modality by reducing empty kilometers, the improvement of vehicle utilization rates, and scale increases in transport modes (vessel scale, train length, and tonnage, truck platooning).
- Implement smart planning by bundling cargo within a company or between companies.
- Support the transition to a **greener energy input** for transport by imposing minimum emissions standards on vehicles entering the port area (e.g. the Clean Truck Program, part of the San Pedro Bay Ports Clean Air Action Plan) and giving incentives for the use of non-fossil fuels.

- Promote the role of inland terminals and dry ports and port-hinterland concepts in GSCM, for example, by incorporating inland terminals as extended gates to seaport terminals.
- Develop advanced and integrated traffic management systems for rail, barge, and truck.
- Implement pricing mechanisms and other instruments to make fleets greener or to spread traffic in time and space. These include appointment systems, peak pricing, or extended (night) opening hours of terminals.
- Develop pipeline networks (intra-port, inter-port, and port-hinterland) to transport liquids over short and long distances.

## 5.4 Seaports and the circular economy

There are three circular scales in which ports and maritime shipping are embedded (Box 2.15). At the largest scale, the circular economy is all about restructuring industrial systems to support ecosystems by adopting methods to maximize the efficient use of resources by recycling and minimizing emissions and waste. In a port context, the main fields of action at that scale are:

- Promote **industrial ecology** to optimize waste management through interactions between stakeholders within the same geographical area, such as exchanging materials, water, and by-products.
- Develop seaports as **hubs for recycling flows** where flows are delivered, transformed into new products, and re-exported worldwide.
- Use **renewable energy sources** through hydro and offshore power installations.

The second scale concerns the circular processes directly related to **shipping and port operations** and their supply chains. The third is related to the specialized container market with circular processes involving the repair, repositioning, and recycling of discarded containers. By design, containers are circular goods that can be constantly reused and exchanged on transport markets.

A circular system is not necessarily sustainable as reusing or recycling costs may exceed linear procurement costs. For instance, recycling goods such as waste paper and some plastics is more expensive than sourcing from new resources. Under such circumstances, circularity becomes a political or societal choice requiring regulations and subsidies, which results in higher costs and potential disruptions related to the availability of resources.

### Box 2.15 The circular economy in ports and maritime shipping

*The port and maritime shipping industry have unique forms of circularity. Both shipping lines and terminal operators rely on their linear supply/procurement chains, with the outcomes being the setting up of shipping networks (A) and investments in port infrastructure (B). Four principles common to the circular economy can be integrated into the port and shipping sectors (Figure 2.32).*

## FIGURE 2.32 The Circular Economy in Ports and Maritime Shipping

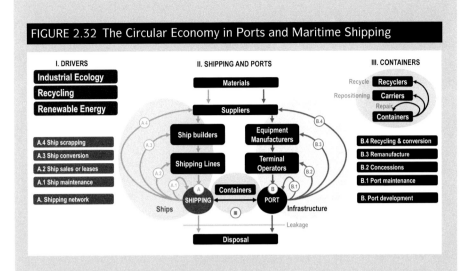

*Maintenance*. This basic form of circularity ensures that the product can be recurrently used and have its life cycle extended. To maintain acceptable operational conditions, both ships (A.1) and ports (B.1) require recurring maintenance. For capital-intensive assets, maintenance is a common aspect of extending their life cycle, in opposition to several consumer goods not designed to be repaired. Therefore, the port and shipping industry are based on substantial repair and maintenance practices where cost-effectiveness and predictability are at the forefront of their commercial viability. Maintenance is a particularly challenging issue for port terminals as operations have to continue while maintenance is taking place.

*Reuse*. There is an extensive market for ship sales or leases (A.2), allowing shipping assets to be shared and remain optimally used. For instance, several of the largest shipping lines can lease more than half of their ship assets. At the end of the lease, the ship can return to the leasing market and be 'reused'. Another circular characteristic concerns the cascading of ships from deepsea to regional feeder services when new and larger ships are introduced. Since ports are fixed assets, concessions (B.2) can be perceived as circularity mechanisms where port authorities offer terminal assets to be leased. Once the concession is over, the terminal asset can be leased by another terminal operator. Terminal equipment can also be leased to cover periods of high activity or to remove excess capacity.

*Remanufacture*. Ships can be converted to new uses and new propulsion technologies (A.3). For instance, the first containerships were converted bulk and break-bulk ships, and the first cruise ships were converted liners. Low sulfur bunker fuel requirements implemented in 2020 are encouraging many shipping lines to reconvert their ship engines with technologies such as scrubbers. In the port sector, changing the function or operational characteristics of a port terminal by upgrading the existing equipment (B.3) is a form of circularity. For instance, cranes and yard equipment can be upgraded for automation.

> *Recycle. There is an extensive industry that scraps ships and recycles their components, particularly metals (A.4). India and Bangladesh are the most significant locations where ships are scrapped. Once at the end of its life cycle, terminal equipment can be discarded and recycled (B.4). A more complex issue concerns the land footprint of a terminal that can be converted for other uses, such as residential. For instance, if the nautical profile of the terminal is no longer suitable for port operations (lack of depth), the site can be 'recycled' into urban redevelopments.*
>
> *Containers represent a specialized form of circularity as container shipping is designed as a recycling system. A container is a reusable unit constantly being repositioned by carriers who own or lease container fleets. Another segment involves container leasing companies allocating their assets to maximize returns. Thus, the container is an interchangeable transport unit, with its carrying capacity being traded on transport markets. To remain a suitable asset for carriers, containers need to be cleaned, maintained, and repaired. At the end of their useful life (about 15 years), containers can be discarded and recycled for their components or other uses (e.g. storage, office space).*

## 5.5 Knowledge development

The last possible field of action for GSCM in ports includes measures that facilitate knowledge development, information sharing, and exchange of best practices. A non-exhaustive list of some areas for initiatives include:

- Develop interactive **environmental and energy information and management systems** that enrich business processes with new knowledge about energy consumption and emissions. This can help set up benchmarks and standards.
- Cooperate in the framework of **port-related associations**, such as WPSP (World Port Sustainability Program) and Ecoports, that provide a forum to discuss strategies and best practices.
- Develop **sustainability and CSR programs** to improve the social and environmental performance of the port cluster and to improve communication and exchanges with a broad range of stakeholders.
- Implement **sustainability reporting** at the corporate, port authority, or port industry level. Larger port authorities are the main actors that have started producing sustainability reports.
- Develop the **local knowledge base on GSCM** in ports by setting up incubators and smart-labs for start-ups and scale-ups, Hackathon events, and creating a good business environment for R&D-focused firms, research centers, consultancy firms, and start-ups.

# PART III

# Port terminals

## Chapter 3.1  Terminals and terminal operators

*Ports are composed of specialized terminals designed to handle a specific cargo type. An increasing number of port terminals, serving either cargoes or passengers, are managed by operators maintaining an international portfolio.*

### 1 PORT TERMINALS

Ports are mainly **multifunctional entities**, but this characteristic is often the result of the combined activities of a number of specialized terminals, each dealing with specific goods and commodities such as containers, grain, oil, or iron ore. Thus, a port is the combination of terminal facilities, each developed to fulfill a specific function and sometimes serving a single user such as a petrochemical plant. The main types of port terminals include:

- **Break-bulk**. Concerns cargo that is carried in drums, bags, pallets, or boxes. Also referred to as general-purpose facilities that have a combination of open storage space and warehouses. Historically, most port terminals were built as multipurpose facilities as most commercial cargo was carried in a break-bulk form. It is only in the late nineteenth century that ship specialization became dominant, allowing specialized terminal facilities.
- **Dry bulk**. Relates to cargo that is not packaged and transported in large quantities that are limited by ship size or existing demand. The main commodities involve coal, iron ore, and grain, which require specialized equipment and storage facilities. This specialization level implies that the terminal cannot handle bulk products other than those it was designed and equipped to handle. Thus, a grain terminal cannot handle other commodities even if the pier can accommodate any ship class.

DOI 10.4324/9780429318184-3

- **Liquid bulk**. Commodities transported in liquid form requiring specialized transshipment equipment and storage facilities. The most common liquid bulk terminal facilities are designed to handle oil and petroleum products.
- **Containers**. Terminal facilities are designed only to handle a single break-bulk standard transport unit, the container. Container terminals have come to dominate the port terminal landscape because of the large variety of goods that can be carried in containers. They are capital intensive and require a large footprint due to the storage requirement of containers.
- **RoRo**. Handles vehicles that are rolled on and off a vehicle carrier. Require ramps, but standard vehicle carriers commonly have their own ramps. The most important footprint of a RoRo terminal is the parking space used to store vehicles. Also includes ferries that carry a combination of vehicles and passengers and, as such, require rather extensive parking space while vehicles are waiting to roll onto the ferry.
- **Passengers**. Historically, passengers were handled at multipurpose facilities as liner ships also carried freight. The emergence of the cruise industry has been associated with the setting up of cruise passenger terminals that can be extensive at turn port facilities such as Miami and Barcelona.

Although terminals may share a related port site, they often have no particular commonality in terms of the supply chain they are servicing. There is the potential that a multi-terminal port may not be an integrated entity with their presence merely being coincidental. Still, terminals share common maritime and inland infrastructure.

Outside commercial issues related to the demand for cargo, port terminals depend on a specific range of equipment, and this equipment requires a footprint and a configuration. Terminal equipment is highly commodity-specific as some terminals can only handle one commodity or a limited range of cargoes. For instance, an oil terminal can only handle crude oil bulk shipment through specialized equipment and storage facilities. This equipment would not be able to handle other forms of liquid cargo.

Three fundamental categories of port terminals, equipment, and design characteristics can be found (Figure 3.1):

- **General cargo**. Unitized cargo that can be carried in batches and handled by three specialized terminal types with specific equipment and design considerations. Since break-bulk and container terminals handle unit cargoes, they are designed around the lift-on/lift-off principle requiring cranes and storage areas. Vehicle terminals, a type of neo bulk terminal, are operated on the roll-on/roll-off principle and are dominated by parking areas.
- **Bulk cargo**. Loose cargo carried in loads that are limited only by demand, ship size, and storage capacity. The bulk terminal is where this system is synchronized. Liquid bulk and dry bulk depend on different transshipment and storage techniques and are two distinct categories of bulk terminals with design considerations. Bulk terminals tend to be specialized to handle a single commodity, such as coal, grain, iron ore, natural gas, or petroleum. Each of these commodities has unique equipment, storage, and design considerations.
- **Passengers**. Ferry and cruise terminals are a small segment of port terminals. Ferry terminals are mainly roll-on/roll-off facilities with direct connectivity to the road system. Larger facilities require significant parking areas, but infrastructures and equipment are simple with mooring

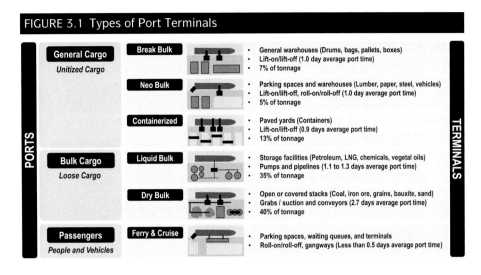

FIGURE 3.1 Types of Port Terminals

areas and ramps. Recently, the growth of the cruise industry has led to the emergence of specialized cruise terminals that include passenger handling facilities and parking areas. Cruise terminals might also be involved in freight activities with the procurement of cruise ships.

Each terminal acts as a key node in the maritime/land interface, allowing maritime and inland systems to interact. The balance between market demand, ship capacity and frequency, and hinterland distribution requires a variety of footprints and design considerations.

## 2 GLOBAL TERMINAL OPERATORS

### 2.1 Private involvement in port terminal operations

As late as the 1980s, **public ownership and operation** were the dominant models. While the forms of port governance differed greatly, from the municipally-owned ports in Northern Europe and the United States to the state-owned ports in France, Italy, and much of the developing world, public ownership was dominant, and publicly managed port operations were prevalent. The institutional entry barriers for port terminal operations were remarkably high and limited to specific services. This contrasted with the shipping industry, where private ownership was almost universal. Containerization particularly underlined how operationally deficient public port authorities adapted to growing time and performance requirements imposed on intermodal transport chains. The changes, slow at first, came from two directions:

- First, there was the belief that the transport industry as a whole should be divested to the private sector to promote competition. Ports were among the many sectors targeted by economic liberalization policies.
- Second, there was a policy recommendation from the World Bank that developing countries would do well to free their highly controlled port industry by issuing concessions to organizations able to modernize their port industries and better manage operations. To facilitate required changes, the World Bank created a Port Reform Tool Kit.

FIGURE 3.2  Forms of Port Terminal Privatization

| | |
|---|---|
| **Sale** | • Terminal is transferred on a freehold basis.<br>• Requirement that it will be used only to provide terminal services. |
| **Concession** | • Long-term lease of terminal land and facilities.<br>• Concessionaire undertakes specified capital investments to build, expand, or maintain the cargo-handling facilities, equipment, and infrastructure. |
| **Capital Lease** | • Private sector is not explicitly required to invest in the facilities and equipment.<br>• Normal maintenance and replacement over the life of the agreement. |
| **Management Contract** | • Private sector assumes the allocation of terminal labor and equipment.<br>• Provides services to the terminal users in the name of the public owner.<br>• The public sector retains control over all the assets. |
| **Service Contract** | • Efficient and transparent procedures. |
| **Equipment Lease** | • Involving leaseback arrangements or supplier credits.<br>• Amortize the costs for new equipment.<br>• Ensure a reliable supply of spare parts and, often, a guaranteed level of service/reliability from this equipment. |

These developments helped create what has become a global snowball of port government reforms, commonly known as **port devolution**, as the public sector relinquished its role in a function it had formerly assumed. It made governments more open to considering reforming port governance and offering better conditions to ensure privatization. The growing demands for public and private investment in ports, precipitated by the growth in world trade, and the limited abilities of governments to meet these needs because of competing investment priorities, were key factors. Thus, while few were willing to go as far as the UK in the total privatization of ports, many countries were willing to consider awarding concessions as an intermediate form of privatization, leading to various forms of **public–private partnerships**.

There are several forms for port terminal privatization (not to be confused with port privatization), ranging from the outright sale of a terminal facility to a service contract where a private operator performs specific operational tasks. In contrast, the port authority retains ownership of the facility and equipment (Figure 3.2).

## 2.2  Typology of port holdings

Privatization has stimulated an almost global trend towards awarding port operational concessions, especially for container terminals. The reasons why container terminals were particularly prone to concessioning were related to the fast growth of international trade requiring massive and rapid capital investments. If the opportunities to award operational concessions can be seen as an increase in demand, growth has also been greatly affected by an increase in the number of companies seeking concessions, with many becoming large port holdings.

> *Port holding*. An entity, commonly private that owns or leases port terminals in a variety of locations. It is also known as a port terminal operator.

The rise of and diversity in global terminal operators is having a structural impact on the port industry. As terminal operators move towards better integration of terminals in supply chains and shipping lines acquire container terminal assets worldwide, leading terminal operating companies are developing diverging strategies towards controlling larger parts of the supply chain.

Transnational terminal holding companies are grouped into three categories (Figure 3.3):

- **Independent stevedores**. Port terminal operators that expanded into new markets to replicate their expertise in terminal operations and to diversify their revenue geographically. PSA International with headquarters in Singapore is the largest global terminal operator coming from a stevedore background, followed by Hutchison Ports with headquarters in Hong Kong. Stevedores account for about 50% of the hectares controlled by terminal operators worldwide (Figure 3.4).
- **Maritime shipping companies**. Invested in port terminal facilities to help support their core maritime shipping business. In many cases, hybrid structures are formed with separate business units or sister companies active in liner shipping or terminal operations. The terminal facilities can be operated on a single-user dedicated base or alternatively also be open to third-party shipping lines. APM Terminals, a Maersk Line sister company, is the largest global terminal operator from a maritime shipping background. Shipping lines account for about 31% of the hectares controlled by terminal operators worldwide (Figure 3.5).
- **Financial holdings**. Include various financial interests ranging from investment banks and retirement funds to sovereign wealth funds attracted by the port terminal sector as an asset class, and with revenue generation potential. The majority have an indirect management approach, acquiring an asset stake, and leaving the existing operator to take care of the operations. Others will directly manage the terminal assets through a parent company. DP World, a branch of the Dubai World sovereign wealth fund, is the largest global terminal operator coming from a financial background. The main reason why financial holding companies became interested in having port terminal assets in

**FIGURE 3.3 Typology of Global Port Operators**

| Stevedores | Maritime Shipping Lines | Financial Holdings |
|---|---|---|
| Horizontal integration | Vertical integration | Portfolio diversification |
| Port operations is the core business; Investment in container terminals for expansion and diversification. | Maritime shipping is the main business; Investment in container terminals as a support function. | Financial assets management is the main business; Investment in container terminals for valuation and revenue generation. |
| Expansion through direct investment. | Expansion through direct investment or through parent companies. | Expansion through acquisitions, mergers and reorganization of assets. |
| PSA (Public), HHLA (Public), Eurogate (Private), HPH (Private), ICTSI (Private), SSA (Private). | APM (Private), COSCO (Public), MSC (Private), APL (Private), Hanjin (Private), Evergreen (Private). | DPW (Sovereign Wealth Fund), Ports America (AIG; Fund), Macquarie Infrastructure (Fund), Morgan Stanley Infrastructure (Fund). |

Source: Adapted from Notteboom and Rodrigue (2012).

FIGURE 3.4 Container Terminals Controlled by Independent Stevedores, 2019

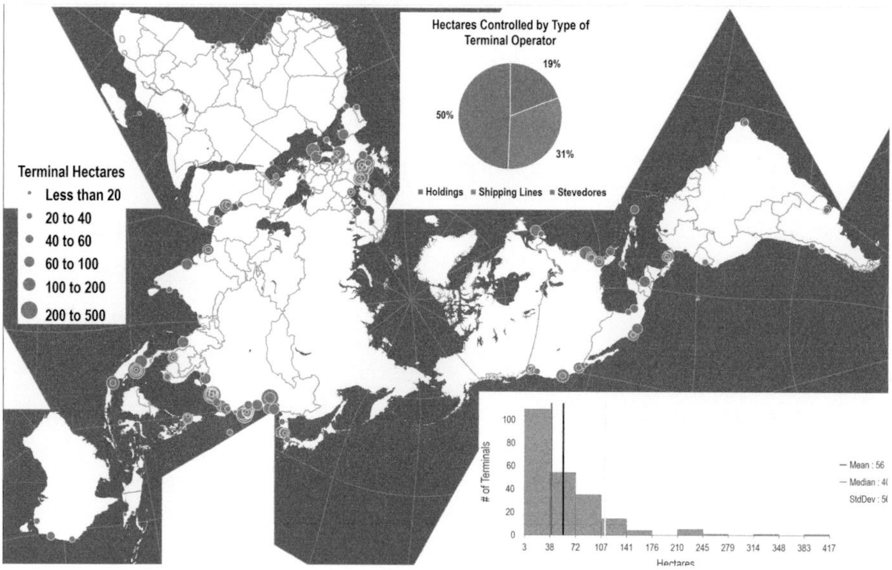

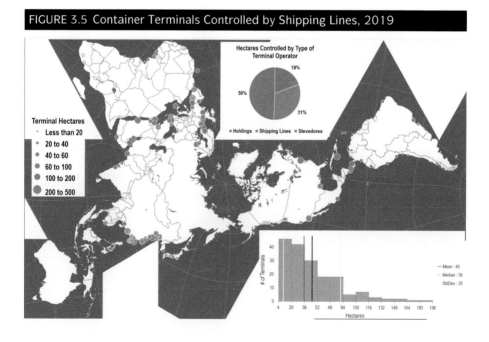

Source: Authors' compilation based on data from Drewry Shipping Consultants.

FIGURE 3.5 Container Terminals Controlled by Shipping Lines, 2019

their portfolio is that they were perceived to have a high-value proposition (Box 3.1). Holdings account for about 19% of the hectares controlled by terminal operators worldwide (Figure 3.6).

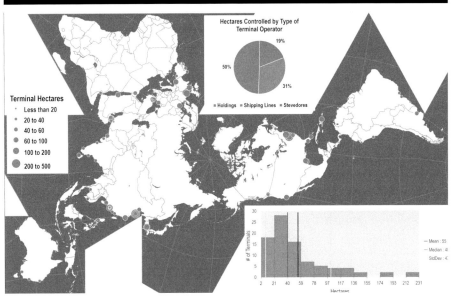

FIGURE 3.6 Container Terminals Controlled by Financial Holdings, 2019

The setting up of specialized terminal operating companies is not a recent phenomenon. Many ports in Northern Europe and the United States had already awarded terminals to local cargo handling companies through concessions and lease agreements. Because they were relatively small and locally based with only a few exceptions, they did not participate in the global growth of concession awards opportunities. The exceptions were Stevedore Services of America (SSA), already active in several US West Coast Ports, which obtained concessions to operate facilities in Panama and several other smaller ports in Central America; Eurogate, a joint company formed by terminal handling companies from Bremen and Hamburg; and Contship Italia, that obtained concessions in Italy and Morocco.

Beyond the three main categories, other types of companies are also involved in container terminals operations:

- **Freight transport companies**. They are involved in a wide range of freight services such as shipping agents, freight forwarders, road and rail transport companies, and third-party logistics service providers. Examples include Bollore, Arkas (Turkey), Wilson (Brazil), Kuwait Gulf Link, Rennies (South Africa), Korea Express, Nippon Express, Severstahltrans (Russia), and Kontena Nasional (Malaysia).
- **Construction companies**. Primarily large engineering firms that have become involved in container terminal concessions through Private Finance Initiatives or attempts to secure terminal construction contracts. Examples include Acciona (Spain), Gammon (India), Tribasa (Mexico), Tucuman (Brazil), Samsung Corp, and Hyundai Development.
- **Equipment manufacturers**. Small specialist companies that have moved into concessions from their original base in equipment servicing. It is worth noting that none of the major manufacturers of container terminal equipment (quay cranes, RTGs) have been involved in bids for terminal

concessions. Being involved in terminal operations could be perceived as an unfair competitive practice since they would be providing equipment to competing operators. Examples include Portek (Singapore), ABG Heavy Industries (India), and Mi-Jack (USA).

- **Property developers**. These are companies based mainly in Hong Kong and Southeast Asia and have diversified from commercial/residential developments into the provision of concessioned infrastructure. Examples include New World, Fairyoung, Henderson (HK), Metro Pacific Investment Corp, and Brisas del Pacifico (Colombia).

- **Industrial conglomerates**. These are either diversified holding companies or large manufacturers (such as steel or cars) regarded by their governments as national champions with the management ability to develop strategic assets. An important sub-set of this group comprises wealthy or well-connected individuals or families who have become involved because of their links to governments. For example, the Motta and Heibron families in Manzanillo (Panama), the Suharto family in Indonesia or Dato Ahmad Sebi at Westports in Port Klang. Other examples of industrial conglomerates include CITIC (China), Syanco (Saudi Arabia), FIAT, Mitsui, Tusdeer, CSN (Brazil), Razon Group (Philippines), Evyap Group (Turkey), and John Keells Holdings (Sri Lanka).

Several of the companies operating container terminals are multi-faceted, often belonging to larger corporate entities covering a wide range of economic activities. Their categorization depends on how far back one goes in tracing the chain of ownership. The farther back the beneficial ownership of a concession is traced, the more complex and fragmented the ownership structure becomes. APMT, for example, whilst trading as an independent terminal operator, has close links to Maersk Line. Similarly, until its sale to institutional investors, Dradagos, the Spanish port and logistics services company, formed part of the ACS Group. ACS's activities include construction, energy supply, environmental engineering, industrial services, and concessions in other modes of transport. In addition, some corporate structures are deliberately opaque to minimize commercial risks, taxation, or exposure to publicity.

### Box 3.1 Value propositions behind the interest of equity firms in transport terminals

*The rationale for the growing involvement of the financial sector in port terminals is mainly that terminals are increasingly capital intensive since the asset has an intrinsic and operational value. The substantial levels of productivity brought by containerization have resulted in a much more capital-intensive industry depending on financing not just for asset acquisition but also for their operations. Since terminals occupy strategic waterfront locations, their value as real estate assets is expected to increase. In turn, there is the expectation that terminals are relatively liquid assets, implying that they can be sold and a buyer readily found. However, such an expectation can change rapidly in periods of recession where terminal assets can become rather illiquid. The amortization of investments tends to occur over longer time periods, implying a more direct involvement and oversight of financial firms. Terminals in landlord ports became particularly attractive investments because land lease arrangements in these ports allow investors to acquire exclusive user rights on prime port sites for the entire duration of the lease term, typically between 25 and 40 years for larger terminals (Figure 3.7).*

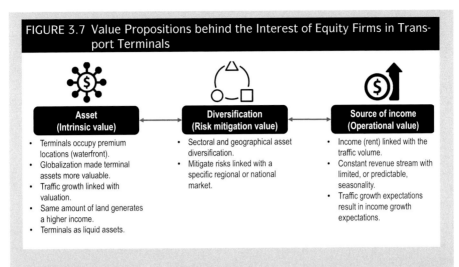

FIGURE 3.7 Value Propositions behind the Interest of Equity Firms in Transport Terminals

**Asset (Intrinsic value)**

- Terminals occupy premium locations (waterfront).
- Globalization made terminal assets more valuable.
- Traffic growth linked with valuation.
- Same amount of land generates a higher income.
- Terminals as liquid assets.

**Diversification (Risk mitigation value)**

- Sectoral and geographical asset diversification.
- Mitigate risks linked with a specific regional or national market.

**Source of income (Operational value)**

- Income (rent) linked with the traffic volume.
- Constant revenue stream with limited, or predictable, seasonality.
- Traffic growth expectations result in income growth expectations.

*With the growth of international trade, the volume handled by terminals grew accordingly and with it their revenue. This attracted the attention of financial firms, such as banks, insurance companies, and even pension funds, seeing transportation assets, such as port terminals, as an investment class part of a diversified global portfolio permitting* **risk mitigation.** *Pension funds became interested in terminal assets because the time horizon of an investment such as a concession agreement corresponded to their time horizon, which is long term. This helped to provide large quantities of capital to develop intermodal assets and increase their value. Scale factors were also important. Global financial firms were looking at opportunities large enough to accommodate the vast quantities of capital at their disposal, and terminals represented an asset class that suited the scale of this allocation well. Therefore, both the capital time and scale prospects of the maritime industry were in synchronism with the prospects of the financial industry. With the growth of international trade, transactions between commercial actors became increasingly complex and reliant on financing.*

## 2.3 Global terminal operators

Like many multinational corporations, global terminal operators are market seekers that expand their business opportunities through an entry into new markets. A terminal can grow organically, but this is a rather slow process. A much faster growth rate can be achieved through the acquisition of terminal facilities in new markets. From the 1990s, a few companies were able to become major global terminal operators controlling a multinational portfolio of terminal assets. They mostly originate from Asia, with four large companies dominating, three coming from a stevedore background and one from a shipping line:

- Hong Kong-based firm, **Hutchison Ports** (HPH), part of a major conglomerate, Hutchison Whampoa.
- **PSA International** (PSA), the government-owned operator of the port of Singapore. Note that the Port of Singapore Authority (PSA) was formed in 1964. In 1997, PSA corporatized and was renamed as PSA Corporation Limited. The company kept the name PSA but it is no longer an

acronym. In 2003, PSA International Private Limited became the main holding company for the PSA Group.

- **DP World** (DPW), which is mainly part of a sovereign wealth fund created by the government of Dubai to invest the wealth derived from oil trade.
- **APM Terminals** (APM), as a parent company of the world's largest shipping line; Maersk.

The setting up of global terminal operators took place in three main waves:

- The **first wave** included companies like HPH, P&O Ports, and SSA, who expanded their operations on a geographical scale, thereby benefiting from the port privatization schemes in many regions across the world. HPH, which originated as a terminal operator in Hong Kong, first purchased Felixstowe, the largest UK container port. It developed a portfolio of more than 50 terminals worldwide, including in Rotterdam and Shanghai.
- As soon as the strategies of the pioneers proved to be successful, the **second wave** of companies started seeking expansion internationally, such as PSA, CSX World Terminals, and Eurogate. PSA has been active in securing concessions in China and Europe, including Antwerp and Genoa. Like HPH, PSA takes its origin from globally-oriented ports offering limited local terminal expansion opportunities. Local operators were thus encouraged to manage the constrained assets efficiently and to look abroad for expansion opportunities.
- The **third wave** of terminal operators emerged when major container carriers entered the terminal industry in an effort to support their core business. This also included financial holdings such as DPW that have grown through acquisitions, such as P&O Ports and CSX World Terminals, and by securing concessions in new markets. Shipping lines have also participated in terminal concessions but to a lesser extent. The most important is the in-house terminal operating company of Maersk; APM Terminals. Besides, Evergreen, COSCO (via COSCO Shipping Ports), MSC (via its majority shareholding in TiL – Terminal Investment Limited), and CMA-CGM (via its majority shareholding in Terminal Link) hold port terminal leases. Between the dedicated terminal operating companies and the shipping lines, a global pattern of concessions is evident.

A **concentration of ownership** among four major port holdings is taking place. While mergers and acquisitions are usually successfully completed, there are cases where they have triggered a regulatory response. Despite being global, large terminal operators have a strong regional orientation, which indicates their transnational level. Global container terminal operators show varying degrees of involvement in the main cargo handling markets around the world. Complex and geographically diversified portfolios were established in virtually every freight market of the world. The container terminal has become a fundamental node in global freight distribution, with the managerial and operational expertise offered by global holdings an important element in its performance in terms of capacity and reliability.

## 3 THE STRATEGIES OF CONTAINER TERMINAL OPERATORS

The rapid expansion of terminal operating companies is a strategy that reflects two economic forces. First, the entry of former terminal operators into the global system represents a **horizontal integration process** (Figure 3.8). The companies, constrained by the growth limits of their own ports, seek to apply their expertise in new markets and seek new income sources. Second, the entry of shipping lines into terminal operations is an example of **vertical integration**. The companies seek to extend their control over other links in the transport chain. There is a third strategy, mainly followed by holdings having a strong financial orientation, **portfolio diversification**, in which terminal assets feature.

Port holdings, such as Hutchison Ports or DP World, are attempts at horizontal integration by acquiring stakes at port terminals in a variety of markets. A maritime shipping company that ventures into the management of port terminals simultaneously performs a process of vertical and horizontal integration since it is expanding geographically but also from maritime towards inland services (e.g. Maersk/APM Terminals). In all cases, the outcome is a more integrated and efficient transport chain that includes maritime shipping, port terminal operations, inland access, and even freight distribution centers (as a service to customers). If inland facilities such as inland (dry) ports and corridors develop, port regionalization is emergent.

Several strategies explain the growth of global terminal operating companies and their diffusion as key stakeholders in port terminals:

- **Profitability**. By modernizing port operations, mainly through better equipment, information systems, and management, port holdings can increase the profitability of their terminal assets. Because of their scale, management, and efficiency, global terminal operators tend to be more profitable than a single terminal operating firm. For instance, HPH achieved a 35% per year return on investment in the early 2000s. Port management was very lucrative, stimulating others to expand existing assets and encouraging new players to enter the field. Since 2010, profit

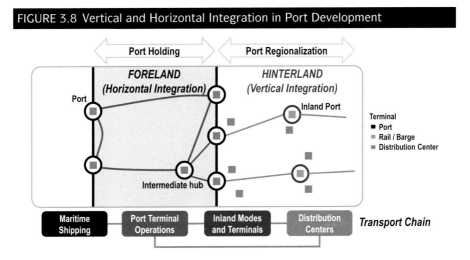

**FIGURE 3.8** Vertical and Horizontal Integration in Port Development

margins in terminal operations have become thinner, further underlining the advantage of efficient terminal operation practices.

- **Financial assets**. Port holdings have the financial means to invest in infrastructures as they have a wide variety of assets and the capacity to borrow large quantities of capital. They can use the profits generated by their profitable terminals to invest and subsidize the development of new terminals, thus expanding their asset base and operating revenues. Most are listed on equity markets, allowing access to global capital, which supports the freight transport sector as a source of returns driven by traffic growth fundamentals. This financial advantage cannot be matched by port authorities, even those heavily subsidized by public funds. In other cases, terminals have become financial assets that can grow more valuable as the traffic they handle increases (additional revenue). Financial holdings, such as retirement funds, have considered transport terminals and port terminals assets for their portfolios.

- **Managerial expertise**. Port holdings excel in establishing procedures to handle complex tasks such as the loading and unloading sequence of containerships and all the intricacies of terminal operations. Many have accumulated substantial experience in terminal design and the management of containerized operations in a wide array of settings. Therefore, they are able to transfer managerial expertise to new terminals. Being private entities, they tend to have better customer service and considerable flexibility to meet the needs of their clients through service differentiation. This also includes the use of well-developed information systems and the capacity to quickly comply with legal procedures related to customs clearance and security.

- **Gateway access**. From a geographical standpoint, most port holdings follow a strategy to establish privileged positions to access hinterlands. Doing so, they secure a market share and can guarantee a level of port and often inland transport service to their customers. This can also be seen as a commercial strategy where a 'stronghold' is established, limiting the presence of other competitors and creating a situation of monopoly. Gateway access thus provides a more stable flow of containerized shipments since gateways tend to endure as global connectors. The acquisition of a new port terminal is often accompanied by the development of related inland logistics activities by companies related to the port holding.

- **Leverage**. A port holding is able to negotiate favorable conditions with maritime shippers and inland freight transport companies, namely around rates, access, and level of service. Some are subsidiaries of global maritime shipping lines (such as the A.P. Moller group controlled by the shipper Maersk). In contrast, others are directly controlled by them (such as Evergreen) so they can offer a complete logistical solution to international freight transportation. They are also better placed to mitigate pressures from port authorities to increase rents and port fees. The 'footloose' character of maritime shippers has for long been recognized, with the balance of power more in their favor than it is of the port authorities they negotiate with.

- **Traffic capture**. Because of their privileged relationships with maritime shipping lines, port holdings are able to capture and maintain traffic for their terminals. The decision to invest is often related to knowing that the terminal will handle a relatively secure number of port calls. Consequently, the level of traffic and revenue can be secured more effectively.

- **Global perspective**. Port holdings have a comprehensive view of the state of the industry and are able to interpret political and price signals to their advantage. They are thus well placed to influence the direction of the industry and anticipate developments and opportunities to offer global solutions to terminal requirements in ports around the world. Under such circumstances, they can allocate new investments (or divest) to take advantage of new growth opportunities and new markets.

The growth of transnational terminal operating companies has resulted in a concentration of ownership. In 2018 the top seven global terminal operators accounted for 34.5% of global container port activity in terms of equity-based throughput. Perhaps most important is that they are now dominant in the most important container ports in the world and wield monopoly power in many smaller ports. There is strong evidence that performance has improved in most ports due to concessioning to global terminal operators. The question is whether to regulate the further concentration of power, leaving several maritime ranges having to deal with a limited number of terminal operators that are in a position to impose oligopolistic fees and charges.

## 4 CRUISE TERMINAL OPERATORS

### 4.1 The emergence of cruise terminal operators

Until the COVID-19 pandemic, the cruise industry experienced remarkable growth rates. Since the 1990s, the global growth rate of the cruise industry has endured in spite of economic cycles of growth and recession or other events disrupting cruise tourism, such as hurricanes. This growth is rapidly reshaping the cruise industry, with **private operators** entering the business. Liberalization and internationalization in the cruise terminal business have become a trend similar to that which occurred in the container terminal sector. Ports started to see cruises as more than an ancillary activity of secondary importance.

The presence of **specialized cruise terminal operators** has expanded. Along with service and other upgrades, the essential infrastructure for cruise terminal operations is also changing rapidly. Specialized cruise terminals replace multipurpose or temporary docking facilities. The bigger cruise ports develop via a **terminalization** strategy – the evolution of autonomously operating terminals of considerable size; the terminals at Cruise Port Barcelona, the biggest port in Europe; and the size of cruise terminals in North America provide illustrative examples. New cruise terminals are built and existing facilities are upsized and upgraded, imposing additional investments on the host port or terminal operator. Aiming to effectively respond to calls for upgrading cruise terminals while safeguarding public spending, port authorities started to seek the active involvement of third parties to finance, construct, operate, and commercially develop cruise facilities. Private entry in cruise terminals has been facilitated by the port governance reforms applied to all port activities, with governments establishing a more commercialized environment for port operators.

---

**FIGURE 3.9 Cruise Terminal Operators: Typology and Drivers of Entry**

| Entry Frequency | Terminal Operator | Main Drivers of Entry |
|---|---|---|
| HIGH | Cruise lines | • Vertical integration (cost control, service quality and reliability improvements); Promotion of assets (size of vessels); Increase of bargaining power; Exploiting business opportunities. |
| | Cruise terminal operators | • Horizontal integration; Economies of scope; Geographic diversification; Exploiting business opportunities. |
| | Container terminal operators | • Concentric diversification; Incidental entries in non-core activities. |
| | Port companies | • Economies of scope; Exploiting business opportunities and formal/informal ties. |
| | Third party service providers | • Shipping agencies, travel operators, & logistics companies. Concentric diversification; Support to own tourism activities. |
| | Chambers of commerce | • Promotion of local business and identity. |
| | Shipping companies | • Concentric diversification; Vertical integration; Financial defense of assets (size of vessels); Increase of bargaining power; Exploiting business opportunities |
| | Conglomerates | • Conglomerate diversification. |
| LOW | Financial institutions | • Financial diversification of the portfolio of assets. |

Source: Adapted from Pallis, Parola, Satta and Notteboom (2018).

This development has resulted in new opportunities for several firms, such as cruise lines and specialized cruise terminal operators, wishing to undertake new or additional investments in the cruise business, and sometimes to follow a path of internationalization (Figure 3.9). The **concessioning of cruise terminals** to third parties and the **development of new terminals** have become common practices. In some ports, cruise lines are directly involved in the financing, building, and operations of terminals. In other ports, local cruise terminal operators, which are often also port agents, are progressively joined by other companies that have developed interests in taking control of cruise ports and specialized purpose vehicles (SPVs) built by terminal operating companies. Eventually, international players emerged. As cruise activities in ports gain additional operational autonomy, public authorities are pursuing partnerships with third parties to finance and develop growth strategies.

## 4.2 Strategies of cruise terminal operators

The growing commitment of investors in the funding and management of cruise ports has reached levels comparable to what is being experienced in cargo ports, particularly container terminals. In the long-term, this might affect the interactions between ports and cruise lines, changing bargaining power relations between cruise lines and port authorities and the structure of cruise itineraries, as well as development strategies such as initiatives to address the existing seasonality of cruise activities or attract higher spending cruisers. The leading actors involved in cruise terminal operations include:

- **Cruise lines** that are expanding vertically into terminal operation to support their core activity.
- **Pure cruise terminal operators** that are expanding horizontally in new markets.
- **Third parties** such as Chambers of Commerce, shipping agencies, travel operators, and logistics companies entering for a specific opportunity, such as local economic development and simple diversification.

Cruise lines exploit the opportunities offered and undertake aggressive growth strategies, often entering overseas locations. In the Mediterranean market alone, Royal Caribbean Cruise Lines has emerged as the most active. The company operates cruise terminals in four different countries, such as Italy (Civitavecchia, La Spezia, Naples, Ravenna), Portugal (Lisbon), Spain (Barcelona), and Turkey (Kusadasi). Costa Crociere is present in France (Port of Marseille) and Spain (Port of Barcelona), and MSC Cruises operates cruise terminals in both France (Port of Marseille) and Italy (Port of Naples).

Cruise lines prefer to focus their terminal investments in turnaround (home) ports with a high level of transport accessibility for tourists and cruisers. The key facilities are airports and high-speed rail stations from which most cruisers arrive. This has resulted in the 'fly and cruise' model where cruise passengers are directly picked up and checked in at the airport. In contrast, transit ports (ports of call) are selected for their touristic highlights and landmarks. The interest of international cruise lines in the financing, building, and operating of terminals, which emerged in the early 2000s, is part of a vertical integration strategy. The main drivers of their strategies include the need for cost control and improvement in service quality and reliability, the need to defend their core assets financially, and the search for additional bargaining power in negotiations with local public authorities. Such vertical integration is experienced in other shipping sectors and is a means for achieving competitiveness along the supply chain.

Pure cruise terminal operators are investors who pursue horizontal integration and internationalization strategies to reach economies of scope and geographic diversification. Similar drivers trigger the entry of real estate and infrastructure managers, which rely on technical and managerial competencies developed in their core business to generate cross-sectorial synergies.

### 4.3 The internationalization of cruise terminal operators

More recently, cruise terminal operators started expanding overseas.

> *International Cruise Terminal Operators (ICTOs) are companies holding at least a share in one cruise facility located in a foreign country, and emerging as the main actors driving industry privatization.*

Global Ports Holding (GPH) is a major ICTO established in 2004 as an international port operator with a diversified portfolio of cruise and commercial ports. It started as a cruise terminal operator in Turkey and now operates 21 ports in 13 countries, including nine ports in six Mediterranean countries. As of 2019, GPH facilities handled 14 million passengers, accounting for a 24% market share in the Mediterranean. The group also offers commercial port operations that specialize in container, bulk, and general cargo handling. Another ICTO, Creuers Del Port Barcelona S.A., was established by the Port of Barcelona and then extended its cruise terminal portfolio to Asia (Singapore). The internationalization of cruise terminals might create an array of international actors managing global portfolios of facilities, comparable to what has happened with the rise of global container terminal operators (Box 3.2).

### Box 3.2  Cruise terminals operated by Global Ports Holding (GPH), 2020

*Established in 2004, Global Ports Holding (GPH) has become the world's largest cruise terminal operator. Its growth is similar to the expansion in the container terminal industry two decades earlier with the setting up of global terminal operators. As the cruise industry grew and gained a critical mass of passengers, cruise terminals became increasingly profitable but complex to manage. Further, the development of new facilities, particularly at turn ports, requires capital investments that port authorities may not be able to provide. This has opened up a window of opportunity for the development of portfolios in the cruise terminal operations (Figure 3.10).*

**FIGURE 3.10  The Cruise Portfolio of Global Ports Holdings**

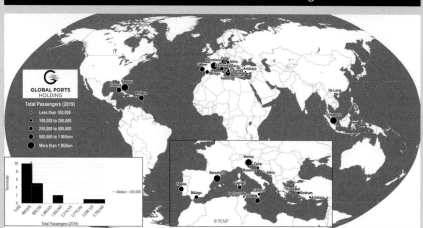

Source: Global Ports Holding (GPH) website; various sources of cruise passenger movements per port.

*GPH has positioned its assets in three major cruise markets:*

*   **Mediterranean**. *From its initial operations in Turkey, GPH was able to acquire a portfolio comprising the most important cruise ports, particularly Barcelona (a major turn port) and Venice (a major destination).*

*   **Caribbean**. *Represents the most important cruise market in the world, with year-round use. HPH was able to secure Nassau, a major hub and destination. It is unlikely that HPH will secure concessions in Florida since major cruise lines such as Royal Caribbean and Carnival are already terminal operators in hubs such as Miami and Fort Lauderdale. Still, many cruise ports in the Caribbean are potential targets for acquisition, which has already begun with Antigua and Havana.*

*   **Southeast Asia**. *Represents a fast-growing market for the cruise industry. HPH established a strong foothold in Singapore, but the development of its portfolio in this region is still in its infancy. Vietnam represents a growth opportunity for the cruise industry.*

*   *Since mid-2017, GPH has been a public company listed on the London Stock Exchange. Its portfolio included a 62% majority shareholding in Barcelona, the main cruise port in the Mediterranean Sea. Since then, GPH has announced further acquisitions (Cagliari; Ravenna; Catania, La Spezia, Taranto), with greenfield (Bar in Montenegro), and operating (Dubrovnik) concessions.*

**Global Container Terminal Operators** (GTOs) have recently assumed responsibilities for cruise terminal operations. This has been the outcome of the acquisition of majority stakes and ownership of entire ports. For instance, China Cosco Shipping became the owner of the master concession in Piraeus, and Terminal Link (CMA CGM) took over the concession in Thessaloniki, both ports and important container terminal facilities, but also cruise ports. Further, in 2017, DP World was awarded the concession to operate the port of Limassol, another important cruise destination. This trend is emerging even though cruise terminal activities are not part of their core business but a derived responsibility that may provide an incentive to acquire additional assets.

Given the pivotal role of cruise terminals in touristic global value chains, entities responsible for port destination development, such as Chambers of Commerce, and tourism-related firms, such as shipping agencies and travel operators, have become involved. Cruise facilities operations are seen as a tool to promote local and regional business or to support tourism. In some cases, such entities establish hybrid companies responsible for the management and operation of cruise ports. For instance, CCI Nice Cote d'Azur is an entity operating cruise terminals in several French Riviera ports. Several port companies are corporations with a public-ownership background that paved the way for the cruise business launch and facilitated a higher private equity commitment. Some of them entered the market predominantly in search of economies of scope and new business opportunities. For this purpose, they often exploited formal and informal ties with local public entities and institutions, rejecting the option of seeking foreign investments.

**Financial investors**, who are less present, might be attracted by high growth rates and profitability in the cruise business. Specialized financial institutions such as banks, insurance companies, and private equity (PE) firms, are searching for a reasonable risk, return-maximization, and maturity of investments. They may see cruise terminals as attractive assets for diversifying their business portfolio, contributing to a higher degree of financialization of the port sector. The attractive features of port terminals include the long-term economic life of the assets, the monopolistic or oligopolistic nature of the industry, and the possibility of partially transferring risk to host governments through public-private partnerships.

An emerging trend has been the setting up of **dedicated facilities** where the cruise shipping company is directly involved in the development of the cruise terminal as well as co-located amenities. Examples of this practice are the private islands in the Caribbean which are reserved exclusively for a cruise company (Box 3.3). The most prominent include Labadee (Royal Caribbean) in Haiti, Coco Cay (Royal Caribbean), Half Moon Cay (Holland), Castaway Cay (Disney), Princess Cay (Princess), and Great Stirrup Cay (Norwegian) in the Bahamas. These private facilities are all within one cruise day from the home ports of Florida, offering the option of short 3–4 days cruises to a quiet and safe destination. They are all enclaves within their respective host countries.

## Box 3.3  Private islands in the Caribbean owned by cruise lines

*The acquisition of Great Stirrup Cay by Norwegian Cruises in 1977 marks the beginning of a trend where large cruise shipping lines secure private islands (or beaches) for their exclusive use (Figure 3.11). The acquisition usually takes the form of a long-term lease (up to 99 years according to international law) or an exclusive use agreement for specific periods. This has particularly taken place in the Caribbean and for the following reasons:*

*Revenue capture. Private islands are part of the trend pursued by cruise lines to internalize their sources of revenue. Since the cruise line owns all the amenities of the private island, they can capture all the revenues generated by these amenities (e.g. food, drinks, activities). They thus try to include their private island as a port of call in as many itineraries as possible.*

*Alternative port call. The majority of the private islands are located in the Bahamas, a night sailing away from the major Miami cruise hub (or other Floridian cruise ports), for which they can conveniently be used as first or last port of call during a cruise and as an alternative if the itinerary needs to be modified (e.g. inclement weather). They can thus be easily included in cruise itineraries as a last-minute change in ports of call.*

*Exclusivity. The cruise lines effectively market private islands as exclusive locations that only their customers can access and that are closed to the general public (or the local population). They are thus perceived as less crowded and safe locations, which appeals to many cruisers.*

*Beach experience. Many cruisers expect a beach experience, particularly since the Caribbean is known as a region offering a wide variety of beaches. However, many ports of call along Caribbean itineraries are cities and towns that do not have high-quality beaches in close proximity or have beaches that require transportation (an excursion) for access. The private beach is advertised as part of the experience where cruisers can disembark right at the amenity with minimal effort. The amenity is also comprehensive, with a wide array of services and entertainment options being offered.*

FIGURE 3.11  Private Islands in the Caribbean Owned by Cruise Lines

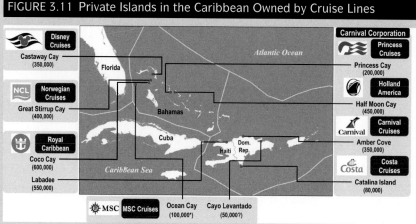

Note: Figures are the estimated average number of visitors per year. Ocean Cay opened in December 2019 and visitor figures are capacity estimates.

# Chapter 3.2  Terminal concessions and land leases

*Most port terminals are leased to terminal operators through concessions involving a bidding process to capture the terminal asset.*

## 1 PRIVATE INVOLVEMENT IN PORT INVESTMENT AND OPERATION

In many countries worldwide, governments and public port authorities have retreated from port operations. The core driver is the belief that enterprise-based port services and operations will allow for greater flexibility and efficiency in the market through more competition and a better response to customers' demands. Ports, which have traditionally been run like a government department, are seeing private money promoting greater competition and higher productivity. Eventually, lower costs are passed on to importers and exporters. Often this involves the transfer of provision of services from public bodies to private enterprises. Ports have become a business attracting the attention of large investment groups and equity fund managers.

Ports are inclined to develop new governance structures, which should be tailored to the specific local conditions in terms of culture and commercial objectives, leading to several options. Four major types of combinations of **port/terminal ownership and port/terminal operations** can be distinguished:

- Public ownership and public participation in operations.
- Public ownership and private participation in port/terminal construction, operations, and management.
- Public ownership and private participation in superstructure installation (e.g. cranes) and operations.
- Private ownership and operations.

The use of the model of **Public Ownership and Private Operations** (POPO) is the most common and typically involves some form of **Public-Private Partnership** (PPP) between the public (in the form of a government agency) and the private sector in providing a specific public service. Such partnerships require that risks, responsibilities, and returns be shared between the public and private sectors.

The use of PPP arrangements is widespread in the seaport industry to structure the responsibilities of terminal operators and port authorities concerning the construction, financing, and operations of the terminal facility. Commonly used arrangements include (Figure 3.12):

- **Build-Lease-Operate** (BLO). The government or port authority leases the construction and operation of the whole port or part of it to a private company through a long-term concession. The private company constructs facilities such as berths and terminals. In turn, the port authority controls the rights throughout the concession period and receives an annual lease payment.

- **Build-Operate-Transfer** (BOT). The government or public authority grants a concession or a franchise to a private company to finance and build or modernize a specific port facility. The private company is entitled to operate the facilities and to obtain revenue from specified operations or the full port for a designated time period. The private sector takes all commercial risks during the concession. At the end of the concession period, the government retakes ownership of the improved assets. Arrangements between the government and the private operator are set out in a concession contract that may or may not include regulatory provisions.
- **Rehabilitate-Operate-Transfer** (ROT). The government or public authority grants a concession to a private company to finance and rehabilitate or modernize a specific terminal or an entire port. This company is entitled to operate and obtain revenue from the rehabilitated port for a specific period. The private company takes all commercial risks, and at the end of the concession period, the government retakes ownership of the improved asset.
- **Build-Rehabilitate-Operate-Transfer** (BROT). The government or public authority grants a concession to a private company to finance, build and rehabilitate or modernize a specific terminal or an entire port. The private partner will build, operate, and obtain revenue from the rehabilitated port for a specific period. The private company takes on all commercial risks, and at the end of the concession period, the government retakes ownership of the improved asset. BROT is a combination of the BOT and ROT mechanisms.
- **Build-Operate-Share-Transfer** (BOST). BOST is similar to BOT. A government grants a concession or a franchise to a private company to finance and build or modernize a specific port/terminal for a designated time period. The revenue obtained from terminal operations is shared with a designated public authority throughout the concession period. The government/public authority should ensure a specific quantity of throughput for revenue. The commercial risks are shared between the government and the concessionaire. At the end of the concession period, the government retakes ownership of the improved asset.

FIGURE 3.12 Main Types of Public-Private Partnerships

| Type of PPP | Mode of Entry | Operations | Investments | Ownership | Duration (years) |
|---|---|---|---|---|---|
| Management contract | Contract | Private | Public | Public | 3-5 |
| Leasing | Contract | Private | Public | Public | 8-15 |
| Rehabilitate-operate-transfer (ROT) | Concession | Private | Private | Public | 20-30 |
| Rehabilitate-lease/rent-transfer (RLRT) | Concession | Private | Private | Public | 20-30 |
| Merchant | Greenfield | Private | Private | Public | 20-30 |
| Build-rehabilitate-operate-transfer | Concession | Private | Private | Public | 20-30 |
| Build-operate-transfer (BOT) | Greenfield | Private | Private | Semi-private | 20-30 |
| Build-own-operate-transfer (BOOT) | Greenfield | Private | Private | Semi-private | 30+ |
| Build-lease-own (BLO) | Greenfield | Private | Private | Private | 30+ |
| Build-own-operate (BOO) | Greenfield | Private | Private | Private | 30+ |
| Partial privatization | Divesture | Private | Private | Private | 30+ |

Source: Adapted from Hammami, Ruhashyankiko and Yehoue (2006).

Critical success factors for a sound implementation of PPPs in the port context include the accuracy of the PPP contract, the ability to allocate and share the risk appropriately, the technical feasibility of the project, the commitment made by partners, the attractiveness of the financial package, a clear definition of responsibilities, the presence of a strong private consortium and a realistic cost/benefit assessment.

## 2 TERMINAL CONCESSIONS

> *A concession is a grant by a government or port authority to a (private) operator for providing specific port services, such as terminal operations or nautical services (e.g. pilotage and towage).*

In a terminal concession setting, a concession agreement is signed between, on the one hand, a private terminal operator and, on the other hand, a landlord port authority or empowered government agency. Concessions can take the form of a **long-term lease or an operating license**. Under the long-term lease system, a private company is allowed to operate a specified terminal for a defined time period. The government or a public authority holds the property rights of the facilities throughout the concession period and receives lease payments on the assets. The **concession/lease fees** paid by the private terminal operator are used to upgrade and expand the facility.

The concessioning of land to private terminal operators is a cornerstone of the **landlord port authority model**. Under this model, the landlord port authority usually is a separate entity under public law, established by specific legislation. It has the capacity to conclude contracts (including concession agreements), enforce standards, and make rules and regulations applicable within the port area. Private companies carry out port operations (especially cargo-handling). The landlord port is the dominant port model in large and medium-sized ports.

Concession policy has become a powerful governance tool for port managers in the terminal operating business:

- Through concession policy, port authorities or government agencies can retain some control over the organization and structure of the supply side of the port market.
- Through concession policy, port managers can encourage port service providers to optimize the use of scarce resources such as land.

## 3 THE TERMINAL AWARDING PROCEDURE

The awarding practices in many ports around the world have undergone quite some changes in recent years. While there were often no formal conditions required, the awarding process nowadays typically consists of a thorough inquiry into the different candidates seeking to obtain a terminal. Terminals may be awarded by several methods, including:

- Direct appointment.
- Private negotiation from a qualified pool.
- Competitive bidding process.

National and supranational legislation, port privatization schemes, and legal disputes concerning irregularities in concession policy have made **competitive bidding** the most common procedure used in concession granting. Potential candidates are invited by the managing body of the port, or the managing body of the port publishes an open call for tender. The call could involve a public tendering procedure or other types of tendering, such as an open assessment procedure with room for negotiations and the submission of improved proposals during the process. Any competitive bidding should comply with the principle of equality, which states that every candidate should be equally treated and compared. There should be no favoritism in awarding the concession or no substantial reduction of competition and of the principle of transparency.

In the case of an open call for tender, the terminal typically is awarded based on the offers of the eligible candidates, followed by one or more negotiation rounds. In the remaining cases, the terminal is awarded based on the offers of the eligible candidates without any negotiations or the possibility for candidates to submit a revised proposal during the awarding process. Some ports use different types of tendering procedures depending on specific criteria. For example, a limited or 'light' version for smaller facilities and a full version for larger terminals.

In the cases where terminals are directly appointed, managing bodies of ports do so mainly for strategic reasons which may include creating intra-port competition or securing further expansion possibilities for efficient incumbent firms. Also, a terminal project can represent a marginal extension of an existing facility, such as the extension of an existing container terminal with one berth.

More than one out of four ports have assigned container terminals through some form of competitive bidding or tendering (Figure 3.13 and Box 3.4). As an alternative to competitive tendering, concessions negotiated with a new entrant or a company already operating in the port (the incumbent) have been endorsed in almost half of the ports. Negotiations with incumbents include concession renewals and the involvement of existing general cargo stevedores in the development of container terminals in the 1970s and 1980s. More than 100 of the current concessions have been negotiated with incumbents. Local stevedoring companies form the largest group, but incumbents also include national shipping lines, shipping agents, and freight forwarders. Another category of incumbents can be found in China (Dalian, Qingdao, and Tianjin) where successive terminals in large ports have been built by the existing operators, but with modifications to the consortium ownership structure at each stage to bring in additional partners. A last category is made up mainly of semi-dedicated terminals leased to partnerships of stevedores and container lines on a regular renewal basis. What is striking about this category, apart from the large number of separate terminal leases it generates in each port, is its concentration on the West Coast of the USA and in Japan, with common features on both sides of the Pacific. In Japan, shipping lines and stevedoring companies may be linked through keiretsu, vertically integrated groups of companies with inter-locking share ownerships, such as Mitsui & Co. Ltd. This makes it difficult to establish exactly where management control over terminals resides.

FIGURE 3.13 Container Terminal Concessions in World Ports: Transactions Per Type (%)

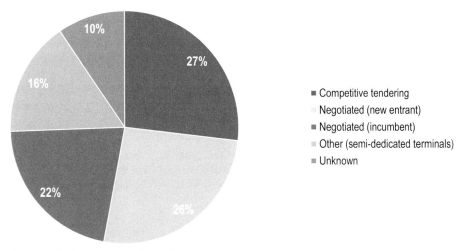

- Competitive tendering
- Negotiated (new entrant)
- Negotiated (incumbent)
- Other (semi-dedicated terminals)
- Unknown

Source: Adapted from Farrell (2012).

## Box 3.4 The geography of competitively tendered container terminal concessions

*The proportion of competitively tendered concessions is highest in Central and South America, where the concessioning process has primarily involved the divestment of public assets. In Brazil and Uruguay, terminal operating rights have been publicly auctioned. Elsewhere, the 'two envelope' system has been more common, with bids evaluated on technical and then financial criteria. The main exceptions to competitive bidding in this region are found in Colombia, where whole port concessions have been awarded to Sociedades Portuarias Regionales, umbrella organizations of local stakeholders.*

*The proportion of competitively tendered concessions is lowest in North America, which has a strongly entrenched private stevedoring industry, access to capital markets and local taxpayers for the funding of new berth construction, and a high level of inter-port competition. Local authorities have been more willing than elsewhere to build new terminals on demand for individual stevedores and/or shipping lines, even though this has resulted in below-average use of port assets. So, until quite recently, there has not been much interest in using competitive tendering to select the most efficient operator.*

*The relatively low proportion of competitively tendered concessions in Asia is due to the large number of new terminals located in China, which has had a strong preference for negotiated deals with large foreign operators based on the creation of joint ventures. India has developed quite elaborate rules for the competitive assignment of concessions in Major Trust Ports but has been slow to implement its divestiture program; new greenfield terminals have been mainly built outside of the Major Trust Ports, authorized by individual State governments which have generally favored negotiated deals.*

*Europe, the Middle East and Africa occupy the middle ground. Europe's long private stevedoring tradition has resulted in a high proportion of leases being assigned to incumbents, particularly in Northern Europe. Although the concessioning process in German ports still favors local operators, terminal operations in the Netherlands and Belgium were opened up to outsiders in the 1990s through competitive bidding and merger and acquisition activity, a process which began in France in the mid-2000s. However, competitive tendering has been an important component of the port reform process in the Mediterranean countries and is now beginning to be used for greenfield projects in Northern Europe as well, in response to shortages of capital and space.*

*In the Middle East, competitive tendering has been important in some countries (Syria, Lebanon, Jordan, Saudi Arabia) but in the UAE, contracts for the management of smaller ports, such as Fujairah and Mina Zayed, have been directly negotiated with DP World. Oman has also preferred negotiation as a means of bringing in foreign expertise and funding to its centrally controlled ports system.*

*In Africa, the World Bank has provided technical assistance to countries wishing to follow the competitive tendering route, but the desire to retain some degree of public sector control over ports has led to an almost equal number of negotiated deals.*

*Since the 2000s, Australia has also endorsed competitive tendering in order to increase intra port competition and break the duopoly of the incumbent terminal operators.*

*Global trends are less clear, however, as the increase in competitive tendering generated by divesture programs in Africa and Central/South America has been largely offset by the number of new terminals in China which have been non-competitively concessioned.*

A typical terminal awarding procedure consists of three phases (Figure 3.14):

- **Pre-bidding phase**. The awarding authority (typically a port authority or any other managing body of the port) makes the necessary preparations for the award process taking into account prevailing regulatory conditions. The awarding authority has to decide on key issues related to the awarding procedure and make this information available to interested candidates. In this phase, the rules of the game are defined.
- **Awarding phase**, which includes a selection phase and, if considered necessary, a prequalification phase. Candidates are screened, bids are evaluated, and the most appropriate candidate is selected. The challenge for the awarding authority lies in making the right choice given the parameters set up in the pre-bidding phase.
- **Post-bidding phase**. A legally binding contractual agreement is signed with the selected candidate, with the performance of the operator monitored during the contract term. If necessary, corrective measures are taken and disputes are settled.

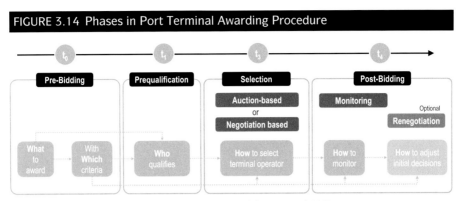

FIGURE 3.14 Phases in Port Terminal Awarding Procedure

Source: Adapted from Theys, Notteboom, Pallis and de Langen (2010).

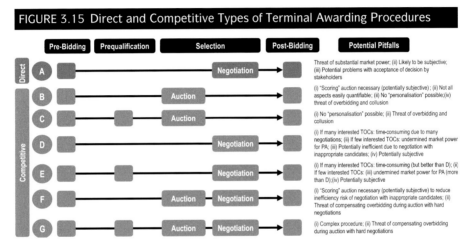

FIGURE 3.15 Direct and Competitive Types of Terminal Awarding Procedures

Source: Adapted from Theys, Notteboom, Pallis and de Langen (2010).

**Prequalification** is often, but not always, a first step in the awarding phase and consists of the selection of qualified companies out of the pool of interested candidates. It is based on a set of conditions developed by the awarding authority before the start of the awarding phase. Companies that have met these conditions are then allowed into one or more selection rounds in which the terminal concession is awarded.

The different phases can be combined in various ways to end up with different types of direct and competitive terminal awarding procedures, each with specific strengths and pitfalls (Figure 3.15).

## 4 THE PRE-BIDDING PHASE

Key decisions during pre-bidding include what to award and under which conditions the awarding will take place. The following **questions** need to be addressed during this phase:

- Should the commodity to be handled be specified, or should bidders have the freedom to identify what cargoes they wish to handle?

- What plots should be concessioned: one large plot or a number of smaller ones?
- What are the key conditions of the concession, and how should these be determined (e.g. duration, fees, and fee structure; performance targets, bonuses, and penalties; final asset compensation, right-to-end)?
- What should be the risk division between the port authority and terminal operator?
- What should be the investment division between the port authority and terminal operator?
- What should be the responsibility division (e.g. maintenance dredging)?

## 4.1 Object of the concession

Once the decision has been taken to concession the operation of a (future) terminal, the awarding authority will have to describe the **object of the concession**. The port site that will be given in concession should be carefully delimited to avoid any potential conflicts over land jurisdiction. Moreover, the technical and geological characteristics of the site and the physical, operative, commercial, juridical, and labor aspects of the proposed concession have to be analyzed and filed. Such information typically ends up in later documents related to the awarding procedure, such as public auctions, tender documents, or requests for proposals in a competitive bidding process. The purpose is to avoid information asymmetry in the awarding process. If the port authority does not provide due diligence, candidates will have to verify the state of the premises and possibly perform surveys and field studies to prepare their bid. This incurs transaction costs and may reduce the number of bidders. In addition, any gaps left by the awarding authority during this stage provide the winner of the concession with opportunities for maneuvering during the later stages and even after the finalization of the process.

## 4.2 Main use of the terminal

An awarding authority might want to decide on the main use of the terminal in the pre-bidding phase. Alternatively, the awarding authority might decide to invite bids for a certain plot rather than specifying how it should be used, as long as its use lies within the functions allowed by the port authority. If the awarding authority clearly defines the use of the terminal (e.g. plot to be used for container handling only), then the port authority will, later on in the process, have an easier task in evaluating the technical and economic proposals of the candidates on an equal footing.

## 4.3 Splitting and phasing of the terminal site

The size of a terminal site to be concessioned is a complex issue as the footprint must be sufficient for expected activity levels. In the pre-bidding phase, the port authority will have to make key decisions concerning whether the development footprint is to be split and phased (Figure 3.16). On the assumption that a port authority has 200 hectares of port land available for container terminal development:

**FIGURE 3.16** Options Related to the Splitting and Phasing of a Terminal Site

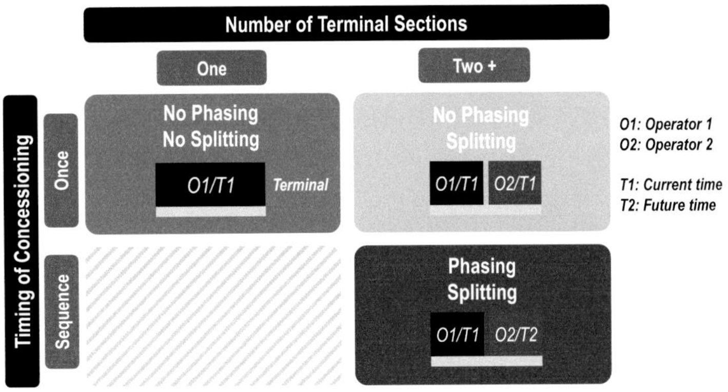

Source: Adapted from Theys, Notteboom, Pallis and de Langen (2010).

- **Splitting option**. Is this site best concessioned as one terminal, or is the plot to be split into two or more sections to be concessioned separately? This option must take into consideration the expected market demand and minimal optimal terminal size.
- **Phasing**. The concession process can be phased. A port authority could decide to award the first section of 100 ha in year 1, 50 ha in year 3, and the remaining 50 ha in year 5. This option must consider the expected growth in demand and the financial and technical capabilities available for terminal construction.

While the strategic options on **splitting and phasing** seem straightforward, solutions are challenging to implement, given the far-reaching impact they may have on the competitive profile of the port. Two key challenges can be identified in this respect:

- **Manner used to phase sections of a terminal plot**. A port authority could organize a separate competitive bidding procedure or auction process for each phase. Alternatively, a port authority might consider a second terminal phase as a mere extension of the initial terminal phase and decide to award the second phase to the incumbent terminal operator by direct appointment, thereby avoiding a competitive bidding process. If the second phase of the terminal represents a marginal extension of the first phase, then a competitive bidding process or auction for the second phase does not make sense, at least when the incumbent terminal operator shows interest in operating the second phase. If the scale differences between the first terminal phase and subsequent terminal phases are small, then a direct appointment to an existing operator is a less obvious choice.
- **Dynamics in intra-port competition**. If the port authority organizes a competitive bidding procedure for the new plot and makes the incumbent firm eligible to compete for the terminal concession, two outcomes are possible. First, the **incumbent firm wins**. The incumbent strengthens its intra-port monopoly position and can extract monopoly rents if there

is insufficient competitive pressure from competing ports. Eventually, the result is high revenues for the port authority but high costs for port users. Simultaneously, the scale of the facilities is likely to generate economies of scale and scope, creating the potential for lowering the handling costs per unit for the operator. Second, a **new entrant is granted the concession**, thereby introducing intra-port competition. Given the scale differences between the existing and new facility, the entrant has a good starting position for outperforming the incumbent firm.

The issues discussed above constitute the core of many legal disputes handled by competition authorities around the world. They inevitably raise further questions about the need and impact of intra-port competition and the minimum efficient scale in terminal operations.

## 4.4 The division of risks and investments

The port authorities will have to decide on the **division of risks and investments** related to the object of the concession. The general principle is that risks should be allocated to the party that can best manage them. In the port industry, **commercial risks** can best be managed by private operators.

For **port infrastructure**, this issue is more complex. In some cases, all risks are transferred to the private sector, and the awarding authority grants a concession to build and operate a terminal. The concessionaire has to make all investments and consequently bears all the risks. This option is especially attractive when the terminal to be concessioned is not part of a larger port expansion project but will need to be built stand-alone. However, when a port authority develops a larger port expansion project with various sites to be concessioned, it is better placed to assume these risks.

The awarding of a concession needs to address risk and reward factors to avoid unrealistic terms that may result in institutional entry barriers and a limited number of bids, or no bids at all.

## 4.5 Duration of the concession period

The port authority will have to decide the **duration, fees, and fee structure** before starting the awarding process. In most cases, the term of the concession is determined by the port authority or government agency. In many parts of the world, legislators have developed rough guidelines on concession durations to safeguard free and fair competition in the port sector. There are hardly any rules of thumb on the concession duration. For instance, attempts have been made by the European Commission to create relevant rules, but these rules have not had the agreement of all stakeholders. In general, the duration of the concession will vary with the amount of the initial investment required, the compliance with the development policy of the port and land lease, and other easement rights.

A port authority might opt for **phased concession terms**, with a typical base duration of 15 years and consecutive renewals every five years, and based on defined criteria. The port authority will also have to develop its views on a possible prolongation of the concession beyond the official term before entering the granting procedure.

The duration of the agreement is of crucial importance to both terminal operators and port authorities. **Long-term agreements** allow private port operators to benefit from learning by doing processes and to achieve a reasonable return on investments (ROI). Port authorities try to find a balance between a reasonable payback period for the investments made by terminal operators on the one hand and a maximum entry to potential newcomers on the other. As long-term agreements act as entry barriers, intra-port competition will only occur among the existing local port operators.

## 4.6  Concession fees and fee structure

The port authority will also have to decide the fees and the fee structure it will use throughout the awarding procedure. On the one hand, port users demand a transparent, uniform, and stable fee system. Such stability in the fee structure is important given the investment decisions of the terminal operator. On the other hand, port authorities are tempted to apply the market mechanism in setting the fees for the use of valuable port land.

The pricing system deployed by the managing body of the port for the use of the port land tends to vary widely among ports:

- The managing body of the port imposes a **fixed rent per year** on the terminal operator for the terminal surface in use (for example, in Euro per square meter per year).
- A **lump sum** is to be paid annually, regardless of the financial results from the operating activity, plus a variable payment (the bigger of the sums: percentage from the total cash flow or coefficient per ton).
- A fixed rent per year on the terminal area plus a **percentage of the revenue earned** (royalty fee).
- A fixed rent for the terminal surface in use, adjusted for a **bonus system**, depending on an annual throughput in relation to the guaranteed volume.

## 4.7  Final asset compensation

Port authorities can follow different paths when dealing with the terminal superstructure, such as sheds, warehouses and fixed cargo handling equipment, at the end of the contract term. Although the decision on what to do with the superstructure is often made at the end of the concession term, it is useful for port authorities to develop views on this issue even as early as in the pre-bidding phase. Common approaches include the removal/destruction of the superstructure by the terminal operator at the end of the contract term or the transfer of the assets to the managing body of the port without any form of compensation. A port authority might opt for financial compensation of the terminal operator for the superstructure that was transferred at the end of the contract term.

## 5 THE PREQUALIFICATION PHASE

A port authority can decide to have a prequalification phase before entering the stage of competitive bidding or auctioning. The prequalification phase aims to reduce the number of potential candidates by developing criteria concerning company size, experience, and financial strength.

## 5.1 Dealing with incumbent terminal operators

An incumbent will generally have the edge over new entrants in additional bidding procedures. In the absence of competitors in a port, an incumbent firm that does not face tight price regulation, or any other barriers (regulatory or not), is likely to win a bidding procedure for an additional terminal. In that case, it would generate some market power that enables extracting economic rents.

Port authorities may decide that incumbent operators cannot hold more than one concession in the same port. Whether they can do so depends on the legal framework in place: the exclusion of potential candidates might be considered anti-competitive by competition authorities. There are also cases where regulation gives an advantage to local/domestic players vis-à-vis foreign candidates.

## 5.2 Experience and financial strength

The experience of the candidate can be demonstrated by the management of facilities for similar cargo in the same or other ports. Thus, the candidate has to demonstrate his experience in the activities related to the project by giving proof of specific **antecedents in the exploitation of terminals**. Defining relevant experience can take different forms depending on the geographical scope followed by the port authority, ranging from experience in the local port up to global experience. The terminal types considered range from multipurpose terminals to specialized terminals such as containers. These requirements are often associated with a particular **minimum handled throughput** in these terminals, occasionally used as a means to minimize the number of bidders due to a (justified?) preference for global operators.

Experience may also be combined with the **technical solvency of the bidder** in the basic port handling services or the ability to fill capability gaps in logistics, broaden the geographical markets served and expand terminal networks. Creative port authorities can design the required experience so that certain terminal operators are well-positioned to enter the selection phase.

The bidding procedure typically contains thresholds on the financial strength of the bidders. For example, it can be stipulated that a certain percentage of the net worth of the bidder should at least equal the estimated project cost. Apart from the financial track record, financial solvency might also be associated with the capacity of the operator to maintain a specific level of reserves that matches a considerable percentage of the total assets and fixed assets throughout the lifetime of the concession.

## 6 THE SELECTION PHASE

Awarding authorities can choose from a variety of different setups, but selection generally takes place based on **negotiations or auction-like structures**:

- Many competitive selection procedures in seaports de facto use **auctions** because the terminal is assigned to the highest bidder – not necessarily in monetary terms but also with the highest 'score' on a number of criteria.
- Negotiations with the highest bidder(s) after the (de facto or formal) auction are not rare and might even result in the reversal of the initial decision.

The selection is based on a **technical and financial proposal or a price bid**. Every qualified bidder will present only one offer, without variants or alternatives. Based on the technical and financial proposal and or the price bid, a bidder is selected from among the previously qualified bidders.

## 6.1 The technical and financial proposal

One way of deciding who will get the concession is to base the decision primarily on the requested technical and financial proposal. Although the required contents of such a technical proposal tend to differ significantly from case to case, it usually consists of the following: implementation details, financing details, a marketing plan, operational and management details, employment impact, an environment plan, and an organizational plan.

Terminal development will follow an **implementation plan** ordered by stages according to the expected growth of the traffic. The implementation plan is backed by the results of a market study. The calculations of handling capacity will have to demonstrate that the installations offered will have the necessary capacity to serve the projected throughput adequately. The timetable of investments will have to include the foreseen cost of works and equipment. Each bidder has to present a complete list of fixed or mobile equipment expected to operate on the terminal, with a definition of the type, capacity, specifications, life span, and the date of entering operation. In case the bidding procedure concerns the development of a greenfield or brownfield terminal by the bidder, each bidder has to present studies and preliminary sketches of the works, estimations of the costs of building, and a plan of investments of all the works that the proposal contemplates.

The **marketing plan** typically includes a market study that defines the demand of services for the terminal and justifies the previsions about the magnitude and requirements of the installations, including projections of yearly throughput for a specified number of years. The candidate might have to indicate the expected prices and maximum charges for any of the services offered to the terminal users and **operation costs** (including labor, equipment, fuels, and other inputs and supplies), maintenance and supervision, and administration.

Each bidder typically has to present **environmental and territorial studies** on aspects such as the impact of the terminal operations on the environment and mobility and the alternatives to eliminate, rate various aspects of the technical and financial proposal reduce or mitigate selected adverse effects.

Further, each bidder typically has to quantify **staff requirements** for the concession and project its evolution according to the cargo projections.

In a well-prepared proposal, there should be a continuous chain of logic, which flows from the market demand and cargo projections through to the physical layout, equipment purchases, manning levels, and operating assumptions. Considering the final selection, it is quite common to rate various aspects of the technical and financial proposal and add up the results in a weighted or unweighted score, based on each of the evaluation criteria related to the elements in the proposal. The weights and passing criteria are included in the bidding documents, if applicable.

## 6.2 Price bid

An alternative way of awarding a concession consists of putting a strong focus on the price. The available alternatives range from a given rent but minimal charges to a maximum rent and freedom to the private operator to set charges. Given a set level of investment and quality requirements, the winner is either:

1. The highest payer for the right to provide terminal services.
2. The bidder who is proposing the lowest price to be paid by the terminal users.

In the first option, the port authority or government agency aims at maximizing revenue. The payments are typically made annually. The second option focuses more on the interest of the port users and ensures price minimization rather than revenue maximization. The concession fee under the first option is seldom renegotiated. In contrast, the fee under the second option is often renegotiated so that the concessionaire ends up with a larger share of the rent created by its efficiency gains.

In some cases, particularly for new terminal developments in developing countries, bidders have to quote the percentage of their revenue passed on to the government. The competition is then based on bidding, and priority will be given to the party that offers the highest percentage to the government share.

## 7 POST-BIDDING PHASE

### 7.1 The concession agreement

The post-bidding phase includes the **drafting and signing of the concession agreement**, the follow-up to the agreement, and the termination and renegotiation, if any, of the contract.

The **design of the concession agreement** or contract, starting with the rights and obligations of the concessionaire, is a key element in any concession. One of the main reasons behind specific contractual arrangements in a concession agreement relates to potential **information asymmetries** described in the principal/agent theory. A port authority (the principal) bases its decisions about granting a concession on the available information. Although the information about the candidate might be very elaborate, such as financial status, performance in other ports, or client base, the port authority has no guarantee that the agent will meet its objectives in terms of cargo generation. As such, concession agreements often take the form of **performance-based contracts** to create incentives for the agent (terminal operator) to act in the principal's interest.

The specific design of the concession agreement, its regulatory regime, the tariff regime, and the way the concession is awarded reveal the priorities of port authorities and government agencies and, as such, play an important role in port governance.

**Renegotiation**, whether due to contract incompleteness or opportunism, can eliminate the benefits of a competitive allocation mechanism. Essentially, an auction winner will be the best negotiator, not necessarily the best infrastructure operator. Efforts should be made to restrict renegotiation to non-opportunistic situations, such as unexpected events outside the control of the parties.

A concession agreement typically contains provisions to protect the terminal operator and port authority against arbitrary and early **cancellation**. However, it can also include provisions that enable the port authority to (unilaterally) end the concession if the terminal operator does not meet certain preset performance indicators.

## 7.2 Throughput guarantees

The most common **performance clauses** in concession agreements relate to **cargo throughput**. The port authority or government agency can indicate upfront a **minimum throughput** to be guaranteed by the concessionaire, especially for existing berths or terminals. This should encourage the operator to market the port services, attract maritime trade and optimize terminal and land usage. In cases where the terminal operator does not meet the objectives as set up in the concession agreement, a penalty will be paid to the port authority (e.g. a fixed amount per ton or TEU short) or, in the most extreme case, the concession will be rescinded.

In principle, throughput guarantees help secure a reasonable level of land productivity, reach high terminal utilization rates, and lower the entry barriers to newcomers. This is particularly the case if the port authority follows a retracting policy or reallocates certain parts of the terminal due to under-utilization.

## 7.3 Effectiveness of sanctions in concession agreements

Concession agreements can have a considerable influence on overall port performance. A poorly-designed lease contract can lead to situations where the port authority has no legal means to penalize inefficient companies or end the contract unilaterally. The resulting **underutilization of valuable land and infrastructure** undermines the growth potential of the port.

Whatever the explicit objectives of the concession may be, each lease contract should contain an explicit list of **penalties** that will be incurred where the rules are infringed. With the emergence of international terminal operators, some of them shipping line branches, port authorities are confronted with influential and footloose players. Fierce competition and the fear of traffic losses might make port authorities less observant and strict concerning the enforcement of the concession agreement rules.

In a well-tailored concession contract, sanctions are such that the parties fail to comply with rules only when non-compliance is overwhelmingly beneficial to them. Excessive penalties give the contract a rigidity that is inefficient, meaning that only **credible penalties** should be included in a concession agreement. Credible penalties are those that the port authority will have an interest in implementing if a violation occurs. For instance, a penalty can be imposed on a terminal operator for not meeting a minimum throughput. Non-credible penalties are not effective because their presence in the concession agreement weakens its reliability and legal certainty. They encourage the terminal operator to violate the rules or try to challenge any decision it does not like. In an environment with powerful and footloose market players, this represents a highly undesirable position for a port authority.

Threats of imposing **severe penalties**, such as **contract termination**, could be detrimental to the relationship between the port authority and terminal operator and may lack credibility. A way out could be to include a range of penalties in the concession agreement. For example, financial penalties can be incrementally imposed with the ultimate sanction of contract termination.

A port authority might also consider rewarding terminal operators that are performing above expectations. **Penalties and bonuses** should ideally reflect the economic costs and benefits of the behaviors the port authority wishes to prevent or promote. For example, penalties may be related to the economic loss caused by not reaching the throughput levels set out in the concession agreement. The economic loss includes terminal-related elements (terminal underutilization) and broader economic elements, such as missed added-value and employment.

# Chapter 3.3  Financialization and terminal funding

*Port terminals are capital-intensive assets that require investments for their construction, expansion, and maintenance. This capital needs to be provided by financial mechanisms on which the port terminal industry relies. Complex relationships between port terminals and the finance industry have been established.*

## 1 THE FINANCIALIZATION OF THE TERMINAL INDUSTRY

Conventionally, terminal ownership and operation were mainly assumed by the public sector through port authorities. The provision of capital for port infrastructure projects was the responsibility of the public sector. However, productivity levels tended to be low, and returns on public investments were limited. As privatization took shape, the dominant model shifted to port authorities being landlords, and the terminal operating business drastically changed. From a situation of fragmentation, the terminal and stevedoring industry expanded substantially with the emergence of global terminal operators controlling large multinational portfolios of terminal assets.

In the early 2000s, the terminal operation business reached a phase of rapid global expansion, on a par with the rapid traffic growth supported by the shipping industry. Some corporate terminal networks were driven by strong demand and new greenfield terminal developments, and by a series of large-scale acquisitions and multiple entries to boost expansion strategies, such as the take-over of CSX World Terminals and P&O Ports by DP World in 2004. This process was accelerated due to **port reforms** across the world and the evolving balance of power between shipping lines and terminal operators.

Simultaneously, the port and maritime industry has been subjected to increased **financialization**, implying that financial institutions play a growing

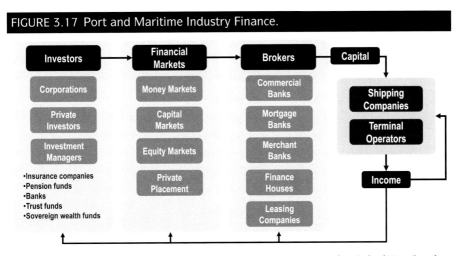

FIGURE 3.17 Port and Maritime Industry Finance.

Source: Adapted from Stopford (1997 & 2009) *Maritime Economics*, 2nd & 3rd edition, London: Routledge.

role. Financial holdings such as investment banks, pension funds, and sovereign wealth funds, entered the market by providing large capital pools unavailable in the industry beforehand. The port terminal sector was seen as an attractive asset class having a potential for revenue generation. In more general terms, the financial sector provided capital for firms related to terminal operations and contributed to their remarkable expansion (Figure 3.17). For example, container terminal operators typically financially outperform container shipping lines, which are also strongly asset-based. An emerging class of terminal operators took the form of holdings backed by large pools of capital, using this capital to rapidly expand, particularly by acquiring terminal assets which became part of a portfolio of port terminals.

The financing of the port and shipping industries comes from several sources, but it is commonly the responsibility of specialized brokers with close relationships with the industry. The income is used to directly finance the operational and capital requirements of shipping companies and terminal operators as well as payback dividends to the institutions providing capital. In such a context, the maritime industry most shapes the allocation of investment capital, and the financial sector provides this capital based upon merit and expected levels of return. Those are strongly derived from existing trade volume and its growth potential. In recent decades globalization has expanded maritime trade substantially, which has attracted large capital sums. Containerization in particular increased the capital intensiveness of the industry, which again stimulated additional investments. Another important trend has also been the more direct involvement of investors, such as insurance companies and pension funds (sovereign wealth funds). The conventional link between brokers and the maritime industry is becoming more tenuous.

> *Financialization refers to the increasing role of financial motives, financial markets, financial actors, and financial institutions in port terminals, ranging from the provision of capital to involvement in terminal operations.*

When ports face terminal capacity constraints, financial holdings, independent terminal operators, and carrier-related terminal operators are willing to pay premium prices to acquire or develop terminal assets. The unintended consequence of financialization was that an increasing quantity of capital was chasing an asset class that could only be expanded at a slow pace, which resulted in **asset inflation** within the terminal industry during the 2000s. Financial bubbles have historically characterized sectorial investments such as real estate and high technology, and the terminal industry experienced such a process in the 2000s. The 2008–2009 financial crisis that resulted from cross-sectorial asset inflation and the resulting defaults led terminal operators and their financial actors to reassess risks and move away from previous aggressive expansion strategies.

After the financial crisis, **financial institutions** became more cautious and more demanding about terms and project characteristics. Terminal operators are also more prone to selling stakes in terminal assets for financial relief while keeping their role as operators. This commonly involves a financial holding seeking an opportunity to acquire terminal assets while leaving the existing terminal operator taking care of operations.

## 2 RISKS AND TERMINAL INVESTMENTS

### 2.1 Port terminals as financial risk factors

The terminal operating sector has its own set of risk factors to be considered in capital investment, some of them related to the financial sector, but many related to its inherent business and operational conditions. The overall risks are (Figure 3.18):

- Pure **financial risks** include **capital and currency risks**. There is a risk of losing the **investment capital** through devaluation or default, particularly since a terminal requires a large capital investment. The amortization of this capital takes at least a decade. The higher the margin taken on the asset, the higher is the risk of this asset becoming illiquid. Since

FIGURE 3.18 Risks Associated with Terminal Investments

| | |
|---|---|
| **Financial** | • Capital and currency risks.<br>• Lost of investment capital. |
| **Market** | • Changes in supply or demand.<br>• Traffic fluctuations and contestability.<br>• Energy costs. |
| **Political & Regulatory** | • Changes in commercial environment.<br>• Changes in regulatory framework. |
| **Concentration** | • Dependency on a specific region/market.<br>• Availability of a large cargo base. |
| **Moral Hazard** | • Embeddedness with public sector.<br>• Misallocation of public funds. |

terminals are used as co-laterals for capital investment, the capital risk is low if one expects that the value of this asset will rise and that a buyer could be found. However, there is a risk of the situation changing. Moreover, terminal operators generally face currency risks due to fluctuations in exchange rates, including in the case of major currencies.

- **Market risks** include unforeseen changes in demand and supply. This risk is strongly embedded within the **regional economic and commercial geography** of the terminal portfolio as well as the **structure of maritime shipping networks**. Intermediate hub ports with a strong focus on transshipment operations are particularly vulnerable and are among the riskiest terminal investment projects. With increasing competition for port hinterlands, the contestability of gateway traffic is also more acute. Thus, market risks may equally be considered as **revenue or investment risks**. They compound capital risk in a terminal by impacting the length of the amortization and the intervening changes in demand due to **traffic fluctuations and contestability**. Market risks are very explicit in **concession contracts**. For example, terminal operating companies often face high throughput guarantees in concession agreements. Additional internal micro-level market risks, such as **energy cost risks**, affect a terminal's position. Energy is one of the main operating costs for shipping and terminal assets. Terminal operators have conventionally not applied energy costs hedging, compared to shipping lines that typically try to protect themselves through either hedging operations or bunker fuel surcharges.

- **Political and regulatory risks** concern international trade and manufacturing issues. For terminals, these involve the risk of arbitrary changes in the commercial environment due to political expediency, favoritism towards a carrier or operator, and even confiscation (nationalization). Even if recent decades have seen an environment more open to trade and liberalization, there are risks that countervailing forces such as protectionism can emerge. Entering the market at a specific point in time means that longer term regulatory changes are unforeseeable, particularly since terminal concessions can last for over 20 years. Regulatory risks refer to unexpected changes in the competition, such as in the incumbents or changes in the market strategy of competitors. It can also involve regulatory changes and planning conditions or more expensive operational models. For terminal operators, the regulatory framework for concession renewal increases the risk in relation to the committed investment during the early stages of operation.

- **Market concentration and specialization risks** are common when a player focuses on a specific region or a type of service. Containerization and economies of scale in mega-ships have expanded specialization risks, as they assume the availability of large freight volumes. In contrast, concentration reduces port of call options. With better hinterland access, the traditional markets of many terminals are highly contestable. A concentration of a portfolio in a specific market may lead to high returns if economic prospects are better than expected but to negative multiplying effects if economic conditions are even slightly lower than expected.

- **Moral hazard risk.** Many port terminals are either public or have strong relationships with the public sector since governments and sovereign wealth funds can be stakeholders. Several are perceived to be of national strategic interest. If they face financial difficulties, they have the opportunity to use their political embeddedness to access public capital or private capital guaranteed by the public sector. This can potentially lead to **misallocations** (being 'too big to fail'), enabling less high performing operators to remain in business who, otherwise, would have been forced to rationalize their assets. There is a link between **moral hazard risk** and **political risk**. Policymakers can have strategic reasons to protect a terminal operator from defaulting, such as maintaining operations at a port judged to be crucial for a national economy.

## 2.2 Port specific risks for terminal operators

The size of the infrastructure and superstructure for terminal development adds to investment risks. To develop a terminal, an operator might have to invest in developing or improving the infrastructure and the superstructure of a terminal, which is capital intensive. The larger these infrastructures, the higher the sunk costs in the facility. The risks associated with port or terminal investments vary depending on the nature of the market and the stage of the development of the port. Public actors decide about the terms of a concession, and terminal operators decide to bid and assume responsibilities of terminal operations for a period that commonly exceeds two decades.

The probability of occurrence of terminal-specific risks relates to the stage of development of the terminal site to be operated by a private actor, which might invest in:

1. An **undeveloped site** where the operator will have to develop infrastructure.
2. A **greenfield site** with infrastructure developed to the site boundary.
3. An **improved site** with a quay line and paved yard but without buildings or handling equipment.
4. A site with **all civil works completed** but the operator supplies quay cranes and yard handling equipment.
5. A **fully developed site** including quay cranes but the operator supplies yard handling equipment.

This condition is closely related to the technical, as well as the financial and market risks assumed, with the first option (1) being associated with the highest technical risk, and a declining risk as we head towards the last option (5) where technical risk transfer is the lowest. **Technical risks** ultimately result in delays and cost overruns or both, including in relation to:

- The application of innovative techniques and technologies.
- Design changes, including terminal function.
- Land acquisition and availability.
- Delays in project approvals and permits.
- Changes in construction legislation and default by the contractor.
- Archaeological findings.
- Construction contract variations or default from one of the contractors.
- Availability of finance (cash flow) and force majeure such as a natural disaster.

Market risks may depend on the size of the investment. Still, their level also reflects the uncertainty in predicted traffic volumes, transport demand, and the willingness of users to call at a particular terminal and pay for services rendered. Demand predictions and forecasts are sensitive to uncertainties and strategic or optimism bias facilitated by less established markets. Due to underestimated traffic volumes, terminals in these markets are very sensitive to income, industrial production, economic growth, and disruptions due to economic shocks, such as the financial crisis of 2008–2009 or the COVID-19 pandemic.

The probability of risk exposure depends on the nature of the market for the particular port or terminal and results from the presence of alternative conditions:

1. **No established regional trade** with projections based on unproven market expectations, such as those associated with a new free trade zone.
2. **Established regional trade** with substantial transshipment.
3. **Established hinterland general cargo** trade but with a low market penetration factor.
4. **Established regional and national trade** but open to competition from other terminal operators within the same or a nearby port.
5. **Established container trade** and need for facilities upgrade.

The probability of market risk, in general, varies from highest in the first case (1) to lowest in the last (5). Given the intervening changes in demand due to traffic fluctuations, and contestability on the supply side (intermediate hubs are particularly contestable), market risk is directly connected to investment risk in a terminal due to the amortization length. In recent years this risk was abated by the surge in transshipment throughput as maritime shipping companies organized the networks to cope with the growth in long-distance trade and economies of scale. With emerging hinterland access regimes, the contestability of gateway traffic is also more acute.

An environmental component of risks is also present in all terminal investments, though not unique to the industry. Project design, environmental impacts assessments, and respective approvals and permits are the norm. The risk associated with prerequisites in securing construction, maintenance, and expansion of a terminal is common in all transport projects. Addressing environmental risks might be costly and, perhaps more importantly, result in unnecessary delays in terminal operators' strategies. Also, growing environmental concerns increase the risks of new environmental legislation, which may influence the operation and maintenance of a terminal. Environmental risks are related to the size of the terminal, with more complex operations being exposed to greater risks. At the same time, they are associated with the location, which is connected with the country and its respective national and international obligations.

## 2.3 Implications for concessions

All risks are well known to the industry and embedded in its **business strategies**. A common risk minimization strategy is to launch large terminal projects in phases, following developments in port services demand. These phases can be planned to accompany expected volume growth, and financial support can be secured accordingly. While capital could not have been readily secured for a large terminal capacity development project, such capital can be made available on an incremental basis and based on realized outcomes from investments in prior phases.

Global terminal operators follow a careful and selective approach when bidding for new terminal concessions, acquiring terminal assets, and selecting partnerships. They are also hedging risks by opting for more complex ownership and partnership structures with shipping lines, financial holdings, and other organizations.

## 3 FUNDING AND FINANCING OF TERMINAL DEVELOPMENT

Terminal capacity investments are very costly given their capital-intensive nature. Because of the costs involved, port managers and terminal operators are typically inclined to first stretch existing capacity via measures leading to better terminal planning and more optimized port operations. It is easier to provide superstructures such as better equipment for improving the stacking density than expand the terminal footprint. It is only when capacity stretching has been exhausted that additional capacity should be made available. Such projects require large sums of capital from various public and private sources through funding and financing mechanisms.

> *Funding entails the provision of money at no interest for developing the port project (e.g. state grants, internal reserves). The capital is not necessarily expected to be recovered.*
>
> *Financing implies that the money lent is regarded as an investment and comes at an interest rate (e.g. commercial and investment banks, bond financing) or required rate of return for the investor. The capital is expected to be recovered.*

In practice, matching demand and supply is not an easy task given the long lead time to plan, construct, and start up new port and terminal infrastructure. Finding a suitable timing to initiate the planning and implementation phases of new port infrastructure is, therefore, a challenge prone to risks. There is always the imminent risk of creating overcapacity in cases where a port extension project does not induce growth in port demand. The timing of capacity expansion and a good assessment of future demand is crucial to position the port for sustained growth and secure suitable funding sources for capacity extensions.

Funding strategies for costly port investments are primarily constrained by a port's institutional position. Pure public or tool ports, for example, are limited to funding sources obtained from national funds. Developing countries face increased constraints on the level of public funding sources available to develop port infrastructure due to other national infrastructural and social priorities. In these circumstances, the port must compete in the political arena, where political interest groups influence priorities, to secure capital in competition with other projects.

There are five major sources of funding and finance available for port terminal infrastructure development (Figure 3.19):

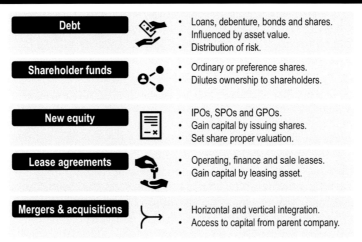

FIGURE 3.19 Sources of Funding and Finance for Port Terminals

- **Debt** can comprise conventional loans, debentures (loan certificates), bonds, and convertible preference shares. Interest payments (the cost of debt) can be expensive, and defaulting on contractual repayment obligations can result in the forfeiture of assets, depending on the terms of the debt agreement. In general, banks or other lenders are susceptible to the project assets and their potential market value. In evaluating an investment project, they assess the extent to which the project assets remain within the operating authority or company. Banks and other lenders are also strict when it comes to risk distribution. They favor a setting where all risks associated with the port infrastructure project are assumed and passed on to the appropriate actor. For example, lenders might insist on passing the risk to the other project participants through contracts, such as a construction, operation, and maintenance contract.
- **Shareholder funds** in the form of ordinary shares or preference shares. They are similar to debt but with equity characteristics or shareholder reserves that are re-invested retained earnings. A diverse shareholding dilutes ownership, relinquishing control to majority shareholders. The cost of a share is essentially measured as the required rate of return on the investment from shareholders. However, in the case of retained earnings, these funds are not a free source of finance, and the required rate of return is essentially the cost of equity because funds belong to equity investors, not the firm.
- **New equity issues**, in the form of initial public offering (IPO; the first issuance of shares on a stock exchange) or a seasoned public offering (SPO) or a general public offering (GPO). Methods of issuing seasoned equity include the private placement of shares to a single or small group of investors, employee options, or a rights offering (a right to purchase shares with a price concession). A GPO is similar to an IPO but with generally lower underwriting costs. A most noteworthy feature of a GPO is that, generally, the market identifies a GPO as a

signal that management thinks the firm is overvalued. The required rate of return is lower than the correct rate of return, implying a cheap source of funds or the market has overestimated the firm's future free cash flows. Risks for shareholders associated with shares as a finance source reside in how value is affected (gain/loss value) on the share trading market.

- **Lease agreements** comprise pure operating leases, finance leases (in substance a loan), or sale and leaseback agreements. Terminal operation concession agreements are essentially long-term operational leases used extensively for private participation in ports. The government or a public authority holds the property rights of the facilities throughout the concession period and receives lease payments on the assets. The private partner bears the production and commercial risks, so it has an incentive to innovate, optimize, and improve its services. Terminal concession and lease-operate arrangements are common in landlord ports. The financial side of a concession agreement remains a balancing act. High concession fees, royalty payments, and revenue sharing stipulations are detrimental to returns on investment. They could decrease the investment potential of the incumbent terminal operator and deter future investors. Low payments could negatively affect the revenue base of the public (port) authority, so it can no longer support its landlord functions. Finance leases are becoming more difficult to justify due to advances in accounting practices and vigilance against tax avoidance. The accounting treatment and favorable tax concessions are less evident with the adoption of international financial reporting standards.
- **Mergers and acquisitions**. These comprise horizontal integration mergers with firms in the same line of business and vertical integration mergers with firms higher or lower in the value chain, such as between suppliers and customers. Besides, there are also conglomerate mergers whereby a merger occurs with a completely unrelated firm to realize diversification benefits and management buyouts. This can also involve a management buyout (MBO). MBOs are an extreme form of divestiture. The overriding objective of a merger is to create synergy, where the sum of the merged firm is greater than the sum of the individual (firm) parts. Economic value is generated through efficiencies, increased expertise, and greater access to funding. Notably, mergers and acquisitions have come under increased scrutiny because of anti-competitive and antitrust legislation.

Excluded from the above five sources of port terminal finance are **fiscal and government funds** associated with public policy and national commercial strategic objectives.

Recent decades have seen a substantial expansion of terminal facilities that required the injection of capital coming from various public and private sources. The port terminal industry has privatized and internationalized to cope with this demand, establishing partnerships with financial institutions. As global trade matures, investment priorities are likely to shift towards upgrading existing facilities, particularly automation and digitalization.

# Chapter 3.4  Container terminal design and equipment

*Container terminals have design considerations and equipment uses that vary according to their function.*

## 1 THE DESIGN OF CONTAINER TERMINALS

Once they started emerging in the 1960s, container terminals brought an entirely new era in port development and terminal design. One of the first impacts concerned the **required footprint**, which expanded. A large container terminal occupies a substantial area, mainly because of storage requirements, even if this storage is short term, usually three to five days (Box 3.5). Where possible, early container terminals were created from converting existing general cargo terminals by tearing down on-dock warehouses to provide stacking yards. The outcome has been a wide variety of terminal configurations and a diversity between the available nautical profile and the yard footprint.

Many ports did not have enough available space to accommodate the footprint for container terminal operations, which required the setting up of new facilities and new port areas. This gave opportunities to experiment with container terminal design to improve its operations. The design and operations of container terminals take into consideration the following constraints:

- The **available land footprint** that will limit terminal capacity, particularly yard storage.
- The **nautical profile** of the site that will command maximum ship size and the number of ships that can be serviced at a given time.
- The **available transport infrastructures** supporting the connectivity of the terminal with its hinterland.

### Box 3.5  Terminal footprint, selected container ports

*The optimal shape of a container terminal is a rectangle that allows sufficient berthing space and a corresponding yard footprint. However, such an ideal footprint is rarely found, particularly in older terminals, due to physical and site constraints. The outcome is a variety of container terminal footprints that are relatively rectangular if the site allows, but each terminal has faced specific constraints in its development (Figure 3.20). The following footprint development strategies are noted:*

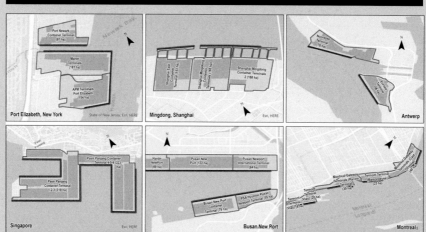

FIGURE 3.20 Terminal Footprint, Selected Terminals in a Sample of Container Ports

**Reconversion.** *A container terminal can be created by reconverting existing port facilities that have been abandoned or are seen as less profitable. This tends to be a common and low-cost option for existing ports, but the challenge is an effective reconversion. For instance, the Port Elizabeth complex (New York) is among the oldest container terminal facilities and began operation in the 1960s. The terminals were built over reconverted break-bulk and warehousing facilities that were gradually torn down as container traffic grew. For this complex, the port did not expand its total footprint but reconverted towards containerization by removing marginalized port activities. In the 1990s, an on-dock rail facility was added between the APM and Maher terminals, which reduced the yard footprint but allowed better hinterland access. The case of Montreal underlines unique reconversion challenges as the container terminal facilities were forced to expand laterally due to the limited availability of adjacent real estate. This led to terminal footprints that are narrow and elongated.*

*Adaptation. A new terminal footprint can be adapted to mitigate the physical, technical, or real estate* limitations of a site, *leading to unique footprints. In the late 1980s and 1990s, two major container terminals were added to the port of Antwerp at a downstream location of the Scheldt River (Europa Terminal and Noordzee Terminal). These facilities were constrained by the available real estate footprint and the inability to expand into the Scheldt River through land reclamation. In the early 2000s, the port of Shanghai was expanding rapidly with new facilities downstream along the Yangtze River. For the Mingdong complex, shallow depths along the river banks and siltation made dredging costs prohibitive. To the container yard facilities were added a series of jetties and piers separating the berth areas to the yards, allowing use of the complex as a container port. The drawbacks of this adaptive footprint are longer pier to yard movements.*

*Land reclamation. The construction of new terminal facilities through the creation of an entirely new footprint, which allows for mitigating technical*

*limitations such as depth and the lack of real estate. These facilities tend to be rectangular and closer to optimal design but require substantial engineering and capital investments. They are common on mega port development projects where a suitable and available land footprint does not exist. In the late 1990s and early 2000s, both Singapore and Busan engaged in massive land reclamation projects to expand their transshipment facilities in new areas. The Pasir Panjang (Singapore) and Newport (Busan) terminals were designed to mainly serve the function of transshipment, implying that they are more rectangularly-shaped, which allows for more berth space as containers tend to spend less time in the yard.*

## 2 CONTAINER TERMINAL EQUIPMENT

To perform its operations, a container terminal relies on an array of **intermodal equipment**, including straddle carriers, gantry cranes, and portainers. The choice of equipment and its mix is related to a number of factors in terms of capital investment, volume, stacking density, and productivity.

- The **forklift** can be considered the most basic piece of intermodal equipment but has limitations and can handle only loaded 20-foot containers or empty containers of other dimensions. This is not a piece of equipment suitable for intermodal operations.
- The **holster truck** is designed to move containers loaded on chassis within terminals. Although it represents a low capital investment and can move containers at high speed, it is restricted to moving containers already loaded on chassis and therefore requires other equipment.
- The **straddle carrier** is a flexible piece of equipment that can be used for all intermodal operations such as loading/loading railcars and trucks and stacking containers up to three in height depending on whether the straddle carrier is a 3-high or 4-high. So, depending on the straddle carrier type, the stacking density may vary between 500 and 700 TEU per hectare. Straddle carriers are often used to move containers from piers to stacks.
- The **front-end loader** is a more restricted piece of equipment that can reach stacks of up to three full containers and can be used for double-stack intermodal rail operations. It can also be used to manage empty stacks by reaching up to eight empty containers in height.
- The **reach stacker** (also known as a side loader) is also a flexible piece of equipment performing intermodal operations for rail and trucks as well as the stacking of containers. Since reach stackers are limited to stacks of three full containers (four or five empty), they can support a stacking density of 500 TEU per hectare. They are often used in intermodal rail terminals and in maritime terminals for specialized moves (e.g. reefers).
- The **rubber-tired gantry** (RTG) is a fixed intermodal piece of equipment that is used for loading and unloading railcars from trucks in high-density terminals as it can span over up to four rail tracks. It is also used for stacking operations to manage densities of up to 1,000 TEU per hectare with stacks of up to four full containers or five empty containers. It can service eight to nine trucks per hour, which involves 30–40 container

movements since containers need to be reshuffled within their stacks. The RTG has higher acquisition costs but lower operational costs and fits well into regular container yard operations.

- The **rail-mounted gantry** (RMG) is a fixed piece of intermodal equipment that is widespan and can be used for intermodal operations over six to ten rail tracks. While they tend to be mostly used at port terminals for operations over large container stacks, new intermodal rail terminals are increasingly relying on RMGs to perform intermodal operations over a series of train tracks, often with some below crane space for track-side stacking. Several RMG models can swivel, allowing for perpendicular crane side loading and unloading. An RMG used solely for stacking can accommodate densities above 1,000 TEU per hectare (four full or five empty containers).

- The portainer or **ship-to-shore crane** (STS) is a gantry crane strictly used to load and unload containerships and comes in different sizes based upon the ship class they can accommodate. While a Panamax portainer can accommodate ships up to 13 containers in width, a Post-Panamax portainer reaches up to 16 containers alongside each other. The latest class of portainers is dubbed 'Ultra Post Panamax' and can handle the latest generation of containerships of 24,000 TEU by spanning up to 24 containers. The latest cranes can lift more than 150 tons at a time. Containers have to be brought to the portainer by holsters using tractor/chassis combinations, straddle carriers or automated guided vehicles (AGV).

The basic structure of portainers consists of the following parts:

- The **main boom** is the part that is hanging over the ship. Manufacturers provide the market with many and different types of main booms. Low profile STS cranes exist where the boom is able either to push forwards or to push in above vessel deck. These cranes are suitable for maximum crane height restrictions (for example, near airports) and reduced visual impact.

- The **trolley** is the part of the crane that drives over the mean boom. The trolley is the supporting structure for the spreader and the cabin. Trolleys have to support the hoisting mechanism and the mechanism that enables the trolley to ride over the main boom.

- The **spreader** is the device that picks up the containers and is mounted on the trolley with cables. Spreaders have twist locks on each corner to secure the container during hoisting. Spreader technology has evolved, with quite a few portainers now able to perform twin and tandem lifting. Equipment manufacturers have also tested triple lifting and systems that can handle even more containers in one move.

- The **cabin** is the part of the crane housing its operator. The cabin can be accessed by stairs or elevator. A remotely operated STS does not have a cabin.

- The **legs** (waterside leg or WS and landside leg or LS) of the crane generate the height. The height of the cranes has been increasing over the years due to the increasing stacking height of containers above the ship's deck (now up to 11 containers above decks and 12 below deck). In general, the

WS leg is thicker than the LS leg. This is because the WS leg has to support more moment forces. Legs can be vertical, but some of the WS legs have a slight angle in the LS direction.

- **Cable reel** and power-supply allow flexibility during loading and unloading of the ships and are necessary for the cranes to move along the quay. STS cranes are commonly powered by two types of power supply. The first is a diesel engine-driven generator located on top of the crane and the second is electric power provided from the dock by the terminal facility. Most STS cranes are electrically powered and therefore need to be connected to a power grid. This connection is realized by huge cables that lie in gutters over the quay. The voltage that they require may range from 4,000 to 13,200 volts. When the crane needs to move, the cable must roll on-roll off by the motorized reel.
- **A boogie set** and wheels support the crane on the quay. The boogie set is the part of the crane that is under the leg of each corner, meaning that a crane has four boogie sets. Typically, a crane has eight wheels per corner.

The ongoing **automation** of terminals is replacing the manually operated conventional equipment with semi or fully automated improvements. This is particularly the case for portainers, gantries, and straddle carriers, which can be remotely controlled.

## 3 MARITIME OPERATIONS

The first segment of the container terminal concerns maritime operations. Ship turnaround times are expected to be short, and the terminal must accommodate the schedule integrity of shipping lines. The **docking area** is a berth where a containership can dock, with technical specifications such as length and draft. These specifications have been under pressure in recent decades as the size of containerships increased, demanding longer piers and deeper drafts. A standard post-Panamax containership of 8,000 TEU requires about 325 meters of docking space as well as a draft of about 45 feet (13 meters). Ships of the Neo-Panamax class (12,500 TEU) require 370 meters and a draft of 50 feet (15.2 meters). Thus, a pier length of 400 meters is expected to be the right size to accommodate the largest containerships. The largest container vessels have a length overall (LOA) of some 400m, requiring a berth length of 450m. Some terminals have separate facilities for handling barges (such as Antwerp and Rotterdam), although most barges can be handled alongside the deepsea quays.

Terminal depth represents the available draft at existing terminals that can differ from channel depth, which is the draft of the port access channel(s). Docking depth and pier length may limit the number of slots that can accommodate a deep draft vessel within a port. The drafts of a large sample of commercial ports reveal two major clusters (Figure 3.21). The first is around the Panamax standard of about 12 meters, and the second is around 15-16 meters. The introduction of larger containerships, namely the post-Panamax plus class (draft above 12 meters), imposes limitations on available port calls. Draft considerations have become a key component in the commercial viability of ports.

FIGURE 3.21 Terminal Depth at Selected Ports

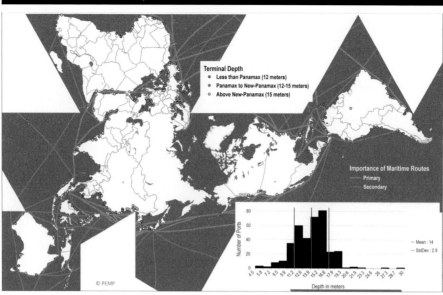

© PEMP

**Container cranes** represent the interface between the containership and the dock. Cranes have technical specifications in terms of the number of movements per hour, maximum weight, and lateral coverage. A gantry crane can perform about one movement (loading or unloading) every two minutes. The larger the number of cranes assigned to the transshipment process, the faster it can take place. However, significant portside capabilities must be present to accommodate this throughput.

**Aprons** (loading/unloading areas) are directly adjacent to the piers and under the gantry cranes (portainers). They are the interaction between the cranes and the storage areas where containers are either brought in to be lifted on the containership or unloaded to be immediately picked up and brought to storage areas. This is mainly done with straddlers or holsters. In the case of straddle carriers, the containers are left on the ground, while with holsters, the containers are loaded from or unloaded to a chassis. The usage of straddle carriers is more common as it enables movement of containers directly from dockside to the stack (or vice versa). Still, terminal automation has seen the introduction of automated holsters that carry containers from the dockside to stacking areas.

## 4 YARD AND AUXILIARY OPERATIONS

**Container storage** represents a temporary buffer zone where containers are left while the assigned containership is available to be loaded or while waiting to be picked up for inland distribution. The larger the containerships handled by a port, the larger the required container storage yard. Container storage can be arranged by shipbound (export) and landbound (import) stacks of containers. For shared terminal facilities, stacks can even be sub-divided according to

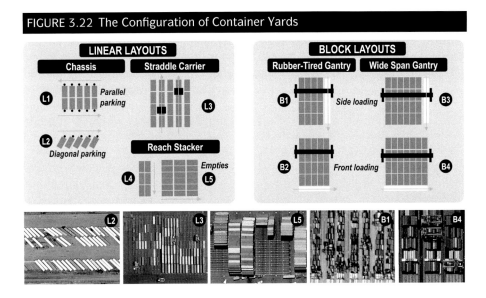

FIGURE 3.22 The Configuration of Container Yards

shippers. The stacking density of container storage varies depending on the selected equipment and the yard configuration (Figure 3.22).

For **linear layout** configurations, containers are either stored on a chassis (rare for port terminals but more common for rail terminals) or on linear stacks of two or three containers in height that can be circulated over by straddle carriers. **Block layouts** are serviced by rubber-tired gantry cranes or by rail-mounted (wide span) gantry cranes, enabling a higher storage density of at least four containers across (seven or eight for a wide span crane, if not more) and five full containers in height. However, higher stacking densities are linked with additional repositioning and rehandling of containers, requiring effective yard management systems. Rows of containers can be parallel or perpendicular to piers depending on the configuration and operations of the terminal.

Most terminals have a dedicated reefers (refrigerated containers) storage area where they can be plugged in, which represents, on average, about 5% of a terminal's stacking area. Specific storage areas are also assigned to empties, which can be stacked up to seven or eight containers in height due to less stringent weight limitations. Empty container stacks are easily distinguishable from loaded container stacks because of different stacking configurations; empty stacks are higher and denser. For terminals facing capacity pressures, the tendency has been to have empty container depots outside terminal facilities. The majority of container yards also have storage for refrigerated containers, which requires specialized equipment, namely electric plugs.

A series of on-site activities support a container terminal. The **management facility** (administrative building) of the terminal often has a control tower to ensure a level of visibility of the terminal area. This is where many complex logistical functions are performed, such as the assignment of delivered containers to a storage space location as well as the location and the loading or unloading sequence of containers by straddlers and holsters. Additionally, the complex task of designing the loading and unloading sequence of a containership is performed. With digitalization and automation, the administration building has become the information and telecommunication nexus of the terminal.

**Repair and maintenance** areas are where the regular maintenance of the terminal's heavy equipment is performed. **Chassis storage** areas are where empty chassis are stored while waiting to be allocated to a truck or a holster. While in North American terminals, chassis storage can take a notable amount of space because chassis are owned by pools, in the rest of the world trucking companies own the chassis and bring them to the terminal. The outcome is less space allocated for chassis storage. Usually, chassis are stored outside the terminal facility since chassis storage is a poor use of valuable terminal real estate.

## 5 HINTERLAND CONNECTIVITY

Port terminals are *connected to their hinterlands* through inland transportation modes. The **gate** represents the terminal's entry and exit point, handling up to 25 trucks at once for a large terminal facility. Truck drivers present proper documentation (bills of lading) for pick up or delivery. Most of the inspection is done remotely with cameras and intercom systems. An operator can remotely see the container identification number and verify if it corresponds to the bill of lading. Modern management systems no longer require paperwork since all the documentation is kept in an electronic format that is transmissible through secure connections. With appointment systems, the priority is to verify the identity of the truck driver, the truck, the container, and the chassis, which are all registered.

For a delivery, the truck is assigned to a specific slot at the **truck drop/pick up area** where the chassis holding the container will be left to be picked up by a holster, a straddle carrier, or a gantry crane for more recent terminal designs. For a pickup, the truck will be assigned to a slot in a waiting area while the container is being picked up from a storage area, put on a chassis (if the truck does not bring its own chassis), and brought to the proper slot. The truck will then head out of the terminal, be inspected to ensure that the right container has been picked up, and head inland. If this is well managed (such as by use of an appointment system), the container will already be available for pick up (on a chassis in the truck drop/pick up area). However, delays for pick up can sometimes be considerable (hours) when a large containership has just delivered a significant batch of containers, and there is a 'rush' to be the first to pick them up. Therefore, substantial efforts have been made by terminal operators in recent years to improve the throughput of terminal gates through better design and with the application of information technologies, including appointment systems.

Many large container terminals have an adjacent rail terminal to which they are directly connected. **On-dock or near-dock rail terminals** enable the composition of large containerized unit trains that reach long-distance inland markets through inland ports. An important advantage of on-dock rail facilities compared with near-dock rail facilities is that the container does not have to clear the gate of the marine terminal. In North America, since container unit trains can be very long (longer than the container port terminal facility), segments are assembled in the port on-dock rail facility and brought to a near-dock facility for full unit train assembly.

## 6 CONVENTIONAL VS. AUTOMATED TERMINAL CONFIGURATION

There are two major port container terminal configurations: **conventional and automated**. The impacts of automation are not fully implemented on terminal operations, leading to changes in terminal configurations.

Although the function of both conventional and automated container terminals is the same (ship to shore transfer), their operations differ (Figure 3.23). In a conventional terminal, containers are brought to a pickup/drop-off area, where they will be moved to the stacking area by a holster truck or a straddle carrier. Then, they will be brought quayside by another holster truck or straddle carrier when ready to be loaded onto a ship. The emerging automated container terminal paradigm relies on block layouts that are perpendicular to the piers. These stacking blocks are serviced by automated stacking cranes (ASC), allowing quick storage and retrieval. On the gate-side, stacks are serviced by trucks that have their containers picked up by an ASC. On the pier-side, containers are retrieved by straddle carriers or automated guided vehicles (AGV; for fully automated terminals) and brought to the end of a stack. The main differences between conventional and automated container terminal configurations are that the latter reduce horizontal ground movements and remove vehicles from the stacking areas, enabling a higher stacking density.

Areas close to container terminals tend to have a high concentration of activities linked to freight distribution, such as distribution centers, empty container storage depots, trucking companies, and large retailers. This is commonly associated with high congestion levels around the port terminal facilities. To deal with the issue, the design of several container terminals has been modified to include coordination between on-dock rail facilities and satellite terminals as well as container depots. The goal is to transfer a part of the footprint to another less constrained location.

FIGURE 3.23 Conventional and Automated Container Terminal Configurations

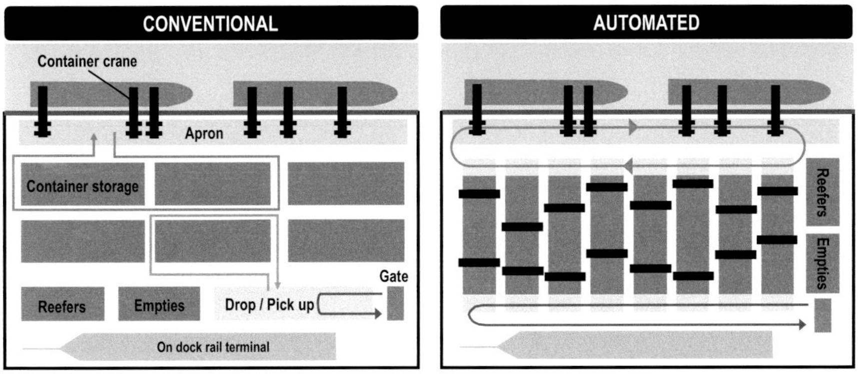

## 7 TERMINAL CAPACITY USE AND OPTIMIZATION

Terminal equipment is combined to form an integrated container terminal system. The total terminal capacity is determined by the interaction between three levels, which are the quay, the yard, and the gate system (Figure 3.24):

- **Ship or quay-related operational challenges** include the berth allocation problem (BAP), the vessel stowage planning problem, and the quay crane assignment/scheduling problem (QCAP). In most cases, berth and quay crane planning are combined in the integrated berth allocation and quay crane assignment problem (BACAP).
- The **yard allocation problem** (YAP) involves the design of the stacking area (in terms of stacking height, slot capacity, etc.) or the optimization of container storage and stacking operations as a function of container type (reefer, dry, etc.), container flow (import, export, transshipment, empties) and dwell time characteristics. Yard-related issues also deal with intra-terminal transport, such as the transport between the quayside and the stacking area and the intra-terminal reshuffling of containers. Here, the optimization of yard operations usually involves an integrated approach, such as by simultaneously determining the yard crane schedules and the vehicle parking positions.
- **Gate optimization** deals with the connectivity of terminals to landside transportation modes, such as rail transport, inland barges, and trucking. Typical operational challenges in this field include the truck gate process optimization problem, gate appointment systems, the equipment assignment problem, and the modal separation on a terminal in space and time.

The optimal container terminal design is rectangular, but the relationship between water, yard, and gate capacity varies according to the terminal function. Gateway terminals tend to be more square-shaped (more yard space),

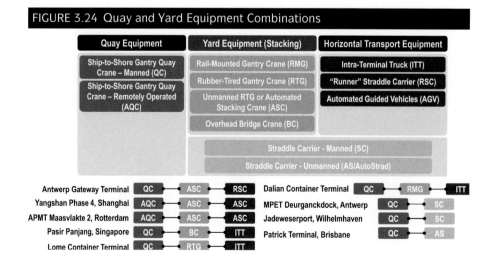

FIGURE 3.24 Quay and Yard Equipment Combinations

while transshipment hubs tend to be elongated rectangles (more berth space) (Box 3.6). Terminal optimization is about optimizing the quay, yard, and gate operations individually and finding an optimal balance between the three capacity dimensions. For example, terminal operators can find a better balance between quay and yard capacity by focusing on hardware investments (infrastructure, equipment), software (optimizations using IT solutions), and orgware (for example, through pricing incentives).

In the past decades, terminal operators have developed a more integrated view on container terminal optimization, often relying on simulation approaches to analyze terminal operations from a system-based perspective combining BAP/QCAP/BACAP with YAP. Discrete-event simulation remains one of the most popular techniques in terminal operations modeling. Other techniques have been used, such as agent-based modeling, network-based modeling, simulation-based education, and web-based simulation. These optimization techniques are incorporated in terminal design applications and Terminal Operating Systems (TOS). Artificial intelligence (AI) and advanced machine learning have also found their way to terminal optimization.

## Box 3.6 Balancing water and yard capacity

*An important element of container terminal design and configuration concerns the ratio between the water and the yard capacity. The desired outcome is related to the function of the terminal within shipping networks and its hinterland. Therefore, there is no optimal ratio as the ideal design is context-specific (Figure 3.25).*

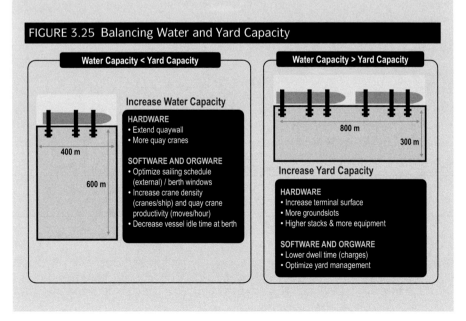

FIGURE 3.25 Balancing Water and Yard Capacity

*Water capacity lower than yard capacity. This mainly concerns ports that act as gateways to major commercial hinterlands, implying that the containers may spend more time in the yard (longer dwell time). It could also involve ports that have a constrained nautical profile, leaving limitations in piers. Increasing the water capacity can involve both the port's hardware and software, and also its orgware. From a hardware perspective, quay walls can be expanded, and more cranes can be added. From a software perspective, a series of optimizations can be attempted, mainly involving better management of berth windows and an increase in crane productivity. The term orgware refers to organizational and process-related adaptations.*

*Water capacity higher than yard capacity. This mainly concerns ports that act as transshipment hubs and where several ships need to be handled at any given time. It could also involve ports that are constrained from the landside, such as those with limited land for expansion and proximity to urban activities. From a hardware perspective, increasing port hardware implies expanding the yard surface (plus more ground slots) and adding yard equipment. From a software perspective, yard operations can be optimized, resulting in lower dwell times and more throughput for the same yard surface.*

*Still, container terminals can rarely have an optimal configuration due to the commercial environment in terms of foreland and hinterland activity and port site limitations regarding nautical profile and available land footprint.*

# Chapter 3.5 Bulk and break-bulk terminal design and equipment

*Dry bulk, liquid bulk, roll-on/roll-off (RoRo), and break-bulk terminals have a diversity of terminal designs and functions and a broad range of quay, yard and warehousing equipment.*

## 1 MAJOR DRY BULK TERMINALS

The term **major bulk** refers to commodities that are transported in very large quantities using bulk carriers. Three major components impact bulk terminal design:

- **Supply characteristics**. Resources carried by bulk are extracted according to geographic (minerals and fossil fuels) and climatic conditions (agricultural goods and wood products). Some, such as coal, iron ore, and petroleum, have a high level of concentration, while others, such as agricultural goods, are collected over extensive areas.
- **Demand characteristics**. Each bulk market has a demand-pull related to intermediary processing and manufacturing activities. The location of these facilities, usually adjacent to port sites, considers the demand for the resources over an extensive market and a material index (ratio of inputs over outputs). The demand for bulk commodities is usually managed by large commodity traders and brokers able to consolidate purchases and distribution in large quantities.

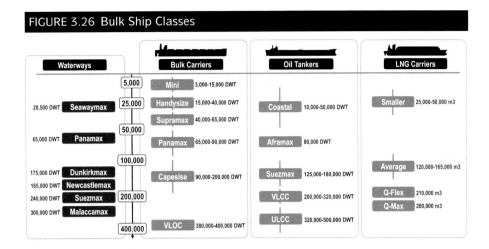

FIGURE 3.26 Bulk Ship Classes

- **Potential for economies of scale**. The economic rationale in using the largest ship size possible considering the geographical distribution of the supply and demand is fundamental in the bulk market. This potential is limited by the characteristics of the waterways at the port of origin, in transit (e.g. Panama, Suez), and at the port of destination. The outcome is a wide range of bulk ship classes trying to reconcile supply, demand, and economies of scale (Figure 3.26).

Major dry bulk commodities include iron ore, coal, and grains. They are not homogeneous as there are several grades of coal used for making steel (coking coal) and energy generation (steam coal). Each represents a different market, implying a segmentation of the bulk trades. Further, there is an important directionality to bulk trade, implying that export bulk terminals are designed rather differently from import bulk terminals:

- **Export terminals** for coals and iron ore combine stacker reclaimer systems and ship loaders to connect the yard to the bulk carriers. A good example of a major export terminal for dry bulk is Port Hedland in Australia, the world's largest coal export port. Export terminals facilitate outgoing cargo flows and are strongly synchronized with the inland transport system (mostly rail-based) that connects the mining areas to the terminal. Export terminals try to limit stocks but sometimes have to keep a large (unsold) stock to support commodity trade pricing. In most cases, export terminals handle a limited number of material types due to their location in relation to mining areas or due to their ownership, as many export terminals are owned by traders or mining companies. The location of many export terminals is a compromise between the hinterland and maritime accessibility.
- **Import terminals** for coal and iron ore use unloaders equipped with large grabs to discharge the commodities. There are several types of quay cranes and grabs available. The choice of the crane type depends on the operational needs of the terminal operator in terms of ship sizes to be served and minimum cargo handling productivity in tons per hour. Conveyor systems transport the discharged commodities along the quay and

on to the yard. As import terminals usually handle multiple types and grades of major bulks, stockpiles of bulk material are spread across the yard. The terminal surfaces of import terminals are quite large to avoid cross-contamination between stockpiles and comply with necessary certification requirements. Stacker reclaimers are used to transport the bulk products from the yard to the loading stations for seagoing vessels, inland barges, and railcars. A good example of a major import terminal for dry bulk is EMO in Rotterdam, one of the largest dry bulk terminals in Europe. Import terminals for handling major bulks rely heavily on rail and barge (where available) for hinterland transportation. They have to match services to both the waterside and the landside modalities. The most advanced bulk terminals are equipped with automated railcar loading/unloading systems. Terminal planning is quite challenging as vessels usually arrive in a stochastic manner, and the consignee selects landside services and inland modalities.

Bulk commodities are usually discharged using grabs attached to a crane. High capacity clamshell grabs offer high unloading rates and high efficiency. The bulk handling cranes can be positioned along the quay (quay crane), on a platform/pontoon (floating crane), or on the ship (deck crane):

- **Common quay crane types** include portal cranes (mounted on rails), jib cranes, and balanced hydraulic cranes. Lifting capacities can range from a few tons up to 85 tons. Slewing cranes are built with single jib and double jib designs. The main advantage of the double jib crane is the horizontal path of the load. During the luffing of the crane, the grab stays at practically the same height. Luffing is the vertical motion of a crane. Slewing is when a crane rotates around its vertical axis.
- **Floating cranes** can be used for cargo handling when few quays or no quays are available or the water depth alongside the quays is too shallow. Large bulk terminals might use floating cranes for direct ship-to-ship or ship-to-barge operations. Floating cranes can also be deployed for 'topping off' or 'lightening' operations on large bulk carriers (Panamax or Capesize) using ship-to-barge transfers (river) or ship-to-ship transfers (coast or river). In this manner, the vessel draft decreases to a level that allows entry in a port with restricted nautical access.
- **Deck cranes or derricks** are cranes installed on the vessel. They are particularly used in regions where ports lack the necessary cargo handling devices.

In some cases continuous unloaders and loaders are used:

- **Continuous ship unloaders** are equipped with an L-shaped, bucket-elevator-type unloading device that is suspended from the boom. The material to be unloaded is scooped up by the bucket elevator and transferred to a belt conveyor.
- **Ship loaders** are mounted on rails that are parallel to the ship and are fed by a conveyor belt. A belt conveyor is utilized on the boom and usually, a shuttle head provides complete coverage of the ship's hold. The discharge spout incorporates a rotating spoon, which allows the operator greater flexibility when placing the material.

Occasionally, the offshore handling of dry bulk cargo takes place which ranges from simple floating cranes to floating transfer stations with large offshore storage. Cranes are placed on one or more pontoons and connected to a cargo handling system consisting of hoppers, conveyors and ship loaders. The ship loaders have a large outreach and sufficient air draft to be able to deliver cargo into the holds of a large vessel, on ballast. In some cases, the transshipment equipment is placed on a ship which is anchored next to other dry bulk carriers.

Coal and iron ore terminals might offer additional services such as washing, screening to separate the bulk material into different grades, blending silos, and compacting to prevent spontaneous combustion. Terminals limit environmental effects by investing in technology to save energy and reduce noise and dust emissions.

**Dust control** is a key concern at dry bulk terminals. Whenever a transfer of coal or iron ore occurs, there is a potential to break the lumps, resulting in dust, which can be spread by crosswinds. Once the coal or iron ore is stockpiled, dust can still be a problem. Even if it arrives wet, wind across the stockpile can evaporate the moisture and dust will be lifted. Any vehicles driving over crushed lumps will also raise dust. Several measures are taken to reduce dust emission, such as:

- **Dust covers** on grabs and conveyors.
- **Fogging systems** that release small droplets of water into the air, forcing dust to precipitate.
- **Sprinkler systems** spray water on stockpiles to keep them damped down. This includes an adapted drainage system and on occasion a water recycling station.
- Optimized **stockpile design** such as avoiding edges that can dry quicker than a rounded surface.
- Add a **protective layer** over the stockpile such as a skin formed by a water additive.
- In case of loading operations in the vessel holds, **loading chutes with heavy-duty dust skirts** can be used in order to prevent dust cloud formation arising from the product falling onto the peak of the product pile in the hold.

The capacity of a dry bulk terminal to transload coal or iron ore is determined by many factors, such as the quay length, the yard dimensions, the quay and yard equipment, the stockpile patterns and heights, the storage time distribution of the bulk material, the number of types and/or grades handled, the terminal operating hours (waterside and landside), the arrival patterns, types and sizes of ships and land transport modes. The use of an existing terminal can be further optimized by improving berthing/unberthing procedures, optimizing vessel traffic rules, synchronizing vessel and landside operations, reducing downtime (caused by hatch changes, shift changes, or breakdowns), and installing provisions that allow all-weather operations. In some cases, dry bulk is not handled at terminals but using offshore handling facilities.

**Grain terminals** are designed to handle and store wheat, soy, and other grains and oilseeds. There are many models of both discontinuous systems (such as those using grabs) and continuous ship unloaders (CSU), including pneumatic chain, screw, or twin-belt machines. Grain elevators stockpile or store grains using bucket elevators or pneumatic conveyors that scoop up grain from a lower level and deposit it in a silo or other storage facility. Large grain terminals can have dozens of large silos located next to each other. Many grain terminals offer additional services such as cargo sieving in order to calibrate the grain, and fumigation. Many factors influence the performance of unloading systems, such as ship type and size, type of product, the number of product impurities, product density, adverse weather conditions, and down-times.

## 2 MINOR DRY BULK TERMINALS

Minor bulks include cargoes such as fertilizers, bulky agricultural products, cement, sand, petroleum coke, and metal scrap. While major bulks are often loaded in large bulk carriers (such as Capesize and Panamax vessels), minor bulks are usually transported by sea in smaller and more versatile vessels such as handymax ships and coasters. The term **minor bulk** is derived from the potential economies of scale that can be realized due to market size and demand patterns that are more dispersed than for major bulk trades. Just like for major bulks, minor bulks are placed or poured into cargo holds. The terminal superstructure includes:

- **Cranes and conveyors**. Portal quay cranes, jib cranes, mobile cranes, floating cranes, and loader/unloader systems are deployed to load and discharge minor bulks, combined with conveyor and elevator systems where required. The cranes are equipped with specialized grabs, mostly of the clamshell type. The grabs can be operated by ropes (single-rope, two-rope, or four-rope clamshell buckets), electro-hydraulically or diesel hydraulically.
- **Yard and warehouse vehicles**. The cargo handling operations are supported by different types of yard and warehouse vehicles such as bobcats, tractors, trailers, forklifts, and front-end loading shovels (fitted with a pusher).
- **Other equipment** at the yard and the covered storage facilities can include weighbridges, hoppers (where the product is loaded into trailers or trucks), blending silos, and bagging plant facilities.
- **Minor bulk storage facilities** can be in the open air or covered in warehouses and are typically sectioned off into separate bays to enable various products or grades to be stored.

Minor bulk terminals face a wide range of possible **operational risks** such as cross-contamination of cargo types, water ingress, and fire/ignition/explosion hazards. The handling of bulk ships can be rather dangerous, with specific rules and regulations related to cargo movement and immersion.

## 3 LIQUID BULK TERMINALS

**Liquid bulk terminals** are equipped to handle cargoes in liquid and gaseous forms, such as crude oil, oil products, LNG, and LPG. These products are shipped by oil tankers, chemical tankers, parcel tankers, and gas carriers. The **oil tanker fleet** consists of various ship sizes and has been particularly prone to economies of scale considering the global demand for petroleum, one of the most extensively traded commodities. A common size is the Very Large Crude Carrier (VLCC) of around 200,000 dwt. **LNG carriers** can be grouped into different sizes depending on the trade route concerned and service a market that has seen rapid growth. **Chemical and parcel tankers** are designed to carry an assortment of liquids, such as chemicals, or different grades of a liquid, like petroleum, at one time. They usually have a capacity in the range of 25,000 to 80,000 dwt, although smaller units are used for coastal trade.

The loading and unloading of tankers needs special equipment such as loading hoses or loading arms. These **loading arms** include safety accessories and are often geared with remotely operated quick couplers. Loading arms consist of a piping assembly with moveable pipes. The flexibility is achieved by swiveling joints. Because of the high weight of the steel piping, the moveable pipes are counterweight balanced. The loading arms can have one or two liquid lines and, if needed, can be equipped with a vapor line. The loading arms can be installed on jetties or regular quay walls.

The capture and recovery of hydrocarbon vapor or volatile organic compounds (VOC) to reduce emissions is vital in modern oil and gas terminal handling and storage. The requirements for the **vapor recovery systems** depend on the type of product handled and stored. Vapor from the cargo tanks passes through a vapor head to a recovery unit. Sulfur components in the vapor are removed before entering the vapor recovery system.

The yard of a liquid bulk terminal usually contains a mix of tank storage facilities and other technical installations such as pump stations. Many liquid bulk terminals are directly connected by pipeline to chemical or petrochemical production sites.

## 4 RORO TERMINALS

There are several types of roll-on/roll-off (RoRo) terminals, each focused on specific market segments. First, there are terminals equipped to handle **RoRo and ropax vessels** (ferries), which operate on end-to-end type services with a port of call at either side of the route. The ferry capacities tend to vary greatly. For example, in Europe, large units deployed on the English Channel and parts of the Baltic can handle 120 trucks per voyage. In contrast, vessel capacities on services in smaller markets (e.g. the Irish isles) tend to be more limited.

The short-distance RoRo services market can involve **accompanied transport**, where truck-trailer combinations go onboard with drivers, or **unaccompanied transport**, where trailers make the crossing without drivers. In the latter case, the trailer is positioned onboard using a special tractor, which allows for more capacity, but requires more handling at the terminals. It is also possible for a 40- or 45-foot container to be positioned on a chassis and then loaded on board, which allows ferries to support containerized trade.

Terminals used for ferry crossings are designed for the fast turnaround of the vessel. The apron is usually equipped with fixed ramps. Simultaneously, the yard includes extensive parking facilities for trucks and cars waiting to board and an administrative building, including a ticketing office and customs office if applicable. A good example of a large ferry terminal complex is the Calais Ferry Terminal on the French side of the English Channel. The terminal specializes in cars, accompanied trucks, and passengers making the crossing to the UK.

The required shape of the quayside of a RoRo terminal depends on the type of ramp the visiting vessels have. In most cases, a straight quay wall suffices. However, when the vessel uses a **bow or stern ramp**, the quay wall might have a small outward extension to facilitate vessel handling.

Second, there are terminals specialized in handling new (and second-hand) cars and rolling material. The **deepsea and shortsea car carrying trade** is an important segment in the RoRo market as it supports an active international trade of motor vehicles with Germany, Japan, and South Korea as the lead exporters. On long-distance routes, operators deploy Pure Car and Truck Carriers (PCTC) with capacities of up to 8,000 CEU (car equivalent units). A number of large car ports have successfully combined deepsea services with intra-regional shortsea services. The resulting hub-and-spoke network configuration is combined with growing local clusters of automotive logistics companies. While road haulage is by far the dominant mode of inland transport for car terminals, rail and barge, particularly in the Rhine and Yangtze river basins, play an ever more important role in securing the inland access of the larger car ports.

New car terminals usually cover large surfaces. Vans bring dock workers on board, after which they each pick a car to be driven down the ramp and parked on a designated spot on the yard. The yard is designed as a large parking area with small distances kept between cars. Specific parking configurations are deployed to maximize terminal land productivity without limiting access to the parked vehicles. For example, a five by four block configuration implies that a maximum of one car needs to be moved to reach any car within this block. Different types of parking configurations can be combined at the same terminal, such as five by four blocks for longer-term storage and a fish-bone configuration for the pre-sorting of cars in view of loading operations onto trucks or rail wagons. Some terminals have opted for multi-deck car storage facilities to reduce their spatial footprint. These multi-deck facilities come at an additional cost and are mostly found in ports with land availability issues and high concession fees. The automotive customer might specifically request multi-deck storage for economic, safety, or environmental reasons.

Car terminals are usually equipped with one or more **PDI centers** (Pre-Delivery Inspection). PDI activities are performed at the request of the car manufacturer or importer. They can include car inspection, repair of transport damages, installing car options, dewaxing, cleaning, and removing the transport wrap or foil. Advanced terminal operating systems (TOS) assist the terminal manager in tracking individual vehicles during their arrival at, stay, and departure from the terminal.

To cater for the increasing electrification of cars and the rise of fully electric vehicles (EVs), a number of larger terminals have invested in **battery** charging facilities at the yard, often powered by green energy such as wind turbines.

Many car and truck terminals combine RoRo activities with break-bulk or container handling and storage. This is particularly the case when the terminal is visited by **conro** (container/RoRo) ships.

## 5 BREAK-BULK TERMINALS

*Break-bulk is general cargo, loaded into a ship or transport mode as individual or bundled pieces, not stowed into a container, or not transported in ship-sized liquid or dry bulk loads.*

Conventional general cargo or break-bulk cargo encompasses a myriad of different commodities:

- **Project cargo**, including power generation equipment such as generators, turbines, wind turbines, equipment for the oil and gas industry, cables on reels, gas tanks, modules, petrochemical plants, mining equipment, building, construction equipment, brewery tanks, silos, and heavy machinery.
- **Iron and steel products** such as coils, plates, steel bars, slabs, plates, steel wire, pipes, and tubes.
- **Forest products** such as lumber and paper products.
- **Parcels and bags** such as malt, fertilizer, sugar, and rice.
- **Reefer vessel trades**, including fruit and meat.
- **Break-bulk shipments of smaller lots** such as large bags, skidded and palletized cargoes.

The wide range of break-bulk cargoes implies there are also many types of terminals and handling equipment available. Many break-bulk terminals are highly specialized to handle one specific type of break-bulk cargo and cannot be readily converted to other uses.

Break-bulk cargo is handled by cranes on the quay, floating cranes, or the ship's own cargo gear (deck cranes, derricks). On the docks, various types of **dockside cranes, level-luffing cranes, and mobile cranes** are used for moving and lifting packages. All the vertical cargo movements are conducted by the lifting gear (lift-on/lift-off equipment). Attached to such lifting gear is a shackle that links the crane or derrick with the cargo-handling equipment being used. For most lifts, a **hook** is used. There are numerous types of tools or loose gear that can be attached to the shipboard or shore-based lifting gear:

- **Sling or strop**, which is probably the most common form of loose gear. Such equipment, generally made of rope, is ideal for hoisting strong packages, such as wooden cases or bagged cargo, which is not likely to sag or be damaged when raised.
- **Snotters or canvas slings** are suitable for bagged cargo.
- **Chain slings** are used for heavy slender cargoes, such as timber or steel rails.
- **Can or barrel hooks** are suitable for hoisting barrels or drums.
- **Cargo nets** are suitable for mail bags and similar cargoes that are not liable to be crushed when hoisted.
- **Heavy lifting beams** are suitable for heavy and long articles such as locomotives, boilers, or railway passenger coaches.
- **Cargo trays and pallets**, the latter being of wooden or steel construction, are ideal for moderate dimension cargoes, which can be conveniently stacked, such as cartons, bags, or small wooden crates or cases.

**Forklift trucks** are frequently used on break-bulk terminals. This type of equipment can be mechanically or electrically operated and fitted in front with a platform in the shape of two prongs of a fork. Lifting capacity varies from 1 to 45 tons. Clamps for reels and bales are provided on some forklift trucks.

In the case of palletized break-bulk cargo, **pallet jacks** are used as well to lift and move pallets. The front wheels are mounted inside the end of the forks and, as the hydraulic jack is raised, the forks are separated vertically from the front wheels, forcing the load upward until it clears the floor. The pallet is only lifted enough to clear the floor for subsequent travel.

Many commodities such as coffee, cocoa, tobacco, and bananas used to be transported and handled as break-bulk. At present, these commodities are *mostly containerized*. Once the container has been discharged, it is transported to a specialized terminal in the port area or the hinterland. The container is stripped for storage, distribution, and value-added logistics activities (VALS) regarding its content.

In some cases, a commodity is discharged at a terminal equipped to handle both **break-bulk vessels and containerized cargo**. For example, this is the case at many banana import terminals where reefer container trade meets traditional reefer vessels carrying palletized banana boxes in their holds.

# Chapter 3.6 Cruise terminal design and equipment

*Cruise terminals have a unique set of characteristics and operational considerations since they need to handle a large number of passengers and cruise ship supplies.*

## 1 CRUISE TERMINALS

Cruise terminals are designed to serve the requirements of cruise vessels and their passengers. At the same time, they have to be integrated with transport, tourism, and the urban planning strategies of the port–city and nearby destinations. From a maritime viewpoint, cruise terminals need to fulfill minimum requirements for draft, berthing lines, and navigation channels for cruise ships. Inside the cruise terminal, there are provisions for various spaces, including the apron area, terminal building, and ground transportation. Due to the nature of their customers and the nature of cruise operations, connectivity to the city, car parking, and public transport facilities are particularly important.

**Operational considerations** are a critical factor in implementing the design of a cruise terminal at a specific port. The cruise port's function as a home-port, a transit port, or a hybrid port, implies different needs and design considerations:

- In a **home-port**, the cruise vessel that begins or concludes its itinerary commonly arrives early in the day so that passengers proceed to customs and immigration, have their luggage (un)loaded, and make their flight connections (more an issue for arriving passengers). Provisions for the next cruise need to be loaded, baggage from arriving passengers scanned and loaded, passengers processed through ticketing, spare parts, deck supplies, and bunkers (potable water and fuel oil) taken aboard. Minor repairs may also be undertaken. A portion of the crew visits the port-city and returns before the ship departs. All these activities need to take place within up to 24 hours and preferably within 12 hours. Handling a large number of passengers in a short amount of time requires a terminal

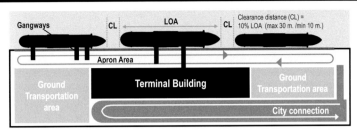

**FIGURE 3.27** Cruise Terminal Configuration

Source: Adapted from PIANC Working Group 152 (2016).

building, parking areas, and good access to the local transport system, particularly airports. The conditions and performance of the cruise port terminal are strongly linked with home-ports selection by cruise lines.

- A **port of call** (transit) is visited for only a few hours within a day, or overnight, and requires a fast and efficient system for transporting passengers to points of interest or recreational spots.
- **Hybrid cruise ports** are used for both home-porting and transit activities. The terminal is designed to handle home-port and visitor flows at the same time.

Once designed and constructed, the operating costs of cruise terminals are generally smaller than in other port terminals, as cruise terminals do not require heavy equipment and do not consume much energy. The main operating cost items are the staff for managing the terminal, security, and luggage handling. These are frequently outsourced owing to the seasonal nature of the industry. On the other hand, security is a fundamental issue as cruise ships and passengers at ports might be vulnerable. A large number of passengers concentrated in a small restricted area might be considered a potential risk. Cruise ships also have high symbolic and economic value. Consequently, cruise port design and operations must comply with several security regulations, while cruise lines and regulatory agencies constantly audit port security (Figure 3.27).

## 2 MARITIME INFRASTRUCTURE

The core consideration for cruise terminal design is related to the expected technical characteristics of the cruise ships. Indicators, such as the tonnage, overall length (LOA), beam, and draft of modern cruise ships, along with the passenger capacity, and the number of crew on board, are the most considered. The maritime infrastructure of a cruise terminal depends on several factors:

- The **number, size, and class** of the cruise vessels that could utilize the terminal. Since the 2000s, the average size of cruise ships has increased in all dimensions (i.e. larger, wider, and higher passenger capacity) (Figure 3.28). The average cruise ship capacity has increased from 1,300 to 3,100 passengers, and the average length from 200 to over 300 meters.
- The **characteristics of the vessel types** that could call at the port are key aspects. Due to design changes and technology, the mass and dimensions

| Name | Year | Cruise Line | # Passengers | Tonnage (GT) | Length (m) | Beam (m) | Draft (m) |
|------|------|-------------|--------------|--------------|------------|----------|-----------|
| Queen Elizabeth II | 1968 | Cunard Line | 1,778 | 70,327 | 294 | 32.0 | 6.0 |
| Carnival Destiny | 1996 | Carnival Cruises | 2,642 | 101,353 | 272 | 35.4 | 8.2 |
| Navigator of the Seas | 2002 | Royal Caribbean | 3,386 | 138,000 | 311 | 48.0 | 8.8 |
| Queen Mary II | 2004 | Cunard Line | 3,056 | 151,400 | 345 | 41.1 | 9.8 |
| Freedom of the Seas | 2006 | Royal Caribbean | 3,782 | 160,000 | 339 | 56.1 | 8.5 |
| Allure of the Seas | 2010 | Royal Caribbean | 6,780 | 225,282 | 361 | 47.0 | 9.1 |
| Harmony of the Seas | 2016 | Royal Caribbean | 6,780 | 227,700 | 362 | 47.4 | 9.3 |

FIGURE 3.28 Evolution of Representative Vessels in Cruise Shipping

of cruise vessels include a variety of deck designs. These features contribute to the design of shoreside infrastructures like shore-power location, gangway placement, and cruise terminal building dimensions and facilities.

- **Operational conditions** imposed by weather. Some cruise ports may be exposed to the seasonality of weather risks, such as hurricanes in the Caribbean.
- The **operational needs of stevedoring** for activities such as mooring, bunkering, and stores.
- The **desired potential berthing patterns** and the average number of cruise ships expected to be docked.
- For home-ports, the **number of crew members** is also significant. Depending on the size and market segment of the cruise, the ratio varies from one crew member per passenger in a luxury cruise ship to one crew member per three passengers in a standard ship.

Entrance **channels to berths and maneuvering** areas provide safe clearance during vessel movements and operational loading conditions. Their minimum depth incorporates the maximum draft and allowances for technical and wave conditions anticipated during vessel approaches. Modern cruise vessels are very maneuverable in most sea conditions. The berth area length required for safe mooring and securing the vessel allows for a minimum clearance of 10% of the vessel's overall length (LOA). Where turning basins are required, a diameter of two times the LOA plus an allowance for adverse weather conditions is necessary. In home port operations, the port maintains contingency plans in case of extreme weather due to the need for passengers to connect to the various modes of transportation from the terminal. Ports of call do not need such plans, as ships have the option of skipping a port of call in the case of inclement weather.

**Mooring of cruise vessels** generally uses arrangements where the maximum pier frontage adjacent to the vessel offers loading/unloading efficiencies. In some transit ports, vessels are moored to piers shorter than the vessel, using dolphins to secure the offshore end of the vessel. Cruise vessel facilities are typically provided with fender systems along the full frontage of the berth area to absorb the energy of an impact during vessel berthing and provide a soft buffer between the pier and vessel while moored.

## 3 APRON AREA OF THE CRUISE TERMINAL

Aprons are fenced secured areas immediately adjacent to the cruise building and vessel service doors. While cruise vessel loading can occur with small widths of apron surface, the wider and less obstructed the surface in the area is, the better. The apron area provides space for any of the following operations:

- **Stevedoring services** including line-handling, baggage movement, utility connections, and waste processing from the vessel. Luggage is moved by forklift and baggage handling carriages from/to the ground floor of the cruise building to/from the vessel luggage doors.
- **Supplies** to the vessels to serve the needs of passengers, crew, systems, and equipment. The provisions arrive on trucks soon after the ship arrives at berth. With larger ships served by a total of between 20 and 40 tractor-trailer size trucks, managing this flow and providing proper maneuvering, unloading, and turn-around space is critical to the success of this process. In addition to space, two other factors are important, connectivity with the ground transportation area, and storage areas where certain perishable provisions can be placed before being loaded onto the ship in order to avoid any damage.
- **Access for vehicle** circulation, parking, unloading, and access for load/unload equipment.
- **Emergency vehicle access**.
- **Provisions for site-specific needs** of terminal operations, such as vehicle controls.

All these operations take place in the apron area via the various service doors of cruise vessels. Within the apron, the operational pier service loading area for vehicles servicing cruise vessels, such as containers and tanker trucks, is separated from the cruise terminal passenger areas. **Gangways** are the single most important passenger processing element of the entire terminal as they are crucial for turning vessels around quickly and efficiently.

> *The gangway is the means of getting on and off a ship. In general shipping terms, it refers to a walkway or bridge connecting the vessel to land. Because access varies widely from one port to another, a cruise ship gangway refers to the place on the ship where passengers enter and exit.*

Gangways transfer passengers from the vessel doors to the terminal building through the boarding corridor (boardwalk). For example, on embarkation and debarkation days, the gangway will often consist of an enclosed raised bridge like a jetway in an airport. For larger vessels, the embarking and disembarking processes entail the need for two fully automated mobile gangways per berth to move in excess of 1,000 passengers per hour. Cruise terminal operators might select one of the various types of cruise gangways available to meet these needs and provide safe boarding in all conditions.

For home-ports, the demand for some or all of the following **vessel utilities** might require further infrastructure that might even extend beyond the facility property in order to provide sufficient capacities to allow vessels to be serviced during their limited time at berth:

- **Bunkering** for ship refueling.
- **Waste reception facilities** such as oily wastes, garbage from ships, and sewage.

- **Potable water**. A 3,500 passenger vessel can use approximately 1.40 million gallons during a seven-day excursion. Most of this water demand is provided through onboard desalination systems. However, it is not uncommon for cruise vessels to take on water while at the pier.
- **Ballast water**.
- **Energy** such as shore power (cold ironing and LNG provisioning.

## 4 CRUISE TERMINAL BUILDING

The presence of a **cruise terminal building** is part of the evolution of the cruise business. As the market matures, cruise ports have started developing purpose-built terminal buildings to serve cruise passenger movements. Still, for ports where cruising activities are in their initial phase, the terminal is often a temporary structure, or a building primarily having a non-cruise use and is convertible on the days a ship calls. A range of structures is used:

- **Temporary cruise terminal buildings** exist in cruise ports with few calls and are managed only when a ship is calling. This includes vessel navigation and berthing, provisioning, passenger debarking, ship hoteling, passenger embarking, and vessel deployment. The methods of handling these needs rely primarily on essential services only, and on occasion, there is no building dedicated to being a cruise terminal. In these cases, organizing and segregating functions are handled on-site with temporary event-type facilities with movable barriers, traffic control elements such as bollards and cones, and tape lines.
- **Convertible cruise terminal buildings** focusing on hospitality, civic, commercial, retail, or warehousing as the primary function. As these facilities are not specialized cruise terminals, passengers, baggage, and supplies are managed on a day-of-cruise basis. Before a ship berths, specific cruise use elements such as signage, furniture, equipment, and space-dividing material will be set up for a cruise and then removed after the ship departs. Several processes (including immigration) may be handled on the vessel rather than in the terminal.
- **Purpose-built cruise terminal buildings** address the entire needs and functionality of cruises on both disembarkation and embarkation. On occasion, some of the building spaces may be designed for dual-use (embarking and debarking). Most often, each space is designed and built for specific functionality. These buildings can also have secondary uses such as event space for shopping areas, cafeterias, and restaurants. Sill, cruising remains the primary design and operational driver. Embarkation and disembarkation spaces, equipment, furniture, signage, and agency requirements are all are designed to optimize flow, heighten passenger satisfaction, minimize staffing levels, and maintain security. Often these buildings are part of a larger port community, or combined waterfront context, but they stand alone, not usually offering other uses when no ship is at berth.
- **Mixed-use cruise terminal buildings** are the most developed response to cruise tourism, along with the need to serve a waterfront community. Recognizing the multi-functionality that a single building can provide, such mixed-use buildings include all the necessary elements

of a purpose-built terminal. They also add other uses, such as shopping areas, commercial areas, theatres, and convention centers. As with other mixed-use buildings, the economics of capital investment, operating cost, and revenue stream are combined in order to benefit from multiple uses. This creates a beneficial cycle of increased use, greater revenue, heightened visibility, and a stronger tourism market. Simultaneously, regardless of whether or not cruising is the dominant purpose of the mixed-use building, the cruise market must perceive that the building is successfully serving the core cruise terminal mission.

Cruise terminal buildings are either single-story or multi-story. A single-story terminal has the advantages of fitting on an open site, especially in relation to the length of a cruise vessel and the need for ground transportation, and the absence of vertical core elements such as stairs, escalators, and elevators. On the negative side, the operational distances are longer on one level than in multi-story terminals. Multi-story terminals are becoming the more common form of cruise terminal buildings, especially in the bigger home-porting cruise ports. This format takes advantage of the inherent differences between embarkation and disembarkation processes to segregate them by floor level, a design common in airport facilities. The stacking of spaces on different levels has greater advantages when co-locating other activities, such as parking. Most often, a multi-story terminal will have the majority of disembarkation spaces on the ground floor and most of the embarkation space on the upper level. This has the operational advantage that embarking passengers are brought upstairs to check-in and wait to board while disembarking passengers flow through immigration check, baggage pickup, customs, and ground transportation pickup.

## 5 EMBARKATION AND DISEMBARKATION PROCESSES

The embarkation process of cruise passengers begins upon arrival at the cruise terminal. In home-ports, a number of different spaces and services are provided to facilitate the process:

- **Entrance space** is a gathering space for passengers arriving at the terminal, a shelter from the weather, a place to seek information, and a place to queue for the next step in the process.
- **Bag drop space** where bags are brought for the security check and organizing prior to loading onto the ship.
- **Luggage security controls** (X-ray scanners) that allow thorough luggage monitoring, and detecting objects that are not allowed on board.
- **Queuing space** that includes multiple lanes for passengers to process through security controls boarding the vessel.
- **Passenger security controls** (passenger X-ray lanes), with operating schedules adapted to the size of traffic, peak hours, and other local and cruise-ship requirements.
- **Ticketing** where passengers pick up their tickets before the check-in if not available through prior arrangements.
- **Ticket area queue** where passengers queue before checking in so that people can move quickly from ticketing to boarding.

- **Check-in area** with counters where cruise-line staff process passengers for the designated cruise trip. The use of new technologies like mobile applications or bar-coded wristbands in the check-in process is already bringing changes in the layout of this area.
- **Waiting areas** for checked-in/ticketed passengers to wait until boarding can begin. This space is large enough to allow for ample seating and circulation area, as well as space for cruise information and other pre-travel material the cruise lines have.
- **Boarding corridors** where passengers move toward the vessel.
- **Staff offices** for cruise operator staff, cruise line staff, and port security.
- **Other spaces**, such as spaces where passengers can have their pictures taken, VIP lounges separated from the general embarkation experience, and even wedding and other special group spaces.

The size and location orientation of each of the above spaces and respective services varies from one cruise terminal to the other. Not all of the spaces listed will be found in every terminal or found in similar arrangements. Security might take place at the entrance of the terminal building or after check-in. Well-developed VIP spaces do not exist in all terminals, as the configuration is determined to meet the needs of all stakeholders (port, cruise lines, operator, customs, and port security). In any case, the terminal needs to offer a positive experience to passengers, as it might provide the first impression to the embarking passengers and it is thus valued significantly by cruise lines.

The **disembarkation process** in the home port begins before a passenger leaves the vessel to enter the terminal, aiming at reducing the processing time to a minimum and maximizing this final experience for the passenger. The different spaces and services that are provided in home-port terminals include:

- **Boarding corridors** for disembarking passengers.
- **Customs, immigration, quarantine, and police spaces** and processes.
- **Baggage lay down**, which is often the single largest space in the building. Luggage is brought directly from the ship according to deck level and grouped via a 'lay-down' process that takes place before passengers enter the space. While in most cases separation refers to baggage waiting in different spaces per group of passengers, more sophisticated processes of managing bags also exist, the most obvious being carousels such as those used in airports.
- **Customs areas** for passengers to proceed after luggage collections to processing counters, and to conclude applicable procedures.
- **Meeting spaces** where passengers gather and meet with others and move to ground transportation.

In ports of call, the disembarkation/embarkation processes are less complex, particularly since passengers do not carry luggage. The terminals do not usually have or need a building to host passengers since the (dis)embarkation time is normally short, lasting less than an hour, with access to the local means of transportation or to the walkways and back to the ship having to be as fast and simple as possible. In the absence of a terminal building, the port provides an open space along the quay to enable passengers to gather comfortably. If a terminal building exists, transit terminals do not require spaces for the check-in process or luggage operations.

## 6 GROUND TRANSPORTATION

The ground transportation area of a cruise terminal is where passengers arrive from all transport modes to embark on the cruise. It is also where they disembark to take any transportation mode to travel inland, usually through public roads and transit systems. Since the passengers of a single cruise generate large numbers of inland trips, ground transportation is an important function of the cruise terminal. As traffic needs to move quickly, safely, and efficiently from and to the terminal and from and to the city, this area must be located close to the terminal building. The ground transportation area includes spaces for:

- **Coach parking,** such as shuttle buses provided by the port or the cruise lines and tour buses provided by the ship and independent excursion buses.
- **Taxi lines** with comfortable space around the cars to facilitate loading and unloading.
- **Drop-off spaces** such as a short-stay car park earmarked for people dropping off or picking up passengers.
- **Parking spaces** for passengers who drove to the terminal to take a cruise.
- **Regional and local connectivity** to both the local and regional intermodal system, such as the airport, needs to be connected to the home port by rail or road.

The modal distribution of cruise passenger mobility differs by port. Passengers can decide to take a coach, a taxi, a private car, or go on foot depending on factors such as proximity to major hotels and connectivity to the regional transport system. Space assigned to ground transportation services at a cruise terminal depends on:

- **Type of cruise vessel** operations at the port of call, with buses and shuttles being the main transport mode. In a home-port taxis and private transport are the most used transport mode, together with transfers and connections with the airport.
- **Port–city distance.** Where the cruise terminal is within a metropolitan district, most of the passengers might go into the city by foot, depending on the presence of pedestrian corridors. However, if the city is far off a shuttle system of transport is provided.
- **Transport systems available.** Several transport modes and services near the terminal area, such as car parks, train connections, and airport connectivity, are considered.
- **Other factors** such as local, regional, and environmental considerations may affect the design criteria. A terminal in an area of recurrent high temperatures may need to provide air conditioning in most ground transportation areas. In contrast, a terminal in an area prone to security risks will need to ensure that these areas are secured.

In addition to infrastructures such as quays construction, dock expansion, dredging of channels and basins, waiting areas, and gangways that improve traffic flows and accessibility, modern cruise terminals also involve **shoreside projects**. In many cases, land reclamation, retail, restaurants, and hotels are of equal importance. The multi-purpose use of the cruise terminals is of a different type. Due to their service and touristic orientation, the terminals are 'people-friendly', rather than 'cargo friendly'. Thus, they might be used with open access to the public for events or other usages. This is especially the case as the seasonality of cruise activities implies that several terminals host cruise ship calls for only a few months each year.

Beyond the change in usage of existing infrastructure or the development of greenfield projects, recent developments have also revolved around the adaptive reuse of brownfield assets. Such cases can be found in the United States, on both the East (Brooklyn and Galveston) and the West (San Francisco and San Diego) coasts. In all cases, cruise port infrastructure development takes far longer than building new cruise ships, meaning that ports may lag behind in trying to meet vessel capacity developments in the market.

# Chapter 3.7 Port labor

*Dockworkers are essential to terminal performance and overall port competitiveness. They are challenged by changing market requirements, which results in dock labor reform and adaptations in working practices.*

## 1 EMPLOYMENT EFFECTS OF CARGO HANDLING

Cargo handling operations at terminals lie at the core of the function of ports. They create jobs for terminal and stevedoring companies in the form of dockworkers, management, and administrative positions. Dock labor needs are very dependent on the cargo flows handled in the port. Other cargo service-related jobs include cargo survey, land transport and storage, port-related storage, and conveyor/pipeline transfer between berths and storage facilities. Generally speaking, the handling of break-bulk typically has the highest dock labor intensity. This is also confirmed when analyzing the intrinsic cargo handling tons (Box 3.7).

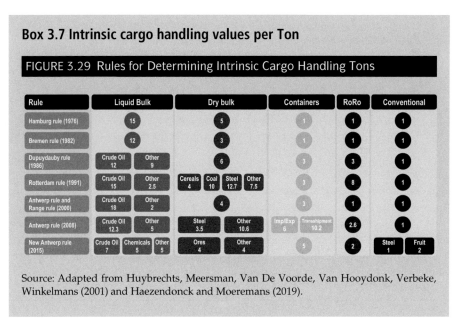

**Box 3.7 Intrinsic cargo handling values per Ton**

FIGURE 3.29 Rules for Determining Intrinsic Cargo Handling Tons

| Rule | Liquid Bulk | | | Dry bulk | | | | Containers | | RoRo | Conventional | |
|---|---|---|---|---|---|---|---|---|---|---|---|---|
| Hamburg rule (1976) | 15 | | | 5 | | | | 1 | | 1 | 1 | |
| Bremen rule (1982) | 12 | | | 3 | | | | 1 | | 1 | 1 | |
| Dupuydauby rule (1986) | Crude Oil 12 | Other 9 | | 6 | | | | 3 | | 3 | 1 | |
| Rotterdam rule (1991) | Crude Oil 15 | Other 2.5 | | Cereals 4 | Coal 10 | Steel 12.7 | Other 7.5 | 3 | | 8 | 1 | |
| Antwerp rule and Range rule (2000) | Crude Oil 18 | Other 2 | | 4 | | | | 3 | | 1 | 1 | |
| Antwerp rule (2008) | Crude Oil 12.3 | Other 5 | | Steel 3.5 | Other 10.6 | | | Imp/Exp 6 | Transshipment 10.2 | 2.6 | 1 | |
| New Antwerp rule (2015) | Crude Oil 7 | Chemicals 5 | Other 5 | Ores 4 | Other 4 | | | 5 | | 2 | Steel 1 | Fruit 2 |

Source: Adapted from Huybrechts, Meersman, Van De Voorde, Van Hooydonk, Verbeke, Winkelmans (2001) and Haezendonck and Moeremans (2019).

Several studies have attempted to measure intrinsic cargo handling values by presenting the relative added value associated with the handling of one ton of cargo (Figure 3.29). The methodologies deployed range from bottom-up to top-down approaches:

- The Port of Hamburg presented the **Hamburg Rule** in 1976, which became the reference standard.
- The **Bremen Rule** was presented in 1982 by the port of Bremen. It was based on the differences in labor costs for handling cargo and provided the following relative weights: one ton of general cargo equals three tons of dry bulk or 12 tons of liquid bulk.
- The Rotterdam Port Authority introduced the **Rotterdam Rule** in 1985 and refined the method further in 1991 with more detailed dry bulk classes.
- In 1986, the **Dupuydauby Rule** came with revised relative weights in cargo handling value per ton. It particularly underlines that containerization was becoming less labor-intensive, with an intrinsic value changing from one to three.
- The **Antwerp** Rule is based on data from the Antwerp port and distinguishes 13 traffic categories. Based on these figures, the highest added value per ton in the port of Antwerp is created by the handling of fruit. As the Antwerp Rule is only based on Antwerp data, the University of Antwerp also developed a **Range Rule** based on data for ports in the Hamburg-Le Havre range.
- The Antwerp rule was updated and refined in 2008 and 2015 (**New Antwerp Rule**). It clearly underlines the growing productivity of containerization from a labor perspective.

Many service companies involved in the booking, consolidation, and tracking of vessels and cargo, such as freight forwarders and ship agents, are located in the seaport area. The **consolidation of cargo** is an important port activity, which generates added value and employment and contributes to efficiency improvements in terms of loading rates and the balance between incoming and outgoing goods flows. Ports often act as consolidation points for partial loads, such as **Less than Container Load (LCL) cargo and groupage** activities. However, disintermediation in the supply chains and the increasing globalization of the maritime and port industry can imply that some ports face a relocation of some of the decision-making power over cargo flows to inland centers or major (maritime) cities. When cargo control centers are set up outside the port area, the role of the local service providers is narrowed down to specific operational tasks or back-office functions.

**Employment and added-value per ton** increase when goods undergo logistics or industrial transformations in the port area. For example, the stuffing and stripping of containers are up to five times more labor-intensive than the loading or discharging from a vessel. **Storage, distribution, and other logistics activities** in industrial subcontracting or postponed manufacturing in the port area also boost employment levels for a given cargo throughput level. The gateway position of major seaports offers opportunities for the development of **value-added logistics** (VAL). Many seaports have evolved from pure transshipment centers to key nodes within a logistics system. The rise of port-based activities in the hinterland can pressure logistics activities in ports and spread logistics job creation from the port to the wider hinterland.

## 2 DOCK LABOR

Port labor can be defined in different terms. Within a narrow definition, port labor refers to the loading or unloading of ships. Broadly defined, port labor refers to all forms of cargo handling in a port zone, including the stuffing and stripping of containers, the loading and unloading of inland waterway vessels, lorries, and railway wagons, and the storage and semi-industrial processing of goods in warehouses and logistics areas.

The term port/dock worker is a generic term that includes general workers (operatives) working on board ships and those on land and specialized workers. Specialized workers are operators (or drivers) of various types of machinery such as forklifts, straddle carriers, reach stackers, bulldozers, bobcats, conveyor belts and cranes (also called winchmen); signalmen (hatchmen, hatch tenders, or deck hands); lashers; tallymen (also called tally clerks or checkers); (gang) foremen, and chief tallymen and chief foremen (supervisors). Signalmen are stationed at the hatchway opening, give the necessary signals to the winchman and supervise the raising and lowering of slingloads. Lashers are men who lash, unlash, secure and release cargoes stowed in the ship's hold or on deck. Checkers or tallymen keep a tally of quantity or weight of goods shipped or received and check for apparent damage and shortages. Foremen are responsible for the management and supervision of a gang of workers. Typically, one gang of workers is used per ship's hatch or hold, or per shoreside crane. In many ports, cargo handlers also employ mechanics (also called maintenance or repair men, including electricians) responsible for keeping equipment in running condition; these workers often have the same or similar status as port workers proper. Cargo handling companies also employ office staff involved in administration, sales, marketing, information technology, and legal matters.

Port workers are employed by a variety of employers, including private terminal operators, and public port authorities (especially crane drivers), or by companies controlled by a state-owned entity. Other port workers are self-employed and hired by ship owners or their agents; these workers may at the same time act as employers of other workers. Port workers include **permanent workers** employed under an employment contract for an indefinite or a definite term that is fully governed by general labor law and permanent workers are registered as port workers under specific port labor arrangements. Many ports rely on **registered pool workers** who are hired on a daily basis (or for a shift or a half shift) and who are entitled to an unemployment benefit while they are not working. Finally, many ports use various categories of more or less **irregularly employed supplementary workers** (occasional or auxiliary workers, including, in some ports, seasonal workers and temporary agency or interim workers).

### 2.1 Market requirements

Dock labor is a key production factor for terminal operators, next to terminal land and capital goods such as cranes, yard equipment, and terminal management system hardware and software. While the dock labor force typically represents a modest portion of total direct jobs in quite a number of ports,

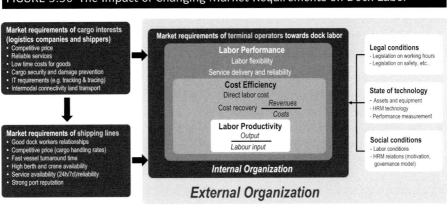

**FIGURE 3.30** The Impact of Changing Market Requirements on Dock Labor

Source: Adapted from Notteboom (2018).

it is a key production factor of port terminals. Dock labor is part of the supply profile of the port or terminal. Dockworker relationships are listed as a separate port/terminal selection criterion. However, dock labor performance also has an impact on several other criteria. For example, impacts might be found concerning supply profile factors such as container handling rates, service reliability, vessel turnaround speed, and berth availability. Factors related to the market profile of the port can also be strongly affected by dock labor performance. A dock worker strike negatively affects the factor port reputation. Furthermore, dock labor can affect inland transportation, particularly in ports where registered dock workers handle rail and barge cargo. Large port customers and large cargo handling companies can significantly impact dock labor arrangements as they try to apply best practices throughout their terminal network.

Shippers, third-party logistics service providers, and shipping lines exert pressure on terminal operators to meet their market requirements. The requirements of these market actors push terminal operators towards the maximization of the performance of dock workers (Figure 3.30). This objective can be deconstructed into three underlying dimensions, such as labor productivity, cost efficiency, and more qualitative aspects of labor performance. These dimensions are part of the 'internal' organization as they are largely under the control of dock labor management actors.

Dock labor arrangements and systems should be designed so that dock workers meet the market needs. However, these internal dimensions related to the organization of dock work take place within a wider set of legal and social conditions and the current and future state of technology. These more external dimensions form framework conditions for the development of dock labor systems.

## 2.2 Productivity

*Labor productivity is an economic interpretation of labor performance and can be defined as the total output divided by labor inputs. Labor productivity captures the extent to which the human capital is delivering value to the firm.*

The **dock labor input quantity** can typically be expressed in the number of person-hours worked and or the size of the docker workforce deployed to handle cargo. The output quantity can relate to the cargo volume handled per time unit (i.e. an hour, shift, week, month, or year) or the created value-added for the terminal operating company. In a supply chain context, the value-added of dock labor is the enhancement added to the supply chain by the workforce of the terminal operating company. From an accounting point of view, value-added is the sum of wages, amortizations of capital goods, and loss/profits. With the increasing importance of integrating ports and terminals in value-driven supply chains, many ports and terminal operators have developed a stronger interest in creating value-added, next to the more traditional approach aimed at maximizing cargo tons handled.

When using the output per person-hour or tons per gang shift, one should consider the technology used to handle the cargo and the nature of the cargo. **Benchmarking dock labor productivity** thus requires indicators that combine handling rates with the technology used, for instance, by looking at output per person-hour produced with a certain stock of fixed capital of a given technology and operational characteristics. The identification and use of relevant measures and key performance indicators (KPIs) on labor productivity also pose challenges in other industries where capital-intensive assets are used to produce outputs in the form of products or services.

## 2.3 Cost efficiency

Cost efficiency is the second dimension of labor performance. **Dock labor costs** (blue-collar) typically represent between 40% and 75% of total terminal operating costs of general cargo terminals. Next to a base wage, the labor costs include bonuses and wage supplements that are widespread in the port industry. Even in the capital-intensive container handling industry, the share of dock labor costs in total operating costs can be as high as 50%. The handling of dry bulk (i.e. major bulks such as iron ore and coal) requires less dock labor due to the presence of conveyor belt systems throughout the bulk terminals. Therefore, the share of labor costs at dry bulk terminals typically ranges between 15% and 20% of total operating costs.

**Cost recovery** is an important consideration for terminal operators in the context of labor cost efficiency. To reach cost recovery, terminal operators should design terminal pricing schemes that generate revenues above the total fixed and variable terminal operating costs related to capital, land, and labor (i.e. dock workers and white-collar workers involved in terminal management and administration).

## 2.4 Qualitative aspects of labor performance

The performance dimensions of labor productivity and cost efficiency are affected by the more qualitative aspects of **labor flexibility and service reliability, quality, and dependability**. Low service reliability, quality, and dependability (i.e. the quality of being counted on or relied upon) of dock workers expose terminal operators and the wider maritime and logistics community to all sorts of **indirect and unanticipated costs**. It can negatively affect productivity and cost recovery targets:

- The service reliability is undermined when there is a shortage of gangs or dock workers, leading to substantial delays in vessel loading and discharging operations. Shortages can be caused by sudden non-anticipated peaks in demand or a (short-term) significant drop in the availability of dock workers (due to holiday periods, weekends). Structural long-term shortages are an incentive to enlarge the docker workforce.
- Service quality is partly reflected in damage-free terminal operations. Cargo damage incidents at the terminal can result in an interruption of normal operations and generate costs for the cargo owner. A high incidence of damage cases might point to a lack of training or a low commitment of the dockworker (i.e. the absence of a 'we care' attitude).
- **Strikes** negatively affect service reliability, quality, and dependability. Short isolated strikes and long port-wide strikes by dockworkers reduce labor productivity (sometimes to zero) and impose costs on the port and logistics community, trickling down to an entire economic system. Strikes cause port deviation costs for ship-owners, time costs for ships in port, lost revenues for inland transport operators and other port-related companies, time costs and broader logistics costs for cargo owners, and potentially high costs to factories linked to major disruptions in the production line (stock-out). Strikes are typically a result of disputes about labor conditions with potentially detrimental long-term effects on the port's reputation. Labor disputes have been endemic in the history of the port industry. Most of the time, strikes resulted from disputes between labor unions (representing the interests of the dockworkers) and employer organizations concerning the terms and conditions for the renewal of collective bargaining agreements.
- **Accidents and absenteeism** can confront a port or terminal with service reliability challenges, lower productivity, and additional costs. The reasons for absenteeism can be company-related (e.g. ineffective selection and placement procedures, excessive fatigue, ineffective use of skills, poor supervision, inadequate training or promotion programs) or personal causes (e.g. dual occupation, alcoholism, or drugs). As in other industries, absenteeism can relate to job satisfaction and an indicator of a worker's responsibility in fulfilling his/her contractual obligations.
- Lower service quality can also result from operational inefficiencies due to a lack of communication between the vessel and the terminal, possible breakdowns of equipment, or the late reception of the load plans. These will, in the end, affect cost efficiency and labor productivity.

Next to service reliability, quality, and dependability concerns, there are the needs of terminal operators in terms of **labor flexibility** which take several forms:

- **Flexibility in working hours**. A distinction should be made between passive and active flexibility. Passive flexibility implies that the employer establishes schedules considering legal provisions and breaks, and holidays. Active flexibility gives employees much flexibility. A dock labor employment system with many casual workers typically generates a high degree of operational flexibility. The dockworkers have, within certain limits, freedom of choice for specific tasks. When the dock labor employment system does not impose a work obligation at specific moments in time (for example, for weekend work or work on holidays), finding enough volunteers is often a matter of providing generous bonuses for performing such tasks.

- **Flexibility in terms of total labor quantity.** This refers to the possibility of adapting the size of the workforce to the amount of work that needs to be done. In terminal operations that suffer from peaks in cargo handling demand, this kind of flexibility is crucial for a good business operation. Another flexibility is linked to recruiting workers outside dockworkers pools (for instance, via temporary labor offices) when there are shortages.
- **Operational deployment of dock workers** or the extent to which dockworkers can be used for different tasks (multi-skilling or multi-tasking). When dockworkers are assigned to specific job categories, such flexibility is only guaranteed when a system of qualifications (based on certification or training) allows dockworkers' mobility between categories. When dock workers strictly adhere to their specific **professional category**, then the multi-skilled nature of the categories is typically low. This can lead to discrepancies whereby shortages in one category cannot be compensated by surplus dockers in other (higher-ranked) categories.
- **Flexibility in the assignment of gangs/teams, the size of the gangs, and the shift system in place.** In principle, the employers benefit most when they have the widest possible freedom in switching gangs between vessels during a shift, vary the size of the gangs to match the desired productivity per hour, and deploy every dock worker to work in the most appropriate shift. In practice, there are limits to such forms of flexibility.

## 2.5 Legal and social conditions and state of technology

The internal organization of dock labor is taking place within a wider setting involving **legal and social conditions** and the **state of technology**.

The legal constraints are embedded in regulation and legislation and industry-wide labor and safety regulations. Both national governments and international/supranational organizations, such as the International Labour Organization (ILO), have a role to play. For example, the Dock Work Convention (No. 137) of 1973 is a convention on the social repercussions of new cargo handling methods in docks. This convention assigns great importance to the worker-technology relationship in ports, particularly regarding efficiency and training. Article 6 stipulates that each member shall ensure that appropriate safety, health, welfare, and vocational training provisions apply to dockworkers. The ILO Occupational Safety and Health (Dock Work) Convention (No. 152) of 1979 includes several mandatory training requirements. ILO also brings out recommendations that set out guidelines that can orient national policy and action and often complement corresponding conventions.

The theme of **social conditions, including labor relations**, is complex, difficult to delineate, and hard to measure. Dockworkers have a strong preference for **employment systems** that combine job freedom with labor conditions that are found in permanent contracts (such as job security and guaranteed wages).

The overall state of technology determines to what extent terminal operators can deploy new technology to improve the three dimensions of dock labor performance. These new technologies can be applied in terminal management, terminal equipment and automation, performance measurement and management, and human resource management (e.g. electronic hiring systems for dock workers).

## 3  MEETING MARKET REQUIREMENTS

### 3.1  Deployment of new technology

The use of advanced terminal equipment and planning technology is one way for terminal operators to increase terminal performance and meet market requirements. Technological advances in cargo handling facilities have led to labor productivity increases and quality improvements but also brought new requirements in terms of the skills and qualifications of the workforce. Technological innovations and developments in cargo handling increase labor productivity expressed in tons handled per docker per time unit. The unloading of bananas is a good example. With the introduction of pallet cages and containerization, the number of banana boxes handled per minute per crane increased from 50 when using a spiral unloader to 385 for the pallet cage and 480 when pallets are containerized.

The willingness of stevedoring companies to invest in new cargo handling technology and automation is partly related to the perceived labor productivity benefits and cost savings at the level of dock labor. If a technical innovation would, in principle, reduce the workforce per gang (or, in case of full automation, even eliminate workforce), the terminal operator will only benefit from the labor cost savings if the gangs are indeed reduced in size. If such a reduction in workforce is not possible within the contours of the dock labor employment system, then the stevedoring company will be far less eager to introduce technological innovations.

### 3.2  The legal status of dockworkers

**Dockworkers** can be civil servants in state-owned service ports, directly employed by a private terminal operating company, or employed through dock labor schemes. Quite a few dock labor employment systems require that only registered dock workers perform dock work in the port. This obligation can be imposed by national or regional legislation or is the outcome of collective bargaining agreements between port employers and trade unions.

Though not ratified by many Member States, **Article 3 of ILO Convention 137** makes explicit reference to the registration of dockworkers:

> *Registers shall be established and maintained for all occupational categories of dockworkers, in a manner to be determined by national law or practice* and *registered dock workers shall have priority of engagement for dock work.*

Where employers must use registered dock workers, the criteria for recognizing dockworkers and the entities involved in the recognition process might differ between ports. Port reform processes often envisage loosened preferential relations between registered dockworkers and port employers and introduce competition among registered dock work services providers.

## 3.3  Open and autonomous labor pool systems

A large variety of dock labor schemes can be observed among ports. Dock labor schemes are in some cases based on a centrally managed pool of registered dock workers. The use of registered dockers through such a pool can be mandatory, or not. This obligation can be de facto or imposed by law. **Dock labor pool schemes** generally involve three elements:

- The designation of an 'in-group' of officially registered (in effect, licensed) dockworkers.
- Registered workers are not permanently employed at particular stevedoring enterprises but hired through a central pool or hiring hall, which stevedores are obligated to use for their primary source of casual labor.
- A system of minimum pay guarantees or unemployment benefits for registered dockworkers who are left idle by a shortage of ships to be worked during a particular day, week, or month.

One of the main incentives behind the establishment of dock labor pools in quite a few ports is to guarantee flexibility in labor quantity. Employers and employees then jointly determine the size of the docker workforce size of the docker workforce based on current and future needs.

In an increasing number of ports, dock workers are **directly employed by terminal operators** instead of contracted via pools. In some cases, such as in Germany and the Netherlands, employers can hire permanent company employees directly from the **external labor market**. Still, any additional (casual) labor must be hired from a regulated labor pool.

There is a general trend towards open and autonomous pool systems with the back-up of temporary employment agencies. Over the last 50 years or so, the **collective bargaining process** in many ports has progressively been decentralized to the company level.

## 4  IMPROVING PORT WORK CONDITIONS

### 4.1  Increased training initiatives and modalities

Labor performance is impacted by **training and experience levels**. A customized training plan can provide dock workers with a future career path based on experience and proven competence. Many ports use occupational categories of dock workers combined with clear rules regarding the flow from one category to another higher category. The regulation of the **influx of new dockers** is also relevant in this context. Key issues in this respect relate to the 'screening' of potential candidates, training facilities, the modalities for trial periods, and the characteristics of labor evaluation systems.

Many ports have set up **dedicated training centers** for dock workers. These training centers offer voluntary or obligatory professional training courses for newly registered dockers and special schooling for dockers willing to move to another job category.

## 4.2  A push for continuous work

Terminal operators are pushing for changes in labor arrangements with a view to boosting labor productivity, cost efficiency, service quality, and labor flexibility:

- **Continuous work**. The high time costs of vessels make high quay productivity and 24/7 operations indispensable.
- **Performance improvements in terminal operations**. There is a general tendency towards individual rather than collective breaks, flexible start times, and variable shift lengths.
- Dock labor schemes show various ways of dealing with **overtime, night shifts, and weekend work**. For example, in some ports, weekend work is, to some extent, considered a normal shift. In contrast, dockers in other ports have the freedom to accept weekend shifts (voluntary basis) with provisions in place for overtime money if they do.
- Implementation of the so-called **'hot seat' change** or the seamless transition from one shift to another, resulting in continuous work on a ship which thereby reduces the idle time of the handling equipment.

## 4.3  Composition of gangs or teams

A competitive spirit between **dock worker gangs** and a strong social control within a gang enhance labor performance per shift. Strong and highly motivated supervisors typically create an atmosphere of coherence and a focus on solid teamwork. High flexibility in the deployment of gangs (e.g. movement of a gang between vessels during a shift) also contributes to optimal use of available dock workers.

Ports show a large variety in how the respective dock labor employment systems deal with the composition of and flexibility within gangs or teams of dockers. There are systems advocating semi-autonomous and multi-skilled team working with a high degree of freedom given to allocating tasks within specific shifts and over longer shift cycles. Other ports strongly rely on rather fixed gangs as the central entities responsible for achieving high productivity through experience, teamwork, and a spirit of competition among the gangs.

## 4.4  Changes in hiring systems

Hiring methods are guided by the provisions of local dock labor schemes. Even in ports with a pool of registered dock workers, hiring systems can vary greatly in terms of:

- The **hiring moment**, such as hiring at fixed moments per weekday or continuously.
- The **persons involved in the hiring process** such as foreman and company officials.
- The **characteristics and governance** of the supervisory system.

- The **interaction between docker and hiring person/entity** such as physically in a hiring hall or by electronic systems.
- The **control given to the docker**, such as matching voluntarily or controlled externally with or without taking into account the preferences of dockers.

Technological advances in mobile communication have facilitated the **modernization of job assignment systems** towards electronic dispatching of dockworkers in ports or terminals, which have a high demand for a flexible workforce.

## 4.5 Specialization, categorization and qualification

Dockers in ports are generally **not a homogeneous group**. Significant differences between their members can relate to the tasks carried out, the required skills, the way they are hired, the training arrangements, and career planning.

One of the foundations for the categorization of dockworkers is the division between permanent and non-permanent workers. Global terminal operators, particularly in the container business, increasingly demand direct employment for many of their own workers, especially crane drivers and other heavy yard equipment operators (the **regulars**). Casual workers are deployed during periods of peak demand. Even when a labor scheme is in place that includes a pool of registered casual workers, local port employers often hire a large proportion of dockers on an almost continual basis (the **quasi-permanent workers or semi-regulars**). Labor schemes often include a **continuity rule** where a docker hired on a particular day can be rehired for the next day(s) without having to be rehired every day in a central hiring place. The rule also gives new dockworkers the chance to become acquainted with the routines in a gang.

Some labor systems rely on the **job categories** of dockers, with varying degrees of labor mobility between categories. Other employment systems are based on **job qualifications**, allowing a (casual) docker to be deployed for any dock work, subject to them having the right qualifications. Dock labor employment systems show various types and degrees of **multi-skilling among dockers**. Multi-skilling programs can be organized at the company level, by the pool, or provided by the state. In some cases, multi-skilling arrangements allow functional combinations of several jobs to be performed within the same shift, which adds to labor flexibility.

There is a push for terminal operators to move away from job categories and opt for job qualification systems.

## 4.6 Enhancing motivation and commitment

Some intrinsic and extrinsic motivators can be used in a dock labor context to promote motivation, a high labor spirit, and commitment:

- **Extrinsic motivators** include wage levels and a performance-based bonus system with a view to stimulating labor performance and job loyalty. For example, the most straightforward way to increase labor flexibility is to increase the remuneration of dockworkers through higher base wages or, more commonly, by installing bonus systems linked to flexible tasking and irregular working hours.

• **Intrinsic motivators** include non-financial employment motivation and mental well-being aimed at increasing job satisfaction. When the societal status of the profession and professional pride are low, the port might face difficulties in finding motivated dockworkers.

Industry relations between employers and employees also impact the motivation and commitment of workers. Consultation and social dialogue enhance employee-employer relationships. Labor unions are typically very visible at the dock labor front, although major differences in union power can be observed across seaports and countries. Most ports have a long tradition of social dialog, via both formal and informal channels. In case of disputes, a **dispute-resolution procedure** sets in to resolve problems and to avoid strikes. Through effective joint consultation bodies, social dialog is considered the key to a sustainable relationship between employers and trade unions. A climate of constructive dialog enhances social peace in ports. In 2005, the International Labor Organization published a **practical guide to social dialog** in the process of structural adjustment and private sector participation in ports.

# Chapter 3.8  Terminal automation

*Terminal automation is a full or partial substitution of terminal operations through the use of automated equipment and processes.*

## 1  AUTOMATING TERMINALS

Since the emergence of containerization, mechanization has been an ongoing process for freight terminals as more efficient intermodal equipment was developed. Still, all that equipment needed to be operated by trained labor, such as crane operators and drivers. Since the 1990s, there has been a push towards automation as global trade surged. In combination with growing ship sizes, this has encouraged ports to improve their productivity, namely throughput and ship turnaround time, to in the range of 30% more than standard terminals. Another important driver has been the large diffusion of information technologies, making it possible to integrate information and physical systems that automation depends on.

Both port and intermodal rail terminals can be automated according to similar principles and technologies since automation revolves around handling containers; a standard load unit (Figure 3.31). The container thus becomes the unit around which physical and information handling systems are built and organized. Automation can be comprehensive when involving several stages of terminal operations or specific when only one stage is involved at a time. For greenfield terminals (new projects), comprehensive automation is becoming standard, while existing terminals electively automate part of their operations as comprehensive automation could be highly disruptive and costly. Automation involves three main dimensions; within the terminal (yard), its interface, and the foreland and hinterland.

FIGURE 3.31 Freight Terminal Automation

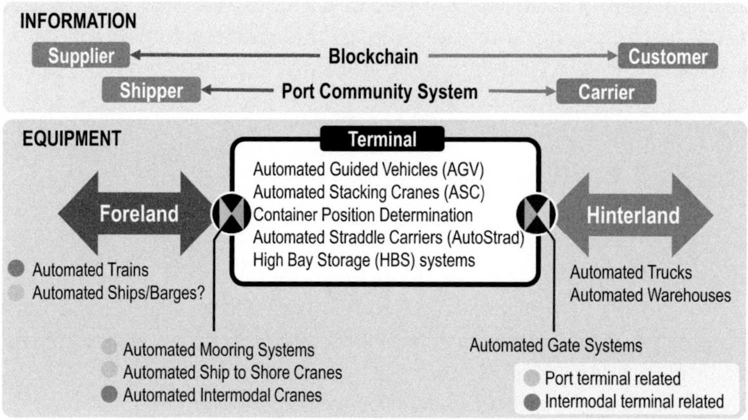

INFORMATION

Supplier ← Blockchain → Customer
Shipper ← Port Community System → Carrier

EQUIPMENT

**Terminal**
Automated Guided Vehicles (AGV)
Automated Stacking Cranes (ASC)
Container Position Determination
Automated Straddle Carriers (AutoStrad)
High Bay Storage (HBS) systems

**Foreland** — **Hinterland**

Automated Trains
Automated Ships/Barges?

Automated Trucks
Automated Warehouses

Automated Mooring Systems
Automated Ship to Shore Cranes
Automated Intermodal Cranes

Automated Gate Systems

Port terminal related
Intermodal terminal related

Freight terminal automation involves a **physical** (equipment) and **information** component. It involves the configuration of freight terminals that need to be adapted to automation, particularly the processes of handling containers with automated equipment.

## 1.1  Yard automation

Within a freight terminal, several processes can be automated. Container yard management has been automated for decades, using information systems to manage the stacking of inbound and outbound containers. Thus, **automated yard planning** allows for more effective positioning of containers and equipment to increase throughput with the same assets. Horizontal movement automation involves using **Automated Guided Vehicles** (AGVs) and automated straddle carriers (AutoStrads) or shuttles. These vehicles bring containers back and forth from **Automated Stacking Cranes** (ASCs), which are rail-mounted gantry cranes managing stacks of containers that are usually aligned perpendicular to the pier. The pier-side of the stack is used for loading and unloading containers coming from the pier, while the gate side of the stack is used for pick up or deliveries of containers to or from the terminal gate. Such movements are usually done with trucks and chassis. Yard automation requires container position determination systems that make the location of all the containers within the terminal known at any time through sensors. This enables their effective management, making them available to be quickly retrieved for loading on a ship or picking up for inland distribution.

## 1.2  Terminal interface automation

Automated mooring systems are able to quickly dock and undock a ship, improving ship turnaround time. **Automated Ship to Shore Cranes** (ASSCs) are automated versions of standard portainers that are remotely controlled. An operator can control several cranes instead of one. For intermodal terminals, Automated Intermodal Cranes are a modified version of ASCs and are usually wider since they service as loading and unloading, and stacking equipment.

**Automated gate systems** (AGSs) have received wide diffusion because of the substantial benefits they provide for terminal access. They need to have documentation electronically provided before picking up or dropping at the terminal, which improves processing time and reduces the risk of errors with their associated delays.

AGSs commonly rely on optical character recognition and radio frequency identification to quickly capture data about inbound and outbound containers. Photos of containers and equipment can also be automatically taken and stored. This has substantially accelerated gate time, which is a common hurdle in terminal operation. Further, truck drivers are able to use mobile technologies to schedule appointments to pick up or drop containers and even swap equipment such as chassis. This is linked with demand planning and prediction, allowing for a better understanding of terminal gate access time and frequency distribution.

### 1.3 Foreland and hinterland automation

Foreland and hinterland automation relates to processes that are not directly linked with terminal automation but can support its benefits **upstream** (foreland) or **downstream** (hinterland) along the transport chain (Figure 3.31). Although automated ships are not to be envisioned within the foreseeable future, many aspects of ship operations have been automated (propulsion and power monitoring, ballast), reducing crew size substantially. The same issue applies to rail transportation (control systems, signaling, crossings). Automated trains are a distinct reality since they operate on their own guideways and automated trains are already common for public transit systems. The introduction of automated trucks carrying containers between terminals and their hinterland is a distinct possibility, particularly along selected high-volume corridors. Warehouses with automated storage and retrieval systems have also been introduced in recent years, which has improved distribution efficiency, particularly for e-commerce.

Terminal operations require equipment such as portainers, gantry cranes, straddle carriers or reach stackers, all of which can be automated. Since terminal equipment requires maintenance, predictive maintenance technologies, supported by sensors, allow for a better assessment of the wear and tear terminal equipment is facing, irrespective of whether this equipment is automated or not. The equipment life cycle is improved through better maintenance as well as a reduction of the frequency and duration of equipment downtime due to unanticipated failures.

Like mechanization previously, automation is promoting a further standardization of terminals over three main dimensions:

• The **configuration** of the terminal to make it suitable for automation.
• The automation of the **processes** handling containers.
• The automation of the **systems** controlling the equipment.

## 2 THE PORT AUTOMATION DRIVE

There is an increased interest in the automation of container terminals to improve **quayside and land productivity**. Port terminals are particularly prone to automation since they directly improve cost, efficiency, safety, and reliability performance indicators. Terminal operators are trying to realize productivity leaps to deal with the scale increases in container vessel size and increased container volumes. Advances in port productivity have resulted in disproportionately lower growth of port turnaround times as a function of vessel size. The potential port-related diseconomies of scale linked to larger vessels have been fully or partially absorbed by terminal operators. Therefore, shipping lines are encouraged to pursue consecutive rounds of scale increases in vessel size.

Automation is often aimed at reducing generalized costs per unit handled in terminal operations. The expectations are that automation can reduce operating expenses by 25% to 50% and increase productivity by up to 30%, but these expectations remain unfulfilled. This is further underlined by handling standard container box sizes using conventional equipment, which is susceptible to automation. Terminals facing severe **land availability issues** show a higher willingness to consider automation. Still, automation takes place at different rates depending on the technology involved.

The drive towards automation can partially be explained by a **cost/benefit perspective** where the least costly and most beneficial forms of automation will be adopted first. Adoption is a risky proposition since it often involves untested systems with uncertain outcomes but, if successful, it can lead to substantial benefits. The willingness of stevedoring companies to invest in new cargo handling technology and automation is partly related to the perceived labor productivity benefits and cost savings at the level of dock labor. Technological innovations and developments in cargo handling should increase labor productivity expressed in TEUs handled per docker per time unit, as typically fewer dock workers are needed. If a technical innovation allows a reduction in labor per gang (or, in the case of full automation, even eliminating labor), then the terminal operator will only benefit from the labor cost savings if the gangs are reduced in size. If such a reduction in labor is not possible within the terms of the dock labor employment system, then the stevedoring company will be far less eager to introduce technological innovations. The trade-offs that need to be made when introducing new automated cargo handling technology can lead to disputes between labor unions and the terminal operator.

Automation usually involves **new terminal developments** since there is an opportunity to automate terminal-wide without disrupting existing operations. As automation is implemented, it creates further pressures on other components of the terminal to improve productivity in order to keep pace (Figure 3.32). Eventually, the whole terminal can be automated. Further, effective automation technologies promote their adoption by other terminals needing to remain competitive and keep up with the most efficient operational practices. Once about 25% of the terminals have adopted a form of automation, a rapid diffusion is expected since the technology has proven to be effective from a cost and an operational standpoint. By the time it reaches 50%

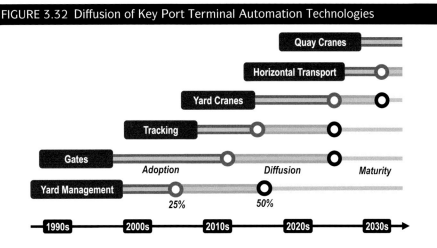

**FIGURE 3.32** Diffusion of Key Port Terminal Automation Technologies

of terminals, automation will enter a maturity phase with well-established equipment, standards, and modes of operation. It will cease to offer a competitive advantage and be a standard mode of terminal operation.

The push towards automation appears to be an irrevocable trend, further increasing the **capital intensiveness of container terminals**. This is likely to consolidate the competitiveness of the largest terminals able to first invest in automation or afford existing solutions. If the cost of automation goes down as expected, it will diffuse into smaller terminals and the competitive advantage of automation will recede. Automation will become an industry standard for freight terminals.

Still, automation creates an **asynchronism in terminal operations** since it may not be implemented at the same rate in terminals being reconverted. For instance, improving gate access may place pressures on yard operations (and vice versa), so careful consideration must be given to the impact of automation on the whole terminal operations.

Despite the possible advantages of automation, only a limited number of terminals are fully or partly automated (Figure 3.33). As of 2018, about 8.8% of all the major container terminals were fully or partially automated. Several terminal operators show a **reluctance concerning automation** and adopt a wait-and-see approach. The main reasons for such behavior are associated with the high irreversible investment costs of automation, the availability of skills, resources, and equipment, governance issues (labor contracts), and implementation time. While the risks for automation can be substantial, the rewards in terms of productivity and lower operational costs may not be entirely evident.

Up to the late 2000s, only a few terminals implemented automation strategies since they involved unproven technologies. Then, from the early 2010s, the number of automated terminals increased rapidly as equipment was standardized and as automation costs declined.

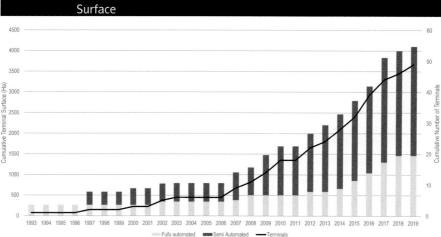

FIGURE 3.33 Cumulative Number of Automated Terminals and Automated Surface

## 3 AUTOMATED CONTAINER TERMINALS

Automation is taking place at different scales, paces, and locations. There are various degrees of automation. In many ways, automation is present in a large number of terminals depending on how it is defined and whether it focuses on infrastructure (e.g. stacking cranes) or information systems (e.g. yard management or port community systems). The most common definition classifies terminals as fully or semi-automated, but this definition is partial.

- A **fully automated terminal** is when the stacking yard and horizontal transfers between the quay and the yard are automated. This implies that a container is handled automatically from the dockside to the pickup area.
- A **semi-automated terminal** only involves an automated staking yard.

Such a definition does not consider automated terminal gates and other softer forms of automation such as appointment systems and yard planning systems. Further, as portainers become automated, the need to provide a more comprehensive perspective about port terminal automation will become even more salient. Therefore, comparing terminals by their level of automation is not a straightforward endeavor. Eventually, a term such as a **completely automated terminal** will be required to define a terminal where automation occurs from the portainer to the gate (and beyond).

As a capital-intensive and complex process, automation is thus more prevalent among large commercial gateways and transshipment hubs (Figure 3.34). An overview of existing terminal automation facilities underlines three main contexts in which automation is taking place:

1. When an existing terminal facility has a footprint that is difficult to expand, automation becomes a strategy to increase throughput, cope with higher operating costs, and remain competitive.

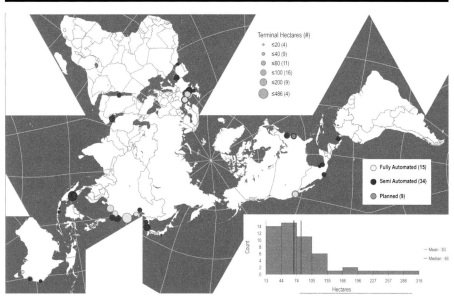

**FIGURE 3.34** Fully and Semi-Automated Container Terminals, Total Hectares, 2020

Source: Adapted from Drewry Shipping Consultants and Port Equipment Manufacturers Association.

2. When a terminal acts as a **major transshipment hub**, automation becomes a strategy to increase the transshipment throughput. The hub can perform its function more effectively, particularly in light of larger containerships.

3. When a **new terminal facility is developed** with the latest automation technology, automation becomes a strategy to attract customers in a competitive environment while reducing the necessity to train a port terminal workforce.

An inventory of terminal automation reveals a rapidly evolving situation. Although the information is likely to be partial and incomplete, 55 container terminals around the world were either fully or partially automated as of mid-2020. Considering that there are about 750 container terminals, this represents 7.3% of all main container terminals, but 12.2% of the total global footprint in terms of hectares. While the average container terminal size was 51.7 hectares, it was 85.5 hectares for fully automated terminals and 69.9 hectares for semi-automated terminals, underlining the scale propensity for automation.

A positive impact of automation concerns safety since automated terminals are less prone to accidents with fewer (or no) workers directly present. Automated equipment also tends to be electrically powered, **reducing local environmental externalities** such as pollution and noise. Further, terminal automation can be effective in a context where labor is expensive or difficult to find and train.

A major challenge in automating an existing terminal facility is how to phase the process with existing operations. The removal of old equipment and installing automated equipment requires a temporary loss of capacity and operational efficiency. The implementation period for an automated terminal is typically longer than for conventional terminals. Terminal operators have to invest large sums of money for a longer time period before any ROI can be achieved. The long implementation time is caused by extended terminal construction and testing periods. Converting an existing fully operational terminal to an automated facility can be complex. The operator will need to temporarily give up some of its terminal capacity and be faced with managing two operational systems (automated and non-automated) during the transition period. This may involve a decision to lose revenue while automation is taking place, but with the expected benefit of improved efficiency.

Since automation is a relatively recent process starting to diffuse through the container port system, its impacts are not well understood (Box 3.8). Shipping networks, terminal operations, and the footprint of containerization, as well as the interactions between key stakeholders such as shipping lines, cargo owners, and logistics service providers are all impacted. It also remains to be seen what are the applicable limits of terminal automation and at what level it does not generate significant additional value.

---

### Box 3.8 Potential impacts of container terminal automation

*The automation of container terminals may impact several aspects of maritime shipping, terminal operation, and logistics.*

*__Shipping network__. Terminal automation may encourage shipping lines to call at automated ports with their largest ships since these terminals may be able to provide higher throughput, allowing them to use their assets more effectively. An additional form of competition for transshipment hubs could emerge, imposing a rationalization of shipping networks along a hierarchy where automation plays a role.*

*__Terminal facilities__. Automation promotes the design of new terminal facilities with new arrangements of stacking yards and interactions with the piers and the gates. This changes terminal operations in terms of the availability of terminal capacity, work cycles, and turnaround times. In turn, the velocity of the respective terminal flows changes, requiring adjustments, particularly with inland distribution.*

*__Terminal footprint__. Terminal automation allows for higher density use of terminal space. If automation becomes a dominant force in shipping terminal development, then a decline of the terminal footprint could be expected as the same amount of traffic (or more traffic) could be handled with less footprint. In ports having several container terminals, this could imply the closure of less productive terminal facilities.*

*__Vertical integration__. The digitalization aspect of automation encourages a better integration with the providers of logistical services, from carriers, cargo owners, and distributors, as well as regulatory stakeholders (port authority, customs). Therefore, both automation and its associated digitalization increase the velocity of freight and provide new forms of interactions (such as freight markets) between actors (Figure 3.35).*

**FIGURE 3.35** Potential Impacts of Container Terminal Automation

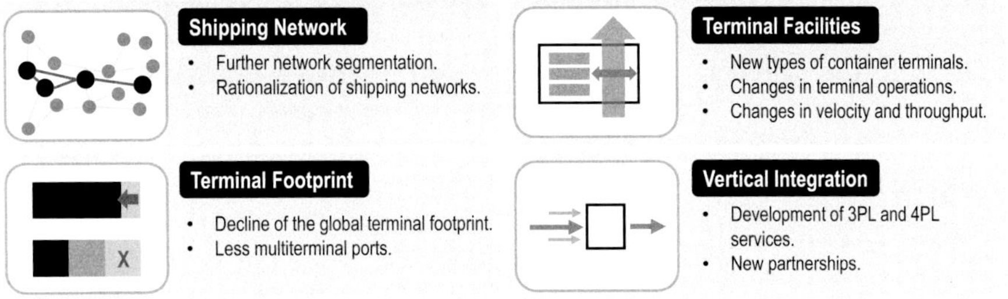

**Shipping Network**
- Further network segmentation.
- Rationalization of shipping networks.

**Terminal Facilities**
- New types of container terminals.
- Changes in terminal operations.
- Changes in velocity and throughput.

**Terminal Footprint**
- Decline of the global terminal footprint.
- Less multiterminal ports.

**Vertical Integration**
- Development of 3PL and 4PL services.
- New partnerships.

# Chapter 3.9  Port terminal construction

*Ship and terminal demand characteristics determine the requirements for terminal construction in terms of nautical access conditions, quay walls, and terminal layout and equipment.*

## 1 GREENFIELD AND BROWNFIELD SITES

Terminal construction techniques and procedures are influenced by the topological and technical characteristics of the site, such as its situation and geology and the intended use of the plot. It occurs under greenfield or brownfield conditions.

*Terminal development on a **brownfield site** involves reconverting an existing (mostly industrial) site for terminal use.*

Brownfield port construction usually involves large-scale clean-up operations of contaminated soil and the renovation and deepening of the quay walls. It results in the **rehabilitation and reuse** of existing port real estate, thereby avoiding lengthy and difficult port extension procedures. Redevelopment of port brownfields produces numerous environmental, social, and economic benefits. By cleaning up and returning these lands to use, communities can remove dangerous structures and stop or stabilize contamination near waterways. Port redevelopment presents valuable opportunities for waterfront redevelopment, and it may catalyze revitalization in the broader community. Brownfield redevelopment frees space for various uses and creates a more available property for sale or lease, providing ports with additional sources of revenue. Besides, redevelopment of previously used sites can help alleviate pressure on undeveloped wetland and coastal areas, thus protecting important coastal habitats.

*Construction of a terminal on a **greenfield site** mostly involves extending a port on a vacant site along a river, estuary, or coastline.*

Historically, the majority of port development projects were labeled greenfield, which often goes hand in hand with port migration. The vacant site might be located in a green zone, wetland, or agricultural area. Getting permission for a greenfield development usually takes a long time given existing spatial planning and environmental rules and regulations, and the required extensive project evaluation. For example, the Bird and Habitat Directive and the Water Directive of the European Commission impose a complex regulatory condition on greenfield development for ports. Such developments can imply small- or large-scale land reclamation works along a coastline or riverside or the digging of a dock on dry land connected to a river or existing dock system.

> *Land reclamation is based on hydraulic fill, a process whereby sediment or rock excavated by dredgers from the seabed or other borrow areas is transported and placed into the designated reclamation area.*

Well-graded quartz sands are the preferred material for landfills. Before the hydraulic fill can commence, extensive preparatory engineering studies are conducted to collect bathymetrical (a measurement of the depth of bodies of water), topographical (physical features of the area), geological (soil and rock), and geotechnical data on the reclamation site and the borrow areas. This step also includes an examination of the hydraulic, meteorological, and environmental conditions. Based on these studies, a method and the right equipment are chosen to obtain the desired mix of soil/sand and water to facilitate the dredging, transport, and placement of fill material, and to meet the load-bearing and stability requirements of the reclaimed site. The quality of the landfill will be determined by its stiffness, strength, density (liquefaction resistance), and drainage capacity. The nature of the fill will influence the type of equipment, the means of transport, the reclamation method, and the possible need for ground improvement. Much used ground improvement techniques include vertical drains and vibratory, dynamic, or explosive compaction with or without admixtures.

## 2  NAUTICAL ACCESS TO TERMINALS

Terminal construction often involves an adaptation of the nautical access to guarantee a **minimum nautical draft** for seagoing vessels. These adaptations can deepen the **water depth** near the quay wall and **capital dredging work** on the nautical route (river or sea) from the main shipping lane to the terminal site. Further improvements to the nautical access to the terminal might be needed, such as the widening of the fairway to allow two-way vessel traffic, the widening of the breakwater entrance to the port terminal, or the widening of the turning basin for vessels. Once the deepening or widening of the nautical access has been realized, regular maintenance dredging must ensure that nautical access conditions remain the same.

> *Capital dredging involves dredging to deepen and widen existing rivers or nautical access routes or create a new port or terminal.*
>    *Maintenance dredging is done to maintain an existing waterway or channel.*

There are four phases in the dredging process: excavation, vertical transport, horizontal transport, and placement or use of the dredged material. Since dredging is an ad hoc activity linked to temporary projects, it is often contracted to specialized companies that position their equipment from one project to another. Dredging equipment operated solely by a port would likely remain idle for long periods of time. Therefore, land reclamation and dredging works are performed by **dredging companies** using specialized equipment:

- **Mechanical dredgers**: backhoe dredger, bucket ladder dredgers and grab
- **Hydraulic dredgers**: trailing suction hopper dredger
- **Hydraulic/mechanical dredgers**: cutter suction dredger
- **Hydrodynamic dredgers**: water injection dredger.

The **dredged material** can vary greatly (peat and organic soils, cobbles, clays, boulders, silts, broken rock, sands, rock and gravels, cemented soils and corals), and dredging depth can vary from a few meters to more than a hundred meters. Each type of equipment has different characteristics that determine the suitability for a particular type of soil, rock, or sediment in a particular setting, accounting for the waves and swell, the currents, and the water temperature. Other elements that guide selecting the right equipment include the location of the borrow area or dumping area (distance, vessel traffic intensity at location) and water depth.

Contaminated dredged material can be treated in situ or ex-situ:

- **In situ ('in place') remediation** refers to the clean up of contaminated soils and groundwater without removing contaminated media from the subsurface, typically through the use of physical and/or chemical processes.
- **Ex situ remediation** involves the removal of contaminated media, either for off-site disposal or for on-site treatment and subsequent return to the subsurface.

The treatment mechanisms can range from physical/chemical, or biological to thermal treatment technologies:

- **Physical/chemical treatment technologies** can potentially remove high levels of metal contaminants in situ. Many metal species can be simultaneously removed. Despite their effectiveness, they generally cost a lot, due to the specialized devices, machinery, and chemicals. This category of treatment includes soil vapor extraction, solidification/stabilization, chemical oxidation, soil flushing, and electrokinetic separation.
- **Biological treatment technologies** use a process whereby contaminants in soil, sediments, sludge, or groundwater are transformed or degraded into innocuous substances such as carbon dioxide, water, fatty acids, and biomass, through the action of microbial metabolism. This technology is commercially available for treating fuel contamination. This category of treatment includes bioventing and phytoremediation.
- **Thermal treatment technologies** raise the temperature of the contaminated soil to approximately 260°C for a specified period of time by exposing it to hot gases (i.e. heated air), volatilizing the contaminants, and destroying them in an afterburner. The techniques available include electrical resistance heating, steam injection, and extraction, as well as conductive heating, radio-frequency heating, and vitrification.

Many dredging companies have developed into comprehensive organizations specialized in offshore, marine, civil, environmental, and project development.

Some of the largest in this field include the Belgian companies DEME and Jan De Nul Group, the Dutch companies Van Oord and Boskalis, National Marine Dredging Company (UAE), Great Lakes Dredging & Dock Company (US), and Penta Ocean (Japan). Other dredging companies are part of large construction conglomerates, such as China Communications Construction Company (CCCC).

When designing or upgrading **port approach channels and ship maneuvering and anchoring areas**, engineers have to consider a multitude of factors associated with the channels and the expected and future generations of ship dimensions and maneuvering characteristics, such as:

- **Draught-related factors** such as under keel clearance (and related requirements), wave-induced motions, and squat (hydrodynamic effect of a ship moving through shallow waters).
- **Wind effects**.
- **Air draught** for vertical clearance under bridges and overhead cables.
- **Support craft** requirements, such as towage.
- Existing and required **aids to navigation** onboard and as part of the Vessel Traffic Management System (VTMS) of the port or channel.
- **Environmental factors**.
- **Safety risks**.

The World Association for Waterborne Transport Infrastructure (PIANC) has developed **design guidelines** for harbor approach channels. They relate to vertical (channel depth, air draught) and horizontal (channel width) dimensions. Also, they contain guidelines on squat, under keel clearance in muddy channel beds, methods for predicting vertical ship motions due to waves, and tools for ship maneuvering simulation and capacity simulation modeling. Although there is a wide variety of port sites and physical constraints, construction and engineering techniques have been standardized.

In some ports, terminals can only be reached when seagoing vessels pass through a **lock or tide gate**. The largest locks in seaports can be found in ports such as Antwerp (Belgium, Box 3.9) and Amsterdam (the Netherlands). Some major canals, such as the Panama Canal, also feature lock systems that set ship size standards around which ships and port terminal characteristics are designed.

---

### Box 3.9 Locks in the port of Antwerp, Belgium

*The port of Antwerp in Belgium is located along the river Scheldt which gives access to the North Sea some 80 km downstream. As a result of three capital dredging programs on the river and the estuary, completed in the periods 1970–1975, 1997–1998, and 2010–2011, Antwerp can now accommodate vessels with a draught up to 16 m sailing up-river and 15.2 m down-river on a tide-dependent basis. The tide-independent draught is 13.1 m. The Scheldt river is a tidal river with a tidal range (low tide vs high tide) of 3.5 m near the northern part of the port and 5.7 m near the city center. Large parts of the port area have historically been developed in dock systems behind locks in order to provide a constant water depth to the berthed vessels and facilitate cargo handling operations (Figure 3.36).*

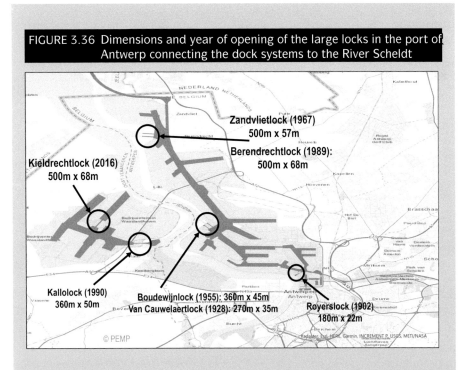

FIGURE 3.36 Dimensions and year of opening of the large locks in the port of Antwerp connecting the dock systems to the River Scheldt

*Some of the largest sea locks in the world are found in the port: the Zandvliet-lock opened in 1967, and the Berendrechtlock opened in 1989. The Kieldrechtlock is the latest addition: this large lock was opened in 2016 and provides a second nautical access to the left bank port area, next to the smaller Kallolock. Construction of the Kieldrechtlock required nearly three times the amount of steel used to build the Eiffel Tower. In the 1990s, the port of Antwerp decided to start developing terminals on the river (tidal terminals Europa Terminal and Noordzee Terminal and the tidal Deurganckdock), as container ships are time-sensitive and lock operations take time and form a risk (collision). Today all major container terminals in Antwerp have direct access to the river without sea locks (including the planned open tidal Saeftinghe dock). In this way, container vessels are not subjected to lock operations, reducing risks and port turnaround time. The tidal difference at the container terminals implies that the vessels go up or down several meters when handled. To cope with that the systems/ropes used to fix the ship to the quay are adjusted continuously. The height of quay cranes is calculated for high tide.*

## 3 QUAY WALL CONSTRUCTION

> *A **quay wall** is a soil retaining structure that provides a mooring place for ships, bearing capacity for crane loads, goods and storage, and sometimes a water-retaining function.*

The basic role of a **berth structure** is to accommodate a particular vessel or range of vessels as well as cargo handling operations. There is a wide variety of berth structures with different characteristics with a variety of engineering considerations. More specifically, the method and sequence of construction, the availability of construction materials, and the support of major construction plants such as cement making can determine the type of structure finally selected. This structure and the availability of construction equipment can significantly influence the construction schedule in view of factors such as weather downtime and the availability of contractors.

General parameters that are considered when choosing an appropriate quay wall type include:

- **Dredging and filling** in order to minimize the environmental impact of those operations.
- **Access and safety** during all the stages of the construction and operation of the structure.
- **Berth orientation**, berth geometry, and berth length.
- **Required depth** alongside the berth.
- **Seabed conditions**.
- **Local construction materials**, method of construction, and construction difficulties.
- **General site considerations** such as drainage and filters, wave pressures on walls, scour protection, the risk of earthquakes, paving and surface water drainage, the chance of ice formation.

Furthermore, the effects of marine propellers and bow thrusters, waves, and currents on the **stability of the seabed** and any underwater slopes near structures should also be taken into account. Where scour is considered likely, protection, such as a rubble anti-scour apron on the seabed, should be provided in front of the quay walls, particularly at berths where vessels will generally berth in the same position. The size of rock protection for the underwater slopes should not be less than that needed to resist the wash of propellers and bow thrusters.

The possible failure or malfunction of a quay wall can be caused by the failure of the sheet pile wall, too much groundwater flow, not enough soil stability, or failure of the supporting points.

Quay walls are typically equipped with quay wall **fenders**, ship mooring **bollards**, crane **rails**, cable **gutters**, and other technical features.

## 3.1 Embedded retaining walls

Embedded retaining walls include **sheet-pile walls** and **in-situ concrete pile walls**. The latter are embedded retaining walls of in-situ concrete bored piles usually built on the existing ground or an artificial embankment, using either a contiguous or a secant pile system. This type of wall is generally most suitable for cohesive soils and weak rock and where heavy vertical loads are accommodated. There may also be built-in granular soils when a casing or support fluid is used during excavation. However, environmental issues connected with the use of support fluids or pumping of concrete in water-bearing soils need to be considered. A common method is the diaphragm wall, which consists of an embedded retaining wall in the form of in-situ concrete diaphragm walling. Diaphragm walls are used for high walls or where heavy vertical loads are imposed on the wall.

Sheet pile walls are among the most commonly used types of quay walls used in port construction. They are widely used in the construction of container and bulk terminals, as well as for sea walls and reclamation projects where a fill is needed seaward of the existing shore and for marinas and other structures where deep water is needed directly to the shore. Different materials might be used for the sheet piles:

- **Steel sheet** piles are the most widely used embedded retaining wall elements in quays. They are relatively light and easy to handle, can be supplied in long lengths, and can be extended and cut without undue difficulty. This type of pile can be driven to a considerable depth with low displacement in a wide range of ground conditions and into the weathered rock. With various forms of pre-treatment, steel sheet piles may also be installed in solid rock in a trench backfilled with concrete, by pre-splitting the rock. The principal disadvantage of steel sheet piles is corrosion, which should be allowed for in the design. Some types of floating fenders can cause abrasion of steel sheet piles or their protective coatings, and this should be taken into account in selecting the form of fendering to be adopted.
- **Concrete sheet piles** may be used to construct moderate height walls and where driving is not too hard. The penetration required might have to be achieved by pre-boring or jetting. In rock, the piles may be installed in a trench backfilled with concrete. The main advantage of properly designed concrete sheet piles is their durability. However, the weight of the sheet piles, the care required during handling, the difficulty of forming extensions, and the usually poor interlock at joints are all factors that, in many cases, will dictate against their use. If there is a danger of losing material, the joints may be sealed by providing a filter behind the wall or grouting after driving.
- **Timber sheet piles** can provide an economical wall for moderate heights of retained material and where driving conditions are not too severe. Examples of suitable applications are bulkhead walls behind suspended decks and quays for small craft. Most timbers require protective treatment against rot and marine borers. Rubbing strips should be provided where abrasion is expected.

**Fill placed behind embedded retaining walls** should be granular material capable of free drainage. Loss of material through joints in the wall should, where necessary, be prevented by providing a suitable filter behind the wall.

**Combi-walls** are retaining walls composed of primary and secondary elements. The primary elements are normally steel tubular piles or built-up boxes, spaced uniformly along the length of the wall. The secondary elements are generally steel sheet piles of various types installed in the spaces between the primary elements and connected to them by interlocks.

## 3.2 Gravity walls

Gravity walls are built behind a **cofferdam** in the dry and are usually constructed in situ. Still, most walls are constructed in water by a method used only in maritime works, in which large precast units are lifted or floated into position and installed on a prepared bed underwater. It is common to use rubble or a free draining granular fill immediately behind a quay wall so that the effects of tidal lag are minimized and earth pressures are reduced. Gravity structures are usually used where the seabed is of good quality. They may be used where the foundation near the dredged level is of rock, dense sand, or stiff clay. The main types of gravity quay walls are (Figure 3.37):

- **Concrete block walls** consisting of heavy precast mass concrete blocks. This type of construction is suitable where a rock foundation exists since differential settlement cannot easily be accommodated by this form of gravity wall. Blocks are placed vertically above each other.
- **L-walls** obtain their stability through their structural weight and soil weight that rests on the horizontal part of the L-shaped structure. L-walls can be built in-situ in dry conditions (i.e. an excavated building pit, as was the case for the Deurganckdock in the port of Antwerp) or prefabricated ex-situ and then brought to the waterside.
- **Concrete caissons** are based on the caisson method. A pressurized chamber underneath the structure is created to keep the water out of this chamber. From this chamber, the soil under the structure can be removed. By carefully and evenly removing the soil from under the structure, it will submerge gradually until its final depth. During this process, verticality is monitored continuously, and the place where the soil is removed from under the structure is adjusted accordingly to maintain verticality. Concrete caissons consist of **open-topped cells prefabricated in the dry** (on land, in a dry dock, or in a floating dock), usually floated to their final location and then sunk into position on the seabed. Concrete caissons may be built in a wide variety of shapes, such as rectangular, circular, or cloverleaf. Caissons are usually limited to about 30 meters in width in the greatest plan dimension. They are usually designed so that, after sinking, the top is just above low water level with due allowance for waves. The cells are filled, usually with sand and sometimes with concrete or gravel. The superstructure may consist of a solid in-situ concrete capping or a reinforced concrete edge retaining wall, which is backfilled, and the top surfaced with concrete paving. Caissons, after filling, form self-stable structures that can be used to support heavy construction equipment. Large caissons will generally need to be strengthened with internal walls.

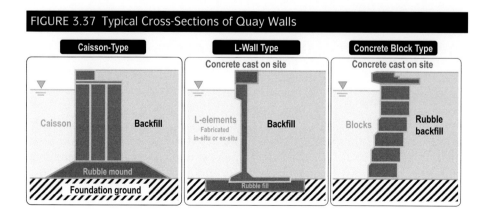

FIGURE 3.37 Typical Cross-Sections of Quay Walls

### 3.3 Suspended deck structures (piles)

Suspended deck structures may be of steel, concrete or timber, or a combination of more than one of these materials:

- **Timber piles** are easy to handle and cut to length; they require only simple driving equipment, and their flexibility can be useful in energy-absorbing structures. The length of timber piles is generally restricted, varying from 12 to 18 meters. Lengths up to 24 meters are sometimes available. Timber should generally be treated or cased with concrete muffs to prevent attack by marine borers.
- **Pre-cast reinforced concrete piles** may be driven in many ground types and may also be placed in pre-bored holes in the seabed. If the piles are to be cast at a yard remote from the site, their maximum length might be restricted to about 20 meters. If necessary, provision may be made for extending the piles using an interlocking joint.
- **Steel piles** are relatively light and easy to handle and can be driven in most ground types, including many types of rock. External corrosion may be minimized through protective coatings or cathodic protection or may be allowed for in the design.

Suspended deck structures will usually be the most suitable type in the following circumstances:

- Ground consisting of **weak upper materials**.
- Ground immediately below the seabed consisting of **suitable material for bearing piles**.
- Non-availability of **suitable backfill** for use in a retaining wall type of quay.
- **Great water depth**.

With the rapid growth of port activities worldwide, including the emergence of global terminal operators, a wave of construction projects has taken place. The **standardization of terminal design**, particularly in the container sector, has been associated with **standard construction techniques and equipment** along with well-designed guidelines.

# PART IV

# Port governance

# Chapter 4.1  Port governance and reform

*Port governance issues have become central to the port policy agendas. Governments revisited the objectives of ports and reformed existing structures and strategies to match the contemporary economic environment.*

## 1 PORT GOVERNANCE

### 1.1 Defining port governance

Governance principles are most important in the case of ports. Ports are critical infrastructure for an economy, contributing to the realization of trade and movement. At the same time, port management, operations, and development are capital intensive, consume scarce (public) land, generate externalities (noise, emissions), and involve **many decision-makers and stakeholders** such as the port authority, terminal operators, rail operators, trucking companies, logistics providers, and port-cities.

> *Port governance is the adoption and enforcement of rules governing conduct and exercising authority and institutional resources to develop and manage port activities to benefit society and the economy.*

Port governance concerns the public as well as the private sectors but tends to apply differently depending on whether public or private interests are at stake. Its features are imposed by governments or adopted voluntarily by entities, groups, or associations. Its principles apply to relationships between businesses, public/private agencies and their stakeholders, organizations, and those who establish them to undertake activities on their behalf.

The trends in (global) trade and in transport are vital for port governance, as they define the environment within which ports operate. Since the 1980s, port governance has become central to the agendas of many governments. A changing economic environment produced by the globalization of production

DOI 10.4324/9780429318184-4

FIGURE 4.1 Transport, Trade and Port Governance

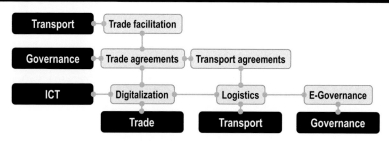

and distribution, changing cargo transportation forms, and technological breakthroughs ended a long period of stable, state-controlled (public) port governance models in most countries. As economic circumstances changed, so too were changes, albeit slowly, made to port governance structures. Many governments entered a port reform period to adapt to a new context, changing applicable governance structures.

The objectives of port governance are decided within a given economic context, where trends in global trade, the facilitation of this trade, transport organization, and related agreements and logistics inform the decisions of policymakers at the national, regional, or local/port level (Figure 4.1). Besides, the applications of Information and Communication Technology (ICT), along with the resulting e-governance mechanisms, readjust the operational and commercial relationships within the port community, increasingly informing port-governance changes.

In the absence of a perfect port governance prototype, the features of the applied port governance models differ. In fact, the variety increases as decision-makers adjust port governance and reevaluate the existing configurations within broader perspectives that involve (Figure 4.2):

- A **multi-modal vision of ports and their governance** considers the importance of logistics integration and inland freight distribution. This requires stakeholder management approaches as the scope of coordination beyond price between actors involved is essential, and opportunistic behavior could limit trust and infrastructure for solving collective action problems. Within such a multi-modal perspective, the notion of port governance includes spatial-jurisdictional scales, stakeholder relations (internal, external, public policy, and community), and logistical capabilities.
- A **broader stakeholder engagement** aiming to address all economic, operational, social, and cultural variables linked with port management, operations, and development.

A port governance model seeking to optimize the management, operations, and economic development prospects of the port while considering social and cultural variables might be achieved by thinking in concentric circles about those who need to be engaged in a multi-modal perspective. The logistics integration in ports and the regionalization of port functions, as well as the importance of inland freight distribution, have a major impact on port governance.

**FIGURE 4.2** A Multi-Modal Port Governance Vision

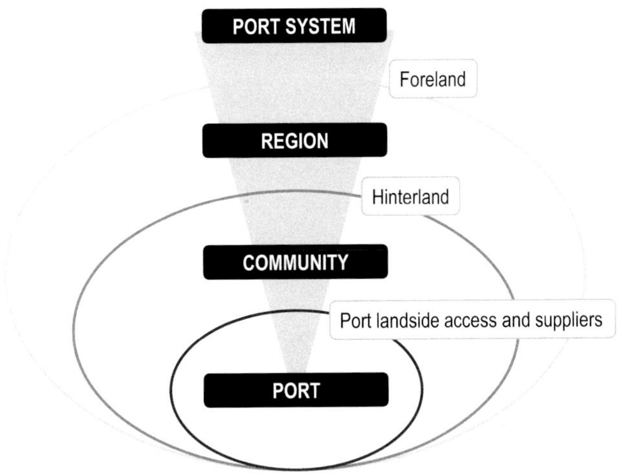

Source: Adapted from Brooks and Pallis (2012).

## 1.2 Port governance objectives

Governments or other relevant policymakers impose structures of port governance with particular policy objectives in mind. The **strategic objectives** that may drive the choice of port governance model involve maximizing:

- Traffic throughput.
- Return on investment.
- Profits for shareholders.
- Traffic throughput subject to a maximum allowable operating deficit.
- Economic development prospects at the local or national levels.

The full range of objectives varies across the world as ports are as much interested in **economic development** as they are in serving **commercial and trading interests**. Most ports see their roles as complex, with multiple objectives, and as having national and regional, and local impacts. They serve more than just their customers or their communities. They are in the business of balancing multiple roles and expectations. Ports determine their objectives to cope with government regulators (or owners), customers, local community stakeholders, and managers (or shareholders).

**Optimizing economic development** prospects is the objective most frequently chosen by major ports, as well as by small ones with ambitions to grow. Ports owned and managed by the government most commonly seek to enhance the contribution of the port and shipping related activities to the economy or to advance and safeguard national strategic maritime interests. Private ports focus on profit, sale, and development opportunities or on increasing financial value for their shareholders. Yet, even private ports consider the economic value they may generate for their local community.

## 1.3 Port governance tasks

With ports being multifaceted organizations depending on numerous functions, port governance involves decisions regarding the execution of several different tasks. These tasks are frequently interlinked and might be responsible for one or more public or private entities operating at the port or another level. Each of them is related to one of the following groups of port governance tasks (Figure 4.3):

- Port policy formation.
- Public authority functions.
- Technical management of the port area.
- Market and price regulation (including competition).
- Management of concession agreements.
- Management of emerging issues.

The **formulation of port policy** incorporates several port governance tasks. The definition, development, and adoption of a (national) port policy are just some of them. The adopted port policy has to be implemented via a number of activities such as the coordination of actors involved in the sector; the coordination of transport and other policies related to it; the adoption and approval of master plans or business plans submitted by the terminal and port operators; and the development of relevant environmental legislation in line with the principles of port policy. Both the formation and implementation of port policy also include the representation of ports at the international fora that shape and adopt regulations applying at port level (e.g. the International Maritime Organisation (IMO)), and the development of a framework (i.e. consultation with stakeholders, maintenance of port statistics, carrying out strategic studies) that provide the background for any needed adjustments of the port policy in place. These decisions regarding port policy formations, and thus the choices regarding their governance, inform and therefore are strongly related to the other types of port governance tasks.

The **management of port operations** is subject to a number of functions that are commonly undertaken by public authorities. Depending on the port governance model, these authorities might be national, regional, or at the port level. Some of the functions might also be undertaken by the harbor master or the coastguard. Private entities tend to be less involved. Port authorities also adopt and enforce security regulations for marine traffic, speed limits, the safety of operations, berthing, movement of hazardous materials, accessibility of the port area, substance abuse, recreational boating, and licensing personnel.

The functions included in this category of port governance tasks are the **adoption and approval of regulations** concerning the safety of operations and the provision of maritime services, such as pilotage, towage, and mooring, or infrastructures (lighting, channels, buoying, navigability, radar). Further responsibilities are the implementation of local or international safety and security codes (i.e. ISPS Code) and protocols; the provision of waste reception facilities in line with international conventions; Port State Control according to international regulations; and the organization of a number of auxiliary services ranging from customs formalities, immigration control, and veterinary checks, to policing, fire-fighting, search and rescue services and emergency and contingency plans.

Port governance includes decisions regarding the performance of different types of tasks. This includes various responsibilities linked with the

FIGURE 4.3 Port Governance Tasks

## A  Port policy formulation

A.1 Define, develop and implement national ports policy.
A.2 Co-ordinate all public sector agencies exercising port-related competences.
A.3 International representation (e.g. IMO).
A.4 Adopt national strategy / master plan.
A.5 Approve master plans (submitted by operators).
A.6 Approve development plans (submitted by operators).
A.7 Co-ordinate local and hinterland transport policies.
A.8 Coordinate structure and budget of port authority.
A.9 Adopt environmental legislations.
A.10 Organize and facilitate consultations on port policy.
A.11 Maintain port statistics.
A.12 Carry out strategic studies.

## B  Public authority functions

B.1 Adopt and enforce security regulations.
B.2 Adopt pilotage regulations.
B.3 Adopt towage regulations.
B.4 Approve mooring regulations.
B.5 Provision of vessel traffic services.
B.6 Lighting, marking of channels, buoying etc. including inspections.
B.7 Inspect & survey navigability of maritime access routes.
B.8 Works to maintain navigability outside the port (including dredging).
B.9 Erect and maintain shore-based radar system.
B.10 Providing nautical weather information.
B.11 Management of ISPS compliance.
B.12 Management of mandatory ship reporting regimes.
B.13 Waterborne safety and security patrols.
B.14 Inspect waste reception facilities.
B.15 Port State control.
B.16 Immigration control.
B.17 Land-based health and safety inspections.
B.18 International sanitary control / Veterinary inspections.
B.19 Fire-fighting.
B.20 Adopt emergency / incident / contingency plans.
B.21 Adopt Safety Management Systems.
B.22 Adopt plans to prevent damage to submarine pipelines.
B.23 Intervene and assist in emergency situations.
B.24 Investigation of and reporting on incidents.
B.25 Provision of search and rescue services / MRCC.
B.26 Granting and refusing access to places of refuge.
B.27 Enforce heritage laws / Protect underwater heritage.
B.28 Customs formalities, inspections and enforcement.

## C  Technical management of port area

C.1 Decide on modifications of the public land assigned to ports.
C.2 Issue building permits.
C.3 Approve proposed compulsory acquisition of land.
C.4 Issue environmental licenses and authorizations.
C.5 Provide berths for public authority or public services.
C.6 Manage and operate special customs warehouses or areas.
C.7 Maintain and manage real estate left outside commercial port area.
C.8 Manage heritage in port areas.
C.9 Redevelop real estate left outside commercial port area for new uses.
C.10 Provide public transport to and from the port area.

## D  Market and price regulation

D.1 Issue and monitor licenses & authorizations
D.2 Issue guidance/Approve structure of tariffs for infrastructure charges
D.3 Issue guidance/Approve structure of tariffs for certain service charges
D.4 Regulate fees for sub-concessions granted to third parties
D.5 Monitor port market, competitiveness and price levels
D.6 Ensure validity of PO's reports on quality of service
D.7 Receive, investigate and act on complaints
D.8 Issue prohibitions / impose fines for breaches of competition law
D.9 Receive and investigate complaints
D.10 Open ex officio investigations
D.11 Manage arbitration cases between operators and users

## E  Mngt of concession agreements

E.1 Monitor general compliance with and manage concession agreements.
E.2 Monitor compliance with Service Level Agreements.
E.3 Monitor compliance with public service obligations.
E.4 Monitor implementation of business plan of concessionaire.
E.5 Manage financial aspects of concession agreements.
E.6 Evaluate functioning of concession agreements.
E.7 Receive and respond to requests for amendments / re-negotiations.
E.8 Enforce concession agreements in case of breaches.
E.9 Receive / investigate complaints, breaches of Concession Agreement.
E.10 Organize and/or facilitate consultations on port operations.

technical management of the port areas. The operation of a port is subject to decisions related to the land used by the port (e.g. land assigned to the port, acquisitions), the type of use for parts of this land (e.g. type of cargoes/passengers to be served, land to be used for building, warehouses, commercial reasons, the provision of building permits), and the provision of any licenses and authorizations needed for port operation and development.

Ports require the performance of a number of tasks related to **market conditions**, the tariffs applied, and the rules governing sub-concessions to service providers. Public authorities (national, port level) might have a major or minor role in setting various tariffs applying at the port (e.g. infrastructure, service charges). Depending on the governance model, private service providers may require approval, or can set tariffs independently. Governance tasks also include market monitoring, quality of the offered services, the application of competition rules, the undertaking of competition-related investigations, handling and complaints, and arbitration. All these functions, and thus the choices regarding their governance, are interdependent with the other types of port governance tasks.

Concessions of rights to operate and provide port services, with the public sector retaining port ownership and authority, have been the most common practice worldwide. Commonly, concessions are granted for specific terminals (i.e. container terminal, cruise terminal) and for providing specific services. Beyond determining the main terminal characteristics such as size, location, and waterside and landside access, and the conditions and the process of granting such concessions, (public) port authorities or other public agencies need to monitor and manage the implementation of concession agreements. Monitoring general compliance, service level agreements, public services obligations, and implementations of business plans by concessionaires are tasks that are as important as the evaluation of the concession agreements, their renegotiation, the investigation of any breaches, and the organization and facilitation of consultations on the port operations provided.

The management of emerging issues and the efficient and effective adaptation of port organization and operations represent an additional group of key port governance activities. Within a dynamic economic context marked by business model adjustments by carriers, transportation companies along the supply chains, as well as port terminal operators and other service providers, the themes of this group expand. Responses to the continuing consolidation and alliance formations of the shipping industry or the coordination of the integration of ports and landside transport modes are two of the most illustrative examples of such issues. Technological trends add further emerging issues, including the advancement of collaboration in innovation and new technologies implementation, generation of blockchains, and cybersecurity. While the specific themes may, and will, change in the future, the allocation of responsibilities regarding the leadership and implementation of strategies and specific plans to address emerging issues remains a core part of port governance models.

## 1.4 Port governance configuration

The interactions between the responsible government department (ministry or other relevant policy actors), the entity responsible for the management and operation of the port, and the involved private actors offering services are key for the governance model. This model is defined by the configuration of three inputs:

- The **strategy**, namely objectives, decisions about its market scope, and the business plan, as developed by the port authority (PA).
- The **structure**, which is implemented as a result of government regulations and policies, and the strategy selected by the PA.
- The **contextual environment** in which a port operates, which has both controllable and uncontrollable factors.

Establishing a port governance model is a process unfolding over time. Governments, or other relevant policymakers, usually impose governance structures with particular objectives in mind. These objectives are set at the national, regional, or port level as economic circumstances change. The scope of governance is to adjust strategies and corporate goals in order to align with the **contextual economic environment**.

Informed by the performance of a port or a port system, and changes in the economic context, the responsible institutions initiate changes in the structures and strategies of the respective ports aiming to generate a **matching framework**. In the absence of a better framework, these inputs produce an output (performance), the quality of which results from the consistency of the considered inputs. When considering the environment-structure-strategy triptych, two configurations emerge (Figure 4.4):

- **First configuration**. Characterized by an environment of low uncertainty, low complexity, and dynamism. It is an efficiency-oriented strategy that focuses on delivering the essential services and a mechanistic structure of centralized decision-making characterized by procedural standardization.
- **Second configuration**. Characterized by a highly uncertain environment with an effectiveness-oriented strategy offering peripheral products and services in addition to essential services. It is an organic structure of decentralized decision-making.

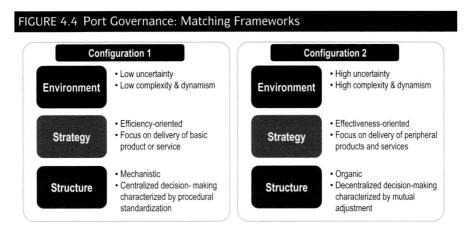

FIGURE 4.4 Port Governance: Matching Frameworks

Source: Adapted from Baltazar and Brooks (2006).

## 1.5 Realignment of port governance

Once in place, a port governance model can be reevaluated and subject to realignments. Governance models are revisited to fix any misalignment in the framework or fit changing economic circumstances. Another reason is to incorporate feedback from the port or its regulators as the reforms unfold in practice. Two conclusions can be drawn from the examination of port governance models in place around the world. First, combining inputs does not always result in a fit of the objectives based on optimal performance. Second, while governments may have had the best intentions in establishing a more commercialized footing for port operations, port governance reforms have not always delivered the full benefits sought.

Correcting these mismatches requires that a port links its governance model and its performance (Box 4.1). Port performance is the output of a governance configuration. Performance deficiencies are partially the by-products of inconsistent governance frameworks, either because of their flaws or because frameworks appropriate to particular objectives have not been imposed as anticipated. This misallocation encourages a realignment of the components of governance models. Therefore, decision-makers must know how the models have failed to deliver if this was the conclusion drawn in a particular context. A prerequisite is developing indicators that detail the exact components of this performance, the agents involved in measuring these components, and, at a port level, prioritizing the performance components.

Linking outcomes to objectives enables a **feedback mechanism** for the next cycle of port governance review. The process of evaluating port performance begins by understanding the objectives of both the port reform process and the configuration of objectives carried by the port authority. The full consideration of efficiency and effectiveness performance can be used to inform future port reform decisions. When all stakeholders are satisfied with the outcomes, there is little impetus to move further. If, on the other hand, some stakeholders are dissatisfied with the outcomes, governance objectives have not been met. This prompts changes to the imposed port governance model, how the PA configures itself in response to the imposed model (and accompanying regulation), or to the management team. Governments can also be tempted to intervene if they are not pleased with performance. In the same way, stakeholders can lobby governments if they are dissatisfied, and port users can stop using the facilities.

### Box 4.1 Linking port governance and performance

*Once in place, a port governance model is under re-evaluation and subject to realignments. The scope is to fix any misalignment in the framework imposed or to fit it to changing economic circumstances, but also to incorporate feedback from the port itself or perhaps its political masters as experience with port reform unfolds in practice (Figure 4.5).*

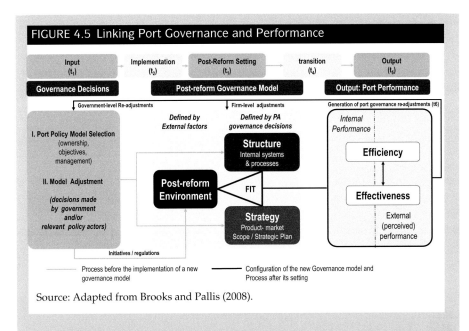

FIGURE 4.5 Linking Port Governance and Performance

Source: Adapted from Brooks and Pallis (2008).

*A feedback loop is generated through the evaluation of performance to the contemplation of opportunities for readjustment. Within a process that unfolds over time, the output (performance) and the contextual environment provide the background for the initiation of further adjustments aiming to adjust minimally, or comprehensively reform, the specifics of the governance model in place. Motivated by the conditions of a port, relevant policymakers decide to initiate change at (t1). These decisions are made in the light of a specific environment, with decision-makers having a vision of what they would like to see as port performance output. These decisions generate a process wherein port authorities (PAs) act at t2 to develop their objectives and implement the systems and processes to execute the decisions.*

*Even when the governance model is fully implemented (t3), estimations of its output are needed to fine-tune adjustments. All these changes are accompanied by transition times (t4). Measuring the performance (output) at time (t5) and informed by any changes in the economic environment (defined partially by previous governance decisions that reform objectives and regulatory frameworks, and partially by exogenous variables), PAs and relevant government agencies and/or other actors can reach decisions for adjusting previous governance choices. Governance modifications will then continue to result in performance changes and vice-versa. Of course, to complete the process, PAs and other relevant actors need to establish essential performance monitoring practices.*

## 2  TOWARDS MODERN PORT GOVERNANCE

### 2.1  Waves of port reform

Successive waves of port governance reforms, management, and organization have taken place worldwide since the 1990s. They have been the response to the globalization of production and consumption, the ongoing growth in maritime trade, and, more specifically, the booming demand for container transport and its supporting infrastructure provided by container ports and terminal operators. These reforms have increased the autonomy of port-level authorities to act and introduced a more active role for private firms in providing port services.

The first wave of port reforms took place in the 1990s and early 2000s when a number of developed and developing economies expanded the involvement of private actors in port operations and management. The core theme was the devolution of port management and operational responsibility and, to a lesser extent, the transfer of port assets from local public (decentralized) entities to private commercially driven corporate port entities. Some of these port entities are today listed on international stock markets. Commonly, the public sector retains a supervisory and monitoring role, disassociated from the provision of services and port operations, beyond the ownership of the port. In some cases, though (like the UK), there is no national agency monitoring ports. In the absence of consensus on the most appropriate governance model, implementing the planned reforms proved to be excessively challenging for many governments.

The second wave of port governance reforms is in progress. The restructuring of national port systems continues, as does the quest for identifying the most appropriate allocation of governance structures and management responsibilities, and this for two main reasons. First, ports continue to seek suitable models for optimum performance outcomes, how best to lower entry barriers to acquire the benefits of intra-port competition, reform port labor, and best engage local stakeholders in efforts to improve port hinterland access. Second, despite the best intentions, the first wave of reforms has not always delivered the expected benefits. Even though port governance configurations are rarely in place for long enough to observe clear consequences or outcomes, decision-makers implement adjustments ranging from relatively simple fine-tuning to complete reversal of previous decisions.

The **broader macroeconomic circumstances** informed these reforms. The global economic crisis of 2008 provided the impetus for many port reforms, in particular the transition towards the full implementation of the landlord model, in order to devolve operational responsibility to the private sector and cut costs, often with the specific objectives of improving efficiency, increasing volumes and enhancing profitability.

Recently, legislative adjustments have been more complex. As reforms in several countries in Asia and Europe illustrate (Figures 4.6 and 4.7):

- There is no longer a single port reform theme, such as devolution or opening the market to private terminal operators, as was the case in the 1990s. For instance, Italy is now encouraging the merger of port authorities, Greece has changed from corporatizing the state-owned enterprises managing ports to their full privatization. In countries such as Korea, and China, the national port system is still very dependent on government policies and action plans. Canada is exploring ways to enhance transparency in the port sector while Colombia seeks to re-establish authority in the national port system that was privatized in the early 1990s.
- Ports, governments, and stakeholders have moved away from a belief in a single port governance model. Some commonalities exist in terms of

FIGURE 4.6 Recent European Port Governance Reforms

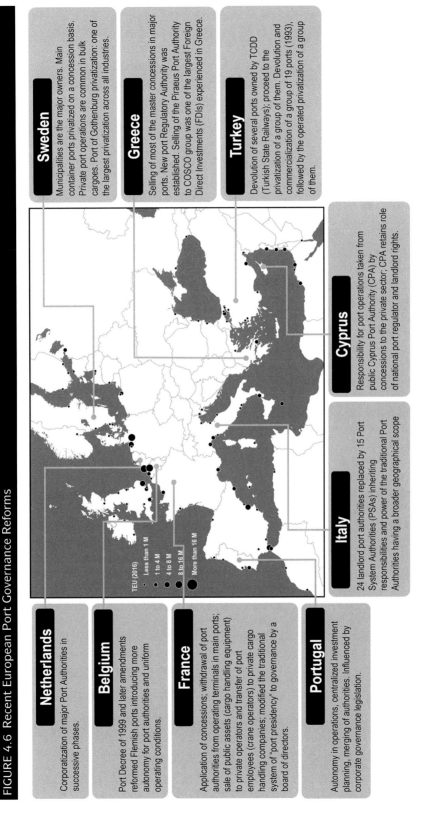

**Sweden**

Municipalities are the major owners. Main container ports privatized on a concession basis. Private port operations are common in bulk cargoes. Port of Gothenburg privatization: one of the largest privatization across all industries.

**Greece**

Selling of most of the master concessions in major ports. New port Regulatory Authority was established. Selling of the Piraeus Port Authority to COSCO group was one of the largest Foreign Direct Investments (FDIs) experienced in Greece.

**Turkey**

Devolution of several ports owned by TCDD (Turkish State Railways); proceed to the privatization of a group of them. Devolution and commercialization of a group of 19 ports (1993), followed by the operated privatization of a group of them.

**Cyprus**

Responsibility for port operations taken from public Cyprus Port Authority (CPA) by concessions to the private sector; CPA retains role of national port regulator and landlord rights.

**Italy**

24 landlord port authorities replaced by 15 Port System Authorities (PSAs) inheriting responsibilities and power of the traditional Port Authorities having a broader geographical scope

**Netherlands**

Corporatization of major Port Authorities in successive phases.

**Belgium**

Port Decree of 1999 and later amendments reformed Flemish ports introducing more autonomy for port authorities and uniform operating conditions.

**France**

Application of concessions; withdrawal of port authorities from operating terminals in main ports; sale of public assets (cargo handling equipment) to private operators and transfer of port employees (crane operators) to private cargo handling companies; modified the traditional system of "port presidency" to governance by a board of directors.

**Portugal**

Autonomy in operations, centralized investment planning, merging of authorities. Influenced by corporate governance legislation.

TEU (2016)
- Less than 1 M
- 1 to 4 M
- 4 to 8 M
- 8 to 16 M
- More than 16 M

Source: Based on Brooks, Cullinane and Pallis (2017) and various contributions in the same volume.

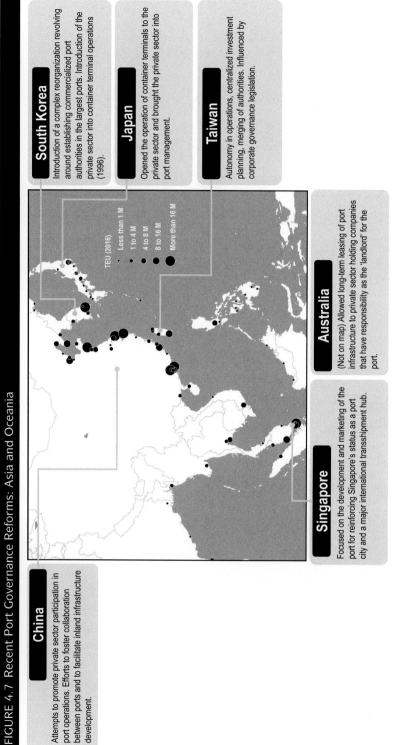

FIGURE 4.7 Recent Port Governance Reforms: Asia and Oceania

**China**

Attempts to promote private sector participation in port operations. Efforts to foster collaboration between ports and to facilitate inland infrastructure development.

**South Korea**

Introduction of a complex reorganization revolving around establishing commercialized port authorities in the largest ports. Introduction of the private sector into container terminal operations (1996).

**Japan**

Opened the operation of container terminals to the private sector and brought the private sector into port management.

**Taiwan**

Autonomy in operations, centralized investment planning, merging of authorities. Influenced by corporate governance legislation.

**Singapore**

Focused on the development and marketing of the port for reinforcing Singapore's status as a port city and a major international transshipment hub.

**Australia**

(Not on map) Allowed long-term leasing of port infrastructure to private sector holding companies that have responsibility as the 'landlord' for the port.

TEU (2016)

Less than 1 M
1 to 4 M
4 to 8 M
8 to 16 M
More than 16 M

Source: Based on Brooks, Cullinane and Pallis (2017) and various contributions in the same volume.

both the issues that decision-makers have attempted to address and the observed reforms in anticipated response. The precise level of desired state intervention in the port sector remains a theme of utmost controversy and discussion in several countries.

In the early 2020s, the COVID-19 pandemic, rising international trade disputes (e.g. China–USA trade relations) and tensions in existing trading blocs (e.g. Brexit in Europe) add to the observed volatility in international trade and cargo volumes in ports. Beyond economic factors, the growing role of environmental and social considerations shapes the behavior and strategies of port-related actors, with a greater role attributed to setting and achieving sustainability goals and to rolling out initiatives in the field of corporate social responsibility (CSR), stakeholder relations management and green supply chain management, All these, along with the consequent (de)regulatory pressures and the growing emancipation of individual citizens and stakeholders, might result in further revisits of port governance principles and details.

## 2.2 Types of endorsed reforms

A **full spectrum** of port governance models ranging from public to privately managed port activities remains in place, even after the second wave of reforms since 2000. The typology of the different paths endorsed can be summarized as follows:

- **Privatization**. The full transfer of asset ownership (including land) to a privately-owned for-profit entity. The retained role of the government is to regulate the transferred entity. Very few countries, such as the UK and New Zealand, have applied a fully privatized port governance system, including the privatization of the port land. In other cases, privatization is commonly used as a term for the long-lived transfer of management rights of ports to private entities by selling the (corporatized) public governing port authority to a private company.
- **Commercialization**. Governments have withdrawn from the operation of transportation infrastructure while retaining its ownership. The most commonly endorsed port governance model worldwide is the concessions of rights to manage and operate terminals or provide port services to third parties and is a form of commercialization.
- **Decentralization**. Decentralization of oversight responsibility from the national to the local level increases local responsiveness and flexibility, and often accompanies commercialization. In some cases, this reallocation of responsibility within the public sector includes transferring ownership to a local government entity. A few countries have chosen to either commercialize or decentralize their port infrastructure. However, most have moved towards more commercial approaches by adopting concessions.
- **Corporatization**. A particular form of commercialization involves creating a separate legal corporate entity, which takes on the legal responsibility to provide the functions or services mandated in its charter or by-laws. The distinguishing feature of corporatization is the creation of a legal entity with shares. Corporatization has been a key governance model imposed in many countries. Considerable debate exists about whether corporatization, either through the issuance of share capital or via the creation of purpose-driven entities for the state), has been particularly successful.

The majority of the largest ports have implemented **commercialized or corporatized** governance structures. They have also endorsed ways to increase the participation of the private sector via the provision of public activities and public-private partnerships, including infrastructure development through build-operate-transfer schemes or the operation of terminal facilities through concession agreements. Mixed governance models incorporating contracted management are also present. Many ports continue to remain government-owned and government-managed, although they may have been decentralized.

A few ports are listed on stock exchanges. In Europe, this is the case of some ports in the UK and the two major Greek ports, Piraeus and Thessaloniki. In many cases, corporatization has taken place with the issuance of share capital. Still, the government has retained a majority of the shares, and the issuance has not been accompanied by public listing.

## 3 CONTEMPORARY PORT GOVERNANCE MODELS

### 3.1 Public and private roles in port management

There are five main models based upon the respective responsibility of the public and private sectors in port management (Figure 4.8):

- **Public service ports**. The port authority of public service ports performs the whole range of port-related services and owns all the infrastructure. They are commonly a branch of a government ministry, and most of their employees are civil servants. Some ancillary services can be left to private companies. Because of the related inefficiencies, the number of public service ports has declined.
- **Tool ports**. Like every aspect of a public service port, the tool port differs only in the private handling of its cargo operations, albeit the port authority still owns all or part of the terminal equipment. In several cases, a tool port is a transitional form between a public service port and a landlord port.
- **Landlord ports**. Represents the most common management model where infrastructure, particularly terminals, is leased to private operating companies with the port authority retaining control of the land where the port develops either by owning it or via retaining the rights for exclusive exploitation (as granted by the competent public authority). The most common form of lease is a concession agreement where a private company is granted a long-term lease in exchange for a rent that is commonly a function of the size of the facility as well as the investment required to build, renovate or expand the terminal. Private port operators provide and maintain their superstructure, including buildings (e.g. offices, sheds, warehouses, container freight stations, workshops), and private terminal operators employ dock labor. The private operator is also responsible for providing terminal equipment so that operating standards are maintained. Today this is the dominant port model in larger and medium-sized ports. The popularity of the model, particularly within Europe and the Americas, is undoubted. Still, it has a number of variants, depending upon the level of decentralization and autonomy of the port authority involved, the cultural disposition of the country considered, the division of infrastructure investments (such as

FIGURE 4.8 Public and Private Roles in Port Management

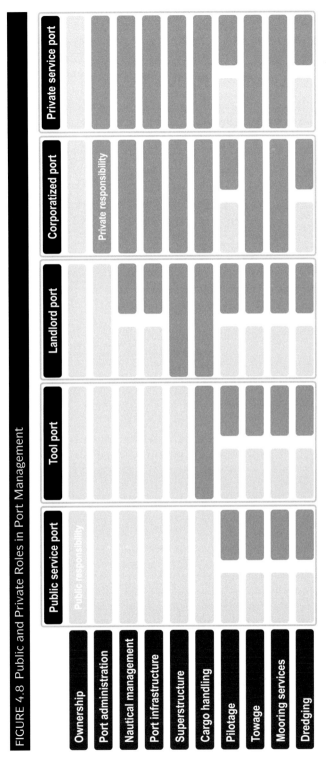

Source: Adapted from World Bank (undated, 2005) World Bank Port Reform Toolkit.

quay walls, terminal surface, etc.) between the PA and the private terminal operators, or the level of involvement of the landlord in furthering and enhancing port activities.

- **Corporatized ports**. This concerns ports that have almost entirely been privatized, with the exception that ownership remains public and is often assumed as a majority shareholder. The port authority essentially behaves like a private enterprise. This management model is unique since it is the only one where ownership and control are separated, which lessens the 'public good' pressures landlord port authorities face and the 'shareholder value' pressures private ports face.
- **Private service ports**. This is the outcome of complete privatization of the port facility with a mandate that the facilities retain their maritime role. The port authority is entirely privatized, with almost all the port functions under private control, with the public sector retaining a standard regulatory oversight. Still, public entities can be shareholders and thus gear the port towards strategies deemed to be in the public interest.

These models are applied to ports with different characteristics concerning the ownership of infrastructure, equipment, terminal operation, and models for port services provision. While service and tool ports mostly exist to promote public interests, landlord ports attempt to balance public and private interests. At the other end of the spectrum, private service ports are maximizing the interests of their shareholders.

## 3.2 Public ownership remains dominant

Public ownership of ports is still a dominant feature of port governance, with few fully privatized ports, especially amongst the largest. There are five types of port governance associated with port ownership approaches, moving from the most centralized public ownership and management to the most private sector-oriented:

- **Central government-owned** with central government management and control.
- **Government-owned** but management and control are **decentralized to a local government** body.
- **Government-owned** (national, regional, or municipal) but managed and controlled by a **corporatized entity**.
- **Government-owned** but managed by a **private sector entity** via a concession or lease arrangement, or owned and managed via a **public-private partnership** agreement.
- **Wholly privately owned**, managed, and controlled.

In some cases, government ownership means that there is no port authority but a government department responsible for port policy. In contrast, some countries have created a single port authority as the custodian of all major seaports (i.e. South Africa's Transnet National Ports Authority or TNPA, one of the divisions of state-owned company Transnet) or several ports (i.e. Romania) with no port-level port authority.

The presence of port authorities governing more than one port is a port governance approach that has recently been applied in Italy, where the national government decided to merge the managing entities of several ports in geographical proximity, forming what is now called 'Port System Authorities', which have the responsibility for governing multiple ports.

## 3.3 The extensive use of concessions

Port governance models based on concessions of rights to operate and provide port services, with the public sector retaining port ownership and the landlord port authority role, are the most common practices worldwide. This trend has been accelerated by containerization and the development of container terminals. It has progressively expanded in other types of terminals, such as cruise ports. Still, the extent of concessions differs, depending on traffic type, and remains common for container terminal management. This is perhaps because bulk terminals often serve captive users, and competition policy concerns are in play.

Commonly, concessions are granted for **specific terminals** (see Chapter 3.2 for an extensive discussion). Public port authorities (or occasionally other public agencies) generally develop a port master plan detailing the layout of port development, such as breakwaters and terminal areas, and invest in general port infrastructures such as port real estate, access roads, and rail tracks. Port authorities grant private terminal operating companies concessions to operate a terminal and receive a concession fee. The responsibility for investment differs between concessions. In some cases, the port authority invests in quays and terminal footprint, while in other cases, the private terminal operator has to make these investments. The government usually determines the main terminal characteristics such as size, location, waterside, and landside access.

In most cases, terminal operation is only undertaken by terminal operating companies. When port authorities are involved in container terminal operations, a terminal operating company might be present. In most cases, port authorities assume the role of the overseer that initiates and monitors the operator. Port authorities no longer engage in developmental activities within their port boundaries but are engaging in various coordination or cooperation activities.

Contemporary port authorities face a dilemma as the delivery of local benefits may not match the objectives of those who are granted the terminal concession. This dilemma has become more acute for several reasons. First, the **consolidation of terminal operations** has continued. Second, several ports act as **transshipment hubs** serving destinations outside the economy that hosts the port. Thus, the immediate benefits for the local economy are neither visible nor of the expected magnitude. Third, the **financialization of terminal operations** continues even after the global financial crisis of 2008–2009, as financial infrastructure funds remain active in acquiring terminal operations.

This focus on the business of terminal operations has led to divergent directions. One is that ownership by global financial interests has separated terminal operations from the community. They focused their interests on delivering returns at a time when governments were seeking even greater social returns. These have boosted rather than limited the consolidation and dominance of a few private interests in terminal operations.

## 3.4 Lessons from full port privatization

Port reforms have been a response to a broader agenda of streamlining government as a means of dealing with deficits and the result of a shift in macroeconomic thinking towards greater private sector involvement in public goods delivery. The process gained strength when the full impact of the UK decision in the 1980s to reform its public sector changed the way governments saw the way forward on the governance of most transport activities, including ports.

The British experience has informed thinking in port privatization. Port devolution in the UK often involved outright sale, regulatory functions, listing on the stock exchange, deregulation of the port labor market, and transfers often at discounted prices. The outcome is that there is no port regulator. Privatization was used to unwind nationalizations that took place during World War II. That reform was as much about reversing public ownership as it was about selling companies that should not be publicly owned. What made the UK reform model unique was that the privatization of UK ports was complete because they included the sale of port land. The British case was about selling ports (removing public ownership and accountability) rather than creating new and improved port infrastructure and facilities, which was the goal of most other countries.

Only a few countries have gone so far as to change the ownership status of both port authority and port land from public to private. The UK continues to lead the world in full privatization of the port sector, with 15 of 20 major ports and a group of other privately owned and operated ports handling 69% of total tonnage. This has been the outcome of a tradition beginning with Felixstowe in 1886 and enhanced by port reforms instigated in the 1980s and 1990s. Still, no other UK ports have been sold since 1997, despite a voluntary privatization application made by the Port of Dover in 2012, which the UK Secretary of State for Transport rejected. The only recently implemented model approaching full privatization was adopted in Australia, whereby long-term leaseholds over the port assets (including land) are sold to the private sector, usually for 99 years.

Full privatization is rarely endorsed as experience suggests that it has not been without challenges. For example, UK ports have been sold at undervalued prices; there was less investment than might have otherwise occurred. Furthermore, when private interests responded to improved trade, and financial institutions began to acquire infrastructure holdings, the loss of an oversight or monitoring role created discontent in the UK port industry and business. Other ex-post assessments of these reforms have questioned the effectiveness of the realized developments. Such criticism includes the relevant legislation that accompanied reforms and empirical evidence that corporatization does not 'a priori' result in improved financial performance. As a result, few other governments have considered copying the UK model in its entirety.

Another key problem in the case of private entities owning assets under full privatization is that in several cases, the same private company is the harbor authority, the owner of the land on which the port sits, and the port operator. This situation is also observed in Turkey, where the control of operations and management is transferred to contractor companies together with new capital assets that are expected to be transferred back to the government at the end of the concession contract. Similarly, in the mid-2010s, Greece endorsed the master concessions model, selling 51% of the shares of its major ports, Piraeus and Thessaloniki, to a third party.

## 3.5 Governance approaches across port sizes

Port governance models and reforms are **not uniformly applied** to all ports. Different treatment for secondary or peripheral ports, which are generally of small sizes, is not uncommon. Successive reforms in Europe (i.e. Spain and Italy, France and Greece) or the Americas (i.e. Canada) have followed a distinctive approach for ports of national interest from that applied to peripheral ports, which were granted a certain degree of autonomy but within a public framework of management and operation. The reason is the very different conditions and challenges faced by these ports compared to major international ports; the former group prioritizes local and regional transportation of goods to/from the local community, the need to serve as axes of regional development and poles attracting investments that would boost the prospects of local economies. Besides, even in the smaller ports alone, the variety of public service obligations, geographical constraints, or economic development aspirations is remarkable.

The size effect is an important factor in explaining the heterogeneity of port organization. Port governance regimes comprising at least two tiers are common, particularly in nations where port operations are highly concentrated within just one or a few key ports. To give some examples, in the UK, where 20 ports account for 87% of total throughput, the UK Trust ports were allowed to privatize in 1991, yet all have remained in the public sector, except for one. In Sweden, Gothenburg dominates the country's container handling. Its privatization in 2010 represented one of the biggest ever in Sweden, across all sectors. Still, numerous small ports remain public entities, while three significant container ports have been privatized through concession. In Greece, where the privatized Piraeus and Thessaloniki account for virtually all of the country's container throughput, local and municipal ports remain under strict public control. In Canada, the port reform process introduced a three-tier approach, with the largest strategic interest ports given greater autonomy (Canada Port Authority ports), second-tier local and regional ports divested to local interests, and 'remote' ports retained by the federal government.

It is not only the size of operations that limits the prospects of a port reform. It is also the structure of the regional and national market within which a port operates. While sufficient size is required for reaping economies of scale, there may not be sufficient scale remaining within the system to ensure either intra-port competition or inter-port competition, or both. These circumstances might compromise or limit the potential benefits to be derived from port governance reforms.

## 3.6 The role of the institutional setting

**Institutional and cultural differences** across nations might result in the different treatment of ports. Institutional conditions restrict port governance choices and lead to diversified outcomes and development trajectories.

Port governance structures follow a path largely affected by the characteristics of local/national institutional frameworks and the political traditions in place. Path-dependent decisions preserve the system, resulting in implementation asymmetries, even when different governments seek the same generic port governance solution. For example, in the Netherlands, private law allows for the different treatment of corporatized (even non-profit) entities by the government compared to what is allowed in France or Belgium. Cultural traditions might also result in different practices. The advanced tariffs negotiation model with port user associations in the case of the biggest European port, Rotterdam, is not common elsewhere.

Besides, while port governance frameworks are the subject of specific legislation that exclusively addresses the organization of the port sector, they are often shaped by policy and legislation that more directly relate to other sectors, such as the legislation on **corporate governance and public management**.

Changes in dominant political tenets around the world are also significant. On occasion, the confidence in public management has been eroded. Following the financial crisis of 2008, populism gained ground, and port reform was explicitly instigated as part of a wider political strategy to help extricate nations from economic decline, or it was imposed on governments as a condition of bailout packages. Cyprus, Greece, and Portugal are examples where recent decisions on port governance have been externally imposed by international institutions monitoring adherence to imposed bailout conditions.

The influence of national/local **political factors** is important. Port governance reforms are subject to drafting, approving, implementing, and fine-tuning that involve different port communities and stakeholders reacting to national and global changes. The negotiating power held by stakeholders such as terminal operators, concessionaires, ship agents, freight forwarders, and unions is likely to result in the idiosyncratic nature of national reform patterns. The port reforms that eventually emerge may be different from what was originally intended. This outcome is inevitably the case within any long political process. A heavily politicized process not only delays reforms but also changes targets and models. To give an example, Greece shifted from concessions of activities to the selling of master concessions.

The introduction of policy and legislation enabling port reform and establishing a new port governance system is the outcome of a long process extending the timeline beyond expectations. In some countries, such as in the Netherlands, reforms have not been subject to delays . In France, it took three years to implement transfer to new port entities. In other countries (i.e. Brazil, Greece, Italy), the process has been prolonged. The cause of delays during the implementation stage is systematically linked to the embeddedness of ports in specific institutional and economic domains. This embeddedness results in the institutional divergence between the objectives set at the governmental level and the interests and objectives at the regional/port level. In the absence of both local acceptance and a bottom-up perspective on the implementation of port reform, the presence of multilevel organizations and associated interests and motivations may constitute a potential barrier to the successful implementation of a new port governance framework.

Consequently, there is still very little evidence on best practices in port governance. In general terms, the heterogeneity of models and the lack of consistency in the roles of public sector agents and stakeholders precludes a comparative analysis of the outcomes achieved by port reform in relation to the objectives which are set for the reform. The middle ground between centralized control and full privatization is extremely complex, and there are no clear and transparent models. In Europe, for example, every country does port governance differently. For many years, a European Union Common Port Policy failed to emerge. It was only in 2016 that a framework was adopted, and even this is limited in application to only some port services within the core European ports. As in other parts of the world, the endorsed port governance models relate to national circumstances, traditions, and, frequently, the economic situation of the hosting country.

# Chapter 4.2  Port authorities

*Port authorities are involved in port management and the promotion of the port they manage. With the increasing presence of private operators, the role of port authorities has evolved.*

## 1 PORT AUTHORITY: A DEFINITION

Any given seaport around the world is typically managed by a port authority.

> *A port authority is a public or a private entity that, whether or not in conjunction with other activities, under national law or regulation is empowered to carry out the (i) administration, (ii) development, (iii) management, and, occasionally, (iv) operation of the port land and infrastructure, and (v) the coordination and control of port operation activities.*

Historically, port authorities were governmental or quasi-governmental public institutions established in order to address:

- The need to **manage property rights** in waterfront areas.
- The need to **plan port development**.
- The **provision of public goods**, which, like navigation safety, cannot be denied to users who refuse to pay while consuming services that are unlikely to be provided by the market.
- The need to take into account both **positive and negative externalities**.
- The need to promote the **efficiency of local monopolies** in port services provision, which have the potential to generate economic rents.

As part of the port policy formation tasks, national or state legislation defines ownership, institutional structures, level of autonomy, level of strategic freedom, and, frequently, the composition of the governing body of a port authority. Within the given powers and strategic freedoms, port authorities define their goals and activities in order to fulfill objectives set by their regulators. Port authorities generally have specific strategic goals that relate to their responsibilities and functions. Given the differences in institutional structures (i.e. the norms and the rules of an economy) and market environment, the strategic goals may differ. The common strategic goal of port authorities is

**competitiveness**, but a number of other strategic goals are either explicitly or implicitly linked with this primary goal:

- Contribute to local, regional, and national **economic growth**.
- Create **employment**.
- **Facilitate trade**.
- Maximize **throughput volumes**.
- Maximize the **added value** of the port as a whole or individual companies.
- Generate **income and profits**.
- Integrate ports with their **foreland and hinterland**.
- Promote **sustainability**.

As entities, port authorities combine public and private goals and can be characterized as **hybrid or shared value organizations**. Fully public institutions or private port authorities are uncommon, but secondary ports generally have public port authorities. The absence of a port authority is rare. There have been cases where ports, including the real estate, were fully privatized. These ports are managed by the private companies that have bought them (e.g. the United Kingdom), the centralized national management and regulatory authorities (e.g. Colombia), or public institutions assigned to provide oversight (e.g. Hong Kong). Port authorities are bodies that might manage one or more ports in one or more geographical location.

In the twenty-first century, the role of port authorities is evolving with its importance remaining high. Extensive **port governance reforms** devolving powers at the port level and rearranging public and private roles in port management, an expanding presence of private operators and owners, and a changing economic context and technological environment have altered both port functions and the role of port authorities. This has led to the introduction of other more generic terms to describe them, including the widespread use of the managing body of the port.

## 2 FUNCTIONS OF PORT AUTHORITIES

The conventional roles of a port authority are those of a landlord, a regulator, and an operator of the port:

- As a **landlord**, a port authority manages the port assets under its jurisdiction. This commonly concerns the provision of infrastructure such as piers and the dredging of waterways. This was commonly done with public funds that port authorities were able to levy.
- As a **regulator**, a port authority sets the planning framework, namely fees, subcontracting services, and safety, as well as the enforcement of national and port-related rules and regulations.
- As an **operator**, a port authority provides day-to-day services to ships (e.g. pilotage and towage) and merchandise (e.g. loading/unloading and warehousing).

Traditionally, port authorities performed one or more of these functions, with the variations defined by local port development traditions. The determining variables were the **centralization level** of port governance-related decisions and the extent of private operations. Since the late 1990s, changes in the

## FIGURE 4.9 Recent Changes in Port Authority Functions

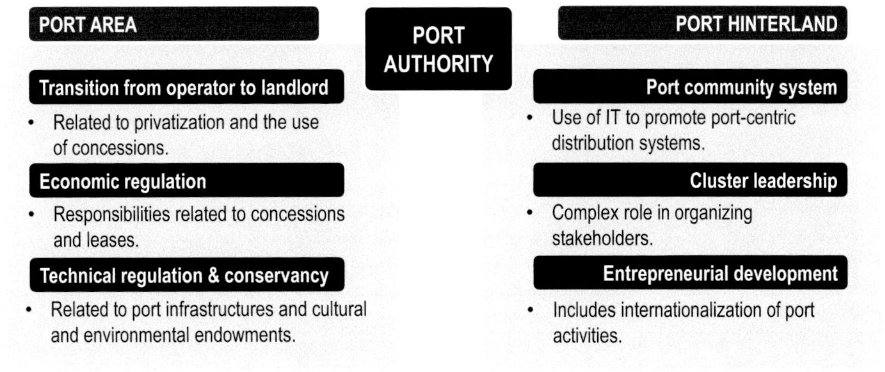

**PORT AREA**

**PORT AUTHORITY**

**PORT HINTERLAND**

**Transition from operator to landlord**
- Related to privatization and the use of concessions.

**Economic regulation**
- Responsibilities related to concessions and leases.

**Technical regulation & conservancy**
- Related to port infrastructures and cultural and environmental endowments.

**Port community system**
- Use of IT to promote port-centric distribution systems.

**Cluster leadership**
- Complex role in organizing stakeholders.

**Entrepreneurial development**
- Includes internationalization of port activities.

business and political environments within which ports operate transformed these functions (Figure 4.9):

- **Devolution of governance** has supported the notion that port authorities act as corporatized and/or commercialized entities that define autonomously at the local level the planning, development, and management of activities at the respective port(s) under their responsibility.
- **Concessioning** has reduced the port authority role as an operator since this role is increasingly assumed by specialized terminal operators renting terminal facilities over long periods of time (frequently for more than 30 years). The dominant rationale behind this process was that port authorities tended to have poor performance levels in their terminal operations. As a result, port authorities have to manage ports where operations are provided by several service providers including global terminal operators having terminal assets in a wide variety of markets.
- **Cluster governance** is an emerging and extensive trend where the port authority assumes leadership in activities that conventionally were outside its jurisdiction. These include the setting up of inland terminals and logistics zones (directly or in partnership), various strategies to monitor and improve performance (such as stakeholder relations management, marketing strategies, and internationalization activities), setting up port community systems, promoting environmental and social initiatives, and being involved in training and education for port-related employment as well as facilitating relations with its surrounding urban areas.
- **Growth of port activities and port regionalization** have introduced further goals related to economic, social, and environmental sustainability and the need to secure the social acceptance of port operators; a practice commonly referred to as 'securing the port's license to operate'.

Along with new business-oriented approaches in public management, these changes progressively altered the strategic role of port authorities. This revision refers to two strategies. The first is the **positioning of port authorities** within the new institutional setting of port governance (Figure 4.10). The second relates to the functions and activities of the management entities in order to

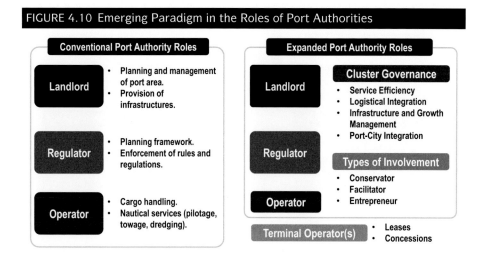

FIGURE 4.10 Emerging Paradigm in the Roles of Port Authorities

advance their competitiveness. In many cases, the involvement of port authorities in operations lessened or was even abandoned. Port authorities started undertaking a number of additional functions. Like many organizations, ports now have environmental, social, and governance obligations, in addition to their responsibility for the promotion of trade. Environmental responsibilities (including mitigation measures) have led to greater coastal planning involvement, the management of inland traffic flows, and urban land-use planning. Social responsibilities increased concerns about the distribution of the costs and benefits of port development. The existence of multiple stakeholders leads to gradual changes in port governance arrangements and how decisions are made. There has been a significant increase in the functions that port authorities can be called upon to undertake, although not all of them do this.

The centrality of port authorities in the management of ports remains intact. Within the new governance settings it is further upgraded as they are at the core of the landlord model. Port authorities, which might be corporatized or not, assume responsibilities for handling commercial and financial affairs, investments in new development projects, mid-term business planning and implementation, and autonomous setting of long-term strategies and objectives. This centrality expands their role well beyond that of the port development company or that of the conflict manager.

When performing these functions port authorities might opt to act as:

- **Conservators** of the existing port ecosystems.
- **Facilitators** of broader interaction between economic and societal interests within the port and beyond the port perimeter, trying to engage in strategic regional partnerships.
- **Entrepreneurs**, combining the main features of the facilitator with a more outspoken commercial attitude, with the potential to advance the prospects of the port(s) they manage.

The facilitating or entrepreneurial roles of port authorities are associated with:

- Adopting a corporate culture based on **transparency, entrepreneurship, and accountability** that is free of political interference and encourages an entrepreneurial approach coupled with strict financial discipline and sound risk management. This has even led port authorities to developing a function supporting new service development by private port companies and knowledge-based institutions.

- A strategy of increased **flexibility and adaptability**, that is moving beyond long-term infrastructure plans and is endorsed by critical stakeholders.
- A permanent and **constructive relationship with stakeholders**, including the business community, government agencies, non-governmental organizations, and local community interest groups. This relationship provides the social acceptability that the managing entities of the port need to get the permits necessary to operate and expand.
- A **port development strategy** that is not confined to within the geographical boundaries of the port but builds partnerships and networks beyond the port boundaries to enhance port competitiveness.

## 3 PORT AUTHORITY RESPONSIBILITIES

### 3.1 The port authority as a landlord

The **landlord port model** involves private sector operations in the port area. The port authority manages public infrastructure and advances the prospects of the entire port cluster (Figure 4.11). Among its many other responsibilities, the port authority is the curator and the authorized manager of the port land and adjacent aquatic surfaces to be leased to the private sector. The port authority acts as the landlord, and is commonly the regulatory body responsible for the technical management of the port area and several public authority functions. In contrast, port operations (especially cargo handling) are carried out by private companies. Infrastructure is leased to private operating companies and industries such as refineries, tank terminals, and chemical plants. Private port operators provide and maintain their superstructure, including buildings (e.g. offices, sheds, warehouses, container freight stations, workshops) and dock labor. This has become the dominant model in larger and medium-sized ports.

**FIGURE 4.11 The Main Activities of Landlord Port Authorities**

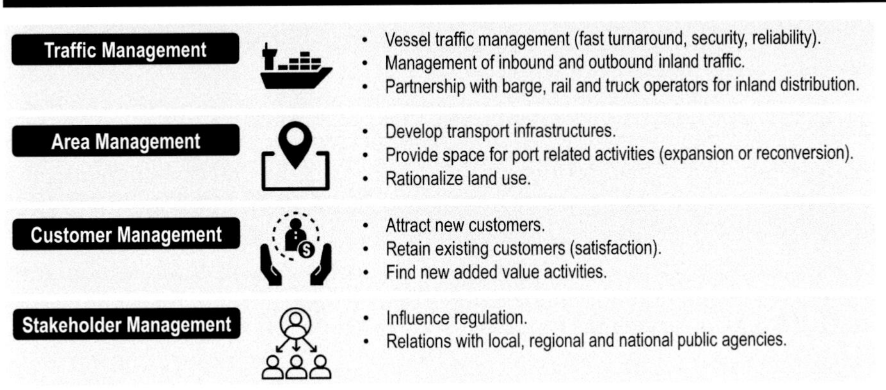

**Traffic Management**
- Vessel traffic management (fast turnaround, security, reliability).
- Management of inbound and outbound inland traffic.
- Partnership with barge, rail and truck operators for inland distribution.

**Area Management**
- Develop transport infrastructures.
- Provide space for port related activities (expansion or reconversion).
- Rationalize land use.

**Customer Management**
- Attract new customers.
- Retain existing customers (satisfaction).
- Find new added value activities.

**Stakeholder Management**
- Influence regulation.
- Relations with local, regional and national public agencies.

As a landlord, the port authority must optimize the use of its domain (the total area, land and aquatic, under the statutory responsibility of the port authority) by earmarking port areas for specific uses, awarding concessions and authorizations to a selected mix of companies, monitoring and managing the implementation of concession agreements, and adopting an appropriate pricing system.

A landlord port authority might opt to perform its roles acting as the **conservator** that focuses on passive traffic, real estate, and area management. It can decide to be the **facilitator** who operates as an active broker that mediates business-to-business relations with other actors, including customers (users) and stakeholders. Within a regional approach, it develops strategic partnerships inside or beyond the port perimeter. In the largest ports, a port authority might be the entrepreneur landlord that acts as the active developer. Simultaneously, it is directly involved in commercial business-to-business negotiations and investments beyond the port perimeter, collaborating with other port authorities as part of an internationalization strategy.

The situation is far from being uniform. On the one hand, the port authority is a **concessionaire**, managing leases port areas. Often, leasing accounts for 50% of the total port revenue. In these instances, the port authority has fairly limited autonomy in setting concession prices, port operator authorization fees, wharfage charges, and other dues. At the same time, it does have the responsibility for generating a fiscal surplus. On the other hand, many other port authorities are still described as landlords but often provide services and develop strategic activities that are not generally associated with this role. These port authorities act with more autonomy and a more business-like structure, with a broader strategic scope and more business-like goals. The shift of focus from macro-level goals to goals at the firm level underlines their entrepreneurial role.

## 3.2 The port authority as an operator

In ports that continue to have a predominantly public character, known as **service ports**, the port authority acts as the operator offering a complete range of services required for the functioning of the seaport system. The port owns, maintains, and operates every available asset (fixed and mobile), and cargo-handling activities are executed by labor employed directly by the port authority. They are under the direct jurisdiction of public agencies such as a transport ministry or a maritime one, a Chair (or Director-General), and a Board of Directors, including civil servants appointed by and directly reporting to the public agency.

Port authorities also retain **operating functions** in some ports where the private sector has assumed, via concessions, leases, or outright selling, the responsibility to operate terminals. In these cases, the involvement of port authorities in operations maintains a shareholding in private companies providing services and the provision of public or specialized services. Otherwise, Port Authorities do not act as operators. They are limited to either applying or even to monitoring the implementation of mechanistic or dynamic concession policies of terminals to third parties.

## 3.3 The port authority as a regulator

Port authorities are the **port level regulators**, undertaking and monitoring several public authority governance functions. Acting as conservators of a given port, or port system, they take care of the application and enforcement of regulations set by other policy-makers, such as national administrators responsible for port policy set by international organizations, such as the International Maritime Organisation. These include regulations concerning operational safety, the implementation of local or international safety and security codes (i.e. the ISPS Code), and protocols and rules governing the provision of auxiliary services. Often, port authorities adopt port-specific rules aiming to secure the implementation of these regulations. In several cases, and for specific regulations like navigation, and law and order, they are assisted by the Harbor Master or the coastguard. Port authorities also regulate financial revenues by having full or partial control of port tariffs.

Beyond being active in creating mechanisms that facilitate implementation and monitoring compliance, port authorities can develop their own rules. Environmental management is one such field where port authorities are increasingly active in developing initiatives to advance sustainability. The adoption of differential charging methods (i.e. offering lower charges to environmentally friendly ships) is an example of a method currently used to promote the sustainability of port operations.

As part of **internationalization strategies**, port authorities have tried to capitalize their expertise as regulators. They are moving towards an entrepreneurial role linked with the commercialization of their expertise and tools available into other ports and creating financial revenues on a commercial basis.

# 4 THE PORT AUTHORITY AS A CLUSTER MANAGER

## 4.1 Cluster leaders

In a contemporary setting, port authorities are hybrid organizations that act and develop beyond the management of the activities within their jurisdiction. Port management entities are increasingly acting as **community and port cluster managers** engaged with stakeholders and investing in facilitating activities like information technologies, promotion and marketing of the port, and training and education activities.

While cargo handling is the core of port activities, geographically concentrated and mutually related transport, logistics, production, and trade activities in the port zone and the surrounding areas, forming a port cluster. These activities, centered around a distinctive economic specialization, develop in each port, with all stakeholders benefiting from competitiveness improvements. Port authorities increasingly have an active role in improving this competitiveness by increasing the cluster's internal cohesion and generating agglomeration effects and competition with the hinterland.

Port clusters consist of a substantial number of firms and their evolution, producing **cluster externalities** such as port marketing, labor inflow, education and training, and hinterland access. Some of these externalities might be addressed on an ad-hoc basis, yet most require shared investments. This is because the threat of free-riding prevents the cooperation of competing firms and, as a consequence, insufficient investments with joint benefits are made. The need for collective action follows, with the port authority standing as the institutional arrangement to address these collective action problems.

Within a port cluster, the port authorities act as the **leading firm and the broker**, who is trusted to resolve the emerging collective action problems. These initiatives would not be present otherwise, either because the scale of operations is small and natural internal monopolies exist in many seaports, or because specific actions might not be taken on by firms that operate within the cluster but prioritize their very own interests. The role of the port authority is to increase investments in collective action problems and secure capital. The port authority might advance public-private partnerships, joint responsibility, and joint funding with other stakeholders to achieve this goal. The trust stakeholders have in the port authority can lower transaction costs, enable cooperation and investments, and also innovation.

Ideally, for a port authority to effectively perform its cluster manager role, it should be self-sustaining, have the autonomy to set prices, make investment decisions and prioritize the goal of maximizing the performance of the port cluster. While port authorities might seek to advance the competitiveness of the cluster, the situation differs between ports. In some cases, the optimal amount of joint investments is very substantial, while in other ports, private industries may invest relatively more, and the extra investments needed are relatively limited. The better the cluster governance, the more competitive the port cluster is.

## 4.2 Stakeholder relationships management

Stakeholder relationship management practices are important in advancing the prospects of the port cluster. They cover monitoring critical topics, involving stakeholders, and implementing strategies. According to their priorities, port authorities proceed to identify and classify various stakeholders, evaluate their potential influence on port operations development and planning, prioritize stakeholder relations, and then manage the ties between the organization and the most influential stakeholders.

A port stakeholder's classification includes ten different categories that refer to both internal and external groups that are part of the broader port cluster. Community groups and civil society organizations are also included through their increasing attention to port activities, expansion patterns, and development plans. The main stakeholders include:

1. **Shareholders** such as public or private organizations, firms holding an equity share in the port authority or allowed to appoint directors and executives of the port authority board.
2. **Port services providers** such as pilots, mooring and towage operators, customs, and the coast guard.
3. **Concessionaires** such as terminal operators with concessions in the port areas, or other concessionaires related to warehouses, industrial areas, logistics platforms, malls, and commercial areas.
4. **Carriers** such as shipping lines and tramp operators.

5. **Employees and trade unions** such as people working at the executive and operational level in the port authority, and in public institutions, labor pools, and port-related firms, such as forwarders, ship agents, and customs brokers.

6. **Port users** such as freight forwarders, ship agents, brokers, road hauliers, railway companies, and logistics providers.

7. **Passengers** such as people using port facilities for commuting, travel (ferries), and tourism (cruising and yachting).

8. The **financial community** such as credit and financial institutions providing financial resources to support port investments and development.

9. **Local community and societal groups of interest** such as people and organizations located in the vicinity of the port areas and affected by port operations and business. The category also includes individuals or groups defending specific social or environmental causes.

10. **Regulators** such as local, regional, national, and international institutions setting up the institutional and governance frameworks within which ports operate.

To achieve their growth targets, port authorities interact with stakeholders and other ports, developing coordination and cooperation strategies:

- First, the growing complexity of supply chains is encouraging port authorities to undertake strategies aiming at a better level of **coordination of their hinterland**. Port authorities act as leaders in bringing together the various supply chain actors to provide, through coordination strategies, an integrated transportation service beneficial to all the actors but especially to the port.

- Second, ports develop **cooperation strategies with other ports** (Chapter 4.3), which might be competing ports located in geographic proximity or ports located in different port regions. In the context of the latter strategy and within an entrepreneurial approach, port authorities of the largest ports are involved in internationalization strategies as well.

## 5 PORT AUTHORITIES' ROLE IN CRUISE PORTS GOVERNANCE

Port authorities have assumed a different role within each of the cruise port governance models. They perform as either entrepreneur, facilitator, or conservator. The role of the facilitator is qualified as less or more active, depending on several port strategy and structure variables, including the role of the port managing entities co-existing at the cruise port.

Four cruise port governance models are present in the Mediterranean and its adjoining seas, the second major cruise market in the world (Figure 4.12). Each model assumes a different role for the managing entity of the cruise port. All models co-exist with a contextual environment of apparent complexity and dynamism.

The port authority can be an **active leader and an entrepreneur** on all different fronts (model A). These are primarily large ports, in terms of passenger movements, without the presence of a cruise terminal operator. The

FIGURE 4.12 Cruise Ports Governance Models

| | Model A | Model B | Model C | Model D |
|---|---|---|---|---|
| **Terminal(s) Operated by** | Port Authority (PA) | International Container Terminal Operator (ICTO) | Terminal Operator (TO) | Port Authority |
| **Role of Port Authority** | Entrepreneur | Facilitator | Facilitator | Conservator |
| **Role of terminal operating entity** | Active Leadership | The Investor | The Marketer | Passive |
| **Port Structure** | PA operates; PA plans; PA develops | ICTO operates; PA and ICTO develop, or ICTO develops; PA & ICTO plan, or ICTO | TO operates; TO plans, or PA and TO plan; PA and TO develop, or TO develops | PA operates; PA plans; PA develops |
| **Port Strategy** | PA in charge of marketing; Cancellation policies; Public funding; Feedback received (passengers) | Direct investments; TO decides on investments; Feedback received; No strategic partnerships | TO in charge of marketing; No direct investments by TO | PA in charge of marketing; Strategic partnerships; No berth allocation / No feedback; no contemporary cruises |
| **Port Type** | Large cruise port; Marquee destination; Many terminals | Large cruise port; Marquee destination; Many terminals; homeport | Any type of cruise port (large/small; one/more terminals) | One terminal; Small Non marquee; Transit [port |

Source: Adapted from Pallis, Arapi and Papachristou (2019).

port authority is responsible for the planning, development, and operation of the cruise port. It is also the entity leading overall promotion and marketing efforts. These ports tend to target premium cruise lines more than those that belong to other groups. Their strategy usually includes receiving feedback from passengers, applying cancellation policies for cruise lines that do not call according to schedule, and seeking public funding to develop infrastructures supporting cruise activities.

Large marquee homeports can be marked by the presence of an active investor (model B). Commonly, an International Cruise Terminal Operator (ICTO) manages and operates the terminal. The port authority is closer to the role of the **facilitator** of the ICTO strategic actions. The operator also acts as an investor and develops the port, either alone or with the facilitation of the port authority. The latter is more likely to have made direct investments, while the operator decides autonomously on new investments in capital assets. Just like model A, these are ports receiving feedback from passengers as part of their strategy. At the same time, they tend to develop without establishing partnerships with other cruise ports, terminals, or cruise lines.

The role of the port authority can also be that of **facilitator**, though less active (model C). Ports in this group usually have the terminal operator leading marketing and promotional activities. There is no significant relationship of this model with particular port features (i.e. port type). Instead, both the port authority and the cruise terminal operator jointly advance port planning. The entities operating cruise terminals tend not to make direct investments, with such investments remaining a public sector responsibility.

There are smaller cruise ports where the port authority maintains a **passive managerial role** (model D). This is the entity that, in practice, assumes the role of the conservator by taking responsibility for all marketing and promotional activities. It also tends to develop strategic partnerships with other cruise ports, terminals, or cruise lines. The strategy of these ports is also rather conservative. They usually do not apply berth allocation policies, nor do they receive feedback from passengers. These ports rarely target hosting the contemporary mass cruises market segment, and most of them do not have a formal collaboration with those responsible for other transport modes. Even if terminal operators are involved in port operations, they usually do not decide autonomously on new investments.

## 6 OWNERSHIP OF PORT AUTHORITIES

Seaports remain **predominantly under public ownership**, and this is reflected in the ownership of port authorities. For most port authorities, particularly in North America and Europe, full ownership by the state or the municipality remains predominant. Only a few port authorities combine ownership of different government levels, such as state-municipality or province-municipality. Mixed public-private ownership is rare, with the public sector owning the majority of shares and limited private shareholder participation. Port authorities listed on the stock exchange remain an exception. Full private ownership, where one or more private parties owns both the port authority and the land, is only found in the UK and New Zealand.

Despite perceptions, successive port governance reforms in recent decades have opened port services to private actors, but ownership of port authorities has not changed substantially. In Europe, financial and economic crises put pressure on national budgets in the 2010s and impacted port ownership, leading to the privatization of some port authorities. In 2016, the major Mediterranean port of Piraeus in Greece was acquired by China's Cosco Group, which took a 67% stake in the shares of the listed Piraeus Port Authority. In 2018, the second largest port of Greece, Thessaloniki, was acquired by a consortium led by a German investing Fund (Deutsche Invest Equity Partners), Terminal Link (a company owned by CMA-CGM), and China Merchant Holdings International (International Terminal Operator), which also bought 67% of the listed Thessaloniki Port Authority. Similar trends were observed in Koper in Slovenia, and Constanza, in Romania.

Port authorities are also moving towards more **independent private management**. European ports provide several examples illustrating this trend. The Port of Amsterdam was officially corporatized in 2013 to a limited liability company with the City of Amsterdam as the main shareholder. Finnish ports have been limited liability companies since 2015 and, as of 2016, the Port Authority of Antwerp, the second-largest port in Europe, became a corporation under public law. According to a 2016 survey of the European Sea Ports Organisation, 51% of the port authorities in Europe were already structured as independent commercial entities companies, and 44% were still independent public bodies with their own legal framework and different degrees of functional and financial dependency from public oversight. While operating under different legal forms, these two main categories may share similarities such as self-financing and commercial and entrepreneurial behavior to increase market share and attract private investment. They may also share the same levels of influence from public authorities through participation in the governing board of the port. At the same time, four out of five port authorities were fully or partially subject to commercial law and governed by specific laws and acts.

# Chapter 4.3 Port coordination and cooperation

*Ports can develop cooperation and coordination strategies providing an integrated transportation service beneficial to actors involved in port supply chains.*

## 1 COORDINATION OF PORT ACTIVITIES

The purpose of port coordination and cooperation strategies is for a port authority to formalize its expansion through a more active landlord function. The key drivers for the setting up of coordination mechanisms include capital investments to accommodate increased traffic through the involvement of supply chain actors at the port and in the hinterland. Land scarcity, oligopoly in terminal operations, and negative externalities of port development, such as environmental impacts, further stimulate port authorities to a more active role. Port authorities have designed coordination strategies in order to align

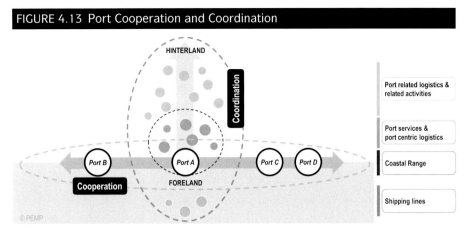

FIGURE 4.13 Port Cooperation and Coordination

Source: Adapted from Brooks, McCalla, Pallis and Van der Lugt (2010).

the various supply chain actors using integrated approaches and to develop cooperation strategies with other port authorities.

There are two types of competitive strategies for ports: (1) the concept of **cooperation** between different ports and (2) the concept of improving the integration and **coordination** in hinterland transport networks (Figure 4.13). Ports may cooperate to serve shippers and shipping lines, or a port may coordinate with other port services, logistics providers, and carriers, aiming to provide better services in linking overseas forelands with inland destinations.

Globalization and the growing complexity of supply chains are encouraging port authorities to undertake strategies aiming at a better level of coordination of their hinterland that involve:

- **Usage of incentives**. Coordinate operations of freight actors so that the usage of transport chains and the underlying assets is improved. It can involve using a preferential rate structure for customers that provide a minimum volume or meet a reliability level. Others will be encouraged to follow since the reward is lower-cost access to the infrastructures.
- **Inter-firm alliances**. They concern two types of alliances. The first is vertical integration (along transport chains), where a maritime shipping company and a terminal operator can agree to coordinate their services. The second is horizontal integration (between competitors), where an equipment or container pool can be established to improve asset utilization.
- **Organizational scope**. A vertical integration process where an actor decides to penetrate a new market to expand or add value to its activities. For instance, a maritime shipping company can be involved in port terminal operations. Also, a port authority could be involved in developing an inland port as a strategy to alleviate congestion and expand to the market potential of its hinterland.
- **Collective actions**. A series of strategies under the port authority leadership, such as setting up public/private partnerships to create a logistic zone. Each actor contributes to its realm of expertise. The development

of port community systems is also a collective action relying on information technologies.

The development of **inland ports and logistical zones** is an emerging paradigm. Still, port authorities tend to be reluctant to undertake partnerships with inland ports, mostly out of concern for losing added value activities and employment. Inland ports may also promote port competition by offering access to new freight corridors, thus challenging the fundamental hinterland of a port and its related cargo.

However, there is an increasing level of coordination between port authorities and inland ports, particularly among the largest ports. The latter tend to have more congestion issues as well as the volume and the financial and technical capability to undertake these initiatives. In Europe, the dominant strategy is the setting up of dedicated rail or barge services towards the inland port. In North America, port authorities tend to set up logistical zones within their adjacent areas to better anchor traffic.

## 2 COORDINATION IN CONTAINER TERMINAL OPERATIONS

Coordination also occurs **within port terminals**, as terminal operators attempt to improve productivity through coordination with terminal users. In the case of vessel operations, this coordination focuses on:

- **Berthing and the start of work on vessel arrivals**. Terminal operators and carriers share information to coordinate berth allocation and work schedules.
- **Planning for delays**. Terminal operators and carriers coordinate to protect schedule integrity through communications with local shipping line agencies and ports along the liner call sequence for real-time information regarding schedule delays.
- **Planning maximum crane allocation** and adherence to berth windows, such as reaching agreements on available cranes, volume forecasts, allocations, and dock labor order.
- **Organization of bunker and store deliveries**. This coordination refers to sharing information and plans for deliveries so that they do not conflict with operations at the terminal and are completed before or during port operations.
- **Late ordering of services** (pilot, tugs, linesmen) by the carriers.

Terminal operators also collaborate with shippers and other cargo interests with a focus on:

- The latest possible **delivery window** to receive cargoes.
- **Load information** (volumes, weights, container numbers, destinations).
- **Documentation** (customs information, dangerous goods, incorrect weight, seal details).
- **Stow plans** on what is received in the terminal or will be loaded/stowed/restowed (i.e. empties, cargoes with special needs).
- **Last-minute and unplanned stows** or empty loads.
- **Roll-over cargoes** from a vessel to the next vessels in the case of transshipment, with last-minute priorities set on major customers and provisions for specific loads, such as reefer, dry, and empty containers.

- **Late provision of discharge information** and next modality information (e.g. latest possible connections to/from trucks, barges, rail, feeder, vessels).

These approaches facilitate qualitative improvements concerning asset planning and utilization. Understanding the needs of shipping lines might result in improvements of the stowage layout to match the needs of prioritized vessels, so they are ready for other discharge ports. Understanding the need of shippers might increase **cargo discipline**, minimizing the potential for excessive dwell times and empty storage entitlements. In any case, even when terminal users share similar visions for operational standards (on-time performance, high data quality), terminal operators are taking care of adequate serviceable equipment levels with sufficient excess capacity for flexibility and appropriate labor levels to service demand peaks.

## 3 COOPERATION BETWEEN PORTS

### 3.1 Emerging cooperation schemes

Cooperation between port authorities governing different ports, as well as cooperation between terminal operators and between other service providers, does not exclude intense competitive behavior. Since the 1990s, cooperation is increasingly common, aiming at more flexible traffic distribution patterns. An early example includes Rotterdam and Baltic Region ports that began cooperating in the early 1990s to strengthen their competitive positions.

Cooperation expanded to a strategy including a broad spectrum of initiatives aiming to:

- Better use assets in terms of efficiency, scale, and scope.
- Improve competencies.
- Gain a positional advantage by offsetting the undesirable effects of competition.

All these societal gains were made primarily through increased efficiencies. As in other businesses, cooperation between ports might be multi or single function and might even reach the form of coopetition, defined as cooperation with competitors to reach decisive benefits that cannot be reached otherwise.

Port cooperation is a strategy to improve port performance. Due to port regionalization, imbalances in port capacity and the competition in broader geographical regions form the key drivers of cooperation between ports, especially between those in proximity. Port cooperation sustains existing maritime links or establishes new services integrated into door-to-door logistics chains. It is also perceived to lead to specialization in cargo or ship types, and organization and pooling of hinterland transport facilities, and, in many cases, to an improvement in output.

For larger ports, cooperation might facilitate **landside coordination of hinterland connections** through neighboring load centers. The centrally located load center ports may face difficulties in maintaining their competitive position. A key reason is a continuously changing port–hinterland relationship. The advent of port regionalization, where the performance of major seaports is interrelated with the development and performance of inland networks and value-added activities in the port hinterland, brings port development to a larger geographical scale beyond the port perimeter. Many load centers face local land scarcity and the infrastructure needed to make efficient inland connections, conditions exacerbated by diseconomies of scale (i.e. inland congestion), environmental constraints, and local opposition to port expansion. Competing services in terminal, rail, and barge operations have brought challenges in terms of the provision of effective regional operations and efficient infrastructure use. Coordination leads to the more effective bundling of container volumes towards the hinterland. This allows deeper hinterland penetration and promotes intermodal transportation through higher service frequency and better utilization of shuttle trains and barges.

For smaller ports on the periphery, the rationale for cooperation is to bring more centrality to those ports and the region in which they are located. This can be achieved by increasing the volume of the specific hinterland and maritime transport services and a better configuration and working environment for maritime operations and hinterland transport chains.

### 3.2 Port networking

Port networking for market segmentation and the coordination of functions can prevent port authorities from wasting scarce resources on inter-port competition. For a port range serving a limited overlapping hinterland, there are two reasons why ports might cooperate. First, there may be substantial duplication in the services leading to over-competition. Second, there are gaps in the ability of the port range to serve the specific needs of shippers. In the latter case, developing a common regional public policy might be mutually beneficial, or a common marketing strategy could drive growth in total traffic for the port range. Alternatively, cooperation may mean an agreement to specialize in service at one port while not duplicating that service at another. Cooperation benefits lead to strategic alliances among ports premised on the belief that seamless customer service does not require ownership of all the assets and results from managerial values that accept cooperative behavior. In this context, in several parts of the world, such as the European Union, public funding has made cooperative port development projects popular and even led to more permanent forms of association between ports.

Cooperation takes several forms, with the typology of port authorities cooperation underlining that there is no optimal approach (Box 4.2 and 4.3).

---

**Box 4.2 Examples of cooperation between adjacent ports**

*Examples of port cooperation provide a typology or classification of cooperation practices (Figure 4.14). As a first division, differentiation between formal and informal cooperation is noted. Formal would apply to legal agreements or written contracts, including memoranda of understanding (MoU); informal would be ad hoc in nature in response to a specific issue or as a trial before formal arrangements are agreed. The different forms of cooperation can then be grouped under four headings: marketing and business development, operations, administrative, and regulatory.*

FIGURE 4.14 Cooperation of Port Authorities: A Typology

| | Marketing & Business Development | Operations | Regulations | Administration |
|---|---|---|---|---|
| **Formal** | • Establishing a joint marketing agency<br>• Joint advertising activities | • Common training<br>• Joint application of new communications technologies[1]<br>• Port development planning[1]<br>• Partnerships with stakeholders[1]<br>• Joint development of similar operating practices[1] | • Joint environmental protection initiatives<br>• Coordinated investment in safety and security | • Port representatives participating in other ports<br>• Joint investments in hinterland infrastructures<br>• Joint management of port expansion<br>• (inter)national cooperative organizations |
| **Informal** | • Seeking joint clients<br>• Exchange of experts<br>• Promote the use of each other's facilities | • Information exchange on terminal management<br>• Sharing of information on port development<br>• Exchange of experts<br>• Joint studies | • Information sharing on environmental programs | • Technical assistance in port management<br>• Common positions at international forums |

Source: Adapted from Brooks, McCalla, Pallis and Van der Lugt (2010).

*In North America, Los Angeles and Long Beach cooperate to apply environmental initiatives (i.e. PierPass) and coordinate cargo storage fees to reduce congestion. Seattle and Tacoma cooperate on infrastructure, promotion, and environmental issues. The infrastructure projects are operational and administrative in scope, involving road and rail, to improve access to port areas.*

*In northwest Europe, the port authorities of Rotterdam, Antwerp, Hamburg, Bremen, and Le Havre meet regularly to discuss, amongst other matters of shared concern, financial, environmental, and security issues. Rotterdam and Amsterdam have merged their independent port data systems to exchange data between themselves, their customers, and customs. The formal creation of one single port community information system is both an operational and administrative initiative resulting from the demand of the international business community operating in both ports.*

*Regional cooperation in intercontinental marketing and operations is also evident in the Mediterranean region. Algeciras and Tanger Med cooperate with northwest European ports Dover and Calais in marketing, commercial development, and RoRo terminal management. Barcelona cooperates with the Tunisian Maritime Authority in enhancing the quality of port services, as do Las Palmas and several ports in Morocco.*

*In Asia, the term 'port co-opetition' has been used to describe the collaborating relations developed between competing neighboring ports in China and Hong Kong.*

Cooperation includes training, technical exchanges, port management assistance, sharing information on port development and environmental programs, promoting mutual logistics services, and articulating a common position at international forums. This occurs between ports in the same geographical region, aiming at the joint development of infrastructure, regional promotion and marketing, and common approaches to environmental issues. Cooperation between larger and smaller ports is also frequent, as regional cooperation aims to enhance particular trade corridors.

### Box 4.3  Examples of non-proximate ports cooperation

*Collaborative efforts between non-proximate ports are scattered across continents and take on different types of relationship formats. These range from collaborations (formalized via mutually signed agreements or not), Joint Ventures/investments, and port alliances with the signing of Memorandum of Understanding (MoU), to consultancy services, where one of the port authorities involved acts as the consultant (Figure 4.15).*

*Several port authorities have created subsidiary companies that develop such partnerships. The corporatized Port of Rotterdam Authority established the Port of Rotterdam International (PORint) department to promote trade by developing a global port network. In a similar pattern, Port of Antwerp International (PAI) is an investment subsidiary of the Port of Antwerp Authority. The Port of Amsterdam has also been involved in a collaboration.*

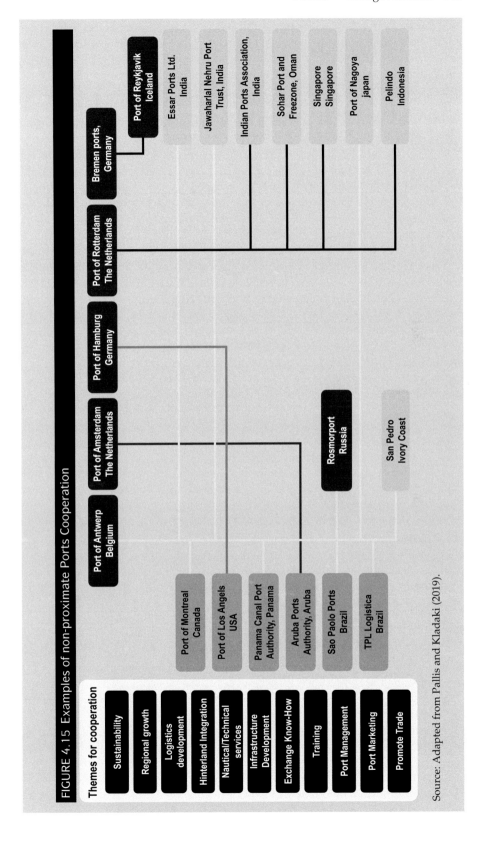

FIGURE 4.15 Examples of non-proximate Ports Cooperation

Source: Adapted from Pallis and Kladaki (2019).

In the early 2000s, **strategic alliances between adjacent container ports** emerged as a countervailing option against the growing market power of shipping lines. Within an economic environment of seagoing trade, ports are 'pawns in the game' of facilitating efficient and effective maritime flow, with cooperation between ports gaining, in several countries, anti-trust immunity so that cooperation may be used to facilitate counterbalancing carrier power but also to deal with the most pressing congestion problems facing ports.

Since the early 2010s, the collaboration between non-proximate ports has expanded. Port authorities develop partnerships to establish a commercial representation abroad, transfer know-how, and occasionally invest abroad. The motives relate to diverse goals ranging from marketing the port worldwide to 'promote and/or sell the port' (the customers-seeking principle), to controlling international transport networks a port forms part of (the efficiency and effectiveness principle) or gaining a competitive advantage via additional knowledge, cutting-edge technologies, or new business opportunities. There are at least two ways that port cooperation expands beyond adjacent ports. The first is **cooperation between the two ends of a logistics corridor** to optimize freight flows between the two regions. The second is **agreements to exchange information** on port activities, management, organization, and technology. Port authorities with autonomy and a more business-like structure move towards a more entrepreneurial role that, apart from business development, involves internationalization strategies and partnerships that develop informally, such as signing memorandums of understanding.

At the same time, it is worth noting that the ongoing restructuring of liner shipping through alliances formation, acts as an incentive for collaboration between both proximate and non-proximate port authorities. For instance, Savannah and Norfolk port authorities on the American East Coast recently requested from the Federal Maritime Commission its permission to present to newly formed liner shipping alliances a united front on several vital issues. These port authorities are on the same coastline but 500 miles apart. As they do not directly compete on their captive local cargo markets, only on the longer distance discretionary intermodal markets, they are seeking to collaborate on a range of topics such as coordinating vessel calls and berthing arrangements, marketing, and procurement, and for the efficient use of their facilities. There are also adjacent ports forming alliances, such as the ports of Seattle and Tacoma forming the SeaTac Alliance, or neighboring terminals forming cooperation agreements.

## 3.3 Merging of port authorities

In some cases, the cooperation between port authorities can reach an advanced stage and take the form of **port authority mergers**. Port authority merger or full integration is the most far-reaching form of cooperation.

Port authority mergers at the national or regional level can be found worldwide. In some cases, these involve mergers between ports of similar sizes, such as the Ningbo-Zhoushan port in China or Hamina-Kotka in Finland. In other cases, a larger port authority merges with smaller ones such as for Port Metro Vancouver in Canada (Vancouver and Fraser), Valencia-port in Spain (Valencia, Sagunto, and Gandia), the integration of the port of

Dordrecht in the Rotterdam Port Authority (the Netherlands) and the 2022 merger between the ports of Antwerp and Zeebrugge (Belgium). There also exist particular cases of regional integration of port authorities at a regional level, such as the creation of port system authorities in Italy (Box 4.4) and the integration of Chinese ports at the provincial level (Box 4.5).

Cross-border mergers of port authorities are rare. The formation of **Copenhagen Malmo Port (CMP)** was the first cross-border merger in Europe. One of the main drivers behind the merger between the Danish port of Copenhagen and the Swedish port of Malmo was the realization of the fixed Oresund link between Denmark and Sweden, basically wiping out all short-distance ferry activity between both ports. Another cross-border merger is the creation of **North Sea Port** following the 2017 merger between Ghent Port Authority in Belgium and Zeeland Seaports (Terneuzen and Flushing) in the Netherlands.

In addition to full port authority integration schemes, a range of far-reaching port alliances is emerging. Examples include the Northwest Seaport Alliance between Seattle and Tacoma in the U.S. and the structural cooperation platform HAROPA in France involving the seaports of Le Havre and Rouen and the inland port of Paris. The latter turned into a fully-fledged merger in mid-2021.

Port authority mergers can result from a decision or policy imposed by the national, regional, or provincial government (**top-down** such as in Italy or China) or be initiated by the port authorities themselves (**bottom-up**). Compulsory or voluntary top-down mergers are thus mainly driven by (national) policies. The core goal is to reduce the administrative burden and the recurrent jurisdiction overlap when port authorities are in proximity. The merged entity is expected to be more effective. Bottom-up mergers are more a response to market pressure, inter-firm ties (global terminal networks, vertically integrated carriers), and common threats or market challenges. The Rhine-Scheldt Delta region in Belgium and the Netherlands provides a good example of bottom-up mergers between port authorities (Box 4.6).

---

### Box 4.4  Italian Port System Authorities

*The merging of the 24 existing port authorities and other smaller ports into 15 Port System Authorities (PSAs) has been the foundation of the 2016 Italian port governance reform (Figure 4.16). The stated aim for this merging of port managing entities was to eliminate the major weaknesses threatening Italian ports, such as sub-optimal port size, insufficient financial and funding resources, low competitiveness, and inefficiencies related to hinterland connections.*

*The 15 PSAs inherited the duties and the power of the traditional port authorities, with a broader geographical scope. Existing port authorities have been grouped into PSAs according to historical backgrounds, political pressures, port characteristics, and hinterland profiles. For example, the three Ligurian ports (Savona, Genova, and La Spezia) were included in two different PSAs, and the three Apulian port authorities acted similarly (Bari and Brindisi formed a single PSA with a couple of minor ports, but Taranto formed a PSA on its own).*

*With this being a top-down initiative rather than a port-level decision, challenges remain. The most significant relates to the presence of a multi-layer port governance system and the role sustained by the central government that*

FIGURE 4.16 Italian Port System Authorities

*does more than appointing the head of each PSA. The PSAs play a coordination role, while for each former port authority, a special Port Directorate (PD) remains in charge of port-level tasks and duties. The PD also proposes the implementation of different actions to the President of its PSA.*

*As a consequence, the introduction of coordination mechanisms through the formation of PSAs is predicted to bring a rationalization of small ports. The simultaneous presence of two diverse entities (PDs and PSAs) with overlapping functions might reduce the positive effect of the new organization, especially as a third layer was also introduced, and a special ministerial department was assigned to rationalize and coordinate investments and financial resources of the different PSAs, as a whole. In a nutshell, the central government retains a great influence on the financial aspect, the PSAs playing the critical planning and coordination role, and the PDs managing local resources.*

## Box 4.5 Port reform and integration in mainland China

*The past 65 years have brought significant changes to China's economic and political landscape. The changes in China's economic policy brought by Deng Xiaoping in 1978 were followed by a long transition period towards a market-based economy. Chinese national reforms and the transfer of power from the central government to local governments had an impact on the governance of seaports which evolved in several phases:*

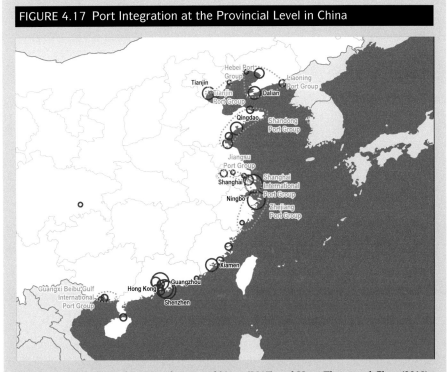

FIGURE 4.17 Port Integration at the Provincial Level in China

Source: Compiled based on Notteboom and Yang (2017) and Huo, Zhang and Chen (2018).

- ***Period 1979–1984***: *The first phase was characterized by a centrally planned economic system with strongly centralized decision-making. The combination of insufficient funds for port development and lagging efficiency improvements caused severe port capacity problems in the early 1980s.*
- ***Period 1984–2004***: *The second phase brought a process towards decentralization. With the exception of Qinhuangdao, which stayed under central government control, all other ports ended up being controlled either by central and local governments or by the local government alone. The port authorities received regulatory powers, but at the same time their status as state-owned enterprises (SOE) pushed them to become more market-oriented, for instance in terms of investment decisions. The new governance system resulted in a gradual entry of foreign private investors in Chinese ports, particularly in the container business as exemplified by the investments of HPH and PSA. However, the government de facto remained in the driver's seat when it came to port planning and secured the biggest share of the revenues collected from port terminal operations.*
- ***The Port Law of 2004*** *forms the cornerstone for today's port governance. The new policy led to a further decentralization of port governance in China and opened the path to the corporatization of port authorities and the introduction of modern corporate governance principles in the seaport system. In order to end the dual role of port authorities as both regulator and port operator, the new governance framework aimed at strictly separating these functions via the establishment of so-called Port Administration Bureaux*

*and separate port business companies or groups. Moreover, the Port Law put an end to port ownership by the central government. The ceiling of 49% for foreign investors was abolished, which in theory opened possibilities for foreign players to invest in and operate ports, even without needing a local Chinese partner. Policy formulation and strategic port planning fall under the responsibility of the central government and the respective provincial governments, so any plans of local governments need to be approved by these higher authorities.*

In more recent years, the decentralization policy brought by the 2004 Port Law shifted to large-scale port integration at the provincial level (Figure 4.17). **Port cooperation and integration** has become a hot topic in China against the background of slower traffic growth, increased competition and growing international opportunities. We can interpret this result in two ways. One approach concludes that the port devolution process to the more local level has not resulted in the excessive self-interest and ambitions of individual ports, but has actually enhanced their sense of cooperation and coordination. Another possible perspective is that the port devolution process made government agencies at higher levels (i.e. national and provincial) work out schemes to avoid duplication of facilities, overcapacity and excessive competition in a seaport system characterized by a highly decentralized governance structure. In our view, both perspectives have played a role, although regional differences exist in the relative contribution of each perspective.

Integration and cooperation schemes are currently rolled out in almost all coastal provinces:

- **Liaoning Province**: Dalian port group and Jinzhou port, both located in Liaoning Province in the Northeastern part of China, began to cooperate in 2006. In June 2017, it was announced that Liaoning province would form a new company to run its ports, with China Merchants Group purchasing a controlling stake. The new **Liaoning Port Group** was set up to integrate the coastal ports in Liaoning province.
- **Hebei Province**: Hebei Port Group Co. Ltd, the largest bulk cargo handling company in the world, owns Qinhuangdao port, Caofeidian port, and Huanghua port. The company is controlled by Hebei province. In December 2015, the Tianjin Port Group Co. Ltd and Hebei Port Group Co. Ltd signed an agreement to form a 50/50 joint venture company Jinhaiyi port investment. The company is planning to purchase some berths in Tianjin port and Huanghua port. In May 2016, Hebei Port group subsidiary Qinghuangdao Co. Ltd and Tianjin Port Group established Bohai Jinyi port investment development Co. Ltd.
- **Shandong Province**. In April 2009, the ports of Qingdao, Rizhao and Yantai signed a strategic alliance agreement. It was agreed that Qingdao port act as the leading port and Yantai port and Rizhao port act as assistant ports with a view of establishing a regional shipping center. The resulting **Shandong Port Group Co Ltd**. is not only active in the Shandong Province. Through Shandong Port Overseas Development Group Co Ltd, the company concentrates on overseas development. Its overseas involvement includes Vado Ligure Port in Italy and Kimbo Port in Guinea, and it also

*has projects on a fiduciary basis such as Qasim Port in Pakistan and Boffa Port in Guinea.*

- *Jiangsu Province. In 2017, Jiangsu Port Group Co. Ltd. was established by integrating Nanjing port, Lianyungang port, Suzhou port, Nantong port, Zhenjiang port, Changzhou port, Taizhou and Yangzhou port.*
- *Zhejiang Province. At the end of September 2015, the port complexes of Zhoushan and Ningbo in Zhejiang province merged to form the largest port group in the world. The Ningbo port group was renamed to Ningbo-Zhoushan Port Group Co Ltd. Next to the creation of Ningbo-Zhoushan Port Group, Zhejiang Province has set up a company named Zhejiang sea-port group, which is devoted to integrating the five ports of Zhejiang province (i.e. Ningbo- Zhoushan port, Wenzhou port, Taizhou port, Jiaxing port and Yiwu International Dry Port).*
- *Guangxi Province. In 2007 the Guangxi Beibu Gulf International Port Group Co. Ltd. was established, including Qinzhou port, Beihai port and Fangchenggang port.*

## Box 4.6  Port authority mergers in the Rhine-Scheldt Delta

*The Rhine-Scheldt Delta includes all ports located in the estuary systems of the Rhine, Meuse, and Scheldt rivers. In 2020, this port system handled about 878 million TEU and about 28.7 million TEU. The two largest ports in Europe, Rotterdam and Antwerp, are located in this Delta as well as Europe's fourth-largest*

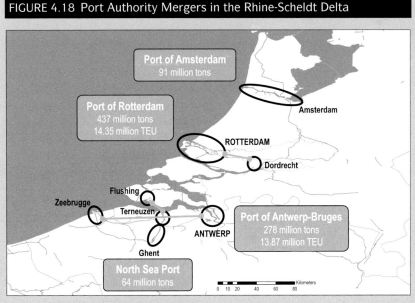

FIGURE 4.18 Port Authority Mergers in the Rhine-Scheldt Delta

Source: Adapted from Notteboom (2018).

*(Amsterdam). Antwerp, Rotterdam, North Sea Port, and Moerdijk are home to large interconnected (petro)chemical industry clusters. At the same time, steel plants can be found in North Sea Port (ArcelorMittal) and Ijmuiden/Amsterdam (Tata Steel). The port of Amsterdam is strongly specialized in liquid bulk and dry bulk and has very limited container traffic. The coastal port area of Zeebrugge (by late 2021 managed by Port of Antwerp-Bruges) is the largest car handling port in the world, with about three million new cars handled each year and a major energy hub for gas transported by pipelines and LNG carriers.*

*The region is home to several 'bottom-up' mergers and cooperation agreements between port authorities (Figure 4.18):*

- *The cross-border port authority **North Sea Port** was formed in 2017 after the merger between the port authority of Ghent (Belgium) and Zeeland Seaports (ports of Flushing and Terneuzen in the Netherlands).*
- ***Port of Antwerp-Bruges**. This merger port authority was announced in February 2021 and formally installed in 2022. It is the result of the merger between the Antwerp Port Authority and MBZ, the port authority of Zeebrugge. It is one of the largest port mergers in Europe in terms of volume. Discussion about the merger started in early 2018 between the City of Antwerp and the City of Bruges with a view to closer collaboration. However, there have been several other attempts to reach a closer collaboration between both ports in the past decades, particularly focusing on the container business. Next to further strengthening its position in cargo handling and logistics, the merged entity also aims to become Europe's most important hub for hydrogen, a center for energy transition and the circular economy, and overall a resilient, sustainable, and diversified port ecosystem. The ports combined handled 278 million tons in 2020 and 13.8 million TEU. The port area (i.e. Antwerp right bank, Antwerp left bank, and Zeebrugge's inner and outer port area) covers just over 14,000 hectares. Direct employment amounts to 72,000 jobs, and direct and indirect value added reached 20 billion euro (or 4.5% of GDP in 2019).*
- *In 2013, the Port of Rotterdam Authority adopted responsibility for the operation and development of Dordrecht's port area. The port authority is working closely with the Municipality of Dordrecht and local companies to exploit the full potential of the 290-hectare port area and the neighboring industrial estate, under the brand name **Dordrecht Inland Seaport**.*
- *The **Port of Amsterdam** can be considered the main port in a cluster of ports along the North Sea Canal, which includes Amsterdam, Velsen/ IJmuiden, Zaanstad, and Beverwijk.*

The percentage of port authorities that are responsible for the managing of more than one port is increasing. This is evident in both commercial and cruise ports. The number of European port authorities that govern more than one port increased from 38% of the total in 2011 to 46% in 2016. In the second-biggest cruise region of the world, the Mediterranean and its adjoining seas, the percentage of Mediterranean cruise ports where the responsible authority governs more than one port reaches almost 30% of the total.

There are numerous possible drivers for port authority mergers, including:

- To avoid duplication of facilities and unnecessary competition through a more comprehensive planning process that rationalizes the use of assets of the merged authorities. Recognizing that land use planning and rationalization of existing terminals often become political in locally controlled ports, the merger of the cargo operations of the Ports of Seattle and Tacoma purposely avoided some of these challenges, focusing instead on challenges faced in governance. The creation of the Liaoning port group in Northeastern China provides another example. Dalian and Yingkou separately undertook strategies to maximize their competitive position against each other. These strategies included integrating terminals within their jurisdiction, developing relationships with inland ports, promoting port-related industries, and working with shipping companies on financing infrastructure. As these strategies did not reduce over-competition between Dalian and Yingkou, a second round of integration was implemented by China Merchants Holding. Competition between Japanese and Korean ports for trans-pacific cargo has prompted the Japanese government to create port alliances within key bays in Japan, such as the Osaka Bay (Ports of Osaka and Kobe).
- To respond to mounting market and financial pressures and opportunities. For example, consolidation among the ocean carriers has brought pressure on individual ports to make investments to handle larger ships and remain competitive, while port sustainability and energy transition present unique opportunities for merged ports. Corporatized port authorities might resort to mergers to improve their financial status.

While port authority mergers have become a clear trend, many attempts have failed. For example, the adjacent ports of Los Angeles and Long Beach never succeeded in merging despite several attempts. This case shows the necessity of having a transparent process involving all stakeholders, and economic studies that identify clear benefits to both sides. A failed merger is not necessarily a negative outcome as it may force each port to behave more strategically, which can enhance their performance.

Overall there exist several possible impediments to port authority mergers:

- **Administrative and cognitive borders** at the national, provincial, and even local level underline differences in port governance models in terms of socio-economic effects on decision-making (political and commercial) combined with top-down government interference. Cross-border mergers are challenging to match with national or regional port policy.
- **Unfounded pressure on ports to specialize** their activities after a proposed merger.
- No clear win-win situation with unclear or unfair **distribution of costs and benefits** of the proposed merger.
- Inter-personal factors such as the **lack of trust** between key decision makers.

- **Lack of decision-making power** of initiators.
- **No clear business case**: internally (profitability, development potential) or externally (towards port users and broader port community).
- **Belief in expanded cooperation and coordination** efforts to address the common issues instead of a merger.

# Chapter 4.4  Port clusters

*Ports clusters consist of geographically concentrated and mutually related business units centered around transport, logistics, trade, and industrial production.*

## 1  PORT CLUSTER FORMATION

Ports are clusters of companies and economic activities. Port clusters exhibit strong scale and scope advantages linked to physical cargo flows. The concentration of activities opens more opportunities to the bundling of cargo flows via intermodal transport (shortsea, barge, or rail) and to achieve higher connectivity to the rest of the world via frequent transport services. The process of cluster formation takes place at two scales. The first concerns the **clustering of ports** around a maritime range, and the second concerns the **clustering of activities** around a port.

There are important geographical attributes behind port cluster formation., which varies substantially by maritime range, mainly owing to the following constraints (Figure 4.19):

- **Availability of port sites**. Coastal geography varies across ranges, impacting the number of suitable port sites because of factors such as protected bays, river deltas, and tidal ranges. Such characteristics are related to the distribution of cities where a coastal cluster of cities is more prone to forming port clusters reflecting the urban system. Also,

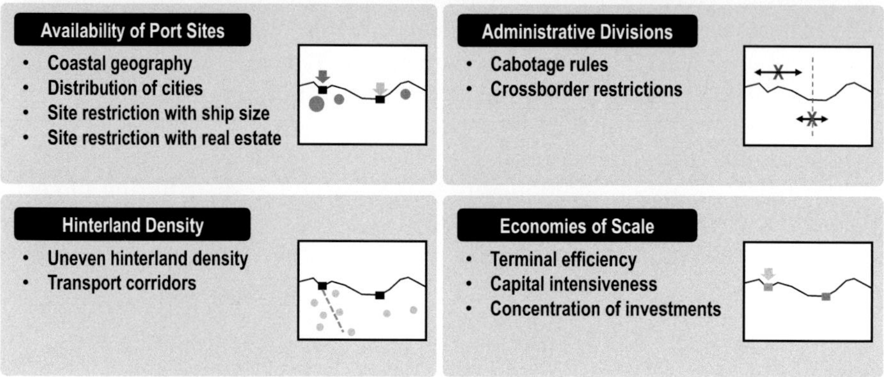

FIGURE 4.19 Maritime Ranges and the Propensity for Cluster Formation

container terminals require a substantial amount of real estate for piers and yards, that is challenging to find. Coastal geography attributes along a maritime range are generally prone to cluster formation.

• **Administrative divisions**. Nation states commonly have their own cabotage rules and restrictions, which can impact how hinterlands are serviced. In a context of limited economic integration, adjacent national states, or even administrative divisions, a dedicated container port can be serviced with the level of activity constrained by the size of the administrative unit. This can also encourage the over-supply and duplication of port infrastructure, giving the illusion of a port cluster. Simultaneously, the absence of administrative divisions would have generated fewer ports, or even a single large port, to service this hinterland.

• **Hinterland accessibility and density**. Economic development, urbanization, and the distribution of resources imply an uneven hinterland density. As major economic regions are structured along corridors, this concentration favors specific container ports and port groups servicing these areas. The higher the density, the greater the propensity for clustering. Therefore, the nature of the hinterland influences cluster formation.

• **Economies of scale and infrastructure**. The growing average size of containerships tends to restrict port choice because of draft limitations and underlines the capital intensiveness of containerization. In turn, this encourages a concentration of investments and infrastructure in a specific number of efficient container ports in order to generate enough traffic and economic return. Technical and technological developments lean towards cluster formation.

The above constraints result in the geographical distribution of the world's major container ports along several large clusters of port activity (Figure 4.20) as 62% of all the activity is accounted for by 22 clusters. Clusters allow a high level of inter-port competition as well as a simultaneous complementarity of options to service hinterlands. The two most important container port clusters globally are the Yangtze River Delta (Central China) and the Pearl River Delta (Southern China), jointly accounting for about 20% of all the throughput. The importance of these port clusters is associated with the clustering of manufacturing and logistics activities of their hinterland. Other clusters such as the Strait of Malacca and Dubai/Gulf are mainly the outcome of shipping lines selecting transshipment hubs. Containerization has allowed for the setting up of massive economies of scale and agglomeration that have become prevalent in port geography.

## 2 ACTIVITIES IN PORT CLUSTERS

### 2.1 Transport and cargo handling

Ports use infrastructures to channel ships and vehicles and to accommodate cargo and information flows. While other typologies might be found, a distinction can be made between basic nautical infrastructure (such as access channels and locks), commercial port infrastructure (such as quay walls), and port superstructure (such as cranes, warehouses). The **construction, operation, and maintenance** of these infrastructures constitute a key activity in ports. For example, dredging companies execute most of the capital and maintenance dredging works in seaports and are involved in land reclamation projects. The

FIGURE 4.20 World's Largest Container Port Clusters, 2016

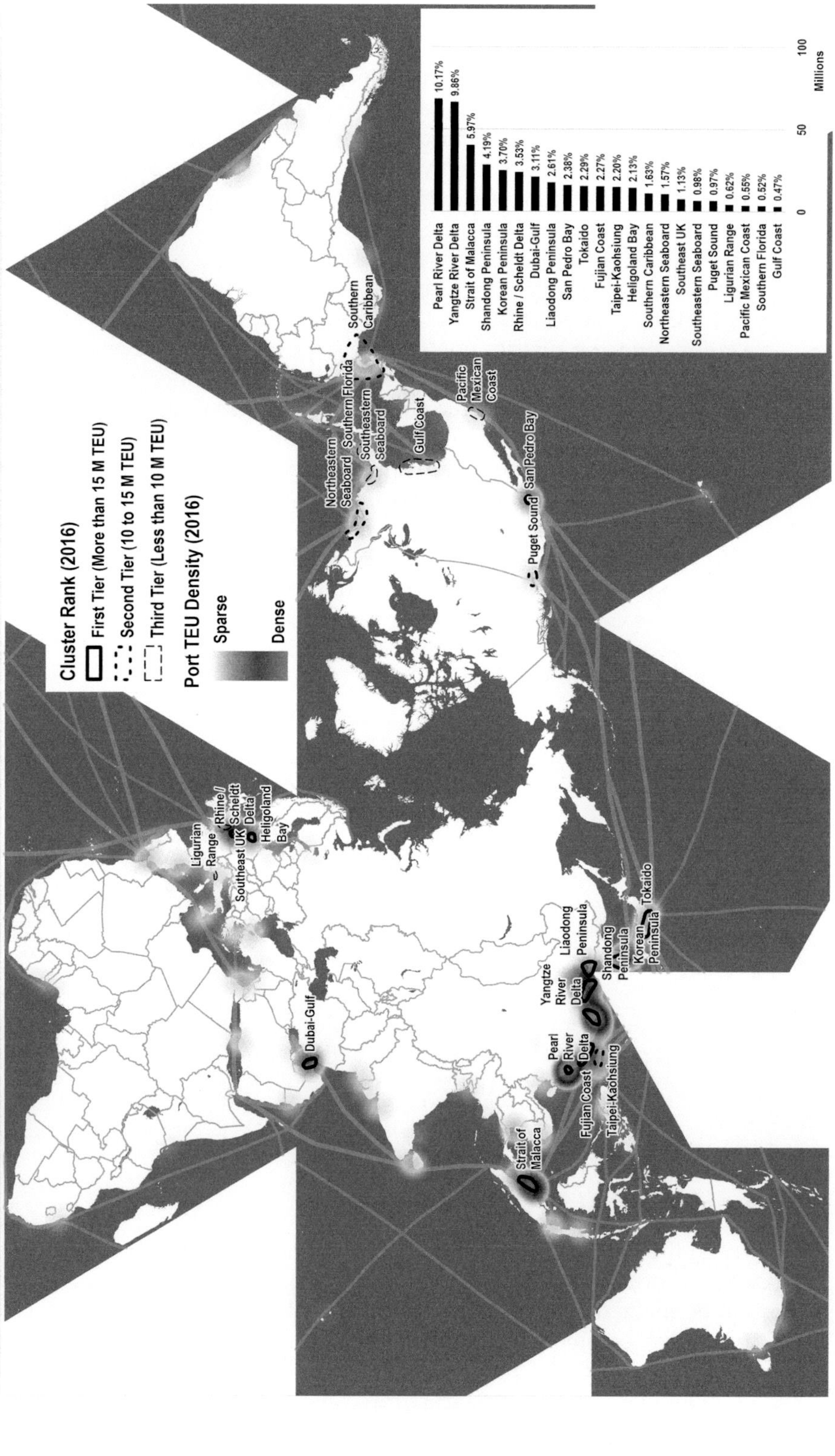

development of new terminals, port zones, and intra-port and inland access infrastructure offers project work to consultancy firms, contractors and construction firms, to engineering firms, and to all sorts of suppliers of technical equipment and services.

The call of a vessel in a port generally requires the involvement of towage companies, pilotage services, mooring/unmooring services, the harbor master's office (part of the port authority or government department), lock operators (if any), ship agents, companies involved in signaling and shipping services, waste reception facilities, ship suppliers and chandlers, marine surveyors, bunkering firms, classification societies, safety contractors, and security firms. Quite a number of ports also offer ship repair facilities or are home to shipyards.

**Cargo handling operations** in ports can relate to different types of goods: liquid bulk cargo (crude oil, oil products, LNG), dry bulk cargo (coal, iron ore, grain), roll-on/roll-off cargo (new cars, used cars, rolling material, trailers), containerized cargo, and conventional general cargo. Conventional general cargo encompasses a myriad of different non-containerized commodities such as project cargo (power generation plants, steel mills, wood-pulp factories, gas power plants, road construction equipment), power plant equipment (gas turbines, power generators, transformers, turbines, heavy machinery, industrial equipment), iron and steel products (bars, coils, plates, wires), forest products (wood and paper products), parcels (malt, fertilizer, sugar, rice), reefer vessel trades (fruit, meat) and breakbulk shipments of smaller lots.

The efficiency and effectiveness with which **loading and discharging activities** occur in a port are important cornerstones for the port's competitiveness and its ability to generate broader economic effects in employment and value-added creation. Cargo handling in the first place involves terminal and stevedoring companies that employ or use dock workers. The dock labor needs are very dependent on the cargo flows handled in the port. Other cargo-related service jobs include cargo survey, land transport and storage, port-related storage, conveyor/pipeline, and transfer between berths and storage facilities. Generally speaking, conventional general cargo handling is confronted with ever-tighter handling space in many seaports (containers consume more and more square meters). Given the strong labor intensity, it is also sensitive to labor-related issues.

**Government agencies and organizations** develop activities linked to cargo and vessel operations in ports. Semi-public or public managing bodies of ports are important players in the port arena, depending on the tasks the port authority adopts. Government agencies typically include customs, sanitary and food inspection, environmental offices, harbor police, the pilotage service, state-owned tugboat companies, navigation aids, and vessel traffic systems (VTS), firefighters, and maritime courts.

**Military activities** such as naval bases can also be found in seaport areas. The permanent stationing of naval fleets in a seaport or visits by foreign naval vessels may affect a regional economy in the form of purchasing fuel and provisions and the expenditure by crews in the local economy.

Many seaports also act as important nodes for **passenger traffic**. These passenger flows might be linked to cruise vessels, ferries, and regional river or coastal passenger services. Passenger terminals create direct value-added and employment, but also have an impact on other activities that might be located elsewhere. Examples include tourism agencies, hotels, restaurants, museums, taxi and bus companies, and airports.

## 2.2 Logistics

Goods can undergo logistics transformations in the port area, which is defined as **port-centric logistics**. Examples include storage, distribution, and other logistics activities in the framework of industrial subcontracting or postponed manufacturing in the port area. The gateway position of major seaports offers opportunities for the development of **value-added logistics services** (VALS). Many seaports have evolved from pure transshipment centers to complexes of key functions within a logistics system. A mix of pure stevedoring activities and logistics activities occurs.

Ports are not only nodes handling goods flows. They also deal with large quantities of **information flows**. Many service companies involved in the booking, consolidation, and tracking of vessels and cargo (freight forwarders and ship agents) are located in the seaport or immediate vicinity. The consolidation of cargo is an important port activity, which generates added value and employment and contributes to efficiency improvements in loading rates and the balance between incoming and outgoing goods flows. Ports often act as consolidation points for partial loads, such as LCL (less than container load) cargo and groupage activities. However, disintermediation in the supply chains and the increasing globalization of the maritime and port industry can imply that some ports face a relocation of some of the decision-making power over cargo flows to inland centers or major (maritime) cities. When cargo control centers are set up outside the port area, the role of the local service providers is narrowed down to specific operational tasks or back-office functions. Therefore, the role of the port in supply chains is increasingly dependent on factors and actors outside the port area.

The branch associations of economic sectors in the port (i.e. freight forwarders, ship agents, industrial firms) and umbrella associations (e.g. Deltalinqs in the port of Rotterdam) are involved in promotion of their respective port sectors. Numerous jobs are created in training and education, not only at the public level (universities, schools of higher education, technical schools) but also in private training centers. A wide range of advanced trade service firms (such as banks, other financial institutions, investment firms, insurance firms, law firms) realize a part of their turnover in ports.

## 2.3 Industrial activities

There exists a wide range of industrial activities that typically locate in port areas. Industries that are part of **maritime clusters** include shipyards (ship repair and shipbuilding), marine equipment companies, crane and terminal equipment producers, salvage companies, offshore companies (offshore survey, exploration, production, installation, supply, pipe laying), marine construction firms, dredging firms, naval bases, and the fish processing industry. Non-maritime cluster industries that are often found in ports include chemical plants, power plants, steel plants, car assembly plants, paper mills, food production companies, and firms producing building materials (cement, bricks, tiles).

**Petrochemical and chemical companies** and large integrated centers of industrial activities in seaports constitute an essential part of the economic activity in ports, exemplified by the large petrochemical and chemical clusters in Singapore, Houston, Rotterdam, and Antwerp. These clusters are integrated upstream into primary raw materials, feedstock, commodities, or intermediates and downstream into other chemical industry sectors or key customer industries (automotive, packaging, construction). The petrochemical industry is strongly based on oil refinery activities, many of which are located in ports:

- First, there are the **basic chemicals** which include polymers (e.g. polyethylene (PE), polyvinyl chloride (PVC), polypropylene (PP), polystyrene (PS) and fibers such as polyester, nylon, polypropylene, and acrylics), bulk petrochemicals and intermediates (i.e. primarily made from liquefied petroleum gas (LPG), natural gas and crude oil and used for the production of ethylene, propylene, benzene, toluene, methanol, styrene), other derivatives and basic industrials (e.g. synthetic rubber, surfactants, dyes and pigments, resins, carbon black, explosives), inorganic chemicals (e.g. salt, chlorine, caustic soda, soda ash, acids) and fertilizers (phosphates, ammonia and potash chemicals).
- Second, the **life sciences** include differentiated chemical and biological substances, pharmaceuticals, diagnostics, animal health products, vitamins, and crop protection (herbicides, insecticides, and fungicides). These products tend to have very high prices and require substantial investment in research and development.
- The third group concerns **specialty chemicals** such as electronic chemicals, industrial gases, adhesives, sealants, coatings, cleaning products, and catalysts.
- The fourth group consists of **consumer products** that are directly sold to the consumer, such as soaps, detergents, and cosmetics.

The successful development of the **chemical clusters in seaports** depends on various factors such as:

- The availability of skilled labor at competitive prices.
- Good training and educational facilities.
- The role and support of port authorities and government agencies in providing incentives and support in the development of infrastructure.
- The availability of land.
- The availability of raw material supplies at competitive prices.
- Competitive prices for energy and utilities.
- A low-risk and stable business climate and stable regulatory environment.
- Co-siting and partnering opportunities (industrial cascades).
- Relative proximity and easy access to most important customers.
- The availability of efficient services (logistics, finance, IT, packaging, security, marketing, promotion).

Industrial clusters in ports often rely on **sustainable industrial symbiosis** or **sustainable industrial ecosystems**. Raw materials are extracted locally, and finished products and secondary flows are used locally. By-products of the production process (for example, oxygen, heat, or water) are recycled and reused locally. This ensures far-reaching industrial and circular integration and the creation of so-called **ecologies of scale**. Such symbiosis requires supporting infrastructures, such as pipelines and storage tanks, to transport raw materials and finished products to the correct location. Thus, a competitive cluster requires good inter-company infrastructure (e.g. pipelines), product diversity, the sharing of utility services and infrastructure, and strong cluster governance. Chemical clusters are increasingly overcoming regional boundaries by developing pipeline systems and other mass transport infrastructure that link chemical clusters in several ports (e.g. pipeline linkages between Rotterdam, Antwerp, and Terneuzen) and also link the ports to major chemical clusters in the hinterland (e.g. links between the Rhine-Scheldt Delta ports in Belgium and the Netherlands, the chemical axis along the Albert Canal to Liège in Belgium and the German Ruhr area).

Many of the world's **steel plants** are located in seaport areas. The steel industry operates in a highly competitive environment globally, where rigorous cost management is imperative for maintaining and strengthening its competitiveness. Therefore, steelmaking processes have been developed and refined over the years. Steelmaking is capital intensive, and the average plant life is very long, which makes changes to new technologies possible only in a timeframe of several decades. Many steel plants are located in seaport areas. A good example is ArcelorMittal. ArcelorMittal operates several maritime flat carbon steel mills (e.g. in Europe: Dunkirk, Ghent, Fos Marseille, Gijon, and Bremen). Most other mills are located less than 100km from major import ports. On the import side, steel plants generate large iron ore flows, pellets, coking coal, metal scrap, and steel slabs. The outgoing cargo flows typically include steel coils, steel booms, steel wires, and related products.

The same applies to the **automotive industry**. While assembly plants mostly do not locate in seaport areas (for example, only about 10 of the 150 European assembly plants are located in seaport areas), they often locate quite close to seaports for reasons of ingoing and outgoing flows of parts and finished cars.

## 2.4 Energy

Many seaports are home to large **energy plants**. Electricity is produced in conventional steam-electric plants (coal and lignite), conventional steam-electric plants (other fuels), combined-cycle and gas turbine plants, conventional hydroelectric plants, pumped-storage hydroelectric plants, nuclear power plants, waste-to-energy plants, biomass power plants, diesel and gas-engine power plants, wind energy plants, geothermal power plants and solar power plants. The availability of land and cooling water and the presence of large industrial customers are some of the reasons for energy-producing firms to set up business in seaport areas.

Depending on the set-up, conventional steam-electric plants are massive consumers of coal. Growing trends in electricity production include plants that produce electricity based on gas, pellets, waste, or biomass. Stations powered by these fuels present economic advantages, are often faster to build and are more environmentally friendly when compared to electricity production from other (fossil) fuels. There is also an increased interest in **wind energy**. While most wind farms are installed offshore (mostly on sandbanks) or in open plots in the hinterland, a number of seaports are also home to wind farms. These wind farms are typically installed on breakwaters or narrow stretches of land close to the sea, thereby benefiting from favorable winds in coastal areas.

Many seaports also play an essential role in the **distribution of natural gas**. The gas comes in either via vessels (LNG carriers) using specialized deep-sea terminals or via pipelines that land in the seaport area. The presence of power plants and power distribution infrastructure not only generates direct jobs and value-added in power plants, energy distribution platforms, and the terminal operating business (i.e. handling of coal, gas, and other fuels), but is also a major creator of jobs and value-added in other industries and services such as engineering firms, construction companies, maintenance and repair companies, survey and inspection firms, and security services.

## 3 PORT-CENTRIC LOGISTICS

The clustering of ports is associated with the clustering of logistics.

> *Port-centric logistics refers to the range of freight transportation and distribution activities that are directly related to port terminals.*

Port terminals handle three types of flows, which are inbound (imports), outbound (exports), and transshipment (mostly for containers), each of which is associated with different forms of port-centric logistics. These come into two tiers (Figure 4.21):

- **Port cargo logistics** (first tier). The set of activities that directly affect the load unit of the cargo handled at the port. The first is the function

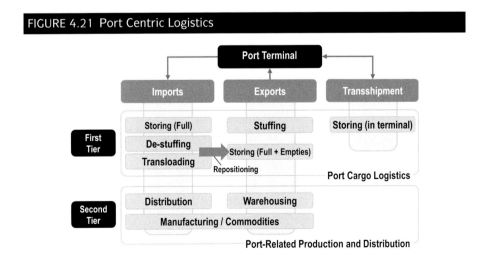

**FIGURE 4.21 Port Centric Logistics**

of storing where the cargo is waiting to be picked up or transshipped. This usually occurs within the terminal facility (for transshipment, a container rarely leaves the terminal facility), with the dwell time an important consideration for supply chain managers to organize pickup. The de-stuffing (and often palletization) of container loads is an important activity that takes place at nearby specialized facilities. Transloading is also commonly associated with de-stuffing activities as it transfers loads of maritime (ISO) containers into domestic containers. Empty containers are then repositioned either back to the container terminal or to an empty depot. Containers are then available to be picked up for stuffing and then exported.

• **Port-related production and distribution** (second tier). Activities that perform a level of transformation (in whole or in part) to the cargo that is either imported or exported through a port. Inbound cargo, particularly finished goods, must be consolidated and sorted in distribution centers for hinterland customers. Outbound cargo is usually warehoused waiting to be loaded (break-bulk cargo) or stuffed (containerized cargo). Manufacturing activities that are closely dependent on global markets, either for inputs (suppliers) or outputs (customers), will tend to be located in the vicinity of port areas. The commodity sector has traditionally shown a high association with port terminals (e.g. petrochemicals), which has usually endured. However, the growing use of containers to transport commodities such as agricultural goods, including refrigerated goods, conveys a new dynamic to port-centric logistics.

Moreover, instead of using the stacking area as a facilitator for a smooth synchronization between transport modes, shippers and logistics service providers started to use terminals as places for the temporary storage of consignments. Terminals thus serve as **buffers in logistics chains**. This has allowed them to develop value-added logistics activities such as:

• Paper-cutting operations at forest products terminals.
• Steel-cutting operations and packaging of project cargo at general cargo terminals.
• Quality control and packaging at fruit terminals.
• Sorting and blending operations at major bulk terminals.
• PDI activities (pre-delivery inspection) at car terminals.
• Bagging at minor bulk terminals (e.g. plastics).

Containerization had enduring impacts on the relationships between ports and their hinterlands. These relationships shifted in time with **dissociation** in the earlier phases of containerization and the recent **reinsertion** phase with port-centric logistics. Port-centric logistics is not a uniform strategy because it is a function of the position of a port within the global maritime transport system and the dominant direction of the flows they handle. In this regard, three main types of port-centric logistics can be retained, export-oriented, intermediate, and import-oriented (Box 4.7).

## Box 4.7  Functional types of port centric logistics

*The first functional type illustrates the standard **export-oriented paradigm**, where the container port is the pivot for an export-oriented platform. This is particularly prevalent in East Asia, where offshoring has substantially influenced port development towards the setting up of large manufacturing clusters. First-tier port-centric logistics are predominantly focused on the consolidation of loads and container stuffing. Since there are more exports than imports (in addition to the different composition of imports versus exports), an important component of first-tier logistics is the repositioning of large pools of containers between importers and exporters, many of them empty. Second-tier logistics are oriented along with manufacturing activities, having a close relationship with the port to provide for their inputs (parts) and outputs (finished products).*

*The second functional type of port-centric logistics is the least common but represents a value proposition in a global economy where the importance of connectivity is increasing. It relates to major transshipment hubs as intermediary locations that connect deep sea and feeder shipping networks. Notable examples include Dubai, Singapore, and Panama. Under such circumstances, the port becomes a distribution platform servicing a region by stocking parts and finished goods, assembly and customization services, and light manufacturing. New forms of interactions can also occur, particularly when maritime and air cargo operations are jointly used in supply chain management. The joint connectivity of both air and maritime networks creates multiplying effects since there are additional sourcing and distribution options through air/maritime transloading.*

*The third functional type of port-centric logistics is import-oriented, which is common in North America and Europe. Since the import of retail goods dominates, first-tier port-centric logistics rely on container destuffing and the deconsolidation of loads for specific distribution centers. Like export-oriented platforms, there is an active container repositioning market trying to reconcile inbound and outbound logistics. Transloading is also an important logistics activity with the contents of container load units transferred into domestic units, such as between 40-foot ISO containers and 53-foot domestic containers in North America. Since inbound logistics has a significant retail orientation, second-tier port-centric logistics involve assembly and customization and various forms of distribution, such as fulfilment and postponement (Figure 4.22).*

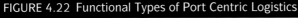

FIGURE 4.22  Functional Types of Port Centric Logistics

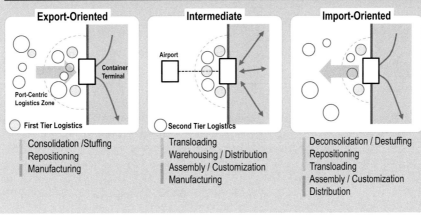

## 4 PORT CLUSTER GOVERNANCE

The governance of hinterland access regimes is linked with **cluster formation**. It refers to the agglomeration effects and the degree of internal cohesion and competition within a hinterland. This governance concept not only applies to ports, but can also be inferred for airports, inland ports and logistical zones, or any freight distribution construct where a closer integration of the involved actors could lead to performance improvements. An emerging paradigm concerns the **city as a terminal and a hub**, which means it acts as a functional freight region. This paradigm is fundamental because:

- A metropolitan area is the **origin, destination, and point of transit** of large volumes of passengers and freight. They are embedded within their respective supply chains with a wide array of flows.
- All regional transportation assets are **interrelated** and contribute to the regional, national, and global economy. They are embedded within their respective transport chains with an array of modes and terminals.
- Existing governance and regulatory structures are ill-placed to reflect this **jurisdictional, functional, and operational reality**.

**Cluster governance** is a business strategy that relates to the mix of, and relations between, organizations and institutions that foster coordination and pursue projects that improve the cluster as a whole through regional strategies and the coordination of their hinterland. The main advantages of cluster governance are better access to competencies and innovative ideas, better access to suppliers and customers, better access to capital, and an overall reduction of transactional costs. Although there is no single cluster governance model, as each port (or terminal) region has a different set of geographical, economic, regulatory, and operational characteristics, the following four issues tend to be common to all clusters:

- **Service efficiency**. Concerns a series of initiatives to improve the quality and reliability of terminal assets. This goes beyond infrastructural issues, as it involves some operational commitments to standard levels of service, often through certification by external agencies. An emerging strategy in this direction consists of developing port community systems that are making available information to manage terminal-related supply chains, commonly through a web portal. Service efficiency can also involve technical and managerial training to improve labor quality. A standard is thus set among the terminal users regarding what level of quality and efficiency is expected. In turn, this promotes the marketability of all the terminal users.
- **Logistical integration**. Concerns strategies that aim at better embedding terminals within their regional supply chains. For a port, this can involve the setting up of satellite terminals or inland ports that are accessed through dedicated corridors. The setting up of co-located logistics zones is also common in proximity to the port, rail, or airport terminal facilities.
- **Infrastructure and growth management**. Although port authorities conventionally undertake both infrastructure and growth management, the emerging paradigm concerns a higher level of intermodal integration

with, for instance, on-dock rail facilities. Infrastructure development also takes place more in a public-private partnership form with terminal operators and other private stakeholders such as rail operators and logistical firms.

- **Terminal-city integration**. Concerns various strategies that help mitigate the frequently significant environmental and social externalities that terminals have on their surrounding communities. As terminal facilities, notably ports, tend to be in proximity to high-density urban areas, environmental management, and corporate responsibility are perceived as tools helping to promote better coordination and avoid possible conflicts. On the other end, airport terminals are typically located away from central areas implying that their integration can lean on the setting up of transit corridors and adjacent retailing, office, and housing activities.

The full implications of cluster governance remain to be assessed, particularly the extent to which they generate added value to the terminal region and if such strategies are linked with the attraction, or at least the retention of customers and the traffic they generate. There are also impacts on competition within the cluster as firms undertake collaborative strategies to improve their respective efficiency. It is to be expected that better access to international markets will be achieved, which would indirectly promote the globalization of the companies within the cluster. This also has an impact on competition between clusters over discretionary traffic, namely transshipment.

# Chapter 4.5  Green port governance

*The greening of port management is a process affecting port authorities, safeguarding their license to operate and increasing their economic and environmental competitiveness.*

## 1 PORT AUTHORITIES AND GREEN PORTS

### 1.1 Sources of environmental pollution in ports

Since ports are generators of externalities, environmental concerns linked to port activity are mounting. The focus on environmental issues is especially keen for vessel and cargo handling operations, industrial activities in ports, port planning and extension initiatives, and hinterland accessibility. The prime sources of the environmental impact of seaports include pollution related to **port-related construction and operations**. These include air emissions of ships at berth, terminal handling equipment (such as cranes and yard equipment), and logistics and industrial activities in the port. There is also noise associated with port-related operations and the environmental effects and potential congestion associated with landside operations of barges, rail, and trucks.

There are **nine groups of environmental facets** in port development and construction, including water quality, coastal hydrology, soil contamination, marine, and coastal ecology, air quality, noise and vibration, waste management, visual intrusion, and socio-cultural impacts such as the relocation of communities. This classification provides possible realms of engagement, mitigation, and policy-making and requires **precise measurements** of respective impacts and externalities.

**Air pollution** is one of the major environmental impacts generated by ports, particularly greenhouse gas (GHG) emissions, leading to climate change since GHG traps heat. This, in turn, distorts the natural ecosystem. There are also health effects impacting the residents of the local community surrounding ports which include asthma, other respiratory diseases, cardiovascular disease, lung cancer, and premature mortality. The main sources of air pollution in ports include:

- **Ships port calls**, which are a source of air pollutants such as $CO_2$, $SO_x$, $NO_x$, $PM_{10}$, $PM_{2.5}$, HC, CO, and VOC. The maritime shipping industry contributes 2.5% to 3% of annual human-produced carbon dioxide ($CO_2$) emissions, in which the largest portion is derived from container shipping. Without countermeasures, the emissions of sulfur oxide ($SO_x$) and nitrogen oxide ($NO_x$) of the shipping industry would exceed all other emission sources in transport and result in poor air quality in ports and their surroundings. To reduce, and eventually halt emissions, some important steps have already been taken. They include the judicial implementation of the International Maritime Organisation (IMO) Convention for the Prevention of Pollution from Ships (MARPOL) (Annex VI) that imposes limitations on the main air pollutants contained in ships' exhaust as well as plans for implementing additional requirements, the Energy Efficiency Design Index (EEDI) for new ships, and the Ship Energy Efficiency Management Plan (SEEMP) for all ships. The Convention places a cap on sulfur within particular areas (Emission Control Areas – ECAs). For example, in the SECA (Sulfur Emission Control Area) in the North and Baltic Seas area, the mass fraction of sulfur in bunker fuel has to be less than 1% from 2010. North America installed similar arrangements in 2012. This limit was decreased to less than 0.1% from 2015. The worldwide sulfur limit of 3.5% in bunker fuel was reduced to 0.5% in early 2020. Specific sulfur caps exist when ships are in port. Alternative fuels are considered (Liquefied Natural Gas (LNG), and hydrogen; see Box 4.8 for a discussion on LNG) to reduce ship emissions at sea and in ports. Onshore power supply solutions (or cold ironing) can help to reduce ship emissions in port significantly.
- **Land side activities**, particularly cargo operations at terminals, which form another source of airborne emission. Emissions of dust from bulk cargo handling, electricity consumption, and gases from cargo handling equipment and trucks adversely affect air quality. Regarding **landside operations** connecting inland transport, environmental impacts caused by intermodal connections and congestion lead to adverse effects, particularly air pollution emitted by internal combustion engines. Depending on modal choices and the associated cost and transit time requirements from shippers, such environmental effects vary and can be mitigated.

## Box 4.8 Supporting LNG as a ship fuel – port authority initiatives

*Liquefied Natural Gas (LNG) serves as an attractive fuel for ships to meet the stringent environmental regulations enacted by IMO, particularly in sulfur and NOx emissions. Dual-fueled ships are entering the market. An example is the new generation of LNG containerships introduced by CMA CGM in 2020, which are emitting up to 25% less $CO_2$, 99% fewer sulfur emissions, 99% fewer particulates, and 85% fewer nitrogen oxide emissions than ships using heavy fuel oil (HFO). The orderbooks suggest that by 2025, more than 650 LNG-powered ships of all types will be in operation.*

*LNG bunkering facilities still remain more the exception than the rule. On the one hand, the drivers for ports to provide LNG bunkers are extensive. They include the location of the port relative to an ECA, the number of ship calls at the port, the pricing of LNG fuel comparable to alternative fuel options, the provision of infrastructure and facilities for LNG bunkering, the demand from cruise lines for LNG bunkering, the development of a positive public perception of the port and the status of the port as a major bunker port, and the existence of other competitive bunkering ports along the itinerary. The EU has endorsed a directive addressing LNG bunkering terminal availability in ports, stating that refueling points for LNG at maritime and inland ports of the TEN-T core network should be available by the end of 2025 and 2030, respectively.*

*On the other hand, it can be argued that LNG may not be the ship fuel of the future as, compared to fuel oil, the savings in $CO_2$ are quite limited. There are unresolved questions about the impact of methane slip (unburned natural gas) on climate change. Several crucial barriers, such as the lack of bunkering infrastructure and operational standards, have slowed down its development. However, rising environmental concerns give an incentive for the public sector to provide policy support in removing any remaining obstacles. The competitive environment supports the widespread application of LNG as a ship fuel with global LNG supply chains already in place. Still, the use of LNG as a ship fuel is expected to first gain momentum in niche markets, like small ferry routes and regular liner traffic. LNG carriers are pioneers in using LNG as a ship fuel as they typically burn a portion of their boil-off gas. In the longer run, the adoption of LNG as a ship fuel on a global scale rests on three main factors:*

- *The price differences between LNG, low sulfur fuel (LSFO), and scrubber technology.*
- *The dynamics in the global emission regulations.*
- *The availability of LNG bunkering facilities.*

*In the past decade, investments in LNG bunkering infrastructure in ports have taken off. Quite a few public port authorities play a proactive role in facilitating LNG use as a marine fuel, often in close partnership with industrial actors. Port authorities are also using various types of financial instruments to promote the market development of LNG facilities, including:*

- *Building joint ventures or PPPs with private actors to invest in bunkering facilities.*
- *Providing funding or applying for subsidies to support investment.*

> - *Developing a differential port tariff favoring ships powered by clean fuels, like LNG*
> - *Providing funding for ship conversion (e.g. in the port of Stockholm).*
> - *If applicable, establishing pilot projects, such as owning LNG-powered port vessels, kick-starting LNG market development, and solving the chicken-and-egg problem.*

- **Industrial and logistics activities** in and near port areas. These also contribute to total air emissions but tend to be considered outside port emissions.

Another major environmental concern is **water pollution** and the effects on marine ecosystems. Water pollution comes from ballast water, fuel oil residue and waste disposal from ship operations, and cargo residue. These marine pollutants are harmful to natural habitats located around port waters, which would upset marine and coastal ecology and lead to the damage and loss of coastal ecology and fishery resources. The need for navigation channel deepening and widening would lead to contaminated sludge from dredging.

Untreated **water and waste disposal** from port operations, industrial activities, construction, and expansion projects causes another major category of environmental externality. This includes solid, liquid, and hazardous wastes. Waste lubricants, oily mixtures, solid waste (garbage), wastes from cargo operations, daily administration, and buildings also create pollution. Disposal of these contaminated materials on land may cause destruction of plants, leakage of contaminated materials, unpleasant sights, and other nuisances to the local community. Hence, improper waste control and treatment can be a significant strain on the natural environment surrounding the port area. An international policy agenda has already developed referring to the availability and adequacy of port reception facilities for ship-generated waste and cargo residues. Together with establishing systems that provide incentives for ships to use, these facilities reduce ship discharges into the sea.

Relevant provisions have been adopted in Annexes V and VI of MARPOL. These provisions define which wastes can be discharged into the sea and impose obligations to provide facilities for the reception of ship-generated residues and garbage. They also target inadequate reception and handling and inadequate delivery by ships of their waste cargo residues. Regional initiatives (i.e. the European Union Directive 2000/59/EC on port reception facilities for ship-generated waste and cargo residues) align legislation with the international initiatives and address the legal, financial, and practical responsibilities of the different operators involved when operating at ports.

Waste management in ports implies a hierarchy containing several steps in a preferred order of priority, with the first three of the following being the most desirable ones:

- **Reducing** the use of resources and minimizing the quantities and hazardous qualities of the waste generated.

- **Reuse.** Using products or items again for the same or different purposes.
- **Recycling.** reprocessing valuable components/materials of waste for use as a feedstock to manufacture the same or a different product.
- **Recovery.** obtaining value from wastes by composting, energy recovery, or other technologies.
- **Disposal.** If there is no other appropriate solution, waste disposal by land filling and incineration without energy recovery. Waste disposal has various options depending on the type of waste and according to acceptable environmental standards.

Two initial steps allow for achievement of better results:

- **Waste segregation** separates waste, making it useable or less difficult to dispose of. Waste segregation at source is a prerequisite to securing separate fractions of sufficient quality for different treatment processes.
- **Waste treatment** to reduce hazards or nuisance, preferably at the site of generation. The need for treatment and the level and type of treatment is determined by the requirement of its use or disposal.

## 1.2 The greening of port management

The **greening of port management** is attracting growing attention in business practice as the growing green reflex is mirrored in the many green initiatives of individual ports and the coordinated actions of the wider port community (see Chapter 2.5 for an overview of initiatives), **Port authorities** show increasing concerns about the impacts of noise pollution, waste disposal, water pollution and air emissions on the sustainable functioning of the port since they represent the externalities that have the most identifiable impacts on the health of people working or living around ports. Limiting pollution is not only an environmental goal for port authorities. It has also become a clear mission in **corporate social responsibility** (CSR) and **stakeholder relations management** in port areas.

It has become evident that any port infrastructure project can be constrained by environmental factors and the public response they can generate. Thus, ports are facing higher pressure from the public in terms of performing their social responsibility. Ports must demonstrate an ever-higher level of environmental performance to ensure **community support**. Ports need to comply with ever-higher regulatory and societal requirements in the fields of environmental protection, which can impact on the footprint for the ports to grow, not only in terms of hectares but also in terms of so-called **environmental space**. This challenges seaports to minimize emissions of existing and future activities in the port areas and the wider logistics area. Environmental aspects also play an increasing role in attracting trading partners and potential investors. A port with a strong environmental record and a high level of community support is likely to be favored.

As such, **green port governance** is considered a key strategic challenge to port authorities and the wider port communities. Without proper environmental governance, tools and policies in ports, there is an increased risk of having a clear imbalance between the benefits and costs of ports for the local community. Such imbalances potentially form a breeding ground for major socio-economic confrontations related to port development and operations.

## 2 INSTRUMENTS AND TOOLS FOR PROMOTING GREEN PORTS

Given the potential environmental impacts of port development and operations, port authorities or any other managing bodies of a seaport are challenged to avoid and or reduce effects through a range of **green management tools and instruments**. In the following sections, three groups of tools and instruments are discussed in more detail: (a) penalty and incentive pricing, (b) monitoring and measuring, (c) market access control and environmental standard regulation.

Instruments can also be grouped into two categories, which are instruments that directly limit environmental impacts and instruments that do not (Figure 4.23). Such a range of instruments in a port terminal context can be used to influence the green behavior of a terminal operator.

### 2.1 Penalty and incentive pricing

Port authorities can use **port pricing** (Chapter 5.4) as an **environmental incentive tool** in ports. Motivating or giving an incentive pricing to the good doers and punishing or giving a penalty pricing to the wrongdoers is an effective tool to promote environmental awareness. Pricing control by port authorities is most commonly used in shipping traffic, followed by industrial activities at ports. Voluntary schemes aimed at cleaner ships, such as rewarding the use of low sulfur fuel oil (LSFO), are the most common. A pioneering example is the Port of Long Beach which implemented the Green Flag Speed Reduction Program. By slowing down, ships can reduce airborne emissions and shipowners, in return, are granted a discount the following year as an incentive.

Another good example is green port dues, such as the Environmental Ship Index (ESI) program. Ship operators typically embrace such voluntary schemes, particularly when the implementation and further refinement/ updating of such programs go hand in hand with a proactive and constructive collaboration between the maritime industry and the respective government agencies or port authorities. However, since prices paid by shipping companies and other port users affect their commercial behavior and decisions, price regulation may lead to market distortions if not uniformly applied among competing ports.

### 2.2 Monitoring and measuring

Ports are highly vulnerable to unfounded claims of environmental damage. To deflect such claims, ports need quantifiable and detailed information on the impacts of their operations on the adjacent environment. Port authorities and wider port communities should communicate how environmental impacts associated with port operations are being effectively managed. By monitoring the air quality, water quality, and policy development, the port authority

FIGURE 4.23 Instruments for Port Authorities to Reduce the Environmental Impacts of Terminals

**INSTRUMENTS THAT DIRECTLY LIMIT ENVIRONMENTAL IMPACTS**

**Setting of fixed impact reduction targets**

**Single-source instruments ("command and control")** Terminal operator (TO) needs to comply with an emission limitation or face penalties

**Harm-based standards** — Description of required end results (e.g. cap on $CO_2$ emission of terminal)

**Design standards** — Description of required emission limits based on model technology

**Technology specifications** — Specification of the technology the TO must use to control its pollution

**Bans and limitations** — Ban or restrict equipment or operations that present unreasonable risks

**Multi-source instruments (limits on cumulative impacts from multiple sources)** Terminal operator has some compliance flexibility with environmental targets

**Integrated permitting** — Multiple requirements into a single permit

**Tradeable emissions** — Trade emission control responsibilities given an aggregate regulatory cap on emissions

**Challenge regulations** — Responsibility for designing and implementing programs to achieve imposed target

**INSTRUMENTS THAT DO NOT DIRECTLY LIMIT ENVIRONMENTAL IMPACTS**

**Pollution control without setting specific emission targets**

**Pollution charges** — TO pays fixed amount for each unit of pollution (no ceiling)

**Liability** — TO pays compensation to those that are harmed by impacts

**Information reporting** — TO needs to report impacts publicly

**Subsidies/discounts** — Knowledge support to TOs (good practice guide, training, information centre)

**Technical assistance** — Financial assistance or discounts to TOs as an incentive/carrot to change their behavior, or to help defray costs of mandatory standards

Source: Adapted from Notteboom and Lam (2018).

could keep track of the port's environmental performance, and subsequently formulate or modify its targeted strategies and policies.

Many port authorities have increased **transparency on environmental impacts** and broader sustainability aspects by publishing annual or bi-annual sustainability reports. The practice of sustainability reporting, beyond mere environmental reporting, started in the late 1990s. More recently, the port industry has adopted this sort of reporting to conceptualize sustainability and as an essential basis for the license to operate. Mainly larger port authorities have started producing sustainability reports or integrated reporting voluntarily in the past decade (e.g. Antwerp, Hamburg, Rotterdam). In contrast, others have been obliged to adopt the practice due to enforced legislation by governments when it comes to example-setting by state-owned enterprises (e.g. Swedish ports). Ports increasingly follow global guidelines and standards for sustainability reporting (such as the Global Reporting Initiative – GRI).

In 2016, the first Sustainability Report at the level of the European Port Industry was presented in the context of the European Commission POR-TOPIA project. Using datasets present within the European Seaports Organisation (ESPO) and the ECOPORTS project, it revealed that many unsolved conceptual issues and differences in approach among ports remain when it comes to sustainability reporting:

- The scope and the boundaries of the reporting, i.e. organizational, functional, or geographical boundaries.
- The perspectives of performance and the calculation/definition of indicators.
- The integration of stakeholder perspectives.

## 2.3 Market access control and environmental standard regulation

Access regulation controls how terminal operators and other port actors access the facilities they need to compete in the market. Access regulation can include elements concerning emissions and overall environmental performance. A good example is how environmental criteria can be used in the competitive bidding procedure for a terminal concession (Box 4.9).

Port authorities might have varying degrees of regulatory jurisdiction to restrict market access and stipulate environmental standards. In other words, the discretionary powers of port authorities in environmental matters have their limits. In most cases, the bulk of the regulatory power can be found at the regional, national or supranational level. For example, international conventions, like MARPOL, give each signatory nation the accountability to enact domestic laws to implement the convention and to comply with it.

Other than international regulatory control, legislation is at various levels depending on the country/port. It could be a stated law from national government, a law stipulated by the municipality, certain rules set by the port authority, or a mutually binding agreement between the port authority and market players, such as concession agreements. Although regulations are usually strict, their implementation and enforcement might be slow and weak due to a lack of local legitimacy caused by conflicting interests of stakeholders. They might also come at a high regulation cost for both

## Box 4.9 The greening of terminal concessions

*One emerging field of action for landlord port authorities relates to the **inclusion of green factors when awarding terminals to private terminal operators** (Figure 4.24). Land for port development is scarce, making the concessioning of terminals to private stevedoring companies a primary task of landlord port authorities. Key issues in the concessioning of terminals include the allocation mechanisms used for granting seaport concessions, and determining the concession term and concessions fees. The inclusion of special clauses in the concession contract aimed at assuring that the terminal operator will act in the interest of the port authority and the wider community (for example, throughput guarantees) is common. A well-designed concession policy allows port authorities to retain some control on the organization and structure of the supply side of the port market while optimizing the use of scarce resources such as land.*

*When deciding what site to award, port authorities could more explicitly look at the **environmental quality of the port site**. Brownfields might be more expensive to redevelop but often lead to higher spatial quality and regeneration of older port sites. Port authorities could also include more stringent construction guidelines for port infrastructure and superstructure. Such measures could consist of using a minimum percentage of green energy or installing cold ironing facilities.*

*In the **awarding or selection phase**, port authorities often include a pre-qualification stage. The number of candidates is narrowed down based on minimum requirements related to their financial strength and relevant experience in operating facilities for similar cargo in the same or other ports. **Environmental performance** can constitute a new additional element in the qualification phase of a terminal awarding process. By doing so, possible candidates are rewarded for their market scale and financial potential and they will have taken initiatives previously to develop a green policy at other terminals in their portfolio. There is scope to more explicitly integrate environmental performance in the selection*

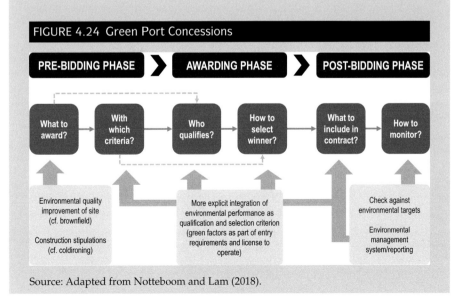

FIGURE 4.24 Green Port Concessions

Source: Adapted from Notteboom and Lam (2018).

*process next to more traditional criteria such as throughput expectations, financial performance, the price bid, and socio-economic impacts in terms of value-added created and employment effects.*

*Port authorities should also consider the inclusion of green elements in the post-bidding phase, including **environmental clauses** that go beyond simply stipulating that the terminal operator will have to comply with local, national, and supranational environmental legislation.*

*A small number of recent terminal contracts include **modal split specifications**, particularly in a container terminal context. This mostly takes the form of some **technical specifications and compulsory investments** to be done by the terminal operator in hinterland transport infrastructures on the terminal site. In only a few cases, the modal split clauses explicitly impose a **specific modal split** on the terminal operator to be reached by a specific year (for example, 40% road, 40% barge and shortsea, and 20% rail by 2025). The modal split target is often formulated as a soft objective (an intention). However, soft targets are best kept outside the contractual setting as they cannot be legally imposed on the terminal operator. The port authority can encourage terminal operators to reach soft targets through favorable pricing or awarding systems (the 'carrot' approach).*

*The setting of **hard targets** in the concession agreement implies a 'stick' approach with binding clauses and enforcement (penalties for non-compliance). In following such a stick approach, port authorities often face the problem of posing credible threats. For example, terminal operators confronted with 'hard' modal split clauses will argue that the distribution of cargo over the various inland transport modes is largely affected by exogenous factors such as the supply chain practices of their customers, the pricing and quality of rail and barge services and the infrastructure policy (of the government) outside the port area. However, terminal operators can positively influence the modal split on their terminal through pricing (for instance, a dwell time fee system or pricing of moves to inland transport modes), actions to increase the transparency of information flows (which makes cargo bundling towards rail and barge easier) and extended gate solutions in the hinterland (for instance by setting up satellite terminals in the hinterland).*

implementation and enforcement. While the environmental level playing field among ports continues to be considered, attention has shifted to the need to cooperate, both nationally and internationally, to push the green port agenda forward.

## 3 CHALLENGES TO GREEN PORT GOVERNANCE

Port authorities have realized that further greening is required to maintain their competitive edge and their license to operate, but it can also create **earning opportunities**. In practice, the attitude of port authorities can range from **reactive monitoring** of general environmental management programs to more **proactive approaches** aimed at value creation and revenue-making.

However, port communities also understand that the challenges remain immense and progress made is not at the same level in all domains of action:

- Reducing the environmental footprint commonly requires **drastic and large-scale solutions** such as Carbon Capture and Utilization (CCU) and Carbon Capture and Storage (CCS), a further push towards greener shipping and modal shift.
- The greening of ports also demands a shift in **perspectives, values, and a joint commitment and dedication** of the parties involved. More than ever, port authorities and market players will have to call out to other partners in the chains to achieve green corporate and societal objectives. Success typically depends on coordination and cooperation between the involved actors and the availability, use, and **sharing of data** through appropriate platforms and systems.
- As many landlord port authorities have been corporatized, **investment recovery** is often cited as a critical aspect of green initiatives.

Like private companies, port authorities have become very sensitive to the **coherence, continuity, and legal certainty of developed government policies**. As many investment decisions have a medium to long-term payback time, any changes in government policy can have huge implications for the soundness of the initial decision related to a green initiative. This is particularly the case for the abolition of a subsidy scheme for specific green investments. Thus, government policies and regulations should provide legal and investment certainty to the affected port authorities and private businesses.

Instead of opting for a one size fits all approach in environmental initiatives, landlord port authorities are invited to evaluate carefully:

- Whether they have **a role to play**, such as will their involvement likely lead to a superior outcome compared to no involvement?
- What **tools or instruments to use**, such as pricing, knowledge development/sharing, and investment?
- Whether they should act as **facilitator or entrepreneur**. In some cases, port authorities move beyond the pure facilitation role by entering into key investments, particularly when private investors show more reluctance to do so.

While many port authorities are very active in implementing the green port concept, **progress remains challenging in some areas**, such as the large-scale implementation of cold ironing solutions for deep-sea vessels or the greening of terminal concession procedures and agreements.

Given the position of seaports as crucial nodes in global supply chains and logistics networks, it is tempting to push port authorities to take up a role as **tax collectors for the related environmental damage**. Policymakers should not force port authorities to act as the convenient tax collectors for greening supply chains at the supranational or national level. Any **internalization of environmental costs** should target the polluter at source and cannot lead to an obligation for port authorities to punish for externalities or to reward environmental performance. Obviously, the above point does not imply that port authorities should refrain from launching such **schemes on a voluntary basis**, either individually or in collaboration with other ports.

## 4 GREEN PORT GOVERNANCE AND STAKEHOLDERS

**Stakeholder relations management** has become an important part of port management and strategy. In dealing with stakeholders, port authorities can resort to **effective environmental management**, which includes:

- An **environmental management system**. In essence, this is a documented process that describes a structure for the management of environmental impact processes and continuous improvements, such as environmental risk assessment and management actions to address those risks.
- **Environmental monitoring and reporting**. Ports are extremely vulnerable to unfounded claims of environmental damage, such as those related to dredging. To deflect such claims, ports need quantifiable and detailed information on the environmental impacts of their operations. Examples of environmental reporting are environmental impact assessment studies associated with port expansion, reports related to dredging impacts, and monitoring of natural resources such as wetland conditions and bird populations, and migration. A growing number of ports are developing sustainability reports on an annual or regular basis.
- **Community consultation** forms a key component of environmental management. Ports should communicate how environmental impacts associated with port operations are being effectively managed. If a port starts a dialogue with the local community only in response to a problem, a negative perception in the community could be the outcome. The key is to identify what aspects of port development are negotiable and then communicate this to the community.
- **Land use strategies** should identify plans for future port operation and strategies to conserve and protect conservation value areas, such as buffers and wildlife corridors. By coming to terms with both the community and the government on future port activities, a port can reach a higher level of certainty that it will grow and meet changing trade needs.

When ecosystems are damaged or lost due to port development, port authorities should interact with stakeholders to find answers to some important questions about the **restoration of environmental assets**:

- What is to be restored; the resource itself or resource services?
- How much restoration is required to compensate for the loss?
- What alternative does the cost-effective restoration option provide?
- Do the benefits to be obtained from the restoration justify the costs?
- Who pays, or how can the costs be shared equitably?

These questions raise real concerns for green port governance as mitigation and compensation measures can add between 10% and 20% to the port project cost.

## 5 GREEN CRUISE PORTS

### 5.1 The cruise environmental challenge

Not only cargo ports are challenged to **reduce environmental impacts**. The aspirations to host more cruise activities are increasingly combined with the strategic importance of sustainability and **green cruise governance**.

A condition to enable local communities to extract the greatest benefit from cruise market growth is the endorsement of best practices and policy options to mitigate the externalities produced by cruise shipping. The challenges to be addressed relate to three pillars, one of them referring to the *environment*. Addressing the externalities produced by the provision of cruise shipping and the hosting of vessels and cruise passengers at cruise ports stands today as a priority. Environmental externalities refer to the handling of waste produced, water quality, air emissions, noise, and soil, as well as to other issues (i.e. constructions that alter natural or built environment, fauna, energy resources). Two key externalities are waste management and the various forms of emissions, including air and noise emissions. Their importance and global presence have led to discussion and conclusions on measures to occur at the international level.

## 5.2  Waste management

A key issue on cruising and the environment is developing effective policies and practices for collecting and handling the waste and garbage produced onboard (Box 4.10). As a cruise ship carries several thousand passengers and crew in an enclosed facility, an array of municipal utilities such as water supply, electricity generation, sewers, and waste management are found onboard. The amount and types of waste might vary from one cruise ship to another, yet cruises are generators of the highest amount of garbage compared to other shipping markets. A cruise ship with 3,000 passengers and crew generates about 50 tons of solid waste in a single week and an average of 50 tons of sewage (black water) per day. IMO uses a figure of 3.5 kg/passenger/day, while the U.S. Department of Transportation data estimates that the generated waste during a typical one-week voyage includes 25,000 gallons of oily bilge water; 210,000 gallons of sewage (or black water), one million gallons of non-sewage wastewater and eight tons of solid waste (i.e. plastic, paper, wood, cardboard, food, cans, glass).

Most cruise lines and port authorities have implemented environmental management systems to ensure improved **waste reception operations**. Cruise lines have put effort into reducing, selecting, and managing the garbage generated onboard in compliance with MARPOL requirements. An environmental policy goal of 'zero discharge' for solid waste at sea has been endorsed by several of them, putting pressure on cruise ports to go beyond the environmental regulatory obligations. Waste management at the port is vital, as is shipboard recycling, oil wastes treatment, management of hazardous wastes, and ballast water management for cruise companies. Similarly, cruise ports implement solid waste management processes. They develop facilities, technologies, and services to allow for continuity in a cruise ship's garbage life cycle that is more efficient. Today, port reception facilities are generally available and the volumes of waste delivered, compared to that discharged at sea, have increased.

A significant concern for cruise ports, operators, and involved third parties is developing **efficient information and monitoring systems** allowing for the best use of the mechanisms present. Reducing solid waste and increasing recycling via the availability of garbage reception facilities at all berths, 24 hours a day, seven days per week, demands stakeholders' cooperation to manage better ship-generated waste and, not least, the application of innovative technologies. Cruise ports need to promote handling services such as segregation, biological reprocessing, inactivation and composting, recycling, and storage. Together, these actors can explore waste treatment possibilities on ships via investment in advancing innovative new technologies. These efforts could

---

**Box 4.10 Cruise ports waste reception facilities: ownership and fee schemes**

*In the second major cruise market of the world, the Mediterranean Sea, the available waste reception facilities in port are under different proprietary status, private ownership being dominant, yet the extent of this happens per type of facility differs. In the case of recycling plants, over half of the available facilities are privately owned. This percentage reduces to one-third in the case of incineration and biological plants and storage areas and one quarter in the case of energy recovery plants. Public proprietary status is comparatively high in storage areas, while public-private partnerships are on the rise in all types of waste reception facilities.*

*The fee selection schemes aim to enable ports to establish cost recovery systems to encourage the delivery of waste on land and discourage dumping at sea. The most commonly applied fee selection scheme is collecting indirect fees irrespective of the actual use of facilities. The direct fee selection scheme is applied at almost one-quarter of the ports, while the remainder apply a combination of direct and indirect fee schemes. Given the remarkable variation in fee payment methods, it is worth focusing on the main principles of fee selection schemes applied at five major ports in different countries:*

- *Barcelona (Spain). The largest European cruise port applies a fixed waste tax per call. A private company provides the service requested by ships, and the port authority is responsible for the payment for the services offered.*
- *Dubrovnik (Croatia). The ships are charged different fees based on the type of waste. The disposal of solid waste carries an obligatory fee based on ship gross tonnage. Ships that are less than 500 grt pay a fixed fee, and those over 500 grt pay a fee based on the quantity of the disposed waste. Other wastes received are fluid wastes and oil waste, with a quantity based charge for both disposals.*
- *Kusadasi (Turkey). All cruise ship vessels are subject to a compulsory contribution fee that is designated according to the gross tonnage of the vessel. This compulsory contribution fee allows each vessel to deliver a certain amount of waste (m3) without any charge while it is charged for any additional m3 of garbage.*
- *Piraeus (Greece). Two categories of waste fees apply to cruise ships calling. The first one is a contributory fee that covers the delivery, treatment, and final disposal of a maximum permitted quantity of waste per ship call. This fee applies to cruise ships whose deployment includes frequent and regular calls at the port of Piraeus, i.e. those realizing a minimum of three calls per month. The second type of fee is a fixed fee per call. This applies to cruise ships without scheduled itineraries and is structured to cover food waste and domestic waste only. For the operational waste and the excessive*

> *quantities of domestic waste that are not covered by the contributory fee, the additional applicable charge depends on the waste quantity.*
> • *Venice (Italy). The fee selection scheme is based on the division of the respective fees into two different types of rates. The first type is a fixed rate that covers the costs necessary to carry out the collection and disposal service by ensuring at least 35% of the fixed costs. The current legislation requires the payment of this fee even from vessels that do not discharge waste at the Port of Venice. The second one is a variable rate that covers costs directly related to the actual delivery of wastes based on tonnage. This variable rate is also subdivided into an hourly rate, a fee per cubic meter, and a fee for the service provided.*

decrease the significant disparity between waste management ashore and disposal services at the destination.

Improving wastewater treatment capacities is a process of importance. In this case, the IMO has already designated 'special areas' for passenger ships (i.e. the Baltic sea) where the discharge of sewage from a cruise ship will be prohibited through a gradual process. Stakeholders undertake initiatives to ensure that facilities for the reception of sewage are provided in ports and terminals where coastal countries can report that the sewage reception facilities in their ports fulfill the criteria of adequacy.

### 5.3 Emission control

**Cruise port and cruise shipping-related emissions** have attracted great interest among decision-makers and in port-cities that experience port and port-related operations' negative externalities. Cruise shipping is a relatively large emitter due to the large hoteling load. Even though the average emissions in a port account are comparatively low, cruise terminals are often close to city centers, meaning that population exposure might be on the higher side. Significant differences in $CO_2$ emissions can be observed between individual cruise ships depending on the size, the age, and the ship's capacity configuration (i.e. high-end luxury cruise ships vs 'mass' cruise ships). The largest ships show the lowest $CO_2$ output, partly because of the high occupancy rate in the number of beds per surface unit and their relatively young age.

The need to control emissions, along with the international regulatory frameworks restricting the use of fueling options, has triggered interest in alternative forms of powering cruise vessels. Liquefied Natural Gas (LNG) has emerged as the primary alternative fuel for the shipping industry as many new buildings have dual-fuel engines that allow them to use heavy oil or LNG. Cruise ships have the highest adoption build rate among the different types of seagoing vessels; LNG will power 19 out of 105 cruise ships to be delivered between 2018 and 2026, and more cruise lines are committing to LNG-fueled cruise ships. This increase creates for the cruise port industry the need for the provision of LNG bunkering facilities. Cruise ports can also use LNG to fuel their handling and transport equipment and serve the energy needs of the

## Box 4.11 Shoreside power facilities at cruise ports

*Cold ironing or shoreside power facilities are being installed in several urban cruise terminals to reduce the environmental impact of docked ships. In 2001, the port of Juneau in Alaska was the first in the world to offer shoreside power for cruise vessels. Seattle followed with two installations in 2005 and 2006. In 2009, Port Metro Vancouver also introduced a system to connect ships to the power grid so they could turn off their engines while docked. It is estimated that for an average cruise ship, some 17,000 liters of fuel can be saved in a 10 hour docking period. In October 2010, San Francisco became the first port in California to offer clean shore power for cruise ships. Los Angeles, San Diego, and Long Beach now provide similar facilities. Also, in Europe, a number of ports have taken initiatives in this area (e.g. Gothenburg, Venice, Barcelona, La Spezia, Civitavecchia, and Hamburg).*

*A cruise ship requires a fast store loading process since port turns between cruises are relatively short (8 to 12 hours on average). Because the pier is higher than the cargo door, a lift system is used to lower cargo pallets (mostly food) to the cargo dock level. To mitigate the environmental impacts of cruise ships docked at the cruise terminal adjacent to its central business district, Port Metro Vancouver installed cold ironing facilities in 2009 to provide electric power to ships. This enables a cruise ship to cut its bunker engines and considerably reduce its emissions at the cruise port. Alaskan cruises rely the most on cold ironing, particularly in light of the environmental sensitivity of the region visited. About 5% of the energy spent on Alaskan cruises is from cold ironing.*

cruise terminal buildings, such as air conditioning. Cold ironing or shoreside power facilities are also installed in several urban cruise terminals to reduce the environmental impact of docked ships (Box 4.11).

The application of measures to reduce emissions, including onshore power for cruise ships, remains subject to **regional variations**. For example, it is further developed in North America than in Europe, with future technologies, such as wind and solar power, also options under consideration.

Regarding **noise emissions**, there are different noise sources on ships during their dockage at ports, classified as diesel generator engine exhaust, ventilation inlets/outlets, and secondary noise sources, e.g. pumps or reefers. Cruise ship operations generate disturbing noise for nearby areas and the crew, and they are also sources of low-frequency noises. The IMO has already defined a Code on noise levels on board ships detailing limits for the different types of noise and setting limits for the noise emitted into the surroundings. However, the existing international framework covers only the noise onboard ships but not in a port or during maneuvering. While the latter activities are, in some countries, subject to additional regulations, an international discussion for global rules would facilitate an effective and sustaining answer concerning the limits of noise emissions produced by cruise vessels at the port.

## 5.4 Regulating an emerging industry

In environmental challenges, **international regulations** are highly appropriate when a legislative approach is found wanting. The most appropriate way to deal with environmental externalities uniformly, hence securing a level playing field for the entire cruise industry, is the endorsement of international policy instruments. In the significant parts of the market (i.e. North America, Europe), legislation is already endorsed as the main driver of the need for environmental management tools. In emerging areas, such as Asia, environmental considerations remain, for the moment, of secondary importance. Beyond legislation, agreements on associated issues – such as the presence of remote monitoring systems as tools for improving the level of cruise and port environmental conditions – which demand complex and expensive processes are better addressed at the international level, rather than being causes of distorting competition.

The industry has implemented several **self-regulatory practices** that have secured growth and remarkable operational achievements. Even on the environmental front, self-regulation at the international level is not rare. Cruise companies spend heavily to install exhaust gas cleaning technology (scrubbers) to reduce air emissions from cruise ships. Receiving support from governmental organizations (i.e. Carnival has established links with the U.S. Coast Guard and Transport Canada on this issue, while Royal Caribbean International has developed similar initiatives) and through discussion would help develop and implement environmental technology to comply with existing regulation or even pre-empt future ones. Cooperation aims to advance innovation and alternative approaches at the international level to facilitate adjustments and solutions meeting the challenges related to shore power for cruise ships. Similarly, meaningful international cruise emissions inventories would provide information on several unknown factors, such as the actual emissions of ships while docked compared with when they are at sea or comparison with emissions from other shipping sectors. All these would inform adjustments of the related regulatory frameworks.

Environmental externalities have been the theme of initiatives collectively developed by the port industry within respective port associations. Individual ports use environmental management systems compliant with ISO14001 and other practices and tools available to manage environmental issues. Incentive pricing is also applied as a means to address environmental challenges. Ships producing reduced quantities of ship-generated waste are subject to lower dues, as discounts are offered based on green award certificates or on the basis of an Environmental Ship Index. However, even in this case, the presence of common principles would facilitate the identification of such ships. Simultaneously, it would limit questions on the effectiveness of the tools in application, and not least the potential for cross-subsidization between ship types depending on the markets served.

Overall environmental issues regarding cruise shipping and those regarding cruise ports are strongly interconnected. Thus the tools, measures, and policies to combat the externalities caused by these two industries require a holistic study and approach to be developed internationally. Reports, studies, and essential inventories of internalizing external costs are another field beyond regulation that international level discussions might advance, facilitating the growth of cruise activities.

# Chapter 4.6 Port management, governance and leadership

(Chapter authored by Dr. Geraldine Knatz, USC Sol Price School of Public Policy, USC Viterbi School of Engineering, University of Southern California. Executive Directors, Port of Los Angeles, 2006-2014.)

> *Port leadership is subject to a complex setting related to port governance, the socioeconomic environment, and the main goals of reconciling interest groups.*

## 1 LEADERSHIP CHALLENGES FOR PORT DIRECTORS AND EXECUTIVE STAFF

Port directors work in an environment that is complex and constantly changing. The chief executive of a port, whether the position is called **Executive Director** or CEO, sometimes both, juggles competing demands from customers, board members, stakeholders, staff, and in some cases, one or more overseeing governmental authorities. The role and functions of a port director and a port's executive management team reflect the **port's governance structure**. This section examines the role of a director at a public port (e.g. U.S. ports) or corporatized port which is still publicly owned but administered and operated by a corporate entity (e.g. Rotterdam, Dublin, Canadian and Australian ports). While there are other governance models, such as entirely private ports (e.g. United Kingdom) or publicly-listed ports with a majority of private corporate shareholders (e.g. Piraeus, Greece), executives of these organizations do not have the added complexity of being controlled fully or partially by government authorities.

One of the most significant differences between the CEO of a private corporation and a public port leader is that port authorities may be subject to significant political influence. The public ownership of the port property and the extent of government control make the port director position unique and differentiate it from a private sector CEO position. A desire to quickly make changes and get things done often butts up against the realities of the pace and process of government authority decision-making. While a port executive might share some common characteristics with a private sector CEO position, such as prestige and salary, the growing public awareness and participation in port activities, coupled with greater diversity among port board membership, has resulted in **increased politicization of the port director's position**.

To ensure decisions about port assets and investment were market-driven without political influence, a move to privatize ports took off globally in the 1990s, after some initial actions by Great Britain and Malaysia in the 1980s. A corporatized port, purportedly, is one that can focus on commercial interests with the overriding public interest being served through the government assuming a regulatory role or dictating shareholder policies. The negative externalities of port expansion on local communities have led to the recognition that the government needs to maintain some modicum of control. Thus some efforts to corporatize ports, such as in Indonesia, have resulted in a hybrid situation where the government authority still appoints the director, and the board members are political appointments. During this reform period, some ports shifted from operating to landlord ports or were corporatized to a limited degree, with the government entity still retaining some control. The majority of the world's ports are a hybrid combination of public and private control.

The intent here is not to elaborate on the merits of different models on port governance but to examine how the governance model affects the role of the chief executive. What characteristics of a public port authority make its chief executive different to their equivalent in other business enterprises?

1. The public port director is typically a **government employee**. For example, the director of the Port of Long Beach, California, is an employee of the City of Long Beach. In contrast, the director of the Port of Baltimore, Maryland, is an employee of the Maryland State Department of Transportation. Depending on transparency laws where the port is located, the public port director's salary may be a matter of public record.

2. The director of a landlord port may have **limited control over operations within the port**. The director may not have a direct relationship with the dockworkers (i.e. no seat at the collective bargaining table between management and labor). This presents some interesting quandaries for port directors, especially during labor disputes which can shut down the port. In most cases, the public landlord port director has no authority to resolve labor disputes and only acts as a facilitator.

3. The general public and media often **do not distinguish between the 'port' and its users, tenants, or customers**, especially when there is bad news.

4. Unlike the corporate world, where board members are generally appointed to a Board of Directors for their expertise in a given business field, the port Board of Directors may be **political appointees or elected officials**, typically with little or no background in ports. This presents an additional responsibility for the port director – educating the board members.

5. The port director may have to **wear multiple hats and serve multiple masters**. For example, the Port of Los Angeles is a municipal enterprise. To the outside world, it is the Port of Los Angeles. To the City of Los Angeles, it is the Los Angeles Harbor Department, one of its three proprietary departments — like the Water and Power Department and the Department of Airports. The California State Lands Commission serves as a watchdog over Los Angeles port spending to ensure that port revenues are consistent with the state grant that established the port in 1911.

6. **Decision-making can be laborious**. The public port Board of Directors may not be empowered to make major decisions. For example, to effect an agreement of longer than three years and over a specific dollar threshold, it is necessary that the port director in Los Angeles seek approval from its Board of Directors, then from the City of Los Angeles Chief Administrative Officer, then from a committee of the Los Angeles City Council, then from the elected City Council. Unless the mayor's office approves of the agreement or expenditure, this process does not

even get started. Los Angeles probably represents one extreme as far as a bureaucratic decision-making process is concerned. Like the Port of Long Beach, other port boards are empowered to make a final decision and only require annual budget approval from their City Council. Regardless, decision-making by public port boards often has political connotations that require the executive team to balance competing interests and coordinate extensively with their overseeing government authority.

7. Decision-making and investments may not be market-based but may be **responsive to the local community or political influence**.

8. Port pricing may be **a political versus a business proposition** as port customers will lobby government authorities to keep rates low. Depending on how politicized the port is, its pricing may lag behind the market.

9. A port that is not financially sustainable and must rely on tax assessments or voter-approved general-obligation bonds will have **less independence in spending** than a port that has the ability to issue revenue bonds. The ability to make longer-term investments that port customers want can be affected by this lack of autonomy in financing.

10. Employees of a public port may **be hired and fired in accordance with the policies of the government authority** of which it is a part. However, some ports have the right to operate their own personnel departments.

The above list illustrates the types of challenges or limitations that a public port director may face. Depending on the specific structure of a corporatized port and the residual powers retained by the government authority, the director of a corporatized port may also experience some of the above challenges as well.

## 2 THE NEED FOR ALIGNMENT ON THE PORT MISSION

The ability for a port to undertake activities is related to its board composition, economic trends, ability to finance, and its relationship with its customers and stakeholders. The director and executive team must navigate **competing interests to advance the port's mission**. Success in that venture necessitates alignment on the port's mission between the port executive team, its Board of Directors, and, if applicable, the overseeing government authority. While this may sound like a straightforward concept, a lack of alignment on the port's mission can lead to potential conflict.

The prevailing view for most of the twentieth century – that ports were financially independent, politically insulated, and highly autonomous – no longer exists. It would be naïve in today's world to assume the mission for a public port is only to move people and cargo, or even to move people and cargo in a sustainable manner. As the trend for more public participation took hold in the 1980s and 1990s, port boards became more diverse, and board members felt compelled to represent not only the interests of the port but also the **community and underrepresented minority groups**. Today port commissioners are often appointed or elected to serve a particular constituency. Board members may have campaigned for the position to remedy an ill they saw in the port or represent a specific constituency, such as organized labor or environmental interests. Alternatively, they may be focused on economic development opportunities for local businesses or visitor-serving activities. Board members have a loyalty to the constituency that elected them, the government authority that appointed them, or their neighbors in the community. Their personal agendas might conflict with the executive teams' vision of the port's mission.

## 2.1 Alignment between the port executive team and the board members

Most ports have **published mission statements**, while others provide mission, vision, and values or a complete copy of their strategic plan online. A strategic planning or a visioning process that helps create alignment among board members and the executive staff can be crucial to minimizing conflicts. A comprehensive process would also engage customers and stakeholders.

Alignment should be sought not just between the port director and the Board but among board members. A board with split philosophy on mission fundamentals presents a significant challenge for the director. In many cases, decisions represent a **balancing act** to address the needs of multiple constituencies because a port's mission may be multi-faceted. Ensuring that the port's mission, vision, and values reflect a broader constituency is not as challenging as implementing a diverse range of projects to satisfy multiple constituencies. A budget-setting process with board participation can be a tool used to prioritize investment.

Port mission statements evolve over time and may be updated as frequently as every few years. Often the turnover in port directors or board leadership will prompt a review of the mission. An update to the mission statement may also be triggered to reflect current business conditions and changing times. A port mission may focus on contributing to the economic development of the local economy and job creation (Maryland, U.S.). The port may view itself as a steward of a particular geographic region (Oakland, CA). The Port of Gladstone, Australia's mission statement incorporates the principle of reducing social inequality, in their case, specifically to address the needs of indigenous peoples. Gladstone Ports Corporation in Queensland Australia, was one of the first ports to develop a Reconciliation Action Plan to raise the living standards of Aboriginal and Torres Strait Islanders. The importance of their relationship with the indigenous population is reflected in the mission statement: 'facilitate the prosperity of others'.

The challenges of remaining competitive have caused many ports to consider expanding beyond their traditional roles. Landlord ports have begun to address shortcomings in the supply chain that affect their customers. Rather than being an observer of the supply chains, landlord ports are becoming **supply chain participants** to help boost performance through their port. This is evidenced by ports increasing their role in facilitating digitization to support the logistics needs of their customers and evolving into 'smart' ports (Port of Hamburg, Germany). Reversing a global trend in governance, Jurong Port, a multi-purpose port in Singapore, had transitioned from a landlord port into an operating port. By developing 'port-centric ecosystems' or clusters, they have successfully brought elements of the bulk cargo supply chain closer to their port to improve efficiency and competitiveness. One example is the construction materials supply chain, particularly cement. Jurong now operates the largest common user cement terminal in the world. While they have not published a mission statement, their website emphasizes their commitment to 'extend seamless, integrated solutions for the most complex of projects and logistics operations'.

Some ports are expanding their mission beyond their traditional geographical boundaries through the development of inland ports and marine 'highways' (marine 'highways' revive underutilized navigable waterways for shipping goods). Beyond the potential competitive benefits of these actions, ports that move beyond their traditional geographical boundaries find they have increased the size of their constituency, which can often bring with it political, environmental, and financial implications.

Whether they be extreme weather or natural and anthropogenic disasters, disruptive events have resulted in many ports considering energy production as part of their mission. Ports are examining their dependence on external energy sources as part of their resiliency planning. While a decade or two ago, solar panels were just being considered for installation on port facilities, ports today are more active in the energy transition necessary to do their part to reduce the production of greenhouse gases. For example, the Port of Marseille, France, is preparing for energy independence and transition by initiating one of the first industrial-scale projects to convert excess green energy into hydrogen gas (Jupiter 1,000 project).

**Environmental management and sustainability** are two additional concepts that figure in many port mission statements. Even if there is no direct link to the ports' mission statement, many ports link their vision and values to one or more of the 17 United Nations Sustainable Development Goals.

## 2.2 Alignment of port mission with customer and stakeholder goals

Even if the port executive team and board are in alignment on mission, port business customers typically expect that the port's primary focus is on them and their business objectives. A port cannot be successful unless it recognizes the needs of its customers. Usually, the maritime industry is fully aware of the importance of addressing community and environmental concerns, especially if it puts the port board in a position to be able to advance capital projects in support of customer needs. Yet, port customers will be concerned if their terminal improvements are delayed because they perceived that the port placed a higher priority on the community over customer projects. The port executive team will find the need to achieve a balance that satisfies customer needs, protects their revenue sources, and maintains a positive relationship with the surrounding communities. Engagement with community stakeholders by port executives is necessary to understand community values. Residents near a large urban port may be concerned about air pollution and traffic. Smaller ports or ports in rural areas may serve a niche market that may be closely tied to the economic vitality of the surrounding community or provide a disproportionate share of jobs in the local community. In these cases, the local community may prioritize a port mission of providing jobs and supporting economic development.

Inherent in this balancing act is whether or not the port is financially self-sufficient or relies on taxes or subsidies paid by residents of the surrounding communities. Many ports like to tout that they do not rely on tax subsidies or, if the port has taxing authority, that it has not had to assess taxes, as a reflection of the prudent and successful management of the port by its current leadership. However, some ports, like the ports of Seattle and Tacoma, do have the ability to assess taxes on surrounding residents. They also have elected commissions. Ports that rely on the ability to raise taxes from the general public or on general obligation bonds needing voter approval may have **far less independence** in their decision-making than ports that are financially self-sufficient.

Public ports in the United States have regular board meetings open to the public. Thirty-nine percent of U.S. public ports have their board meetings webcast. Or, board meetings may be memorialized by video and available on the port's website. In Canada, ports have one open meeting per year, called the 'annual meeting'. European ports follow the private sector approach and are not open to the public. Based on a 2020 survey of 26 European ports, only 12% opened their board meetings by invitation. In Latin America, only 5% of the 21 ports surveyed have board meetings open to the public. So it is primarily in the United States and occasionally in Canada where the actions of the board members and the executive staff are on public display.

When conflict arises between a customer-oriented project and community values, or over environmental impacts of a proposed port action or development project, typically, more of the general public will attend a board meeting than port customers or industry associations. The business perspective can often be drowned out by a well-informed, organized, and even emotional display of community concern or opposition. Often, industry advocates will orchestrate attendees from labor organizations who benefit from the construction or operational jobs a port project might provide. Board members, whether appointed or elected, want to 'look good' in public. They are often compelled to try and satisfy the speakers who come before them.

At the core of surviving public board meetings is a prior understanding of community issues and being **prepared for opposition**. A senior port executive tasked with the job of external affairs should have done sufficient outreach to all stakeholder groups to be prepared for the issues that will arise and be ready to respond to them. Board members need to be kept up to date and not blind-sided by public speakers. This is easier said than done because, at times, both port executives and board members are blind-sided by public comments about an issue they may have no knowledge of. Often, the only remedy is holding an item over to a later meeting so the port and board members can take the time to educate themselves about the issue.

## 3 THE VIEW FROM THE TOP: THE PORT DIRECTOR POSITION

When, in the 1960s, containerization drove a wave of port construction across the globe, it was not unusual to find that a port director might have held the top position for decades. Often the director had an **engineering or construction background** as the race was on to build modern facilities to attract customers as globalization took hold. Not surprisingly, all the port directors were male.

It was not until the 1970s that **environmental and stakeholder concerns** began to influence the activities of the ports after many countries adopted forms of environmental impact assessment legislation. Ports were suddenly faced with addressing impacts on the environment and building a relationship with community stakeholders. The ports did not adopt this philosophical change lightly as one can find statements made by port directors in the 1970s that a port's purpose was to serve commerce, and create jobs, not mitigate for environmental impacts. Some port directors were better than others in making the transition from a 'build it' perspective to one that gave validity to stakeholder concerns. Those that could not were retired and replaced by a new breed of port executive, better equipped to navigate the complex relationships necessary to succeed in the position. Port boards began to look for leadership that could implement **change management** in a historically conservative industry.

The educational background and work experience of today's port director is diverse. Today's port director is someone who may have come from within the port industry, hopscotching from smaller port to larger port, or have come from the shipping industry or another closely related field in the logistics business. Port boards have also looked outside the maritime industry to select a director. The director may have a background in information management, technology, science, engineering, law, or policy.

**Gender issues** are gaining importance. Since the 1970s, when females were rarely found on port boards, the ports have made inroads in addressing the gender bias on board appointments but less progress has been made for top leadership positions. Data for female seafarers indicates even less progress than at the ports. The International Maritime Organization maintains statistics on the number of women seafarers. Today only 2% of the world's 1.5 million seafarers are women, and 94% of them work in the cruise industry. Recognizing the need to prepare women for leadership positions within the maritime industry, the IMO launched its Women in Maritime program in 1988 to help foster the training and recruitment of women in the maritime fields, including ports. Similarly, in 2013, the International Association of Ports and Harbors launched the Women's Forum, providing scholarships to assist women in advancement within the port sector. Individual ports have also developed their own initiatives to increase diversity among their employee ranks.

All positions of leadership rely on **relationships**. The public port director does not always rule from a position of authority depending on its governance structure. The director may face obstacles in achieving their vision for the organization. These might be political, bureaucratic, lack of resources, competing interests, stakeholder opposition, or something else. Any project or policy might need acceptance or approval by a multitude of individuals and organizations. To ensure that a leader's focus is directed appropriately, a director may want to map the necessary relationships in a power wheel.

The power wheel is a graphic representation of relationships that the director needs to have with other organizations or individuals – where they exist and where they need to exist (Figure 4.25). The port director is at the center of the wheel, surrounded by all the constituencies where relationships need to be **cultivated and maintained**. Understanding which groups or individuals interact with each other, also represented on the graphic by lines between the groups, is a necessary step in creating a wheel. The exercise of drawing lines

**FIGURE 4.25** Port Power Wheel for a Port Director Leading a Locally-Controlled Public Port

to identify those known or assumed relationships will clarify the influence of different organizations.

Not all corporate executives can make the transition easily to a government-controlled agency. Regardless of how talent requirements in the technical and functional fields have evolved for port executives, **leadership** becomes the dominant trait for the senior executive. The director has to operate in a highly complex and political environment. This individual has to translate vision into reality and problems into opportunities. The director also has to select and forge a high-performance management team and do it to ensure the **continuity of leadership**. Moreover, the director needs to survive long enough to get something accomplished.

## 4 BOARD RELATIONS

Relationships between members of the Board of Directors and the chief executive can be beneficial to achieving the mission. It is not uncommon for the director to have to deal with one or more board members who begin to stray from their policy setting and the fiduciary role and locate themselves in functions that are more appropriately within the purview of the director and staff. Board members tend to do this when they feel 'out of the loop' or are caught off guard by the press or their associates about activities at the port. No board member wants to be stopped on the street and asked by a friend or colleague about something at the port and realize a community member knows more about a port issue than the board member does. This may prompt a director to go directly to the staff for information or to give direction. One mechanism for minimizing the desire of board members to circle around the chief executive is to ensure that board members get the information they need in a timely manner. Some port boards only meet once a month, but the board members are in the community on a daily basis.

Management needs to have a sense of what issues will rise to the level of board involvement, certainly of any that are community concerns or are likely to appear in the press. Not all board members will want the same level of information, and some board members will require more attention from the port director. Generally, a strong board chairperson can set the direction for interactions between board members and lower staff levels. Another strategy is the establishment of board committees that can meet and interact with staff on specified topics. Board committees may hold open or closed meetings, depending on how many board members are appointed to the committee and the board quorum for decision-making. In the United States, if the committee is sized at a number lower than a quorum for decision-making, board committees do not have to meet in public. Some committee meetings are thus more informal and allow for board members to interact with staff at various levels.

# PART V

# Port competition

# Chapter 5.1 Inter-port competition

*Port competition is competition for trades, with terminals as the competing units, logistics, transport, and industrial enterprises as the chain managers of the respective trades with port authorities and port policy-makers as co-developers.*

## 1 THE PORT COMPETITION CONCEPT

The globalization of production and consumption, the emergence of a global transport network, and changes in inter-port relations, port-hinterland relationships, and logistics have created greater competition among ports. Shippers, logistics service providers, and shipping lines do not necessarily choose a port, but they select a chain in which a port is merely a node. In order to respond to the requirements of trade and international supply chains, ports need to accommodate and handle more and larger ships and hinterland transport modes faster. These trends and the expansion of the role of the private sector in port activities have forced ports to become more market-oriented, more innovative, and more responsive to the needs of all actors involved in the trades that pass through the port.

Port competition has become a complex and multi-faceted concept. The nature and characteristics of competition depend, among other things, upon the type of the **competing ports** (e.g. feeder port, hub port) and the **cargo group** (e.g. containers, liquid bulk, dry bulk, non-containerized general cargo). In container transport, a distinction has to be made between the large load centers or main/hub ports and the smaller regional or feeder ports. The load centers are primarily competing for deepsea intercontinental liner services, in which large ships of up to 24,000 TEU are being deployed. Regional ports strive for connections to as many nearby load centers as possible and have good regional hinterland connectivity.

DOI 10.4324/9780429318184-5

*Port competition can be defined as competition for trades, with terminals as the competing units, logistics, transport, and industrial enterprises as the chain managers of the respective trades and port authorities and port policymakers as co-developers of the broadly defined port complex.*

**Terminals are the major focus** of the competitive strategy, not ports. Competition between ports has increasingly been replaced by competition among market players who often are present in more than one port (cf. global terminal operators such as PSA, DP World, Hutchison Ports, and APM Terminals) or multimodal logistics and transport service providers who, in addition to operating various transport modes, have also combined stevedoring, storage, forwarding and other activities in one 'bundle' for shippers. Port competition can also involve rivalry among port authorities with a view to offering the best facilities (both material and non-material) to all actors involved in the supply chains of the various trades (e.g. stevedoring companies, shipping companies, shippers, and multimodal operators).

## 2 GEOGRAPHICAL AND FUNCTIONAL LEVELS OF PORT COMPETITION

### 2.1 Intra-port competition

Private port companies often compete to handle cargoes (terminals) and provide other port services (e.g. towage, bunkering). For the port authority or the port itself as a whole, such competition can serve as a management method to improve the efficiency of port activities. Competition between operators or providers of facilities within the same port can generally increase port efficiency and improve services. However, the need to realize economies of scale and reach the so-called Minimum Efficient Scale (MES) and the existence of competition from operators in other ports may justify an operational monopoly of port activities.

The playing field for intra-port competition is very often influenced by basic infrastructural investment decisions by port or regional authorities. For example, in many larger ports, not all container terminals have the same draft conditions, reducing choice for very large container vessels. Therefore, even if there are a handful of terminals in a large port area, the largest container vessels might be able to call at one terminal only.

### 2.2 Inter-port competition within a multi-port gateway region

The multi-port gateway region concept provides an extended framework for inter-port competition. Many stevedoring companies are expanding their activities over more than one port in the same maritime range or port region. The increasingly footloose character of shipping companies pushes port authorities and port companies into fierce competition. On the port authority level, the battle is mainly focused on offering the best basic infrastructural (docks, quays) and 'infostructural' (IT) facilities, the best logistic/distribution facilities, and the lowest port user costs. At the terminal level, the competition mainly focuses on price, handling time, and productivity.

When ports in the same gateway region do not fall under the same national government, government policies can impact the conditions and level of competition among sub-groups (e.g. Dutch ports against Belgian ports or the port of Singapore against Malaysian ports). Regional authorities often aim to secure complementary product-market developments in neighboring (rival) ports of the same port region. They therefore try to provide a framework in which each seaport can manage its port-specific advantages, while at the same time encouraging cooperation.

### 2.3 Inter-port competition within a port range

The third level of competition is the port range which can be defined as a group of ports situated at the same seashore and **sharing a similar hinterland**. Within port ranges, fierce competition can be observed, particularly for discretionary cargo bound to an inland destination. For example, within the Hamburg-Le Havre range, the most important port range in Europe in cargo throughput terms, port cooperation initiatives are primarily based on the exchange of information (aimed at improving mutual understanding) instead of real structural cooperation. The vigorous intra-range competition in the Hamburg-Le Havre range is reinforced by the fact that the ports are spread over different countries (Belgium, Germany, the Netherlands, and France), each following their own port policy. Several main ports situated in different countries are competing for the status of nodal point of nodal points within a European transport network.

### 2.4 Inter-range competition

The fourth and last level of port competition involves the **rivalry between port ranges**. For example, the gradual completion of one European transport network and the growth in hub-feeder port relations has intensified inter-range competition in Europe, e.g. between the Hamburg-Le Havre range and the Mediterranean ports. Inter-range competition requires a common approach to port development, as different policies distort the playing field and thus lead to inefficient freight flow patterns. However, such a common approach is often complicated even when supra-national authorities, like the European Commission, are involved.

### 3 PORT COMPETITIVE ADVANTAGES

The **competitive position of a port** is determined by its competitive offering to the host of shippers and shipping lines for specific trade routes, geographical regions, and other ports to which the port is connected. However, at the broader dimension, the competitiveness of a port is determined by the range of **competitive advantages** that are acquired or created by the port over time.

A port's competitiveness will be high if it possesses the best **array of resources** for its business and strategy. Resources are the source of the **port's capabilities**, which is the capacity of a set of resources to perform an activity. These capabilities are indirectly the main source of competitive advantage. In order to become or remain competitive, ports and their actors have to identify, cultivate and exploit their **core competencies**.

> *Core competencies are the collective learning in the organization, especially how to coordinate diverse skills and integrate multiple streams of technology.*

The ability to consolidate the port's capabilities and skills into competencies that enable adapting to changing opportunities is an important source of competitive advantage for port management. A competency can only be considered as a core competence and can only provide a solid basis for sustainable competitive advantage, and thus for effective strategy, if it exhibits the following five characteristics:

- **Inimitability**. If it is difficult for a rival port or actor to imitate a port's competence, the probability of generating a sustainable competitive advantage is increased. However, inimitability normally does not last forever. A port can forestall its competitors by focusing on resources that are inimitable by nature or by process. A number of core competencies are practically unchangeable or inimitable by nature, simply because they are physically unique (e.g. geographical location) (Box 5.1). Other core competencies can only be built through a process of continuous improvement and enhancement. If a core competence is based on the complexity of technologies and skills, it will be difficult for competing ports to imitate. Therefore, it will have a higher probability of generating a competitive advantage. Core competencies can relate to location-bound or non-location bound port-specific advantages depending on the possibilities for transferring the competence to other ports or locations.
- **Durability**. The sustainability of a port's competitive advantage depends upon the rate at which the underlying resources and capabilities depreciate in time. A core competence should therefore possess a high degree of durability. For example, as port technology evolves very rapidly, a competitive advantage purely based on technological competencies is less durable than one based on the port's reputation. Therefore, port management will have to invest relatively more in the former competence in order to retain its durable character.
- **Transparency**. If competing ports are able to identify the different underlying resources and capabilities of a port's competitive advantage, they may be able to learn about the port's strategy rather rapidly. Therefore, a competence with high transparency is less likely to lead to a sustainable competitive advantage. In contrast, port competencies based on a continuous process of improvement and a multitude of skills and capabilities (cf. port productivity) show little transparency, whence they are fairly sustainable.
- **Transferability**. This element is related to location-bound as well as port-specific advantages not bound to a location. The higher the immobility of resources and capabilities needed for building up competitive advantage, the lower the transferability. High immobility can result from geographical factors, high transaction costs, or imperfect information. It discourages competing ports from imitating strategies. If a competing

port faces little or no difficulty acquiring the necessary resources and capabilities to imitate a competitive advantage, that advantage will be short-lived.

- **Replicability**. If a competing port cannot or does not wish to 'buy' the valuable resources and capabilities needed to gain success, it can always try to acquire these resources by internal investments. However, the non-replicability of resources reflects the difficulties associated with successfully developing resources and capabilities internally.

Besides these five elements, the port's ability to appropriate the returns of a specific resource or capability is important for building sustainable competitive advantage. This means that a resource or capability of a particular port will be more valuable if the port succeeds in directing all resulting returns and profits to the port and not to third parties.

A broad array of **core competencies** form the breeding ground for (further) development of the port's **core services**, each offering the necessary ingredients for a range of **specialized port services**. In fact, a port's core services are the physical embodiment of one or more core competencies and contribute to the crucial input for specialized port services. For example, a port that develops core competencies in general port productivity and covered storage facilities will be able to use these core competencies to develop core services in covered storage of general cargo. These core services themselves will form the cornerstone for specialized port services, like the handling and storage of forest products.

---

### Box 5.1  Classification of the core competencies of ports

*Based on the parameters of source of inimitability and character of the core competencies, a matrix can be constructed (Figure 5.1).*

*A core competency purely based on the geographic location of a port is a typical example in quadrant 1. A port's high productivity can usually be situated in quadrant 2. This requires a continuous building process based on an interaction between technology and human skills that cannot be easily transferred to other ports. Both maritime and hinterland accessibility can partly be positioned in quadrant 1 (the part which can be attributed to natural geographic conditions) and partly in quadrant 2 (the part which is the result of a dynamic building process aimed at consolidating good accessibility such as the progressive development of a hinterland network).*

*A competence purely based on port technology can be positioned in quadrant 4. For example, a fully automated container terminal results from a technological process that might be difficult to imitate. Still, the technology itself can rather easily be transferred to other ports. However, the patent on this technology could be positioned in quadrant 3 as it is by definition inimitable.*

*Core competencies situated in quadrant 4 are rather important to defend, which may demand enormous efforts. Fierce port competition on the level of the development of core competencies primarily exists in quadrants 2 and 4.*

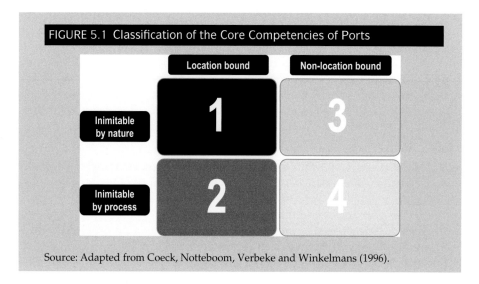

FIGURE 5.1 Classification of the Core Competencies of Ports

Source: Adapted from Coeck, Notteboom, Verbeke and Winkelmans (1996).

## 4 DETERMINANTS OF PORT COMPETITIVENESS

The competitiveness of ports can only be understood by following a supply chain approach. Port and route selection criteria are related to the entire network in which the port is just one node. The ports that are being chosen will help minimize the sum of seaport and inland costs, including inventory and quality considerations of shippers. Port choice becomes more a function of the overall network cost and performance. A well-coordinated logistic and distribution function of seaports with the cooperation of various service providers facilitates the integration of ports in advanced logistical and distributional networks through a new range of high-quality value-adding services. The traditional view on a port's competitiveness primarily considers **standalone physical attributes** of a port such as:

- **Physical and technical infrastructure** (nautical accessibility profile, terminal infrastructure, and equipment, hinterland accessibility profile).
- The **geographical location** (vis-à-vis the immediate and distant hinterlands and vis-à-vis the main shipping lanes).
- **Port efficiency**.
- **Connectivity** of the port on seaside and landside.
- **Quality and costs of auxiliary services** such as pilotage, towage, customs.
- Efficiency and costs of **port management and administration** (e.g. port dues).
- Availability, quality, and costs of **logistic value-added activities** (e.g. warehousing).
- Availability, quality, and costs of **port community systems** (PCS) and other digital solutions.
- **Port security**/safety and **environmental profile** of the port.
- **Port reputation**.
- Reliability, capacity, frequency, and costs of **inland transport services** by truck, rail, inland barge, and pipelines.

The focus on standalone physical attributes of a port when assessing its competitiveness does not mirror the reality of (global) supply chains. Ports compete not as individual places that handle ships but as crucial links within global supply chains. Ports and terminals are forced to seek effective integration into these supply chains. The main selection criteria of logistics companies and shippers include:

- Competitive **price of port services**.
- **Reliable services**.
- **Low time costs** for goods.
- **Cargo security** and damage prevention.
- Facilitation through the use of **information platforms**.
- Good **intermodal connectivity** to the hinterland.

The **out-of-pocket costs** of transporting goods between origins and destinations and the port (including cargo handling costs) constitute just one cost component in supply chain routing decisions by shippers or their representatives. The more integrated supply chain decision-making becomes, the more the focus is shifted to the **generalized logistics costs**. The implications on port and modal choice are far-reaching. Shippers or their representatives might opt for more expensive ports or more expensive hinterland solutions in case savings overcompensate for the additional port-related and modal out-of-pocket costs in other logistics costs. These other costs typically consist of:

- **Time costs** of the goods, such as the opportunity costs linked to the capital tied up in the transported goods and costs linked to the economic or technical depreciation of the goods.
- **Inventory costs** linked to the holding of safety stocks.
- **Indirect logistics costs** linked to the aggregated quality within the transport chain and the willingness of the various actors involved to tune operations to the customer's requirements, namely in terms of responsiveness to variable flows, information provision, and ease of administration.

However, the out-of-pocket costs do not fully explain routing decisions. **Connectivity** via liner services and connectivity via rail or barge (where available) remain important factors for route decisions since they imply higher frequencies and better connectivity to the foreland and the hinterland. In practice, a port with high connectivity is typically able to attract more cargo for the distant hinterland, even if there is another port with much lower connectivity which also offers solutions for the hinterland routing of the goods.

The logistics actors and transport operators have designed more complex networks that need a high level of **reliability**. The current development and expansion of global supply chains and the associated intermodal transport systems rely on the **synchronization of different geographical scales**. The efficiency of transport systems can be seriously hampered if shipments are significantly delayed, albeit with low transport costs. But when the synchronization level increases, the sea-land network as a whole becomes more unstable. This leads to extra costs to find alternative routes. In the context of reducing risk of major disruptions, logistics players tend to opt for a **flexible network design** offering various routing alternatives. This 'not all the eggs in one basket' approach implies that a specific port-corridor combination rarely finds itself in a position where the market will forgive major flaws in system performance.

To add to the complexity, it is worth mentioning that the competitive position of a port cannot always be narrowed down to cost and quality factors alone. Historical (the so-called 'memory' effect), **psychological, political, and personal factors** can result in a routing of flows that diverges from a perfect market-based division. Bounded rationality, inertia, and opportunistic behavior (Box 5.2) are among the behavioral factors that could lead to a deviation from the optimal solution.

The last cost dimension concerns the **external costs** (congestion, traffic safety, and environmental damage) generated by port and inland transport activities. When major differences exist in external costs between modes or when these external costs are not internalized in a balanced way, the resulting **market imbalances** might enhance port and route choices that deviate from a situation in which external costs are more balanced and equally internalized in the generalized logistics costs.

---

**Box 5.2  Behavioral factors influencing cargo routing decisions and port choice**

*Humans do not always behaving in a fully rational way and this could affect the choice of a route, a transportation mode or a port:*

- *Incorrect and incomplete market information on the possible alternative routes available to supply chain managers and shippers results in '**bounded rationality**' in the transport chain design, leading to sub-optimal decisions. Shippers sometimes impose bounded rational behavior on freight forwarders and shipping lines, as in the case where a shipper asks to call at a specific port or to use a specific land transport mode, even if this port or mode might not be the most efficient solution from a rational economic point of view.*
- ***Opportunistic behavior** of economic actors or informal commitments to individuals or companies might lead to non-cost minimizing decisions.*
- *Some customers might not consider using other ports or other transport modes because they assume that the **inertia and transaction costs** linked to transferring activities to other ports or modes do not outweigh the direct and indirect logistics costs connected to the current non-optimal solution.*

---

# Chapter 5.2  Intra-port competition

*Intra-port competition refers to the presence of two or more firms competing to provide the same services in the same port complex.*

## 1 INTRA-PORT COMPETITION

Intra-port competition is beneficial for the competitiveness of ports, local and national economies, and consumers and exporting industries. Its presence is conditional and might be facilitated by specific initiatives. This is most commonly observed in terminal operations, where a terminal operator has jurisdiction over an entire terminal area, from the berth to the gate, and competes with other terminal operators responsible for other terminals. Intra-port competition might also be observed in providing other services, either at landside (warehousing, logistics, value-added services) or maritime side (pilotage, towage, mooring) of the port.

A variation is **intra-terminal competition**, which is the case of entities competing to provide the same services within the same terminal. Intra-terminal competition exists in the largest ports. Together, these two types of competition form an inclusive definition of intra-port competition as the competition between two or more similar production units that provide competing services in the context of the same port complex.

## 2 BENEFITS OF INTRA-PORT COMPETITION

Intra-port competition is beneficial for the competitiveness of ports, for local and national economies, and for consumers and exporting industries. Particularly:

- It prevents the potential of monopolistic excess **rent-seeking** by port service providers who enjoy excess market power.
- It acts as an engine of **innovation and specialization**, allowing for achievement of economies of scope and flexible multi-service organization structures that are essential in modern seaports.

These positive effects guide policy initiatives at local, national, or supranational levels aiming to lower **entry barriers** in the market and generate conditions that enable intra-port competition in the provision of port services. However, in most market segments and ports, market concentration remains remarkably high and rising, partly because of the emergence of **global terminal operators**.

### 2.1 Rent-seeking behavior by service providers

Intra-port competition suppresses monopolistic market power and, thus, economic rent-seeking by port service providers. **Economic rents** in seaports consist of the savings on the generalized transport cost that the use of a port offers over the next best available routing. Their level is related to the price difference compared to a second-best port. It may accrue to a variety of actors, including the owner of the port, port service providers, labor (high wages or minimum workforce use), governments (local or national), and the users of (trans)port services. In the worst case, a port user has no other alternatives and is forced to assume the fare structure dictated by the port.

The actual benefits of intra-port competition are positively related to when a port faces imperfect or limited inter-port competition, with substantial economic rent. Monopolistic power enables service providers to discriminate according to demand elasticity, and port users experience abnormal pricing and rigid operational conditions. When intra-port competition exists for all port services, including competitive hinterland transport markets, all port charges are based on cost recovery and provided efficiently (Figure 5.2). A similar case is when port service providers are constantly under threat from

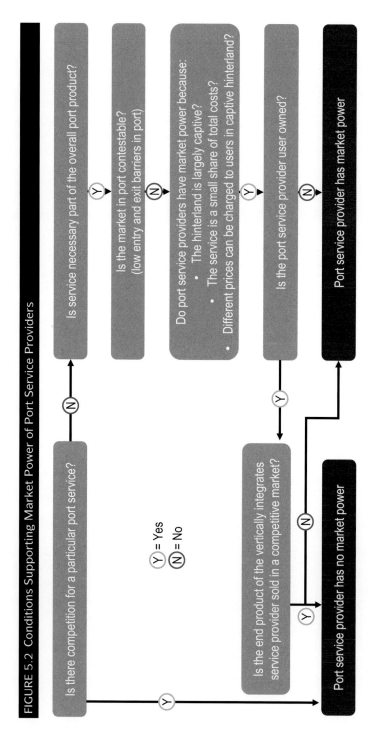

FIGURE 5.2 Conditions Supporting Market Power of Port Service Providers

Source: Adapted from De Langen and Pallis (2006).

potential new entrants. Existing providers do not have market power as long as there are low barriers to entry. Even if there is only one service provider, the threat of potential entrants as soon as profit opportunities arise suppresses excessive prices. This is known as the **principle of contestability**. In port ranges with acute inter-port competition, such as the European market, economic rents are improbable. Increased competition prevents intra-port monopolists from acquiring any supra-normal profits even if high barriers to entry to the port exist.

Intra-port competition is most important for port services that are a necessary part of the overall port product. In other words, the service cannot be purchased in another port. This is not the case for some port services such as bunkering or ship supplies, as competition for these services is commonly fierce. Then, the level of economic rents depends on the competitive advantage of a port for serving a particular hinterland. Thus, the distinction between captive and contestable hinterlands is useful. **Captive hinterlands** are all those areas where a port has such a competitive advantage because of low generalized transport costs to those regions and handles the vast majority of all cargoes. For most ports, captive hinterlands are less prevalent. **Contestable hinterlands** consist of all those regions with no single port having a clear cost advantage over competing ports. If the vast majority of cargo originates from or is destined to a contestable hinterland, economic rents are small or non-existent. A similar distinction applies in relation to **primary hinterlands**, the area where the port is well established, and **secondary hinterlands**, with rivalry among ports.

If parts of the hinterland are captive and markets are not contestable, opportunities for rent extraction by the port service provider exist when any of the following three conditions are met:

- **The share of the port services in total port costs is not substantial**. The overall port product consists of various services, such as terminal handling, towage, pilotage, and ship handling. Port services providers that are of relatively minor importance for the overall costs will hardly lose business when they raise prices, as port users are sensitive to total port costs, rather than their individual components. Thus, such service providers have market power.
- **The captive hinterland is large compared to the contestable hinterland**. In this case, monopoly pricing is possible since many port users cannot shift to an alternative port without facing substantial additional costs. Monopoly prices increase revenues for service providers, even if a part of the port's users in the contestable hinterland shifts to another port.
- **Opportunities to differentiate prices in the captive hinterland exist**. Even when the captive hinterland is not sufficiently large to maximize profits via monopoly pricing, it may be possible to charge port users in the captive hinterland higher prices, since they can hardly shift to other ports. Three different types of port users purchase port services: shippers (cargo owners), shipping lines, and forwarders (or other transport intermediaries). Unless they are located in a perfectly contestable hinterland, shippers have the worst bargaining position since switching to a second-best port leads to higher transport costs. Port service providers have market power versus captive shippers located in the captive hinterland as

they can charge higher prices than those applicable for contestable shippers. This explains why large shippers in captive hinterlands frequently invest in user-owned port facilities. However, most shippers do not have direct contracts with port service providers. Instead, they have contracts with either shipping lines or forwarders. The bargaining position of port service providers vis-à-vis shipping lines or forwarders is substantially weaker because these users might consolidate cargo with different origins and destinations. Consolidation and the development of transshipment hubs and the increasing efficiency of inland transportation limit geographical powers and increase the cross-elasticity of demand for ports. Price differentiation related to the origin/destination of the cargo is not viable when shipping lines or forwarders purchase services. In short, port service providers do not have market power vis-à-vis shipping lines and forwarders in ports where the contestable hinterland is so large that the loss of volume (volume effect) offsets the additional revenues from the price increase (price effect), and the port service is an important component of total port costs.

The experience from the privatization of terminal operation suggests that due to the lack of intra-port competition, port users rarely face high tariffs and request regulatory institutions to limit the monopolistic position of terminal operators. Such regulation (whether created and monitored by a government agency or by a port authority) incurs costs, such as monitoring costs, including productivity and tariff controls. Furthermore, due to **information asymmetry** between the regulator and the port industry, regulation is unlikely to be ideal for the purpose of preventing all efforts to extract monopoly rents. Intra-port competition is potentially a more effective way to ensure competitive port tariffs.

The threat of rent-seeking by port service providers accelerates **vertical integration** in seaports. By providing their own port services, port users can prevent abuse of market power. Two kinds of port users, shippers and shipping lines, frequently own and operate dedicated facilities. The involvement of large shippers in port services is mainly aimed at preventing exposure to market power. This explains why many shippers in liquid and dry bulk (such as Shell, Exxon, BP, Corus Steel) own terminal facilities. Shipping lines also own terminals, and these investments may be partially explained by the above considerations, as they also stem from a strategy to offer door-to-door transport services. In any case, user-owned port facilities prevent rent extraction if the end products of the vertically integrated firms are sold in a competitive market. This is the case for most user-owned oil, iron ore, and steel terminals as well as most user-owned container terminals. Only very large port users have the scale to develop dedicated terminals. In other cases, terminals are owned by joint ventures of a limited number of port users. For port users with only small cargo volumes, vertical integration as a strategy to prevent rent extraction is not viable. Therefore, in several cases, the problem of market power is not fully solved through vertical integration. Under such circumstances, promoting intra-port competition remains essential.

## 2.2 Specialization, flexible adaptation and innovation

Intra-port competition fosters specialization, innovation, and diversity in the provision of port services. It is, in principle, competition on a level playing field. Competitors face cost curves that are similar and operate within the same regulatory framework, labor market conditions, trade costs, and supplier bases. In such an operating environment, specialization of services is more likely. This is especially important since the contemporary port product is a chain of (specialized) interlinking functions that, in most cases, is better offered by a network of firms potentially operating in different organizational forms rather than as one single corporate hierarchy. In an environment marked by flexible specialization and globalization of production as well as the transportation of intermediate goods, port activities retain their competitiveness by understanding user expectations and adjusting their actions accordingly. This includes interactions between those involved in the production and exchange of port services, such as service providers, labor, users, and institutions.

Ports need to provide both **generic services** via a standardized process defined in advance and **dedicated services** responding to individual demand and based on the mobilization of specialized resources. Therefore, some port network actors focus on standardized services, price competition, and increased volumes of services. In contrast, others focus on an increased range of services, concentrating on economies of scope and competition based on the quality of products and services. Increasing the quality of services, high flexibility and adaptability levels, close integration with other transport modes, service and process innovation, better management, more efficient labor regimes, and adaptability to users' needs, are all goals whose achievement requires ports that exhibit organizational structures incorporating the following elements and principles:

- The traditional **industrial world**, focused on the efficient mass production of generic (such as pre-defined by the producer) services aiming to decrease average cost and achieve large-scale operations in conditions of certainty.
- The **market world**, based on standardized services, economies of scale, and differentiation, competition centered on price flexibility in conditions of uncertainty.
- The **interpersonal world**, based on dedicated specialized services, economies of variety, competition centered on quality, skilled labor, and developing in conditions of uncertainty.

Intra-port competition creates conditions for the design of organizational structures based on **economies of scale and economies of scope**. The competition between several port services providers facilitates entrepreneurship and creativity. This ensures that innovations are introduced (and copied) and competing firms constantly aim to improve services to their customers, a dynamic process that keeps ports competitive. Internal competition leads to dynamism in the entire port cluster. Differentiation and specialization enhance the performance of the cluster as a whole because port users can purchase products and services that match their specific demands.

## 3 CONDITIONS AND EFFECTS OF INTRA-PORT COMPETITION

The viability of intra-port competition depends on the presence of entry barriers into a particular port market, with size an important consideration. The relevant market should be at least twice as large as the **Minimum Efficient Scale (MES)** for providing a port service (Box 5.3). In the absence of this size, intra-port competition may be desirable but impossible to introduce. Once the size of a port service market is double the size of the MES, facilitating entry, and exit, in the port market by lowering any other **entry barriers** is an additional strategy. Lower entry barriers increase the level of intra-port competition by enhancing market contestability, putting pressure on existing port service providers and also on new and potential entrants.

A potential adverse effect of intra-port competition could be **facility duplication** leading to a wasteful allocation of resources. However, under the assumption that governments, including public port authorities, create a level playing field and do not grossly subsidize port investments, it is hard to see how such a wasteful allocation could persist in the long run under free-market conditions. Furthermore, it is by no means apparent that such over-investment would be more likely to arise in an environment with intra-port competition.

The second potential negative effect is that intra-port competition could generate additional externalities, such as pollution and congestion. This negative effect is related to the issue of scale economies in port services and may be present in specific cases. However, there are no compelling arguments for a negative structural relation between intra-port competition and negative externalities.

---

### Box 5.3 Minimum Efficient Scale (MES)

*In economic theory, the Minimum Efficient Scale (MES) is a particularly difficult notion to define. One possible way of defining MES in a port context is by linking terminal scale to operational efficiency as reflected by the average cost function (Figure 5.3).*

*The MES is the smallest terminal provider scale at which output can be produced at a minimum average long-run cost under the assumption that the terminal is operating with a given technology.*

*The Long Run Average Cost (LRAC) cost curve defines all the possible options and represents the expected distribution of average costs. The LRAC curve will normally have an L-shape or a stretched U-shape. The L-shape assumes that economies of scale will gradually diminish and eventually disappear, whilst the U-shape requires the appearance of diseconomies of scale after the Maximal Efficiency Scale (MaxES). Since each terminal has different configurations and equipment, there is a range of terminal-specific MES (Terminal 1, 2, and 3). For instance, Terminal 1 is likely to be a small facility with limited equipment, while Terminal 3 is likely to be a large well-equipped, and managed facility.*

*From the perspective of the terminal operator, MES is the capacity beyond which there are no more significant unit cost advantages because economies of scale have been exhausted. Empirical evidence suggests that a unique MES might not exist given the observed diversity in terminal scales worldwide. Essentially, one can expect MES variations rather than a unique MES for the entire terminal industry.*

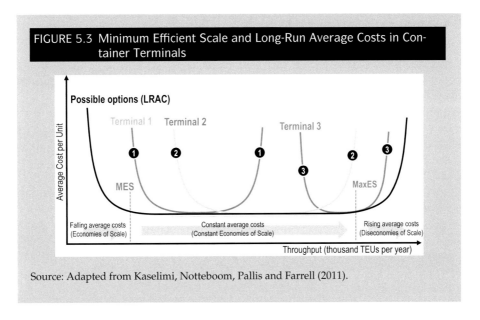

FIGURE 5.3  Minimum Efficient Scale and Long-Run Average Costs in Container Terminals

Source: Adapted from Kaselimi, Notteboom, Pallis and Farrell (2011).

# Chapter 5.3  Port marketing

*Intra-port competition refers to the presence of two or more firms competing to provide the same services in the same port complex.*

## 1 PORTS AND THEIR CUSTOMERS

Marketing and customer **relationship management** are among the 'beyond the landlord' functions of port authorities that are gaining momentum. The various forms of communication, trade and business development, local community liaison, and customer relationship management are major components of the overall marketing effort. A fact-finding report that surveyed port authorities in Europe revealed that 81% of them lead promotion and marketing activities for the ports under their management. A study of 70 cruise ports in the Mediterranean Sea found that 71.4% of the port authorities are leaders in port marketing.

Marketing is the process of defining, developing, and delivering **value to stakeholders** depending on distinctive competencies. By adopting a market-driven approach, a port authority provides various marketing solutions for each stakeholder in the port community and beyond. Marketing strategies developed by port authorities deal with networks of stakeholders, the members of which are categorized into three groups:

1. **Business-related stakeholders** (e.g. shipping lines, shippers, terminal operators, logistics and forwarding companies, transport services providers). These are market players affecting (and being affected by) port authority strategies to pursue marketing objectives.
2. **Societal groups and local communities** seeking sustainable port growth in harmony with the territory and its citizens.

3. **Institutional stakeholders** are involved in meaningful interactions with port authorities on matters linked to several policy issues, legislative interventions, and public interests.

Each stakeholder represents a **target for marketing activities**, whereas groups of the latter (portfolios of marketing actions) head towards specific marketing objectives. A successful marketing strategy focuses on identifying the key business relationships through which a port can deliver value to (internal and external) stakeholders based on its distinctive competencies. When such marketing actions are not effective, ports are probably unable to cope with an additional demand.

The potential value for stakeholders generated through marketing efforts develops in line with the main functions that a given port authority undertakes, such as landlord, regulator, operator, or community/cluster manager. Following the evaluation of internal strengths, competitors, the business ecosystem, and the social community, the endorsed marketing strategies are associated with a **portfolio of actions** based on the capabilities of the port authority. Port authorities define value propositions via actions that might relate to one or more marketing processes aiming to:

- **Define value** (e.g. identifying the needs, positioning the offers).
- **Provide value** (e.g. products/services development, defining the price, selecting and choosing the distribution channels).
- **Communicate value** (e.g. sales force messages, promotion, advertizing, PR, media planning).

Port authorities deal with a multitude of public and private stakeholders, frequently dispersed over a wide geographic space, who exercise a multi-directional influence on their action. The borderless nature of modern supply chains and port clusters evolution have their own implications for port marketing strategies:

- It is rarely the case that actors **operate or develop alone** within the port cluster. Irrespective of size, the bundling of operations and the clustering of activities facing related issues by endorsing a collective action logic is essential, irrespective of the market niche.
- Even though port authorities are physically **bounded in their own territorial jurisdiction**, they deal with players in distant and multiple locations. They want to influence their behavior and generate business opportunities. This occurs regardless of any physically limited extension of port operations or the intrinsic normative limitations of port authorities.
- The fuzzy geography of the decisional chains of some stakeholders, such as multinational corporations, might interact with port authorities through **multiple decisional units** based in geographically distant locations. The existence of multi-layered decisional units (i.e. local offices, national branches, regional and global headquarters) complicates marketing interactions, given diverse representatives within the same multinational corporation.
- Marketing has reference to actors with **diverse cultural backgrounds** as well as economic and institutional environments. Port authorities interact with players having diverse legal natures (e.g. public bodies, public

companies, private companies, individual citizens, trade associations), interests (private vs public), geographic location, and strategic ambitions (local, national, international). Such diversity might generate problems of market adaptation and make the dialogue with stakeholders less fruitful and constructive.

Thus, marketing efforts developed by port authorities are increasingly complex and require the commitment of specialized and highly qualified managers.

## 2 MARKETING OBJECTIVES AND ACTIONS

Ports pursue a **spectrum of marketing objectives** (Figure 5.4). The scope of port marketing encompasses five mainstream categories of objectives (Box 5.4):

1. Secure additional investments.
2. Enhance additional demand.
3. Exploit non-core business opportunities.
4. Build solid community liaisons.
5. Enhance institutional dialogue.

The first three refer to **business-to-business** relations. Another objective resides in **business-to-community relationships**. The fifth refers to the port **relations with institutions and their administrators**. These marketing objectives are mutually linked, whereas marketing actions are often required to support each other for achieving objectives that, despite appearances, are not stand-alone.

With marketing objectives closely interconnected, the interplays developed between port authorities and major stakeholders might have further implications compared to what their geographic and functional positioning might imply. A port authority may generate cross-fertilization effects that materialize due to the synergies and economies of scope in **committing resources and capabilities to marketing actions**. At the same time, any given stakeholder might be involved as a co-creator in marketing actions.

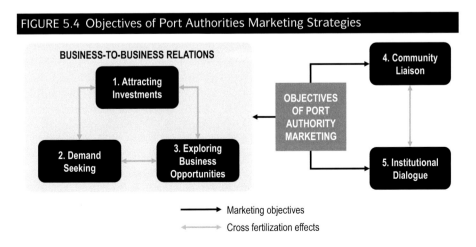

FIGURE 5.4 Objectives of Port Authorities Marketing Strategies

Source: Adapted from Parola, Pallis, Risitano, and Ferretti (2018).

The port authority might select from multiple combinations of stakeholders and marketing actions, emphasizing the distinguishing features of their value proposition and market image (Figure 5.5). With port marketing efforts targeting different market segments and combinations of stakeholders, the set of marketing actions to be used is complex. The port authority can potentially select any combination as an objective and then serve it via suitable marketing actions, committing core resources, skills and competencies, and physical and financial resources, as well as time constraints. With marketing objectives inextricably linked and marketing actions often supporting each other, the generation of cross-fertilization effects might be produced due to synergies and economies of scope in committing resources and capabilities to marketing actions.

The intensity of the overall positioning and the corresponding marketing efforts depend on the specifics of each port:

1. When a port is active in shipping markets, marketing focuses on a **single segment**. To understand the needs and wants of a specific segment, the port authority focuses on a homogeneous group of stakeholders with limited geography. This approach typically ensures cost flexibility for service production and promotion and leads to specialization. This might increase the chances of achieving a strong market presence in a particular segment. As a limitation, the port authority is more exposed to risk, given the absence of diversification, such as from unforeseen contextual changes.

2. **Selective specialization** occurs when the port authority identifies a number of target segments and then undertakes varied marketing actions directed to several stakeholder groups. This strategy has the advantage of risk diversification. The port authority can achieve economies of scale and scope and gain existing synergies in marketing action. Drawbacks relate to the need to cater to more than one segment in a complex and dynamic environment. Hence, it is necessary to develop multi-market knowledge and competencies in sophisticated marketing activities.

3. **Marketing action specialization** means that the port authority utilizes a set of similar marketing actions to deal with several different stakeholders across its foreland and hinterland. The advantage of this approach is that the port authority caters to different segments with a single marketing action and can thus internally develop unique resources and capabilities.

4. In the case of stakeholder specialization, the port authority interacts with **one specific market**, trying to match the needs of a particular stakeholder group. This is particularly the case for the container shipping market dominated by alliances of few companies or the cruise market dominated by few brands. The advantage of this pattern is that in the case of a monopolistic/oligopolistic environment, the port authority has the potential to adjust. The geography of stakeholders is limited, reducing the complexity of marketing actions. The weakest point of this positioning is that the port authority becomes stakeholder-focused. If the specific segment weakens, the port authority risks a profound downsizing or even a market exit.

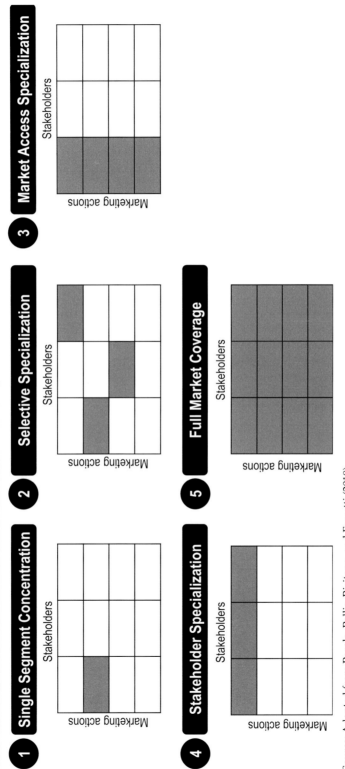

FIGURE 5.5 A Taxonomy of Strategic Marketing Positioning by Port Authorities

1 Single Segment Concentration

2 Selective Specialization

3 Market Access Specialization

4 Stakeholder Specialization

5 Full Market Coverage

Source: Adapted from Parola, Pallis, Risitano, and Ferretti (2018).

5. **Full market coverage** implies that the port authority covers all market segments. This strategy requires committing a large amount of financial and technical resources and the capacity to face diverse contexts and stakeholder categories. The advantages are that a large-scale diversification (multi-geography of stakeholders) reduces market and other types of risk, minimizing the chances of failure. The main drawback is the implied lack of focus on any particular stakeholder market. Marketing actions have to intercept stakeholders in multiple geographic regions, and port markets add further complexity to the overall picture.

---

### Box 5.4 Marketing objectives of port authorities

*Attracting investments. A key marketing objective is to secure suitable financial resources in order to enhance the competitiveness of the port in a fast-changing environment (Figure 5.6). The demand for upgraded and modernized infrastructures and services and the provision of fast and reliable operational performances is considerable, especially as economies of scale in different port markets (i.e. gigantism of container and cruise vessels) results in various dimensions of port operations and a quest for more advanced supply chains and logistics. Yet, the mobilization of third parties to invest should not be taken for granted. Marketing strategies are devoted to attracting salient stakeholders, such as investors, logistics, and industrial firms, which bring financial, technical, and human resources, and potential organizational and managerial capabilities to ensure high service quality.*

*Demand seeking. A second major marketing objective for port authorities is to enhance additional demand for the port. Demand refers to cargo and passenger volumes boosted by the presence of superior hinterland and maritime connectivity. Given the increasing importance of terminals as units with their own dynamic, different settings exist within each port. Thus the precise nature of the demand-seeking port authority strategy is detailed accordingly. For example, Mediterranean port authorities work collectively to generate demand source markets for cruising. Notably, port authorities are leaders in such marketing activities even in ports that have concessioned terminal operations (i.e. Naples, Malta, Barcelona, Cyprus). In the case of cargo ports, the port authorities of the biggest three European ports (Rotterdam, Antwerp, Hamburg) are active in overseas markets aiming to bring cargo traffic to the ports they govern.*

*Exploring business opportunities. Enhancing additional demand and securing suitable endowments are two strongly interdependent marketing objectives that may produce synergies. A successful attraction of investments and resources creates pre-conditions for a competitive port, with a solid market reputation and capabilities to deliver reliable services. In turn, a port that generates growing traffic volumes is considered attractive by port operators and draws the attention of business and financial players seeking investment opportunities in logistics facilities.*

*The objectives of marketing activities by port authorities include catching up with other business opportunities in areas beyond their core objectives, which are the handling and serving of cargoes/passengers in the port and adjacent areas. Here the reference is not only to logistics and supply chain integration but also to*

FIGURE 5.6 Port Marketing Objectives

| | Focus | Target / co-creators | Value proposition and marketing actions |
|---|---|---|---|
| **1** **Attracting Investments** | Attract **national and foreign investments** for port, dry-port and inland port infrastructures. | Concessionaries, terminals, financial institutions, logistics firms, ICT firms, construction companies. | **Product** (concession areas, common areas, logistics services, tax regimes); **Pricing** (concession fees, contractual clauses); **Promotion** (press days, visits, foreign representatives, annual reports). |
| **2** **Demand Seeking** | Attract **additional demand** for the provision of port services and logistics. Look for additional cargo demand along the entire logistics chain. | Terminals, ocean carriers, logistics firms, road / rail / barge operators, cargo owners. | **Product** (port services, customization, hinterland access); **Pricing** (terminal charges, port charges, dwell time); **Promotion** (press days, visits, foreign representatives, annual reports) |
| **3** **Exploring business opportunities** | Identify **new business opportunities.** ICT, safety/security, green operations, investments in foreign ports and providing logistics consulting services. | New markets (terminals, ocean carriers, logistics firms, road / rail / barge operators, cargo owners, financial institutions, ICT firms, construction companies) | **"Global port" proposition** *(customers-seeking)*; Control of port logistics network *(efficiency and effectiveness)*; Provide **innovative logistics skills**, additional revenues, access to new technologies, new business *(competitive advantage)*. |
| **4** **Community liaison** | Manage **global/local/region business ambitions and local interests** (social responsibility). Engage local community in strategic decisions. | Community committees, local firms, tourism actors, trade unions, associations. | Identify core benefits (safety & security, employment, externalities,) and communication campaign; Build a **maritime culture** (Image, Reputation, etc.); **Create consensus and confidence** through participatory meeting; **Communication tools** ( advertising, reporting, port days, school visits, press day) |
| **5** **Institutional Dialogue** | Create **networks** between port authority and main public stakeholders. Manage the local community more effectively. | Municipality, region, province, ministries, consulates and embassies, Government agencies, universities, other port authorities. chambers of commerce. | Coordinate horizontal (and vertical) relationships with stakeholders to manage: Strategic port planning; Port reform and regulations; Administrative decisions and business strategy; Lobbying actions. |

Source: Adapted from Parola, Pallis, Risitano, and Ferretti (2018).

*activities such as ship-repairing or hotel management. Such emerging initiatives are strategically related to the more traditional port authority marketing objectives (Objectives 1 and 2) but take place through comparatively uncommon strategies that exploit the resources and capabilities accumulated in mainstream activities.*

*Community liaison. Business-to-business marketing coexists with business-to-community objectives, as the environmental complexity and spatial issues incentivize ports to establish a trustworthy relationship with their local stakeholders. The building of solid community liaisons with the societal backyard is increasingly necessary for internationalized ports, where the disconnection between global (business-driven) ambitions and local interests becomes critical. Port authorities promote the related port by effectively communicating with the main local community stakeholders. Such promotional activities aim to make the population aware of the beneficial presence of the port, projecting an appropriate image. Marketing activities aim to build the consensus and trust of citizens and local economic clusters on port planning, securing the satisfactory co-existence and coherent co-development of urban and port areas.*

*Institutional dialogue. Good relationships with public administrations are a fundamental business marketing building block that, inter alia, enhances community liaisons. These activities stand at the intersection between marketing activities and lobbying. To maintain the pace of port and business development, port authorities have to efficiently deal with political and administrative counterparts at various levels. Generating balance within a given institutional architecture is tuning in the decisions of public administrators to the evolving needs of private firms. In this regard, vertical and horizontal coordination with public organizations enables dealing with key issues such as port planning and development, port reform and regulatory implementation, the execution of administrative and business decisions, and the implementation of political actions. Vertical coordination refers to effective institutional dialogue and distribution of competencies between port authorities and public actors. Horizontal coordination instead requires a sound and integrated dialogue among port authorities concerning the prioritization of investments and the avoidance of overcapacity concerns in port planning. These dialogues generate lobbying effects, exert political pressure to raise additional funding, moderate conflicts with the local community, and obtain a fast-tracked approval of key projects.*

## 3 INCREASING CUSTOMER LOYALTY

Despite the best of intentions and efforts when developing relationships, customers may defect to other ports. The main reasons behind this change in port choice are related to inadequate service or often just the impression of being treated with indifference. **Retaining or reclaiming customers** can be accomplished through a number of **complementary strategies**.

### 3.1 Communication with customers

It is of paramount importance to occasionally survey customers, preferably via direct verbal communication, to discover satisfaction levels about the port and find out how the port service compares to the competition. This form of **market research** should be approached systematically and regularly to understand changes in customer satisfaction levels. Issues to discuss include the degree of satisfaction with the services provided, perceptions of value for money, views on port efficiency, feedback on the available information (e.g. web site), establishing potential growth in terms of tonnage through the port as well as changes to their needs and requirements, feedback on customer service, and in general, the day-to-day issues creating operational problems for customers.

To further assist with customer communications, some ports have developed a **visitation program** for the chief executive, board members, and senior managers to meet and gather information with current and prospective customers locally, nationally, and internationally, with the objective of better understanding customer requirements.

The formation of **port user groups** is another effective means of communicating with a broad range of customers. These groups tend to be consultative and information-sharing mechanisms to provide feedback and maintain communication between the port and its customers that may include stevedoring companies, tenants, shipping companies, shipping agents, and community groups. Matters discussed at these meetings may range from operational and policy issues, infrastructure developments, strategy, and environmental management.

## 3.2 Listening to front-line people

The customer contact people are often the first to hear what bothers customers and are better positioned to identify customer needs and concerns. They are not only physically or virtually close but may have developed a personal bond with the customer. Understanding that front-line employees continually interact with customers and influence customer satisfaction levels should highlight the importance of employing customer-focused staff and providing them with at least fundamental training in marketing.

## 3.3 Service failure recovery

The true test of commitment to customer satisfaction is how the port responds when mistakes are made or there is poor customer service. A complaint may arise because the business has not delivered on the promises made in marketing communications. Labor strikes in ports or severe delays due to operational issues are typical events triggering poor customer service. When assessing poor performance, the reality is conditioned by customer perception. Three major **types of service failures** exist:

- **Failures of the core business** where there have been inadequate responses to service delivery system errors.
- **Poor or no responses to customer needs and requests**.
- **Unsatisfactory employee behavior** such as being abusive, poor attitudes, being discriminatory, and not considering cultural norms.

A **recovery from poor service delivery** can convert even frustrated customers into loyal customers. Companies should invest in implementing problem-solving, and follow-up on service recovery strategies since both significantly enhance corporate image. However, the opportunity for service recovery is sometimes missed because employees are not empowered or have insufficient training to address the error in a timely and appropriate manner.

## 3.4 Identify potential defectors

Observant ports can detect potential defectors early in the process. There are **several indicators** that a customer might defect:

- Slower returns of customer approval requests.
- Access to upper-level management decreases.
- The flow of customer data slows down.
- Plans for future work become progressively shorter-term.
- One or more of the products or services are discontinued.
- The volume of business (TEUs, cargo tonnage or passenger numbers) is gradually reduced.

Effective inter-port competition creates opportunities for customers to defect. In many cases, a triggering event causes a customer to leave, often coinciding with a window of opportunity created in a rival port. When competition levels are low, and no alternative ports are available, the customer becomes **captive**, making defection very difficult.

In the port industry, port executives should invest in research to understand the **real reasons why their customers leave or stay**. Price, changing needs, and customer service levels are common reasons.

## 3.5 Complaint management

Loyal customers tend to be more forgiving. Therefore the port can occasionally make a mistake and still not lose customers. Receiving customer complaints can be **considered positively** because they provide an opportunity to address the problem, solve it, and retain customers. Essentially a customer who complains indicates to the service business that it wishes to remain a customer and is willing to give it a second chance. Therefore, ports should make it easy to complain. Complaints can be encouraged by providing customer feedback surveys and speaking to customers directly about any concerns they may have. Asking for feedback from the customers is itself a **loyalty-generating process**.

Furthermore, good complaint management can only be achieved if the service provider uses a **formal system** to monitor, process, and follow up on customer complaints. This assumes, for instance, a corporate environment in which employees are encouraged to report on customer complaints instead of an environment in which employees are hiding complaints because they fear penalization from senior management.

## 3.6 Capitalize on positive communication

A benefit of retaining highly satisfied customers loyal to the business is that they spread positive word-of-mouth communication (WOM). This factor, along with a critical reputation in the port industry, is a key source of information for new clients. **Social media** and new communication tools have increased reliance on online information seeking, leading to the growing importance of electronic word-of-mouth or **eWOM**. If many customers are spreading positive word-of-mouth communication, promotion costs to attract new customers are lowered. Customers believe word of mouth communication to be **less biased and more credible** than traditional marketing communications. However, concerns have been expressed on the reliability of eWOM due to possible manipulation, disinformation by rivals, and the utilization of fake eWOM. Negative eWOM can lead to so-called online firestorms, which can seriously undermine a port reputation.

## 3.7 Usage of exit barriers

One way to give the port authority a chance to respond is to make it difficult for the customer to leave. Erecting a simple **barrier to departure** allows a port manager to determine what is wrong and fix it before the customer leaves. However, trying to lock customers in does not guarantee port loyalty.

A similar outcome may be achieved by using **service guarantees and customer service charters** to offset the difficulties of service recovery. Although this may represent a potential cost to the port, service guarantees may increase customer loyalty.

Port authorities confronted with a highly competitive market environment might use concession agreements as a way to lock in terminal operators or consortia between terminal operators and shipping lines. The granting of **dedicated terminals** combined with favorable port dues and strict throughput guarantees can also reduce the risk of defection.

## 3.8 Customer differentiation

Customers **do not have an equal value** to the port business. Ports become increasingly dependent on external coordination and control by actors who extract a large share of the economic rent produced by ports and are often motivated by creating shareholder value. Given the increasingly **footloose** character of its traffic, it might be inappropriate for a port to try to keep traffic at any cost. If powerful actors in a specific logistics chain exert strong pressure on a port because of economic rents generated elsewhere in the chain, it might be relevant for the port to opt out of this chain.

Due to changes in the competitive environment, current positioning, and desired target markets, customers should be assessed to ensure they match the stated objectives and value proposition. **Segmentation analysis** can assist in distinguishing between customers and ensuring the port can serve customers efficiently, effectively, and – importantly – profitably for mutual value.

Port managers can attribute a **risk profile to each of the customers** (Figure 5.7). Certain customers can be very valuable for the port as a whole. Losing them could trigger effects on other customers because of vertical linkages between companies (e.g. a feeder company might stop calling because a mother vessel is changing the port of call) or leader/follower dynamics (e.g. if a leading company leaves a port, some followers in the market might be eager to do the same).

Port managers should determine the **lifetime value of the customers** and divide them into high, medium, and low lifetime value segments. They

**FIGURE 5.7 Risk Profile of Port Customers**

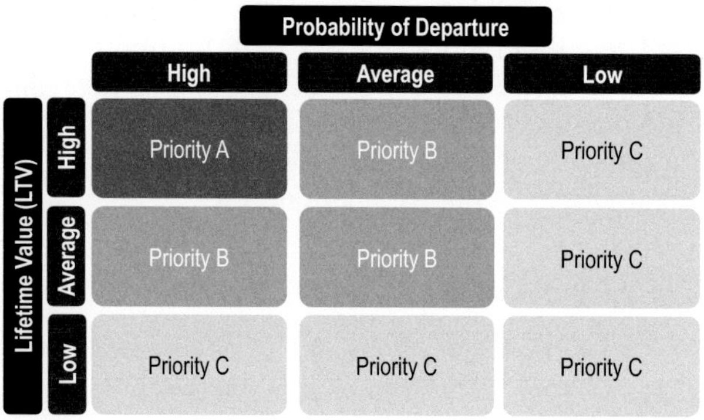

| | | Probability of Departure | | |
|---|---|---|---|---|
| | | **High** | **Average** | **Low** |
| **Lifetime Value (LTV)** | **High** | Priority A | Priority B | Priority C |
| | **Average** | Priority B | Priority B | Priority C |
| | **Low** | Priority C | Priority C | Priority C |

Source: Adapted from Hughes (2003).

should also determine the **likelihood that the customer will leave** by dividing the customers into three **defection classes**.

The customers a port should be most concerned about are the four most important boxes, priorities A and B. Those with the highest lifetime value and the highest probability of defecting are the priority A customers. Priority C customers are the low lifetime value – or very loyal customers who will never leave. Once the port manager has identified those customers the port most wants to retain, the manager can do something as simple as making sure those customers are key accounts.

### 3.9 Pricing strategies

A **pricing strategy** tailored to the individual needs of the customer is a key factor in developing relationships and loyalty. This implies the economic perspective on port pricing should be complemented by elements from marketing and relationship management linked to different requirements of each major segment.

# Chapter 5.4  Port pricing

> *Port pricing is subject to the variety of charges and fees that ports and terminals levy on their users.*

## 1 PORT PRICING STRATEGIES

Pricing is an important aspect guiding the **interactions between economic actors** in the port industry. The port authority (usually a public entity), other public bodies (state or municipally operated departments or enterprises), and private companies are the three economic actors that offer services and facilities in a port. Therefore, they are responsible for setting the pricing structure for the port users. The services that these actors offer include:

- **Infrastructural services** related to the use of docks, quays, locks, port sites and concessions.
- **Services to vessels and cargo** such as terminal operations, warehousing and distribution activities, mooring, lashing and securing, surveillance, tallying/marking/weighing, inland transport operations, forwarding and supply chain management, shipping agency activities, ship and cargo surveying, customs, sanitary services, veterinary inspection, waste disposal, bunkering, and water supply.
- **Nautical services** such as pilotage, towage, and vessel traffic management.

The basic principle is that port users pay a price or tariff for the services offered to them and the facilities they use. Price has the greatest effect on the profitability of both the providers and the users of the service and is one of the **'P'** components of marketing (product, price, promotion, and place).

Port actors engaging in port pricing need to be aware of some critical foundations:

- **Formal contractual relationships between port actors**. Not all port actors have direct contractual relationships that involve the charging of prices or tariffs. For example, container shipping lines pay container terminal operators for the handling of containers at the terminal. The pricing strategy of the terminal operator is thus focused on shipping lines. Cargo owners or their representatives (such as freight forwarders or 3PLs) do not pay the container terminal operator for container handling. Instead, the shipping line leads in recovering the paid terminal handling costs from its customers (cargo owners, freight forwarders) through the freight rate and relevant surcharges, particularly Terminal Handling Charges (THC). Understanding the contractual relationships between port-related actors is a prerequisite for developing effective pricing strategies.
- **The interaction between the pricing strategies of different actors**. The pricing strategies of different port-related actors have a mutual influence. The pricing system used and the level of fees set by one actor can affect the competitiveness of other actors and the entire port. For example, a port authority that levies high land fees to terminal concessionaires might force the latter to charge higher cargo handling fees to the shipping lines, negatively affecting the port's attractiveness and the competitiveness of local firms.
- **Cost structure**. A **cost center** is an accounting device used to group port costs satisfying a given criterion. Such cost centers facilitate a proper analysis of port costs and are indispensable when building up a pricing system.
- **The benefits and added-value created**. If a port is operating economically, then the flow of benefits will equal or exceed the flow of costs (i.e. cost recovery principle). Pricing systems are designed to transfer the advantages gained by the recipients of the benefits, wholly or in part, to the service providers in the form of a revenue flow. It is useful to use **revenue centers**, such as accounting devices that allow the grouping of all revenues of the same nature. The definitions of cost and revenue centers should be related to each other in order to facilitate their comparison. If a port actor tries to charge its customers more than the benefits offered to them, the relationship is not sustainable. However, certain **indirect**

**benefits of port services** cannot be readily quantified and expressed as a financial flow, which complicates the setting of fair price levels.

- **Market segments and port users might have a different price elasticity**. Not all port actors react in the same way to price changes. Some port users are relatively **captive** to the port. This is either because of the lack of alternative ports or because a decision to use another port would result in high switching costs. Other users are comparatively footloose and very sensitive to changes in prices and tariffs. Furthermore, with ports embedded in supply chains, some port users attach greater value to the available capacity, reliability, and overall quality of the port services than to the price. Port service and facilities providers should understand the customer base and figure out the role port-related prices play in explaining the behavior of current and potential users.

- **Measure and analyze**. Port actors should measure and analyze how specific pricing schemes affect the revenue/cost variation by product, customer, segment, channel, and geography. Such exercises help segment users understand how different prices can affect user segments and develop customized **key performance indicators** (KPIs) to facilitate the right pricing decisions. Data-driven technology supports pricing analytics.

- **Balance between standard pricing/tariffs and individualized pricing**. Despite observed differences in price elasticity, it is often not advisable to design customized prices for each port user or cargo flow. Port actors typically try to balance tailored approaches to specific users and market segments and a simple, standardized pricing or tariff structures. Simple pricing structures rely on a limited number of charges and the use of a limited number of variables in the basis for each charge.

- **Balance between penalties and incentives**. Pricing can be used to influence the behavior of port users. Pricing can act as a penalty to customers who do not perform well or do not follow the rules. Examples include fines to shipping lines that do not respect the waste disposal rules and the penalties for terminal operators who do not meet the pre-set throughput guarantees included in the concession agreement. **Incentive pricing** gives a bonus or benefit to users who meet certain thresholds in performance or compliance. The endorsement of price differentiation practices based on the environmental performance of port users and specific services is part of this approach (a good example is the **Environmental Ship Index (ESI)** program, Box 5.5). Port-related actors can also apply a system whereby the collected penalties from underperformers are used to reward those who comply.

---

**Box 5.5 Green port dues – the Environmental Ship Index (ESI)**

*Ports can implement voluntary programs to incentivize ship operators to green their ships. Green ship operators, in return, receive a benefit, such as a discount in port dues.*

*An example is the Environmental Ship Index (ESI). Under the auspices of the **IAPH's World Ports Sustainability Program**, the Environmental Ship*

*Index (ESI) Portal enables ports and other interested parties to incentivize ships to use cleaner engines and fuels with preferential treatment offered either through discounts on port dues, bonuses or other benefits commensurate with a specified level of cleanliness. ESI is a voluntary tool which includes a formula-based evaluation of vessels' nitrogen oxide (NOx) and sulfur oxide (SOx) emissions. The calculation also rewards vessels that are equipped to use available onshore power and which demonstrate fuel efficiency improvements over time, reducing carbon dioxide (CO$_2$) and particulate matter (PM) emissions.*

*In early 2021, IAPH signed a contract with the **Green Award Foundation** to administer and manage the more-than 8,400-strong database of ships and 59 incentive providers already registered on the index. The strongest representation comes from the container shipping sector, with over half of the world fleet registered. Tankers (gas, chemical and oil) are also well represented with 28% of the world fleet. The focus is on growing the number of registered dry bulk and general cargo vessels as well as RoRo and cruise vessels. Green Award is a global, independent, non-profit quality assurance organization with the primary task of certifying ship managers and vessels that go beyond the industry standards in terms of safety, quality and environmental performance. The foundation works closely with maritime authorities and classification societies, and provides data to **Equasis** (the database containing safety-related information on the world's merchant fleet).*

*The ESI has become the **established standard** upon which port authorities and maritime administrations incentivize ship owners and ship owner/operators to continuously improve the environmental performance of the fleets calling at their terminals.*

*While ports or other public authorities could, in principle, also decide to implement **strict regulation on emission criteria for ships** entering the port (i.e. dirty ships are not granted access), such access restrictions have only been implemented in a few ports around the world.*

## 2 PRICING AND ASSET UTILIZATION

There is a relation between pricing and the **utilization level of resources or assets** such as land, facilities, or equipment. Prices should ensure that port land and facilities are used most efficiently. When land or specific port facilities are in short supply, prices are likely to increase so that only those users who utilize the asset efficiently have a net benefit sufficient to make such a use worthwhile. When a port has ample space available, there is an incentive to lower prices to attract additional business. The dwell time charges used by container terminal operators provide a good example:

> **Dwell time charges** *are applied by container terminal operators when containers are stacked on the terminal yard. Container terminal operators typically provide a 'free time' period for containers stacked in the yard (for example, the first five days). Once a container stays longer than the free time, the cargo owner has to pay a dwell time charge per day, which increases exponentially for each day above the free time.*

Such pricing schemes give an incentive to some cargo owners to pick up their containers on time. They also enable the terminal operator to optimize land productivity, such as the number of TEU per hectare per year. Terminal operators who face land availability issues or high throughput guarantees are more likely to impose a short free time period and high dwell time charges.

In practice, port-related prices might not always change much in case of capacity shortages. Still, the behavior of port users changes as a consequence of an increase in **indirect costs** caused by additional time costs for cargo and vessels or additional charges imposed by other actors in the supply chain. For example, a container shipping line may impose a congestion surcharge on cargo owners when calling at a congested port.

The objective of ensuring the most economical utilization of assets cannot always be achieved through port charges alone. The pricing system can only influence the utilization of assets as far as the demand for the services of those assets is elastic. When demand for a service is inelastic in relation to the price, other measures, generally more authoritative than pricing, have to be found and implemented.

## 3 PRICING AND CUSTOMER MANAGEMENT

Many port-related studies on pricing take an economic perspective rather than a marketing and relationship management point of view. The pricing strategy appears to be dealt with in isolation and is not necessarily based on market research linked to the different requirements of major segments, nor is it integrated with other strategic marketing decisions. For example, pricing methods used by port authorities often do not seem to be driven by commercial considerations, even though many port authorities increasingly act as commercial undertakings.

Three pricing strategies can be used in a marketing context depending on the customer segment and type of relationship required:

- **Satisfaction-based pricing strategies** are useful for risk-averse customers as they assist in reducing their aversion by providing more certainty in pricing structures. This can be done by offering **service guarantees**, using **benefit-driven pricing** where customers are charged only for the services used, and **flat-rate pricing**, decreasing uncertainty.
- **Efficiency pricing** appeals to customers requiring the lowest available prices. The strategy requires an internal focus on streamlining operations to enable cost reductions, which are then passed on to customers.
- **Relationship pricing** encourages the customer to develop further relationships with the port. Ports should not use this strategy with all customers, but only with those that are either profitable in the long-term or have a clear growth potential. Two methods are available to achieve a relationship pricing strategy. The first is by using long-term contracts to encourage customers to move beyond a transactional approach. The second is by adopting price bundling, where multiple services are combined and offered for a single price. Price bundling is also an effective means of making comparability between services provided by ports more difficult.

# 4 PRICE INCENTIVES FOR PORT CUSTOMERS

Price incentives are designed to promote certain desired customer behaviors. Four categories can be distinguished:

- Volume incentives.
- Service incentives.
- Utilization incentives.
- Gain-sharing incentives.

Incentives could be granted by all port-related players in an effort to attract activity to the port and should preferably meet several criteria:

- **Effective**. They should make a difference, tangibly or perceptively.
- No effect on the **general price levels**.
- **Sustainable and defendable**, and **not easy to copy** by competitors.

To illustrate the above, the following sections will apply the four types of pricing incentives to the pricing strategies of a **container terminal operator** for services delivered to container shipping lines. The target audience of these types of incentives depends on the focus of the container terminal:

- When **transshipment volumes are high** and carrier haulage is substantial, the relative focus will be on the shipping lines because they dominate the container flows.
- When the **deepsea carrier decides on feeder routes**, the incentives will be towards the deepsea lines. Where the feeder operator is the leading party, these lines will be discounted.
- Granting discounts to shippers and forwarders creates **direct commercial relations with the customers** of the line and the (real) decision-makers in merchant haulage markets or markets where merchant-inspired carrier haulage is involved.
- Where **competitors can easily copy discounts**, the terminal should ensure that additional logistic added value is created through aligned connections, warehousing, distribution, or other logistic activities.

## 4.1 Volume incentives

A container terminal operator can implement **volume incentives for shipping lines**. The growth of deepsea volume is discounted by some percentage. Ideally, the customer share is taken as a measure, possibly in conjunction with volume growth objectives, although measuring this ratio is complex. Volume incentive can also relate to service strings or loops. The terminal operator can also use a discount sum or a discounted rate per container when a line or alliance introduces a new liner service or considers moving a liner service from one port or terminal to another. These volume incentives do not alter the rate structure and rate level of the already existing volumes. The average rate level only decreases when the liner service calls at the terminal. The withdrawal of a string will automatically lead to higher revenues per box.

For attracting cargo-specific volumes, an amount per container or a special dwell time arrangement can be developed to bring in a specific shipper in partnership with its preferred shipping line. A terminal operator can develop volume incentives for **specific market segments**. Some examples of **rate incentives for feeder traffic** include:

- **Start-up incentives**. Fixed sum or an amount per container and possibly limited to a pre-defined utilization percentage of the capacity of the targeted service.
- A **specific discount** can be applied for a particular feeder route the terminal wants to promote.
- A **separate rate** for handling full or empty containers from a container feeder vessel.
- A **rebate** for each container handled from a container feeder vessel.
- Rebates in **volume brackets** (0 to 29,999 moves, 30,000 to 39,999 moves, etc.).

## 4.2 Service incentives

A container terminal operator can rely on **service incentives for shipping lines**. The most common service incentive is a penalty for **under-performance** and a **bonus for over-performance**. The rate incentive can be structured as a discount (a certain percentage on the handling) or as an amount per hour above the agreed or contractual berthing time.

Bonuses tend to be unsustainable because of the fact that repeating over-performance automatically develops into new, perceived service standards. **Penalty systems** are also challenging to implement because under-performance is often the result of both sub-optimal input and process quality of the shipping line and terminal.

**Specific incentives** can be generated for input variables of the shipping lines where they actually influence or even determine the service level:

- Incentives to avoid **late arrivals on the landside** (for example, an add-up) and vessels arriving out of the schedule window.
- Incentives to **avoid additional administrative handling** due to changes in container weights or calling vessels.

## 4.3 Utilization incentives

In a container terminal context, **utilization incentives** are designed to promote terminal utilization or reduce capacity demand peaks. A good example is **dwell time incentives**. A conventional way of applying dwell time incentives is allowing for a free number of storage days, after which a certain amount per TEU per day is charged. More sophisticated schemes differentiate by the direction of the container flow, such as for import, export, or transshipment containers. **Progressive rate levels** are applicable after the free period, in successive periods increasing the applied storage rates.

Other incentives to reduce peak capacity requirement include:

- **Pre-notification** bonuses for truckers.
- Bonuses for arrival **outside peak periods**.
- **Gang waiting-hours charges** when vessels arrive out of the scheduled window.

Utilization incentives can aim at avoiding terminal congestion. There are essentially two types of congestion:

- Congestion mainly caused by **cycles/seasonality** in the traffic volumes. In peak periods, a terminal operator can consider having **peak season surcharges**, like those applied by shipping lines with peak season surcharges to their customers.
- **Structural congestion** caused by chronic underinvestment by the terminal operator. For this type of congestion, shipping lines are not eager to pay more since capacity supply lags behind demand. Shipping lines will then start to consider imposing congestion surcharges and not peak season surcharges on their customers. This is a situation that should be avoided.

### 4.4 Gain-sharing incentives

A **gain-sharing program** consists of a documented and agreed project plan to reduce costs at the terminal or the shipping line with the assistance of both parties. Examples include:

- A change of schedule windows reducing terminal personnel in-hire.
- Improving schedule window reliability.
- Improving cargo distribution over the vessel, allowing for higher berth performances.
- Arranging additional equipment for improving flexibility.

In the gain-sharing program, the **financial effects** should be determined. Cost reductions should be shared between the terminal and the line. This can be a simple 50/50 on cost reductions related to the actual cost of the improvement. Gain-sharing requires **mutual trust** in the relevant calculations and discussions on establishing and measuring the cost reductions.

## 5 PORT PRICING BY PORT AUTHORITIES

### 5.1 General considerations

Landlord port authorities provide infrastructural and other services mainly to three groups of port users; the cargo owner, the shipowner/operator, and the concessionaires (if applicable). The typical revenues of a landlord port authority are directly linked to the benefits created for cargo owners, shipowners, and concessionaires, such as **cargo dues, marine charges, and concession/land fees**. The cargo dues and marine charges combined form the **port dues**.

In setting the prices for the port dues and land fees, port authorities might follow different objectives:

- **Macro-economic**, such as to support the economic development of the region or maximize port employment.
- **Economic-logistic**, such as to insert the port in supply chains in an efficient manner.
- **Port-centric**, such as to guarantee a high utilization of port resources and assets.

- **Financial**, such as to build up financial reserves for future investments and/or cushioning the port against unexpected falls in revenue or rises in costs.
- **Sustainability**, such as to support green supply chain management and energy transition.

There are some general factors to consider when designing and implementing pricing systems:

- The pricing structure (number of charges, type of charges, charging base) of a port should be **designed to last for many years**, although each port charge level may be modified as conditions change. It is a complex procedure for a port to change its pricing structure, and too frequent changes may be a source of confusion for port users. Simple pricing systems may interfere with the achievement of the pricing objectives.
- The pricing system should, ideally, be **cheap to build and operate**. The charging base should also rely on measures or data that can be accurately determined and easily provided by the customers. For example, the traditional charging units for ships (as a basis for marine charges) are the gross tonnage (GT) or net tonnage (NT) of the vessels, as this information is readily available and supported by official ship measurement documentation.
- Pricing systems should be **understandable and ideally comparable between ports**. In practice, there is still quite some diversity in the various pricing systems and bases for calculating port charges throughout the world, hampering comparisons and benchmarking. In some parts of the world, supranational institutions (such as the EU) or national authorities have endorsed strict rules or general guiding principles for pricing by port authorities. These include common methods of calculating charges with tariff levels left to the discretion of the local port authorities.
- Port authorities should **clearly explain each charge**, specifying which services are included and which are excluded. Many port authorities have developed **tariff books** with a view to providing (public) access to the pricing system used and its components.

## 5.2 Port dues

Shipowners or operators have to pay port dues when calling at a port and staying in the port. There are different types of port dues, such as **marine charges** and **cargo dues**.

> *Tonnage dues* or *marine charges are indivisible charges calculated on the basis of the ship's tonnage.*

The **basis for calculating marine charges** can be the gross tonnage (GT) or net tonnage (NT) of the vessel. However, it is also possible to use other ship measurements, such as the deadweight tonnage (DWT). In order to determine the marine charges, the ship operator, the shipowner, the charterer, the master, or the authorized representative must submit the vessel's **international tonnage certificate** when the vessel calls at the port for the first time or when changes in the ship's measurement occur. Payment of the marine charges entitles the vessel to stay at the port for an **uninterrupted period** (for example, ten or 20 days) from the day of arrival at the port. Upon expiry of that period, additional marine charges will be due. The time a vessel spends in a dry dock is usually excluded from the official port time.

The marine charges to be paid per GT or NT can vary, and discounts might apply:

- The charges may vary per **ship type** and, occasionally, also per **ship size**. For example, several ports apply lower marine charges per capacity unit for container feeder vessels compared to mainline container vessels. The tariff setting for specific ship types and sizes is influenced by the **level of competition** exerted by competing ports for accommodating the same vessel class.
- It is quite common to have different marine charges for **liner ships** (i.e. vessels operating in regular liner shipping services) and vessels operating in **non-liner trade**.
- Discounts might apply to shipping lines that exceed a certain threshold in terms of the number of vessel calls (**frequency-based discount**), or the ship-related cargo volume handled in the port (**traffic-based discount**) per time period (**seasonality discount**).
- Many ports have developed voluntary programs to promote green shipping. Within the framework of such programs, the port authority usually grants a discount on the marine charges for ships that meet certain **minimum environmental standards**. A good example of such a voluntary program is the Environmental Ship Index (ESI), see earlier Box 5.5.
- Reduced marine charges or discounts might apply to sea-going vessels entering the port for a short period solely for **non-terminal uses** such as bunkering, repair, or disinfection purposes, sea-going vessels entering the port because of perils at sea, or vessels entering the port exclusively for transit purposes when a ship passes through a port to reach another port upstream.

The port authority might decide to exempt some vessel types from paying marine charges. Training ships, naval ships, sea-going vessels that remain inactive at the roadstead, sea-going vessels that call into port solely for tank cleaning and/or degassing purposes, and sea-going vessels involved in operations on behalf of the port city or other local or national government agencies typically fall into this category.

> *Cargo dues, berthing dues, or wharfage dues are indivisible charges calculated based on the goods unloaded or loaded by the vessel in port, expressed in tons.*

The **calculation of the cargo dues** is based on the number of loaded or unloaded tons as reported on the manifest and registry. Port authorities usually charge a different tariff depending on the type of cargo. For example, separate cargo dues per ton might be applicable for containers, non-containerized general cargo, and bulk cargo.

The **total port costs** for the port user are **not limited to the port dues** collected by the port authority. Other major cost factors linked to a port call include:

- **Costs associated with ship cargo handling at a terminal**. The terminal operator collects these cargo handling fees, tariffs, or costs.

- Costs paid by the shipping line for compulsory marine and nautical services such as pilotage, berthing, and towage (tug assistance). These costs are usually incurred when entering and leaving the port and based on vessel size. Depending on the port, these types of services are offered by the central or local government, the port authority, and one or more private companies.
- Most ports also have **separate charges for waste reception** at port reception facilities. These can be fixed, floating, or mobile facilities which carry out the reception of waste or cargo residues, such as remnants of any cargo material on board in cargo holds or tanks). Shipping wastes include oily waste such as sludge, bilge water, and used engine oil, as well as garbage such as food waste from the crew, domestic waste, and maintenance waste from the engine room.

## 5.3 Port concessions/land fees

The port authority or government can set the **fees and the fee structure** for port land concessioned or leased to terminal operators and other companies active in the port area (Figure 5.8). On the one hand, port users demand a transparent, uniform, and stable fee system. Such stability of the fee structure is essential in view of the investment decisions of the terminal operator. On the other hand, port authorities are tempted to apply the market mechanism in setting the fees for the use of valuable port land.

The pricing system deployed by the managing body of the port for the use of port land tends to vary widely among ports. The options available include:

- The managing body of the port imposes a **fixed rent per year** on the operator for the land surface in use, such as per square meter per year. This rent is usually determined on the basis of used footprint, infrastructure investments made by the port authority, location of the site, and activities that are performed on-site.
- A **lump sum** to be paid annually regardless of the financial results from the operating activity plus a variable payment.

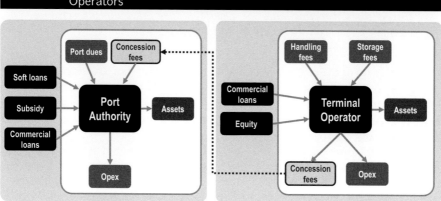

FIGURE 5.8 Concession Fees and Financial Flows of Port Authorities and Terminal Operators

Source: Adapted from Uyttendaele (2012).

- A fixed rent per year on the land area plus a **percentage of the revenue earned** (royalty fee).
- A fixed rent for the land surface in use adjusted for an **incentive/penalty system**, depending on an annual throughput or activity in relation to the guaranteed volume/activity.

Concession fees can change based on a substantiated review and are typically adjusted annually in line with inflation. Payments are to be made in advance every month, quarter, or year.

## 6 STRUCTURES OF PORT CHARGES

### 6.1 Charges at container terminals

Several different tariffs apply at each container terminal. **Terminal handling rates** for the ship to shore works include different charges for (Figure 5.9):

- **Unloading a container**, such as discharging a container from the vessel, move a container from the wharf to the container yard and subsequently loading onto a chassis.
- **Uploading a container**, such as lifting a container from a chassis to the container yard and subsequently moving the container to the wharf and loading onto the vessel.

Depending on the port, the loading/uploading charge might differ between **import and export containers**. The charges vary per **container size**, with the 20-foot containers charged differently from 40-foot containers or high cube 40-foot containers. They also vary depending on whether the container is fully loaded or empty.

Different charges apply to **transshipment services**, with a cargo handling fee applying for the discharge of the transshipment container from the inbound vessel, the move of the container from the wharf to the container yard, the move of the transshipment container from the container yard to the wharf, and loading onto the outbound vessel.

A surcharge is imposed for handling containers, including dangerous goods demanding extra safety measures. Further surcharges apply in the case of specific containers containing cargoes demanding extra care, such as those classified as IMO containers including mass explosion hazard, or explosives with projection hazard, or radioactive substances, which demand the use of qualified handling personnel.

Additional charges also apply:

- When an **empty or a fully loaded container** is received from the chassis and is not shipped but subsequently delivered back to the chassis.
- For **late container arrivals**.
- For the movement of a container from the container yard for **inspections**, such as by customs, or for health or agricultural reasons.
- When an empty or fully loaded container is received but subsequently shipped via another vessel.
- For any additional container movements not stated above, extra movement charges are levied.

FIGURE 5.9 Container Terminal: Cargo Handling Charges

### Loading/Unloading Works (Ship to Shore)

| Size | Full load | | Empties | Transhipment | |
| --- | --- | --- | --- | --- | --- |
|  | Import | Export | | Empties | Full load |
| 20" | * | * | * | * | * |
| 40" | * | * | * | * | * |

### Surcharges (Loading / Unloading works) (Ship to Shore / Shore to Shore)

| Transversal (putting the container abeam) | Wires | Hazardous | Waste |
| --- | --- | --- | --- |

### Additional Vessel Work

| Hatch covers | Shifting regardless of size, full load - empties | Delay (per hour) | Gantry Crane Shift cancelling | Additional dockworker (per day) |
| --- | --- | --- | --- | --- |

### Landside Works (Lift-on, Lift-off) (Shore to Shore)

| Size | For import | Local for Exports | In transit | Empties |
| --- | --- | --- | --- | --- |
| 20" | * | * | * | * |
| 40" | * | * | * | * |

### Container moves

| Size | Inside Terminal | | Outside Terminal | | Electrification |
| --- | --- | --- | --- | --- | --- |
|  | Full load | Empties | Full load | Empties | |
| 20" | | | | | |
| 40" | | | | | |

| Customs Control | Dockworker (per hour) | Connecting reefer containers in plugs | Container weighing |
| --- | --- | --- | --- |

Charging/ Discharging of Containers for deliveries directly to transport means or to storage areas

FIGURE 5.10 Container Terminal: Cargo Storage Charges

## Storage rights

| | | | | | |
|---|---|---|---|---|---|
| Imports (full load) | First 4 days | 5th – 6th day | 7th - 10th | 11th - 20th | 21st & longer |
| Exports (full load) | First 4 days | 5th – 6th day | 7th - 10th | 16th - 25th | 26th & longer |
| In Transit | First 4 days | 5th – 6th day | 7th - 10th | 16th - 25th | 26th & longer |
| Empties | First 4 days | 5th – 6th day | 7th - 10th | 21st - 30th | 31st & longer |
| Transshipment | First 4 days | 1st - 15th | 16th - 30th | After the 30th day the container is subject to category "IMPORT" | |
| | | 20"/40"/45" | | | |

## Surcharges on storage rights

| Open Top | Flat Racks | Waste | Hazardous |
|---|---|---|---|

## Surcharges for extraordinary - overtime works (applies in landside operations)

| From land transport mode to storage areas | weekdays | weekends |
|---|---|---|

## Dues (vehicle clearance) per vehicle

| | Full load (general cargo) | | Empties |
|---|---|---|---|
| | kg < 2,500 | Kg > 2,500 | 20" or 40" |
| Up to 2 days | | | |
| Longer than 2 days | | | |
| Sat - Sun - Holidays | | | |

© PEMP

Onboard shifting of containers involves additional charges as well. They include distinctive categories for:

- **Hatch cover handling**, such as opening and closing hatches and lifting of hatch covers and lids.
- **Container shifts**, such as landing and subsequently reshipping containers on the same vessel and shifting of containers from one location on the vessel to another.

Beyond terminal cargo handling fees, a container terminal user pays charges for **acquiring storage rights** within the port terminal area. The user is also charged for landside operations. Both fully loaded containers and empties have a certain number of days of free storage at the container yard, calculated from the date containers are stacked in the yard to the date the containers are removed from it. The size of the container, and its direction, whether it is imported or exported, imply different charges. Thereafter, stacked containers carry a storage charge, which increases as the containers remain in the yard. Surcharges on storage services apply in the case of specialized container handling, such as refrigerated containers.

In addition, container terminal users pay port dues for maritime services, and potentially for the use of other utilities, with these dues defined by the managing body (Figure 5.10).

## 6.2 Cruise terminals

A variety of fees are charged regularly in cruise ports. In addition to the different tariffs applied at cruise terminals for either maritime or land-side services, fees can be levied for waste disposal and supplies (Figure 5.11). Port fees increase with the ship size and differ depending on the type of call, with the fees for a transit cruise call approximately half the port fees for a turnaround call, regardless of ship size.

The major economic benefits for the port result from the dues paid for the cruise call and from the disembarking and embarking passengers. Typical fees collected from cruise ships are the entrance fees, generally calculated based on gross registered tonnage, and the berthing fees, generally calculated per day and vessel length. There are many other potentially applicable dues, such as the pilot fees or the handling of onboard-generated waste. These might also be calculated according to the vessel's gross registered tonnage or according to use. However, they might be collected by third parties providing services rather than by the port itself.

A **cruise passenger fee** is imposed for transit as well as homeport passengers but, in the latter case, the fee is higher. Passengers (dis)embarkation is also subject to other fees such as the passenger security fee to use the International Ship and Port Facility Security (ISPS) Code provisions. This charge is usually a fixed rate per cruise passenger embarking, disembarking, or transiting through the cruise port. Apart from the charges mentioned above, there are also charges based on providing specific port services, such as bunkering, provision of water and electricity to the cruise ship, and cruise ship supplies. When levied, the compulsory fees include passenger fees, port dues, fees for mooring and unmooring, dockage/

FIGURE 5.11 Categories of Port Fees at a Cruise Terminal

## Maritime Activities

- Anchorage dues
- Dockage/anchorage fee
- Light(house) Dues
- Mooring and unmooring
- Navigation Dues
- Pilotage
- Tender
- Terminal dues
- Tug / Towage
- Port Dues (Utilities)

## Landside Activities

- Chamber of shipping / commerce fee
- Crew fees
- Customs / clearance
- Gangway fee
- Immigration
- Passenger fees
- Passenger luggage handling
- Passenger luggage storage
- Sanitary dues
- Security costs
- Shuttle bus

anchorage fees, navigation dues, tender fees, and passenger luggage storage. Other fees are applicable in some ports, including chamber of shipping/commerce fees, gangway fees, immigration and navigation dues, passenger luggage storage fees, and fees for shuttle bus services, tenders, and crew, as well as customs/clearance and sanitary dues. Ports typically apply discount policies for cruise ships and passengers as a promotion tool for attracting cruise traffic. These discounts are based on the number of passengers per year or the number of cruise ship calls.

The ratio of cost components of port fees differs for transit and turnaround calls. The main difference is that fees for passenger luggage handling are only levied for turnaround calls. This also creates differences in the ratio of other cost components between transit and turnaround calls since for turnaround calls, passenger fees need to be paid twice. For transit calls, passenger fees are on average substantially higher in large ports than in small ports. This difference decreases with an increase in ship size. Also, for turnaround calls, passenger fees are on average substantially higher in large ports than in small ports. However, for small and medium-sized ships, passenger fees are similar or higher in smaller ports.

A fee for **pilotage** is frequently compulsory. The percentage for which a fee for pilotage is compulsory increases slightly with the ship size. Similarly, a fee for **tug/towage** is compulsory in many ports and increases slightly with the ship size, except for mega-ships. In some ports, the fee for tug/towage is fixed and independent of ship size. Therefore these cost components have a relatively more significant share in the total port fees for smaller ships than they do for larger ships. This also involves variable costs components (like passenger fees), which have a relatively smaller share in the total port fees of smaller ships than they do in larger ships.

There are differences in port fees applied in cruise ports between weekdays and weekends. Some ports levy higher costs on the weekend for cost components involving overtime labor costs.

# Chapter 5.5  Entry barriers in seaports

*Entry barriers comprise the placement of economic, regulatory, and locational impediments in seaports.*

## 1 ENTRY BARRIERS IN SEAPORTS

Although the port industry has become a more open market in the last decades, entry barriers for those wishing to provide port services remain substantial. A barrier to entry is anything that prevents an entrepreneur from instantaneously **creating a new firm in a specific market**. In contrast, a long-run barrier to entry is a cost that must be incurred by a new entrant that incumbents do not, or have not had to, bear. In some cases, port reforms have introduced a few private port operators, yet they have failed to lower the entry barriers for more firms interested in providing port services.

Barriers to entry in seaports are classified into three categories (Figure 5.12):

FIGURE 5.12 Entry Barriers in Seaports

| Type of Barrier | Entry Barrier | Contributing Factors |
|---|---|---|
| **Economic** | **Structural cost advantage of existing provider(s)** | • Incumbent enjoys a better location in the seaport.<br>• Minimum efficient scale is large compared with port size.<br>• Incumbent benefiting from accumulated public investments. |
| | **Switching costs** | • Carriers need capital expenditure to switch port facilities.<br>• Services bundling by incumbents increases switching costs.<br>• Reciprocity in partnerships leads to switching costs. |
| | **Required investments in networks** | • New firms need time, capital, and knowledge to join spatial and functional networks. |
| **Institutional (Regulatory)** | **Entry conditions / permissions** | • Restricted entrance for political and commercial reasons.<br>• Subjective entrance (allowing for discrimination) controlled by PAs that are both regulators and operators. |
| | **Exclusive concessions** | • Regulation serving the benefits of politicians, bureaucrats, and existing firms that can extract rents. |
| **Geographical (Locational)** | **Unavailable land for entrants** | • Natural, environmental, and capital constraints to port capacity protecting incumbents. |

Source: Adapted from de Langen and Pallis (2007).

- **Economic entry barriers** such as the need to make long-term, capital intensive, and fixed investments.
- **Regulatory and institutional entry barriers** such as no license given to new firms willing to operate in a particular port.
- **Locational** (geographical), space-related, entry barriers such as having no attractive site in the port for an entrant.

## 2 ECONOMIC ENTRY BARRIERS

The first type of economic entry barrier in seaports is **the absolute cost advantage** that might be enjoyed by an existing port service provider. This advantage might be the result of one or more of the following factors:

- **The scale of operations is not big enough to allow the presence of additional service providers**. This issue is relevant when the minimum efficient scale (MES) for providing a port service is large compared with specific market size. This phenomenon frequently happens in the case of seaports. In such conditions, potential new entrants face a competitive disadvantage resulting from a smaller scale or need to create a capacity similar to that of the incumbent firm. This option would be unlikely if it were to result in substantial excess supply, the prospect of a price war, and losses for both the incumbent and the entrant.
- **The existing service provider (incumbent) enjoys a better location in the port**. When the incumbent is perfectly located, for instance regarding access to hinterland transport modes such as rail, road, and inland waterways, or at a site with good maritime accessibility, the entry of competitors in less attractive vacant sites is unlikely to materialize.
- **Incumbents benefit from accumulated public investments**. In most seaports, public port authorities have invested in infrastructures such as rail terminals and quays. In some cases, they have also invested in the superstructure. Furthermore, the opportunity costs of the land are not always included in the land price paid to the landlord by port-service providers. Thus, existing leaseholders may benefit from accumulated public investments. Incumbents have a long-term cost advantage if such benefits from public investments are no longer available for entrants, for example because of changing policy guidelines. Consequently, new entrants face costs that incumbents have not had to bear. If such subsidies are not available for new entrants, that is clearly a barrier to entry. The incumbent has had lower initial investments and enjoys relatively high profits.

Specialized equipment and high capital requirements alone are **not an entry barrier**. Entrants are, in many cases, multinationals (such as Hutchison Ports); others are affiliated to large state-owned conglomerates (such as the Chinese COSCO), or might even be groups of investors with access to the capital markets.

### 2.1 Minimum efficient scale of port services

*The **Minimum Efficient Scale** (MES) for providing a port service depends on the cost curves for this provision. MES is the smallest scale at which the output can be produced at a minimum average long-run cost (i.e. it is* *reached when marginal and average costs no longer decrease when capacity is expanded) under the assumption that the terminal is operating with a given technology.*

For port services such as a container terminal, or an iron ore terminal, the MES is quite large. In a small market size relative to the MES, economies of scale are only fully realized with one supplier of port services. A second, smaller competitor may have a structural cost disadvantage that prevents profitability. It may exit, leaving the market to one operator with a sufficient scale. The large size of the MES might explain the relatively high concentration of most port services.

The MES in a port market might be reduced by a public authority, mainly the port authority, that owns assets and leases them to private firms. In such an arrangement, the public authority can **secure scale economies**, such as equipment purchasing, maintenance, port planning, and terminal layout, and let relatively small firms provide port services. Policy options also include tender procedures to ensure the economic rent accrues to a public organization, and tariff monitoring and benchmarking of port service providers. Furthermore, access to port services can be regulated based on essential services access regulation. Port services and port facilities can be termed essential if they are necessary components of transport chains and economically viable alternatives (e.g. outside the port or other ports) are not available. Such essential facilities include towage, pilotage, mooring, stevedoring, and shore handling and are strategies to introduce port competition.

## 2.2 Switching costs

The second type of economic entry barrier is **the magnitude of switching costs**. These are costs associated with the decision of a port user to switch from the incumbent port service provider to the new entrant. They can come in several forms and often determine the capability of new entrants to start operations in a port:

- Switching from one port facility to another may require the **investments of port users**. In some cases, such costs are insignificant; for example, shipping lines can easily switch containers from one transshipment facility to a competing facility. In other cases, switching costs may be substantial. For instance, port users (shipping lines, forwarders, or shippers) may have long-term contracts with rail or barge companies or may be invested in dedicated transport equipment. Other port users may have invested in facilities at the site of the port-service providers (for instance, car manufacturers that carry out pre-delivery inspection and small repair activities at the site of a terminal operator). Such port users cannot easily switch to another port service provider. For most bulk transport flows, switching is prohibitive because of the specific investments made to create an efficient overall transport chain (including hinterland transport). This also explains why cargo owners frequently invest in terminal facilities: to avoid being exposed to independent terminal operators with dominant market positions.
- Switching costs may also be high through the **bundling of the services** of the incumbent port-service provider. For instance, a terminal-operating company may also provide pilotage, towage, and hinterland transport

services. Such an arrangement creates a barrier to entry in each of the separate markets, especially when some of the bundled services are natural monopolies. The bundling of port services is partly due to the geographical and functional integration of ports in wider regions and networks. With the rapid restructuring of the supply chains in which ports are embedded, ports are now elements in value-driven chain systems, not simply places with particular functions. In the emerging flow-based system, the various supply phases are closely synchronized, and the various transport services are frequently bundled.

## 2.3 Sunk costs

Sunk costs, such as networking, marketing, and advertizing costs, cannot be recovered once a firm decides to leave the market and, thus, might stand as the third type of economic barrier to entry. Sunk costs include the essential investments in embeddedness in specific networks in order to achieve integration in maritime transportation and supply chains. The quest for **long-term relationships** with partners to reduce uncertainty and improve coordination leads port authorities to implement strategies to strengthen partnerships with other players by offering incumbent firms the conditions to develop strategies to succeed. Embeddedness in such a strategic network enhances the competitive position of a firm. For new firms entering the market, inclusion in such networks may demand resources and be costly to achieve because of the importance of reputation, trust, and experience, for example. Should a firm decide to leave the market, the investments required for inclusion in strategic networks cannot be recovered.

## 3  REGULATORY, INSTITUTIONAL AND GEOGRAPHY ENTRY BARRIERS

Regulatory and institutional entry barriers might make entry into a market costly, time-consuming, or impossible. In a substantial number of ports, policy-makers or port authorities **effectively limit the number of terminal-operating companies**, towage companies, and other port-service providers. Sometimes these limits are set by explicit entry criteria that effectively limit the number of competitors. In other cases, the port authority or some other relevant policy-maker decides about an entry based on its interpretation of the rules, such as those regarding compliance with local, national, and international environmental requirements and the development policy of the port.

In some cases, not only do port authorities grant authorizations, but they also **provide port services**. This provision presents fundamental obstacles to market openness. Furthermore, in a situation where the state in one of its various forms (national, regional, local) owns a port-service provider, this operator enjoys an implicit state guarantee: the state would not allow a state-owned operator to go bankrupt. This situation is a deterrent to new entry, as the state-owned operator can potentially engage in predatory pricing: that is, set prices below cost to remove competitors from the market.

Provisions in leases, concessions, and other operating agreements, particularly those involving **long-term investments by private operators**, often provide these operators with some degree of protection against new entrants. For example, a terminal operator who has been given the concession to operate a container-handling facility might have exclusive rights to handle containers in the port during the concession period. Furthermore, lengthy concessions, even though they provide benefits in the short run that are often passed on to the users, can also provide opportunities for rent-seeking.

The existence of regulatory entry barriers can be understood, at least in part, with insights from **public choice theories**. They are the result of the lobby efforts of incumbent firms to persuade policy-makers to deter further entry and secure profits or serve the wish to extract rents. Both of these explanations underline the adverse welfare effects of entry barriers, with the latter associated with higher levels of informal economies rather than better quality goods and services.

These public-choice theories suggest that the emergence of legal and institutional entry barriers to serve the interests of incumbent firms, public port authorities, or state agencies may not be ruled out in advance. Ports are traditionally strong, locally-oriented communities with close relationships between the port authority and port service providers. In such an environment, entry barriers may develop to serve the interests of the incumbent port community. An alternative explanation along the same lines, namely that legal and institutional entry barriers are the result of the lobbying of interest groups, is that a public port authority creates entry barriers in order to **collect economic rents**. In many ports, port authorities offer additional services such as pilotage, towage, and port labor. Entry barriers for such services increase the market power of the port authority in these markets.

Natural barriers that constrain port capacity can limit entry, particularly firms requiring land in the port. In many ports, there is simply **no space for additional berths, warehouses, and other facilities**. The lack of suitable locations and environmental regulations constrain expansion to protect incumbents from new entrants. Such entry barriers are particularly relevant if alternative ports are imperfect substitutes, for example if there are differences in hinterland infrastructure or nautical access, including deviation from main routes. Such deficiency is the case in many ports and for many commodities. Greenfield port development (building port infrastructure in a completely new location) is not usually a viable strategy for entry. Large investments are often required for dredging, quay construction, access roads, and port superstructure. In most existing ports, public authorities have contributed a large share of these investments without direct cost recovery. Thus, private greenfield port development is unlikely to emerge. This supposition further strengthens the case for low entry barriers in existing port complexes.

## 4 POLICIES TO REDUCE ENTRY BARRIERS

Lowering entry barriers is desirable from a public-interest point of view:

- First, it enhances **market contestability**. The relevant issue is how accessible (contestable) a market is for entrants. If entry to (and eventually exit from) the market by new competitors is easy, the market is contestable. Such contestability puts pressure on incumbent firms not to charge excessive prices. This contestability is particularly relevant given the increased market concentration arising from economies of scale in modern cargo-handling technologies, the rise of global players in the terminal-handling industry, and horizontal and vertical integration in the shipping industry through the investments of shipping lines in dedicated terminals. Often just the **threat of entry** (potential entry) is enough to persuade incumbents not to abuse their dominant market position. The possibility of entry introduces an element of competition. Although there may not be many operators in the market, it is competitive, with prices not far from social opportunity costs.

- Second, lower entry barriers increase the **level of intra-port competition**. As abuse of market power is curtailed, and port-service providers have incentives to specialize and differentiate their services from competitors in the same port, real intra-port competition is more beneficial for port users (and thus consumers) than contestable markets with only one incumbent. However, owing to the large minimum efficient size of many port services, such intra-port competition is not always viable.

- Third, lower entry barriers allow for the **faster implementation of new technologies and business models**. Even when intra-port competition is established, the entry of additional competitors can be an essential engine for introducing innovations. New firms often generate business dynamism and economic growth, particularly when exogenous changes in demand challenge the current activities of incumbent firms. New firms are thought to be particularly innovative. There is evidence that the process of entry (and exit) plays a part in reallocating resources from low to high productive units. Firm entry plays an important part in **creative destruction** as a mechanism that helps shift resources from less to more productive units, as in a Schumpeterian model with entrepreneurial learning under uncertainty. When incumbents fail to exploit exogenous shifts in costs or demand (perhaps because the required innovations would be rent displacing), entry is an important determinant of industry performance.

**Policies to reduce entry barriers** concentrate on creating conditions that allow entry without hindering the survival and growth of profitable firms (Figure 5.13). Some of the potential policy options to reduce entry barriers may not be applicable or necessary in all seaports but may well be useful in some. While some of these options require national policy initiatives, port authorities can implement others:

- **Structural cost advantages** held by the incumbent can be prevented by using effective pricing mechanisms, such as tender procedures, to grant the right to provide a service or a terminal concession. In such procedures, all cost (dis)advantages are internalized in the price.

- Another policy capable of reducing entry barriers is to **split a terminal into parts**, forming separate concessions. The existence of different market segments increases the viability of intra-port rivalry. Dividing facilities to accommodate various port service providers may be difficult. Much depends on the geographical layout of the port, the available

FIGURE 5.13 Policy Options to Reduce Entry Barriers in Seaports

| Type of Barrier | Entry Barrier | Policy Option |
|---|---|---|
| Economic | Structural cost advantage of existing provider(s) | • Fair and transparent pricing.<br>• Splitting up a terminal in two parts to be concessioned separately. |
| | Switching costs | • Investments in sunk costs by PA and costs passed on to private firms. |
| | Required investments in networks | • The PA might act as a cluster manager that enhance the networking of different operators. |
| Institutional (Regulatory) | Entry conditions / permissions | • Minimum and transparent procedures that ensure the absence of discrimination. |
| | Exclusive concessions | • Licenses for shorter periods, no exclusivity contracts. |
| Geographical (Locational) | Unavailable land for entrants | • Long term, but flexible port planning |

Source: Adapted from de Langen and Pallis (2007).

traffic, and the minimum capacity additions taking into account the lumpiness of port investments.

- In the long term, many physical/locational entry barriers can be overcome by **building in adjacent locations**, extending out into the sea, and so forth. Furthermore, new concepts and technologies can be introduced to limit the need for space in the port. For example, an inland container depot can help create additional space for terminals in the port.

- In most cases, having a public agency, the port authority, which invests in **port-specific and site-specific assets** and **leases these assets to the private sector**, is a policy option to reduce entry barriers related to switching costs and sunk investments. A further role for the port authority to reduce entry barriers is that of a smart coordinator enabling networks of stakeholders. Such a coordinator can help overcome decisional and operational fragmentation. The port authority acts as a cluster manager by coordinating the integrated port services provided by various actors. Such an active port authority can increase opportunities for the entry of small and medium-sized companies.

- Policy reforms that promote **transparent concession procedures**, forbid exclusive contracts, and ensure the absence of discrimination are also relevant for reducing entry barriers. Reducing the (maximum) duration of authorizations and concessions also lowers entry barriers and rent-seeking opportunities. Concessions and authorizations need to be sufficiently long to allow companies to recover their fixed investments and earn a normal return on their investments. However, excessively long durations limit opportunities for entry and reduce the dynamism in the sector. In many European countries, durations of concessions of 50 years in the case of limited investments, 75 years for significant investments in movable assets, or 99 years for immovable assets are common practice. The reduction of maximum durations would certainly lower entry barriers.

- Entry barriers can be further reduced by the **stability of the regulatory regime** and the presence of mechanisms for dispute resolution. Uncertainty and transaction costs are reduced and lower entry barriers ensue.

- Additional regulation, such as **antitrust policies and merger regulations**, can be targeted to prevent incumbents from benefiting from high entry barriers. Most countries, economic zones (like NAFTA), and supranational entities (like the European Union) have developed a general legal framework to ensure low entry barriers. Such regulation is not industry-specific but applies overall. In most countries, competition regulations protect entrants from predatory pricing by incumbents, such as exclusive contracts with suppliers. Mergers and acquisitions are also subject to regulatory oversight. These are relevant in the container-handling market, given its strong consolidation. The question arises whether operators have established a dominant position, limiting the potential of market competition and discouraging newcomers. The general competition law can and often does go hand in hand with industry-specific regulations.

# PART VI

# Port performance

## Chapter 6.1  Port performance

*The concept of port performance is formed by two interconnected components; efficiency and effectiveness. Resilience to disruptions emerges as the additional third component.*

### 1 PORT PERFORMANCE COMPONENTS

The quest for performance measurement has always been a key issue for ports. Port managers, whether port authorities or terminal operators, need to organize complex processes efficiently and effectively to find the best ways to capture value for their customers and address the concerns of stakeholders. In combination, these port performance components provide port operators and government policy-makers with essential feedback for assessing whether they meet their strategic objectives.

Performance refers to the execution of port activities in a manner that **meets targets** set by the owners and service providers and **fulfils the expectations** of the port customers (users). Operating in a given economic context, and with the broader structures defined by the port governance models endorsed and the targets set, ports and their operators develop their strategies. This involves organizing the use of available resources, the planning of their expansion, and the interactions between ports and their users to improve the offered services. The outcome of these efforts will help the port (or a specific actor) reach the set targets. It will inform any needed realignment of the governance model and the reorganization of the available resources, with the aim being to improve the recorded performance of the port further.

Performance is a broad concept covering almost any **objective of operational management and competitive excellence** of a firm and its activities. In the case of ports, based on the complexity of the contemporary port product, each actor (authorities, operators, and stakeholders) engages in multi-faceted examinations of **different performance components**. These are based on the

DOI 10.4324/9780429318184-6

development of several, occasionally unique performance indicators grounded on the distinction between terminal operations, cargo transfer operations, port logistics, and production and postponed manufacturing activities. The users of these products and the respective selection criteria for each specific service offered at a port differ substantially. Given the spatial and functional expansion of ports, such as port regionalization, linking and integrating operational design and strategy within the multi-institutional and cross-functional port sector has become an emerging dimension of port performance. Tailoring performance measurements and communication of performance measures to specific objectives are increasingly common.

The addition of **performance indicators** is a key development in recent port performance measurement. Depicting the taxonomy of the applied performance measurement dimensions, efficiency and utilization interact with quality and effectiveness. Service quality is a measure of how the customer is experiencing the expected level of service. Thus, a simple and effective view of service quality matches what the customer expects and what the customer experiences. For a port to respond to stakeholders satisfactorily, performance measures need to focus on the linkage between expectations and performance.

> *The concept of port performance is formed by two interconnected components, namely efficiency and effectiveness.* **Efficiency** *has been noted as 'doing things right' while* **effectiveness** *is 'doing the right things'. In combination, these port performance components also provide government policy-makers with essential feedback for assessing the governance structure of ports in meeting national strategic objectives.*

Ports use several indicators to measure each of these performance components and their various dimensions. Indicators are quantitative or qualitative factors or variables that provide a simple and reliable means to measure achievement, reflect the changes connected to an intervention, or help assess the performance of an actor.

**Resilience to disruptions** emerges as the third component of port performance. Along with the changing economic environment, unexpected events, such as economic crises, political events, natural disasters, cybersecurity incidents, and health crises, all challenge the infrastructural and operational integrity of ports, their terminals, and their industrial and logistics sites. When such events take place, extended supply chains are put at risk. Thus, efforts to enhance port efficiency, effectiveness, and ultimately competitiveness provide an additional port performance component. Resilience is defined as the capability to anticipate, prepare for, respond to, and recover from significant multi-hazard threats affecting and disrupting maritime networks. Differences in resilience are the outcome of diverse strategies, policies, governance practices, or simply different approaches to terminal operations.

## 2 PERFORMANCE MEASUREMENT: INDUSTRY LEVEL INITIATIVES

Each port measures its performance. It then uses the outcome of this measurement to make any necessary strategic, structural, operational, or other adjustments to improve its competitiveness. In addition, interest in measuring performance at the port industry level is expanding, with efforts to measure port and related supply chains' performance at the industry level developed by two different groups of actors. This reverses a past situation in which this interest was been relatively low compared to other infrastructure industries, like the airport industry where several independent industry performance management initiatives already exist. However, widely accepted measurements providing opportunities to benchmark against industry averages to individual companies, aggregated industry performance figures to industry stakeholders, and linked industry performance to macro-indicators of country performance remain absent in the global port industry, despite efforts referring to either port, or port authority, or operational terminal performance.

The first group of actors developing indexes measuring aspects of port performance at a global or regional scale includes intergovernmental **international organizations** such as the World Bank (Box 6.1), UNCTAD (Box 6.2), OECD (Box 6.3), and the European Commission (Box 6.4). These initiatives aim to empower decision-makers to better understand the missing links in improving the competitiveness of an industry of critical importance for trade prosperity by monitoring and comprehending trends occurring in ports worldwide or within broader constituencies.

---

### Box 6.1 The World Bank and port performance measurement

*The World Bank had already started to report on port indicators in the early 1990s, focusing also on operational issues as it proposed three broad categories of indicators: (1) asset performance indicators, (2) operational performance indicators, and (3) financial performance indicators. A 1993 report simply proposed the indicators but did not include any data on specific world ports.*

*In a 2016 report on the performance of container ports in South Asia (i.e. main ports in India, Sri Lanka, Pakistan, Maldives, and Bangladesh), the World Bank reported and compared data on **operational indicator**s such as average turnaround time, average pre-berthing waiting time and the average percentage of idle time at berth.*

*A well-known, more general indicator published by the World Bank is the **Logistics Performance Index (LPI)**. The World Bank also provides an online tool to show the evolution in the **quality of port infrastructure** in a country (1=extremely underdeveloped to 7=well developed and efficient by international standards) and compare this figure with other countries. The quality of port infrastructure is one factor (as part of transport infrastructure) in the **Global Competitiveness Index** developed by the World Economic Forum.*

*The World Bank is also very active in port governance and reform aspects and their related port performance dimension. The **Port Reform Toolkit** (now in its second version) is a well-known online set of documents aimed to provide policymakers and practitioners with effective decision-making support in undertaking sustainable and well-considered reforms of public institutions in developing countries. A 2017 **World Bank Viewpoint** on 'Achieving Full and Effective Corporatization of Port Authorities' also delivered detailed insight on port governance.*

*In recent years, the World Bank has published several reports on maritime networks, port efficiency and hinterland connectivity, such as the 2019 report on the Mediterranean. In cooperation with other organizations, the World Bank is also advancing the development of other port-related performance metrics related to environmental issues, digital transformation and port time. In 2021, the World Bank launched the Container Port Performance Index (CPPI), which was developed in co-operation with IHS Markit.*

---

### Box 6.2 UNCTAD and port performance measurement

*United Nations Conference on Trade and Development (UNCTAD) is a permanent intergovernmental body established by the United Nations General Assembly in 1964. Its headquarters are in Geneva (Switzerland). UNCTAD supports developing countries in accessing the benefits of a globalized economy more fairly and effectively by providing analysis, consensus-building, and technical assistance. Its focus is predominantly on trade, investment, finance, and technology as vehicles for inclusive and sustainable development. Nevertheless, national and international port systems constitute a privileged field of research and activity for this organization:*

- *In 1976, UNCTAD developed one of the first studies on port performance by providing 18 indicators divided into two broad categories: financial (seven indicators) and operational (11 indicators).*
- *UNCTAD has developed Port Management Monographs, gathering in-depth reports on national and international port systems addressed through various analytical perspectives. In some cases, the reports are focused at terminal level while in others they deal with the port as a whole.*
- *Published in 2016, the report 'Port Performance Linking Performance Indicators to Strategic Objectives' (Port Management Series, volume 4) defines a focus on management benchmarking across a cooperative network of ports and aims to build a port performance scorecard. The document contains country-level port performance measures, which are an average of many disparate port environments. The report attempts to select measures for port services at cargo mode level, which also provides a product mix profile for the port. A port performance scorecard is presented based on four strategic dimensions, i.e. finance, operations, human resources and market. This port-wise scorecard is analogous to the Kaplan and Norton balanced scorecard, a tool that is used to link strategy with performance. The UNCTAD report also addresses additional issues related to port authorities, such as finance and human resource management.*
- *Since 1968, UNCTAD has published 'Review of Maritime Transport' on an annual basis. This review provides an analysis of structural and cyclical changes affecting seaborne trade, and ports and shipping, as well as an exhaustive collection of statistical information. Several port performance indicators are reported in the annual reviews as well as on its website: port throughput, vessel calls, liner shipping connectivity, ship size indicators, container berth productivity and vessel turnaround times in ports.*

## Box 6.3  OECD and port performance measurement

*The Organisation for Economic Co-operation and Development (OECD) is an alliance of 36 member states. Most of them have an above-average economic level with a higher income. Several port-related research initiatives are worth mentioning, most of them published by the OECD research team at International Transport Forum (ITF):*

- *In 2013, OECD developed a meta-study of approximately 150 port impact studies worldwide to compare the **socio-economic impacts of ports** worldwide. While the OECD explicitly mentions that the methods used in these studies differ in many ways, they draw a number of high-level conclusions on the economic impacts of ports.*
- *Another source of more case-based information on port performance can be found in the **OECD Port-Cities Program**. This program aimed to identify how ports can be assets for urban development. The program primarily assessed the impact of ports on cities and regions. It also compared policies aimed at increasing positive regional impacts of ports and limiting negative effects. While the focus is mainly on the port–city interaction, the reports also contain case-based data on the aspects of the performance of the ports under consideration. The OECD has published a large number of case study reports as part of the port-cities program.*
- *The OECD has authored several other reports on the measurement of the socio-economic impact of seaports, the efficiency of world ports for containers and bulk cargo, port migration, the hinterland connectivity of ports, port automation and the impact of the Belt and Road Initiative (BRI).*
- *OECD has developed several discussion papers specifically dealing with the (container) shipping industry with some references to port performance, such as on the impact of mega-ships on ports and supply chains, the role of alliances in container shipping (as input for the evaluation of the EU Consortia Block Exemption), the Northern Sea Route (NSR), the decarbonization of shipping, and maritime subsidies.*

## Box 6.4  The European Commission and port performance measurement

*In addition to publishing port traffic data via its statistics office EUROSTAT, the European Commission (EC) funded two projects focused on the development of Europe-wide performance measures:*

- *The **PPRISM project** aimed to identify a set of sustainable, relevant and feasible port performance indicators to be implemented at EU level in order to measure and assess the impact of the European Port System on society, the environment and the economy. To this end, a typology of port performance indicators was created, validity and data availability was assessed and the indicators were proposed to key stakeholders for assessment in terms of their suitability to be implemented at EU level. The final result of PPRISM was a set of port performance indicators that provide an overview of the environmental, socio-economic and supply chain performance* *of the European Port System. The project was the first systematic attempt at EU level to determine a set of relevant port performance indicators that is widely accepted and commonly defined by the entire port sector and other relevant key stakeholders (such as port users, societal groups, etc.).*

- *The* **PORTOPIA project** *ended in November 2017. The project had two main objectives: (1) To support the European Port Industry with meaningful performance data to increase individual port and port transport system performance; and (2) To support policy formulation and monitor policy implementation. The PORTOPIA project resulted in the creation of an integrated knowledge base and management system of European port performance focusing on five categories of port performance indicators: (1) market trends and structure, (2) socio-economic performance, (3) environment and occupational health and safety and security, (4) logistic chain and operational efficiency and (5) governance and finance and user perceptions of quality. Inland ports were also covered in the project. The project also aimed at enhancing a culture of performance management in the European port sector.*

Among the most influential indicators developed by international organizations to compare countries across economic performance criteria and provide evidence of the **performance of ports**, either at port or country level, are:

- The **Global Competitiveness Index** (GCI) of the World Economic Forum. Seaports contribute to the country scores through the dimension of infrastructures and the adoption of information and communication technologies (Figure 6.1).
- The **Liner Shipping Connectivity Index** (LSCI) released by UNCTAD which incorporates many port-related characteristics related to the connectivity of port systems, such as the number of shipping lines offering services to the national port system and the largest ship sizes (Box 6.5).
- The **Logistics Performance Index** (LPI) released by the World Bank which included as a component the availability of efficient seaports.

The **Global Competitiveness Index (GCI) is** a composite index of four groups of indicators: enabling environment (institutions, infrastructure, ICT adoption, and macro-economic stability), human capital (health, skills), markets (product market, labor market, financial system, market size), and innovation ecosystem (business dynamism, innovation capability).

The Liner Shipping Connectivity Index (LSCI) aims at capturing the **level of integration into the existing liner shipping network** by measuring liner shipping connectivity. It can be calculated at the country and the port level. LSCI can be considered a proxy for accessibility to global trade through the shipping network. The higher the index, the easier it is to access a high capacity and frequency global maritime freight transport system and effectively participate in international trade. Therefore, LSCI can be jointly considered as a measure of connectivity to maritime shipping and as a measure of trade facilitation. It reflects the strategies of container shipping lines seeking to maximize revenue through market coverage.

The distribution of the port LSCI reveals a high concentration level among a small group of highly connected ports that are the gateways and hubs of global trade. In the early 2020s, the countries that have the highest LSCI values

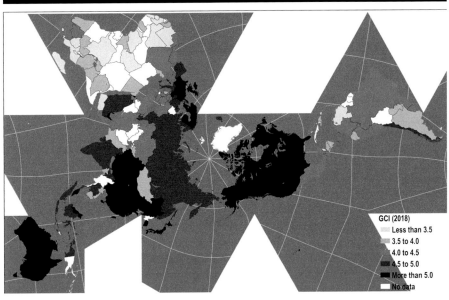

FIGURE 6.1 Global Competitiveness Index, 2018

are actively involved in international trade. Namely, the export-oriented economies of China and Hong Kong rank first, with the Singapore transshipment hub ranking third. Large traders such as the United Kingdom, Germany, South Korea, the United States, and Japan rank among the top 15. Countries such as Malaysia, Spain, the United Arab Emirates, Egypt, and Oman also rank high because of the major transshipment function their ports perform.

## Box 6.5 Country and port level Liner Shipping Connectivity Index

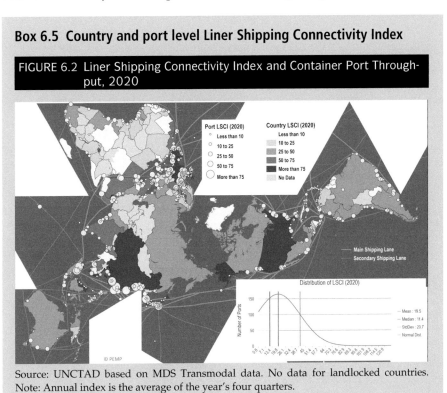

FIGURE 6.2 Liner Shipping Connectivity Index and Container Port Throughput, 2020

Source: UNCTAD based on MDS Transmodal data. No data for landlocked countries.
Note: Annual index is the average of the year's four quarters.

*The index is calculated based on six major components (Figure 6.2).*

*__Scheduled ship calls.__ This concerns the number of ships that are calling on a weekly basis. These calls can involve imports, exports, or transshipment activities. In the case of a high level of transshipment calls, the number of ship calls can be somewhat misleading as those calls are not related to connectivity to the global trade system but to the presence of a transshipment hub. Still, maritime services remain available for importers and exporters.*

*__Deployed capacity.__ The previous measure is mainly linked with the frequency of services, while adding the total capacity of these services enables a link between port calls and the related physical capacity. The higher the capacity, the greater the potential to trade on global markets. However, it does not necessarily mean that the capacity is available for imports or exports.*

*__Number of shipping companies and liner services.__ This relates to how many shipping companies are servicing the country or the port as well as how many scheduled services they are using to provide this coverage.*

*__Maximum container vessel size.__ A proxy to the available economies of scale since they convey lower shipping costs per TEU. A limited number of ports are able to accommodate ships in excess of 8,000–10,000 TEU – those who can have higher connectivity.*

*__Directly connected ports.__ This is the number of ports that are directly connected to the reference port. Due to the structure of maritime shipping services oriented along a sequence of port calls (loops), a direct connection implies that a port is connected to another as long as they are part of that loop and that any container carried between them does not need to be transshipped.*

*The country or port that received the highest score in the reference year of 2006 is assigned a value of 100, which serves as a benchmark to assign value to other ports and countries.*

The **Logistics Performance Index** (LPI) is released by the World Bank. In it, the availability of efficient seaports supports a higher score. In November 2007, the World Bank published its first report, which ranked 150 nations according to their logistics performance based on a metric labeled the Logistics Performance Index (Figure 6.3). The LPI is a composite of a country's rating across seven criteria: customs clearance, logistics infrastructure, ease of international shipments, logistics competence/internal skillsets and service providers, tracking and tracing capabilities, domestic logistics costs, and timeliness/consistency. Countries that are able to connect to the global logistics network have access to vast new markets.

The second group of actors developing industry-level performance measurement initiatives are **regional or global associations** representing ports and port authorities, such as:

- In the Americas, the **American Association of Port Authorities (AAPA)** which has implemented a Customer Service Initiative for East Coast U.S. ports to measure user perceptions of service quality. In addition, AAPA has managed to collect traffic data on American ports. These datasets on trade and traffic flows are made freely available via its website. AAPA also reports on the economic importance of ports to the U.S. economy.

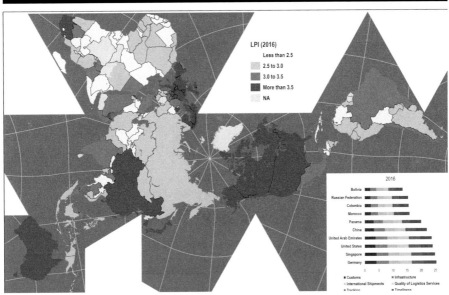

FIGURE 6.3 Logistic Performance Index, 2016

- In Europe, the **European Sea Ports Organisation (ESPO)** has mainly focused on the environmental performance of European ports via the ECOPORTS initiative. ESPO has also been involved in the successive European projects PPRISM and PORTOPIA, exploring how to detail the different dimensions of port performance and the best ways that the related measurements might develop within a balanced, integrated, and objective approach. **National or sub-regional port associations** and committees also collect port performance data. Examples include Puertos del Estado (Spain), Assoporti (Italy), the Baltic Ports Organisation (BPO), Danske Havne (Denmark), and the Finnish Ports Association.
- In Asia, the **Indian Ports Association (IPA)**, which fosters growth and development of all major ports which are under the supervisory control of the Ministry of Shipping, publishes performance metrics on cargo and vessel traffic and port equipment. The **ASEAN Ports Association (APA)** was founded in 1975, with the port performance statistics mainly reported via national websites such as APA Malaysia.

These examples are indicative of the collective interest of ports in increasing the knowledge and awareness of port industry performance and developing a shared vision towards this end.

At the global scale, the International Association of Ports & Harbors (IAPH) is also advancing similar initiatives in the context of its World Ports Sustainability Program that has been in progress since 2017 and was developed with the strategic partnership of other associations. Among these initiatives is the port economic impact barometer that surveys and reports trends in world ports (i.e. vessel calls, hinterland connections, utilization of capacity, availability of workers, investments) and the development of a global port tracker.

# Chapter 6.2 Port efficiency

*Port efficiency is a multi-dimensional concept that refers to operational performance, particularly the maximization of the produced output or the production of a given output with limited possible resources. It has expanded to include additional dimensions of port performance.*

## 1 DIMENSIONS OF PORT EFFICIENCY

Port efficiency is one of the three components of port performance, the other two being effectiveness and resilience.

*Efficiency commonly refers to the operational performance of ports and the maximization of the produced output with given resources or the production of a given output with limited possible resources.*

Operational performance measurements focus on productivity and relate to the physical quantities of items, the levels of effort expended, the scale or scope of activities, and efficiency in transforming resources into some product (or service). Indicators traditionally used to measure **terminal operations efficiency** (productivity) include berth occupancy, revenue per ton of cargo, capital equipment expenditure per ton of cargo, turnaround time, and the number of gangs employed to facilitate cargo operations. Such efficiency measurements span a **performance continuum** from maritime operations to terminal and hinterland operations. This performance is too important to be measured at the terminal level since the facilitation of cargo arriving, staying, and leaving the terminal through various bundled services stands as a vital function in integrated transportation chains. Efficiency performance is measured at the port level as well. On the one hand, the performance of different terminals might diverge. On the other hand, it is not uncommon for users to select first the port they will use and, in the next phase, the terminal.

This list of indicators used to measure port and port terminal efficiency is expanding, with port performance becoming multidimensional (Figure 6.4). Measurements of performance for efficiency-focused ports and terminals also

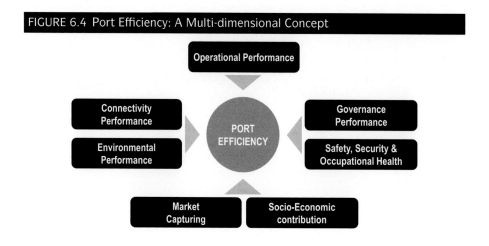

FIGURE 6.4 Port Efficiency: A Multi-dimensional Concept

benchmark financial, system-wide, and production and marketing activities against prior year performance and against competitors' performance to deliver efficiency objectives. Measurements of the **financial performance** of port entities (terminal operators and many port managing bodies) and the **performance of the governance model** in place are essential and present in all ports. The list expands further, given the significance of integrating ports into supply chains and facing environmental sustainability challenges. The **connectivity performance** (in terms of capacity, costs, congestion) and the **environmental performance** of ports are also parts of a comprehensive port performance measurement, as are safety, security, and occupational health performance. Additionally, two dimensions reflecting the very essence of port presence include the performance of the port as regards **market capturing** and its **socio-economic contribution**.

## 2 OPERATIONAL EFFICIENCY

### 2.1 The port efficiency continuum

The efficiency of a port is part of a continuum that includes maritime, terminal, and hinterland operations (Figure 6.5). These dimensions are interrelated since inefficiencies in one dimension are likely to impact the others. For instance, issues in terminal operations are most likely to negatively impact maritime and hinterland operations with delays.

- **Maritime operations**. What happens at the port foreland can impact its performance, mainly because of ship delays. The efficiency of maritime access is a component of port performance, which includes average anchorage time (M1), where ships are waiting for an available berthing slot. Long waiting times at anchorage can be the outcome of a lack of berthing slots able to accommodate specific ship classes (e.g. draft and cargo type) as well as terminal productivity issues. Depending on their site and configuration, ports can have complex in-port navigation requiring pilotage and tugs through access channels and turn basins. The

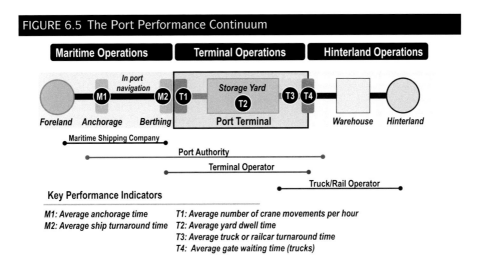

**FIGURE 6.5** The Port Performance Continuum

**Key Performance Indicators**

M1: Average anchorage time
M2: Average ship turnaround time

T1: Average number of crane movements per hour
T2: Average yard dwell time
T3: Average truck or railcar turnaround time
T4: Average gate waiting time (trucks)

average ship turnaround time (or ship dwell time; M2) represents the time it takes to service the ship once it has docked. Enhancing such a system is clearly to the benefit of maritime shipping companies.

- **Terminal operations**. Represent the most common performance indicator to assess port efficiency. For container terminal operations, this commonly involves several key operations. Crane performance (T1) is a common bottleneck in terms of the average number of crane movements per hour. For maritime shipping companies, this is a crucial factor since it is related to the amount of time their ships will spend at the port. How cargo (in containers) is brought back and forth to the storage yard is also a component of port performance and often related to the number of movements per crane hour. Many container terminals use holsters or straddle carriers for such operations. Container storage yard operations involve stacking and related stacking density, an important variable determining terminal capacity. The average yard dwell time (T2) for inbound, outbound, and transshipment cargo is also a common indicator. When trucks enter the terminal to pick up or drop off cargo, space and equipment are required. This is often a critical bottleneck for trucking companies since it dictates the amount of time they will spend at the terminal, reflected in the average truck turnaround time (T3). Gate performance concerns the efficiency of tasks related to document processing and security inspections. A truck is admitted and cleared to pick up or drop cargo at the facility. Gates used above their capacity are characterized by long lines of truck waiting to be processed and enter the terminal for the cargo they are already chartered to handle. Therefore, the average gate waiting time (T4) can be used as a performance indicator. For terminals having on-dock rail facilities, the performance of the rail loading/unloading equipment can also be an important component of the terminal's performance.
- **Hinterland operations**. The efficiency of transport operations beyond the terminal is usually not considered a port performance indicator. It involves all the transport and distribution activities servicing the port's customers, such as an inland port. However, for practical purposes, it generally focuses on inland operations adjacent to the port area (often labeled as the back of port). The key factor in hinterland operations is the capacity of the local road network in areas adjacent to the port. Congestion and bottlenecks at street intersections impair the port's performance in many of the supply chain management strategies of the port's customers. Some ports have near-dock rail yards that must be serviced through the terminals' gates. In many gateway ports, transloading activities that transfer the contents of maritime containers into domestic truckloads (or domestic containers), or vice-versa, are an element of the performance of hinterland operations. Port authorities have an oversight, either directly or indirectly, of port efficiency.

While terminal operations are usually concessioned to private operators, port authorities tend to have direct oversight of maritime operations and several elements of hinterland operations, such as local roads directly connected to the port terminals, some of which are on land owned by the port. Although cities are not directly involved in port operations and commonly have limited, if any, jurisdiction on port land, they commonly provide and maintain crucial road infrastructure connecting the port with its hinterland. They also bear many of the externalities of port operations, namely local congestion. Therefore, the port authority and the city are important stakeholders in the port performance continuum.

## 2.2 Container terminal efficiency

Ports measure performance to monitor their activities, check their efficiency, compare present with past performance, and compare current with targeted performance. Based on the outcome of these exercises they adopt any necessary alignments to structures and strategies (and/or targets) to improve performance. The performance measurement output can also be used to promote the business of the port.

The questions that each port managing entity and terminal operator has to answer are **what to measure**, **how to measure**, and **how to use** this measurement. In general, the list of indicators that ports and terminal operators use to measure their performance includes (a) **production measures**, (b) **productivity measures**, (c) **utilization measures**, and (d) **services measures**. Production measurements differentiate between **traffic measures** where quantity is the temporal unit of reference and **throughput measures** where movements are the reference unit (Figure 6.6).

Regarding the ship/port interface, the (un)loading of each container generates a throughput that exceeds the absolute number of the containers that are unloaded or loaded on the vessel. Several additional **container movements** occur once the container arrives at the terminal so that each traffic container might generate one to three additional movements. At the quay transfer, what is counted includes movements to stack inbound and outbound local containers at the yard, discharged transshipment containers, loaded containers, and shifts and restows via the container yard. Beyond the throughput (un) loaded at the port from/to vessels, quay throughput, and yard movements, the terminal-related performance also includes indicators related to the port gate throughput, such as the number of vehicles reaching the port collecting full and empty containers. Terminal performance improves with the presence of vessels that both deliver and collect containers. Throughput imbalances usually negatively impact terminal performance.

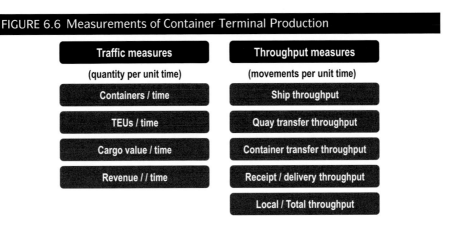

FIGURE 6.6 Measurements of Container Terminal Production

| Traffic measures | Throughput measures |
|---|---|
| (quantity per unit time) | (movements per unit time) |
| Containers / time | Ship throughput |
| TEUs / time | Quay transfer throughput |
| Cargo value / time | Container transfer throughput |
| Revenue / / time | Receipt / delivery throughput |
| | Local / Total throughput |

## 2.3 Performance and the upscale of port operations

The increase in vessel size has changed the scale of port operations across the world. Scale enlargement in vessel size is taking place in different shipping markets, redefining port as well as terminal performance requirements. The most illustrative examples are the cases of container and cruise vessels.

In the container world, **consecutive rounds of container scale increases** led to the introduction of ships of 24,000 TEU. This has resulted in an overall upscaling across the main East–West trade routes, with large vessels cascading to North–South routes. The largest container vessels operate on the Far East–Europe routes, calling in ports in the Gulf and the Indian Sub-Continent (ISC). The biggest vessels might not call in sub-Saharan African, Latin America, or Oceania, yet, since 2010, the size of the maximum container vessel calling has doubled in all regions of the world. The implications are not uniform given the variation in the scale of container operations in world ports. Based on vessel size, three distinctive groups of container ports exist. Larger vessels (18,000–24,000 TEU) call at selected major hubs offering transshipment services. The second group of world ports hosts the New Panamax standard (12,500 TEU), and a third one hosts vessels around Panamax size (4,500 TEU).

The increase in the size of vessels calling at a port is accompanied by a lower number of calls for transporting the same amount of cargo. The trend accelerates further with the reorganization of liner shipping in alliances that allow cargo sharing agreements, in turn enabling the scheduling of fully loaded container vessels sailing fewer voyages. In retrospect, ports and their terminals need to increase their productivity by redefining operations.

## 3 MARKET CAPTURE

The levels of market capture are fundamental port performance indicators. With the monitoring of trends per market and structure having a high practical relevance, many such indicators are already used by the industry. The estimation of market capture levels relates to (Figure 6.7):

- **Maritime traffic.** Throughput levels per type of cargo served by the ports and passenger movements served in a given period (year/quarter/ month).

---

**FIGURE 6.7** Market Capture Performance Indicators

| **Maritime Traffic** (per market) | **Vessel Calls/Size** (per type of vessel) | **Additional Indicators** |
|---|---|---|
| • Total tonnage (metric tons)<br>• Total general cargo (tons)<br>• Total liquid bulk (tons)<br>• Total dry bulk (tons)<br>• Containers (TEU)<br>• Imports / Exports (per type of cargo)<br>• Transhipment/Transit/Local/Empties/ Types (containers)<br>• Passenger (coastal shipping) (number)<br>• Cruise Passengers (number)<br>• Transit/Homeporting cruise passengers | • Container ships<br>• Breakbulk ships<br>• Dry Bulk ships<br>• Tankers and other liquid bulk carriers<br>• LNG carriers<br>• LPG carriers<br>• Passenger ship (coastal shipping)<br>• Cruise ships | • Market share in port region<br>• Modal split of cargo moving in/out<br>• Utilization of the warehousing and Distribution capacities of the port<br>• The cargo served (TEU and/or tons) per hectare,<br>• GPD growth vs tons per type of cargo |

- **Vessel traffic.** Number of different types of seagoing vessels (cargo and passengers) reaching the port in a given time period.
- **Call size.** The average and maximum size of the seagoing vessel calling at the port. This indicator is a combination of the two previous indicators.

There are some common standards in maritime traffic measurements. Container traffic is reported in TEU (20-feet-equivalent units), or the number of containers handled. The most useful of these reports are those detailing these numbers per container category, such as loaded/empties, local/transit/transshipment, dangerous goods, and reefers). Reports of container traffic in tons are occasional, though this indicator is of limited relevance beyond the statistical records. Throughput in the categories liquid bulk, dry bulk, conventional general cargo, and Ro/Ro is reported in tons. Still, there are cases where different definitions exist in the measurement of throughput. Port authorities (or terminal operators) **do not necessarily use the same individual traffic categories or measurement units**. Some ports use net tonnage (net weight of the cargo), others use gross tonnage (the net weight plus first packaging), others gross plus tonnage (gross tonnage plus tar weight of the load unit). Differences also exist among ports when assigning cargo volumes on trailers to either RoRo or conventional general cargo. Some ports add the RoRo based container traffic to the container throughput, while other ports only count LoLo (lift-on/lift-off) operations when drawing up their container statistics.

Some additional performance indicators apply for each shipping market:

- The separate monitoring of the **trends of imported and exported cargoes** is relevant as they represent a clear indication of the capacity of the port to facilitate specific supply chains.
- In containerized trade, ports measure different types of boxes, with the other categories including **sea–sea transshipment, import/export cargoes, and local cargoes**, as well as the number of empty containers and dangerous goods. They also measure the number of containers moved per size (20 feet or 40 feet container) and container type (e.g. standard, reefer).
- In the cruise passenger market, ports monitor the number of **transit passenger movements** (passengers embarking/disembarking for a few hours) and **homeport passengers** (passengers commencing and concluding their cruise at the port).

Vessel traffic refers to monitoring more than the aggregate number of vessel calls or the type of cargo vessels calling at the port. The average and maximum **size of ships calling at the port** also need to be monitored. Whenever possible, compared with trends in those ports considered as competitors, they represent indicators of the capacity that a port has demonstrated to host particular types of vessels.

Additional performance indicators related to market capture are being monitored. They incentivize ports to further analyze throughput in the light of their capacity and thus reach a comprehensive understanding of the potential in capturing further calls and throughput.

## 4 CONNECTIVITY PERFORMANCE

The connectivity performance of a port relates to its capacity to **integrate within maritime supply chains** and the operational function of a port as a **node in transport networks**. This dimension of port performance requires the development of a list of different types of indicators, aiming to measure the performance of the port, and its various activities, within a supply chain perspective:

- **Maritime connectivity**. The connectivity of a port with container services (liner shipping) and other regular services (i.e. Ro/Ro connectivity) to third destinations. Relevant indicators include the frequency of services, the number of operators, the deployed capacity, and the number of ports/countries that maintain direct links with the port.
- **Intermodal connectivity**. The connectivity of a port with intermodal container transport services to and from hinterland destinations. These indicators might be split into sub-indicators referring to how well a port is connected with different transport modes (rail; road; barges). Relevant indicators include the frequency of services per transport mode, truck turnaround time (i.e. in minutes), and the number of rail/truck/warehousing companies linked with the port.
- **On-time performance** (sea-going vessels).
- **On-time performance** (road, rail, inland waterways).
- **Mean-time customs clearance**.
- Availability of **port community systems**.

## 5 ENVIRONMENTAL PERFORMANCE

The environmental performance of any port is a crucial dimension of its overall performance. The expansion of port activities and the increase of the environmental externalities contribute to this trend. Market enlargement results in a greater socio-economic importance of the environmental performance of ports, the greater sensitivity of public opinion, and the development of related legislation aiming to advance and make mandatory, in certain respects, mitigation of environmental externalities produced by port activities. For ports, environmental sustainability has become a **factor of competitiveness**.

There are many drivers for port investments in environmental performance. At the top of the list is **regulatory compliance**. Motives leading a port entity to improve its environmental performance include the response to societal pressures, the resulting direct economic benefits, corporate conscience at either the development and planning stage, improving operations, and gaining competitive advantage. Most likely, each port has its own motivations depending on the executive management philosophy and its local sociopolitical context.

The priorities ports assign to individual environmental issues change with time and as conditions evolve. In the European context, port authorities have developed a periodically revised hierarchy of the top ten environmental priorities, aiming to produce benchmarking regarding key areas of port environmental performance. In 2020, air quality was the top environmental priority, followed by climate change, which first reached the top-10 list of European ports' environmental priorities in 2016. Energy efficiency is the third priority for ports. These priorities have shifted with **climate change emerging as the epicenter**. It was the tenth environmental priority in 2017 and became the second priority for ports in 2020.

There is an apparent increase in the number of ports facing operational challenges due to climate change. Thus they are interested in monitoring these trends to strengthen the resilience of their existing infrastructure to adapt to climate change and take it into consideration when planning the development of their future infrastructure projects.

The culture and practice of identifying, monitoring, and reporting environmental performance indicators are reasonably widely established. Several parameters have been added to the ever-present considerations of the environmental impact assessments for port development projects, such as dredged material management, occupation of natural areas, port enlargement in reclaimed land from the sea. The environmental performance of ports and their expanding activities relates to several parameters. The most substantial include carbon footprint, waste reception and handling, water treatment, and the environmental management practices endorsed by the managing entities of the port or any service providers that are involved.

The necessity for measuring these parameters is commonly accepted by a wide range of ports and maritime organizations. Most of the largest ports have an environmental policy in place and an inventory of significant environmental aspects. Monitoring becomes a managerial issue, such as in managing contaminated soils, water quality, air quality, sediment quality, identifying the source of pollution, and following global standards.

Measuring its environmental performance is one of the most complex exercises a port can undertake. Quantitative and qualitative data are required, with some collected through costly surveys, and with standardization of the indicators still under development. For instance, the 2020 environmental report of ESPO included more than 60 different benchmark indicators used by European ports. Besides, each port has its characteristics, so they use individual exercises corresponding to their structures and challenges.

Although harmonizing tools, methodologies, and techniques remains a challenge, the standardization of environmental practices and performance monitoring is becoming common practice. In Europe, port authorities have developed a self-diagnosis method that acts as a good practice checklist. This port environmental review system provides an international quality standard of environmental management specifically dedicated to ports. In this context, environmental performance indicators are split into two categories (Figure 6.8).

**Environmental management** is an additional dimension of measuring port performance. Environmental performance measurement is closely related to the proper reporting practice. The link is so crucial that it might be argued that environmental management is an integral part of the measurement of environment-related performance. The publicly available environment reports and the communication of environment policy to stakeholders are tools for involving stakeholders in monitoring trends in environmental performance and developing initiatives towards future improvements. For instance, this communication can involve a defined procedure for consulting with the local community on the port's environmental program.

FIGURE 6.8 Environmental Performance Indicators

| Environmental Performance Indicators | Environmental Management Indicators |
|---|---|
| Greenhouse Gas Emissions (NOx, SOx, PM10, VOCs CO$_2$) | Existence of an environmental policy |
| Carbon footprint | Existence of certified Environmental Management System (EMS) |
| Energy efficiency | Inventory of relevant environmental legislation |
| Soil quality | Inventory of significant environmental aspect |
| Water quality | Objectives & targets for environmental improvement |
| Total water consumption | Environmental training program for port employees |
| Amount of garbage/Port waste | Environmental Monitoring Program (EMP) |
| Oxygenation conditions | Documented environmental responsibilities of key personnel |
| Terrestrial habitats | Publicly available Environmental Report |
| Sediment quality | |

An additional group of port performance indicators worth mentioning is **occupational health, safety, and security indicators** (Figure 6.9). While, for occupational health, there is a wider acceptance of its use, the same does not apply for safety and security. These metrics are increasingly implemented by ports, not least because current international standards and conventions adopted by international legislation (e.g. the International Maritime Organisation SOLAS Convention) underline the need to evaluate the performance of ports in these areas as well.

FIGURE 6.9 Safety, Security, and Occupational Health Performance Indicators

| Safety | Security | Occupational Health |
|---|---|---|
| Marine incidents | Security offences | Fatalities |
| Berth incidents | Damage caused by security offences | Major injury |
| Landside incidents | Incidents in security restricted areas | Lost workdays |
| Damaged caused by incidents | Application of advanced security levels in port facilities | Medical treatment injury |
| Pollution incidents | Direct Gross added value per FTE | Occupational illnesses |

## 6 FINANCIAL PERFORMANCE

The financial performance of a port stands as an additional type of performance that is regularly monitored. Its evaluation can offer insights into the bottom-line financial impact of the strategies endorsed by the managing body and by the managerial and operational priorities that have been set. Financial performance indicators contribute to assessing whether the implementation of the specific choices has been successful or if corrective initiatives should come into play.

Focusing on financial aspects and criteria to assess port performance may not be sufficient to reveal the present or future success of port strategies. Port performance depends on a broad spectrum of factors. Yet the financial evaluation of port performance has its own merits for many reasons. **Financial appraisal** directly reflects quantitative and qualitative managerial decisions and policy implications, with such decisions also reflected in the financial results. **Financial profitability** plays a central role in evaluating managerial efficiency as well as successful asset and capital utilization. Then, port financial performance is a critical issue for stakeholders and market participants since it reflects growth prospects and economic robustness. Moreover, port management is judged on the grounds of corporate value maximization rather than simple profit attainment. Especially in the case of port managing entities listed on stock markets, robust financial performance is expected to result in an enhanced firm market value with positive implications for shareholders' wealth.

It might be argued that efficient operations do not necessarily translate to a profitable financial outcome. Financial assessment is better regarded as part of a balanced scorecard approach, considering financial and non-financial performance dimensions. The latter include efficient operating procedures and user satisfaction, internal business processes, learning, and growth perspectives. By including the interests of management, customers (port users), employees, and equity owners simultaneously, such an approach allows comprehensive evaluation of port performance. Port financial performance criteria are still among the most considered part of port performance for managers and investors.

The financial accounts of ports provide the data for a **standardized financial evaluation** (Figure 6.10). The selected summary of key financial ratios might be compared and contrasted to a benchmark level that has been set beforehand. Although arbitrary, such a benchmark ratio level is commonly chosen based on standard empirical practice, related to cumulative conventional corporate wisdom for (conservative) empirical valuation of the firm's financial decisions.

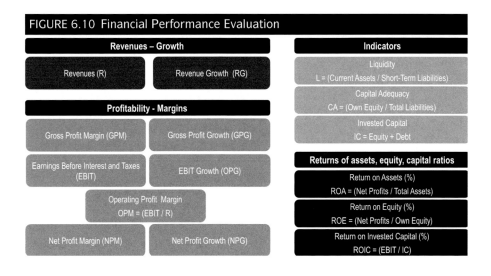

FIGURE 6.10 Financial Performance Evaluation

Focusing strictly on profit maximization policies alone may lead to a partial analysis. Comparing net profits against operating profits, in some cases, net profits might appear to be higher than operating profits. This outcome is mainly associated with the realization of extraordinary one-off earnings that result in a slight improvement in bottom-line results. Improved port profitability arising from irregular factors might lead to skepticism about the robustness of ports' long-term growth potential. For example, port profitability might be due to a lack of investments. **Economic cycles** experienced in the shipping industry affect the port business as well. As a result, profit margins might be constrained, leading to considerable earnings volatility. For these reasons, it is not worth monitoring the financial indicators of any given port alone. Instead the focus should be on the trends observed in ports in the region and beyond.

Financial results are also worth examining in the light of the operating growth rates of each market the port serves. Containers, bulk cargoes, car terminals, cruise, and coastal shipping are all markets with different dynamics and diverse revenue and profitability margins.

In any case, the financial performance of the port is evaluated based on the **priorities that the port managing entity has set**, with these priorities spanning profit generation through to throughput maximization and value creation for the local economy. To extract the greatest financial return, profit-oriented companies focus on measures of asset utilization. The purpose of improved operations is to expand the gross margin extracted. Measurements of performance for profit-focused ports tend to benchmark financial, system-wide, and production and marketing activities against prior year performance and against competitor performance to deliver efficiency objectives. When priority is given to maximizing throughput or adding value, profit generation might be of secondary importance. Balanced or deficit financial accounts are considered a healthy situation as long as they are accompanied by port users' satisfaction and value generation for stakeholders.

## 7 PORT GOVERNANCE PERFORMANCE

Governance performance measurement is a comparatively novel exercise, emerging as more critical following the progress and diversity of port governance reforms. This comparatively novel performance measurement allows a better understanding of the decisions undertaken by those responsible for port management. It contributes towards the better management of a given port. A less sophisticated exercise in terms of data complexity largely depends on realization of its importance by the managing port entity and the setting of priorities regarding which parameters of governance should be prioritized. Dimensions of governance performance that are worth measuring include (Figure 6.11):

- **Serving port governance targets**. The extent that the governance model in place is advancing the main target(s) set by port.
- **Port cluster integration**. The advancement of the expansion and the integration of the port cluster.
- **Port governance transparency**. The levels of reporting verifiable information about the operations in ways that enable stakeholders, including the public sector, to gain knowledge and be involved in the decision-making process.

**FIGURE 6.11** Port Governance Performance Indicators in Port Cluster Integration and Autonomous Management

**Port Cluster Integration**
- PA involved (leader/participant) in solving maritime access operational/service bottlenecks
- PA involved (leader/participant) in solving land access operational/service bottlenecks
- PA involved (leader/participant) in solving terminal operational / service bottlenecks
- PA involved (leader/participant) in solving administrative bottlenecks
- PA operates an Information & Communication Technology (ICT) system for the benefit of the port community
- PA leads the promotion and marketing actions of the port on behalf of the port community
- PA provides training/education for the port community
- PA port community members with the implementation of regulations (safety, security, environment, etc.
- PA is leader in various societal integration initiatives

**Autonomous Management**
- The PA has its own legal status
- The PA is directed by a daily management body (e.g. management board or management committee)
- The PA develops a port masterplan
- The PA is able to contract port land to third parties (e.g. terminal operators) in order to permit these parties to provide port services
- The PA is responsible to set the rules of agreements with third parties
- The PA issues safety regulations in addition to (obligatory) national/international regulations
- The PA issues security regulations in addition to (obligatory) national/international regulations

- **Autonomous management.** The extent that the port managing body maintains and improves its capacity to act autonomously in developing and implementing its strategies.

In all cases, the selected performance measurement indicators need to be realistic and workable, providing meaningful information to the port authority or any other entity that is involved in the management of the port, as well as to all the related stakeholders.

**Transparency** refers to port governing entities making visible meaningful information, enabling stakeholders to gain access to the operations and structures of a given port. The devolution of port management to more autonomous, frequently corporatized, ports and related entities aims to reach the reform goals through increased transparency. Transparency in port governance is an expectation associated with accountability, responsibility, trust, inclusivity, legitimacy, justification, good governance, and socially responsible outcomes. It is also linked with improved performance as it enables comparison of a port's stated goals with its actual performance and supports the enhancement of performance by comparing results with those of other ports in the same market.

With ports being multifaceted entities, transparency is a multidimensional concept associated with information flows, formal disclosure policies, publication approaches, discussions and meetings with stakeholders, the related governmental departments, and the general public. Transparency applies to the various stages of a decision-making process from the **conceptualization** to the **initiation of port development**, **operation and management strategies**, the **planning details** of the decided actions (i.e. business plans, master plans, port works, environmental impact assessments, and governance resolutions), and then during the **implementation phase**, and the **evaluation of the produced outcomes** that could result in a restart of port reform. The levels of transparency at each of these stages define the involvement and contribution of service providers, users, and stakeholders, determining the effectiveness of the decisions taken.

Four different dimensions need to be considered to realize whether the existing levels of transparency facilitate improvements in the governance, and ultimately the performance, of a given port (Figure 6.12):

- First is the **visibility** of information, such as the degree to which information is released and can be found with relative ease. A characteristic of transparency is the degree of completeness of the information. For instance, a summarized unaudited financial report makes the financial results of a port visible. However, it does not reveal a complete picture, and without the auditor's opinion, it may not be considered verifiable.
- An additional dimension of transparency is **inferability**, which refers to the quality of the disclosed information and data and the extent to which information can be used to draw accurate conclusions.
- The third dimension is **verifiability**. With transparency being a matter of information disclosure, the quality and quantity of information permit one to observe organizational action fully and provide a means of solving organizational and societal problems by improving the effectiveness and quality of transparency efforts. Not all information that is visible is verifiable or even intelligible.
- The fourth dimension is **performativity**. This is the extent that transparency enactment (i.e. acts of making things visible) stands as a process with (un)intended dynamics that induce action, such as agreements, conflicts, tensions, and negotiations, leading to the improvement of management in organizational settings.

Decision-making transparency differs depending on whether the model is a private, corporatized, or public port. The governance model must **balance the diverse expectations** of several stakeholders. The challenge in hybrid models (those featuring selected elements of public and private models), is that the reporting structure may not be clear, as the role of shareholder (private) or taxpayer (public) may not be adequately articulated in the governing legislation, regulations, or by-laws. Consequently, transparency in ports varies across regions and governance models and requires more than publication and disclosure of information.

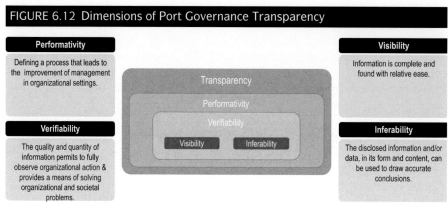

FIGURE 6.12 Dimensions of Port Governance Transparency

Source: Adapted from Brooks, Knatz, Pallis and Wilmsmeier (2020).

The transparency level of a port authority is frequently imposed by national legislation and regulatory mechanisms, which are subject to the cultural dynamics of the political economy within which they are embedded. Publicly accountable organizations have to be available for the general public to assess the rationale behind certain decisions and allow stakeholders to participate in the oversight process, making the board of directors and management accountable for outcomes. The information has to be timely, available, and understandable, and has to be an accurate representation of what the organization is accountable for.

## 8  SOCIO-ECONOMIC PERFORMANCE

Indicators such as direct employment and direct gross added value provide some evidence of the **socio-economic contribution** of a port or a port system (Figure 6.13). Other indicators revealing the socio-economics impact of a port include indirect employment, indirect gross added value, and fiscal revenue generated by the port.

Monitoring the socio-economics performance of a port allows the involved authorities to improve planning, financing, and funding of port infrastructure. Employment, added value, and private investments in ports are economic impact indicators resulting from (public) investments in ports infrastructure. If this (public) investment is made efficiently and effectively, the outcome is optimized allocation of resources, resulting in better socio-economic performance. Socio-economic indicators can be used for evaluating the mechanisms and principles underlying relevant decisions.

While these are significant dimensions of port performance, their measurement is commonly part of **ad hoc exercises** which are occasionally part of port-initiated projects. This is partly because socio-economic indicators are strongly linked to data availability that remains mainly outside the strategic control of the port authority or a port operator. There is no real pressure to measure the socio-economic impact of port operations from stakeholders who are more focused on other dimensions of port performance. The dependence of these indicators on resources for compiling or measuring data (either extensive annual surveys or annual account databases) and quality and consistency control of input data should not be underestimated.

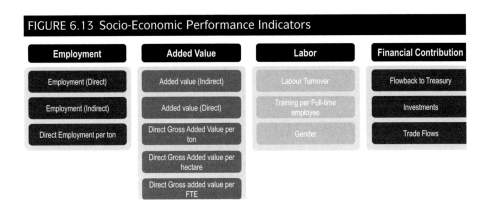

FIGURE 6.13 Socio-Economic Performance Indicators

| Employment | Added Value | Labor | Financial Contribution |
|---|---|---|---|
| Employment (Direct) | Added value (Indirect) | Labour Turnover | Flowback to Treasury |
| Employment (Indirect) | Added value (Direct) | Training per Full-time employee | Investments |
| Direct Employment per ton | Direct Gross Added Value per ton | Gender | Trade Flows |
| | Direct Gross Added value per hectare | | |
| | Direct Gross added value per FTE | | |

# Chapter 6.3 Port effectiveness

*Port effectiveness refers to the performance of a port in fulfilling expectations and delivering the desired services to its users.*

## 1 EFFECTIVENESS COMPONENT OF PORT PERFORMANCE

Port competitiveness is related to **effectiveness in delivering the desired services to users** (Figure 6.14). Desired services are those that are important to the customer, who remain the users of the port. If a negative and significant gap exists between the importance of desired services and their performance, dissatisfaction is the by-product.

Effectiveness and efficiency are two **interdependent components** of port performance. Improving technical efficiency is only a partial solution. A terminal operator wishing to improve its cargo-handling efficiency could enhance berth utilization through faster vessel turnaround. In that case, it may also improve its effectiveness as vessel time at berth drops and customers may be more satisfied. However, a terminal operator may improve its asset utilization by leaving more vessels at anchor so as to minimize downtime. In that case, its utilization is improved but customer service expectations may not have been met, as more cargoes might be stored for more extended periods, increasing congestion at the yard. In this case, efficiency has come at the expense of effectiveness as different stakeholders may have **different performance objectives**.

Efficiency measures alone do not provide a full indication of how well a port manages its assets or serves its customers, such as providing reduced container dwell times or faster vessel turnaround. Even when efficiency indicators are positive from a port perspective, complaints from port users may still arise since they are not reflected in the efficiency indicators used. Effectiveness measures relate to how well the firm or agency uses its strategies, structures, and tasks to meet its mission and stated goals. For an effectiveness-oriented port authority, if one of the goals is profit-maximizing, there will be

**FIGURE 6.14 • Parameters Shaping the Perspectives of Port Users**

**Quality of port infrastructure**
1. Number of berths
2. Total length
3. Operational depth

**Availability of services**
1. Port services to vessels
2. Port services to containers
3. Port services to land transport modes

**Responsiveness**
1. Response to user requests
2. Response to innovativeness
3. Response to regulation changes

**Quality of port superstructure**
1. Total area for cargo storage
2. Number of positions for specialized cargoes

**Connectivity - Landside**
1. Rail / Road connections
2. Number of destinations via rail service

**Provision of adequate information**
1. On-time information
2. Online information
3. Accuracy of information

**Accessibility**
1. Port operating hours
2. Variety of transport means accessing the port
3. Customs operating hours

**Connectivity - Seaside**
1. Deep-sea container services
2. Feeder container services
3. Barge connections

**Costs**
1. Container handling cost
2. Ship-related port costs
3. Cost of ship-related auxiliary services
4. Warehousing cost

**Availability of machinery equipment**
1. Number of operational Gantry Cranes
2. Number of operational Stacking equipment

**Efficiency of operations**
1. On-time departure / arrival
2. Efficiency of auxiliary ship services
3. Efficiency of (un)loading
4. Efficiency of land transport modes

**Efficiency of documentary process**
1. Efficiency of container clearness procedures
2. Transparency of port charges

a companion goal of developing and retaining customers who **generate the greatest margins** while not servicing those that are not profitable. There is no interest within the effectiveness-oriented port authority in serving unprofitable customers unless it is part of its government-imposed mandate. In this case, the port authority will seek a subsidy to offset its losses. However, by meeting the expectations of customers, employees, and stakeholders, profitability will accrue to solutions-driven, customer-focused organizations.

The **perception of stakeholders** is increasingly vital for correcting both operational and governance flaws that a port may experience. Measuring user perspectives helps managers understand current issues and eventually address them to improve experiences with the port. Insights into what is most important to port users provide managers with a two-pronged tool:

- It assists ports in **setting priorities**, such as pointing out areas needing the greatest investment for improvement (against those where investments are less effective).
- It identifies those areas where a port **already delivers value**, and from which it could benefit from marketing initiatives to raise awareness.

For supply chains, effectiveness is related to the objectives of all the involved stakeholders, creating heterogeneous expectations. Port user groups might rate port effectiveness in service delivery differently. A port rated highly by the shipping lines may score poorly when rated by cargo owners or its supply chain partners.

For operators, effectiveness-oriented performance is related to the quality of services provided to transportation users. Quality-of-service measures are essential because they represent the bottom line. While the efficiency perspective is important because it can be used to improve operations, user satisfaction is also one of the critical performance indicators that must be measured in an effectiveness-focused organization.

## 2 EVALUATION OF PORT EFFECTIVENESS

Contrary to other transport sectors, the need to understand efficiency and effectiveness in port performance has been recognized by the industry, with several initiatives being implemented in the last two decades. For example, in 2008, Germanischer Lloyd launched the Container Terminal Quality Indicator, a certification process for quality standards in container terminals. In the European context, consultation on the definition of such indicators was initiated. European port authorities have been involved in collective efforts towards this end, exploring ways to define the relevant indicators and then monitor them.

In all cases, the process applied by a port or operator for evaluating its effectiveness includes three steps:

- **Step 1: Define customer (buyer/user/stakeholder).** Shipping lines are commonly considered as the primary customer (the buyer). In recent years, there has been considerable debate about who chooses a port. The early thinking was that the shipping line chose the port, and the cargo chose the shipping line. The rising power of global cargo interests and the consolidation of lines have meant that ports have less power than before. The power that cargo interests or large logistics providers wield makes it even more important that ports make strategic changes based on the group of users they wish to attract. In cases where a port is specified in the transport contract (or the sales contract), the manufacturer, the freight forwarder (including 3PLs or 4PLs), or the consignee are also buyers depending on who has responsibility for making that purchase choice. Some are actively involved in the supply chain by providing port-related activities in wider geographical locations (i.e. operators of intermodal distribution centers, providers of port-related value-added services, or value-added logistics). Given the incursion of ocean carriers into land-based logistics activities, the role of the carrier in port selection may be even more vital than previously considered. Thus, their perceptions are also of considerable significance, given the emerging geographical and functional integration of ports in wider supply chains and logistics and the transformation of ports to elements embedded in value-driven multifaceted chains, which compete to attract users located in overlapping hinterlands. This second group are included in the category of customers (although they may not be buyers and pay for the services provided) but more frequently are considered stakeholders, parties interested in port activities. This implies understanding the different subcategories of users and actors involved in deciding which port or mode to use to complete a transportation process.

- **Step 2: Identify the decision criteria of importance to the user/buyer/ stakeholder**. Each port wants to understand its user evaluation criteria to improve its performance relative to what its users seek in service delivery. First, the attributes of importance differ per user or group of users. Second, port performance is dynamic. Thus, both the identification and evaluation are periodic activities to be conducted at regular intervals. A dynamic evaluation of the attributes allows the port to better understand changing user perceptions, thereby providing feedback to strategy as it evolves.
- **Step 3: Developing and applying user evaluation of a particular port or service performance**. Once users and their evaluation criteria are defined, attention turns to the development of an appropriate method to regularly assess and, if possible, measure user satisfaction level in a concrete way.

Effective performance by a supplier is measured in terms of what the service user expects. Satisfaction occurs when the performance of a supplier meets or exceeds expectations on the criterion (or criteria) of importance to the user. The purpose is to seek an understanding of the relative importance of each of the criteria for the users of a particular port and conduct a **gap analysis** of the importance a particular user places on the criterion and its assessment of the performance of that port on that criterion. This provides ports with insights about where continuous improvements would pay off from a user and customer perspective. While current satisfaction may not lead to future choice, dissatisfaction will likely lead to rejection for those who are not captive. When a port understands its performance in the context of the expectations of its users, it is able to understand why users are dissatisfied, why business is lost, or how additional business could be gained, particularly if performance is benchmarked against other competing ports.

An effectiveness evaluation program provides a basis for understanding what possibilities exist for **continuous improvement**. It focuses on improving performance on critical factors where performance is poor and investing in resources having the most significant impact. The resulting more efficient allocation of port resources jointly benefits users and operators. Without such understanding, governments are unable to assess when investment decisions in port infrastructure or port policy adjustments are required to meet the needs of the market. Port authorities are less likely to make the optimal resource allocations to improve the competitiveness of their port, and service providers will be frustrated in their efforts to grow and exploit business opportunities.

The relation between the value attributed to specific port activity parameters and the gap between importance and performance provides **actionable data** for developing strategic plans for investment and marketing (Figure 6.15). Ports need to invest in important parameters for users they want to prioritize by identifying gaps between importance and performance. Then secondary attention can be given to parameters that are of lesser importance. Beyond these, there are cases where performance is such that it deserves to be marketed, or it is of little importance to users, and therefore there is no requirement for action.

## 3 SUPPLY CHAIN APPROACH TO EFFECTIVENESS

The **embeddedness of ports within supply chains** underlines the significance of understanding the evaluation of port users concerning the services and processes they judge to be effective. The integration of ports in supply chains and the respective functional and spatial expansion of port-related activities demands increased coordination and synchronization. Relevant interactions include network structures wherein the performance of a firm impacts actors that are upstream or downstream of the supply chain. In light of the extended vertical integration practices and cooperative agreements experienced in shipping and logistics, the limits of these networks are unclear. In the era of information ubiquity, the various actors, service providers, and users have increased information about alternative options. Moreover, differences in size, location, and type of companies have led to a high level of diversity in the requirement of business customers. The difficulty lies in the complexity,

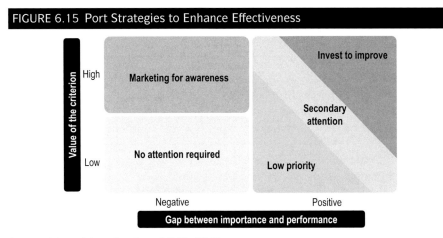

FIGURE 6.15 Port Strategies to Enhance Effectiveness

Source: Adapted from Brooks and Pallis (2013).

diversity, and extended scope that characterizes the relations between port services providers and users.

Conversely, port users refer to choices and satisfaction from a **supply chain perspective**. The **added value** that port activities offer to transportation chains and the fact that those using maritime-related supply chains cannot substitute or bypass them contribute to the influence and control they exert throughout the supply chain. Supply chain interactions are a factor where port interactions play a role. Ports consist of multiple layers of involved entities, with each one pursuing its own goals and strategies and possibly unconcerned about the level of satisfaction that the port, or the supply chain, offers as a whole. These entities are frequently both competitors and cooperating partners, or both users and suppliers involved in a complex internal relationship. The shifting interest towards strategies targeting the control of more extensive parts of transportation chains, such as integration, consolidation, cooperation, and coordination, creates broader business portfolios that blur the classification of market players as competitors or partners. The particulars and the changes in port-specific and closely related activities directly affect the supply chains in which they are nested. Each participant has its own competencies, which are integrated with participants within the supply chain and port setting. It is often within these integrated links that the most value is added within the chain.

In this context, ports search for growth through strategies aiming to attract large corporations, draw extra investments, exploit resources, and attain particular efficiencies. Although such approaches have been proved successful, ports might also outperform competitors by focusing on strategies concerned with searching for unmet needs and discovering and exploiting opportunities for which new services can be created, made available, and sold in competitive markets. Recognizing and fully understanding the needs of port users is the starting point for developing such strategies.

## 4 VARIATION IN STAKEHOLDERS' PERSPECTIVES

Ports commonly **develop tailor-made measurements of their effectiveness**, as the development of usable widespread effectiveness instruments is missing (Figure 6.16). This is partly because each port has its own features, and each user or group of users, such as carriers, shippers, forwarders, might have their own perspectives on effectiveness and port choice.

However, effectiveness is important for most users for the additional reason that ports have developed into functionally and spatially regionalized entities that are embedded in complex supply chains. In this context, supply chain interdependencies (i.e. sequential, pooled, reciprocal) increase with satisfactory port performance as added value for the competitive advantage of the various actors involved.

The criteria that most influence **cargo owners or their agents** (exporters, importers, retailers, and freight forwarders) tend to be those related to customer relationships, responding to and accommodating specific needs, and providing useful on-time information. Criteria such as terminal operator and port authority responsiveness to special requests, the ability to offer tailored services, and the ability of employees to accommodate their needs all have either a strong or medium influence on overall performance assessments.

## FIGURE 6.16 Criteria for Evaluating Port Effectiveness by Levels of Influence per Actor

| Shipping Lines | Cargo Interests | Supply Chain Partners |
|---|---|---|
| **Strong / Medium**<br>• Incidence of delays<br>• Speed of stevedore's cargo loading/unloading | **Strong**<br>• Terminal operator responsiveness to special requests | **Strong / Weak**<br>• Availability of capacity |
| **Strong / Weak**<br>• Quality of rail/truck/warehousing companies | **Strong / Medium**<br>• Port authority responsiveness to special requests<br>• Provision of adequate, on-time information<br>• Capability of employees (can they accommodate our needs?) | **Strong / Medium**<br>• Availability of capacity<br>• Accessibility to port premises for pick-up and delivery (gate congestion)<br>• Availability of labor (do we have to wait to find someone?)<br>• Efficiency of documentary processes<br>• Incidence of delays |
| **Medium**<br>• Availability and capability of dockworkers<br>• Provision of adequate, on-time information<br>• Timely vessel turnaround | **Medium**<br>• Ability to deliver/offer services tailored to different Cargo Interests<br>• Incidence of cargo damage | **Medium**<br>• Terminal operator responsiveness to special requests |
| **Medium / Weak**<br>• Availability of storage capacity<br>• Choice of logistics providers serving the port<br>• Connectivity/operability to rail/truck/warehousing<br>• Invoice accuracy<br>• Port authority responsiveness to special requests<br>• Port security<br>• Quality of maritime services (pilotage, mooring etc.)<br>• Terminal operator responsiveness to special requests | **Medium / Weak**<br>• Availability of direct service to cargo's destination<br>• Choice of rail/truck/warehousing companies<br>• Connectivity/operability to rail/truck/ warehousing<br>• Port security | **Medium / Weak**<br>• Connectivity/operability to rail/truck/warehousing<br>• Port authority responsiveness to special requests<br>• Port security<br>• Provision of adequate, on-time information |

The ability of a port to deliver services tailored to different **cargo interests**, with the choice of inland carriers and intermodal connectivity is also among the criteria critical to achieving high-performance scores. Given the importance of inventory carrying cost to many cargo owners, criteria directly related to the speed of service for cargo interests are also considered. Still, the perspectives of cargo interest vary. Any given port needs to first carefully assess the priorities of those transporting their goods via the use of the port and then prioritize performance improvement strategies.

Some **shipping lines** are influenced by a wider range of criteria than other stakeholders, while these criteria might differ between shipping lines. In contrast, for some shipping lines, the quality of inland carriers stands as the most influential criterion. This parameter has a weak association with the overall port performance when some other shipping lines assess the ports they use. A similar case is the criteria related to time, such as the incidence of delays, cargo loading and unloading speed, and vessel turnaround. On the other hand, empirical evidence suggests that shipping lines attribute a relatively weak influence on overall service performance on incidences of cargo damage, port charges, the hinterland size, and the timeliness of maritime services, such as pilotage and mooring.

Depending on which shipping lines use the port, there are other criteria in which ports need to invest or to market their capacities. They include the availability of storage capacity, the availability and capability of dockworkers, the choice of logistics providers serving the port, the connectivity/operability to inland carriers, port authority and terminal operator responsiveness to special requests, the provision of adequate on-time information, the quality of maritime services (pilotage, mooring), timely vessel turnaround, invoice accuracy, and port security.

**Supply chain partners** are trucking companies, warehouse operators, logistics service providers, and rail lines. The criteria with the strongest influence are the availability of capacity and the efficiency of documentary processes. A common theme is the need for expedient gate operations, the availability of labor, the incidence of delays, and the speed of cargo loading/

unloading. They all strongly influencing the perceived overall service performance. Supply chain partners frequently share concerns with the shipping lines using the same ports as well. On the other hand, empirical evidence suggests that invoice accuracy, ocean carrier schedule reliability/integrity, and cargo damage incidence are among the criteria having weak influences on perceived overall service performance.

There are other areas where ports could invest in improving service and satisfying the requirements of supply chain partners, such as providing adequate, on-time information and timely vessel turnaround. Several other criteria are at play, but their level of influence in supply chain partners' assessments varies from medium to weak. These are the availability of storage capacity, the connectivity/operability to inland carriers (with some of the most significant supply chain partners having their own means to secure bundling services), port authority and terminal operator responsiveness to special requests, or port security.

Three attributes are essential for the implementation of effective performance measurements:

- The first is **customization**. Each port market has unique characteristics and needs. Thus, selecting the market to be assessed by port users and the variables to be measured is a primary implementation step.
- The second attribute is **confidentiality**. As users are reluctant to share business information and data, since such exercise results are sensitive, this information should be accessible only to authorized personnel and decision-makers.
- The third attribute is **flexibility**. A port effectiveness measurement should be applied repeatedly with no specific intervals between two successive measurements. For example, for significant decisions or infrastructure development, the port authority, or the terminal operator, might run the exercise both before the decision (project) to assess perceptions before and after its implementation.

## 5 CRUISE PORTS PERFORMANCE

Effectiveness is a key dimension in the measurement of cruise port performance. There are two categories of criteria applied when assessing the performance of a cruise port (Figure 6.17). The first category relates to the **cruise lines** and the type and quality of services offered when calling at a port. The second category refers to **cruise passengers**, emphasizing the experience when visiting a port and the destination. To these, one might add the level of compliance to an increasing set of relevant regulations, such as on environment-related themes, via the application of best practices.

For cruise lines, **quality port infrastructure, efficient terms and execution of operations**, and **acceptable usage costs** stand as top performance criteria. Addressing infrastructure needs is the major issue with different elements conditioning a competitive cruise port. The terminal (quay, waiting areas, security) and the transport infrastructure in and outside the port offered at both the maritime and landside need to guarantee a good reception for port guests and their mobility. Terminal performance matching frequency or likelihood of demand defines expected turnaround times in a given terminal design. From a cruise line perspective, performance increases through improved flow and

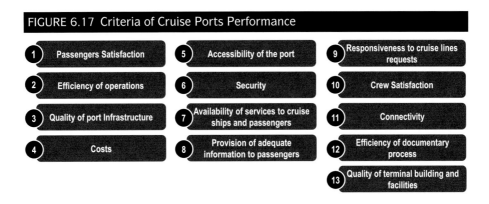

FIGURE 6.17 Criteria of Cruise Ports Performance

capacity, such as providing maximum processing capacity for peak periods. A cruise terminal operator focuses on throughput improvements to reduce the required footprint supporting operations. Providing high standard security measures for cruise passengers is also perceived as a vital performance parameter for cruise ports.

The **passenger experience** is the second category defining the performance of cruise ports. Variables such as time spent, flow during embarkation and disembarkation, absence of queues in procedures, the spaciousness of the area, and the terminal appeal produce positive assessments from passengers. Disembarkation processing time (with customs and immigration) and minimum queue time throughout the terminal are crucial operational performance indicators from a port user perspective. Passenger assessments of the port experience stand as a performance indicator because word of mouth recommendations are vital for generating interest in visiting specific cruise destinations and, consequently, influence itinerary planning.

# Chapter 6.4  Port resilience

*For natural and anthropogenic reasons, ports are subject to disruptions that can impair and even stop activities. The adaptive capacity to recover from disruptions defines the resilience of a port.*

## 1 DEFINING RESILIENCE

The resilience concept is based on the Latin root 'resilire' (to leap back or to rebound), which refers to the ability of an entity or system to **recover from a disturbance or disruption**. There is some level of ambiguity as to the precise meaning of the notion of resilience. The three most commonly used definitions are:

- **Engineering resilience** (physical sciences). The ability of a system to return to, or resume, its assumed equilibrium state or configuration following a shock or disturbance. The focus is on resistance to shocks and stability near equilibrium.

- **Ecological resilience** (ecological sciences). The scale of shock or disturbance a system can absorb before it is destabilized and moved to another stable state or configuration. Focus is on the 'far from equilibrium' behavior of a system.
- **Adaptive resilience** (complex adaptive systems theory). The ability of a system to undergo an anticipatory or reactionary reorganization of form and function to minimize the impact of a destabilizing shock. The focus is on the adaptive capability of a system.

From a transportation and port perspective, resilience allows **reducing the probability of disruption** and, if it occurs, a port will have the ability to **mitigate its impacts**. Therefore, the following definition is used:

*Resilience is the mechanism that allows a transportation infrastructure to cope and recover from disruptions while maintaining operations.*

The more important a transportation node or infrastructure is in supporting trade, supply chains, and the regional economy, the more the concept of resilience is relevant to port planning and operations. As ports can be exposed to a wide array of disruptions, it becomes essential to have infrastructures and operations that are able to recover from a disruption in a timely fashion. This implies that a maritime transport system has the capability to learn from past disruptions and adapt accordingly. More proactively, potential disruptions can be anticipated and mitigated. The new system is expected to be more resilient over three core dimensions (Figure 6.18):

- **Absorptive capacity**. The ability of a mode or a terminal to absorb a disruption while maintaining a level of service.
- **Adaptive capacity**. The ability to route cargo through different nodes and segments during a disruption in order to maintain a level of service.
- **Restorative capacity**. The ability to recover to a level of service similar to, or even above a baseline, prior to the disruption.

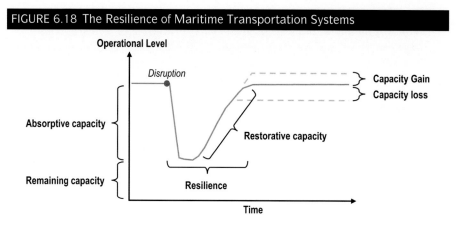

FIGURE 6.18 The Resilience of Maritime Transportation Systems

Since maritime transport networks are composed of nodes and links, the concept of resilience has several implications for components such as modes, infrastructure, and terminals. Depending on the position of the port in the transport hierarchy, its vulnerability and resilience may have different consequences. The vulnerability of maritime networks has different implications depending on whether the port is a **hub or a gateway**. Disruptions at a hub will mostly impact maritime shipping networks, while disruptions at a gateway will mostly impact the hinterland. Logistical networks are also vulnerable to disruptions impacting one element of the supply chain and the connected activities that are upstream and downstream.

The resilience concept is often associated with other related key concepts:

- **Agility** refers to the speed of the adaption process, such as making fast and seamless changes when faced with disruptions. Rapid response and build-in policies and processes that facilitate change are attributes of an agile entity. An **agile supply chain** tries to achieve faster delivery and lead time flexibility. It deploys new technologies and methods, utilizes information systems, technologies, and data interchange facilities, integrates the whole business process, and enhances innovations throughout the chain. An agile port company typically relies on a flat organizational structure to speed up information flows between different departments and develops close and trust-based relationships with its customers and suppliers.
- **Flexibility** is understood as the ability to respond to change with innovative solutions. Within a port context, a flexible port or port company can be altered with relative ease so as to be functional under new, different, or changing requirements in a cost-effective manner.
- **Lean** means a reduction of waste in a system or supply chain. Lean supply chains demand continuous improvement processes that focus on eliminating waste or non-value stops across the chain. Such a lean supply chain leads to superior financial performance for all organizations in the supply chain while reducing redundancy and increasing certain vulnerability aspects. However, reducing redundancies can negatively impact resilience.

## 2 SHOCKS AND DISRUPTIONS IMPACTING PORTS

Disruptions can come from **multiple sources**, some predictable, some random, and others unexpected. They can be **internal** to port operations when related to factors under the control of the port, such as a breakage of equipment due to improper maintenance, a breach in security, or a lack of security measures. They can also be **external** to port operations when related to factors outside the control of the port, such as a hurricane or an economic recession. The impact of a predictable disruption, such as a weather event, can be assessed on the basis of past events and the probability of their occurrence at a certain point in a time sequence such as a year. A random disruption is an event that can occur, but the probability of its occurrence cannot be effectively assessed, particularly over a shorter time period.

An unexpected disruption, at times called a **Black Swan** event, is the outcome of circumstances beyond reasonable expectations considering the information available. The Black Swan concept was first introduced in the finance and managerial world in 2007, just before the major financial events that would unfold in 2008 and 2009. It is an event or occurrence that deviates beyond what is normally expected of a situation, which is extremely difficult to predict. In hindsight, all Black Swans seem predictable, but in practice, they are very hard to identify and are even so rare that they often change perception relative to the context surrounding the event. The term 'crisis' tends to be used afterwards to describe these events.

The resilience of a port is **embedded** within its infrastructure and design. Two types of potential impacts on ports can be underlined. One is **disruptive**, impairing operations and causing delays, but leaving the infrastructure and equipment intact, since the disruption is within design parameters. The other type of impact is **damaging** where infrastructure and equipment are damaged and even destroyed since the disruption is above design parameters. Although some infrastructure and equipment may not have been damaged, the damage that has occurred can prevent regular operations until it is repaired.

Port resilience is associated with the structure of maritime shipping networks. These networks are a **circuitous nodal hierarchy**, implying that services are commonly an arranged sequence of nodes (ports) (Box 6.6). Some hierarchies are simple, such as point-to-point services, while others can be complex with inter-range services that loop back to the port of origin and connected to other networks. While point-to-point services reflect bulk shipping, container shipping is organized between deep-sea and feeder services, with transshipment hubs acting as the interface between network hierarchies. The vulnerability of maritime networks involves different considerations depending on if the node is a hub or a gateway. Disruptions at a hub will mostly impact maritime shipping networks, while disruptions at a gateway will primarily affect the hinterland. This represents the primary consideration when looking at port resilience as to what extent it is related to its foreland or hinterland.

## Box 6.6 Maritime transport networks and vulnerabilities

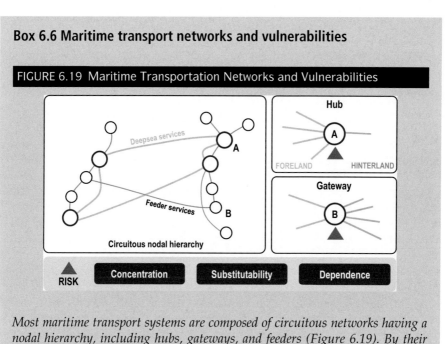

FIGURE 6.19 Maritime Transportation Networks and Vulnerabilities

*Most maritime transport systems are composed of circuitous networks having a nodal hierarchy, including hubs, gateways, and feeders (Figure 6.19). By their nature, ports are associated with three main types of risks:*

- *Concentration*. *A large share of the traffic can become concentrated in a small number of ports, implying that if a disruption occurs at a hub or a gateway, the impact could be significant.*
- *Substitutability*. *If the option of using a specific hub or gateway is temporarily removed, what is the available range of options? The less possible a substitution is, the higher is the associated risk.*
- *Dependence*. *This represents the share of hinterland or feeder traffic that is associated with a single hub or gateway. High levels of dependence are associated with vulnerability as they concern significant cargo volumes that are more difficult to substitute. This is particularly the case for hinterlands associated with a single port and with few if any options.*

*Large transshipment **hubs and gateways** are representative of this vulnerability as the scale and connectivity advantages they are built on can become a vulnerability if they are disrupted in a significant manner.*

## 3 PORTS AND NATURAL DISRUPTIONS

### 3.1 Extreme weather events

Like most transportation modes, maritime transportation can be disrupted by extreme weather events. However, **ports are among the most resilient infrastructures** in the event of weather events. Snowstorms, thunderstorms, and high winds can impair crane operations and may even topple containers, but the chance of infrastructure damage is low. Extreme heat can impair operations by rendering outdoor port work hazardous and can damage superstructures and infrastructures through thermal expansion. The most dramatic weather events are **hurricanes**, which can shut down port facilities for several days while the water recedes from flooded areas and debris is cleared. Ports located within hurricane risk areas have plans that involve tying down cranes and yard equipment to prevent toppling. Loaded containers can be stacked at safer locations within the yard, while empty container stacks can be stacked down to reduce toppling risks.

The growth of the cruise industry has highlighted the risk of hurricanes, particularly in the Caribbean, which is the world's largest destination market. Cruise lines tend to offer fewer cruises during the hurricane season between August and November, with peak hurricane activity in September. Since the path of hurricanes can only be accurately predicted within a day or two of their occurrence, cruises are usually not canceled during a hurricane event. Only the port of call sequence can be altered to take in alternatives that are not at risk. The growth of the cruise industry in Asia is also increasing cruise activity in an area prone to hurricanes (typhoons).

### 3.2 Geophysical disruptions

Tectonic activity is the source of the most serious **geophysical disasters**. Earthquakes are salient forms of geophysical threats since they are difficult to predict but generally occur in areas in the vicinity of tectonic plate boundaries. For ports, this risk is far from being uniform but can be assessed within a reasonable level (Figure 6.20). For instance, about 100 container ports accounting for

FIGURE 6.20  Risk of Earthquake for Global Container Ports

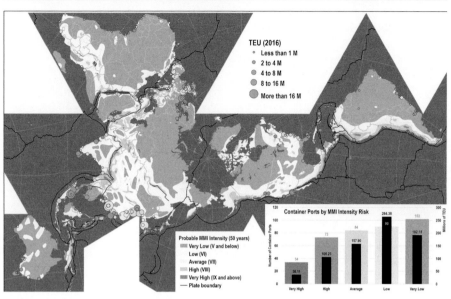

Source: Earthquake risk from "The World Map of Natural Hazards", Munchener Ruckversicher-ungs-Gesellschaft (Munchener Re), Koniginstrasse 107, D-8000 Munchen 40, Germany. Note: MMI stands for Modified Mercalli Intensity scale, which ranks from I (not felt) to XII (extreme catastrophic). Probable MMI is the 20% probability of an earthquake event of a specific scale over a 50-year period.

140 million TEUs are located in areas considered high tectonic risks, implying a 20% risk over a 50-year period of exposure to an earthquake on and above a Modified Mercalli Intensity Scale (MMI) of 8 (severe potential damage). This accounts for about 20% of the current container port activity. The Kobe earthquake of 1995 represents one of the most disruptive geophysical events impacting port activities. Immediately after the event, the port was forced to be shut down, and repairs took about two years. Since Japan is a compact country, there were alternatives to ensure the continuity of maritime services through alternate ports.

Due to the positioning of tectonic plates, ports are exposed to the significant geographical distribution of risk. As container ports have a life span of at least 50 years, it is almost certain that all container ports will be exposed to an earthquake event. What will differ is the intensity of this event. Some areas have a high risk of a high-intensity earthquake taking place over a period of half a century, while for others, only a low-intensity earthquake can be expected for the same time period. Ports bordering the Pacific Plate, also known as the 'Pacific Ring of Fire', are at a particularly high risk since most of the largest earthquake events of the last century took place in that region.

Areas of high tectonic risk are associated with a lower level of economic and port activity. For instance, 34 container ports (19% of all ports) in very high MMI risk areas (IX scale and above) account for only 4.7% of the total TEU handled. Japan and the Pacific Coast of the Americas are areas of particularly high risk. Other areas of high port activity have a very low risk, such as around the Strait of Malacca, Australia, Northern Europe, the Baltic, the American Eastern Seaboard, and the Gulf Coast.

## 3.3 Climate change

Further natural risks to port activity fall under the multidimensional impacts of climate change, many of which will potentially take place in the long term and are difficult to evaluate (Figure 6.21). In addition to the risk of hurricanes, with which it may be associated, rises in sea level are of direct concern to port activity. However, port terminals are resilient facilities designed to handle tidal ranges. Any expected sea-level rise will likely impact surrounding infrastructure such as access roads before disrupting port infrastructure. Climate change can also affect the **hinterland connectivity of ports**. For example, climate change is expected to result in significant water level fluctuations on key inland waterways such as the Rhine in Europe or the Yangtze in China. Extended periods of extremely low water levels jeopardize the continuity in inland barge service operations and negatively affect the utilization level of inland vessels. Vessels have to sail below their actual loading capacity to restrict their draft. A similar risk has been observed over the Great Lakes system with a potential trend of higher water level fluctuations, with periods of lower than average intermixed with periods of higher than average. Navigation and shipping capacity becomes more difficult to plan, impacting investments in new ships and equipment.

Elements associated with climate change have an array of potential impacts on transport operations and infrastructures:

- **Heat waves**. These impair the construction and maintenance of port infrastructure by shortening and restricting work conditions. The cooling equipment of reefer transport is subject to additional loads on the electric grid and the supporting power generation systems. Heat stress can negatively impact port infrastructure, such as the softening of pavements, which can then be substantially damaged by yard equipment such as straddle carriers.
- **Rising sea levels**. In areas near ports, transport operations can be impaired by the temporary flooding of infrastructures accessing port facilities. Port terminals can also be flooded, damaging equipment and disrupting operations.

FIGURE 6.21 Climate Change and its Potential Impacts on Maritime Transportation

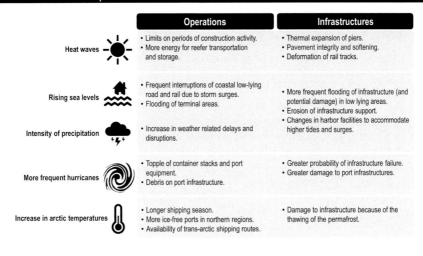

- **Increase in intense precipitation events**. These can damage transport infrastructure through flooding, disrupt maritime shipping operations, and cause delays.
- **More frequent hurricanes**. Hurricanes impose substantial disruptions on port operations, including maritime shipping. The impacts are not confined to just a single port but may affect a series of ports along a hurricane path. For cruise operations, such as in the Caribbean, hurricanes force the diversion of itineraries. Very strong winds can topple container stacks and port equipment such as cranes. The accumulation of debris can delay operations and add to maintenance costs.
- **Increase in Arctic temperatures**. The receding ice cover over the Arctic may extend the shipping season in the region. There is also the potential to use shorter Arctic shipping routes, shortening maritime shipping distances within the Northern Hemisphere.

## 4 PORTS AND ANTHROPOGENIC DISRUPTIONS

### 4.1 Accidents

Anthropogenic disruptions are related to human activities, particularly managerial and operational errors and labor-related disruptions. **Accidents** at terminal facilities can be disruptive but the large majority have a limited impact on total capacity. Errors in ship maneuvering have damaged piers and even toppled cranes, resulting in the loss of terminal capacity and the need for costly repairs. Infrastructure and equipment failures can create sporadic disruptions but can be mitigated with predictive maintenance and operational safety.

Another risk concerns **accidents in the access channel** that could result in a partial or complete blockage of the port terminal facilities or transoceanic passages. The **blockage of transoceanic passages** is rare but can have important ramifications due to the cascading effects created along supply chains. For instance, the closure of the Suez Canal between 1967 and 1975 because of the conflicts between Israel and Egypt led to substantial disruptions in the shipping industry with deviations via the Cape Route. In 2021, the Suez Canal was blocked when the ultra-large containership Ever Given ran aground, causing disruptions on Europe–Asia trade routes and the associated supply chains. Unintentional vessel groundings can have a wide range of causes, but navigation errors remain the most important.

Ports with a long and relatively narrow access channel, such as Antwerp or Hamburg, are particularly at risk of blockage. In the worst-case scenario, an accident or incident on the access route (fairway or lock) can result in a full or partial **port blockage**. The potential impact of a port blockage varies from port to port as options may be available. The direct effect of a blocked entrance would be that no maritime traffic can enter the port for the duration of the salvage of the blockage or repair of the lock. This would mean that normal maritime-related activities would halt for at least a couple of days up to even months. A significant share of all directly employed personnel involved in dock labor would become technically unemployed and logistics companies located in the port would suffer since their main modal transfer point would not be available anymore and they could fail in the long run.

Moreover, **industrial activities** in the port and the immediate hinterland, such as steel plants and car assembly plants, might be seriously affected. They typically rely on the port for incoming and outgoing maritime cargo flows. Rerouting these flows via other neighboring ports is often quite a challenge given the volumes involved and the impact on inter-port land traffic. The probability of such an event occurring is low to moderate. Ships are continuously increasing in size, making for smaller margin errors for pilots. Nautical authorities have worked out stringent conditions for large ships to enter port or navigation channels with a view to avoiding any accident risk as far as is possible. Tests using ship simulators can first evaluate the risks associated with accommodating specific ship sizes in navigation channels and ports. A trial call of a ship can provide empirical verification of the simulation results and a good basis for clearance of the respective ship size and class. Traffic rules and separation schemes, port traffic control, and experienced pilots reduce the risk substantially. Still, a catastrophic failure always remains a possibility even if the chance of occurrence is slim. The risk of accidents and port blockage can further be reduced by providing multiple access ways, such as more locks.

The most disruptive events are linked with the use of the port as a **storage facility for hazardous goods**, such as chemicals and explosives. The Tianjin port explosion of 2015 and the Beirut port explosion of 2020 are illustrative of the massive damage, loss of life, and disruptions a port industrial accident can generate. Both events were the outcome of a fire that set off an explosion in stockpiled explosives and chemicals. While Tianjin was able to resume operations quickly because the explosion took place in the backport area, the Beirut explosion destroyed and severely damaged multiple piers and storage facilities.

Many ports worldwide are home to a whole range of industrial activities such as chemical and petrochemical clusters, steel plants, and automotive assembly plants. These industrial clusters can be the source of **major industrial disasters** ranging from fire, accident, or explosion in a local area to a large chemical spill affecting the entire port. The remote possibility exists for nuclear contamination since many nuclear plants are located in or near port areas. The impact of an industrial disaster depends on its nature. For example, an isolated fire could lay waste to part of a chemical plant and cause temporary problems for surrounding companies but will have no major effect on port operations. On the other hand, a full-scale chemical or even nuclear disaster could damage a large part of the port, causing human losses and blocking or heavily disrupting port activities for an extended period of time. Prolonged reparations and contamination could significantly damage the local economy. To avoid accidents, industrial facilities have to comply with the highest possible **safety norms** and are monitored continuously. Stringent regional and international standards apply in terms of fire prevention, firefighting, and industrial and environmental safety. Furthermore, the port community needs to ensure that extensive **local or regional disaster management plans** are in place to respond effectively in case of any calamity.

## 4.2 Labor disputes

**Labor disputes** resulting in strikes can also hamper port and terminal operations and even result in a de facto port or terminal blockage. Labor unions are typically very visible in a port context, although major differences in union power can be observed across seaports and countries. Labor unions (representing dockworkers and pilots) initiate most port strikes, often disagreeing with planned port reform schemes, reforms of the nautical service provision, wage levels and remuneration, and overall working conditions and arrangements as part of collective bargaining agreement negotiations. The port strikes of 2002, involving 29 ports on the American West Coast, were highly disruptive events for the transpacific trade and a key factor in maritime shipping lines further expanding all-water routes to the East Coast through the Panama Canal. This shift was an important factor in the decision to expand the Panama Canal, which came to fruition in 2016. Terminal automation can also be a source of social unrest. For example, the new APM Terminals terminal development at Maasvlakte 2 in Rotterdam faced strong opposition from local labor unions. They feared the possible loss of jobs and lower wages given the shift from being standard quay crane drivers to remote operators of automated quay cranes.

When a strike lasts several days or even weeks, the disruptions can spread to neighboring ports as many ships deviate to other terminals. Ports affected by regular and extended strikes can incur major **reputational damage** and a **loss of trust** of market players. The impacts can be far-reaching, such as structural shifts of cargo volumes to rival ports and a sharp decline in port investments by international companies. Appropriate **social dialog** structures and effective stakeholder relations management can help to reduce the risk of strikes. Social dialog through effective joint consultation bodies is considered the key to a sustainable relationship between employers and labor unions. When industrial relations are good, labor unions will have the opportunity to contribute to improving the service provision process and labor productivity. Unions can help dock workers and nautical staff participate effectively in improving performance by creating a safe environment in which to critique existing work methods. A climate of constructive dialog thus enhances social peace in ports.

## 4.3 Economic and geopolitical events

Another category of disruptions is associated with the **derived demand of ports**, implying that port activity is bound to external demand factors largely outside its control. Economic and political shocks can indirectly disrupt port activities by impacting cargo demand. For instance, the financial crisis of 2008–2009 was associated with substantial declines in port activity in several regions of the world. For ports such as Los Angeles and Long Beach, it took almost a decade for the traffic to recover to pre-crisis levels. For a large port, such economic disruptions can result in a gap in the traffic generated that can reach millions of TEUs over the years. If infrastructure investments were made in years prior to the economic disruption, a port could face an enduring overcapacity situation that may test its **financial resilience**. Since future traffic expectations are important factors in terminal concessions and infrastructure investments, the lack of return on investments can undermine the viability of ports and maritime shipping. For instance, the Hanjin bankruptcy of 2016 involved the world's seventh-largest carrier, which was forced to cease operations in a market that was in a situation of overcapacity, with most shipping lines posting negative returns. Ports evolving in highly **volatile markets** are subject to constant and difficult to predict traffic fluctuations, for example Argentinian ports like Buenos Aires have seen limited growth over the last 20 years, but with a series of fluctuations.

**Geopolitical events**, particularly conflicts, are acute disrupting factors for the ports involved. As a result of conflicts, port infrastructure can be damaged, pillaged, and unmaintained, undermining the capability to support basic demand for essential goods. Following the Arab Spring of 2011, several countries in North Africa and the Middle East faced social turmoil and, in some cases, the degeneration into civil war. The activity at Libyan (Tripoli, Benghazi), Syrian (Tartus, Latakia), and Yemeni (Aden) ports collapsed and has barely recovered. In the case of civil unrest, ports can become the focus of relief efforts where international aid arrives, creating unique sets of challenges as populations converge towards port facilities. Economic embargos can have negative effects on port activity of both the country subject to sanctions and the ports of its trade partners. Iranian ports have been impacted by successive waves of sanctions that began in 1979 after the Iranian Revolution. The case of Venezuela is also illustrative as economic policy and the associated massive decline in economic activity since 2015 have undermined port volumes, such as in the leading national ports of Puerto Cabello and La Guaira.

## 4.4 Information technologies

A new range of disruptions has emerged in the last decade as ports are increasingly dependent on information technologies for management, operations, communication, and marketing. One type of disruption is related to **information technologies failure** that can undermine operations, particularly management systems, with automated terminals vulnerable. Cyberattacks are an emerging risk, as the 2017 Petya Ransomware Cyber-Attack on Maersk demonstrated. Port Community Systems (PCS) and other port-related platforms for information sharing and exchange are constantly subject to intrusion attempts, in part due to the potential value of the information contained but more for the high ransomware reward if an extensive port system is disrupted.

## 4.5 Pandemics

Pandemics represent an unpredictable but far-reaching risk. One of the largest disruptions that impacted the resilience of ports and maritime shipping was the COVID-19 pandemic. While the 1918–1919 Spanish Flu pandemic was devastating, international trade and port volumes were much more limited, reflecting the regional orientation of most economies. The COVID-19 pandemic took place in a **highly integrated global economy** and was associated with the rapid decline in global port activity in the first half of 2020. Still, ports were able to adapt to the widespread disruption, and many even faced a situation of under-capacity in the second half of 2020 and throughout 2021, as the demand bounced back faster than expected.

## 5 ADAPTATION MECHANISMS

Improving port resilience requires adaptation mechanisms that either lessen the impact of disruptions or allows for a quicker recovery. The following represent the most common:

- **Improving port infrastructure and superstructure** to withstand natural hazards such as from earthquakes or anthropogenic risks from accidents or hazardous materials. The profile of the investment is related to the risks involved, which can be ranked and prioritized. For instance, Japanese and Chilean ports have invested in infrastructure able to withstand earthquake stress at a level much higher than the standard. The risk of earthquakes is so high that the additional investments are perceived as fundamental.

- Planning **traffic diversion strategies** that consider the closure of elements of the port, such as a specific terminal or an access corridor. This can involve contingencies to use different terminals within the port. For hinterland access, this can involve an alternative mode or corridor. The ultimate strategy is to consider a complete traffic diversion if the port is forced to close for a period of time because of serious disruptions and infrastructure damage. This was the case in 1995 after the Kobe earthquake, where traffic needed to be rerouted. It also occasionally happens with short-lived disruptions where a few ships can be diverted to an alternative port, such as in the aftermath of the Tianjin and Beirut port explosions. Cruise lines also redirect cruises to alternative ports of call during a hurricane and, on rare occasions, are forced to switch to a different home port.

- **Preparedness** is commonly advocated as a mitigation strategy and involves the positioning of equipment, parts, and material to replace or repair damaged facilities. It also identifies key personnel that need to be available to operate the terminal and repair damaged infrastructure and equipment. This improves the restorative capacity of the port terminal at the cost of duplication (more parts and equipment than necessary for standard operations) and higher inventory costs. The key challenge is to assess what quantity to store with a view to potential risks and disruptions.

- To avoid industrial accidents, **regulations concerning hazardous materials** need to be rigorously enforced. However, industrial accidents often take place not because regulations are not followed, but because authorities are not aware of the nature, extent, and conditions in which hazardous materials can be stored within port facilities. Therefore, such regulations cannot be effective without a reporting and accounting system.

- Growing concerns about cybersecurity issues have underlined that investments in **information technologies** have become a crucial element of port resilience. This can involve continuous monitoring of breaches and the vetting of key users, as well as secure information exchange protocols and the comprehensive backup of databases.

- The **relocation of terminal facilities** to lower-risk areas represents the most drastic mitigation strategy. It can occur when a terminal has been damaged to the extent that repairs are not cost-effective, so shutting a terminal down becomes an alternative. A new site is selected at a location that is assessed as more resilient and less prone to disruptions.

**Port authorities** can play a vital role in advancing risk mitigation and adaptability. An example of this potential is the variability of the responses and measures that port authorities developed following the outbreak of the COVID-19 pandemic, which built resilience capacities and contributed to avoiding any significant disruptions of operations (Box 6.7). The same example illustrates that appropriate and **timely public policy initiatives** can facilitate the continuation of operations, relief, and recovery in the maritime transport sector.

---

### Box 6.7 Mitigating risks generated by the COVID-19 outbreak[1]

*Port Authorities contributed to mitigate the risks and challenges generated by the COVID-19 crisis."According to UNCTAD and IAPH, responses were multidimensional:"*

- *Operational adjustments. These included the reorganization of operations via (a) the prioritization of essential services; (b) the reorganization of operations and working conditions due to sanitary protocols; and (c) the advancement of digitalization of interactions and information sharing.*
- *Collaboration and coordination among all stakeholders. Communication strategies of the parties involved have been equally instrumental. Existing contingency plans have facilitated quick responses and effectiveness in combating risks and improving resilience. Ports that lacked such plans had to take ad hoc responses or develop strategies in a short period of time.*
- *Sanitary protocols and processes were urgently implemented. Coordinating with national and/or local authorities and communicating with other actors along the chain was critical to the response and coping strategies.*
- *Financial/economic adjustments. For ports, the financial implications of the crisis were manifold and included (i) the difficulties for ports themselves in continuing their financing, (ii) the limited financial capacities of several port providers that are constrained by lockdowns and suppressed demand, and (iii) the challenges imposed on port users. The capacity of ports to adopt urgent and compensatory measures, such as taking advantage of cash flows for early payment of providers, or delay of payments by some of their users, mitigated the adverse effects of the crisis.*
- *Developing guidelines for ensuring a safe interface between ship and shore-based personnel has been critical, not least due to the nature of the crisis. This has taken place at both the local and international levels and with support from relevant industry associations and international organizations. The 'crew changes' challenge highlighted a need for orchestrating an integrated approach by all involved along the supply chain (i.e. airports, public policies imposing restrictions on travel, etc.)*
- *Multidimensional adjustments of working practices were used to limit personnel shortages. Ports were able to diffuse several risks when they allowed for telecommuting, implemented sanitary protocols including*

*social distancing, rearranged working shifts, limited meetings and travel, took advantage of relevant social policies, and made greater use of technology. Similar adjustments were identified in the case of shipping lines. Responses to the crisis and the 'back to work practices' varied in scope and type. Nonetheless, the capacity for active and prompt interventions proved to be crucial.*

As a result, most ports managed to avoid significant disruptions to cargo operations. This was facilitated by the reduced number of vessel port calls and the reduced maritime trade flows.

**Working and operational adjustment measures have been transformational.** Digitalization of processes and the use of technology by much of the workforce have triggered the need to revisit operations and upgrade knowledge and skills.

**Maintaining landside operations has been the most challenging task.** Long queues at borders highlighted the importance of reliable chains when a crisis like a pandemic erupts. These difficulties did not affect maritime countries only. Land-locked and transit countries need to maintain their access to seaports as well. Ports and shippers worked to address landside operations, but the ability to adapt was not always effective. The main instruments used to address these issues were digitalization, enhanced communications, and coordination with other stakeholders and public authorities.

**Public policy initiatives that facilitated relief and recovery** have been both economic and operational. Such measures were adopted at national level, with the challenge in some countries being the need to align federal and state-level initiatives. Supranational institutions and international organizations also adopted a long list of initiatives. Applied on a broader scale, these initiatives facilitated risk mitigation.

The comprehensive goal of the stated adaptation mechanisms is to keep port facilities operational, primarily as a fundamental node supporting supply chains, including any relief effort that may be required. Ports can act as a **stronghold**, which is a secured strategic asset able to ensure the continuity of supply chains and securely access their hinterland (Figure 6.22).

In the case of a major disruption such as a natural disaster, ports can act as strongholds allowing a continuation of supply chains and the availability of transport capabilities for relief. This includes four core aspects:

- **Strategic asset**. As a transport facility, a port provides access and distribution capabilities to global and national markets. This also includes power generation facilities, essential to maintain electric power supply, many being adjacent to port sites.
- **Secure facility area**. The port areas must be secured to promote safe access, which involves setting up a perimeter and checkpoints. The core purpose is to maintain the operational capabilities of the port, which requires the presence of key personnel and equipment.
- **Inventory management**. Ports commonly have co-located logistical facilities (warehouses and distribution centers) that should be considered part of the secure perimeter. These logistical facilities support critical supply

### FIGURE 6.22 The Port as a Stronghold

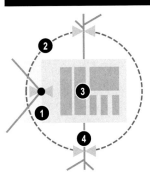

**1 Strategic Asset**
- Port, distribution cluster, energy generation facility.
- Access to global/national resources and markets.

**2 Secure Facility Area**
- Secure area (fences).
- Access restriction (checkpoints).
- Maintenance of basic operations.
- Key personnel on site continuously.

**3 Inventory Management**
- Procurement, storage and distribution of key resources.
- Energy, goods and parts, food, medical supplies.
- Support facilities (maintenance).

**4 Secure Corridors**
- Access to local/regional distribution.
- Setting of secure convoys.

chains by ensuring the procurement of energy, parts, goods, food, and medical supplies. During a disruption, these facilities are expected to assume a larger share in the storage of critical inventory because of the declining availability of resources, safety, and security considerations, including the lack of labor.

- **Secure corridors**. The port must allow access to local areas of production and consumption through the setting of high-priority corridors. Convoys can be organized from the facility to securely bring supplies to local distribution points or important facilities, such as hospitals.

The resilience of global supply chains cannot be assessed without a corresponding overview of the resilience of the port sector and appropriate methods to prepare for uncertainty linked to shocks and disruptions (Box 6.8).

---

### Box 6.8 Tools for managing risk and resilience

*Increased volatility and major external and internal shocks require a focus on risk analysis and mitigation and the avoidance of actions and situations that entail more than moderate degrees of risk. Tools can provide port authorities and port-related companies with a set of actions and alterations to their risk approach. Several modeling tools can be used to deal with uncertainty, such as:*

- *Sensitivity analysis is a method determining how the variation in the output of a model (numerical or otherwise) can be apportioned, qualitatively or quantitatively, to different sources of variation. The given model responds to the information it uses. The goal of sensitivity analysis is to understand the quantitative sources of uncertainty and identify the sources providing the greatest uncertainty.*

- *Error propagation equations assess how the quantified uncertainties in model inputs propagate in model calculations to produce an uncertainty range in a given model outcome of interest. This addresses statistical uncertainty (inexactness) in inputs and parameters.*

- *Monte Carlo simulation is a statistical numerical technique for stochastic model calculations and analysis of error propagation in (model) calculations. The goal of Monte Carlo analysis is to trace the structure of model output that results from the uncertainty of model inputs.*

- **Scenario analysis** *tries to describe logical and internally consistent sequences of events to explore how the future might, could, or should evolve from the past and present. Through scenario analysis, different alternative futures can be explored, and uncertainties thus addressed.*
- **PRIMA** *(Pluralistic Framework of Integrated uncertainty Management and risk Analysis) is a framework for structuring the process of uncertainty management. The guiding principle is that uncertainty legitimates different perspectives on policy issues and that, as a consequence, uncertainty management should explicitly take these different perspectives into account.*
- **Near miss analysis** *is an approach of identifying and analyzing unplanned events that did not result in injury or damage but could have under different circumstances. It helps to create the appropriate corrective actions in order to avoid such events in the future. The purpose of this analysis is to identify systemic or latent errors and hazards and alert the port or enterprise about them.*
- **Adaptive forecasting** *allows a port or port-related company to plug in various variables to gauge the potential outcomes of a single course of action from multiple angles.*
- *A* **SWOT analysis** *is a study undertaken to identify internal strengths and weaknesses, as well as external opportunities and threats. The analysis also examines the degree to which organizational strengths offset threats and identifies opportunities that may serve to overcome weaknesses. SWOT highlights both the positive and negative aspects of a company and its risks.*
- **Diagramming Techniques** *consist of techniques, methods, and tools aimed at graphically representing variables and outcomes of certain decisions or risks. Examples include the cause and effect diagram, the system or process flow chart, and the influence diagram. The last is a graphical representation of situations showing causal influences, time ordering of events, and other relationships among variables and outcomes.*

# PART VII

# Port policies and development

## Chapter 7.1  Ports, policies, and politics

*The setting up, planning, development, and daily functions of ports are subject to public policies and can be part of a geopolitical agenda.*

### 1 MULTI-LEVEL PORT POLICY MAKING

Governments are usually responsible for establishing, developing, and operating ports to facilitate trade, transforming the seaside to facilities where goods are loaded and unloaded. This role is not only limited to port **ownership**, such as owning and controlling wharves and jetties, but includes acting as **regulators**. Seaports are critical infrastructure allowing trade and the movement of goods and persons, with governance and regulation being a matter of public interest. Ports are multifaceted economic arenas that create economic, social, and environmental value at microeconomic (individual firms), meso (sectoral), and macro (economies) levels and are contributors to economic prosperity. Typically, the government or a specialized agent oversees a port and manages its politics to safeguard the public interest.

In the last three decades, **port governance reforms** have resulted in an increasing disassociation of public actors from the management and operation of ports in many countries. However, the public interest in organizing, planning, and regulating port activities remains. This takes shape either through public policies (de)regulating ports or through broader initiatives, such as transportation, competition, environmental, and economic policies that shape the port sector and related activities.

**Intergovernmental organizations** devoted to maritime issues, such as the International Maritime Organisation (IMO), and supranational institutions, such as the European Union (EU), develop initiatives shaping how ports are organized, developed, and managed. This is because of the international

DOI 10.4324/9780429318184-7

character of ports and their importance for serving global maritime trade and the related supply chains. Along with the spatial and functional expansion of port services and the linked supply chains, trade expansion and globalization have reformed the scale of problems and their solutions, generating further interest in adopting related policies implemented at a broader scale.

With ports evolving into clusters of economic activities, port authorities, service providers, entrepreneurs, and stakeholders have established associations representing their interests and seek to shape the content of these port and port-related public policies. Port policies and related decision-making are advancing through public and private actor interactions. These interactions happen at **multiple levels**.

## 2  NATIONAL POLICIES FOR PORTS

### 2.1  National port policies themes

National-level authorities are involved in developing **national port policies** aiming to advance the establishment, planning, development, and organization of ports to ensure that the development of the industry serves the public interest. Such responsibilities lie with regional authorities (e.g. municipal or state level) or city authorities. This depends on the traditions of each country as regards both the organization of ports and the formation of the polity. Federal states tend to delegate such control to the state or municipal level, while more centralized governments create national regulatory agencies having direct oversight.

Government agencies develop initiatives to reach different **targets**:

- The **contribution of ports to the local, regional, and national economy**, as well as to social cohesion.
- The **minimization of any externalities** produced by ports, and environmental protection in line with the applicable legislation.
- The uninterrupted availability and provision of **reliable and quality services** to ships, passengers, cargoes, the users of the port, and the general public without discrimination.

The **themes of the policy initiatives** developed by the competent national authorities include:

- **Definition of the port system** detailing the ports and the related maritime and hinterland infrastructure and connections.
- **Policy formulation** including the definition of the role of the public and private sectors in port governance and operations and the setting of priority targets.
- **Legislation** including design of laws, regulations, and decrees, including competition, and monitoring implementation.
- **International relations** with representation in international forums, negotiations, and agreements.
- **Investment and financial affairs** with assessment and, potentially, financial support for investment projects of national importance.

An additional theme is **port planning**, with the competent authorities commonly responsible for:

- **Designating port zones and establishing** priorities regarding the establishment of ports in the areas under their jurisdiction.
- **Defining property rights** for port land and areas of water where the port(s) develop.
- **Authorizing planning** and, in some cases, executing part of the planned infrastructure.

Many port-related government decisions are contingent on the physical and human geography of the local area. The **ownership and property rights** of the port land and waterside areas are illustrative examples. To develop a port, construction works include breakwaters, quays, piers, anchorage grounds, quarantine areas, large storage areas, and warehouses. Waterfront real estate and water areas commonly cannot be privately owned. Some port facilities extend into the water, often substantially, such as for land reclamations. In most countries, jurisdiction over the waterfront and the water cannot be private. There is no legal recognition of exclusive ownership rights by any third (public and private) entity. Thus, the government controls ownership and the designation of areas for port development. Public authorities establish property rights, concession the land, and authorize port constructions.

Depending on the role of the state in the economy, public control may extend to the **construction of infrastructure**. Elsewhere, the role of public authorities also includes the daily management of the port and even operations. The latter is most common in the case of smaller, secondary or local, ports. Alternatively, in countries such as the UK, even the land on which the port develops and operates is the property of operating companies. These companies develop the port solely on the priorities they set.

Once the jurisdiction and title have been obtained, where ports are placed and how they are to be built is decided. Thus, approach channels, breakwaters, maneuvering areas for ships and harbor water areas, transport links between the port and the hinterland transport network are among the works that are frequently monitored by a public authority. The **planning and execution** of these works are inherently industrial and commercial activities, and in many ports are detailed in the port level master plans. Nonetheless, the authorization to undertake the works in particular sites are actions of a governmental nature, having regard to their consequences for the port use and its natural and human environment.

While departments of transportation, or their equivalent, have the primary role in orchestrating these decisions, they rarely do so alone. The decisions require the **involvement of additional departments**, including those responsible for finance, the environment, spatial planning, civil works, tourism (for passenger/cruise ports), and naval authorities. Port planning requires that the port authority and competent national authorities coordinate all the details and the overall context of investment(s), any authorizations needed for investment plans for industrial and commercial port operations, and the potential inclusion of individual projects in financing plans at the national level. The authorities responsible for finance draw on their financial capacities to support the decisions. The environmental dimension is increasingly present in all major transport projects, with the authorization for any port project set up before its commencement.

Public authorities are also responsible for the **formulation of the port system**, as they define the structures of port governance. In particular, public authorities:

- Set the **conditions for private providers** via decisions expanding (limiting) existing entry barriers into operations.
- **Regulate corporate and financial relations** between the public institutions and port administrations.
- **Establish port authorities** and define whether they will be public, private, or hybrid (at the intersection between public and private) entities.
- Create the **foundations of port functions and responsibilities**, by defining the principles of port governance.

Public authorities monitor the compliance of port activities, which does not mean that they necessarily play any part in performing them. The scope of monitoring is to ensure that activities are carried out in compliance with laws and regulations and contribute effectively to national port policy priorities. In many ports, the public sector maintains a role in providing some nautical services, either because this practice corresponds to the dominant philosophy regarding the role of the state in the economy or because such involvement is considered essential for safety or strategic reasons. A typical example is the provision of pilotage services and their pricing. Dredging and navigational aids, including **harbor master responsibilities**, are examples of port operations frequently undertaken by public authorities.

## 2.2 Competition policies

Part of the public authorities' monitoring process includes the issue of competition. Government agencies are responsible for monitoring that port operations are in line with current competition rules. In some countries (e.g. South Africa, Greece), these responsibilities have been assigned to **independent regulatory authorities** for ports. In many more, for both inter-port competition intra-port competition, the designated national **competition authorities** address related questions, e.g. the Australian Competition and Consumer Commission, Competition Bureau Canada, or the French 'Autorité de la concurrence'. Given the international character of many competition-related issues, such as public financing, the issue of whether this financing should be considered as state aid, and concessioning processes, are increasingly part of the agendas of international authorities, such as the European Commission.

For an extended period, an active presence of national administrations, or their agents, in daily port activities has been based on the perception of ports and port services as public goods. With shifts in global maritime trade, this dimension has gradually declined. Following **port governance reforms**, the presence of the state in port operations has been eliminated, and the rights to provide port services were transferred to the private sector. However, there are still parts of the world, mainly developing countries, where full-service ports remain under public control, with government agents being active in the provision of daily operations.

Despite the decision of governments to devolve the responsibilities of port operations to third parties, ports remain a sector where politics continue to have a significant impact. The conditions for market access stand as a salient example, with national administrations being active in setting entry rules. Government policies aiming to introduce private terminal operations in the container market have led to a concentration of ownership among a few major port holdings. While mergers and acquisitions are usually completed, there are cases where they have triggered a regulatory response. Besides, creating opportunities for more competition through market entry by lowering the legislative and economic barriers is on the agenda of many national and supranational (i.e. European Union) authorities.

## 2.3 Port related policies

State-level authorities exercise control over some **broader issues** that affect port operations and developments, such as:

- **National transport policy** concerning the construction and maintenance of transportation infrastructure.
- **Location** of major industries, as part of industrial policies.
- **Customs and immigration** processes.
- **Safety** requirements and minimum conditions for workers.
- **Environmental** and aesthetic factors.
- **Security** and prevention of unlawful acts.

In addition, **free trade zones (freeport)** with distribution and warehousing activities subject to separate taxation regimes are subject to distinct policies and their development within port zones or adjacent locations. Public authorities also develop policy and **financial initiatives** related to aspects of port investment and development plans.

## 2.4 The Harbor Master

Harbor Masters regulate how vessels conduct their navigation in a port, with the prime consideration being the **safety of navigation** for any vessel. Most regulatory requirements are set out in the form of port by-laws, general directions, and pilotage directions, as these clearly define the terms of safe navigation.

A range and diversity of responsibilities are imposed on those who perform the harbor mastering role. Differing national traditions and structures explain the variations in the job description, which can even exist within one country. Factors such as the size of the port, its specific function, and how the port is owned and administered, also make a difference. There are two primary ways in which Harbor Masters may be appointed. They may be a port employee, or an external appointment, or, as in the USA, an officer of the US Coast Guard.

The Harbor Master is the principal person who typically exercises **jurisdiction over the water area** of a port or port approach. To exercise this jurisdiction, authority is conferred by national law, regulation, or rules, and these duties encompass a legal and operational responsibility for shipping movements to be carried out safely.

From initial information provided by the ship on draft, length overall, and displacement, the Harbor Master will allocate a suitable berth and apply any restrictions necessary for the safe passage of that particular vessel. Ships arriving at a port will typically contact the port control or vessel traffic management systems station to receive instructions on the plan for their arrival and stay in the port. This exchange usually involves confirmation of the time the pilot will board and the berth to which the vessel is proceeding. Harbor Masters use local knowledge to inform their decision-making regarding the manner and circumstances in which commercial vessels are permitted to enter and leave their ports.

Geographical configurations of the port, prevailing weather conditions, port water depths, and the height and strength of the local tides are some of the factors that a Harbor Master considers while formulating an admission policy for commercial vessels wishing to enter and leave the port. Harbor Masters specify their entry requirements in great detail, including the safest approaches to a port, pilot boarding ground, and details of advance notifications to be given to the port before arrival. The arrival of a commercial vessel into a port is always a **planned event**, with notifications of arrival beginning before arrival.

## 3 INTERNATIONAL PORT POLICIES

Policies decided by policy actors go well beyond the boundaries of a single country. Ports serve international maritime transportation and are embedded in **global supply chains**. Thus, ports share several similar concerns and challenges, and addressing them at a local scale can be ineffective or distort competition. An indicative list of these concerns and challenges would include safety, security, labor issues, customs and operational standardization, and competition between the actors involved. International intergovernmental organizations (including United Nations (UN) agents) intervene, taking actions in these areas falling within their competence. Their regulatory decision and other initiatives are, or at least entail the potential to be, more effective than action taken at the national, regional, or local level.

### 3.1 International organizations

The **International Maritime Organization (IMO)** is an intergovernmental organization that, since 1948, has developed and adopted regulations, guidelines, codes of practice, and other initiatives that:

- Set standards for **safety** and security of vessels and ship/port interface.
- Protect the **environment** from shipping activities.

- Establish global provision for **search and rescue**.
- Ensure that all seafarers are adequately **trained** and competent.
- Define liability and ensure **compensation** is available when accidents happen.

Applying **IMO conventions** is subject to ratification and implementation by as many countries as possible. This ratification depends on national technical capabilities and willingness to apply the conventions. The key conventions that have been ratified by countries representing over 95% of the world tonnage already shape the framework within which ports, shipping, and maritime supply chains operate. They include:

- The International Convention for the Safety of Life at Sea (SOLAS) 1974, as amended.
- The International Convention for the Prevention of Pollution from Ships (MARPOL), 1973, as modified by the Protocol of 1978, and by the Protocol of 1997.
- The International Convention on Standards of Training, Certification, and Watchkeeping for Seafarers (STCW) as amended, including the 1995 and 2010 Amendments.

The **International Labour Organization (ILO)** has been active in advancing international port labor standards. ILO is the only tripartite UN agency that brings together governments, employers, and workers of 187 member states to set labor standards, develop policies and devise programs promoting appropriate working conditions. Its port-related activities focus on safety and health, security, training, working conditions, gender issues, and the role of ports in the supply chain. Similar to IMO, the implementation of ILO decisions is subject to their ratification by the participating countries.

Two other international organizations are developing initiatives of relevance. The **World Customs Organization** (**WCO**), established in 1952 as the Customs Co-operation Council (CCC), is an independent body whose mission is to enhance the effectiveness and efficiency of customs procedures. Since 2004, WCO has developed in collaboration with the United Nations Office on Drugs and Crime (UNODC) a global **Container Control Programme (CCP)** to prevent the illicit flow of goods by pooling customs and other law enforcement bodies in coordinating and managing law enforcement responses at seaports in more than 20 countries worldwide.

International Organization for Standardization (ISO) is an independent, non-governmental international organization with a membership of 166 national standards bodies. It develops voluntary, consensus-based, market relevant international standards that support making a product, managing a process, delivering a service or supplying materials. These standards relate to:

- **Quality management** standards to work more efficiently and reduce product failures.
- **Environmental management** standards to reduce environmental impacts, reduce waste, and be more sustainable.
- **Health and safety** standards to reduce accidents in the workplace.
- **Energy management** standards to cut energy consumption.
- **IT security standards** to keep sensitive information secure.

Ports have certified with ISO 9001:2008 the management of container, bulk terminal, passenger, and cruise terminals. The same certification applies for specific services, such as cargo loading and unloading services, mooring, and fewer public procurement and port work cases. A growing number of port authorities and terminal operators have certified their environmental management to terminal operations with ISO 14001. However, the major contribution of standardization, with far-reaching implications for ports and beyond, has been the **standardization of the containers** that are transported (Box 7.1). Standardization enabled the expansion of the containerized seagoing transportation of goods. The usage of standardized containers resulted in a vast reduction in shipping costs. It allowed many countries that were previously isolated from global trade to put their products on the world market and consume imported goods.

---

### Box 7.1 Main physical characteristics of ISO containers

*The container changed the face of globalization, with the box recognized as the 'humble hero' and one of the most influential inventions of the twentieth century (Figure 7.1). Transporting cargo into boxes or bags to shift it around more efficiently as a unit has always been seen as advisable. However, shipping containers were only made possible following the standardization of the dimensions of the different types of containers used in the mid-1960s, when the ISO technical committee on freight containers standardized almost every aspect of containers from their overall dimensions to how they can be stacked, to the twistlocks that securely fasten them to ship decks or truck chassis, to the terminology used to describe them.*

*The **standard 20-foot container** is the most commonly used box for the shipment of goods in ocean freight along with the **40-foot container**. The dimensions are usually measured using the imperial system (feet) and specify both the exterior and interior (usable) dimensions. The standardization of cargo containers ensures containers can be stacked most efficiently, literally one on top of another. Although freight containers are manufactured worldwide, they are built to specific ISO specifications to allow for interoperability across intermodal transportation systems.*

*Many shippers prefer to use the largest load unit possible (e.g. 40-foot containers) because it conveys economies of scale. However, weight restrictions can make the 20-foot a desirable option, particularly for transporting commodities. For instance, the weight restrictions on both the regular and the high cube 40-footers are at around 30 short tons (or 28 metric tons), virtually the same as a 20-footer, so there are no gains in using a high cube container for heavy goods. Payload weight gets even smaller with 45 and 48-foot containers, underlining their specific role in transporting bulky but comparatively light goods. The majority of containers are made with weathering steel (Corten steel), which prevents rusting.*

FIGURE 7.1  Standard Sea Container Dimensions.

| Container Type | Cubic Capacity | Tare Weight | Payload Weight | Gross Weight | Dimensions (L/W/H) |
|---|---|---|---|---|---|
| 20' Standard Container | 33.2 cubic meters (1,170 cubic feet) | 2,400 kg (5,290 lb) | 28,080 kg (61,910 lb) | 30,480 kg (67,200 lb) | 6.058 m / 2.438 m / 2.591 m (20'0" / 8'0" / 8'6") |
| 40' Standard Container | 67.5 cubic meters (2,385 cubic feet) | 4,000 kg (8,820 lb) | 26,480 kg (58,380 lb) | 30,480 kg (67,200 lb) | 12.192 m / 2.438 m / 2.591 m (40'0" / 8'0" / 8'6") |
| 40' High Cube Container | 76.4 cubic meters (2,690 cubic feet) | 4,200 kg (9,260 lb) | 26,280 kg (57,940 lb) | 30,480 kg (67,200 lb) | 12.192 m / 2.438 m / 2.896 m (40'0" / 8'0" / 9'6") |
| 40' High Cube Reefer | 67.7 cubic meters (2,391 cubic feet) | 4,810 kg (10,604 lb) | 29,190 kg (64,353 lb) | 34,000 kg (74,957 lb) | 12.192 m / 2.438 m / 2.896 m (40'0" / 8'0" / 9'6") |
| 45' High Cube Container | 86 cubic meters (3,040 cubic feet) | 4,740 kg (10,450 lb) | 27,800 kg (62,350 lb) | 33,020 kg (72,800 lb) | 13.716 m / 2.438 m / 2.896 m (45'0" / 8'0" / 9'6") |
| 48-Footer High Cube | 98.8 cubic meters (3,489 cubic feet) | 5,140 kg (10,865 lb) | 25,340 kg (56,350 lb) | 30,480 kg (67,197 lb) | 14.630 m / 2.591 m / 2.908 m (48'0" / 8'6" / 9'6 1/2") |

Source: Adapted from Container Alliance.

## 3.2 Supranational port policies: European Union

Economic and political integration in Europe, notably the setting up of a single European market in the 1990s, increased the interdependence of European ports that had historically developed in their own diverse ways, even when located in the same country. The interdependence of European ports intensified due to other factors as well. These factors include economic globalization and containerization; the expansion of transshipment, logistics, and value-added facilities; technological advancements; and the integration of maritime trade in supply chains. The scale and scope of these developments gradually pushed the national boundaries of port policy-making. Since the early 1990s, the search for a long-term **European Port Policy (EPP)** has produced a mix of non-legislative and legislative measures (Figure 7.2). These measures apply to all European Union (EU) ports that together host 37% of the total intra-EU exchange of goods and 75% of the EU trade to the rest of the world by ports directly connected the EU to over 850 ports in the Far East and a total of more than 2,000 ports in the world. Both successes and failures mark this search, as does the associability of port community stakeholders seeking to influence the complex EU policy-making process.

The cornerstone of these initiatives is a regulation on **market access to port services and financial transparency of ports.** Adopted in 2017, it established the entry rules in various port services (bunkering, cargo handling, dredging, mooring, passenger services. port reception facilities, pilotage, and towage) in 319 ports. The regulation **lowers legislative entry barriers**, provides existing and potential port services providers with a **level playing field,** reduces the **administrative burden**, and advances **transparency** of financial interactions. It established the freedom to provide services subject to minimum requirements, conditions for limiting the number of providers, public service obligations, and the presence of an internal operator (i.e. by the Port Authority itself). Financial transparency and autonomy in the use of public funds are enhanced by requirements such as the presence of separate port accounts, transparent and non-discriminatory port service charges, the autonomy of port managing bodies to set port infrastructure charges, and the obligation to inform users about tariffs for port infrastructure charges. Reduction of legal uncertainties is also advanced via the applications of broader rules (i.e. a concession directive) and ongoing discussions on the modernization of applicable state aid rules. The regulation is the outcome of a discussion that lasted 16 years, highlighting both the international dimension of port competition and the difficulties in advancing (de)regulatory measures applying to ports in multiple (in this case 27) countries, as ports vying for traffic shares differ in many ways (markets, governance, geography, rules of entry for third parties).

Beyond this rule that targets the enhancement of EU ports' competitiveness, the EU policies target **improving hinterland connections**. The strategic planning of the transport system in the continent involves developing public co-financing of an integrated **Trans-European Transport Network** that includes a comprehensive list of 319 ports, with a sub-list of core ports. The development of both comprehensive and core EU ports is considered vital for the competitiveness of the European economy, including improving port hinterland connections. European policies aiming to enhance **maritime safety**, improve the relationship of ports and the **environment**, and guarantee **maritime security** are also in place. The list of emerging themes includes initiatives advancing **digitalization**. In all cases, whenever international rules are in place (i.e. safety, security), the emphasis is on their proper implementation rather than new regional initiatives.

FIGURE 7.2 European Port Policy and port-Related Initiatives

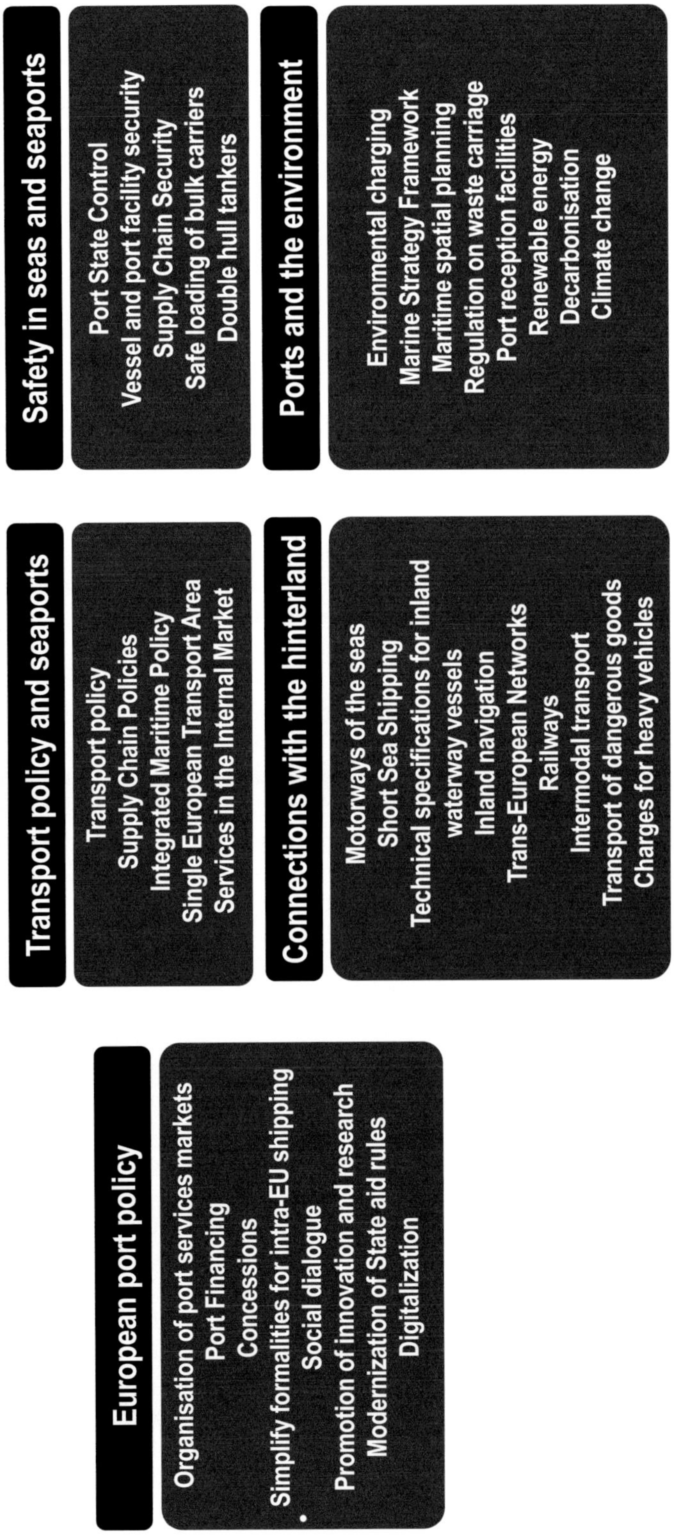

**Safety in seas and seaports**

Port State Control
Vessel and port facility security
Supply Chain Security
Safe loading of bulk carriers
Double hull tankers

**Ports and the environment**

Environmental charging
Marine Strategy Framework
Maritime spatial planning
Regulation on waste carriage
Port reception facilities
Renewable energy
Decarbonisation
Climate change

**Transport policy and seaports**

Transport policy
Supply Chain Policies
Integrated Maritime Policy
Single European Transport Area
Services in the Internal Market

**Connections with the hinterland**

Motorways of the seas
Short Sea Shipping
Technical specifications for inland
waterway vessels
Inland navigation
Trans-European Networks
Railways
Intermodal transport
Transport of dangerous goods
Charges for heavy vehicles

**European port policy**

Organisation of port services markets
Port Financing
Concessions
Simplify formalities for intra-EU shipping
Social dialogue
Promotion of innovation and research
Modernization of State aid rules
Digitalization

## 3.3 Federal port policies: North America

In the United States, the federal government is given exclusive jurisdiction over all navigable waterways. However, due to the nature of the federal system, there is **no national port authority** but a combination of state and municipal port authorities, making policy coordination complex. Early forms of port development and operation were mainly assumed by private companies, particularly railroads. This led to complaints about monopolistic behavior and unfair competitive practices. The public policy response was the setting up of public port authorities in the early part of the twentieth century, particularly when railways led to a gradual deterioration of port facilities due to the lack of investment. A salient example was the creation of the Port Authority of New York in 1921 that placed the role of port infrastructure development and operations firmly in public hands.

Established in 1950, the **Maritime Administration (MARAD)** is an agency of the US Department of Transportation responsible for the waterborne transportation system. MARAD supports the technical aspects of America's maritime transportation infrastructure, including ships and shipping, port and vessel operations, national security, environment, and safety. It also maintains a fleet of cargo ships in reserve to provide surge sea-lift during national emergencies.

In Canada, the federal government has the exclusive jurisdiction over all forms of navigation, forming a national port authority as early as 1868. Although the federal authority can be granted to private or local interests, the majority of large commercial ports remained under close federal jurisdiction. Port policy shifted in 1998 with the Canada Marine Act, that devolved governance responsibilities of a large number of small ports that had been managed by the Ministry of Transport. Under Canada Port Authority, the largest seaports are given a partial level of autonomy for their development and management. From a policy perspective, American port authorities have more latitude than their Canadian counterparts.

## 3.4 National perspectives: China

The past 45 years have brought significant changes to China's economic and political landscape and society. The **changes in economic policy** brought by Deng Xiaoping in 1978 were followed by a long transition period towards a market-based economy. Chinese national reforms and the transfer of power from the central government to local governments impacted the governance of seaports. The period 1979–1984 was characterized by a centrally planned economic system with strongly centralized decision-making. The combination of insufficient funds for port development and lagging efficiency improvements caused severe port capacity problems in the early 1980s. From 1984–2004, the government initiated a **decentralization process**, with ports ending up being controlled either by central and local governments or by the local government. The new governance system resulted in a gradual entry of foreign private investors in Chinese ports, particularly in the container business.

The **Port Law of 2004** forms the cornerstone for today's port system in China, characterized by the corporatization of port authorities and the introduction of modern corporate governance principles in the seaport system. The past decade has brought large-scale port cooperation and integration processes at the provincial level, resulting in large 'port groups' controlling more than one port. Policy formulation and strategic port planning are still the responsibility of the central government and respective provincial governments, so any plans of regional port groups need to be approved by these higher authorities.

Other policies are influencing Chinese ports:

- The actions of the Chinese government in the area of **corporate governance** directly impact the functioning of the Chinese seaport system. For example, the fight against corruption has affected administrative processes, reporting practices, and the mobility of government officials, including in ports.
- The Central Government initiated the **Go West policy** in 2000 to energize local economies and improve people's living standards in the western parts of China. This policy brought higher throughput perspectives for coastal ports and intensified competition among Chinese ports to serve the growing inland regions.
- The **Belt and Road Initiative** (BRI) was launched in 2013 to foster economic cooperation from the Western Pacific to the Baltic Sea and break the connectivity bottleneck in Asia through infrastructure investments. Chinese seaports actively develop strategies to link up to both the maritime and rail-based opportunities brought by the initiative. Furthermore, some provincial port groups are investing in key BRI ports abroad.
- The Chinese government initiated a policy in 2013 to develop pilot **free trade zones** (FTZ) in some coastal port cities. The first FTZ was launched in Shanghai in September 2013. Since 2015, the Chinese State Council has extended the initiative to many other cities. Many of the FTZs are located in seaport areas and have become proving ground for the Chinese government to test new economic policies and governance reforms. The experiences gathered through the FTZ policy can serve as input to formulate further nationwide social, economic, and governance reforms.

## 4 PORT POLICY ISSUES

### 4.1 Emissions control

The need to **control emissions** has led to an IMO regulatory framework restricting several fueling options. The IMO is spearheading sulfur emission restrictions within particular **Emission Control Areas** (ECAs) (Box 7.2). For example, since 2010, in the sulfur emission control area (SECA) of the North and Baltic Sea, the mass fraction of sulfur in a vessel's bunker has to be less

---

### Box 7.2  Emission control areas for maritime shipping

*The International Convention for the Prevention of Pollution from Ships (MAR-POL) established a protocol titled 'Prevention of air pollution from ships' that became effective in 2005. Under this protocol, member nations of the International*

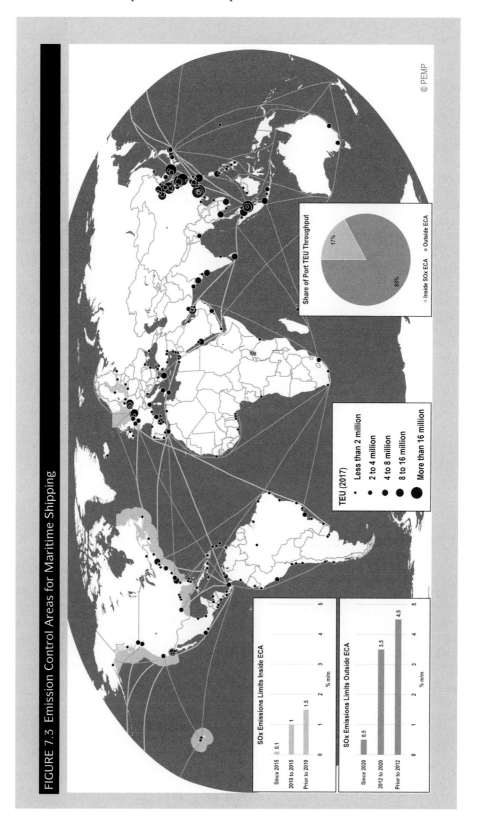

FIGURE 7.3 Emission Control Areas for Maritime Shipping

*Maritime Organization agree to abide by fuel emission standards that are (about three times) more stringent within selected emission control areas (ECA) (Figure 7.3). Emissions are measured by the sulfur content of bunker fuel as a percentage of its mass (% m/m). While SOx standards were 4.5% m/m outside ECAs and 1.5% m/m inside ECAs in the early 2010s, by 2020, they reached 0.5% and 0.1%, respectively.*

*ECA impacts maritime shipping over two dimensions related to **port access** and **shipping lanes**. About 17% of the global port container throughput is within an ECA. Even if this share is relatively small, the ports within ECAs are servicing the wealthiest markets of Europe and North America (e.g. Hamburg-Le Havre range and Eastern Seaboard). Therefore, shipping lines calling at these ports must use lower sulfur bunker fuel, impacting their service network with other ports that have less stringent emission standards.*

*The second dimension is more limited since the existing ECAs are not extensive enough to impact shipping lanes. Traffic going through the English Channel or the North Sea is already bound to ports of the Hamburg–Le Havre range and are thus subject to ECA regulations. Great circle distance traffic passing by the American West Coast ECA, such as Asia–South America lanes, can avoid it through a deviation. The impact of ECAs on shipping lanes could be more significant if the Mediterranean becomes an ECA, as a large volume of shipping transits through the region.*

than 1%. This standard took effect in North America in 2012, with this limit decreasing to 0.5% after 2020. These rules triggered interest in alternative forms of powered vessels. There is considerable interest in ports worldwide using on-shore power supplies (cold ironing) and other similar technologies and practices (use of diesel oil instead of heavy fuel oil or renewable energy sources) to reduce emissions. At the center of these trends is provision of liquefied natural gas (LNG) to ships. The capacity of ports in providing shore power supply or LNG bunkering is also an emerging environmental performance indicator.

## 4.2 Port security

As in maritime safety, some of the essential regulations regarding security in trade and transport have been undertaken by the IMO. In 2002 a security-related amendment to the Convention on Safety Of Life At Sea (SOLAS) was adopted, supplementing it with the **International Ship and Port Facility Security (ISPS) Code**. The initiative changed the way ship and port security is considered. The ISPS Code has two parts. Part A is mandatory for all the contracting countries, while Part B contains recommended actions that have been adopted by a few countries.

The ISPS Code established three security levels denoting the need for normal (Level 1), heightened (Level 2), and exceptional (Level 3) security measures. The implementation of the code's requirements and the respective certification of vessels and shipping companies is the responsibility of the flag state. At the same time, national authorities are responsible for inspecting and certifying proper implementation. These provisions cover all types of ships larger than 500 grt, mobile offshore drilling units, and port facilities serving ships which are engaged in international voyages. Concerning ports, the ISPS Code focuses on the locations of the ship/port interface. Ports have to develop a Port Facility Security Plan (PFSP) detailing the essential actions to prevent, or respond to, a security incident. They also have to designate a port facility security officer responsible for carrying out regular drills, exercises, and seminars concerning port facility security. In addition, Part A makes an explicit reference to identifying and estimating assets and infrastructures that it is important to protect.

The amended IAMO SOLAS Convention (Chapter XI-2) introduced a new technological security measure for ships. This is the **Automatic Identification System (AIS)**, which enables ships to transmit a unique identification signal for the shore operational centers to monitor the ship route. Ships are required to have onboard a security alert system transmitting to a designated competent authority when activated in emergencies, and a Continuous Synopsis Record (CSR) that contains details of the ship, including name, flag, port of registry, IMO number, and owner information.

The **Code of Practice on security in ports** (latest edition: 2004) is another security-related initiative adopted by IMO jointly with ILO. It provides a guidance framework for developing an appropriate strategy for identifying security threats in ports. The main provisions are:

- The development and implementation of a port **security policy statement**.
- The identification and evaluation of the **critical assets and infrastructures** that it is important to protect.
- The development of a **Port Security Plan**, compatible with the ISPS Code for a Port Facility Security Plan.
- Training personnel in **security awareness**.

The WCO Council has adopted the **SAFE Framework of Standards to Secure and Facilitate Global Trade**, an additional international instrument regularly updated to effectively address developments in the international supply chain. The latest (2018) version of the framework focuses on strengthening cooperation between customs administrations through the exchange of information, mutual recognition of controls, mutual recognition of Authorized Economic Operators (AEO)s, and mutual administrative assistance. In addition, it calls for enhanced cooperation between government agencies entrusted with regulatory authority over certain goods, such as weapons, hazardous materials, and passengers, as well as entities responsible for postal issues. The framework also details certain minimum tangible benefits to AEOs.

**International standardization** also plays a role in port security enhancement. ISO 28004-2:2014 identifies supply chain risk and threat scenarios, procedures for conducting risks/threat assessments, and evaluation criteria for measuring conformity and the effectiveness of security plans following standardized (ISO 28000 and ISO 28004) implementation guidelines. An output of this effort is a confidence rating system based on the quality of the security management plans and procedures implemented by the port to safeguard its security and continuity of cargo operations. The rating system is used to identify a measurable level of confidence (on a scale of 1 to 5) that the port security operations conform with standards for protecting the integrity of the supply chain.

## 4.3 International policies for dock labor

ILO has been involved in the definition and organization of dock labor through two **international conventions** on the role of the designated labor pools and the working practices that safeguard the safety and health of port workers. However, the agreed and forwarded ratification by UN member countries 'ILO Convention C137 on the social repercussions of new methods of cargo handling in docks' and 'ILO Convention C152 on occupational safety and health in dock work' have had limited adoption success. The two Conventions were adopted in 1973 and 1981 respectively. The products of international agreements involving both port employees and employers were designed to set the minimum standards for organizing the core elements of port labor. Each convention has only 25 signatory countries that have ratified it.

However, rules included in these conventions have been incorporated into several **international standards** endorsed since then. In recent times, ILO produced relevant codes of practice on safety and health in ports that cover work aspects where goods or passengers are loaded onto or unloaded from ships. ILO has also shifted interest to dockworker training with its objective being to mobilize governments, port authorities, port operators, and training institutes to establish effective and systematic port worker training schemes designed to improve cargo-handling performance, working conditions and practices, safety, and the status and welfare of port workers.

**Labor issues** have also been part of the European agenda. In recent years, there has been a sectoral social dialog involving representatives of all different stakeholders, respecting national, regional, and company agreements and systems, on:

- **Training and Qualifications**. Possible creation of European guidelines for the establishment of training requirements while ensuring greater flexibility and performance standards.
- **Health and Safety**. Establish national health and safety requirements by proper enforcement where high standards exist or raise good practices where standards do not exist.
- **Gender Issues**. Ensure that there are no discriminatory recruitment practices in European ports.
- **Innovation**. Set up a constructive dialog between employers and employees to meet the challenges resulting from technological innovation.

## 5 PORTS AND GEOPOLITICS

Ports have been linked with geopolitical considerations as they are platforms that project commercial activities and military power. Many ports are bases supporting national navies and, as such, **strategic interests**. From the sixteenth century, ports acted as trade platforms in global trade networks, initially supporting colonial empires. Harbor sites were selected on the ground of the protection they could offer and the access they could grant to the resources of a commercial hinterland. Many early port sites were fortified, underlining their contestability.

From the second half of the twentieth century, commercial considerations prevailed in geopolitics. With port authorities adopting the landlord model, this opened the door for private terminal operators to set up a portfolio of privately operated terminals. The nature of the investments in terminal operations, such as the scale of foreign direct investments, the critical infrastructure nature of ports, and sovereign funds in the list of companies that operate port terminals, provide a geopolitical dimension in port development that did not exist before reforms. While, in the majority of cases, private terminal operators are aligned with the national **geopolitics** of the ports they are involved with, there are occasions when this alignment of foreign direct investments can be subject to contention (Box 7.3).

---

### Box 7.3  Geopolitics and foreign direct investments in ports

*Foreign direct investments are controversial since their hold on strategic port facilities may imply a loss of sovereignty and go against long-term national interests.*

*In 1997 HPH was awarded concessions on container facilities on both sides of the **Panama Canal** (Balboa and Cristobal). The reaction by some was that China was now controlling the canal even if the canal itself is under the full jurisdiction of the Panama Canal Commission. This even prompted statements by the CEO of Hutchinson Whampoa, Li Ka-Shing, reassuring the United States that this purchase was strictly a commercial venture fitting the strategies of the holding and that it had nothing to do with the operations of the canal itself.*

*Another salient example took place in 2006. The controversy pertained to management contracts of major American ports to the United Arab Emirates state-owned company DP World. The contracts had already been foreign-owned by Peninsular and Oriental Steam Navigation Company (P&O), a British firm. DP World acquired the terminal assets of P&O, further consolidating its global holdings and managing terminals in **major American ports** (including New York, Baltimore, Miami, New Orleans, and Philadelphia). In a post-September 11 setting where security issues had become highly controversial, the deal stirred a public debate, particularly since Middle Eastern interests control DP World. President George W. Bush argued for approval of the agreement, claiming that the delay was sending the wrong message. Legislation was introduced to the US Congress to delay the sale, and the US House Committee on Appropriations voted 62–2 to block the deal. The settlement involved DP World delegating the American terminal assets of P&O to an American entity. American Insurance Group (AIG) holding purchased assets that included five port terminals and 16 freight handling facilities, which were incorporated in the portfolio of Ports America.*

*Australia overhauled its foreign investment laws in late 2020, giving the government the retrospective power to impose new conditions or even force divestment on deals that had already been approved. Ports were among the first sectors to gain attention. In Spring 2021, the government decided to review the lease of **Port Darwin** to Landbridge Group, which is owned by a Chinese billionaire. Landbridge won a 99 year bid in 2015 to operate the port, the centerpiece of the government's plan to develop its remote north. The Australian government decided to review whether to force the company to give up its ownership due to national security concerns, focusing on its alleged ties to the Chinese military.*

*The news came only weeks after the Australian government's decision to cancel a BRI agreement signed in 2018 between China and the state of Victoria.*

*In Europe, the potential **geopolitical advantage** of the Piraeus port offer led the Chinese government to pursue ownership of the port via its State-owned shipping conglomerate COSCO Pacific. Following **bilateral discussions**, the two governments agreed in the mid-2000s to the involvement of COSCO in Piraeus port operations. When the Greek PM announced the decision during an official trip to China, European institutions sent a reminder of the need for an open tender to secure a level playing field for all parties. In 2008, a 35+5 year container terminal concession was given to COSCO, making Piraeus its port of entry into southern Europe and the Mediterranean.*

*China realized a window of opportunity in a financially struggling country and actively sought to **control the port**. Successive Chinese leaders started official trips in Greece, advocating the importance of gaining control of the major Greek port as part of China's efforts to help Greece overcome its debt crisis. In 2016, an international tender for selecting the preferable investor for PPA SA gave COSCO Shipping Corporation majority share ownership of the Piraeus Port Authority and all operations. Although six parties expressed an initial interest, only COSCO placed a bid at the final stage. The Greek Parliament endorsed the agreement in 2016.*

*The arrival of COSCO Pacific has been catalytic. Piraeus experienced an increase in container throughput due to additional transshipment traffic and moved from the seventeenth largest container port in Europe in 2007 to the fourth by 2020. This was a **political process** balancing the geopolitical interest of a Chinese government developing a presence in the region and Greek interests to ease the pressures posed by the accelerated economic crisis. The public port authority has been replaced by a Chinese entity acting as owner-manager and operator of the whole port.*

*The Greek case also highlights the **importance of politics in port development**. At the beginning of the 2010s, the structural reforms program was accompanied by disagreements between a Troika of international organizations on the desired model. The International Monetary Fund (IMF) favored selling the shares of Greek port authorities. The European Commission and the European Central Bank preferred concessioning to third parties, with the port authorities remaining under public control. Lawsuits followed Piraeus' concession, while COSCO's first arrival in Greece was met with a month-and-a-half-long dockworkers' strike.*

The rapid increase of **Chinese investments** in the operation of container terminals and port management through the purchase of majority shares in corporatized port authorities in many different world regions, and the multinational character of the **Belt and Road Initiative** (BRI), have, in most cases, generated discussion, support, or opposition at governmental level, rather than remaining subject to decisions at port level (Box 7.4). As operators associated with state interests, such as being state enterprises or part of sovereign wealth funds, move into terminal operations in foreign countries, geopolitical concerns about ports as elements of national sovereignty will continue to rise.

## Box 7.4 Belt and Road Initiative

*The Belt and Road Initiative (BRI) was launched in 2013 by President Xi Jinping to foster economic cooperation from the Western Pacific to the Baltic Sea and to break the connectivity bottleneck in Asia through infrastructure investments. It was initially called the **One Belt One Road initiative** (OBOR). The BRI program is a centerpiece of China's foreign policy and domestic economic strategy. In March 2015, the Chinese government unveiled a BRI initiatives action plan. The initiative covers a land-based (in essence rail-based) **Silk Road Economic Belt** (One Belt), including a zone of influence on both sides of the Belt, and a twenty-first century **Maritime Silk Road** (One Road) (Figure 7.4).*

*The land-based Belt begins in Xi'an in central China before stretching west through Lanzhou (Gansu province), Urumqi (Xinjiang), and Khorgas (Xinjiang), which is near the border with Kazakhstan. The Silk Road then runs to Duisburg in Germany via Iraq, Syria, Turkey, Bulgaria, Romania, the Czech Republic, and Germany. From Duisburg, it connects to major north European ports such as Rotterdam, Antwerp, and Hamburg. The Belt runs south to Venice in Italy, where it meets up with the Maritime Silk Road. The Maritime Silk Road begins in the port of Quanzhou in Fujian province and calls at Guangzhou, Beihai (Guangxi), and Haikou (Hainan) before heading south to the Malacca Strait. Then it connects to India/Pakistan (Gwadar port) and East Africa before entering the Mediterranean with key stops in the port of Piraeus in Greece and the port of Venice.*

FIGURE 7.4 The Belt and Road Initiative

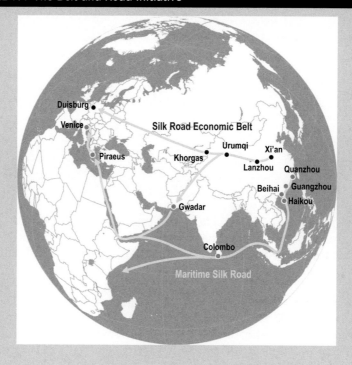

*Meanwhile, the number of routes has been extended. It now covers six economic corridors: the China–Mongolia Russia economic corridor, the New Eurasia Landbridge economic corridor, the China–Central Asia–West Asia economic corridor, the China–Pakistan economic corridor, the Bangladesh–China–India–Myanmar economic corridor, and the China–Indochina Peninsula economic corridor. Since the announcement of the BRI, the number of countries involved has continued to grow.*

*The BRI initiative is supported by a range of funds and financial institutions such as the Silk Road Fund, China Development Bank, and the Export-Import Bank of China (China Eximbank). CIC Capital, a subsidiary of China's sovereign wealth fund, also finances BRI projects, as do other commercial banks. Also, the multilateral Asian Infrastructure Investment Bank (AIIB) has its role to play in financing infrastructure in Asia.*

*China's motives for launching the BRI are of a cultural/historical, geoeconomic, and geopolitical nature:*

- *The **historical and cultural motives** are linked to the ancient trade routes connecting China to the Middle East and Europe that were established during the Han dynasty (207 BCE to 220 CE). Xi'an served as the starting point and endpoint of the historical Silk Road. The geography of the Maritime Silk Road has some resemblance to the historical exploits of Admiral Zheng He (1371–1433) who made maritime journeys between 1405 and 1433 with a reported fleet of some 300 ships. After sailing through South Asia, India, and the Middle East, Somalia and Kenya were reached in 1418.*
- *The **geoeconomic motives** are mainly linked to China's search for economic growth, including for its western and central provinces (Go West policy). Developing stronger economic ties with trading partners and emerging nations in Asia, Central Asia, and Africa, finding new markets for Chinese industries, for example in steel, cement, and alumina, streamlining the foreign investments of Chinese companies and enhancing capital convergence and currency integration of the Chinese Yuan (RMB) are also core motives.*
- *The **geopolitical motives** relate to China's ambition to increase its influence and to adopt a leadership role in the world by making stronger use of economics in shaping diplomatic relationships. There is also a domestic geopolitical component as China is determined to preserve its territorial integrity. The inclusion of Xinjiang province in the BRI as a hub to Central Asia should help to meet this objective.*

*While the BRI offers potential for economic cooperation and development, its implementation is **not without risks**. Some of the key regions involved face political instability. Infrastructure development faces some governance risks such as the need for financial discipline, careful budgeting, and fair tender procedures to avoid any waste of resources. Another key issue is the need to further develop know-how and expertise on infrastructure planning and financing in some of the less developed regions along the Belt and Road.*

*At the seaport level, Chinese companies have proven to be highly instrumental in the realization of key port expansion and rehabilitation projects across Asia, Africa, and parts of Europe, partly in the context of BRI. Still, Chinese*

> *investments are **being scrutinized** regarding the security risk they might pose to national interests, the need for open and fair contracting procedures, and China's credit terms imposed on some of the developing countries involved. Claims and accusations in these areas potentially damage China's reputation. Therefore, the Chinese government and companies are developing a more restrictive and prudent approach. At the same time, the BRI focuses on softer aspects such as cultural exchange to complement the hard economics behind international investments and transactions.*

# Chapter 7.2 Ports and economic development

*Ports are catalysts for economic development as they enable trade and support supply chains. Port investments have economic benefits that can be direct or indirect, and induced.*

## 1 PORTS AND ECONOMIC CHANGE

A port generally offers a value proposition to its region since it confers **economic and social benefits** but is also prone to environmental constraints (Box 7.5). Significant increases in port throughput, particularly in the containerized sector, have put pressure on developing new port infrastructures in existing facilities and entirely new developments when additional capacity cannot be developed on existing sites. Ports are capital-intensive infrastructures that are associated with a wide array of economic impacts. This is particularly apparent because port development and world trade are closely interrelated.

There are numerous expectations in the public sector, which often provides substantial capital investment (through the port authority or general funds), of seeing concrete and measurable economic impacts and benefits resulting from these investments. However, the existing literature is relatively scarce about the formal impacts of ports on regional development. Evidence is usually related to a single port over a narrow range of impacts, making general assessments difficult to achieve.

Economic impacts concern the wide range of changes brought by **infrastructure investment projects**, while economic benefits tend to be directly measurable impacts in terms of monetary value. However, many of these impacts can only be observed after the investments have been made and the benefits measured. An ex-ante (forecasting) exercise is hazardous and commonly leads to inaccurate assessments. Port forecast models are rarely accurate. The bottom line is that estimation of the economic impacts of port investments is an inexact field, which focuses on the effectiveness of transport infrastructure as a catalyst for indirect and induced benefits. Further, these investments are contingent on the scale and scope of changes they generate. Among the most relevant changes that have impacted ports and maritime transport are:

- **Economic changes**. Seaborne trade has increased substantially, in part because of the massive redistribution of manufacturing to low-cost locations (outsourcing) and in part because of ongoing economic growth. This underlines the growing importance of logistics for organizing the resulting complex distribution system. The global evolution of container ports, particularly their differential growth rates, is indicative of the driving force of offshoring and regional economic development.
- **Technical changes**. The growth in ship size to better achieve economies of scale has been a prevalent technical change, particularly since the 1990s, when post-Panamax containerships were first introduced. A growing level of ship specialization (containerships, bulk carriers, car carriers, and even cruise ships) requires dedicated port terminal facilities. A more recent trend concerns automation. All of the above has been placing pressure on ports to upgrade and improve their facilities.
- **Organizational changes**. The maritime and port industry is increasingly controlled by large shipping companies and terminal operators that have engaged in strategic alliances as well as mergers and acquisitions. Their goal is to provide a level of vertical and horizontal integration, which improves the performance of the port transport chain. A number of ports have been able to set up inland terminals.

## Box 7.5  The port as a value proposition

*A port generally offers a value proposition to its region since it confers economic and social benefits (Figure 7.5). The value proposition of a port for its main stakeholders is a combination of its economic, social, and environmental value. The economic value is often expressed as the direct and indirect economic benefits of ports in terms of employment and the support of economic activities. This focuses on the competitiveness of the port in attracting and retaining traffic, which implies a **commercial port**.*

FIGURE 7.5  The Port as a Value Proposition

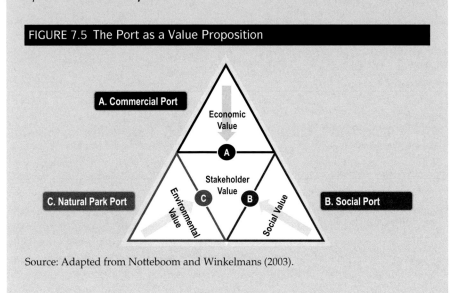

Source: Adapted from Notteboom and Winkelmans (2003).

*Social value is complex to assess since it goes beyond the provision of employment and includes forms of community support that link commercial responsibility (to the shareholders) to social acceptability and accountability. A* **social port** *is viewed as a generator of employment and a source of taxation revenue for the public sector.*

*Since the port is at the interface between land and maritime ecosystems, it is perceived to have an environmental value. Many port-related activities and developments have significant environmental impacts, such as dredging (and the disposal of dredging materials), the loss of coastal and wetlands ecosystems, air and water pollution, congestion on local roads, loss of seafront space, and light and noise externalities, as well as involvement in potential conflicts with commercial fishing and recreational uses. Under such circumstances, the port is a* **natural park** *aiming at mitigating environmental issues.*

*While the economic value of a port is usually well recognized, its social value can be mitigated, and its environmental value is subject to controversy. Ports are facing increasing pressures to demonstrate their value proposition beyond the economic value of a commercial port by encompassing environmental performance in order to ensure community support.*

These changes have involved port developments that are more **capital intensive** while relying on **less labor** and consuming **more land**. The imperatives of maritime shipping companies have been felt by ports as they increasingly tend to compete to attract traffic, particularly since hinterlands tend to be more contested. The industry expects lower tariffs and lower port times in the context of a highly competitive environment and low-profit margins. Ports acting in a monopolistic fashion find themselves with less leverage, negatively impacting their activity and regional economies.

The spatial framework of the port is also changing. Many port areas have seen the relocation of port industries to new sites, either within the region or to another country altogether. These changes have been associated with a dislocation of the relationships of many ports with their localities and regions; this has been labeled as port regionalization. While the port remains a strategically important infrastructure, its economic benefits are less directly apparent within the community, with weaker but more complex relations at the regional versus global levels. Further, ports are subject to different economic functions, such as gateways and transshipment hubs, each having different locational behavior.

The impacts of port infrastructure investments are expected to **positively influence port throughput effects** on local economic development. However, evidence across the world underlines that this **influence is weak**, with elasticity levels between throughput and employment that are typically less than 0.05 jobs per 100 tons. This implies that growth in traffic volumes is not associated with significant direct gains in employment. This elasticity is among the weakest in the transport sector, particularly compared to airports, which are the infrastructure with the highest elasticity. Still, the employment impacts of ports are positive and are usually higher for the service sector than for the industrial sector. Empirical evidence underlines that port infrastructure investment projects foster economic development and are important when a port is nearing its operational capacity. Under such circumstances, the lack of investments will lead to additional externalities, namely congestion, which will undermine the competitiveness of a whole region, if not a nation.

## 2 THE ECONOMIC BENEFITS OF PORTS: DIRECT, INDIRECT AND INDUCED EFFECTS

Like other transport infrastructures, several economic impacts of port infrastructure investments result in economic benefits. Economic theory often refers to ports as important economic development factors, particularly from a historical standpoint as promoters of commerce and the welfare of nations. It is not surprising to realize that most of the world's major cities are port cities, even if, in many cases, port activity now plays a rather small role in the general economic framework of their regions.

The basic argument is that ports **expand the market opportunity** of both national and international firms by expanding the port cargo base and hinterland (Box 7.6). By expanding the market areas of firms, ports increase competition, resulting in lower prices for port traffic users. These involve all economic activity sectors, including manufacturing firms, heavy industries, resource extraction industries, or retailers. Therefore, the economic benefits of ports are specific to the nature of the hinterland they service. They can be straightforward for hinterlands heavily dependent on resources since the output is directly handled by the port, or more nuanced when the hinterland involves manufacturing firms producing intermediate goods.

### Box 7.6 Factors expanding a port's cargo base

*There are three main interdependent factors behind the growth of a port's cargo base, particularly when it is containerized. They are reflective of port competition strategies:*

*Hinterland intensification. A port has a market area over which it assumes the dominance of cargo flows (Figure 7.6). This is often referred to as its main, or fundamental hinterland. Any organic growth in this hinterland, either as imports or exports, results in expanding the cargo base. A port can also be more actively involved in intensifying its fundamental hinterland by developing land for logistics such as port-centric logistics zones.*

*Hinterland expansion. A port also has a market area where it is competing with other ports, often referred to as its competition margin. If this hinterland expands, so does a port's cargo base. However, this requires large investments in infrastructure to increase hinterland connectivity, particularly along corridors. Further, inland facilities such as dry ports are part of a strategy to expand a port's cargo base.*

*Additional transshipment. Many ports have developed a notable transshipment function (ship to ship), some even becoming pure transshipment hubs. This function is often related to the position of a port within the global and regional shipping networks and the outcome of the decision of shipping lines in the organization of their service networks. The challenge remains that transshipment is*

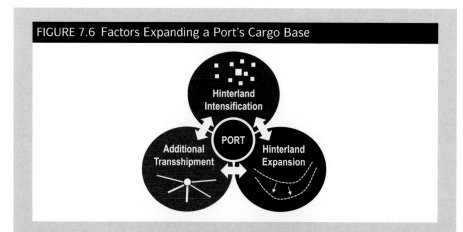

FIGURE 7.6 Factors Expanding a Port's Cargo Base

*complex to anchor and subject to fluctuation if a shipping line decides to change its network configuration. Ports with an active hinterland can expand this connectivity with that of transshipment since they can build additional economies of scale.*

*Thus, the balance between hinterland intensification, expansion, and transshipment can shift during a port's evolution. Typically, a port starts with a local cargo base which can be expanded through the development of its hinterland. However, until recently, the port played a limited role in developing its hinterland. Hinterland expansion was more coincidental and subject to national or regional infrastructure strategies.*

The increasing competitiveness brought by port investments can also be a double-edged sword for a national economy. It enables foreign firms to better access a national economy and compete with national firms, with some sectors being put out of business. However, the benefits of having better access to foreign markets and cheaper goods usually far exceed the risk of having inefficient national firms being undermined. Increasing competitiveness promotes positive economic benefits at the aggregate level, but these benefits are **not uniformly distributed among sectors and geography**.

Ports can be considered **funnels to economic development** since they act as catalysts and encourage development in specific economic sectors and locations near ports or along corridors. The economic benefits of ports are commonly categorized as direct, indirect, and induced. Indirect and induced benefits are far from being clearly identifiable (Figure 7.7).

- **Direct benefits to port**. They involve the revenues that accrue from the port activity and arise from the various charges levied on ships and cargo for the use of the port. Throughput and traffic volumes of a port are thus directly proportional to port revenue. They mainly include fees charged for pilotage, and berthing and towing, charges for cargo handling and demurrage charges. With the emergence of the landlord port model, port authorities are getting additional revenue from terminal concessions. Further, there may be additional rental revenue from the development

**FIGURE 7.7 The Port as a Funnel to Economic Development**

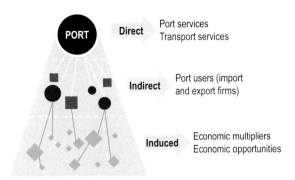

of port land, such as logistics zones or more general real estate projects. However, direct economic benefits tend to be less important than they were in the past, particularly because of mechanization and terminal concessions. Another category of direct benefits concerns the revenue generated by national transport firms servicing the port, such as trucking companies and railways (if present). The direct benefits to port users are generally referred to as economic benefits. These are also generally included in economic appraisals, although which particular benefits are to be included will depend on the given situation.

- **Indirect benefits to port users**. They involve firms that import or export goods from the port. Indirect benefits to port users include cost savings that arise from reduced operating costs, some of which may be realized outside the immediate port area. They involve lower shipping costs due to reduced turnaround time from improvements such as more berth space, better channel access, better terminal productivity, and reduced processing time for cargo at the port. They may also include savings in ship operating costs due to economies of scale from larger ships enabled by deeper drafts and additional volumes. Enhanced port facilities and operations may also reduce inland transport costs due to less congestion, increased productivity, and better turnaround time. Other benefits to users may include savings in insurance costs due to port improvements and savings in interest costs related to inventory, particularly from lower inventory levels, as more efficient port operations enable users to adopt better supply chain management practices.

- **Induced benefits to the economy**. They include the benefits that filter through to the suppliers of input factors, such as income to labor directly employed in port-related activities, and income to industries supplying the port with goods and services, creating indirect employment. In turn, these incomes generate re-spending, which further generates employment and income through the economic multiplier effect. Port investment may also have the effect of stimulating economic activity in industries that use the port. Such benefits, however, are not as straightforward as cost-saving benefits. The induced benefits are secondary and not usually taken into account in economic appraisals. This is partly because it is hard to know where to draw the line in including the successive rounds of induced income and employment. Thus, there is a risk of economic benefit analysis overstating the impacts of port activities by assuming indirect benefits that may not materialize. Besides, in developing economies, the potential induced benefits are often curtailed by lack of capital and skilled labor and are lost through import leakage. Induced benefits can also be assessed from an environmental perspective where less pollution such as noise, particulates, and carbon accrues as a social benefit in terms of quality of life and healthcare costs.

It is difficult to demonstrate that the economic activity and use of the related resources would only occur due to the port investment. When a port investment does lead to increased economic activity, the benefit is properly measured by the net value of the additional output. The direct benefits to the port are financial and would be taken into account in any financial appraisal as well as in economic appraisals. However, the financial benefits would be valued somewhat differently, with economic appraisals using a social discount rate and, for some inputs, possibly valuing them at shadow prices.

## 3 ASSESSING THE ECONOMIC BENEFITS OF PORT INVESTMENTS

The economic benefits of ports are usually measured at an **aggregate level** by indicators such as value-added, employment, taxation revenue, and return on investment. These indicators are primordial for the decision to invest in port development and must take into consideration:

- **Demand forecasts** trying to evaluate the expected traffic that the investment will support and facilitate.
- **Liner shipping strategies**, particularly how they service markets and how the port fits within their service configuration in terms of ship capacity and frequency. While some ports are acting as load centers, others are transshipment hubs. The function of transshipment is often the outcome of the strategy of a shipping company to service-specific regions.
- **Hinterland transport capacity and accessibility** which are contingent on the cargo bound to and originating from the port. They define the existing and potential cargo base that could be handled by the port.
- **Competition between terminals**, since there may be competing terminals within the same port facility. Terminals in a monopolistic situation usually have more pricing power but can be linked with higher returns.
- **Financing of investment** which relates to the capital source and conditions. Large port infrastructure projects are usually financed by bonds issued by port authorities or by investments made by international financial institutions such as development banks, sovereign wealth funds, or pension funds.

Assessing this information can involve different methodologies:

- **Surveys** are based on interviews and questionnaires or microeconomic data on firms. They try to identify and quantify the relationships between the various port actors, often from a qualitative perspective, but commonly in terms of employment. These studies have underlined the important relationships between freight forwarders and agents.

The economic benefits of ports are reflected in the complex system of transactions of the actors involved.

- **Comparative analysis** inferring economic benefits observed at a reference port, particularly its economic base. This approach tries to infer the economic changes that have already taken place in a comparable port setting (similar traffic and composition of traffic) to the port being investigated. Since local and regional economic conditions are not similar, such studies do not provide particularly accurate results. Still, they provide useful guidelines about what could happen to a port and its regional economy once an investment occurs.
- **Input–output analysis models** that seek to identify inter-sectorial multipliers, such as between port traffic and regional employment. They underline the agglomerating effects of port activities, either around the port or around the port region. Such studies have underlined low levels of elasticity between port traffic and service sector employment.

**Input–output analysis** is one of the most commonly used techniques. I–O analysis is based on a set of tables that quantify the linkages and transactions between different sectors of the economy. The quantities of inputs and outputs for a given period are entered in an input–output matrix/ table in order to analyze what happens across various sectors of an economy by performing a **multiplier analysis**.

> A **multiplier** is an index (ratio) that indicates the overall change in activity level that results from an initial change in activity. It effectively adds up all of the successive rounds of re-spending, assuming that major factors such as input prices are unchanged and that there are no resource limitations.

All sector-based multipliers (including direct, indirect, and induced effects) can be calculated when the matrix is complete and includes private consumption figures. The I–O technique can be used to prepare multipliers for a variety of impact measures, such as output, employment, and income. Multipliers can also be estimated for major components, such as by cargo type. Input–output analysis follows a top-down approach building upon comprehensive data per sector. Data collection can also rely on a bottom-up approach which implies the overall impact numbers are computed based on firm-level data. In the latter case, data collection can be based on the balance sheets or annual accounts of individual firms, or data is collected via surveys.

The technique and results of an I–O analysis are relatively easy to understand, and the expertise required is readily available from a large number of consultants and academics. However, the use of the technique also faces some issues:

- It can be **quite costly** if the required input–output base tables are not available at the national and regional level or are outdated. As the structure of a regional economy may change over time, the use of older I–O tables might lead to wrong results. In many cases, new regional tables are generated using survey methods or existing tables updated by incorporating more recent data on production and employment in the region.
- It does not incorporate any **constraints on the supply side**. For example, port development in a tight labor market can lead to crowding effects or

the shift of employees from one industry (e.g. chemical industry) to the port sector. In such a case, the net employment effect for the regional economy stays the same (no net gain in the total number of jobs).

There are also **integrated modeling** techniques available to measure the economic impact of ports. These approaches combine input–output analysis and econometric techniques to analyze the response of an economy to external shocks over time. A very advanced technique is **computable general equilibrium** (CGE) modeling, which estimates the optimal mix of economic variables (e.g. consumption) in response to an external shock. Integrated modeling and CGE modeling are more sophisticated than multiplier analysis, but the data requirements of these methods are very high, so are the costs of performing the analysis.

Port activities have multiplying effects within an economy which are much larger than the port itself. While the economic importance of ports grows, particularly for the sectors they are connected to, their relative importance within the region they are servicing often declines. This diminishes total economic benefits for a regional economy as this economy grows and becomes more complex. The following are the most commonly observed economic benefits of ports for regional employment:

- Port throughput is, in general, **positively related to employment in port regions**, implying that the higher the throughput, the higher is the employment level. Employment impacts are more substantial in the industry than in the service sector.
- Employment impacts vary by commodity sectors. Container and break-bulk traffic usually have **twice the employment impact** of dry and liquid bulk traffic.
- **Private ports** usually have more regional employment impacts than public ports since they usually serve commercial supply chains.
- Each direct port employment is commonly associated with **about three to four indirect jobs**, although such figures vary widely according to the surveys and the context. There is limited empirical evidence about job multiplier figures.

However, the economic benefits per unit of port cargo handled, either in terms of employment or of economic activity, usually **increase with economic growth**. The lower relative benefits of port investments are thus masked by economic growth, while the economic importance of ports is increasing. The economic benefits are less directly related to port activities but more related to the dynamics of the supply chains they support. This support becomes operational and functional, a benefit that is crucial to national competitiveness. Therefore, global trends underline a decline of direct economic benefits of ports but a notable rise in their indirect and induced economic benefits. This trend is challenging because direct economic benefits can be readily assessed, while indirect and induced effects are complex to capture.

## 4 EMPLOYMENT EFFECTS OF PORTS

Ports are important **job generators**. Shipping, cargo, and industrial activities and services in port areas generate direct employment effects. The logistics and industrial clusters in ports employ a vast labor force linked to cargo ship loading and unloading operations, ship operations and services (agencies, pilotage, towage, and bunkering), land transport, logistics activities, cargo services (freight forwarding and customs broking), industrial production facilities and government agencies.

The skills of the port-related employees and the interactions between them contribute to the **competitiveness of seaports**. Port activities are also responsible for a wide range of **indirect employment effects** through the linkages of harbors with other economic sectors and the spatial interactions with large logistics and economic poles outside port areas. Job creation in ports is mirrored in employment levels in education and training, tourism, and even in more cultural segments of the economic spectrum such as (maritime) museums. All the above activities provide people with wages, salaries, and other earnings and are major tax revenues for governments at different geographical levels.

The **employment effects of a port activity** usually extend beyond the initial round of employment generated by that activity. For example, stevedoring companies purchase a part of their inputs from local suppliers. The production of these inputs generates additional employment in the local economy. Suppliers, in turn, purchase goods and services from other local firms. There are further rounds of local re-spending, which generate additional employment. Similarly, households that receive income from employment in stevedoring and related activities spend some of their income on local goods and services. These purchases result in additional local jobs. Some of the household income from these additional jobs is in turn spent on local goods and services, thereby creating further jobs and income for local households. As a result of these **successive rounds of re-spending** in the framework of local purchases, the overall impact on the economy exceeds the initial round of output, income, and employment generated by stevedoring. In essence, seaports create employment impacts in four ways:

- **Direct employment** includes the jobs local firms provide to support services to the seaport. Seaports create direct port employment through all types of activities in the port cluster. These jobs are dependent upon seaport activity and would disappear if the seaport activity were to cease. Typical direct jobs include dockworkers, ship agents, pilots, tug boat operators, freight forwarders, employees of port authorities, ship chandlers, warehouse operators, terminal operators and stevedores, and jobs with railroad, barging, and trucking companies.
- Ports also generate **indirect jobs** due to local purchases by the port-related companies directly dependent upon seaport activity. Hence, port activities are responsible for a wide range of indirect employment effects through the linkages of harbors with other economic sectors and spatial interactions with large logistics and economic poles outside port areas.
- The employees of port-related companies spend part of their wages and salaries. **Induced jobs** are jobs created locally and throughout the wider national or supranational economy due to purchases of goods and services by those directly employed. Induced employment can include grocery stores, local construction industry (housing), retail stores, health care providers, local transportation services, local and state government

agencies providing public services and education to those directly employed, and businesses providing professional and business services in support of those directly employed.

• The last group of employment effects consists of **related jobs**. Manufacturing and distribution firms in and outside the port partly rely on efficient cargo handling operations in seaports. For instance, the steel industry requires the cost-efficient import of iron ore and coal for the blast furnaces and needs the port for exporting finished products such as steel booms and coils. Manufacturers and retail outlets, and distribution centers handling imported containerized cargo rely on efficient port operations. The dependency of related jobs on the port is a function of the location. When industrial activities or distribution centers are located in the port, or in close proximity, the low competitiveness of the seaport could lead to a loss of jobs. In such a case, it is difficult to make a strict distinction between direct and related jobs. When these activities are located in the more distant hinterland, then inefficient operations in one port could lead to a **shift of the cargo flows to a competing port**. A shift of traffic between ports generally preserves employment levels in the related industrial companies and distribution centers in the more distant hinterland. The demand for the final product (e.g. steel products or consumer products) creates the demand for employment with these shippers/consignees that does not involve using a particular seaport or marine terminal.

The extent of the employment effects of port activity is affected by the **boundaries of the economy that is being analyzed**. The increasingly international nature of port and shipping activities and the characteristics of global production networks and global supply chains make the **employment effects of port activities increasingly extend beyond the local port level to a regional or even supranational level**. A few examples underline this trend:

• **Shipping lines** are operational on a global scale. At a local scale, they might generate employment via their liner shipping agencies in the ports of call. However, the jobs related to ship management, container fleet management, and investment and commercial strategies are usually concentrated in global or regional headquarters.

• **Global container terminal operators** such as PSA, Hutchison Ports, DP World, or APM Terminals generate many operational jobs at the local port level but keep some activities, such as equipment purchases, centralized in global or regional headquarters. Terminal operators might purchase terminal equipment not from local operators but from foreign suppliers in Europe (e.g. Kalmar, Gottwald) or overseas (e.g. Shanghai-based ZPMC).

For a particular port activity, the **flow-on employment effects to the national or international economy** will thus generally be larger than the flow-on effects to the regional economy.

## 5 MEASURING EMPLOYMENT EFFECTS

The appropriate technique for analyzing the economic impact of specific port activity is determined by the characteristics of the activity and the region being analyzed and the purpose of the analysis. The availability of data is also an important factor. Measuring the employment impacts of ports is not an easy task. There are **several methodological problems** when evaluating port impacts:

- Identifying **activities that are dependent on the port** and evaluating their **degree of dependency** is potentially exposed to the risk of subjectivity. A lack of exact data can lead to an **overestimation of the degree of dependency** and an overestimation of the employment effects.
- Determining the **intensity of the employment impact of the port**, such as how much of the consumption activities and multiplier effects can be attributed to the existence of the port. Also, an estimation bias can occur when no exact figures are available.

Many of the above problems are structured by differentiation between direct, indirect, induced, and related jobs. However, there is no unique standard methodology for defining the types of impacts, which makes port comparisons difficult. Benchmarking employment impacts of ports is further complicated by the large variety of methodologies applied (mostly bottom-up approaches) and a general lack of recent and port-relevant economic input–output data at the macro-economic scale.

Despite the **lack of a uniform approach** on the issue, many port authorities and (national) government agencies produce figures on the economic impact of their respective ports, including the employment effects. A few European examples are:

- Every year the **National Bank of Belgium** publishes figures on the economic impact of the ports of Antwerp, Ghent, Zeebrugge, Ostend, and more recently, also for the ports of Brussels and Liège. The studies are part of the Working Papers series of the National Bank.
- The Ministry of Transport, Public works and Water Management of the Netherlands regularly commissions a **'Havenmonitor' report** (Port Monitor).
- In the autumn of 2008, Oxford Economics was commissioned by the Chamber of Shipping, British Ports Association (BPA), and United Kingdom Major Ports Group (UKMPG) to prepare two economic impacts studies on aspects of the UK maritime industry. One focuses on ports and the other on the UK shipping industry. These studies are entitled 'The economic contribution of ports to the UK economy' and 'The economic contribution of the UK shipping industry'.

The employment effects are mainly expressed in **full-time equivalents** (FTEs) and a distinction is generally made between direct and indirect/induced effects. Employment impacts are often **disaggregated to the level of individual ports or port regions** and specific economic activities (cargo handling, industrial sector). However, the results are often not comparable among countries or even among ports within the same country as there is a great diversity in measurement methods between countries/ports. There are methodological differences, particularly in terms of the definition of the port area and the economic sectors, the terminology used, the level of aggregation of the data, the approach followed (i.e. top-down via an input–output table with sector data or bottom-up based on firm-level data) and the definitions and methods deployed to analyze indirect/induced employment effects. The observed methodological differences can result in non-transparency and wrong benchmarking exercises. Stakeholders might show some mistrust of the results obtained, even if the methodology is made very transparent. The fact that methodologies differ further fuels criticism of employment studies for being over-optimistic regarding real job creation.

Despite the lack of a standardized methodology, some **common conclusions** apply:

- **Total employment effects of ports** (direct and indirect/induced) are significant and typically represent between 1% and 5% of the total employment in a country.
- In many ports, **local direct employments effects of port activity are stagnating or decreasing** due to a combination of deindustrialization, containerization, and the increasing use of automated port handling systems and technology. As a result, the growth in direct FTEs in many (but not all) port areas is either negative or close to zero while throughput volumes increase.
- **More and more jobs are created outside the port area**. A large variety can be observed in how these processes are materializing in specific individual ports. At one extreme, some ports have succeeded in attracting more businesses and thus more jobs in the port area in recent years. At the other extreme, some seaports have become merely transit centers servicing economic and logistics centers in the immediate or more distant hinterland. When employment effects increasingly extend beyond the local port level, ports might be confronted with a lower direct employment level but higher indirect and related jobs. Potential reasons for less direct jobs include productivity gains, outsourcing activities to companies outside the port, or the delocalization of activities to the hinterland.

## 6 GLOBAL-LOCAL MISMATCH OF THE ECONOMIC BENEFITS OF PORTS

With the setting up of global supply and transport chains, there has been a growing level of **mismatch between the benefits of port activities and the scale and scope of these benefits**. While at the aggregate level, it is clear that port investments have economic benefits, the spatial and sectoral distribution of these benefits is far less evident. One particular mismatch concerns local (community) versus regional/national/global benefits. The following points underline this mismatch:

- **Labor** usually comes from the **local community** and its benefits (mostly wages) are derived in the region, particularly as indirect job multipliers. As port employment has gone down because of mechanization and containerization, so have the local labor benefits. Yet, several port jobs are remunerated at a wage which is much higher than those usually found in the manufacturing sector. The most important employment multiplier of ports is usually related to trucking.
- **Capital** usually does not come from the community but is provided by national and international funding sources, such as investment banks, pension funds, and terminal operators. Thus, the return on this capital

(e.g. loan or operational revenues) does not accumulate in the port region but among global financial centers.

- **Firms** can be local in ownership, but the commercial trends have underlined **vertical and horizontal integration** in the port industry. For instance, this means that terminal operation at one port is usually part of a portfolio of terminals located in different ports across the region or even the world. Thus, profits derived from terminal operations are not necessarily invested in the port where they were generated.
- **Port land use** is usually regulated by leasing and concession contracts, but land prices are often a tool for attracting investors and usually do not reflect real value. This underlines that the impacts of ports on real estate values are not necessarily fully accounted for.
- **Local transport infrastructure**, namely roads, are usually provided for free (or at a fee lower than costs). This represents a form of local or regional subsidy for globally-focused activities.
- **Taxes and customs duties** are only partly allocated to the port region. They are usually a national source of income used to fund other social and infrastructure programs.
- **Environmental** (pollution) and **social** (noise, accidents) externalities are assumed by the community, while the generators of these externalities usually bear only a fraction of them.

Therefore, port benefits are increasingly **distributed across actors** and concern geography that **transcends the local community** and, at times, the region. This trend skews the assessment of the benefits of port investments, where the local economic impacts can be much less significant than those at the regional or national levels. Conflicts or pressures can result from local communities that may be disappointed because their expectations about the economic benefits of port activities may not be met. At the same time, their perception of environmental externalities is present. Still, despite the complexity of assessing their economic impacts, ports remain fundamental to the economic well-being of the nations, regions, and localities they are embedded in.

# Chapter 7.3  Port planning and development

*Port planning and development involve the strategic port planning process, data collection and forecasting, stakeholder relations management in ports, and the evaluation of port development plans and projects.*

## 1 STRATEGIC PORT PLANNING

### 1.1 Port planning in its context

Three different types of port planning by port authorities can be distinguished:

- **Short-term planning** involves the current allocation of the port's resources and services. The resulting decisions aim to solve practical problems related to efficient cargo handling, vessel turnaround, and reasonable utilization of port facilities. Within short-term planning, a distinction can be made between operational and tactical planning. The former usually refers to a time horizon of one year. The latter refers to a planning horizon of one to three years. An important feature of short-term planning is that the time span is too short to allow major changes in the supply of port services, such as by infrastructural investments aimed at increasing port capacity).

• **Medium-term planning** involves both financial and strategic planning, often reported through business plans. The budgeting for the annual allocation of the port's resources to specific activities is part of the financial planning process. Strategic plans, which are usually prepared every three to five years, aim to allocate port resources to different activities and meet specific marketing and financial objectives. This assumes a competitive environment in which the allocation of resources will affect the structure and level of demand.

• **Long-term planning** demands a more fundamental and visionary approach, in most cases embodied in the development of port master plans or strategic port plans. The output is a physical plan (including capital budgeting) for the future development of port infrastructure and other capabilities and capacities with a ten to 30 years planning horizon.

Port management is challenged to maximize consistency between the different types of port planning.

## 1.2 Strategic port planning in a changing market environment

One of the most important differences between strategic port planning and other types of port planning is its **emphasis on evaluating the changes taking place in the environment** and assessing the risks and uncertainties associated with these changes. Ports are affected by larger uncertainties and risks than before. These trends and the expansion of the role of the private sector in port activities have forced ports to become **more market-oriented** and to revise their strategic planning process. This shift can be illustrated by applying the "Corporate Strategy Matrix" to the port sector. The **Port Strategy Matrix** identifies four basic strategies that ports can adopt (Figure 7.8). Port behavior is

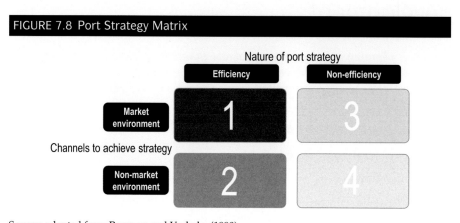

FIGURE 7.8 Port Strategy Matrix

Source: adapted from Rugman and Verbeke (1990)

classified according to (a) the nature of the strategy and (b) the different channels used for implementing this strategy:

- The **nature of the strategy** can either be **efficiency** or **non-efficiency oriented**. The former situation can normally be expected in a competitive environment. In such a situation, a port seeks protection from competitors by creating government shelter or collusive behavior.
- The **implementation** channels of a strategy are situated either in a **market** or a **non-market** environment. In the former context, market forces prevail, whereas, in the latter situation, ports exert strategic behavior vis-à-vis government and pressure groups.

By combining nature and channel elements, the Port Strategy Matrix is constructed, and **four port strategy options** are identified. Non-efficiency-based port strategies aim to achieve an 'artificial' advantage in the form of shelter or protection vis-à-vis rival ports. Unfortunately, such shelter-based strategies are not sustainable in the long run as ports are increasingly subjected to competitive market forces. For instance, ports situated in **quadrant 3** and looking for market sharing agreements may find themselves in an unstable position and may be forced to pursue an efficiency-based strategy.

The **Russian port system during Soviet times** was situated in **quadrant 4**. The Soviet government had a large impact on the economy through state-owned factories and companies and the development of rather rigid multi-year plans affecting all economic activities. As all ports were state-owned, inter-port competition in the Soviet Union was low to non-existent (non-market environment). The ports were developed as strategic assets to serve state-owned industries (steel, mining, manufacturing) and the overall economic system. Given the focus on full employment, port efficiency and overall labor productivity in ports were generally low.

As a result of the changes in the market environment, an increasing number of ports are forced to seek a position in **quadrant 1**, which has a major impact on traditional strategic port planning. Ports operating in highly competitive and volatile markets often develop formal port planning processes involving a larger amount of data collection and analysis. These planning exercises are concerned with directing change rather than responding to it. This involves a proactive rather than a reactive or defensive attitude towards changes in the external environment.

### 1.3 The strategic port planning process

A typical strategic port planning process consists of **five different building blocks** or phases in the development (Figure 7.9).

#### STEP 1: FORMULATE A MISSION OR STRATEGIC INTENT
The starting point in the strategic port planning process is the formulation of the **strategic intent** or **mission statement** of the port. A strategic intent reflects the long-term objective of a port and, by definition, is very **ambitious**. In general, a strategic intent must be valid over long periods of time. In formulating its strategic intent, a port should try to **go beyond extrapolation** of the current status and role of the port. Strategic port planning should aim to identify strategies and

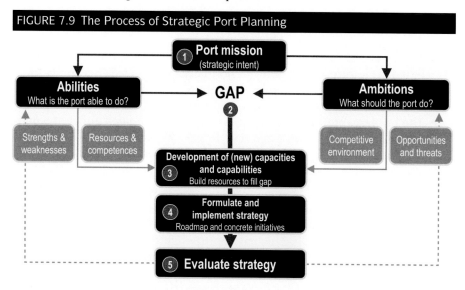

FIGURE 7.9 The Process of Strategic Port Planning

formulate objectives that will provide the port with a competitive advantage to attain its strategic intent when translated into programs and activities. Thus, strategic planning should be focused on the question 'what should we do differently next year or next period to get closer to our strategic intent?'

The **absence of a clear strategic intent** or explicit objectives prevents the port from developing a dynamic strategy. Ad hoc planning often merely results in marginal or incremental adjustments to a current situation and does not allow for building a sustainable competitive advantage. The starting point for future port strategy is too often based on the current strategy without referring to intentions for the future. The entire port sector must accept the port's ambition as specified in the strategic intent. Personal effort and commitment of the individuals involved in the port sector can only be gained if they can identify themselves with the strategic intent.

### STEP 2: ASSESS THE GAP BETWEEN ABILITIES AND AMBITIONS

The strategic intent as defined in step 1 may lead to identifying a difference between what the port can do (abilities) and what the port should do (ambitions). In order to get a complete picture of this gap, a port should assess its port-specific resources and competencies and perform an internal appraisal of its organizational strengths and weaknesses. Further, a port should assess its competitive environment by performing an external appraisal of the environmental opportunities and threats available in the market environment.

### STEP 3: CREATE RESOURCES TO FILL THE GAP

A port can **narrow the gap** between resources (what it is able to do = linked to strengths and weaknesses) and the ambitions set out in the strategic intent (what it should do = linked to environmental opportunities and threats) by creating new valuable resources. Port management should integrate the process of the development of new resources into its strategic planning. Each port is **a collection of physical and intangible assets and capabilities**. The effectiveness of a port is determined by these assets and capabilities. In order to become or remain competitive, port management has to identify, cultivate and exploit its core competencies. Core competencies are the collective learning in the organization, especially how to coordinate diverse skills and integrate multiple streams of technology. The management's ability to consolidate the port's capabilities and skills into competencies that empower the port sector to adapt quickly to changing opportunities is the real source of competitive advantage.

## STEP 4: STRATEGY FORMULATION AND IMPLEMENTATION

After identifying core competencies and resources needed to fill the gap between its abilities (what is the port able to do?) and ambitions (what should the port do?), the next step is to determine strategies to develop a sustainable competitive advantage. The most important resources and capabilities of a port are durable, difficult to identify and understand, imperfectly transferable, not easily replicated, and in the clear ownership and control of the port. Strategy formulation should design a strategy that makes the most effective use of these core resources and capabilities. In the framework of strategy formulation, a port has to:

1. Define specific objectives or goals to pursue.
2. Define specific targets.
3. Develop and compare alternative strategies.

In contrast to the strategic intent, the **objectives** must be dynamic and permit changing external and internal factors. Objectives must be specific in terms of time span and figures and must refer to defined departments or units of the organization. The targets must be more specific than the objectives and apply to smaller units of the organization. Objectives and targets should cover marketing, operation, finance, workforce, and the environment. The ability of a port authority to design and select strategies can be increased by improving communications within the port organization and with the port industry and the relevant public authorities (see Section 4 of this chapter on **stakeholder relations management**). Once a strategic plan has the full support of the entire port organization, the actual strategy implementation can include the following **basic actions**:

- Reallocation of resources (labor skills, technological equipment).
- Reorganization of management or port services provided.
- Investments in new and existing physical (e.g. terminal) or non-physical (e.g. education) assets.
- Implementation of efficiency-oriented measures to lower port user' costs or port operating costs.
- Implementation of measures to improve the sustainability of the port and the supply chains.
- Change in institutional and governance-related aspects of the port.

## STEP 5: EVALUATE THE EFFECTIVENESS OF CHOSEN STRATEGIES

Strategy evaluation should primarily be concerned with whether the port is on the right track for closing the gap between abilities and ambitions and is achieving this at the desired rate. This evaluation must not only consider whether the strategy has been implemented properly and is effective in achieving the objectives and targets. Primarily, it should monitor the process of building a competitive advantage. As the dashed lines in the figure indicate, the strategic evaluation also involves a **constant adaptation of the objectives and strategies** in order to respond adequately to relevant changes in the resources and capabilities of the port (internal appraisal) and its competitive environment (external appraisal).

## 1.4 Approaches to the port planning process

Three basic approaches can be distinguished to structure the port planning process:

- **Top-down planning**. The government or port authority sets the strategic intent and prepares the plan. The main problem associated with this approach is that the port industry might feel neglected while having a better view of the port's resources and capabilities and possessing more information on the external environment.
- **Bottom-up planning**. The port community provides inputs to the strategic plan. The government or port authority integrally uses these inputs to create a strategic plan without critically assessing the views and expectations of the port community. Such an approach can be valuable if the government or port authority wishes to pursue a microeconomic approach to port planning. However, such an approach might be severely influenced by local rationality and opportunism.
- **Goals down-plans up planning**. The government or port authority sets the strategic intent and asks the wider port community to propose ideas and plans that comply with this intent. In most cases, the government or port authority will aim to achieve a structured confrontation by institutionalizing the strategic port planning process. This approach typically envisages a balance between macro-economic objectives and microeconomic goals.

In formulating and implementing a strategy, ports must be able to admit that certain activities could be performed more effectively by other economic actors or in other places, such as inland locations. An effective resource-based strategy does not need to limit itself to the geographical boundaries of the port, but should involve strategic port-network planning.

## 2 DATA COLLECTION IN PORT PLANNING

The strategic planning process demands comprehensive **data about internal resources and capabilities and the external competitive environment of the port**. In collecting the necessary data, a port should keep in mind not only the need to look for **quantitative data** but also the need for valuable **qualitative elements**. A unilateral focus on quantitative data can lead to a narrow-minded analysis of the past and current situation with too much emphasis on marginal developments. For example, a database can track fluctuations in the global steel trade but it is more important for a port to know the general trend and why this trend exists, including the qualitative elements of the evolution. Moreover, some resources such as people-based skills cannot be found in a port database. Such qualitative elements are indispensable in building core competencies and are thus extremely important in the strategic planning process.

There are different ways to collect the necessary qualitative and quantitative information. For the **internal appraisal of resources and capabilities**, a port can get information from port management. A key problem in appraising capabilities is maintaining objectivity. Hence, the people who know most about the port may also be the people whose opinions are likely to be biased. Therefore it is useful to check the information gained against **evidence from**

**outside**. In this respect, customer and competitor surveys can give additional and less biased information about the strengths and weaknesses of the port in question.

For the **external appraisal of the competitive environment**, a port can rely on a multitude of official statistics (e.g. government trade statistics), press reports, and sector studies. More specific information can be obtained through customer surveys, port publications (statistics, master plans), or through the reports of independent experts (consultants, universities, market researchers). However, a major problem remains the reliability and comparability of the information obtained. For example, as the procedure for collecting and presenting port statistics has not been harmonized globally, it remains dangerous to perform port comparisons based on official port statistics. The observation of the external environment should also include changes in technology (port, shipping, and industry), regulations, and public policies (including trade policy, shipping, and port policy). In performing an external appraisal, the tools used for competitor analysis should be focused on the existing resources of the present competing ports and **potential future resources and future competitors**. Regarding customers, special attention should be given to the strategies developed by those clients who determine the routing of the cargo.

If data models are used to assess the internal and external environment of a port, the analyst should keep in mind the **assumptions** that form the basis for the analysis. A **sensitivity analysis** of the results can offer more insight into the value and reliability of the outcomes. Moreover, models must be continuously appraised as to their suitability for the assigned task.

## 3 TRAFFIC FORECASTING AS PART OF PORT PLANNING AND DEVELOPMENT

### 3.1 Rationale behind traffic forecasting

Master plans and port infrastructure projects usually require **long-term forecasts**. As the design and the construction of a port infrastructure may take up to five years or more, and the infrastructure might be around for the next 50 to 100 years, public decision-makers and port authorities are asked to present long-term traffic forecasts. Poor demand forecasts and estimations of future financial flow (revenues and costs) can lead to bad decisions on port investments, wrong timing of such investments, and an overall misallocation of resources, causing both public and private economic and financial losses. Thus, high-quality port traffic forecasts are needed to help **optimize and rationalize investment decisions** regarding their timing and the existing and expected balance between port demand and capacity (Box 7.7).

---

### Box 7.7  Port demand, timing and capacity utilization

*Port planning decisions are taken in a world full of uncertainty. Errors in port traffic forecasts can severely under or overestimate the demand for new port facilities. Therefore, traffic growth rates should be integrated explicitly in the planning model in order to circumvent the error risks in forecasting. Much attention must be directed to the combination of individual risk factors.*

The ***interdependency between port capacity and port traffic demand*** *is one of the main points of attention (Figure 7.10). In general, any port capacity extension will result (albeit not always) in a proportional growth in port traffic.* **Port user costs** *(PUC) rise sharply once port traffic approaches the existing effective port capacity limits (the HEAT or* **highest efficient attainable throughput**). *This creates a real danger of traffic decline or stagnation. The HEAT should be increased in due time to keep demand growth at a high level. An extension and optimization of port facilities will reduce waiting times. A crucial factor is to know whether the demand for new capacity exists.* **Port overcapacity** *is created when a port extension does not induce growth in port demand. In these circumstances, average port costs will be elevated, negatively affecting the competitiveness of the port (Figure 7.11).*

**FIGURE 7.10  Port Demand and Capacity Utilization**

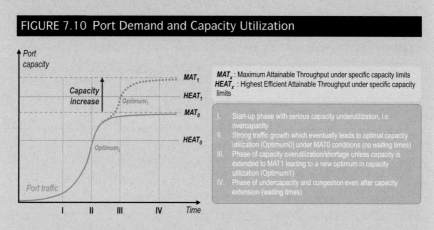

Source: Adapted from Winkelmans and Notteboom (2002).

**FIGURE 7.11  Timing of Port Capacity Extension**

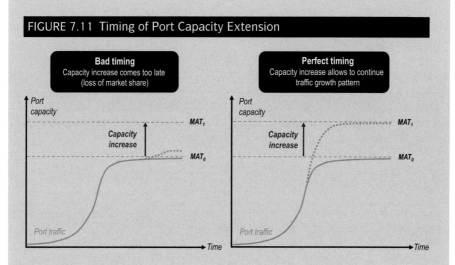

Source: Adapted from Winkelmans and Notteboom (2002).

Port managers are increasingly expected to rely on forecasts and other statistical or quantitative techniques for supporting and justifying the entire decision-making process related to port planning and development. They are required to disclose more information on the assumptions which underlie their strategic planning. This allows them to strengthen the reliability of their development plans. In a port planning context, the port authority has to define the long-term direction of port development, including, among other things, defining the future port size (land and water areas), the portfolio of commodities to be served, and the related destination use of various facilities. The port authority has to plan its own investments in line with demand expectations and forecasting, but also complementarily with the investments planned by individual private actors in their business plans.

## 3.2 Forecasting methods

The port environment exhibits a high level of uncertainty. Cargo flows show variability and seasonality caused by economic cycles (peaks and downturns), seasonal fluctuations and time variations, and economic, social, political, nature-related, or health shocks and crises. The demand for port services is also affected by the evolutionary trajectories of other infrastructures connected to the port. The port choices made by (large) market players such as shippers, shipping lines, and related carrier alliances can also generate traffic volatility. Traffic volumes originate from the service patterns of shipping lines which, in turn, depend upon a number of underlying macro and micro-economic variables. These variables are often characterized by causal relationships, which increase technical concerns related to selecting the most suitable statistical methods for predicting future traffic flows.

A number of factors may affect selecting the appropriate method, such as the context of the forecast, the relevance and availability of historical data, the desired degree of accuracy, and the time period to be forecast. Qualitative and quantitative techniques are two basic forecasting methods, with the latter more reliable and accurate.

**Quantitative estimation techniques** are based on historical data series, that allow for establishment of trends and causal relations between the objective variable to be forecast and other covariates. These trends and relations are subsequently used in models, such as causal and econometric models, to predict future developments. Quantitative methods include a wide range of techniques:

- The first set of quantitative forecasting techniques is exclusively based on **time series analysis**. In time series models, the expected future value of a variable, such as traffic, is obtained by extrapolation or mathematical deduction from the historical pattern of the variable concerned. Scholars also distinguish between parametric forecasting models, such as assuming a model structure that can be described through well-defined mathematical expressions, and non-parametric ones, which are those not based on any definite functional form of the variables. The most used are moving average and exponential smoothing, the ARIMA (autoregressive integrated moving average) approach, and considering or excluding seasonality (SARIMA, X13-ARIMA-SEATS), as well as additional implementations and generalizations (e.g. ARCH and GARCH models). These methods enable the depiction of the main properties of the time series, identification of the underlying data generating process, and forecast estimations on future trends. To overtake the linearity assumption of the data generating process, Artificial Neural Network (ANN) and smoothing splines models are also suggested.

• The second set of more sophisticated quantitative forecasting methods rely on both **causal relationships and time series analysis**. These models start from the assumption that a causal relation can be established between the factor to be forecast and one or more variables. Causal models aim to capture this relationship in mathematical expressions, which constitute the starting point for scenario-based forecasting. Building further on the regression model approach, a large set of econometric models have been implemented (e.g. OLS, GLM, multilevel or hierarchical modeling), supported by longitudinal time-series data.

When data are scarce or ambiguous, **qualitative forecasting techniques** are preferred. They typically rely on expert human judgments and opinions combined with non-complete and non-numerical data. The qualitative forecasting techniques, also known as technological or engineering methods, include **explorative and normative techniques**. In explorative methods, future developments are evaluated based on empirical data from the past supplemented with expert information regarding expected traffic flows. Normative techniques start from future objectives and assess whether these objectives can be met, considering the present resources, capacity, structural limitations, and technologies. Among the techniques, expert opinions are used in the Delphi Method, Panel Consensus Forecast, and Visionary Forecast. Market Research Forecast and Historical Analogy Forecast are based on expert opinions, general trends, and economic knowledge. In general, qualitative methods are not reliable and accurate, but they are useful for drawing approximate scenarios in high variability contexts. As these qualitative methods are based on applying specific procedures, they do not simply reflect the subjective judgments of individuals or organizations viewed as experts.

In some circumstances, qualitative forecasts do not provide port managers and decision-makers with exhaustive data and information for dealing with the challenges impacting port planning and development. In these cases, hybrid techniques might be preferred. In the hybrid case, expert information and judgment are used to complement the outputs of the traffic forecasting models. This might be particularly relevant when considering the exposure of the port industry to economic or social shocks, as demonstrated by the COVID-19 pandemic. It might be useful to mix econometric models with expert judgments and specific commodity insights to provide a solid empirical backbone for strategic decisions.

Given the wide range of port activities and cargo flows, there is a need for a **commodity-wise approach in traffic forecasting**, following a disaggregated forecasting approach at the level of commodity types. Each coherent commodity group has distinct throughput drivers and terminal requirements. For example, inbound, outbound, and sea-sea transshipment flows in the container market may require different model specifications.

The longer the time horizon of predictions, the lower the expected accuracy of forecasts. The purpose of port-related forecasting in such circumstances is to **build scenarios** that help port managers and decision-makers identify the major opportunities and threats going forward and deal with related uncertainties. Uncertainty is tentatively captured using sensitivity analyses and scenario building.

### 3.3 Challenges and pitfalls in traffic forecasting

Traffic forecasting comes with a number of challenge and pitfalls:

- **Lack of know-how**. The forecasting exercise requires a solid knowledge of the port ecosystem and the key variables triggering change, as well as significant technical capabilities in terms of data gathering and data analysis and a good dose of caution in avoiding bias. While port authorities typically present long-term traffic forecasts in the context of port master plans or port (infrastructure) projects, they might not always have the capabilities, know-how, and resources to engage in traffic forecasting. Thus, they might have to resort to experts to support these types of exercises.
- **Stakeholder perceptions**. Despite the advances made in forecasting techniques, the relevance and validity of traffic forecasts are under the scrutiny of port stakeholders, such as market players, government agencies, and community groups. Port authorities are typically challenged to reassess the role and necessity of forecasting exercises in port planning and development processes. Choosing and applying appropriate forecasting methods, interpreting forecasting outputs, and communicating traffic forecasts with stakeholders are also challenges.
- **Complexity**. Traffic forecasts are highly complex exercises, as they should capture uncertainties and the interdependencies between factors that can influence future traffic flows. When engaging in traffic forecasting, port managers or the experts engaged by them often assume that, in predicting future values, uncertainties can be addressed by sensitivity analyses or by considering different plausible scenarios. Traffic forecasts in the context of port planning and development are inherently dependent on these assumptions and scenarios.
- **Ad hoc decision-making**. A number of ports, particularly medium-sized and minor ports, continue to operate on an informal or fragmented basis. Development in these ports often lacks a common backbone, resulting in the evaluation of ad hoc opportunities or political/market pressure. In these cases, port planning activity is not formalized into a comprehensive planning document with a long-term focus and a lack of reliable traffic forecasts.
- **Keep it simple**. Ports might avoid the use of cutting edge forecasting methods, even if these could provide better results. They might fear that using complex methods gives the forecasting exercise a high 'black box' image for stakeholders. Furthermore, sophisticated and complex statistical methods do not necessarily perform better than simpler ones. A lack of reliable data sources or inaccuracies in data gathering, for example, can lead to poor quality forecasts, notwithstanding the sophistication of the forecasting methodology.
- **The life expectancy of forecasts**. As it may take many years to complete a master plan or to implement a port infrastructure project, some of the initial assumptions and forecasts might already be outdated by the

time the plan is presented. This can undermine the validity of the master plans and opens a window of opportunity for decision-makers to justify their actions related to certain port investments on other grounds than the master plan's provisions.

## 4 STAKEHOLDER INVOLVEMENT IN PORT PLANNING AND DEVELOPMENT

### 4.1 Who are the stakeholders?

A large number of actors have interests in the port sector. As a result, (strategic) port planning and development are usually performed in an environment where a multitude of interacting and sometimes conflicting interests are involved. This complexity can create challenges in developing a mission statement, formulating the objectives and strategies for a port, and advancing port development projects.

> In the broad view, **stakeholders** are described as any individual or group having an interest in or being affected by the project. The narrow view only recognizes stakeholders whose relationship is primarily of an economic/contractual kind.
>
> Stakeholder relations management (SRM) aims to balance various groups and take due note of their rights.

In a landlord port, there are internal stakeholders, economic or contractual external stakeholders, community stakeholders, and public policy stakeholders (Figure 7.12).

***INTERNAL STAKEHOLDERS***
They are part of the comprehensive port authority organization. Apart from realizing port authority objectives, the top management of a port authority might also envisage more personal goals such as salary, prestige, and power.

FIGURE 7.12 Stakeholder Groups

The employees are interested in their wages, working conditions, and personal development. The public, semi-public or private shareholders pursue goals such as return on investment, shareholder/stakeholder value, and welfare creation. The identification of the actual shareholders of a port authority is not always an easy task. A large number of landlord port authorities are of the (semi-)public kind, with strong links to a municipality, a city, a region, or province. The true de facto shareholders of a public port authority are the taxpayers on the relevant geographical level. As such, the general public has a dual role to play and in many cases the (local) public is at the same time an external stakeholder and indirect shareholder.

### ECONOMIC/CONTRACTUAL EXTERNAL STAKEHOLDERS

The inter-organizational relationships among economic/contractual external stakeholders are characterized by two forms of interaction: physical (related to the physical transfer of cargo) and incorporeal. The latter type of interaction consists of contractual, supervisory, or information-based exchanges. The interactions between port authorities and the first-order port players are mainly of an incorporeal kind. For instance, port companies involved in physical operations are linked to the port authority via concession agreements.

Different port companies and supporting industries invest directly in the port area and generate value-added and employment. Some of these companies are mainly involved in physical transport operations linked to cargo flows (for example, terminal operators and stevedoring companies, including the carrier/terminal operator in the case of dedicated terminals). Others solely offer logistical organization services (for example, forwarding agencies, shipping agencies). Industrial companies in the port area (for example, power plants, chemical companies, and assembly plants), supporting industries (for example, ship repair, inspection services), and port labor pools also belong to the group of first-order economic stakeholders. Branch organizations and regional associations for specific industries represent a large number of these in situ economic stakeholders. Both the regional associations for specific industries and the existing port cluster umbrella associations play an important role in the governance of the port cluster. They can have a huge impact on the competitiveness of the cluster.

Other economic stakeholder groups include port customers, trading companies, and importers/exporters. These are less directly involved than the in situ economic groups as they do not normally invest directly in the port. Nevertheless, they follow the port evolution carefully because port activity can influence their business results. Moreover, they exert strong demand-pull forces on port service suppliers and, as such, they dictate the market requirements which the port community has to meet. Powerful market players increasingly step to the fore as direct interlocutors at the operational level of port activity and in strategic matters related to port planning and port policy.

### PUBLIC POLICY STAKEHOLDERS

Public policy stakeholders do not include only government departments responsible for transport and economic affairs on a local, regional, national and supranational level. Hence, the scarcity of resources such as land and nature has increased the impact and involvement of **environmental departments and spatial planning authorities** on decision-making processes (particularly in the case of port expansion plans). The potential **overlap in jurisdiction** between the various geographical levels in public policymaking is another issue that needs careful deliberation. A vague demarcation of jurisdiction or bad coordination between the various levels can have a detrimental impact on port development processes, particularly when a court contests the validity of earlier (political) decisions because of procedural errors with respect to public policymaking.

Public policy stakeholders typically follow a political management system based on the **principle of distributional equity**. The organizational structure in a political system is often based on administrative heritage and structural shocks caused by powerful individuals or pressure groups. Port authorities partly rely on political organizations for their survival, as ports are often considered strategic assets in community welfare creation and appropriate tools for achieving higher distributional equity. The challenge is for technocratic port organizations to work constructively with political managers by forming alliances of effective operating organizations.

### COMMUNITY STAKEHOLDERS

Community stakeholders include community groups or civil society organizations, the general public, the press, and other non-market players. They are concerned about the port's evolution, mainly about its expansion programs, for well-being reasons. They pay much attention to both getting and distributing information about port activity trends and port development plans. Environmental considerations are very prominent in the relationships of these groups with port authorities. Some community groups might argue that there is a clear imbalance between the benefits and costs for the local community of having larger and larger ports. This viewpoint is a breeding ground for major socio-economic confrontations related to port development. Local pressure groups often defend their local interests in such a fierce way that the individual well-being of a few people is becoming an even bigger driving force than the well-being of the greater community. For instance, the omnipresence of the NIMBY ('not in my backyard') syndrome can seriously complicate the development of new hinterland infrastructures, even if these infrastructures will generate a positive impact on the modal shift from road to environment-friendly transport modes.

In view of developing sustainable stakeholder relations, port managers and government bodies nowadays (have to) spend much time trying to ensure that new port developments are socially broadly based. Ports cannot and must not take broad **public support for development plans** for granted. This aspect of port competitiveness will undoubtedly become more important in the near future, as resources such as land are becoming scarcer and as broader social and environmental functions increasingly challenge the economic function of seaports. The more international the maritime and port industry becomes, the more energy will be spent on embedding the port in the local community.

## 4.2 Key principles of effective stakeholder relations management (SRM)

As port management is characterized by complex decisions and is regularly confronted with many stakeholders, achieving a **balance between the**

**interests of all stakeholders** is becoming an important job for port managers. Many port managers are well aware that socially responsible behavior can be the basis for a competitive edge in both market and public policy relationships. Stakeholder relations management has close ties with sustainable management. **Sustainable port development** is not possible without a well-balanced and integrated stakeholder approach.

SRM applied to port planning and port infrastructure project evaluation requires simultaneous attention to the **legitimate interests of all appropriate stakeholders**, both in the establishment of procedures and general policies and in case-by-case decision making. However, this principle does not imply that all stakeholders should be equally involved in all processes and decisions. Formal processes might be available that describe how and when **consultation with stakeholders** should take place.

Port authorities and or government departments have to decide about the **role attributed to each stakeholder in the decision-making processes**. They could try to discriminate between those stakeholders with genuine legitimate interests in the process considered and those who only claim to have a legitimate interest. This exercise can turn out to be very difficult because the simple act of classifying a group as not relevant for a specific process can, in itself, become a major source of conflict. For instance, an actor or group with no direct legitimate interest can have a large political influence (for example, an actor who has the capacity to mobilize the press can impact the political level). To avoid such situations, one can opt for a maximum approach in which both the legitimate groups and the non-legitimate groups are invited to take part in the process. In many cases, the active role of the latter groups is limited to information exchange, for example, through (passive) public hearings.

Stakeholders could be classified based on their **involvement in the process/decision** and their possible **impact on the process/decision** (Figure 7.13). Designing a well-balanced planning schedule for the structuring of stakeholder participation throughout the trajectory of port planning or project evaluation is one of the key actions in SRM:

- **Involve all stakeholders right from the start**. The advantage is that no stakeholder will feel neglected. However, a slow start due to long

**FIGURE 7.13 Classification of Stakeholders based on Impact and Involvement**

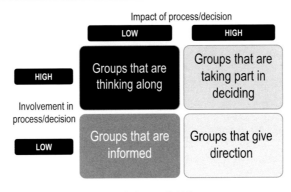

Source: Adapted from Notteboom and Winkelmans (2003).

pre-negotiation rounds in the early phases of the project is a significant disadvantage of this approach.
- **Draw up detailed plans in-house**. Stakeholders will only be involved in the process once these plans have gained maturity. The strength of this approach is that stakeholders are confronted with rather concrete development plans, so there is less room for them to introduce unrealistic alternatives. However, some stakeholders might not feel at ease: such a top-down approach might give the impression that the decisions have already been taken, reducing the stakeholder participation process to a formality or a diversion.

An effective SRM strategy is not possible without suitable **port governance structures**. In fact, stakeholder relationship management partly deals with corporate governance questions, that is, mainly the processes of stakeholder input and participation. The corporate governance framework should recognize the rights of stakeholders and encourage their active co-operation and participation in creating wealth. As effective and efficient governance does not arise automatically, port authorities should develop organizational processes and entrepreneurial cultures that enhance stakeholder satisfaction. Port managers have an obligation to deal openly and honestly with the various stakeholders, thereby avoiding self-serving actions as much as possible. In modern port policy and the concomitant decision-making processes, one should emphasize interdependence among the various stakeholders.

Positive and mutually supportive stakeholder relationships will encourage **trust** and stimulate **collaborative efforts** leading to relational wealth, that is, organizational assets arising from familiarity and teamwork (Figure 7.14). **Conflict and suspicion** among stakeholders will stimulate **formal bargaining** resulting in time delays and increased costs. Formal bargaining often appears when stakeholders demand **compensation for incurred risks or harms**. Compensation claims are often subject to highly politicized negotiation rounds, characterized by a lack of trust and an absence of solid deals/arrangements among the stakeholders. Under these circumstances, port authorities and or government departments might be tempted to use compensations as a tool to neutralize (at least temporarily) some community groups. In contrast, community groups might use the negotiation rounds as a tool to consolidate their position as legitimate interlocutors in port development debates.

FIGURE 7.14 Stakeholder Participation in Port Development Decision Making

| | Early involvement of stakeholders in the process | Delaying discussions with stakeholders until later in the process |
|---|---|---|
| **Problem identification** | • Early identification<br>• Solutions incorporated in initial design process | • Too late<br>• Costly redesign needed |
| **Communication** | • Mutual understanding<br>• Common 'ownership' of the problems requiring solution | • Mistrust<br>• Consultation seen as a cosmetic exercise |
| **Public inquiry or hearing** | • Clearly defined issues<br>• Limited costs | • Opposition/objections<br>• Expensive with a wide range of issues |

Source: Adapted from Notteboom and Winkelmans (2003).

## 4.3 SRM and the port objective struggle

Port managers should acknowledge and, whenever possible, actively monitor the concerns of all legitimate stakeholders. That is, they should take the interests of certain stakeholders appropriately into account in decision-making and operations. However, conflicts of interests among different stakeholders may overshadow the community of interests. Some parties foster the **economic value of ports**. Others are more directed towards the maximization of the **social value** or the **environmental value** of ports. For port managers, there is no alternative but to embark on a quest for a value balance point that satisfies the prevailing market while minimizing adverse effects on the community and the environment.

- **Economic value.** Port managers quantify the direct and indirect economic benefits of their activities, but they might encounter major obstacles whilst communicating the port's economic value to other stakeholders. A part of the population might be ignorant of how the port is organized and operated and how the port contributes to the local economy. The local community might wonder whether it is getting a fair input payback for the scarce local resources used by ports.
- **Social value.** Measuring social benefits is a challenging exercise. Many ports directly support a wide variety of community events and projects through sponsorship in an effort to attract community support. However, it is the indirect social contributions that most benefit local communities. For example, ports might invest in training and education programs. Such forms of social commitment are an important part of the success of ports, linking commercial responsibility to social acceptability and accountability.
- **Environmental Value.** The economic value of a port development project now tends to be taken as a given, so the argument concentrates on the environmental criteria (for example, dredging and dredge disposal, loss of wetlands, emissions into the air, water pollution, congestion, loss of open space, light and noise externalities, potential conflicts with commercial fishing and recreational uses of area waters, etc.). Ports must demonstrate a high level of environmental performance in order to ensure community support. However, environmental aspects also play an increasing role in attracting trading partners and potential investors. A port with a strong environmental record and a high level of community support is likely to be favored.

## 5 ADAPTIVE PORT PLANNING

Current approaches to port planning, design, and evaluation might not take uncertainty fully into account and this could result in plans and designs for port infrastructures that prove **inadequate under fast-changing requirements**. Consequently, the infrastructure has a shortened economic lifetime, which makes payback on the investments risky. Accounting for uncertainty within the planning process should become inherent in all port-related investments.

The **Adaptive Port Planning** (APP) framework tackles uncertainty from another angle (Figure 7.15). Instead of creating a static port plan, this approach

FIGURE 7.15 The Adaptive Port Planning Approach

| | Traditional master planning | Adaptive planning approach |
|---|---|---|
| **Treatment of the future** | Assume it is useful and possible to predict the future | Assume that the future cannot be predicted, or it is dangerous to do so |
| **Treatment of uncertainties** | Via scenarios, but planning is based on single point forecasts | Imagine Black Swans and prepare for them |
| **Planning process** | Static or at most periodic | Continuous |
| **Embedded options** | Single option | Multiple embedded options make the plan dynamic |
| **Focus** | On demand forecasts | On vulnerabilities and opportunities |
| **Approach** | Target oriented | Performance oriented (flexible and integrated) |
| **Reactivity** | Ad-hoc reaction to strong signals | Monitor and react to predefined triggers (mostly performance indicators) |
| **Decision-making** | Decisions based on available information | Decisions based on acquiring new information and evaluating new developments |
| **Solution space** | Limited to physical and operational space | Shape external environment by altering industry structure, creating associations, and restructuring relationships |

Source: Adapted from Taneja (2013).

allows for changes, learning, and adaptation to the constantly shifting environment. These approaches were first created for and implemented in the airport industry, aiming to make plans more robust.

The APP method combines two frameworks, namely Assumption Based Planning and Adaptive Policy Making. The strength of combining these two methods is that uncertainty is not described as a function of possible futures and their respective probability of occurring but rather focuses on the formulation of strategies and actions aimed at minimizing the chance of a catastrophic plan failure.

There are six basic steps in the Adaptive Port Planning process.

### STEP 1A: DEFINE THE PROBLEM

The first step involves studying the objectives of the organization and the needs of the stakeholder in order to formulate the goals of the port project or overall plan. This allows for defining success in terms of the speciation of desired outcomes. This is required in order to be able to decide when the plan needs to be changed. This step also involves identifying various constraints or boundary conditions, the available choices, and the underlying assumptions. There are three major criteria to use when evaluating the success of a project or plan: time, money, and quality. The overall success of a port project or comprehensive port plan is measured based on it meeting a predefined financial criterion, such as minimizing lifecycle costs or maximizing revenues. Even so, criteria related to system effectiveness, such as technical performance, availability, and reliability are specified and need to be met.

### *STEP 1B: DEFINE STRATEGY AND FORMULATE ALTERNATIVES*

The planning time horizon (short, middle, or long) determines the choice of strategy. This includes selecting a forecasting method, planning techniques, tools, and a financial evaluation method. Once the project objective is defined, various alternatives can be formulated. In the case of port projects, these can relate to the various port layouts, infrastructure designs, or the complete master plan. Scenarios play an important role in this step of APP. The alternatives are defined based on numerous assumptions.

### *STEP 2: IDENTIFY LOAD-BEARING AND VULNERABLE ASSUMPTIONS UNDERLYING EACH ALTERNATIVE PLAN*

In this step, the crucial load-bearing and vulnerable assumptions are identified. This requires an assessment of the consequences of failures. Identification of vulnerable assumptions involves thinking about the future and looking for plausible developments that could occur in the lifetime of the plan in question that could cause it to fail. If development is favorable to the plan, it is called an opportunity. Otherwise, the development is called a vulnerability. These vulnerabilities and opportunities are dealt with in subsequent steps.

### *STEP 3: INCREASE THE FLEXIBILITY AND ROBUSTNESS OF EACH ALTERNATIVE*

This step is based on determining the actions to be taken in response to the vulnerabilities and opportunities identified in the previous step. There are two basic ways of preparing a plan for vulnerabilities and opportunities, either by taking action early or by preparing actions in advance that can be taken in the future. The framework identifies multiple reactions to two alternatives, namely shaping, mitigating, hedging, or seizing:

- A **shaping action** either reduces or changes the vulnerability.
- A **mitigating action** is taken to reduce the adverse effects.
- A **hedging action** spreads or reduces the risk of highly uncertain adverse effects of a plan in the current planning cycle. Hedging actions are effective only if a vulnerability appears in the future. Therefore it is important to establish their cost-effectiveness, especially if they entail high investments.
- A **seizing action** enables seizing an opportunity.

### STEP 4: EVALUATE AND SELECT ALTERNATIVE

After the identification and incorporation of each alternative, they need to be subjected to a thorough comparison. Cost being an important criterion in port projects and plans, an economic analysis is always carried out. Often, there is a cost–benefit analysis which includes the future revenues an alternative can generate, and also its direct and indirect effects. The latter may be monetized or assessed qualitatively. Tools such as a Balanced Scorecard can add strategic non-financial performance measures to traditional financial metrics to give managers and executives a more balanced view of organizational performance, thus supporting decision making. The selection from alternatives is generally based on many criteria, combined with other considerations that are often political or strategic.

### STEP 5: SET UP MONITORING SYSTEM FOR ALTERNATIVE

Even the best plans can fail. Therefore there is still the need to monitor the performance of the selected alternative and take action if some of the assumptions are failing. This requires an identification of key values. This is information that should be tracked in order to determine whether the plan is on course to achieving success. The boundaries of these values (**triggers**) are specified, beyond which actions should be taken to ensure that a plan keeps moving the system in the right direction and at a proper speed.

### STEP 6: CONTINGENCY PLANNING FOR SELECTED ALTERNATIVES (TRIGGER REACTION)

In this final step, the plan, based on the selected alternative, is further enhanced by including adaptive elements. Contingency plans are alternative plans that can be used if the baseline plans are going wrong. The measures to treat the uncertainties in step three become a part of the scope of the project. The eventual costs resulting from the risks taken are not included in the project appraisal (except maybe in the contingency budget or the uncertainty reserve of a project). For example, extra container throughput in the event that a new shipping company decides to use a port is not included in the demand forecasts. However, as a contingency measure, land reserves can be used to capitalize on this opportunity.

Next, the selected plan or design can go to the **implementation phase**. Once the basic plan and additional actions are agreed upon, the final step involves implementing the entire plan. The assumptions or the vulnerabilities may have changed after the start of the process. Therefore, APP is an **iterative and continuous process**. After implementing the initial mitigating, hedging, seizing, and shaping actions to make the plan robust, the adaptive planning process is suspended until a **trigger event** occurs.

The **implementation of APP is not easy**. One of the problems is that it requires a change in mentality and approach in the port organization and all stakeholders closely involved in the planning process. For example, environmental and community groups might have some reservations when APP is used to develop a new port area as the new port land is not clearly assigned to a specific port activity (container terminal, industry) upfront. Another difficulty lies in the identification of required actions linked to certain triggers or performance indicators. These actions need to be identified and evaluated on their feasibility, acceptability, and potential impact.

## 6 PORT INFRASTRUCTURE PROJECT EVALUATION

### 6.1 Procedures and guidelines

Port infrastructure projects are under scrutiny due to government budget constraints, increased competition for land, environmental awareness, and the need for integrated transport systems. These considerations are also mirrored in appraisal and evaluation procedures applicable to port infrastructure projects. Governments have to ensure that public funds are spent on activities that provide the greatest benefits to society and are spent most efficiently.

Governments have developed **guidelines and tools** to encourage a more thorough, long-term, and analytically robust approach to the appraisal and evaluation of port infrastructure projects. The **formal frameworks** typically refer to internal arrangements and working procedures. Decision-making frameworks on large infrastructure projects such as major port developments are typically **complex**, both in terms of the procedural aspects and the appraisal and evaluation tools used. The **procedural aspects of the decision-making** on large port infrastructure projects should be designed in such a way that:

- The procedure can be finalized within an acceptable timeframe.
- The involvement of relevant stakeholders throughout the process is guaranteed.
- The quality of the project appraisal results can be guaranteed.

The **time factor** plays an important role in any infrastructure project appraisal. First, there is the timing of the trajectory from the conception of a project to the final decision making. The whole procedure should be finalized within an acceptable timeframe. Guidelines on project appraisal generally might contain clear stipulations on the timing for completion of the project evaluation studies. Deadlines are often put forward for formal steps in the decision-making process.

There is tension between the long-term focus in infrastructure planning/ realization and the short-term developments in business cycles and market developments. Markets change almost overnight, so companies typically use a short planning horizon of a few years. The shorter business cycles and economic cycles make it increasingly difficult to develop a long-term focus in the framework of port projects. Long time series about (cargo) flows are at the core of any port infrastructure appraisal, but the uncertainty of long-term developments becomes more apparent. **Scenario building and risk analysis** have therefore gained importance when considering port infrastructure appraisal.

**Iterative processes** are gaining ground as they are generally considered the way forward to provide a reasonable understanding of whether the project proposal is likely to remain good value for money in the light of changing circumstances. Iterations in a project evaluation procedure often involve a stepwise approach. The detail and accuracy of the data provided increase as the evaluation progresses from the initial steps of identifying and appraising the project alternatives to the final steps in the procedure. Given rising budget constraints, procurement routes are increasingly considered, including the role of the private sector in the financing of the project (public-private partnerships or PPP). This trend poses great challenges to the port project appraisal procedures as potential partnering arrangements and their implications for costs and benefits sharing should be identified early in the process.

Interest in stakeholder approaches to strategic management is growing. The dynamics of investments in port infrastructure do not take place in a vacuum but are articulated by the strategic and operational decisions of the stakeholders involved. Consultation is important. The days when governments or port authorities could unilaterally decide on large port infrastructure projects without the involvement of stakeholders are long gone. At present, a large part of the financial and human resources linked to a project appraisal procedure is linked to consultation with and between stakeholders.

At the appraisal level, there is a greater emphasis on assessing the **differential impacts of port projects on the various stakeholders**, where these are likely to be significant. In other words, project evaluation techniques are geared towards making the distribution of costs and benefits among the relevant groups/stakeholders in society more transparent.

Port authorities, and government departments and agencies are increasingly encouraged to establish formal evaluation or assessment units and formalize access to internal and external auditors. There is an increasing trend to include systematic optimism bias in project evaluation. There is a demonstrated, systematic tendency for project appraisers to be overly optimistic. Optimism bias has played a major role in underestimating construction costs or overrating the indirect benefits of a port project. Dealing with optimism is slowly being internalized in the evaluation process, such as by an explicit adjustment procedure to redress systematic optimism. Sensitivity analyses are now broadly used to test assumptions about operating costs and expected benefits. Project proposals are typically reviewed more than once regarding the impact of risks, uncertainties, and inherent biases.

## 6.2 Evaluation methods

In many cases, the **Social Cost–Benefit Analysis** is an integral part of decision-making trajectories. In most cases, SCBA is combined with other methods, including **multi-criteria analysis, quantitative impact analysis, and qualitative impact analysis**. The latter methods are typically deployed to evaluate effects that one cannot or does not express in monetary values.

The **economic impact study** or **economic effects analysis** can be used as well. In some cases, **input–output analyses**, which form the basis of economic impact studies, are being used to assess indirect economic effects. As such, the economic impact study, where used, is one of the quantitative impact analysis methods that can be used in combination with the SCBA.

A considerable stream of literature has developed over the years on **identifying, managing, and realizing costs and benefits**. This increased focus on methodologies to estimate the effects of port infrastructure projects has led to a multiplication of the kind of effects considered in an SCBA. **Direct and external project effects** that are commonly considered in an SCBA relate to construction costs, costs of maintenance and management, different types of logistics and transport benefits (time savings, vehicle/vessel costs, benefits for goods transportation), and the impact of the project on mobility and connectivity.

The picture is less straightforward in the case of some other **external effects** such as noise pollution, air pollution, and visual intrusion. In quite a number of countries, these latter effects are included in SCBAs and expressed in monetary values using a set of **valuation techniques**. In other cases, **separate quantitative or qualitative analyses** are used with a view to assessing these effects without monetary valuation. Valuation techniques for visual intrusion, vibrations, and community severance have proven to be less robust and less broadly accepted than the methodologies for evaluating noise and air pollution.

Port project appraisal and evaluation procedures and guidelines attach more and more attention to **quality management**. Quality tests can take various forms ranging from assessing compliance with the guidelines on project appraisal to evaluating the basic scenarios and forecasts used. An external expert commission often screens interim and final project evaluation studies, with members typically consisting of central planning authorities and academics.

# Chapter 7.4 Port–city relationships

*Ports are part of a complex urban setting as they provide important economic opportunities, such as access to global supply chains. Divergence can be observed between a port and its city, leading to conflicts over its role and function. Due to significant technological and economic changes, abandoned port areas have been subject to waterfront redevelopment.*

## 1 CITIES AND GLOBAL HUBS

### 1.1 The growing role of megacities in trade

Intra-regional trade and reliance on hub cities continue to play a strong role in facilitating global trade flows. Corporations look to capitalize on new opportunities while managing their exposure in rapidly developing markets. At present, more than half of the world's population lives in cities, with two-thirds of the world population expected to be living in urban areas by 2050 (Figure 7.16). Therefore, the importance of city regions will continue to grow, particularly since more than half of the cities and urban populations are within 100 km of a coastline. Population estimates and predictions indicate the strong growth of metropolitan areas around the world due to increased urbanization. A metropolitan area includes urban agglomerations and surrounding areas of lower density under the direct influence of the city.

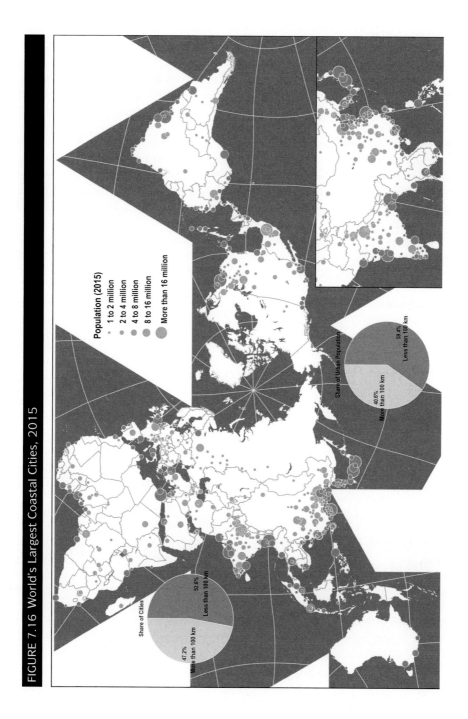

FIGURE 7.16 World's Largest Coastal Cities, 2015

The geography of cities underlines a strong propensity to locate along the coastline, a pattern associated with several factors. Many coastal areas, particularly deltas, are alluvial plains suitable for agriculture and, therefore, for population concentrations. Coastal access is associated with access to trade networks, which historically played an important role as maritime transportation was the least expensive for trade over long distances. The growth of transoceanic trade from the sixteenth century allowed for the setting up of colonial gateways along the coastline of the Americas, Africa, and Oceania. It stimulated a rebalancing of the urban balance from the hinterland to the coast, a process that expanded in the twentieth century with the surge in international trade and containerization.

Cities provide large efficiency benefits, which result in gains in productivity and competitiveness. Cities are the centers of knowledge, innovation, and specialization of production and services. To overcome the challenges of expanding urban structures, such as congestion and emissions, megacities focus on innovation in terms of governance models, cooperation schemes, and technological solutions, for example, in the field of urban (public) transport and logistics systems.

Global cities are generally open to trade and typically strive for **high regional and international connectivity** by air, sea, and other transport means such as rail or barge (Figure 7.17). This connectivity is also apparent in the advanced service sector (e.g. accountancy, advertizing, banking and finance, and law) that select cities in terms of their primacy. This can strengthen the creation of first-tier global transport and communication networks that connect global megacities. Quite a few megacities have reached GDP levels comparable to small or medium-sized countries. For example, Shanghai's GDP is equivalent to the GDP of the Philippines, while the size of Guangzhou's economy is comparable to Switzerland's.

The growth of cities and the connectivity and openness they offer have a significant impact on the distribution of wealth and innovation. A small group of global cities assumes a **commanding role** in a world where cities, not nations, are the key global players. Most of the world's economic power is concentrated in cities, and cities have therefore become the pivotal entities in the world economy. Cities are increasingly leading the way by engaging in direct action in environmental issues, digitalization, and innovation. Cities are increasingly interconnected, leading to a network of (mega)cities. Second-tier cities become more connected to the big cities and often act as economic overflow areas or satellites of the megacities or position themselves as lower-cost manufacturing centers.

## 1.2 Cities as maritime and logistics hubs

The rise of megacities has brought competition among cities to act as **international transportation, logistics, and services hubs** covering the main modes of long-distance transportation, maritime shipping, air passenger services, and air freight services. They are competing to attract the best companies and most talented people. A good example is provided when examining the leading **maritime centers of the world**. The maritime business services sector plays a significant role in quite a few world cities having a heavy commercial

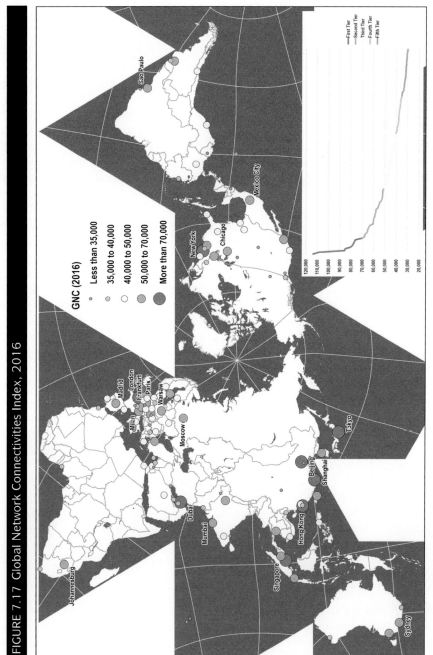

FIGURE 7.17 Global Network Connectivities Index, 2016

Source: Adapted from Derudder and Taylor (2016).

orientation. Maritime and commodity trading services are often located in large world port cities. However, due to the digitalization and financialization of trading and maritime service activities, there is no need for the trader or service provider to be near the physical flows of goods or ships. Therefore, other factors are responsible for attracting maritime services to cities.

The location of **advanced maritime producer services** (AMPS) is correlated with the presence of shipowners, port-related industry, and general advanced producer services, but not with the throughput flow of ports. Specialized producer services tend to agglomerate near other service providers in global cities such as London, New York, Singapore, or Hong Kong. Even non-port cities such as Madrid, Moscow, and Paris show a high concentration of AMPS firms. To a certain degree, a **spatial division of labor** has occurred between the concentration of advanced maritime services and the physical flows of goods and ships. Next to London, New York, Singapore, or Hong Kong, only a few port cities such as Rotterdam, Houston, Shanghai, Dubai, and Hamburg have **successfully combined physical flows** with a considerable scale in APS functions.

Since 2012, risk management firm DNV GL and consultancy firm Menon Economics have identified the **leading maritime capitals** worldwide using 25 objective and 15 subjective indicators to measure the support that different cities provide to maritime business in terms of soft and hard infrastructure in four sectors (shipping, maritime finance and law, maritime technology and ports and logistics) and the overall attractiveness and competitiveness (Figure 7.18). The strategies of these maritime cities are not necessarily the same. For example, Singapore and Hong Kong take very different approaches to maritime center development. Singapore benefits from a dedicated governmental focus on promoting the maritime economy and the comprehensive strategy to develop a maritime cluster. Hong Kong is characterized by a laissez-faire approach and its role as a gateway to the mainland Chinese market.

Many of the global megacities have developed into **major air and maritime transport hubs**. Some of these cities have become major hubs by combining a strategic location in relation to or between key markets with specific policies such as creating Special Economic Zones (e.g. in Shenzhen and Dubai), conferring financial and transactional advantages to an existing manufacturing and physical flows structure.

## 2 PORT–CITY INTERACTIONS: DIVERGENCE

Early civilizations settled in proximity to **commercial crossroads and trading places**. At that time, there was a distinctive correlation between the existence/success of a port and the development of the urban area (Box 7.8). Economic changes in the twentieth century ended with the reorganization of port activities and how they utilize the land. Given the increasing tension between the expanding city and the expanding port, some activities were relocated downstream through processes of port migration, initiating abandonment or diminution of land use intensity on waterfronts in cities. Ancient port areas were abandoned and the link between city and port decayed. Ports usually did not pay much attention to activities concerning reclaiming neglected areas but left them to deteriorate or rented them to industries from sectors unrelated to the main domain of port business.

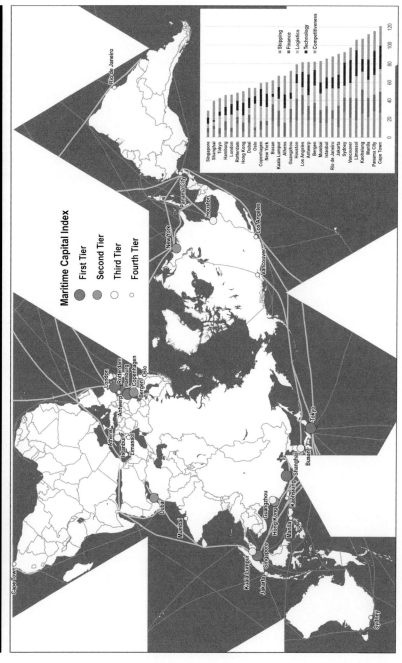

FIGURE 7.18 World Maritime Capitals, 2017

Source: Adapted from Menon Consulting (2017). Note: The lower the score, the higher the ranking. Each selected city was ranked according to a series of criteria within five major categories (shipping centers, maritime finance and law, ports and logistics, maritime technology, and competitiveness). The index is the unweighted summation of the average score for each category.

Many cities worldwide have built an intricate relationship with their port since they owe their origin to their port site. Conventionally, the economic dynamism of cities was linked to their port, which was a source of employment and commercial interactions with the global market. The waterfront still occupies valuable space in proximity to urban activities, which can be a source of dynamism and of conflict. Land and water use along the waterfront, which is a valuable interface zone, requires cooperation between the port and the city so that social and environmental externalities are mitigated. In recent decades, the prevailing trend has been a **growing level of divergence between ports and their host cities**, particularly because of globalization and containerization. The main factors that have favored a port–city divergence are:

- The **migration** of several terminals towards peripheral locations. The need for additional space and deeper drafts has encouraged terminal operators to seek new sites that are located further away from the conventional sites.
- The **containerization** of terminals has reduced labor requirements since a modern container terminal is capital intensive and requires a small quantity of qualified labor to operate. Port terminals thus employ far fewer people than before, reducing a whole array of port/city interactions, such as commuting.
- **Safety and security issues** have become more salient, so that access to port areas, particularly terminals, is restricted. Ports and harbors are gated and protected areas that the public cannot readily access, particularly in container terminals.
- Modern **ship operations** require less labor, and labor sourcing has been internationalized, from managers to ship crews. Under the regime of flags of convenience, ship labor is mostly multinational and therefore not linked to the communities along the ports of call. Further, containerships spend little time in ports, often less than 24 hours, considerably reducing shore leave opportunities.
- **Hinterland accessibility** has improved, meaning that the majority of economic activities using the port are located further inland and much less, as was conventionally the case, in close proximity to port terminals. There is a dissociation with port-related industrial and manufacturing employment.

The outcome is that ports are increasingly economically integrated entities with global supply chains and are environmentally disruptive to and disconnected from their urban areas. However, the same processes that have promoted a divergence between ports and their cities have created opportunities to redevelop older port areas that became abandoned or underused.

## Box 7.8  Typology of port cities

*There is a relationship between the size of a port and the size of the metropolitan area it is located in, particularly for coastal cities having good port sites. Conventionally, because of high inland transport costs, city size and port size tended to converge. Maritime activities were a direct driver of urban growth. With a limited hinterland, port activities were bound to the level of economic activities of a city as a consumption and production center (Figure 7.19).*

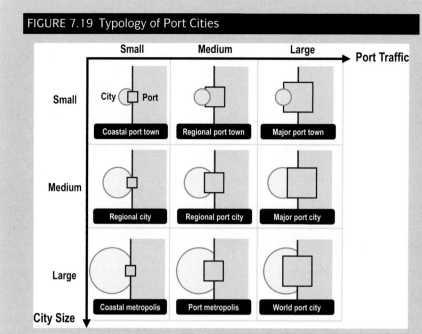

FIGURE 7.19 Typology of Port Cities

Source: Adapted from Ducruet (2003).

*Containerization changed this relationship by supporting the setting up of much larger port terminals and by expanding hinterland access. This allowed a higher level of possible divergence between the level of port activity and city size. Intermediate hubs are the most notable example of such a process since little traffic is bound to the hinterland. Ports such as Algeciras and Freeport are major transshipment hubs near cities of relatively small size. Port size can thus be completely unrelated to city size. The setting up of gateways also contributes to the divergence between port size and city size since they service vast hinterlands. European gateways, such as Antwerp and Rotterdam, are salient examples of medium-sized cities where the port area is larger than the metropolitan area.*

## 3 WATERFRONT REDEVELOPMENT

### 3.1 Waterfront redevelopment as a form of new urbanism

*Given the relocation of port-related activities, the outskirts of port cities often become derelict areas where urban restructuring occurs. Such revitalization of urban areas is called waterfront redevelopment.*

The concept of waterfront redevelopment is related to waterfront sites, but not only limited to these in port cities. Historically, the **first waterfront redevelopment projects** date from the 1960s when cities like Boston, Baltimore, and San Francisco set the trend. In the 1960s, the idea of waterfront revitalization was based upon public access to riverbanks by creating parks and markets. In the middle of the 1970s, attempts at creating new urban activities and multifunctional projects emerged. Since the end of the 1970s, many cities have intensified activities directed towards the functional revitalization of waterfront areas, the rehabilitation of physical waterfront structures, and the creation of new architectural and urban values on the border between water and land. Nowadays, this concept is known all over the world, even in less-advanced developing countries.

Many cities are undergoing major redevelopment of older derelict waterfront areas, intending to turn them into commercial, cultural, tourist, or upmarket residential areas. Cities are using waterfront redevelopment to revitalize urban areas and bolster local economies with new jobs, better housing, improved community amenities, and added tourism opportunities. The redevelopment of the waterfront has also become an opportunity to recover relationships between the city and the port. In some cases, waterfront redevelopment is largely an aesthetic undertaking where the extent to which the projects can revitalize urban areas remains unproven. However, even then, they represent a **shift from industrial to post-industrial land use**.

Most cities have understood that the **industrial heritage** of the port is something that should be reinforced rather than eradicated. As such, they have capitalized on their industrial past to create interesting and inviting waterfronts, reflecting the fact that most people want to see the real working city and not a sanitized landscape stripped of all historical references. Industrial, recreational, commercial, and residential land uses can and do successfully coexist, often with great effect. In fact, their coexistence has proven to be the crucial element in dozens of projects around the world.

Many projects follow the rules of **new urbanism**, which seeks to redefine the nature of metropolitan areas by reintroducing traditional notions of neighborhood design and fitting those ideas into a variety of urban and suburban settings. Some new urbanism principles include walkable neighborhoods, primary orientation to public transit systems, preservation of open space and greenways, and the greater integration of different types of land uses at the neighborhood level. As such, **waterfront redevelopment is one of the most visible manifestations** of a growing appreciation of urban values, which has its roots in specific social, environmental, and cultural factors that have come to the fore in recent decades. These may include environmental concerns, interest in historic preservation, community activism, and changing social values. However, it is clear that waterfront redevelopment should also have the potential to improve the existing economic base of the community and, at a minimum, must not jeopardize this base. In short, successful waterfront redevelopment projects will integrate **economic, societal, and environmental objectives and achieve sustainability**.

### 3.2 Waterfront redevelopment and expanding port activities

Changes in maritime transport and the spatial dimensions of port infrastructures significantly influenced the port–city interface. Whereas the port was formerly known as an area handling commodities, the modern port has evolved into a horizontal cross-section of different supply chains. Because of these trends, the port–city interface has evolved. Whereas the port city is expanding in terms of area occupation, port authorities are driven by the changes in the maritime industry. The maritime industry is looking for available land to meet the expectations of its customers, in this case, terminal operators and shipping companies, and to cope with the shift from a conventional to a modern transport system.

The generic model of port and city extensions demonstrates how the growth of the city, combined with a retreat of port activities to downstream sites, increases the pressure on abandoned port areas to shift the focus to commercial and housing functions. The tensions between city and port are often based on the relative intrinsic land values of areas situated on the border regions between cities and ports. The **evolutionary model** describes how the pressure on the city borders and the need for port renovation schemes (due to limited availability of port extension areas) leads to increased tension between city and port. The outcome will depend on the room given to port activities to expand further downstream or along the coastline (Figure 7.20):

- If **ample space is available**, waterfront revitalization schemes are likely to accommodate different functions that are not really entwined with deep seaport activities, such as new residences, offices, retail facilities, parks, cultural and leisure activities, public spaces, pedestrian routes, transportation systems, marinas, and sporting and recreational areas. In many cases, these functions are fuelled not by ports but by real estate and development corporations that have taken over areas abandoned by ports. They can be ubiquitous and might have little to do with the specificity of the place or maritime culture that would make them unique and sustainable attributes of a city. The main contribution of these non-port-related commercial and residential zones in the redeveloped waterfront area is to relieve some pressure on the city.
- If the port has only **limited expansion possibilities**, a competitive situation will emerge in relation to the waterfront area between port functions and other functions. In that case, a mixed-use scenario for waterfront redevelopment is the most likely outcome, thereby leaving the port with some room to rehabilitate older port areas to form integral parts of the wider port complex.

## 3.3 Waterfront redevelopment as part of stakeholder relations management

Waterfronts often represent a good opportunity for **community enhancement and enrichment**. However, at the same time, waterfront redevelopment can be one of the most highly contested aspects of the city and even of port planning. Waterfronts are often the most valuable resource of a city with many people feeling they are stakeholders; the residents want a beautiful view of marine resources and port industry and everyone wants their interests protected. While changes in the waterfront are hard to implement, rebuilding is essential as waterfronts are often the first part of a port city to be built and may be in the greatest state of disrepair or abandonment.

Most waterfront redevelopment is challenged by city-port relationships that are stimulated by growth. The most common points of conflict and contact are **port growth, industrial growth, land-use competition, and water-use competition**. This comes from a general desire to keep businesses near their markets and customers, keep the waterfront intact, and create an aesthetically

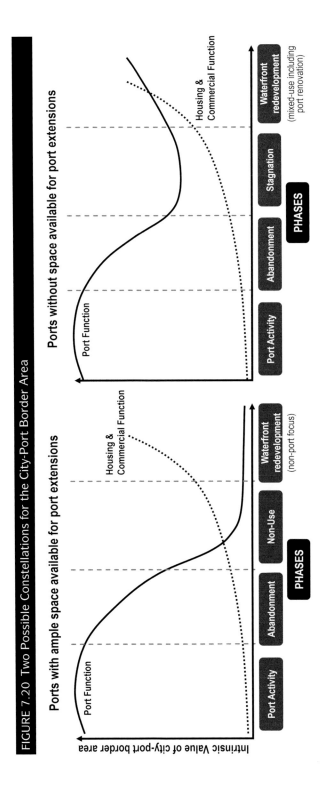

FIGURE 7.20 Two Possible Constellations for the City-Port Border Area

pleasing environment, which is often done through creating corporatist relationships with private owners.

As derelict port areas are situated at the port–city interface, the renewed waterfront attracts economic activities because of its proximity to the city center and at times because of the sense of exclusivity associated with a waterfront location. The redevelopment of the **London docklands** is one of the best-known examples of the attractiveness of a waterfront location in a central high-density area with a scarcity of real estate. The attractiveness is significantly related to the importance of the city in the global urban system and the availability of real estate in relation to demand for it. When evaluating a waterfront redevelopment proposal, a fundamental question arises. Is the project good for the port, and is it beneficial for the city? The final decision of whether or not to develop a derelict port area will be based on **evaluating three elements: physical, economic, and social advantages**.

The **planning of waterfront redevelopment** is usually based upon high-level strategic plans with little detail concerning choice of solutions that enable flexibility in adapting to local market conditions. Usually, the project includes strategic guidelines for redevelopment or a set of simple objectives. Local governments usually play the role of initiators and enter into partnerships with the private sector. Sometimes, elaborating a strategy, management, and finance is given to **specially established institutions or development companies**. These institutions have flexibility in interpreting planning regulations, which allows for a quick response to market impulses. Moving from a conceptual design to implementation can be a complicated task, especially when communities have limited resources. Creating an open implementation program can ensure the ongoing input and involvement of key stakeholders. Nevertheless, orchestrating such an interactive process can be complex and time-consuming, and can lead to **conflicts with stakeholders**. Task forces are often created to keep stakeholders informed and engaged during the development of detailed master plans. With public, private, and government interests, waterfront redevelopment projects often take decades, undergoing many changes in elected officials and public committee members.

Waterfront design can be a successful forum for initiating **community dialog about broader port development plans**. Community groups can have a large impact on port city development programs. Access to and redevelopment of the waterfront is rarely understood in terms of a working waterfront with maritime and port activities. For residents, the perceived negative results of waterfront redevelopment are increased traffic, inadequate parking, lack of privacy, commercial intrusion into residential areas, lack of affordable housing, marine pollution, and non-water dependent uses in the immediate waterfront. In most cases, these negative aspects are counteracted by increased property values, historic preservation, and more public events and amenities. One of the contradictions brought about by renewal is that while property value may increase to benefit some people, most residents cannot afford to live in these areas any more. In contrast to residents, the broader local community typically perceives waterfront redevelopment as a positive action enhancing **local quality of life**.

In some cases, waterfront redevelopment can be used as **compensation** for getting public support for port expansion schemes. These projects can help to activate public acceptance and awareness of seaport activity. Port authorities should take such opportunities to form a sound basis for dialog with community stakeholders, resulting in goodwill and mutual respect. They might even generate more local economic benefit than the renovation of outdated port infrastructure because draft conditions and terminal surfaces of older quays and docks are often too small to allow for modern transshipment activities.

Convincing residents of the benefits of waterfront redevelopment and its possible link to port activity is often not an easy task. When people understand the vision, buy into it, and recognize how it can be used to leverage resources, they are willing to participate in the whole process. Many questions are put to the community to gather views on how a waterfront could be redeveloped and people have a wide range of views. The challenge is to distill from those views the essence that can help to form the **guiding principles** for the core group of planners to understand and follow.

Ports and industrial waterfronts face complex problems associated with **environmental contamination and habitat loss** that affect the ability of local governments to plan and carry out dredging and waterfront development projects. In many parts of the world, separate regulatory programs exist to address source control, the clean-up of contaminated sediments, navigational dredging projects, habitat restoration, and shoreline development projects, each with its own set of agencies, permits, and regulatory requirements. In some areas, these overlapping and often conflicting requirements and interests have led to difficulties in completing waterfront redevelopment and clean-up projects, even when these projects could have substantial environmental benefits. So-called **greenway projects** are important elements of any waterfront redevelopment scheme because they attract people to the shoreline and give them first-hand experience. Such first-hand experience is essential in building support for further source control efforts, brownfield redevelopment, contaminated sediment remediation, pollution prevention, and habitat rehabilitation and conservation.

## 4 PORT–CITY INTERACTIONS: SUSTAINABLE CRUISE GROWTH

The aspirations of many ports to host more cruise activities are combined with the strategic importance of improving port–city relationships. To a great extent, this combination is founded on the remarkable growth already achieved. The **gigantism of cruise ships** and the **multiplication of cruise itineraries** implies an increased number of passengers arriving at a destination for each port call, posing significant challenges for cruise ports and the destinations hosting them. The contemporary cruise segment, which represents more than 75% of cruises, is offered by vessels that exceed 3,000 passengers and 1,000 crew. This implies mass arrivals at destinations, overcrowding, congestion, massive operations, considerable footprint, and the need to cater for receipt of quantities of waste.

Justifiably or not, local communities have started questioning the unqualified growth of cruising, which had previously long been taken as a beneficial development. While the benefits, in terms of spending at destinations, are significant, this growth might be associated with congestion and several related **externalities** to be addressed. Many cruise ports are located in or very **close to urban areas**. This makes them exciting cruise destinations for tourists wanting to discover their amenities and cultural heritage. It also increases the pressure on ports to minimize tensions with the cities that host them.

Nonetheless, not all port cities are struggling with the same issues regarding cruise tourism. For those that struggle with classification, tensions emerge when receiving significant numbers of tourists per year compared to the port-city populations. The challenges to be addressed relate to three elements:

- **Society**. Adherence to social perceptions and work with local communities to reverse misconceptions regarding the impact of cruise activities.
- **Economy**. Expanding in line with local economic development strategies.
- **Environment**. Addressing the externalities produced by providing cruise shipping and the hosting of vessels and cruise passengers at cruise ports.

A critical factor in supporting sustainable cruising is understanding different stakeholder concerns, needs, and expectations. Constructive dialogs, partnerships, synergies, and joint research and development initiatives, are instruments towards this end. International initiatives having an explicit reference to cruising can also facilitate strategies to advance green cruise port governance.

## 4.1 Reversing social perceptions

The expansion of cruise activities has **impacted the image of cruising**. The elite activity of a small number of passengers has been replaced by the mass transportation of thousands of cruise passengers arriving simultaneously. The decision of a community to seek cruise ship visits requires several industries to be involved and has direct and indirect consequences. Besides, a cruise is not dissimilar from the impacts generated by any other tourism development on the visited communities and sites. It might displace current activities, causing changes in costs, access, and variety. These changes can be positive or negative, such as crowded areas near ports, generating additional infrastructure investment to cater to the cruise industry, but not so much for local residents. From a service and real estate standpoint, locals can be priced out of areas near cruise ports. Changes may be viewed as positive by those who benefit and negative by those who do not benefit. All this can lead to societal approaches that conceive of cruise growth as associated with deterioration of the quality of life.

Aesthetics have turned into a significant issue, as did overcrowding of marquee destinations. Venice is one of the most salient cases of a marquee destination that has experienced the negative effect of mass cruising. A ban on large cruise ships passing through the center of Venice was imposed in late 2014, preventing all ships over 96,000 gross tons from sailing to the main cruise terminal and limiting the number of ships doing so to five per day. The debate on this had gained momentum as citizens and local protest groups were unhappy with the presence of the bigger vessels, arguing that they produce pollution and result in substantial levels of emissions. As a world heritage site, Venice is particularly vulnerable to the deleterious effects of air pollution in addition to the tide effects on the sinking lagoon surrounding the city. The image of giant vessels next to traditional buildings led to an heated reaction by local communities. Aesthetics has come to play and cruise liners had to limit the number of big ships calling at Venice and are now considering a complete ban from docking at the port facilities located at the city center.

Other marquee destinations, including Barcelona, Dubrovnik, Santorini, and the French Riviera, have experienced similar issues. The port authority of Barcelona had to substantiate the benefits of cruising using several studies to justify its cruise operations. Dubrovnik decided to limit the number of arriving tourists to a maximum of 8,000 per day at the historic city and Santorini put the same threshold (8,000) on cruise passenger daily arrivals. French Riviera ports limit the arrivals to 5,000 cruise passengers per day.

Whether these challenges are well-founded or not, there are conceptions and perceptions that have to be addressed to achieve sustainable growth. Cruising is inextricably linked with the **carrying capacity of the hosting city**, such as the ability of the destination to absorb tourism before negative impacts are felt. Exceeding the carrying capacity can cause unacceptable changes to the physical environment, or negatively affect the experience of visitors. The need for cruising to take into account the needs of the civil societies that host them is essential due to the periodic overcrowding of cultural sites and historic cities, the limited carrying capacity of certain well-established destinations, the endemic problems of local tourism economies, the dominance of foreign firms enjoying the majority of spending benefits, and the consequent altering of local population perceptions. Estimating carrying capacity in terms of how many cruise passengers can be hosted or how many are wanted raises questions associated with several parameters, such as who decides management objectives, and what exactly are the attributes and capabilities of the destination.

## 4.2 Expanding in line with local strategies

Securing most of the potential local gains by expanding cruise activities requires a consensus on how this might be achieved while also integrated with local economic development strategies. Destinations and cruise ports have **limited spaces and options** for developing the different activities they wish to promote. There are frequently space restrictions, either at the city, at its waterfront, or at the port. Antagonism between actors and industries wanting to maintain or increase the space they use is not rare.

The development of cruise activities or cruise terminals might be associated with **access restrictions to the waterfront**. The growth of the industry is based on the modernization of existing infrastructures, but also on the presence of new facilities and the spatial expansion of the terminals and cruise-related activities. However, waterfront development is appreciated in many cases as preserving alternative uses and the traditions of the cities. Given this appreciation, objections to developing tourist activities or related infrastructures (parking slots, restricted access zones) are not rare. The principles to be adopted and the parameters to be examined should secure a balanced approach.

The same is true for port development. The limitations of a port zone imply the necessity of choices regarding a wide spectrum of activities that could be developed. As multi-purpose terminals are less viable for cruise activity development, cruise-sustaining growth results in a potential interference with other maritime transport markets. Cargo ports also seek to spatially and functionally expand to improve their integration in supply chains. Stakeholders involved in these markets would like to see the biggest parts of the port devoted to their activities rather than to the expansion of cruising. **Balanced port planning** needs to take into account the contradictory potentials of different segments' development.

**Cruise terminal site location** raises issues concerning the site and how it should be planned, which cannot be decided separately from the broader destination or regional planning framework. When several potential port sites are available, broader goals may include spreading tourism to new areas, strengthening infrastructure, creating tourism routes, and providing investment for essential facilities. Plans for other sector development and other forms of tourism create cumulative effects. The forms of involvement of stakeholders in location choice and, when essential, spatial and traffic planning are increasingly important.

Port planning and the hosting of cruise activities do not end at the terminal gate. Passenger transfer from the terminal to the city and transportation related to shore excursions are part of the process. Efficient location choices are conditioned by the efficiency of private or public transport strategies, such as services provided to the terminal. Consideration must also be given to avoiding interference with urban road traffic when a cruise ship arrives or departs. Location choices are also linked with the capacity of several tourism-related industries to connect and also to the urban tourism strategies that tourism organizations and other relevant decision-makers have in place.

Resolving most of these problems demands more than an agreement on some technical issues, such as berth allocation. It also stimulates the development of two types of coordination. The first is the **coordination between cruise ports and cruise lines** to synchronize the system at the port and the operations taking place at the port terminal. The second is the **coordination of tourist destinations**, including local public authorities, museums, retailers and, most importantly, transport service providers (coaches, buses, taxis) and travel-related industries, to create seamless embarkation/disembarkation processes and passenger flow at the destination. Even port arrangements such as berth planning cannot be efficiently implemented if there are no means to involve other actors at the destination in order to orchestrate the entire cruise supply chain.

## 4.3 Sustaining an international agenda

Common problems that cruise lines, cruise ports, and hosting destinations need to tackle, the **international dimension of several sustainability issues,** and the **ongoing globalization of cruising**, underline that efficient and effective strategies might develop at broader international levels rather than relying on local efforts. While sustainability issues are generally of local concern, an international cruise-related agenda would help advance meaningful proposals and minimize concerns about a level playing field. Besides, with local conditions and principles of engagement in cruise differing, an international agenda acts as a facilitator for stakeholders to develop a shared understanding, benchmark existing practices, promote specific solutions, and define actions.

Economic-related challenges refer to the **endorsement of best practices** rather than the necessity, or the potential, of regulatory intervention. Thus, meeting challenges at the international level does not necessarily imply the endorsement of economic and environmental regulatory initiatives. Nor does it mean the absence of any such initiatives. Distinct approaches might be endorsed in an attempt to address each of these challenges separately.

Besides, the requirements and the maturity of cruise markets in different regions of the world are diverse. Destinations, waterfronts, and social acceptability of cruise growth are rarely similar. Seasonality results in some ports and destinations hosting cruises for only a few months, compared to those serving year-round cruises. Technical characteristics and the various hosting capacities of goals and the size of port-cities, such as European cruise port cities being remarkably smaller than their North American counterparts, underline a lack of uniformity. At the same time, they generate opportunities for sharing successful practices. Variations in distances between cruise ports in a given region, and the types of competition that these distances promote, might result in variations in stakeholder strategies. Destinations have their dynamics, and cruise ports are diverse in many respects. Since each port is unique, legislation and incentives for developing cruise activities also differ, making similar practices and policies even more difficult to implement.

Stakeholders seek to enact practices satisfying economic demands and to reduce costs and risks to support sustainable development in compliance with legislation. The scope for international exchanges and resolutions is revealed by interest representation and observed associability. In 2013, Cruise Lines International Association (CLIA) integrated regional branches to represent common interests. Ports in the Caribbean have also formed their regional association. In contrast, cruise ports in northern and southern Europe are organized in respective associations (i.e. MedCruise, Cruise Europe, Cruise Baltic) and collaborate at the pan-European level. The goal is to combine the growth of cruise activities with social responsibility and environmentally friendly strategies. European institutions have also expressed an interest in encouraging stakeholder involvement in promoting an integrated approach between cruise shipping, ports, and coastal tourism stakeholders in the decision-making process.

## 5 PORT–CITY INTERACTIONS: SUSTAINABILITY

The sustainability theme is high on the agenda in shaping the future relations between cities and ports. In 2018, the International Association of Cities and Ports (AIVP – Association Internationale des Villes et Ports) started to develop a **2030 Agenda** covering ten goals to be achieved by 2030. These ten goals specifically focus on port–city relations and are closely aligned with the broadly-used 17 **Sustainable Development Goals** presented in 2015 (Figure 7.21). The AIVP Agenda 2030 thus translates the global governance SDGs into the context of port cities, helping port and urban stakeholders to prepare projects and plans that contribute to sustainable development and port–city relationships.

FIGURE 7.21 The AIVP 2030 Agenda for Sustainable Port Cities

**1. Climate change adaptation**

- Prevent inundation and flooding
- Suitable land management policy
- Give riverbanks and coastlines back to nature to reduce erosion/impacts
- Early warning systems to reduce the impacts of natural phenomena.
- Strategies to deal extreme weather conditions such as drought on ports
- Making resilience and carbon neutrality a priority in the design and operation of city port installations

**2. Energy transition & circular economy**

- Dialogue and cooperation for better management of natural resources.
- Priority for circular economy projects as part of new partnerships between the city, port and civil society,
- Commit to achieving a low carbon, low resources society
- Port community as partners in clean energy, notably when concessions come up for renewal.

© PEMP

**3. Sustainable mobility**

- Focus on multimodal & collaborative mobility, notably for commuting.
- Proximity-based urban logistics
- use of waterways, rail or other non-fossil-based modes
- Reduction of negative impacts of periods of peak activity

**4. Renewed governance**

- Better representation for all stakeholders in decision-making
- Consultation across city port region.
- Transparent management and open information systems.
- Collaborative approaches
- Land management balance between urban uses and the active port

**5. Investing in human capital**

- Life-long professional training and personal development
- Mix of profiles and skills transfers without discrimination
- Training for smart & green technologies in cities and ports
- Interactions between schools, training institutes & professionals
- Collaborative spaces for interaction and innovation

**6. Port culture and identity**

- Promenades and other open spaces in city port interface zones
- Visibility of the port and its activities.
- Creation of Port Centres.
- Daily news and information on port and city life for residents, particularly young people and school students.
- Temporary and permanent cultural events in port areas.

**7. Quality food for all**

- Smart systems for monitoring and controlling food supply chains
- Combat food waste
- Fair trade & organic/local production
- Port areas for commercial fishing
- Innovative food research

**8. Port-city interface**

- Reduce port nuisances into building design.
- Promote port and city heritage
- Public spaces (cultural/recreational) in city port interface zones
- Architectural and landscape integration of port facilities.

**9. Health and life quality**

- Measure air quality, water quality, sound levels, and light pollution
- Management of fresh and sea water
- Greener port facilities.
- Reward the greenest ships
- Regulating cruise ship stopovers

**10. Protecting biodiversity**

- Improve/maintain water quality (port)
- Surveys of biodiversity
- Save sensitive natural habitats when developing port spaces
- Protect fauna and flora
- Biodiversity programs

Source: Adapted from AIVP (2018).

# Chapter 7.5 Representing port interests

*Port and port-related associations represent the interests of the port industry at the local, national, and international levels.*

## 1 PORT AND TERMINAL ASSOCIATIONS

Ports, port authorities, terminal operators, and other stakeholders have formed associations targeting **information**, **best practices**, and **knowledge sharing**, as well as **advocacy** interests in port policy-making processes. Port associations are formed on a global, regional, and national basis to represent common concerns and find an appropriate intervention scale. They are also formed based on special common interests, with regional port associations promoting regional consensus within global port systems. This chapter focuses on international and regional associations, as national level and local port-related business associations, professional organizations, and trade unions exist in almost all countries.

The **International Association of Ports and Harbors** (IAPH) has a global reach. Established in 1955, IAPH is a non-profit-making global alliance of more than 170 ports and 140 port-related organizations covering 90 countries. Its member ports handle more than 60% of international maritime trade and around 80% of world container traffic. IAPH has consultative status with several UN agencies, including the IMO. Through its knowledge base and access to regulatory bodies, IAPH aims to facilitate energy transition, accelerate digitalization and assist in improving the overall resilience of its member ports in a constantly changing world. In 2018, IAPH established the World Ports Sustainability Program (WPSP) together with ESPO, AAPA, PIANC, and AIVP. Guided by the 17 UN Sustainable Development Goals, it aims to unite the sustainability efforts of ports worldwide by sharing best practices through its project portfolio and collaborative partnerships.

**Regional associations of port authorities** with membership expanding in many countries are present globally (Figure 7.22).

- **Port Management Association of Eastern and Southern Africa** (PMAESA). Established in 1973, PMAESA is a non-profit, inter-governmental organization made up of port operators, government ministries, logistics and maritime service providers, and other port and shipping stakeholders from the Eastern, Western, and Southern African and the Indian Ocean regions.
- **Port Management Association of West and Central Africa** (PMAWCA). Established in 1972, PMAWCA associates ports located along the West Coast of Africa, including Mauritania and Angola. The 40 port members handle about 300 million tons of maritime import/export trade for the sub-region, excluding crude oil – which is a major market for many.
- **American Association of Port Authorities** (AAPA). Established in 1912, AAPA represents 150 port authorities in the US, Canada, the Caribbean, and Latin America. AAPA protects and advances the common interests of its diverse member organizations as they connect their communities

FIGURE 7.22 Major Regional Associations of Ports and Terminals

| Association | Continent | Founded | Headquarters |
|---|---|---|---|
| Port Management Association of Eastern and Southern Africa (PMAESA) | Africa | 1973 | Mombasa, Kenya |
| Port Management Association of West and Central Africa (PMAWCA) | Africa | 1972 | Lagos, Nigeria |
| Americans Association of Port Authorities (AAPA) | Americas | 1912 | Alexandria, VA, USA |
| Port Management Association of the Caribbean (PMAC) | Americas | 1998 | Bridgetown, Barbados |
| ASEAN Ports Association (APA) | Asia | 1974 | Manila, Philippines |
| European Sea Ports Organisation (ESPO) | Europe | 1993 | Brussels, Belgium |
| Federation of European Private Port Companies and Terminals (FEPORT) | Europe | 1993 | Brussels, Belgium |
| Ports Australia | Oceania | 1916 | Sydney, Australia |

with the global transportation system. Member ports vary in size, cargo and vessel types, operating structure, and geographic areas served. The association's main goals are to advocate for government policies that strengthen and expand opportunities for member ports, advance professionalism in port management and operations, promote information sharing and relationship-building opportunities for all members, and achieve a greater understanding of the essential role and economic and social value of ports.

- **Port Management Association of the Caribbean** (PMAC). Established in 1988, PMAC fosters operational and financial efficiency and enhances the level of service to the mutual benefit of Caribbean ports and their stakeholders.
- **ASEAN Port Association (**APA). Established in 1974, APA provides to member ports in nine South-East Asian nations regional cooperation in development, operations, management, and promotion of interests. APA promotes and assists in the development and implementation of efficient operational methods, the exchange of data and information on shipping and cargo traffic, upgrade of port personnel skills and knowledge, coordination of port operations and management on an ASEAN basis; it has close relationships with organizations of shippers, shipowners, and inland transport agencies, as well as with other regional or national port associations or international port-related associations.
- **European Sea Ports Organisation** (ESPO). Established in 1993 as an interests advocacy organization, ESPO has been a major contributor to EU port policy discussions and has progressively expanded its role in knowledge, data, and best practice sharing between its members. It represents the port authorities, associations, and administrations of the seaports of 22 member states of the EU and Norway at EU political level. ESPO also has observer members in Albania, Iceland, Israel, Ukraine, and the United Kingdom.
- **Association of Australian Port and Marine Authorities (**Ports Australia**)**. Established in 1916, Ports Australia represents 28 ports that account for over 95% of Australia's imports and exports, a long list of associate members who provide Australia's ports with services, and also several international member ports from across the South Pacific Region. It was initially formed in 1916 as the 'interstate harbour conference in Melbourne' and officially changed its name in 2007.

There are also associations of a **smaller regional scale**, with the participation of ports in proximity that are located in more than one country. An indicative example is the North Adriatic Ports Association (NAPA), established in 2010 to harmonize information systems and the organizational setup of the Croatian, Italian and Slovenian member ports. A more recent one is MEDports Association, created in 2018 by 20 African and European port authorities along the Mediterranean basin, which acts as a business development, cooperation, and promotion platform for its member ports. Another example is the Baltic Ports Organization (BPO), a regional port organization established in 1991 with an aim to facilitate cooperation among the ports and to monitor and improve the possibilities for shipping in the Baltic Sea region.

The Association of Pacific Ports (APP) is a trade and information association promoting increased efficiency and effectiveness. Its programs aim to enhance the technical and governance expertise of commissioners and other port officials through meetings, educational seminars, and the exchange of communications. However, not all regional efforts are successful. In Latin America, public and private ports and terminals from Brazil, Mexico, and Colombia led the formation of the 15 member strong Latin American Ports and Terminals Association, with a head office in Bogotá, Colombia.

Ports are typically associated at a **national level**. Depending on the institutional setting, national associations envisage a different role. In some countries, these are just professional associations aiming to build professional expertise and knowledge sharing. In others, they are also active in, or even focused on, shaping port and port-related policies at the national or even international level. In some cases, these national associations only cover a part of all national ports. For example, the **Indian Ports Association** fosters the growth and development of its major ports, which are under the supervisory control of the Ministry of Shipping.

The **specialization of port activities** inevitably leads to associations representing the interests of ports or terminal operators in specific port markets. One example is the **Association of Bulk Terminal Operators** (ABTO), which aims to provide a forum for its members to discuss the issues impacting seaborne trade and the global transportation of bulk commodities. The most advanced example of this type of association is observed in the cruise port world (Box 7.9).

At terminal operator level, the **International Cargo Handling Coordination Association (ICHCA)**, founded in 1952, is a non-government organization (NGO) dedicated to improving the safety, security, sustainability,

## Box 7.9 Regional cruise ports associations

*With cruise activities based on the presence of itineraries developed in the region where a cruise ship is deployed, cruise ports tend to form **regional cruise port associations**. The membership of these associations expands to include ports and associates located in the same cruise region (Figure 7.23).*

*For most cruise port associations, the primary targets are promoting the respective areas as cruise destinations, linking members with cruise lines, and exchanging best practice. Policy-shaping via the formulation of common positions, policies, or plans on common interest questions and presenting such positions at regional and international forums is of secondary importance. Cruise ports have also attempted to create a global cruise association, but not with tangible outcomes.*

*Another peculiarity of the cruise world is that in the Caribbean, the most important market, cruise ports do not maintain their own association but are linked with the **Florida-Caribbean Cruise Association** (FCCA), a not-for-profit trade organization, established in 1972, with 22 member cruise lines that operate approximately 200 vessels in Floridian, Caribbean, and Latin American waters. This underlines the commanding role of the source market, the United States, in regional cruise interests.*

FIGURE 7.23 Cruise Ports Associations

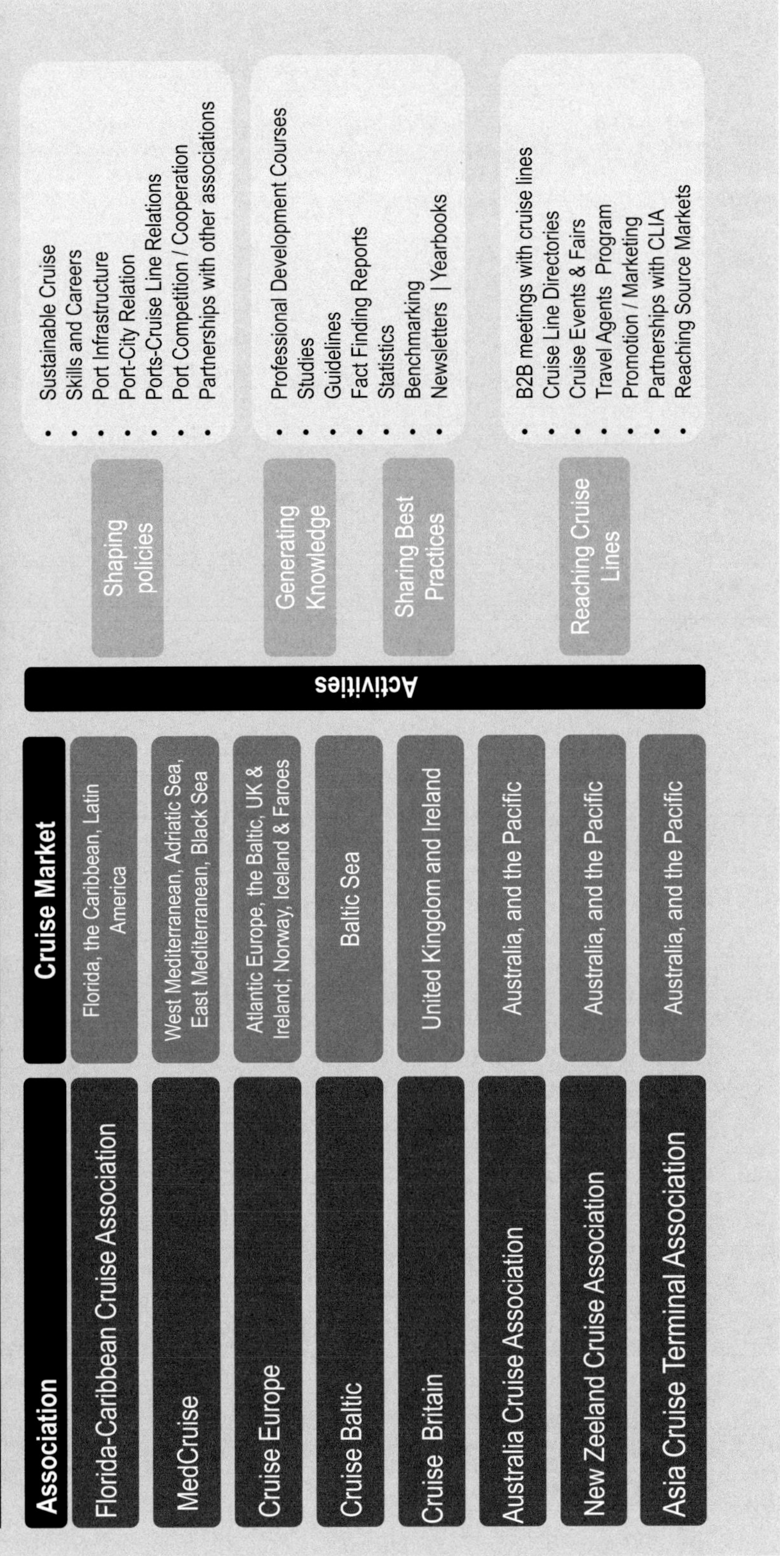

| Association | Cruise Market | Activities | |
|---|---|---|---|
| Florida-Caribbean Cruise Association | Florida, the Caribbean, Latin America | **Shaping policies** | Sustainable Cruise · Skills and Careers · Port Infrastructure · Port-City Relation · Ports-Cruise Line Relations · Port Competition / Cooperation · Partnerships with other associations |
| MedCruise | West Mediterranean, Adriatic Sea, East Mediterranean, Black Sea | **Generating Knowledge** | Professional Development Courses · Studies · Guidelines · Fact Finding Reports · Statistics · Benchmarking · Newsletters | Yearbooks |
| Cruise Europe | Atlantic Europe, the Baltic, UK & Ireland; Norway, Iceland & Faroes | **Sharing Best Practices** | |
| Cruise Baltic | Baltic Sea | | |
| Cruise Britain | United Kingdom and Ireland | **Reaching Cruise Lines** | B2B meetings with cruise lines · Cruise Line Directories · Cruise Events & Fairs · Travel Agents Program · Promotion / Marketing · Partnerships with CLIA · Reaching Source Markets |
| Australia Cruise Association | Australia, and the Pacific | | |
| New Zeeland Cruise Association | Australia, and the Pacific | | |
| Asia Cruise Terminal Association | Australia, and the Pacific | | |

*The major regional cruise port associations include:*

- *MedCruise representing ports and associates in the Mediterranean and its adjoining seas. It is the largest cruise port association in terms of annual cruise passenger movements in its member ports. Membership exceeds 100 ports and spans more than 20 countries in three continents (Europe, Asia, and Africa), and is divided into four local markets: West Med, Adriatic, East Med, and the Black Sea.*
- *Cruise Europe represents cruise ports in Northern and Atlantic Europe. It was the first cruise port network with its membership divided into four chapters: Atlantic Europe, the Baltic, the UK and Ireland, and Norway, Iceland, and Faroes. Three more 'local' cruise networks are particularly active in the region as well. These are **Cruise Baltic, Cruise Britain**, and **Cruise Norway, all of them** being members of Cruise Europe.*
- *Australia Cruise Association represents regional ports, national and state tourism agencies, and shipping agents for Australia and the Pacific region.*
- *New Zealand Cruise Association is another active cruise network operating in Oceania, promoting cruise activities in the region.*
- *Asia Cruise Terminal Association includes some of the major terminal operators in the booming Asian cruise market, with membership from six countries (China, Japan, Malaysia, the Philippines, Singapore, Taiwan).*

productivity, and efficiency of cargo handling and goods movement by all modes and through all phases of national and international supply chains. **ICHCA International** operates through a series of autonomous national and regional chapters, including ICHCA Australia, ICHCA Japan, and ICHCA Canarias/Africa, and working groups. The organization represents its members, and the cargo handling industry at large, before national and international agencies and regulatory bodies.

In Europe, **terminal operators** have formed their regional association, the **Federation of European Private Companies and Terminal Operators (FEPORT)**. Established in 1993, FEPORT represents the interests of a variety of terminal operators and stevedoring companies carrying out activities over 400 terminals in the seaports of the European Union. **Inland ports** are associated in the **European Federation of Inland Ports** (EFIP). In North America, terminal owners and operators in the West Coast of the US have been joined by carriers operating throughout the world in the **Pacific Merchant Shipping Association** (PMSA), an independent, not-for-profit shipping association that is engaged in community affairs and legislative and regulatory processes in the US West Coast states.

The importance of **port–city relationships** and the integration of ports for development purposes has led to a renaissance in port city associations. The **International Association of Cities and Ports (AIVP)** supports the need for dialogue between all stakeholders concerned in port city projects. The 1,900

AIVP stakeholders include city governments, port authorities and administrations, research institutes, and city developers. AIVP promotes international exchanges between port cities and encourages best practices for sustainable city-port projects that meet the aspirations of citizens.

Next to the global, regional, and national level, individual ports usually feature a wide array of **industry and branch organizations** defending the interest of specific professions or activities in the port (e.g. freight forwarders, ship agents, terminal operators, industrial companies) or representing the interests of the entire (private company) port community. Most of these associations strongly focus on operational issues and inter-firm cooperation and exchanges affecting the overall functioning and performance of the port cluster or parts thereof. Still, some of them have widened their focus to include lobby activities at the national and supranational policy level. This is particularly the case for **umbrella associations of large seaports** with a strong and diverse private company portfolio and located in smaller countries (Box 7.10). In larger countries, national private sector associations usually play a more prominent role in the dialogue with policymakers. The representation of port interests in seaports with a strong presence of state-owned port companies relies heavily on consultation between the relevant public actors at the different policy levels.

---

### Box 7.10 Umbrella associations in Rotterdam and Antwerp

*Deltalinqs was established in 2001 to represent the interests of about 700 companies or over 95% of all logistic, ports, and industrial enterprises from 14 different sectors in the **Port of Rotterdam**. Deltalinqs strives to strengthen Rotterdam's competitiveness, sustainable growth, and social and political acceptability in all activities within the port and industrial area. Expertise is shared via knowledge networking groups. The association also develops port-wide initiatives, such as the Digital Safety Passport and the Deltalinqs Training Window. As a lobbying entity, Deltalinqs promotes the interests of its members at many institutions, both locally and nationally, and in European circles.*

***Alfaport Voka** is the platform of and for companies and professional associations from the **Port of Antwerp** within Voka (Chamber of Commerce Antwerp–Waasland). It is the umbrella association of five professional associations in the Port of Antwerp: ABAS (stevedoring companies), ASF (Antwerp Shipping Federation; shipping agencies), Forward Belgium (freight forwarders), RBSA (Royal Belgian Shipowners Association), and KVBG (goods handlers). Unlike Deltalinqs, industrial firms in the port are not represented in Antwerp's umbrella association. The large chemical and petrochemical companies in the port are members of **Essenscia**, the Belgian sector federation of the chemical industry and life sciences. Alfaport Voka strives for an accessible, facilitative, cost-competitive, and sustainable Port of Antwerp with a view to a sustainable anchoring of employment and added value in the port.*

## 2 TRADE UNIONS

**Port labor** has a long history of unionism, which can be traced back as early as the nineteenth century when the first modern longshoremen union was formed in the port of New York. Today, beyond the national level unions, dockers are associated in two umbrella organizations with a global presence:

- The **International Transport workers Federation** (ITF) was established in 1896 as the International Federation of Dock and River Workers, and has become an umbrella organization with affiliated unions from approximately 150 countries. It has a section involved in issues facing port workers and dockers worldwide. The affiliates are unions that are organizing labor directly involved in cargo handling, those indirectly involved in cargo activities (such as those with members employed by port managers, agencies, and freight forwarders), and those representing workers employed by the state, city, or other authority, as well as by private companies. **Regional federations** of these trade unions are also present, such as the **European Transport Workers Federation** (ETF) which represents and advocates for the interests of port and terminal workers all over Europe.
- The **International Dockworkers Council** (IDC) is a trade union federation composed of dockworkers' organizations worldwide. Its basic principles define it as a working-class, unitary, independent, democratic, representative, and assembly organization. Membership is extensive on all continents except Asia. It includes major national unions, such as the **International Longshoremen's Association** (ILA) and the **International Longshore and Warehouse Union** (ILWU), representing dockworkers on the East Coast and West Coast of the US, respectively. In Asia, membership is limited to the Hong Kong Dockers Union.

While national or port level unions might prioritize collective agreements and terms of employment at the local level, the themes of the main activities of the international and regional federations include:

- Health and safety in the port industry.
- Job security for port workers.
- Issue-based campaigns, such as container safety.

The consequences of automation for port labor have generated trade union agendas and discussions on the **future of port work** and the search for a socially sustainable approach to technological developments. ETF is involved in the European sectoral Social Dialogue Committee, where it meets with port and terminal employers to discuss how to shape the future of dock work and promote policies and legislation that ensure jobs and protection of workers' rights along with technological developments in European ports. In this context, ETF has also expressed an interest in promoting research on labor schemes and campaigning for job security in case of a change of port operator.

A notable development took place in 2016 when the ITF set up the **Maersk network** designed to promote the interests of those who are employed either directly or indirectly by this global company, in essence, acknowledging the role of global conglomerates that are horizontally and vertically integrated companies. The network has agreed, among other things, on two other main objectives. First, to put together a union training and development program to support new unions in APM terminals across the Arab World and Africa to build their bargaining capacity and establish strong unions. Second, to assess APM's Latin America growth strategy and identify priorities for the global network terminals campaign.

## 3 PORT SERVICES PROVIDERS

**Providers of services** at ports have their associations, some having a global reach. The **International Association of Dredging Companies** (IADC) is the global umbrella organization for contractors in the private dredging industry. The **International Association of Maritime Pilots** (IMPA), launched in 1971, has over 8,000 members in more than 50 countries, with its principal objective being the promotion of professionally sound and safe pilotage services. The **International Boatmen and Linesman Association** has a similar role. It associates the personnel involved in mooring, unmooring operations and also boatmen, the **International Harbour Masters' Association** with members in more than 50 countries, and the **International Tug Masters Association**.

The members of these associations are also organized at regional and national levels. An example of the former type of associability in Europe is the presence of the **European Dredging Association** (EuDA), the **European Harbour Masters Committee** (EHMC), the **European Maritime Pilots Association** (EMPA), and the **European Tugowners Association** (ETA), with all of them being also active in interactions with European institutions and international organizations.

## 4 PORT USERS

Port users, shipowners, shippers, and freight forwarders are all represented via respective associations at a global or regional level, alongside the many associations at the individual port level. Shipowners maintain a long tradition of being represented globally by either inclusive associations or associations representing specific market segments. One of the former is the **International Chamber of Shipping** (ICS), whose membership comprises national shipowners' associations from 37 countries. Associations in the latter group include **Intercargo**, the International Association of Dry Cargo Shipowners, **Intertanko**, the International Association for Independent Tanker Owners, and **Cruise Lines International Association** (CLIA). To these, one might add BIMCO, whose membership comprises owners, brokers, ships agents, and other operators. Regional level associations are also present, such as the **European Community Shipowners Association** (ECSA), which has been active since the early 1950s, with shipowners maintaining national unions as well.

**Shippers** are also active at the regional level. In Europe, the **European Shippers' Council** (ESC) represents cargo owners from around 100,000 companies throughout Europe, whether manufacturers, retailers, or wholesalers. ESC, together with its counterparts in Asia (the **Asian Shippers' Association** – ASA) and the US (the **American Association of Exporters and Importers** –AAEI), have formed the **Global Shippers Alliance** (GSA).

The **International Federation of Freight Forwarders Associations** (FIATA) is a non-governmental, membership-based organization representing freight forwarders in some 150 countries, with more than 100 Association Members and more than 5,500 individual members, overall representing an industry of 40,000 freight forwarding and logistics firms. Freight forwarders are also associated regionally, with CLECAT (European Association for Forwarding, Transport, Logistics and Customs Services) representing freight forwarders in Europe.

# PART VIII

# Port markets

## Chapter 8.1 Cruise ports

*Ports and destinations have developed an interest in hosting cruise activities. Cruise ports and terminals are undergoing transformation, aiming to achieve growth.*

### 1 AN EXPANDING CRUISE PORT SYSTEM

With the growth in cruise shipping and businesses, cruise ports are gaining importance. The port is vital for assuring schedule reliability and allowing a continuous passenger (dis)embarkation and transfer to onward journeys and day excursions. This highlights the considerable financial contribution of cruising to port cities or nearby touristic destinations. Once cruise lines express an interest in a destination, allowing for economic and geopolitical conditions, its viability relies on port and shore characteristics. The presence of sufficient port-specific and port-related infrastructures, the absence of intense use that might lead to congestion and disruption, and the modernization of infrastructures to provide efficient and effective port services are crucial parameters allowing the usage of a port as part of an itinerary.

Ports also realize the opportunity to provide services to an industry that offers to local economies more than returns to the port itself. With the **direct and indirect impacts** of many cruise-related activities, including passenger and crew spending, on port cities or nearby tourist destinations, interest in increasing the number of cruise passengers has been supported by broader communities and decision-makers. Admittedly, passenger and crew spending contributes significantly to the cruise hosting economies. Cruise line expenditures for goods and services in support of their operations and the many other indirect and induced effects provide additional motivation for hosting cruise activities. The rising importance of port–city integration coincides with the growth of the industry. Cruise activities are part of the agendas promoted by port authorities and other port-managing organizations to link their port

DOI 10.4324/9780429318184-8

with visible benefits for the local economy. All these contribute to the use of different cruise itineraries and reduction in the high level of concentration of the global cruise port system which has been observed in the past.

In the twentieth century, the global cruise port system has been characterized by a high level of regional concentration as well as a clustering of port visits. However, in the twenty-first century this concentration has diminished rapidly, as expansive global itinerary building by cruise lines and a growing interest in advancing cruise activities in many cruise ports has increased the number of ports hosting notable levels of cruise activities.

## 2 TYPOLOGIES OF CRUISE PORTS

Ports offering services to cruise lines vary in many respects as the aim of cruise shipping is different from that of cargo shipping. Cruise lines focus on the provision of amenities to cruise passengers, rather than just transportation services. These two elements, transport and tourism, result in multiple criteria for a typology of cruise ports. The first group of criteria is similar to those observed in cargo port markets. The second group reflects the peculiarities of the cruise market, including the catalytic influence of the tourism element (Figure 8.1).

### 2.1 The port element

Depending on their **role in cruise itineraries**, cruise ports fall into the following categories:

- **Home ports** (turnaround ports or hub ports) are the ports where passengers begin or end their cruises. Most commonly, they are both the commencing and the ending point of a designed itinerary. About 80% of all cruises end up in their port of origin, meaning that cruises are usually set up as loops. There are a growing number of homeports where passengers can begin or end their journey.
- **Ports of call** (transit ports) are an intermediate stop en route to another destination. Cruise vessels call for a few hours before continuing their itinerary, offering their guests the opportunity to visit the port–city and nearby touristic attractions.

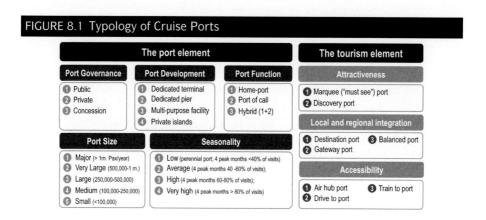

FIGURE 8.1 Typology of Cruise Ports

- **Hybrid ports** blend the two categories as they are the starting and ending point for some cruise itineraries but also act as an intermediate point for other cruise itineraries.

Within the Spanish market, which is the biggest in Europe, Barcelona fulfills the function of a home port. Seville, Valencia, Palma, and Gran Canarias play dual roles. There are even some ports, like Malaga, which can primarily play the role of port-of-call, but have also been used as a home port.

The **state of cruise port development** provides a second typology criterion. The siting and setting up of cruise port facilities are subject to constraints usually not found for cargo port activities. Cruise lines expect specific levels of services and space as more than ten square feet are needed to serve each passenger check-in in less than 15 minutes and disembarkation in less than 20 minutes. Architects and builders are developing specialized terminals with many aesthetic characteristics. This is a major transformation, as most cruise terminals were reconversions of port facilities used for cargo operations, particularly if those sites were adjacent to downtown. However, the move from multi-purpose terminals or temporary docking facilities towards specialized cruise terminals is not universal. Sometimes, scarce port land only allows for one pier to be dedicated to cruises. Alternatively, cruise lines can develop their own ports of call, such as private islands in the Caribbean.

The **terminalization of cruise ports** implies advanced, autonomously operating cruise terminals of considerable size (Box 8.1), accompanied by the presence of cruise terminal operators that assume responsibility for operating and, in some cases, constructing and developing these terminals.

## Box 8.1 Terminalization of cruise ports: Barcelona

### FIGURE 8.2 Terminals at Cruise Port Barcelona

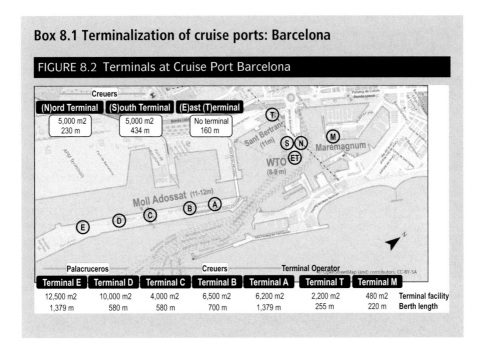

*The port of Barcelona is the major cruise port in Europe and among the biggest in the world. Used for both homeporting and transit calls, the port hosts over three million passenger movements and 800 cruise calls per year. The port facilitates cruise activities via the operation of several terminals of various sizes. The larger terminals accommodating the biggest cruise vessels are concessioned by the Port Authority of Barcelona to terminal operators. The Port Authority only operates some of the smaller cruise facilities (Figure 8.2).*

*Founded in 1999,* **Creuers del Port de Barcelona S.A.** *(Creuers) operates five public cruise terminals at the port of Barcelona. In the second half of the 2000s, it demolished the existing cruise Terminal A and built a new, bigger and upgraded one, which has the capacity to serve mega cruise ships. In 2014, Global Ports Holding acquired the majority of Creuers and became the largest cruise port operator in the World.*

**Palacruceros**, *which is owned by the Carnival group, is the operator of two cruise terminals. Terminal D – Palacruceros was opened in 2007 and the total amount invested in its construction has been wholly financed by the Italian company, Costa Crociere. Since then, the terminal has operated under a private concession that guarantees preference to Carnival Corporation ships. Helix Cruise Center is the newest 12,500 m² cruise terminal of the port. Completed in 2018, it is also concessioned to Palacruceros.*

The uninterrupted growth of cruising has resulted in the opening of a window of opportunity to several firms, including cruise lines and specialized cruise terminal operators such as Global Ports Holding, wishing to undertake new or additional investments in the cruise business, and sometimes to follow a path of internationalization. The leasing of cruise terminals to third parties and the development of new terminals have become common. In some ports, cruise lines are directly involved in the financing, building, and operations of terminals. In other ports, local cruise terminal operators (frequently being port agents) are joined by other companies that have developed interests in taking control over cruise ports and specialized purpose vehicles (SPVs) built by terminal operating companies. This led to the emergence of international operators.

As cruise activities in ports gain operational autonomy, public authorities are pursuing various partnerships with third parties, aiming to finance and develop growth strategies, **Cruise port governance** has in many cases been revisited, with more actors involved than just the managing entity of the port.

Two additional classifications of cruise ports are based on the transportation element of cruising and facilitate a better understanding of the heterogeneity of the cruise port industry. The first is the **size of the cruise ports**. With many ports becoming very large entities handling more than one million passenger movements per year, cruise ports might be classified as being of significant size, or very large, large, or medium, or even a small cruise port — one that hosts very few calls and passenger movements per annum.

The other criterion is the **seasonality of cruise activities** (i.e. low, average, high, very high), which refers to the extent that cruise activities in a region and cruise vessel calls at a particular port occur during just a few months of the year.

## 2.2 The tourism element

Cruise ports also fall into three main categories depending on their role in tourism within their regions. They can be a **destination port** where few, if any, excursions occur outside the port area and the touristic attractions of the linked port–city. They can also be a **gateway port** that mostly serves as a point of embarkation or a **balanced port** offering a combination of port area amenities and inland excursions. Each of these categories implies different development strategies to service the market.

A different classification results from the level of **tourist attractiveness** of each cruise port and its linked port–city and destination. Some of the ports are **marquee ports** that, due to exceptional tourist attractions close by, are essential destinations for cruises in the region. Others are **discovery ports**, commonly seen as having the potential to attract the interest of prospective cruisers.

**Accessibility** stands as another relevant classification of cruise ports. The dominant means of reaching the port, such as flight and cruise, drive and cruise, or train and cruise, influences the type of operations and infrastructure the port needs to provide.

## 2.3 Cruise port services

The services offered to cruise lines at a cruise port differ depending on the **function of the port** along an itinerary (Figure 8.3). The services expected to be on offer at a transit port are a subset of those available at home ports. Generic facilities available at all cruise ports include entrance and berthing facilities. The second group of services is offered to the cruise vessels and cruise lines, and the third group of services is provided to cruise passengers. A home port is expected to provide additional services that assist cruise passengers and their activities.

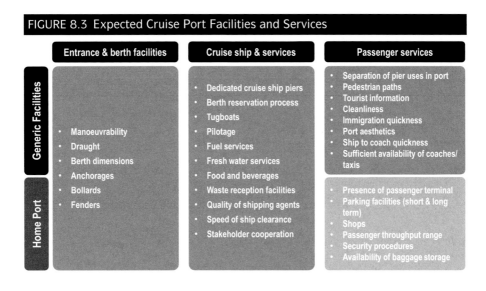

FIGURE 8.3 Expected Cruise Port Facilities and Services

## 3 THE COMPETITIVENESS OF CRUISE PORTS

Cruise ports serve a **derived demand**, such as the wish of cruisers to visit a specific destination. Nonetheless, the **competitiveness** of the infrastructure and services offered at a cruise port can also affect the decisions of cruise lines to include in their cruise itineraries more calls at this port. Seeking to develop a new product, cruise lines have added new cruise ports to itineraries and seek to attract land-based holidaymakers or returning customers. This search continues and is associated with destination features such as tourist attractions, shore excursion potential, and security. However, ports and their facilities, such as berth access, land infrastructure and logistics, maritime services such as pilot and tugs, and landside operation such as security, procedures, and luggage handling, affect the growth of cruising in a given port. Besides, cruise ports do not necessarily have a monopoly in the offered amenities or access to inland touristic attractions. Substitution remains a possibility.

It is less costly for ports to develop a cruise terminal than it is to develop other port facilities, such as container terminals. Superstructures and processes are less demanding in terms of sophistication. However, the quality of port facilities (infrastructure), the efficiency of services and operations, and the levels of port fees (costs) can explain only part of the attractiveness of a cruise port. With cruise passenger satisfaction being the foundation of cruise shipping, a cruise port relies on additional factors if it is to become a port of call and host cruise passenger movements.

First, the extent to which the port is geographically well-positioned for integration into cruise itineraries, which involves the distance between cruise ports. The **location of the port** remains fundamental. Ports located in must-see destinations still need to be part of an appealing itinerary to be a popular cruise destination. A second factor is the **tourist attractiveness of the destination**. This is primarily determined by characteristics of the area (climate, socio-cultural and natural factors, or proximity to tourist attractions), with the port industry and stakeholders having only a secondary influence. The third factor is the **accessibility of the destination**. Port proximity to an airport with airlifts to source markets, a train station with good connections, and highways supporting the increasingly popular drive and cruise concept might determine the potential to host home port traffic.

Taking it for granted that a port has applied all the steps to enhance **security** levels, the next factor is the **quality of port services** and services offered. Port fees stand as a success factor as well. The last two factors are generally the most easily adaptable compared to other success factors. Nevertheless, a cruise port that performs more weakly on location, tourist attractiveness, and accessibility than another port is not likely to match performance by making changes in facilities, services, or fees.

### 3.1 Port choice and itineraries

Cruise ports aim to be part of different cruise itineraries since cruise lines sell **itineraries**, not destinations, implying greater flexibility in selecting ports of call. The selection of an itinerary by cruise lines is the outcome of several commercial considerations:

- **Potential revenue generation and costs**, such as shore excursion revenues plus shipboard revenue, port costs, and fuel costs (including the impact of fuel-related regulations).

- **Operational considerations**, such as geographic location (competing and complementary ports on the itinerary), the distance between ports of call (cruise ships can cover up to 280 nautical miles per night), infrastructure, days of the week that a cruise might call, evening and overnight calls.
- **Brand positioning** (exotic ports of call for premium services).
- **Guest interest and satisfaction** (customer-oriented industry).
- **Marketability** (with itineraries being as strong as the weakest port).
- **Economic trends and market research** include evaluating changes in disposable incomes and the demographics of the customer base.

Once the above criteria have generated a short list of alternative options, attention turns to the cruise ports to be included. Cruise lines are interested in selecting ports that:

- Are not congested.
- Provide quality port facilities.
- Apply transparent berthing policies and other facilities.
- Have the potential to attract cruisers from diversified passenger source markets.

Geographical proximity and connectivity to other cruise ports are vital. **Synchronizing a cruise port location** with the time and speed preferences of cruise lines, particularly the possibility of being included in itineraries involving several ports, is vital. This formula is the outcome of the fact that ships ideally travel at 18 knots for 14 hours. This means that the maximum overnight travel distance is 250 nautical miles, whereas with a speed of 20 knots, the maximum overnight travel distance increases to 280 nautical miles.

Ports are carefully considered with a view to maximizing the commercial potential and utilization of onboard assets. Ships are constantly moving between ports of call, and shore leaves are of low duration, such as 4.3 hours on average in the Caribbean, even if a cruise ship stays at a port for ten to 12 hours. A standard cruise itinerary is a loop beginning and ending at a hub port (also called a turn port or port of embarkation) and typically lasting seven days with three to five ports of call depending on their respective proximity. Cruises of ten to 21 days are also offered, but they tend to have lower profit margins as customers tend to spend less as the cruise progresses.

Analysis of cruises by the number of days duration reveals the characteristics of **cruise itineraries**. The share of cruise lasting seven days is dominant (47%), with other prevalent durations in the range of three to five days. This illustrates a scheduling issue for cruise shipping lines as they maximize their asset utilization through a continuous turn of cruise ships. For instance, a ship usually finishes a weekly cruise early in the morning and begins a new one on the evening of the same day. In the 8–12 hours window between the end of the inbound cruise and the beginning of the outbound cruise, passengers must check out and disembark, facilities are cleaned, waste discarded, stores replenished, the ship refueled, basic maintenance performed, and outbound cruise passengers must check-in and embark. The design variables of itineraries within this time frame mainly concern the number and order of port calls, the synchronization with the (international) air transfers at the turn ports, vessel speed, and vessel size.

Since the cruise industry appears fundamentally to be driven by supply, **supply saturation**, as opposed to demand saturation, often constrains future developments and imposes limitations on an industry that continued to grow rapidly until the COVID-19 pandemic. While large hub ports can accommodate additional port calls, it is the smaller 'exotic' or 'must-see' (marquee) ports that cruisers are seeking to visit that present challenges for additional capacity. Berth availability and the ability of small communities to accommodate large tourist influxes of short duration has become a salient issue. However, the massification of cruise ships is creating a scale and scope challenge for several cruise ports facing the dilemma of the generation of tourism income and the environmental and social disruptions associated with large cruise ships. This leads to further market segmentation between large ports visited by mega-ships and smaller ports visited by smaller ships offering a specialized cruise experience.

This is likely to stimulate further involvement of the cruise industry in terminal operations, a trend that has already started taking place. Irrespective of ownership structure, the emergence of transnational cruise terminal operators (currently observed at a limited scale) might further transform the industry in the coming years. While a further fragmentation of itineraries is likely to occur, closer integration between the cruise port and the cruise shipping industry is expected.

## 3.2 Infrastructure upgrade

The availability of **adequate port infrastructure** and the organization of cruise hosting operations efficiently and securely remain among the conditions for generating the interest of cruise lines in including a port in a cruise itinerary. Cruise ports need docks able to accommodate the new generation of cruise ships efficiently. Requiring new infrastructures poses significant challenges, especially to those ports that face land scarcity or the need for regular dredging of their basin. In the latter case, there is a need to minimize the potential impact on the sea flora and fauna (through land reclamation) and process and use the dredging operation products.

The optimal design and planning of cruise ports and their terminals underline long-term arrangements between ports and cruise lines. When securing the long-term commitment of one or more cruise lines, the cruise port is encouraged to provide adjustments to its operations. Such long-term commitments are defined through negotiations between ports and cruise lines.

Once the port infrastructure is in place, and the port is operational, the managing entity of the cruise port needs to develop a strategy for growing homeporting activities and the desired cruise market segments. Competition for both transit and home port cruise business is growing, with ports and destinations working to evaluate the benefits of each option in order to direct their efforts to the most convenient business opportunity. The most significant **challenges** in the search for competitiveness are:

- Developing **relationships with cruise lines**, with the aim of securing a long-term engagement.
- The accommodation of calls by **larger size cruise ships**.
- The evolution of **relationships with people and businesses around the ports** offering improved services to passengers and cruise ships calling at the port.

- Exploitation of the potential to overcome the **seasonality** of hosting cruise activities via year-round cruising.

A common denominator in these efforts is the need to enhance the economic, social, and environmental sustainability of the cruise activities attracted.

## 3.3 Relationships with cruise lines

Improving relationships with cruise lines is the major challenge for cruise ports. The most important issue to be addressed is the offering of attractive **shore excursions**. Ports and cruise lines need to align their priorities. Subsequently, they coordinate their efforts and engage service providers, authorities, and stakeholders, in organizing transportation infrastructures and tourist services ashore to increase the options available to cruise passengers. The potential for multiple shore excursions encourages itinerary planners to include the port in the offered cruise programs.

The **long-term engagement of cruise lines** to the use of a cruise port is a strong indication of its prospects as a destination. To expand its presence in the cruise market, a port may need to adapt to organizational structures, operational procedures, and governance regimes, or strategies. The presence of cruise lines for more than a few calls, and the commitment for a multi-year presence, appear crucial. The **availability of landside transportation** is another issue creating controversy between ports and cruise lines, with ports and destinations having to collaborate to resolve any bottlenecks.

The demand for port services does not depend on port operations. Cruisers are primarily interested in agile transportation to the port–city or the tourist destination. Less discussed are unexpected call cancelations by cruise lines, which are high on the agenda for cruise ports. Perhaps contrary to what may be expected, other arrangements appear to be more challenging than tariffs. Two significant challenges to be jointly addressed by ports and cruise lines include the **cooperation between ports and cruise lines** when scheduling itineraries and **berth allocation**.

Berth allocation is a long-term planning issue for ports, with vital social implications. The practice refers to the planning of which cruise vessels will visit the given port on a specific day for a particular time span. Ports need to arrange the slot to be reserved for a particular vessel call two years in advance. The reason is that the cruise line needs to define its cruise itineraries and then inform travel agents who will need to sell the cruise to potential customers. For several reasons, such planning does not always happen. Given the limitations imposed by the geographical distances between ports included in an itinerary and the lengths of cruises, having several operators berthing for the same hours is not rare. The problem of berth allocation is even more critical in smaller, secondary cruise ports. In small, picturesque destinations, cruise calls might mean relatively unpleasant situations of a crowded location for certain days or hours, or even distortion of other tourist activities. In bigger ports, this might take the form of congestion at the arrival of bigger ships on which thousands of people are cruising.

The arrival of two average-size cruise vessels at a given port means more than 6,000 passengers disembarking at the same time. Yet, in some cases, congestion in small and medium destinations is produced simply because of a small additional number of calls. Without effective planning, these destinations may be subject to the pressure and the negative effect of too many passengers who can barely be accommodated which does not allow for a positive experience. In several cases, the presence of cruises is marked by seasonality, reducing the problem that smaller tourist destinations face.

However, while the debate on how best to apply berth allocation is at the top of the agenda between key stakeholders, this debate remains in many respects inconclusive. Technical issues related to its application (time scale, details of the berthing allocation) and also the need of all ports included in an itinerary to synchronize with the system, the diverging needs of each cruise line, the treatment of double bookings and cancellations of booked cruise berths, are all vital. With the number of players involved, this discussion is complex to resolve.

## 3.4 Scale of cruise port calls

The early goal of the cruise industry was to **develop a mass market** since cruising was, until then, an activity for the elite. A way to achieve this was through economies of scale as larger ships could accommodate more customers and create additional opportunities for onboard revenue sources. Today, the average dimension of a cruise ship is over 200 meters long, 26 meters beam, and approximately 3,000 passenger capacity. However, the standard deviation is significant and such numbers need to be treated with caution. The current order book suggests a clear stabilization trend regarding maximum vessel size and underlines that there are limits to economies of scale in cruise shipping.

Cruise ships tend to have a low draft since they do not carry cargo; they have **more volume than weight**. This confers the advantage of access to a large number of ports and therefore multiple itinerary options since the setting up of a pure cruise port rests on criteria that are different from commercial ports. Cruise ports tend to be located close to either city centers (cultural and commercial amenities) or natural amenities (e.g. a protected beach). On average, these sites do not have very deep drafts, and dredging would be socially or environmentally unacceptable. For instance, the Oasis-class ships, which as of 2018 accounted for the largest cruise ship class, have a draft of 9.3 meters and a capacity of about 6,600 passengers and a crew of 2,200. Comparatively, a containership of 2,500 TEU requires a draft of 10.6 meters, while a containership of 8,400 TEU requires a draft of 14 meters. Draft issues that have plagued container ports are a much more marginal constraint for cruise shipping. Additionally, cruise ships can anchor and use tendering services, which opens a wide array of ports of call.

The growth in cruise ship size imposes **physical restrictions** on destination ports. Ports must guarantee sufficient draft and berthing lengths, and cruise terminals capable of handling efficiently large volumes of passengers. To receive a mega cruise ship, a cruise terminal must guarantee at least 10 meters of draft, 425 meters of berth length, and a navigation channel 132 meters wide, assuming good weather and other navigational conditions. Limits might also relate to landside operations, such as space for the apron area, the ground transportation area, road communications, the capacity of destinations to serve more cruisers, and the social acceptance of the further growth of cruising. Physical limitations of piers' berth lengths and drafts have historically limited cruise development. Many ports do not meet these requirements and would require major upgrades to host mega cruises.

## 3.5 Seasonality of cruise activities

Despite the remarkable growth of cruise activities, the **seasonality of many cruise itineraries** implies that an array of cruise ports are used during a peak season but may receive limited, if any, cruise ship calls outside the main season. A 40-week cruise season is considered by many as the maximum duration per year, but is uncommon. One of the implications is that cruise terminals remain unused for a lengthy period. Those responsible for developing cruise ports might also be more skeptical about allocating more port areas to cruising. The reason is that this is an activity marked by seasonality when other factors, such as the port land scarcity, and the request for more space by cargo port activities, add pressures to devote available port land to cargo. Societal pressures for year-round utilization, so that the port–city and related destinations that enjoy cruise tourism benefit, put pressure on ports to develop conditions for expanding the cruise season.

Cruise lines set itineraries to maximize customer satisfaction (and revenues) but must consider the seasonality of the demand. The planning of vessel deployment targets maximum capacity utilization in combination with the maximization of earnings per passenger and minimizing expenses (mostly via lower fuel consumption). Seasonality is a fundamental market characteristic, and implies that ports host cruise vessels calls deployed as part of three different types of itineraries (Figure 8.4):

- **Perennial**, responding to a region that is served throughout the year due to the resilient demand (with high/low periods) and stable weather conditions; the Caribbean and, to a lesser extent, the Mediterranean and its adjoining seas, are such markets. Perennial markets can have a seasonality implying that although they are serviced throughout the year, there are periods of lower demand.
- **Seasonal**, to serve periodical market potential in periods with good weather conditions; with the Baltic, Norway, Alaska, and New England standing as typical examples. Ideally, cruise lines would prefer to service only perennial markets since this would represent a close to optimal use of ship assets. However, like the tourism industry in general, seasonality

## FIGURE 8.4 Types of Cruise Itineraries

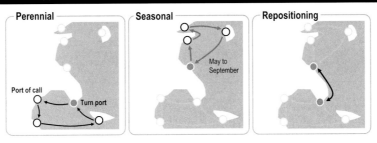

is an important component of the demand for cruises, meaning that some markets are serviced for a few months, mainly during the summer.

- **Repositioning, between perennial or seasonal markets**, a practice evident between the Caribbean and Mediterranean, and Alaska and Hawaii, though following the globalization of the market in recent times this has expanded to additional markets (i.e. the Mediterranean and the Indian Ocean).

The repositioning strategies of cruise lines involve cruise itinerary scheduling based on the **coupling of cruise markets** and deploying a cruise vessel in both markets for specific periods. This coupling is based on the proximity of markets, cost issues, and the sourcing of passenger patterns. For instance, North Asia and South East Asia are two such markets, with their coupling based on the same sourcing of passengers, the demand for the same product, warm alternative weather, and low-cost repositioning. The coupling of North Asia and Australia provides a warm alternative, robust yields, and low-cost repositioning. An Australia/Pacific-Alaska coupling is justified on grounds of the same sourcing of passengers, the same product offered in both markets, and warm alternative weather for cruise passengers at different times of the year. Finally, the coupling of the Mediterranean market and the North America/Caribbean markets is based on the same sourcing of passengers, the offering of the same product, the warm alternative, and the low-cost repositioning of the vessels. For cruise ports, this coupling of markets implies cruise calls by deployed ships and cruise passenger hosting in parts of the year only.

Some cruise regions are less affected by seasonality, with the Caribbean one of the few perennial markets. The number of monthly passengers is relatively stable throughout the year in markets serviced by North American ports with passengers totaling between 800,000 and 1 million per month, with a December/January peak season. However, a closer look reveals specific seasonality patterns. The Caribbean market and its sub-regions dominate to account for more than 90% of the passengers during the high winter season and around 55% of the passengers during the low summer season. The seasonality of Alaska, Bermuda, and Canada/New England is also evident, with cruise lines attempting to optimize the utilization of their assets year-round by repositioning to take advantage of seasonality. An unexpected pattern is a lack of seasonality for the Bahamas, mainly the outcome of the leading cruise lines building private ports reserved for their exclusive use.

Seasonality does not restrict the development of a cruise region, such as for the Mediterranean and its adjoining seas, a most dynamic cruise region. In 2019, between May and October, each month accounted for 10%–12% of the traffic. In total, 75% of the cruise passenger movements that occur annually in this cruise region happen during these six months. The total passenger movements registered during the three winter months (December, January, February) stand at only 7% of the total annual movements. This has stimulated discussions on achieving year-round, but with limited outcomes. Winter activities are linked with single call operations of a different size than in the rest of the year. In the Mediterranean, fewer than 850 calls out of an annual total exceeding 12,500 happen from December to February. However, for these months, each call is associated, on average, with more passengers. January is the month with the highest rate of passengers per call (2,314 passengers), followed by February (2,153 passengers) and December (2,095 passengers). Cruise lines develop fewer itineraries, as repositioning vessels take place, with cruises marked by a substantially higher level of utilization. From a port and destination perspective, respective adjustments of operations are essential.

Due to seasonality, cruise terminals can represent an underutilized asset prone to risks. For many ports, the cruise terminal remains a temporary facility with berth(s) supporting other uses when cruise ships are not calling. An approach is to use a cruise terminal as a multi-purpose facility, often built for another rationale that can include an adjacent hotel, convention center, events hall or any other revenue-generating infrastructure that would gain by being on the waterfront.

## 3.6 Cruise ports: competition and co-opetition

The growth of the cruise industry results in the evolution of **complex relationships between cruise ports**. The central element is the fact that cruising develops based on itineraries rather than destinations. There is an interdependent relationship between competition and cooperation between two or more rival ports competing in a given market.

Ports located in the same region compete to be included in the itineraries scheduled by cruise lines. Yet not all compete for the same market. The reason is the development of distinctive cruise market segments, such as contemporary, premium, and luxury cruises. Either by choice or due to capacity and destination restrictions, several ports target only a specific market segments. Contemporary and luxury cruises stand as the most popular market segments. The competition is more intense between ports of the same category. Cruise lines are interested in creating itineraries that include ports of different sizes. Each port provides various experiences, permitting passengers to select from options for accessing their departing port. For example, competition develops between marquee ports to be part of as many itineraries as possible or between different destination ports. There is also competition between small ports or between ports enabling drive-to-cruise. With the number of ports entering the market increasing, this competition is intensifying. Thus the increase in market size allows for sustenance of a wide range of activities.

In the case of home ports, competition is even more intense than in ports of call. In this case, the geographical location of the competing ports turns out to be of limited importance. Especially when the ports are marquee ports, the geographical concern is limited to the location of other ports able to confirm attractive itineraries. In the case of home ports, features and facilities of the cruise port and the destination are most significant, as are the quality and the variance offered by the existing chain of suppliers (i.e. bunkering, provisioning) having the capacity to serve homeporting calls.

While competing, cruise ports also develop cooperation practices as a critical strategy to establish their market position. This also takes place among cargo ports, but in the case of cruising, ports do so to the extent that their relationship can be described as the perfect case of **co-opetition**. This refers to competing entities generating a number of advantages and opportunities produced through active inter-organizational relationships. The key concept is to collectively benefit from the growth of the cruise industry via networking and promotion of regions as cruise destinations, next to individual ports. Recalling that the size of the market has rapidly expanded and changed in the last decade alone, sharing knowledge on best practices about cruise port development and management is also part of the observable cooperation of cruise ports. Among the drivers behind co-opetition is the knowledge that cruise lines select itineraries, not individual destinations or ports. Co-opetition can lead to some forms of commercial partnerships between ports with a view to improving itinerary attractiveness and promoting certain ports of call combinations. In this vein, co-opetion develops between marque ports and nearby ports-of-call, between boutique destinations, intending to attract the deployment of vessels in the region and the offering of more itinerary building alternatives.

## 4 HOME PORT

A cruise port is, in principle, interested in being a home port for one or more cruise lines, as the total impacts on the port city are generally regarded as more significant. This is due to three reasons:

- The tendency of cruise lines to **purchase goods and services** from port suppliers.
- Passengers are likely to **stay longer in the city** and overnight at local hotels.
- The **spending of crew members**.

A cruise passenger spends six to seven times more at a home port than at a port-of-call. Further, the modernization and upgrade of cruise vessels has resulted in a significant downturn in the average expenditures per cruise passenger ashore and an increase in the share of onboard expenditures. Still, homeporting continues to have a major impact on the selected port and the associated city and tourist destination. Research at Europe's major cruise port revealed that the benefits of homeporting in Barcelona, Spain, were on average €202 spending per cruise passenger hosted with an overnight stay in a hotel, compared to a respective €57 average expenditure of cruise passengers without an overnight stay. Comparatively, a holiday tourist would spend an average €156 in the city with an overnight stay in a hotel. Cruise Lines International Association (CLIA) estimates passenger spending before boarding a cruise at $376 and $101 for a port of call.

The **criteria for selecting a home port** relate to the characteristics of each port and the criteria that a cruise company uses to identify and assess a potential home port (Figure 8.5). Despite the case-by-case approach in determining a home port, there are some major conditions that a cruise port must fulfill.

Cruise lines use sophisticated selection criteria to select a homeport. At the same time, cruise ports and related decision-makers assess their potential and develop their governance, management, and operational strategies, in a way that will fit the expectations of cruise lines. For most users, a cruise involves two travel segments, the first being air travel to the home port airport (with a return trip), and the second is the cruise itself. Therefore, it is essential that a **well-connected airport with significant airlift capacity** services the home port, representing a touristic destination. This is the case for Miami, Fort Lauderdale, and San Juan, which have well-connected airports and act as home ports for Caribbean itineraries. Barcelona and Civitavecchia (near

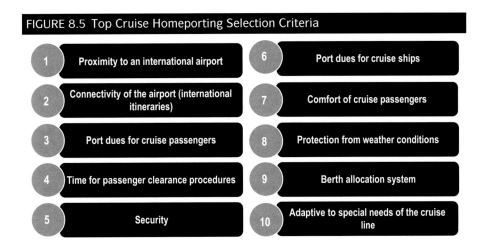

FIGURE 8.5 Top Cruise Homeporting Selection Criteria

| | |
|---|---|
| **1** Proximity to an international airport | **6** Port dues for cruise ships |
| **2** Connectivity of the airport (international itineraries) | **7** Comfort of cruise passengers |
| **3** Port dues for cruise passengers | **8** Protection from weather conditions |
| **4** Time for passenger clearance procedures | **9** Berth allocation system |
| **5** Security | **10** Adaptive to special needs of the cruise line |

Rome) are major home ports for the Mediterranean that are also well serviced by air transportation. Poorly connected airports are commonly associated with higher airfares, which impair the competitiveness of the city for mass tourism. There are several customer benefits linked to having more cruise embarkation points available such as drive-to convenience (particularly in North America) and fewer airport hassles. Availability of more drive to ports also increases the likelihood of cruising, which is why cruise lines will call at ports along the American Gulf Coast and Eastern Seaboard, such as New York, Tampa, Galveston, Baltimore, and New Orleans.

Changes in existing homeporting choices are becoming more common, even in established, comparatively stable cruise markets. The increasing scale of cruise vessels, the larger scale of port operations to serve more visitors per call, and the provision of a new cruise product underscored by **market segmentation**, are all conditions resulting in re-planning existing itineraries or scheduling new ones. Local socioeconomic characteristics might also work towards reforming itineraries. A notable example are the changes in the Adriatic Sea due to new regulations applying to the major home port of Venice. In emerging cruise regions, such as Australia, South America, and the Far East, the planning of new itineraries is even more frequent. The setting and the size of the cruise market might change further following the standstill produced by the **COVID-19 pandemic** in 2020 and the first half of 2021. The new conditions and protocols for serving cruise vessels will probably add to the evolution of new itineraries. They might further alter the criteria taken into consideration when a cruise line decides which port to use as home port.

None of the ports with minimum infrastructure and enhanced in-port and destination experiences for deployed vessels in a specific geographic cruise region have renounced being a home port in this context. Knowing the criteria for being selected by cruise lines is essential for both existing and aspiring home ports. In particular, as few parameters might be taken for granted, the geographical location seems to be of limited importance as vessels deployed in a region have the option to select one of many departing options. Cruise ships might prioritize the attractiveness of destinations or the need to access appropriate port infrastructures, superstructures, supplies, and services to facilitate the ship and the passengers. The deployment of ever-larger cruise ships generates further incentives for homeporting, at least in destinations that have yet to reach their carrying capacity.

A potential home port might decide to invest in increasing cruise traffic and the related added-value supply chains. Favoring cruising and fulfilling a social function may harm cargo activities as homeporting demands space within the port zone. The docking or anchorage facilities are usually limited, and the coexistence of the two industries becomes complicated by individual requirements. A cruise development strategy also demands substantial capital for financing infrastructure improvement as cruise operators demand better facilities to cope with increasing vessel size and passenger volumes. These also put pressure on adjusting operations and strategies. However, although generally described as a placeless business, the offering of cruises relies heavily on local attractions. Cruise lines, ports, and cities are highly interrelated and need to establish collaborations such as joint ventures where cruise lines invest in the ships, while destinations invest in port facilities and tourism attractions. Further strategies that eliminate any challenges associated with the use of public space in port cities hosting substantial numbers of homeporting cruise activities need to be elaborated.

The development of transport and tourism capacities is also critical. These concerns need to be addressed when there is a better understanding about the exact implications of the ever-increasing size and capacity of cruise vessels and its impact on the resulting scale of operations.

Variation exists between regions as regards the **embarkation preferences of passengers**. In the US, driving distance from home, parking, and customs immigration procedures are top of the list, along with a convenient airlift into the port city, cruise terminal facilities, and options for pre/post stays and interest in the surrounding port area. However, while driving up to four hours is acceptable in the US, in Europe, the respective limit is lowered to a maximum of two hours. On the other hand, Europe has shorter train access to ports. Major markets such as the UK and Germany have taken advantage of convenient train-to-cruise patterns of less than three hours, such as at Southampton and Kiel.

Home ports tend to be linked with specific **source markets**. This is due to proximity, access options, and, not least, the preferences of cruise passengers for visits to specific destinations. In Europe where multiple home ports exist, Americans use Southampton, and Dover in the UK, Barcelona in Spain, and Venice, and Civitavecchia in Italy extensively. British passengers depart from the UK (Southampton; Dover), Spain (Malaga, Mallorca), and Malta. Germans depart from Hamburg, Kiel and other nationalities (Italians, Spanish, French, Scandinavians) take advantage of the presence of home ports in their countries.

Each cruising area has its home ports, with the balance of traffic between homeporting and transit passenger movements varying from port to port. The **biggest home ports** in terms of size are located in the USA, the primary source market for cruise passengers. The biggest of all is Miami, with passengers moving in and out of a cruise trip standing at 50% of the total movements. From Miami (southern Florida), proximity favors Caribbean ports, with the frequency of visits declining further into the Southern Caribbean. The ratio of 50:50 of transit/home port passenger movements is observed in two other major home ports, Port Everglades and Port Canaveral. For home ports such as New York and Galveston, passengers beginning or returning from a cruise represent the total of cruise activities.

In the Mediterranean, the leading home port of Venice has the highest level of homeporting (87%). For Barcelona and Savona, the share of home-porting movements is lower, whereas the share is lower than 40% for the Balearic Islands and Civitavecchia. Three of the five major home ports (Venice, Civitavecchia, Savona) are in Italy. The country is strategically located at the center of the Mediterranean Sea, allowing the development of cruise itineraries to both the West and the East Mediterranean. It is a major source market for cruise passengers and well connected to other major source markets, like Germany and France. Regarding the rest of northern Europe, the major home port is Southampton, UK, and Hamburg, Germany. The proximity to cruise source markets plays a vital role in the rising of these home ports, as the UK is the largest source market in Europe and Germany holds second place.

## 5 LOCALIZATION OF CRUISE SUPPLY CHAINS

**Supplying cruise ships** is another important element of the economic footprint of cruising. It relates to both the direct supply of goods and services through local companies and the infrastructure required to support the logistics of non-local supply, usually by container. The dramatic changes in the onboard cruise product, along with the growing size and design of cruise ships have contributed to changes in its **supply chains and logistics**. The latter has been facilitated by technological advancements and re-engineering procurement processes. For instance, prior to the 2000s, the supply chain requirements for most US-based cruise lines were centered around Miami and the Caribbean. However, the cruise industry and its operators now operate in several regions of the world. This, together with the development of logistics and supporting IT management systems, has changed the face of cruise line supply. As a result, in several (major) ports and destinations, the increase in passenger traffic has been associated with a corresponding logistics volume in general.

This new environment creates opportunities for the **consolidation and globalization of supplies**. It also impacts the local and regional supply bases as improvement in the speed and fluidity of logistics operations requires the coordination of several suppliers. Simultaneously, the major cruise lines have also developed their supply chain infrastructure and support so that they now have strategic control points within major cruise destination hubs. Venice and Barcelona are two such hubs in the Mediterranean. However, there is an increasing requirement by the cruise lines to offer more local, regional and specialized products as part of the onboard guest experience. Therefore, local procurement remains a countervailing force to standard procurement. There is also an increased focus on the real cost of supplying goods to the ship, rather than just the commodity cost itself. Increasingly, there is also a focus on the environmental cost related to ship supply.

# Chapter 8.2 Break bulk

*Break bulk is general cargo carried as single or bundled pieces, not stowed into a container, or not transported in ship-sized liquid or dry bulk loads. Containerization has undermined many segments in the traditional break bulk market, which has become highly specialized with custom vessels, terminals, and warehousing facilities.*

## 1 THE ORIGINS OF THE BREAK BULK MARKET

### 1.1 The pre-container era

The **break bulk sector has a long history** closely connected to trade. For centuries, goods have been shipped around the world and across oceans. All major nations and powers arose from the ability to explore the world looking for new treasures, traded food, jewels, and materials that were not available locally. The process was cumbersome. Barrels, sacks, and crates were used in order to haul the cargo across the globe. High risks of accidents, loss of cargo, and theft made the entire process risky and cumbersome. Basic systems were in place in order to increase efficiencies, such as **specialized lifting equipment**, sacks designated for coffee beans, and pallets used to store an abundance of goods. However, the **rise of railways** in the nineteenth century, combined with some major technological advances like steam power and, later on, diesel power, highlighted the serious inadequacy of this system.

It took until the twentieth century for things to change. Before the container era, all transport was transported in the form of break bulk and could be described as general cargo. The term originates in the sentence 'to break bulk' a nautical term with its roots in shipping. It literally means 'begin to unload cargo'. It was a tedious process of loading and unloading, packing, and repacking. Shipping vessels had a mix of cargo on board, often shipments included bulk, liquid bulk, and general cargo all in the same vessel, making it very difficult to estimate the actual general cargo capacity of the world fleet in those days. It also meant that ships had to spend a lot of time in port. **Port turnaround times were very long**, resulting in port times sometimes exceeding the time at sea. Long port times created a situation in which it was not efficient to exploit economies of scale. **Ship sizes** were determined by a balance between the capacity, time, and cost required to handle cargo.

After World War II, some **specialization** appeared with dedicated merchant vessels designed for specific cargoes like bales of wool, wood logs, and liquid bulk. Slowly but surely, economies of scale were gaining importance. However, the bottleneck arising on the dockside kept major advancements at bay. In those days, the cargo was bundled together into pieces or units (bent arrows in Figure 8.6) that dock workers could manipulate, a concept defined as the **man load**, except for gases and some liquids which were transported in bulk (downward arrows in Figure 8.6). Examples of the man load are bags of sugar, cotton bales, and drums of liquids. Dockworkers carried loads of 30 to 50 kg in and out the vessels. In some cases, the single weight to be carried could reach up to 80 kg. The multi-deck Victory and Liberty vessels are textbook

**FIGURE 8.6** The Man Load Concept

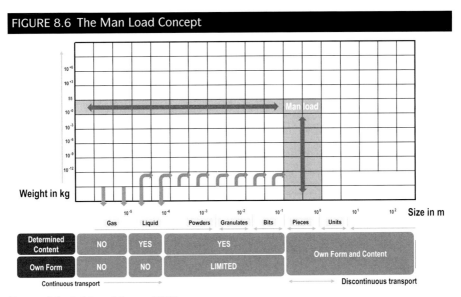

Source: Adapted from Meeuse (1977).

examples of applying the man load concept to vessels. A large workforce, hired daily, was required, given the low mechanization level in the vessel loading and discharging process. Due to the time-consuming nature of all cargo operations, unloading, sorting, clearing, and repacking, had to be done on the dockside. This led to the establishment of covered sheds in ports specifically designed to perform these activities. All this was about to change with the rise of the unit load. The golden era of general cargo shipping would soon be over.

## 1.2 The shift to unit load

Since the 1950s, ports have been facing a **goods explosion model** characterized by a **shift from man load to unit load and bulk cargoes** (Figure 8.7). At one side of the spectrum, bulk commodities (powders, grains) were increasingly carried by specialized bulk vessels and handled on specialized bulk terminals equipped with grab cranes, stackers and reclaimers, conveyor belts, and bulldozers. On the other side of the spectrum, there was a clear trend for general cargo to merge into unit loads such as pallets and containers. The cargo unitization went hand in hand with the development of specialized terminal equipment (e.g. specialized quay cranes, forklifts, terminal tractors, straddle carriers, reach stackers, RMGs, RTGs) and specialized ships (e.g. container ships and RoRo ships). Forklifts, tractors, and other mechanical equipment have been around for more than 70 years.

General cargo was increasingly handled in container ships or RoRo ships. These developments resulted in a spectacular rise in the productivity of labor and port facilities. Vessel turnaround time for a given cargo capacity decreased significantly while far fewer workers were needed. Technology brought new requirements in terms of the skills of the workforce. Up to the late 1950s, dock work basically involved unskilled work requiring little

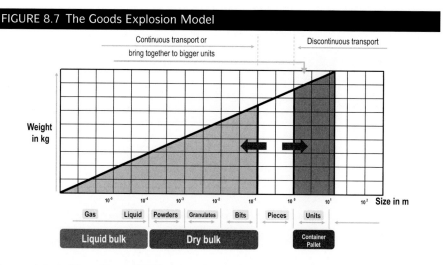

FIGURE 8.7 The Goods Explosion Model

Source: Adapted from Meeuse (1977)

training, except for the operation of the mechanical devices, which at that time accounted for around 10% of the work. Dockworkers were mainly used to handle various bags, and other man loads manually. The multi-skilled nature of dock workers was limited to handling a broad variety of loads, such as bags, bales, crates, and drums.

The goods explosion model increased the need for skilled dock workers who have the **qualifications and experience to operate a more specialized handling superstructure**. A whole new range of crane drivers, straddle carrier drivers, and drivers of other equipment emerged. From an economic point of view, the system dramatically impacted the industry and port economics, even resulting in particular placements of industrial centers around ports and the rise of a specific and highly segmented modern break bulk sector.

## 1.3 The impact of containerization

The current state of the break bulk market cannot be understood without knowing the impacts of containerization. The launching of the **first containership**, the Ideal X, in 1956 is often considered the beginning of containerization. In the early years of container shipping, vessel capacity remained very limited in scale and geographical deployment, and the ships used were converted general cargo ships or tankers. Shipping companies and other logistics players hesitated to embrace the new technology as it required significant capital investments in ships, terminals, and inland transport. The **first transatlantic container service** between the US East Coast and Northern Europe in 1966 marked the start of long-distance containerized trade. The first specialized cellular containerships were delivered in 1968, and containerization expanded over maritime and inland freight transport systems.

Container shipping developed rapidly due to the **adoption of standard container sizes** in the late 1960s and the awareness of industry players of the advantages and cost savings resulting from faster vessel turnaround times in ports, reduction in the level of damages and associated insurance fees, and integration with inland transport modes such as trucks, barges, and trains. Containerization set in motion a cascade of events changing the way transport was conducted. The beauty of the container is that it is handled in the same way no matter which transport mode it uses. This means that handling time and the number of handling moves are significantly reduced. Containers were capturing all the non-specialized cargo in the industry.

How maritime shipping was conducted also changed. The traditional tramp trade evolved towards a **liner system** which has become the norm. Instead of the ships moving from port to port searching for cargo, specific lines were created linking predetermined ports. Containerization also impacted port competition since a larger overlap now exists between different hinterlands, such as a shift from captive to contestable or shared hinterlands.

Initially, **substitution** was the main factor behind containerization with the gradual capture of the break bulk cargo market. This process has been particularly visible in many ports, as illustrated by rising **containerization degrees**, which is the ratio between containerized throughput of the port and its total general cargo volumes.

Many segments of the traditional pre-container break bulk market are already containerized. Many raw materials and food commodity chains are still in the process of being containerized. Some commodities are already fully containerized (e.g. coffee, tobacco), while for others, containerization is still in its infancy. For instance, 95% of all European coffee imports are containerized since coffee is a high-value commodity and its consumption rather ubiquitous. The demand structure of coffee is thus well suited for the benefits of containerization.

Goods that can easily be stuffed in a container have been **massively containerized**, partly because of relatively stable and even declining container shipping costs and a growing number and availability of containers in transport markets worldwide. However, temporal shortages of containers (as reported by market players during the COVID-19 health crisis) and specific container sizes can hamper further containerization in some markets.

The unit load formula of containerization means that container ships typically carry a wide range of containerized cargoes ranging from low-value products (such as waste paper) to high-value consumer electronics. Many of the contemporary break bulk markets still rely on the massification of flows of similar products, such as a reefer ship filled with bananas or a coaster filled with steel coils.

## 2 THE CURRENT BREAK BULK MARKET

It may be inaccurately assumed that break bulk or conventional general cargo is a declining cargo segment, destined to disappear as an outdated way of transporting goods. In reality, this is not the case. The break bulk sector has not disappeared but **changed in nature**, becoming a specialized sector, handling the goods which are too challenging to transport in containers or where containerization does not represent a valid and cost-efficient proposition.

The classic definition of break bulk concerns goods that do not fit into a container. In reality, it is more complicated to propose a comprehensive definition of the modern break bulk sector. The sector moves cargo as big as a 200-ton industrial boiler big enough to occupy the entire deck of a heavy lift ship to palletized cargo, which cannot be transported in containers due to specific cargo-related attributes. The following break bulk definition can be used:

> *Break bulk is general cargo, loaded into a ship or transport mode as individual or bundled pieces, not stowed into a container, or not transported in ship-sized liquid or dry bulk loads.*

Conventional general cargo or break bulk cargo encompasses a **myriad of different commodities**:

- **Project cargo**. Power generation equipment such as generators, turbines, wind turbines, equipment for the oil and gas industry, such as subsea systems, cables on reels, gas tanks, modules, petrochemical plants, mining equipment, building and construction equipment, brewery tanks, silos, and heavy machinery.
- **Iron and steel products**. Including coils, plates, steel bars, slabs, plates, steel wire, pipes, and tubes.
- **Forest products** including wood and paper products
- **Parcels** such as malt, fertilizer, sugar, and rice.
- **Reefer vessel trades** that mostly concern fruits and meat.
- **Break bulk shipments of smaller lots** such as big bags, skidded, and palletized cargoes.

## 3 THE BREAK BULK FLEET

The break bulk fleet is **relatively old** and **declining in total deadweight** compared to other main cargo groups. However, the multipurpose segment is not dying out. Continuous replacement and innovation enable conventional carriers to capture a larger but more specialized market segment, namely project cargo. There is a considerable difference between the old vessels leaving the fleet, and the new specially built ships for break bulk or conventional cargo. A few of the main trends are **increasing lifting capacity**, **greater efficiency**, and an **increase in versatility**, allowing more types of cargo. Compared to the older, less sophisticated vessels, the new general cargo vessels have box-shaped holds, long and wide hatch covers, and increased lifting capacity, and, if installed, flexible decks and open hatch options.

Given the enormous variety that exists when dealing with break bulk cargo, shipments can occur in many different ways.

### 3.1 Conventional liner type concepts

These include a range of options such as:

- Services of a **specific frequency** operated with **dedicated ships**.
- Services offering sailings within a period deploying **trip charters**.
- Services operated on **inducement** but still within a more or less defined trade lane.
- A mixture of two or three of the above options.
- **Parceling or tramping** where the ship is chartered on a trip basis once a specified cargo volume is available.

## 3.2 Barge carriers

In break bulk shipping, a barge carrier system consists of a mothership (mainly a propelled floating dock) that carries barges loaded with cargo over (long) deepsea distances. It services a very small market segment. When reaching the mothership's port of call, the barges are launched from the mothership for the remaining part of their journey, i.e. from anchorage to final destination or vice versa. The barge carrier concept can broadly be divided in two categories, i.e. 'Lighter Aboard Ship' (LASH) and 'Barge Container Carrier' (BACO). Other barge carrier types include Heavy Lift vessels and Naval Auxiliary vessels. Two further designs, i.e. the 'Barge Catamaran' (BACAT) and 'Sea Barge' (SEABEE) are currently not in use. Barge carriers typically transport the following break bulk/neo bulk cargoes: forest products (various types), project, oversized and other cargo (e.g. plant equipment), steel products (various types) and bulk commodities.

## 3.3 Container ships

Some types of break bulk cargo are carried by cellular container ships, although this is the exception rather than the rule. The type of break bulk cargo transported in container ships can roughly be divided into two parts:

- The first type of cargo comprises **large, oversized heavy lift items that do not fit in standard containers**. Instead, they are secured on special container equipment such as flats and platforms and then lifted on the ship using a gantry crane. Another solution includes specially constructed platforms or tops under the deck on which the cargo is lifted. Finally, the cargo can be placed on the hatch cover or tank top, a method only possible on container ships equipped with special 'stoppers' in the cells so that the lowest tier is left free.
- The second type is **small cargo stowed in the containers**, conveniently becoming containerized cargo and not being regarded as break bulk anymore.

## 3.4 Forest product carrier

The forest products cargo segment encompasses a wide variety of wood and paper products, both in raw-material, semi-finished product, and finished product form. Examples include wood chips, wood panels, pulp, sawn timber, plywood, newsprint, paper reels, paper rolls, and paperboard. Nowadays, forest products are shipped in **specialized vessels** such as open-hatch gantry crane vessels (OHGCs) or Totally Enclosed Forest Carriers (TEFCs), which protect against harsh weather conditions, or in more traditional RoRo vessels using trailers.

## 3.5 Heavy lift and project carriers

Operators in this market (e.g. Dockwise) generally deploy purpose-built ships able to carry very heavy and very large cargoes such as powerplants or factories, power plant equipment, or offshore oil and gas facilities. Loading and discharging the vessels is done through various methods, including

**lift-on/lift-off** (LoLo) and **roll-on/roll-off** (RoRo). The greatest demand for specialist heavy lift shipping arises from a wide range of offshore and petrochemical industry projects as well as mining activities, factories, and power plants. Heavy-lift vessels do not operate on fixed routes, but they are attracted to those areas where large investments in the oil and gas industry are made.

## 3.6 Conventional reefer ships

Conventional reefer ships mainly carry **high-value foodstuffs** requiring refrigeration and atmosphere control to avoid spoilage. Examples of reefer cargoes include fresh and frozen fruit (e.g. bananas and citrus fruits), vegetables, fish, meat, poultry, and dairy products. Reefer shipping is a prime example of a one-way (and for some products seasonal) business, with cargoes mainly exported from the southern hemisphere to the northern hemisphere.

Reefer ships tend to be divided into more spaces than conventional dry cargo ships, with several decks. Different commodities can be separated and carried, if required, at different temperatures. Below decks, a reefer ship resembles a large modern warehouse and cargo is usually carried and handled in palletized forms and moved on conveyors or by electric forklift trucks. Reefer ships can usually carry reefer containers on deck, with the more modern vessels able to carry other containers.

As is the case for the forest product industry, the reefer shipping sector is increasingly under pressure from **container shipping**. The **specialist reefer ships**, which are generally operated as tramps rather than in the liner trades, see their cargo base shifting to large container ships, offering more slots for refrigerated boxes. This is very visible in the banana trade, where large producers such as Chiquita are moving towards full containerization. Compared to conventional reefer ships, reefer containers have the additional advantage that they can also be used to transport non-food cargoes which are temperature-sensitive, such as electronic equipment, photographic film, pharmaceuticals, or computer chips, so there is more chance of a full backhaul.

## 3.7 Roll-on roll-off vessels

Although mainly aimed at the transport of wheeled cargo, certain RoRo ships are also used to transport break bulk cargoes on deepsea trade lanes. A distinction can be made between four RoRo vessel types, which are full RoRo cargo vessels, general cargo ships with (auxiliary) RoRo access, container vessels with RoRo capacity (so-called ConRos), and **Pure Car Carriers** (PCCs) and **Pure Car and Truck Carriers** (PCTCs).

RoRo cargo can be either wheeled by itself (i.e. cars, trucks, or rolling equipment) or mobilized (i.e. placed on a trailer-type unit and then towed on board). RoRo thus provides the ability to carry an extensive range of cargo, such as cars (of all kinds), trucks and trailers, (agricultural) machinery, mining equipment, roadbuilding equipment, project cargo, forest products, iron and steel, coils, cables, and oversized cargo. Advantages of RoRo vessels are that there is no need for dockside cargo handling equipment and that they enable fast turnaround times for certain cargo types. On the other hand, stowage productivity for RoRo ships is relatively low, and extensive lashing and securing may be needed to avoid sudden movement of cargo.

# 4 MAJOR BREAK BULK MARKET SEGMENTS

## 4.1 Common market developments

The break bulk sector is **very heterogeneous**. Still, some common developments are affecting the break bulk market:

- **Environmental issues** are having an ever larger impact on break bulk shipping and ports. Shipping lines and terminal operators in the break bulk market must demonstrate a high level of environmental performance in order to ensure a license to operate and attract trading partners and potential investors. Old, heavily polluting plants and transport and cargo handling methods are being phased out and steadily replaced by new units and processes having less environmental impact.
- Markets are characterized by **consolidation**, both on the supply and the demand side. Mergers and acquisitions also shape the contemporary business environment in the break bulk market segments. The consolidation trend puts additional pressure on intermediary parties (such as cargo handling terminals), which now have to deal with large ship operators and shippers or consignees with strong bargaining power. Most sectors are quite susceptible to changes in business outlook or are faced with increased competition and low margins, thus creating an extra incentive for value-added activities in order to raise margins and profitability.
- **Logistics integration levels** in many of the break bulk sectors are increasing. Large logistics operators have emerged with control over many segments of the break bulk supply chain. The integration strategies of the market players have created an environment in which ports are increasingly competing not as individual places that handle ships but within transport networks or supply chains. As the loyalty of port clients cannot be taken for granted, seaports are striving to approach some shippers and carriers who control massive cargo flows and who are in a good position to generate added value for the port region. Seaports are forced to develop a strong customer-oriented focus to secure their position as decoupling points in break bulk supply chains.
- **Seaport competitiveness** in the various break bulk markets is not only dependent on out-of-pocket cost considerations. Reliability, capacity considerations, proven expertise, quality of information services, and a commercial and customer-oriented approach characterized by a clear ability to think along with the customer (not only in the port but throughout the supply chains and networks) are becoming ever more important in competing effectively in the break bulk cargo handling markets.
- Many of the break bulk sectors can obtain major benefits from **clustering**. Not only from an economic point of view with economies of scale and added scope but also for environmental considerations. Closed production cycles are good examples leading to a concentration of industrial activities within ports, benefiting major seaports and allowing for increased use of intermodal options like barge and rail.

## 4.2 The steel market

Steel manufacturing is a competitive global industry, with **consolidation** and **continuous improvements** in manufacturing operations contributing to increased productivity. Mergers and acquisitions, such as the acquisition by Mittal Steels of Arcelor in 2006 and their merger in 2007, have remained an important growth strategy. The Tata Steel and Corus merger in 2008 is another example. The steel industry operates in a highly competitive environment globally, where rigorous cost management is imperative for maintaining and strengthening its competitiveness. Therefore, steelmaking processes have been developed and refined over the years. Steelmaking is capital intensive and requires long average plant life, making moves to new technologies possible only in a timeframe of several decades.

Many of the world's largest steel plants are located in or close to seaports. On the import side, steel plants generate large flows of **iron ore, pellets, cokes coal, metal scrap, and steel slabs**. The outgoing cargo flows typically include **steel coils, steel booms, steel wires, and related products**. Steel trade occurs between the major producers and between countries with a strong steel-dependent manufacturing sector. The most prominent drivers of steel consumption have historically been the automotive and construction markets. The maritime shipment of finished steel products, such as coils and wires, remains one of the largest segments in the break bulk market.

## 4.3 Fresh fruit

The international shipment of fruit is another prominent reefer cargo market, although containerization has significantly reduced this market in the past few decades. In **reefer commodity trade**, a distinction is made between the transport of **living and non-living cargo.** Bananas, exotics (pineapples, kiwifruit, avocados), deciduous (apples, grapes, pears), and citrus (oranges, lemons, limes, grapefruit, others) are a part of the living group. The non-living commodities are fish, seafood, and meat. The dairy (cheese/curd, butter) and other groups (tomatoes, frozen potatoes, stone fruit, berries, melons, frozen vegetables, fresh vegetables) include living and non-living commodities. Making the distinction between living and non-living cargo is vital for the transport mode because of the necessary distinction in temperature setup and atmosphere control. Living commodities will be transported under **refrigerated conditions** with a limited lifespan. Non-living commodities can be **frozen**, resulting in a longer lifespan.

The fruit market is subject to very specific inputs and characteristics, the most important being **seasonality**. November to July marks the peak season in fruit transport. Some specific fruits are transported all year long, like bananas and frozen commodities. Moreover, the volume of these shipments is subject to political, climatic, and economic factors creating uncertainty within the supply chain. One of the subsets of fruit transport is the market of **juice concentrates**, which are transported in bulk, break bulk, or containers.

In some cases, distributors have their own cold storage facilities. In the past decades, supermarkets (the final destination in the chain) have exercised greater influence in the chain as their consolidation resulted in improved purchasing power. Since this benefits the demand side, the supply side is trying to counter this trend with its own consolidations.

An increase in value-added logistics surrounding cold storage can be observed. For instance, packing and washing are performed at the loading and discharging ports. Some major companies have their own warehouses, but these port-based activities are the only financially viable option for smaller producers. This means that the creation and finalization of the consumer product are shifting towards a different point in the supply chain. Originally products were shipped ready for consumption. Now, the final steps often happen at the destination. Ripening facilities for bananas are a typical example.

The rise of reefer containers makes it increasingly feasible to transit a port without stripping the container and only discharging the cargo at the destination, such as an inland distribution center of an importer, retailer, or supermarket chain. Such **bypass operations** could affect the position of dedicated fruit terminals in seaports, particularly in terms of value-added creation at the port. At the same time, retailers are pushing for the perishables transport industry to adopt many of the disciplined supply chain processes common in the hard goods industries. There is a sense that logistics thinking in the container industry might be more aligned with this approach than traditional commodity-focused tramp reefer shipping.

## 4.4 Forest products

The forest products trade is subject to **predefined markets** since large extraction areas such as Canada and Scandinavia have been suppliers for centuries. Overall, the consumption of forest products is still on the rise despite the increased use of synthetic materials and the digitalization of the economy (electronic documentation). International climate change policies, as well as sustainable consumption and production policies, are affecting the forest products industry.

The paper industry is driven by volume generation, also known as the **fill the mill concept**. Waves of consolidation attest to the need for scale increases. Over recent decades, mergers have occurred among producers and buyers alike. Due to this consolidation trend, the power is shifting towards producers that are integrating into complete supply chains. A storage facility near the market is preferred, and integration also promotes logistical and transport concepts unique to the industry. A well-known example is the StoraEnso Cargo Unit (SECU) used for transport between the mills in Scandinavia and the main hub in Zeebrugge. Forwarders and terminal operators are increasingly working for producers and less for traders. The traditional approach was a collection of small independent traders who have now lost their importance. This encourages a consolidation on both the supply and demand sides to deliver added value.

Horizontal integration has become an incentive for vertical integration where wood producers opt for an internal distribution system by investing in terminals and derived activities. The emergence of Just in Time (JIT) in the paper industry creates a need for a central supply. For the maritime shipments of forest products, the number of ports of call is relatively low, reducing the advantages of smaller ports as trade is drawn towards major, better-equipped load centers.

Ports are also experiencing an impact concerning the shift of power towards suppliers. The actual trading is disappearing and ports are becoming storage and distribution facilities. This is why ports have focused on creating specialized terminals and equipment in order to guarantee quality and speed during transport. This includes covered terminals, special hoisting equipment, and climate-controlled areas.

## 4.5 Project cargo

**Project cargo, heavy lifts, and machinery** are among the most important segments within break bulk. As with most other segments, it is a collection of different load units with no common standard since their units are project-related. Project cargo consists, for instance, of knocked down plants, new industrial manufacturing plants, power generation equipment, equipment for the oil and gas industry, diesel engines, mining equipment, and breweries.

Amongst other trends impacting the sector, **shorter build times** prevail. This creates the need for reduced shipping times and a steady flow of components. Also, the risk of penalties is more elevated and the chances of consolidating cargo are slimmer due to the multitude of smaller projects. The shift of assembly activities towards the port area places increased stress on the hinterland connections of ports. In the long run, the physical limitations of hinterland connections could endanger the competitive position of ports.

Due to complex handling activities, the need for added value is relatively high in the project cargo segment. **Cargo consolidation** is happening at ports and requires industrial packaging of goods. This creates the need for intermediaries able to provide transport solutions at sea and in the hinterland. Ultimately this leads to the outsourcing of the logistical process. Industrial and engineering companies focus on their core activities but demand excellence and flexibility, which can only be delivered by a project-based custom approach by the partners responsible for the logistical aspects.

On the whole, the project cargo sector is dependent on a few core main markets. **Energy plants** are on the rise since the search for green sustainable energy is booming. Wind turbines are appearing all across the landscape, driving the demand for the industry. At present, wind blade equipment is estimated to constitute roughly 20% of ocean-borne multi-purpose heavy lift cargo. It has become extremely important for a number of reasons. It moves almost from everywhere to everywhere, and has become a commoditized business in many ways. It has produced a large volume of cargo. These cargoes require specialized vessels due to their dimension, not because they are heavy. They need to stow on vessels in a way that makes transporting them more economically viable. They have thus become a vital component of multi-purpose heavy lift projects. Compared to the blades, some of the turbines and the other structures, such as the towers, can be quite heavy. **Construction projects** are another cornerstone of the sector, with mega-projects in developing countries an important driver. Finally, **mining** is a relatively reliable business delivering cargo on a fairly constant basis.

When there is an economic crisis, project movement lags because of the decline in capital investments. The project cargo market typically has a **lagging**

**effect** that can vary depending on the region but could be eight months or longer for the up and down cycles. This makes it challenging to forecast the demand for projects and thus project cargo.

Within the project cargo sector, a **consolidation and cooperation** wave is taking place in order to offer a larger geographical scope and an adjusted ship tonnage. Some examples of horizontal integration are Spliethoff and Mammoet Shipping (renamed Biglift Shipping in 2000). Despite consolidation, the sector still has many smaller operators that have developed unique skills and equipment. Most ship operators follow a business model that runs on a combination of cargoes. Essentially, almost anything up to and including containers in some cases can qualify as project cargo because a combination of cargoes is necessary to make a successful voyage. This implies that ship operators typically do not build their business around heavy-lift cargoes only. As a result, most of the vessels deployed in the heavy-lift market are multipurpose and suitable for carrying any dry cargo, forest products, steel, containers, and even bulk.

Next to the shipping lines, the **freight forwarding community** plays an essential role in the project cargo market. In many cases, they arrange ocean transportation, clearance in ports, and inland transportation. Ship operators generally do not compete with freight forwarders on a direct basis. However, on specific projects, ship operators might have quotes on cargoes that include services such as barging, rail or trucking (heavy haul), documentation, and packing at the terminal for customers who want to consolidate their cargoes in a single location from multiple suppliers. All these services can be provided either in-house or in collaboration with other freight forwarders in a one-stop-shop approach. Activities can also include extensive engineering for special projects as well as lump sum contracting of integrated projects.

## 4.6 Coffee and cocoa

Coffee and cocoa are products that are both traded in a similar fashion and primarily transported in containers. They are not in the confines of the pure break bulk definition. However, the product is still handled in a very traditional way.

Inside the container, coffee is usually stowed in bags of 60kg. Other stowage options are big bags or container stowage in bulk mode. The bag will remain as a storage and transport unit for three reasons. First, the trade market requires this way of packaging as a unit of measure. Second, coffee is grown in areas that can be difficult to access and represents a unit that can be handled manually. Finally, bags increase the durability of the product. The coffee supply chain consists of cultivators, transporters, processors, traders, and consumers. Most steps in the chain are governed by small corporations, particularly on the production side with farmers and exporters. Traders are mostly grouped into big companies selling coffee to consumers, who are, in most cases, major corporations in the food industry and specialized retailers.

The power in the chain shifts yearly. If the harvest in certain parts of the world is below expectations, farmers in other geographical areas have the opportunity to keep their stocks and raise prices. However, there is a trend of final consumers, namely the big food corporations, integrating along the supply chain. The coffee sector is one where trading remains an essential aspect of the market. Big trading consortia buy shares of the available stocks in warehouses worldwide and try to sell them to the highest bidder. The trader often takes a part of the transport leg for its account. Since the lowest transport cost is looked for, this will influence how the cargo is transported. If break bulk charter rates are below container rates, the coffee (or cocoa) will be transported in break bulk ships.

Major coffee and cocoa producers tend to be located around the equator. Often harvests do not reach the levels that were predicted due to disruptions, particularly weather-related. The major coffee exporters are Brazil, Colombia, Vietnam, and Ethiopia. Although each exporter tries to create a brand name for their coffee, the product is **interchangeable** for most segments of the mass market. The leading importers are the United States, Europe, and Japan, impacting the modes used in major coffee trades. The biggest cocoa exporters are Côte d'Ivoire, Ghana, and Nigeria, with the biggest trade flows between the African continent and Europe.

## 5 BREAK BULK: GENERATING EMPLOYMENT AND ADDED-VALUE IN PORTS

Break bulk cargo handling creates jobs at terminal and stevedoring companies in the form of dockworker and management positions. Dock labor needs are very dependent on the cargo flows handled in the port. Other cargo service-related jobs include cargo survey, land transport and storage, and port-related storage. Compared to the handling of commodities such as crude oil or major dry bulks, conventional general cargo is much more labor-intensive. It generates a substantially higher added value per ton and is the largest generator of dock-related jobs per volume unit, although a significant difference might exist among commodities and ports.

The break bulk market segments, as important sources of employment in ports, impact port labor requirements. Large break bulk customers and large cargo handling companies can exert a significant impact on port labor. As these companies often develop a strong network focus by their presence in several ports, the experiences they gain at different ports is the basis for explicit or implicit port labor benchmarking exercises comparing the turnaround time in each port, terminal productivity, flexibility in working practices, and cost profiles. Increased benchmarking at the company level on an international scale exposes well-established structures and practices in a specific port area to external impulses for change.

The internationalization in the cargo handling industry also facilitates the transfer of new technologies over a wide range of ports. Creating a competitive advantage in terms of terminal productivity is no longer only a question of operating modern terminal equipment but increasingly a matter of ensuring that the most efficient human resource system is in place to operate the terminal equipment. Given the size of some of the break bulk customers, a loss or gain of a large customer can exert a major impact on the port and is directly reflected in the number of dockworkers required.

Employment in ports is also affected by the combination of quay-related cargo-handling activities at terminals and a wide array of logistics activities at warehouses or near the terminals. As such, a mix of pure stevedoring activities and logistics activities occurs, each requiring people with the necessary skills and know-how.

# Chapter 8.3 Ports and energy

*The global economy rests on the consumption of large energy supplies that need to be provided, transformed and transported. Ports have been important complexes supplying and distributing energy.*

## 1 THE ORIGIN OF ENERGY MARKETS

Historically, there was **no energy market** in maritime shipping, Energy in pre-industrial societies faced limited demand, was produced locally, and was not traded. Maritime shipping was a break bulk endeavor not able to support bulk trades effectively. A notable exception was the fuel trade associated with oil lamps relying on animal fats and olive oil, which could be carried over long distances. The extensive trade network of olive oil carried in amphoras during the time of the Roman Empire can be considered one of the early forms of maritime shipping energy trade.

It is not until the industrial revolution that **energy began to be extensively traded**. The rapid growth in energy consumption and a fundamental change in energy supply systems, with the introduction of coal, stimulated the setting up of new supply routes. Coal became a convenient fuel as it could release about four times more energy than a similar mass of wood, did not decay, and could easily be handled and stored. Further, it could be distilled into fuels such as kerosene. The shift from biological energy supply to mineral energy supply entailed locational changes in energy production and consumption and the associated trade flows.

The setting up of the petroleum trade required the design of a new ship class by the late nineteenth century, the oil tanker. Since the first oil tanker began shipping oil in 1878 in the Caspian Sea, the capacity of the world's maritime tanker fleet has grown substantially. From that point, petroleum energy markets expanded to include a network of pipelines, storage areas, port facilities, tanker ships, and refineries. The growing energy demand expanded ports in industrial areas and favored the setting up of new specialized ports near energy extraction areas (coal fields and oil fields).

## 2 MAIN PORT ENERGY MARKETS

Contemporary energy markets supply two complementary transportation systems; **fueling ships** (also called bunkering) and **fueling industrial demand** (plus power generation). The first important characteristic of energy markets is the **concentration of production** and a more geographically **dispersed**

**consumption**. This concentration of production is a direct function of economies of scale characterizing the energy sector more than it does many manufacturing sectors. For energy extraction, processing, and transportation, substantial benefits are realized when additional volumes are handled. Energy represents a significant share of the global shipping markets and accounts for large port volumes.

## 2.1 Coal

Coal is a convenient fuel that is easily combustible to store and transport. It remains an **inexpensive and widely available resource** that is technically simpler to use but is associated with carbon emissions and pollutants such as sulfur dioxide. Since the Industrial Revolution, coal has been the preferred fuel, supporting the massive development of energy and industrial systems. Still, its consumption is declining, particularly in advanced economies transitioning to more advanced fuel sources such as natural gas and alternative energy (solar, wind).

Coal serves two major markets, and **thermal coal** dominates with 90% of demand. It is used mainly in power stations to produce high-pressure steam, which then drives turbines to generate electricity. It is also used to fire cement and lime kilns, supporting the construction industry. This implies that the location of large coal electric plants is associated with transportation capabilities, particularly port infrastructure. Until the middle of the twentieth century, coal was also used in steam engines, with an active steam coal market, which is no longer present. The second coal market is **coking coal** (10% of the demand), a specific type of metallurgical coal derived from bituminous coal and used as a source of carbon for converting a metal ore to metal. Coking coal allows blast furnaces to remove oxygen in the ore by forcing its combination with the carbon in the coal.

The coal industry and its market are facing several challenges and redevelopments. Coal is **becoming less competitive** in relation to other energy sources and its production is on the decline. The industry is subject to a string of environmental regulations and negative public opinion creating pressure to transition away from coal. The efficiency of coal power plants is improving with reduced emissions of ashes and sulfur, and attempts at carbon capture. 'Clean Coal' technologies have been put forward, emitting fewer ashes but releasing the same amount of $CO_2$. Since the 1990s, technology has allowed a reductio of coal-related emissions by a factor of 90%. In many areas in North America and Europe, environmental issues associated with coals, such as acid rains, have ceased to be a major environmental concern. The coal market is subject to comparative prices concerning other energy markets, which can create regional discrepancies. For instance, the Fukushima nuclear accident in 2011 forced Japan to reinvest in coal-based power generation to cope with the lack of alternatives in electric power generation.

## 2.2 Petroleum

Petroleum is the **foremost transportation fuel**. Transportation is almost entirely reliant on refined petroleum products, such as gasoline and diesel for automobiles, diesel for trucks, inland barges and non-electric locomotives, bunker fuel for maritime shipping, and Jet-A fuel for air transportation. While the use of petroleum for other economic sectors, such as industrial and electricity generation, has remained relatively stable, the growth in oil demand (Box 8.2) is mainly attributed to the growth in transportation demand. The share of transportation in total oil consumption has increased and accounts for more than 55% of the oil used with a share of more than 70% in advanced economies such as the United States. Other important uses for petroleum include lubricants, plastics, and fertilizers. The demand for oil has helped shape port development in areas near oil resources, at times introducing entirely new ports and the associated infrastructures. This notably took place in developing economies in the Middle East such as Damman, Kuwait, Doha, Abu Dhabi, and Dubai.

There are limited options for substitution in the medium term, except for the emergence of electric vehicles and a substitution in maritime shipping towards lower sulfur bunker fuels, including natural gas. The largest oil consumers remain in the world's industrialized economies, such as the United States, Western Europe, China, and Japan, which accounted for about 70% of global crude oil imports. Massive port-centric petrochemical complexes such as Houston, Rotterdam, Singapore, and Ulsan have been developed and supply these markets. Still, the share of developing economies is increasing as their transportation systems modernize. Since oil consumption and production are characterized by acute differences in the geography of its supply and demand, international oil transportation is necessary to compensate for these imbalances. The market is divided across crude and refined product tankers, mainly depending on whether oil refining occurs near the source or near the markets.

---

### Box 8.2  The global oil market

*The global oil market is composed of three main elements interacting to set supply, demand, and price:*

- *Production. Oil producers have a level of output related to their physical capabilities in extracting oil as well as market demand subject to seasonality. The geography of oil production shows a high level of concentration and output due to the significant potential for scale economies of the industry and a concentration of oil reserves. In the beginning of 2020s OPEC countries account for 40% of global production.*
- *Consumption. Each economy has a level of oil consumption often expressed in barrels per day. Global oil consumption and production are usually similar since they represent a supply/demand equilibrium.*
- *Reserves (not shown). These reflect medium or long-term expectations about the future level of potential output (Figure 8.8).*

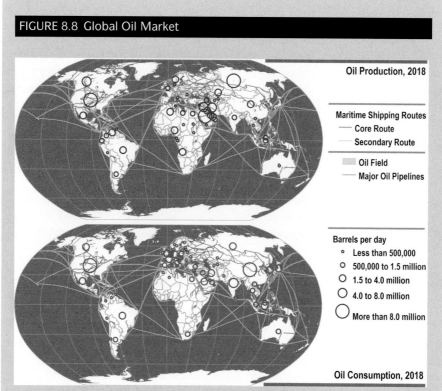

FIGURE 8.8 Global Oil Market

Source: BP Statistical Review of World Energy (oil production and consumption); Lujala, Rød and Thieme (2007) (oil field data); Harvard WorldMap (pipelines).

*There are significant differences in the geography of oil consumption and production, which require distribution infrastructures such as pipelines and shipping networks. In 2018, global oil production was at 95 million barrels per day, but consumption is marginal in a large number of countries. There is a correspondence between the level of oil consumption and the level of economic development. The United States, Japan, China, Germany, Russia, Italy, and France, account for approximately 52% of the global oil demand.*

*The geography of oil production is much more concentrated than its consumption. Eight producers, Saudi Arabia, the United States, Russia, Iran, China, Venezuela, Mexico, and Norway, account for approximately 55% of the global production with a significant share of production in the Middle East. Unlike most countries where oil is domestically produced, a significant portion of OPEC's oil is traded in international markets. The geographical concentration of reserves in the Middle East is also evident.*

## 2.3 Natural gas

Natural gas is composed primarily of fossil methane and other light hydrocarbons. It is a mixture of 50% to 90% by volume of methane, propane, and butane and is characterized as 'dry' or 'wet' based on its methane content and as 'sweet' and 'sour' based on its sulfur content. Natural gas is usually found in association with oil, implying a correspondence between oil and gas fields and the opportunity to combine extraction. The global production of natural gas has been growing with the net result that it is increasingly cost competitive with petroleum.

Natural gas is considered the cleanest fossil fuel to use, particularly for energy generation, and has become a key fuel in electric power plants. Gas turbine technology allows natural gas to produce electricity more cheaply than using coal, implying that the global electric generation market relying on fossil fuels is shifting towards natural gas supply chains. Further, natural gas is increasingly competitive in relation to low-sulfur bunker fuels, particularly in light of ongoing regulations in maritime shipping concerning the sulfur content of bunker fuels. A major challenge concerns the distribution of natural gas, which relies on more complex technologies such as pipelines and its liquefaction.

The growth of the global demand has created requirements to move natural gas over long distances. Liquefied natural gas (LNG) is an ideal form in which to transport natural gas but requires complex technical tasks. Once natural gas is extracted, it is brought by pipeline to a liquefaction plant in the vicinity of a port terminal. Through a cryogenic process, natural gas is brought down to -160°C, implying a volume compression by a factor of 610 times. The LNG product can then be shipped by a fleet of specialized LNG carriers. At the destination port, LNG is stored and re-gasified to be distributed through pipelines.

## 2.4 Bunker fuel

Bunkering is an important energy market for maritime shipping as it involves refueling ships at selected locations. Bunker fuels are the lower cuts from the vacuum distillation tower (higher grade fuels such as gasoline are higher cuts), meaning that they are heavy, low-quality fuels of high viscosity requiring to be preheated to be used for combustion. While bunkering can occur at port docks, the most common process involves a bunkering ship docking alongside the ship to be refueled. Because of the characteristics of the global shipping network, bunkering tends to occur at **major commercial gateways or intermediary locations** where refueling represents an opportunity with minimal disruptions in a ship's path and schedule.

The bunker fuel market is experiencing significant changes as international regulations supported by the IMO (International Maritime Organization) impose restrictions limiting the sulfur content of bunker fuels, from 3.5% to 0.5%. This global implementation has been phased in since 2010 and became fully active in 2020. Existing regulation has pushed a shift to the use of low sulfur fuels, such as LNG, very-low sulfur fuel oil (VLSFO, maximum 0.5% sulfur), ultra-low sulfur fuel oil (ULSFO, max 0.1%), and low sulfur marine gas oil (LSMGO). Alternatively, shipowners can opt to install emission control devices such as scrubbers and selective catalytic reduction (SCR) systems. For the medium term, alternative ship fuels are being considered, such as hydrogen, ammonia, and biofuels.

Singapore remains the most important bunkering market globally, handling around 50 million tons of bunker fuel on an annual basis. This dominance is related to the intensity of the maritime traffic forced to transit through

FIGURE 8.9 Largest Bunker Fuel Markets, 2015

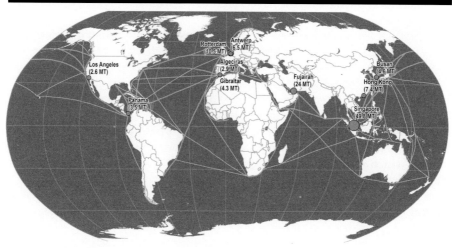

Source: Largest Bunker Fuel Markets (2015).

the Strait of Malacca and the important role Singapore has developed as a major oil refining center. The bunker refueling market has a high level of concentration, with six countries accounting for 60% of global bunker fuel sales (Figure 8.9).

The location of bunkering activity is highly conditioned by geography with two patterns emerging:

- **Major gateways (centrality)**. Ships calling at a major port gateway have an opportunity to refuel. Ports such as Rotterdam, Antwerp, Hong Kong, and Los Angeles/Long Beach are each major diversified commercial gateways experiencing a large number of ship calls.
- **Intermediate locations (intermediacy)**. Locations in the vicinity of major bottlenecks in the global shipping network, such as the Strait of Malacca (Singapore), Ormuz (Fujairah), Gibraltar (Algeciras and Gibraltar), and Panama are active bunkering markets. The proximity effect allows ships passing by or calling at a transshipment hub to refuel.

## 3 THE MARITIME SHIPPING OF ENERGY

The energy transportation market is fragmented, but the dominant modes of energy transportation are complimentary, notably when the origins or destinations are landlocked or when land routes can reduce distances. Like other forms of transportation, energy transportation is often a sequence of modes, with maritime transport and pipelines the most used for large volumes. Such volumes underline the need for economies of scale and the importance of load breakpoints in energy transport chains. The transportation of energy is the activity that is the **most prone to economies of scale** in the transportation industry because of the relatively low value to mass ratio of fuels and the high demand. Therefore, locations adjacent to harbors are usually the primary location of energy storage and processing activities, such as oil refineries, enabling them to access global markets either as an input (crude oil imports) or as an output (refined oil products).

In 2015, about 2.9 billion tons of oil and natural gas products were shipped by maritime transportation, roughly **62% of all the petroleum produced**. The remaining 38% is either using pipelines (predominantly), trains, or trucks. Crude oil alone accounted for 1.77 billion tons. The maritime circulation of petroleum follows a set of maritime routes between regions where it has been extracted and regions where it will be refined and consumed (Figure 8.10). More than 100 million tons of oil are shipped each day by tankers. About half the petroleum shipped is loaded in the Middle East and then shipped to Japan, the United States, and Europe. Tankers bound to Japan are using the Strait of Malacca while tankers bound to Europe and the United States either use the Suez Canal or the Cape of Good Hope, depending on the tanker's size and its specific destination.

The world tanker fleet capacity (excluding tankers owned or chartered on a long-term basis for military use by governments) was about 488 million deadweight tons in 2015, representing about 28% of the world's shipping tonnage. There are roughly 7,000 tankers available on the international oil transportation market. The cost of hiring a tanker is known as the charter rate. It varies according to the size and characteristics of the tanker, its origin, destination, and the availability of ships. However, larger ships are preferred due to the economies of scale they confer. About 638 VLCCs (Very Large Crude Carriers) account for a third of the oil being carried. Transportation costs account for a small percentage of the total cost of gasoline at the pump. For instance, oil carried from the Middle East to the United States accounts for about one cent per liter at the pump. Transportation costs have conventionally accounted for between 5% and 10% of the added oil value, depending on the market being serviced. The growth in oil prices since 2000 makes the transport costs an even lower component of the total costs, sometimes lower than 5%. Thus, oil demand is not related (is inelastic) to its transport costs, but is a factor of effective tanker capacity.

## FIGURE 8.10  Major Oil Flows and Chokepoints

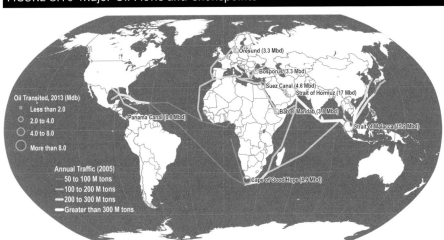

Tanker flows have a high concentration level with different tanker sizes used for different routes due to distance and port access constraints. Larger tanker ships have required the setting up of offshore terminals and even the usage of tanker ships for storage. Tanker ships can also be used as semi-permanent storage tanks. There is thus a **specialization of maritime oil transportation** in terms of ship size according to markets. VLCCs are used primarily from the Middle East in high volumes (more than 2 million barrels per ship) and over long distances (Europe and Pacific Asia). Shorter journeys are generally serviced by smaller tanker ships such as from Latin America (Venezuela and Mexico) to the United States. Transport capacity has a significant impact on market selection. For instance, three-quarters of American oil imports come from the Atlantic Basin (including Western Africa) with journeys of less than 20 days. Most Asian oil imports come from the Middle East, a three-week journey with the halfway location of Singapore being one of the world's largest refining centers. Due to environmental and security considerations, single-hulled tankers have been gradually phased out to be replaced by double-hulled tankers.

The **LNG industry** was originally developed as a niche. It is a highly structured business characterized by **dedicated long term contracts** and regionally based trade flows with shipping tied into special projects for the life of the contract. Due to the large capital requirement of LNG projects and the high risks involved, the leading market participants in the LNG shipping segment used to be limited to the so-called super majors, namely major oil companies. After the 1990s, gas buyers wanted more flexibility in their supplies and started to move upstream, participating in activities such as shipping. Gas sellers also started to move along the chain, becoming minority owners in shipping and occasionally in regasification plants. As a result, LNG shipping came under the control of different parties. In line with the global trend towards the privatization of energy markets, the transformations taking place in the LNG market are heavily influenced by deregulation and liberalization in both the upstream and downstream gas markets.

Nowadays, some **independent shipowners** are starting middle stream activities to integrate their LNG value chain by either cooperating with upstream gas sellers in liquefaction projects or investing with downstream buyers in import terminals. They can also take the role of refrigeration terminals by converting ships to floating gas production or regasification units. Additionally, one of the most noticeable changes in the market structure, which has both contributed to and benefited from a short-term marketplace, has been the emergence of companies that invest throughout the LNG supply chain. These portfolio players have a portfolio of liquefaction interests which they use to supply a portfolio of import terminals using vessels they control specifically for this purpose. This group mainly includes a number of international oil majors (e.g. Shell, BP, ExxonMobil), utility companies (e.g. Suez de GDF, ENI), private companies (e.g. Mitsui), and quasi-government companies (e.g. Sonatrach, Qatar Petroleum and Statoil).

Shipowners can be classified into four categories:

- **LNG integrated projects** with gas suppliers, including national oil companies and their partners.

- **Gas buyers**, like Japan and Korea who are dependent on LNG imports. They own and operate some shipping capacities for diversifying gas suppliers to secure market demand.
- **International oil majors** who are portfolio players, who use their own vessels to sail between the liquefaction and regasification plants where they have portfolio interests.
- **Independent ship owners** who previously secured long term contracts from LNG integrated suppliers or buyers.

With the growth of the LNG trade, additional **LNG projects** are launched with shipping capacity tied in and new tankers are then ordered accordingly.

## 4 ENERGY AND PORTS

Energy products are massive and are carried in bulk, underlining the importance of ports as **energy transport platforms** (economies of scale) and **energy transformation platforms** (economies of agglomeration). Depending on their position within energy supply chains, the clustering of energy transformation activities can either be upstream or downstream of the supply chain. Ports are also **energy generation platforms** (economies of scope) that can provide conventional and alternative sources of energy to their users (Box 8.3).

The relations of ports with energy markets are undertaking an **energy transition** in their functions as providers, consumers, and processors of energy. Even if the port and maritime shipping industry only account for about 2% of global carbon emissions, there are pressures to improve its environmental performance, mainly become of its high level of integration with energy supply chains. The **decarbonization of ports** involves a series of potential strategies clustering around energy generation, electrification, and distribution (Figure 8.11):

- **Transformation of port-centric energy generation**. Ports have conventionally been highly involved in energy generation, such as in coal and gas power plants. Since resources were brought in bulk by maritime shipping, ports were effective locations for energy generation systems built on the principle of economies of scale, including centralized distribution.

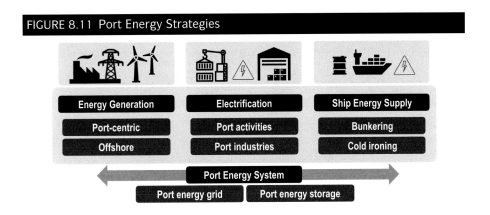

FIGURE 8.11 Port Energy Strategies

Any future energy system relying on this principle will be inclined to use port facilities. Still, ports are not in the business of energy generation. They are convenient locations for energy generation facilities operated by third parties, particularly public or private energy companies.

• **Ship energy supply systems**. The ongoing regulations toward low sulfur bunkering, including LNG, will involve a new energy transformation process and related port-centric activities. The location of bunkering is likely to remain the same, but the transition can offer opportunities to ports able to provide lower-emission fuels first. Another transformation concerns cold ironing, which supplies docked ships with electrical power instead of power generation by the ship's power generator. There is a net cost advantage to using shore-generated power since the electricity is cheaper than the supply generated using onboard generation systems.

• **Electrification of port-centric activities**. These activities include terminal operations, bunkering, logistics, and freight distribution, cold storage facilities, service vessels (e.g. tugboats), and supporting buildings. In addition to reducing carbon emissions, the electrification of port equipment lowers noise emissions and their negative community impacts. However, this requires a network of recharging stations that must be supplied by an energy production system.

• **Electrification of port-centric industries**. Many heavy industries located within port facilities were dependent on fossil fuels as a core energy input. The transition of port energy systems will be accompanied by a transition of the port industrial ecosystem.

• **Offshore wind power generation**. Through the maritime interface, ports can access large coastal oceanic areas that can offer wind generation opportunities. The port and its industries already offer an existing demand for installed wind generation capabilities and can offer port authorities new revenue sources.

• **Integration of port energy systems**. Port clustering allows for different energy systems (conventional and alternative) to operate independently, seeing a better level of integration between supply and demand. This allows for an energy trading system where energy surpluses could be traded between suppliers and users within the port community. A more efficient electric grid and energy storage capabilities have to be developed in tandem.

Once the energy transition of ports has matured, it is expected that ports will play a more strategic role within the respective regional energy systems as platforms to generate and distribute energy.

## Box 8.3 Port-centric energy production and transformation

*Ports are effective locations for energy production or transformation industries such as power or petrochemical plants. The main reason behind this locational behavior is that the material inputs of the energy industry are bulk products prone to economies of scale (petroleum, coal), for which the use of maritime shipping is the most efficient. Still, there are two fundamental choices concerning the port-centric location of energy industries:*

***Upstream cluster.*** *The production or transformation of energy resources is done at a port close to the main material source. The main advantage involves lower procurement transportation costs through a direct connection to energy extraction areas by rail or pipeline corridors. Large energy producers try to build energy transformation facilities to capture additional value along energy supply chains and supply their domestic markets. Dependency on one energy supply source is a risk, implying that if the source is compromised (exhaustion or change in market prices), the cluster could lose its relevance.*

***Downstream cluster.*** *The production or transformation of energy resources is done at a port close to the main market. The main advantage involves choosing the origins of procurement alternatives since energy resources can be brought in from any location, offering a scalable maritime service. This allows flexibility in procurement and a direct outlet to major consumption markets (Figure 8.12).*

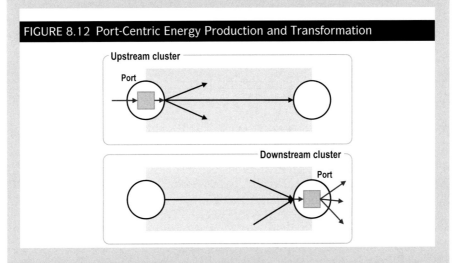

**FIGURE 8.12 Port-Centric Energy Production and Transformation**

*The locational preference is downstream clustering of energy production and transformation, as it confers more procurement flexibility. Ports such as Rotterdam, Ulsan, Houston, and Tianjin are importing energy products, mainly petroleum, from a large array of sources. However, there are several upstream clusters in energy exporting countries such as Saudi Arabia, Iran, Venezuela, and Nigeria. Options for intermediary locations can also be attractive, such as Singapore, one of the world's largest oil refining clusters, taking advantage of its halfway position between the Middle East and major Asian consumption markets.*

# Chapter 8.4 Containers

*Containerization allows for cargo distribution in a unitized form, permitting an intermodal transport system allowing a combination of rail, road, canal, and maritime transport. The provision and management of containers is assumed by shipping lines and container leasing companies, with the repositioning of empty containers mainly the outcome of imbalances in trade flows.*

## 1 THE BOX MARKET

The growth in global trade and freight distribution has led to the **ongoing demand for new containers**. Each year, about 1.5 to 2.5 million TEUs worth of containers are manufactured, the vast majority in China, taking advantage of its containerized export surplus. Top container manufacturers include China International Marine Container Group (CIMC; the world's largest shipping container manufacturer with an annual capacity of 2 million containers), Singamas Container Holdings, CXIC Group Containers (CXIC), China Eastern Containers (CEC), and China COSCO Shipping.

Production peaked at 3.9 million TEU in 2007, with the global inventory of containers estimated to be around 37.6 million TEUs as of 2015. This approximately implies three TEUs of containers for every TEU of maritime containership capacity. The container manufacturing market is **highly volatile**. For example, at the start of the COVID-19 Pandemic in March 2020, there was a massive surplus of boxes, including 3 million empty TEUs available at Chinese ports plus another 1.2 million TEUs in storage at container manufacturers. Orders for new boxes plummeted due to this surplus combined with the expectation that trade would collapse as COVID-19 spread globally. However, the situation reversed in mid-2020 due to a demand surge in North America and Europe. The resulting rise in exports from China led to a flood of orders for new containers, in some cases doubling the price for a standard 20-foot box. Global container production rose to 440,000 in January 2021, far above the average output of 150,000 to 250,000 containers per month.

A 20-foot container costs up to $1.70 per cubic foot to manufacture. In contrast, a 40-foot container costs up to $0.80, which underlines the preference for larger volumes as a more effective usage of assets. Even so, the 20-foot container remains a prime transport unit, particularly for the shipping of commodities such as grain, where it represents an optimal size taking account of weight per unit of volume capacity of containers, around 28 metric tons.

China accounts for about 90% of the global production of containers, which is the outcome of several factors, particularly its export-oriented economy and lower labor costs. Considering that China has a positive trade balance, notably in the manufacturing sector, which highly depends on containerization, it is a logical strategy to have containers manufactured at that location. This enables a free movement since, once produced, a new container is immediately moved to a nearby export activity (factory or distribution center), then loaded and brought to a container port. A long-distance empty repositioning is therefore not required for the newly manufactured container. Every container utilization strategy must thus take into account production and location costs. As container availability has become of strategic importance to trade, several governments, such as the Ministry of Ports, Shipping and Waterways in India, have initiated steps for increasing the domestic production of containers, thereby reducing their dependence on Chinese manufacturers.

The great majority of containers are owned either by maritime shipping companies or by container leasing companies. With the beginning of containerization in the 1970s, a container leasing industry emerged to offer flexibility in managing containerized assets, enabling shipping companies to cope with temporal and geographical fluctuations in demand. Following a period of growth correlated with the ebbs and flows of global trade, the leasing industry went through a period of consolidation in the 1990s, like the container shipping industry. In recent years, an important trend has been the growing share of container ownership attributed to maritime shipping companies, which reached 59.8% in 2008. This growth can be explained by the following:

- Containers allow for clear **brand recognition**, particularly for shipping lines.
- Containers are an asset that maritime shipping companies make available to service their customers. Providing containers helps increase the **utilization rate of containerships**.
- A growing level of **intermodal integration and control** in which maritime shippers interact with port terminal operators (some directly operate port terminals such as APM) as well as with inland transport systems such as railways and inland ports. In such a context, controlling container assets enables more efficient use of the transport chain.
- The rising cost of new containers, the repositioning of empties, and systematically low freight rates along several trade routes have made the **container leasing business less profitable**. Ocean carriers also have a greater ability to reposition empty containers since they control a fleet and can reposition their empty containers when capacity is available. It is also not uncommon for a whole containership to be chartered to reposition empties.

In the beginning of 2020s, about 60% of the equipment available for location is controlled by five leasing companies having fleets exceeding 1 million TEU. If the 13 largest leasing companies are considered, they account for 90% of the global container leasing market and controlled the equivalent of 10.7 million TEU. Shipping and leasing companies often have contradictory strategies in the usage of their container assets. From the point of view of shipping companies, their containers are secondary assets enabling more efficient utilization of their ships through a higher level of cargo control. They consequently maximize their ship usage, which is their primary asset, and the container is a tool for this purpose.

**Chassis fleets** are also an important element of the container market as they are necessary to carry containers by road and sometimes within terminals. In addition to its transport function, a chassis can also be used to store containers at terminals and at distribution centers. Near major intermodal terminals, chassis pools allow for drayage operations by allowing motor carriers to access equipment and return it.

## 2 EMPTY CONTAINER FLOWS

A container is a transport as well as a production unit that moves as an export, import, or repositioning flow (Box 8.4). Once a container has been unloaded, another transport leg must be found, as **moving an empty container is almost as costly as moving a full container**. Irrespective of whether it is loaded or not, a container consumes the same amount of space and therefore requires the same transport capacity. Shipping companies need containers to maintain their operations and level of service along the port network they call. Containers arriving in a market as imports must eventually leave, either empty or full. The longer the delay, the higher the cost.

In an ideal situation, an inbound container would find an outbound load nearby once it has been unloaded. **Repositioning** thus begins after a container has been unloaded, and it involves costs that the shippers must assume. This cost is thus reflected in the costs paid by producers and consumers. Also, empty containers represent development opportunities for export markets as every disequilibrium tends to impose a readjustment of transport rates and can act as an indirect export subsidy. Firms taking advantage of this may reduce, likely temporarily, their transport costs.

An increasing number of containers are **repositioned empty** because cargo cannot be found for a return leg. The outcome has been a growth in the repositioning costs as shippers attempt to manage the level of utilization of their containerized assets. The positioning of empty containers is one of the most complex problems concerning global freight distribution, and a high-lighted issue is that, under normal circumstances, about 2.5 million TEUs of containers are being stored empty, waiting to be used. Empties thus account for about 10% of existing container assets and 20.5% of global port handling. The major causes of this problem include:

- **Trade imbalances**. They are probably the most important source in the accumulation of empty containers in the global economy. A region that imports more than it exports will face the systematic accumulation of empty containers, while a region that exports more than it imports will face a shortage of containers. If this situation endures, a repositioning of large amounts of containers will be required between the two trade partners, involving higher transportation costs and tying up existing dis-tribution capacities.
- **Repositioning costs**. They include a combination of inland transport and international transport costs. If they are low enough, a trade imbalance could endure without much impact as containers get repositioned with-out much of a burden on the shipping industry. Repositioning costs can also get lower if imbalances are acute as carriers (and possibly terminal operators) will offer discounts for flows in the reverse direction of domi-nant flows. However, if costs are high, particularly for repositioning con-tainers inland, shortages of containers may appear on export markets.
- **Revenue generation**. Shipowners allocate their containers to maximize their revenue, not necessarily the economic opportunities of their custom-ers. Given trade imbalances and the higher container rates they impose on the inbound trip for transpacific pendulum routes, shipowners often opt to reposition their containers back to Asian export markets instead of waiting for the availability of an export load. For instance, while a container could spend three to four weeks in the hinterland being loaded and brought back to port, earning an income of about $800, the same time can be used to reposition the container across the Pacific to generate a return income of $3,000. The latter figure could be much higher in cases of peak demand.
- **Manufacturing and leasing costs**. If the costs of manufacturing new containers, or leasing existing units, are cheaper than repositioning them, which is possible over long distances, an accumulation can hap-pen. Conversely, higher manufacturing or leasing costs may favor the repositioning of empty containers. Such a condition tends to be tempo-rary as leasing costs and imbalances are correlated.

- **Usage preferences**. A large number of shipping lines use containers to brand the company name and offer readily available capacity to their customers. This, combined with the reluctance of shipping lines and leasing companies to share market information on container positions and quantities for competitive reasons, makes it very difficult to establish container pools or introduce the 'grey box' concept. Still, as demonstrated by the North American rail system (TTX rail equipment pool), it is possible for transport companies to distinctly separate container assets from modal assets so that efficiency (such as the turnover rate) can be improved.
- **Slow steaming.** Excess capacity and rising bunker fuel prices have encouraged maritime shipping companies to reduce the operational speed of their containerships from 21 knots to 19 knots, a practice known as slow steaming. The resulting longer transoceanic journeys tie more container inventory in transit, promote transloading in the proximity of port terminals and reduce the availability of containers inland.

## Box 8.4. Types of container flows

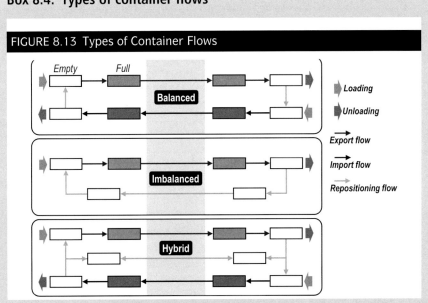

FIGURE 8.13 Types of Container Flows

For long distance trade, three main types of container flow are possible:

- *Balanced. Container flows for exports and imports between two partners are almost similar. Thus, for each full container being unloaded, there is an opportunity for a backhaul movement. This situation is uncommon (Figure 8.13).*
- *Imbalanced. There are container flows in only one direction, implying that once a container has been emptied, the return leg is performed without carrying any load. Again, this situation is uncommon but can happen at the local or regional level.*
- *Hybrid. For various reasons, such as differences in the level of industrialization and development, container flows have a level of imbalance, which requires a specific market for the repositioning of empties. This situation is relatively common, particularly along the Asia–Europe and Transpacific routes.*

## 3 REPOSITIONING SCALES

Container repositioning can occur at three major scales, depending on the nature of the container flow imbalances (Figure 8.14). Each of these scales involves specific repositioning strategies:

- **Local (empty interchange).** Occurs regularly as containers are reshuffled between locations where they are emptied to those where they are filled. They are of short duration with limited use of storage facilities since containers are simply in a queue at the consignee or the consigner, especially if the same freight distributor manages them. The availability of chassis compounds this problem.
- **Regional (intermodal repositioning).** Involves industrial and consumption regions where there are imbalances, often the outcome of economic specialization. For instance, a metropolitan area having a marked service function may be a net importer of containers. In contrast, a nearby area may have a manufacturing specialization, implying a status of a net exporter. The matter then becomes the repositioning of the surplus containers from one part of the region to the other. This may involve a longer time period due to the scale and scope of repositioning and often requires specialized storage facilities. This scale offers freight forwarders opportunities to establish strategies such as dedicated empty container flows and storage depots (or inland ports) at suitable locations. However, locating empty depots near port facilities consumes valuable real estate.
- **International (overseas repositioning).** Is the outcome of systematic macro-economic imbalances between trade partners, as exemplified by China and the United States. Such a repositioning scale is the most costly and time-consuming as it ties up substantial storage capacity in proportion to the trade imbalance. Significant inland freight distribution capacities are also wasted since long-distance trade, especially concerning manufactured goods, tends to involve a wide array of destinations in a national economy. This is paradoxical as maritime container shipping capacity will be readily available for global repositioning. Still, high inland freight transport costs could limit the number of empty containers reaching the vicinity of a container port. It may even force

FIGURE 8.14 Geographical Levels of Empty Container Repositioning

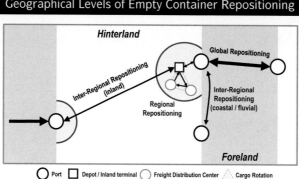

Source: Adapted from Boile, Theofanis, Baveja and Mittal (2008).

an oversupply of containers as the trade partner having a net deficit of containers (exporter) may find it more convenient to manufacture new containers than to reposition existing units, which disrupts the container leasing market.

**Empty container repositioning** costs are multiple and include handling and transshipping at the terminal, chassis location for drayage, empty warehousing while waiting to be repositioned, inland repositioning by rail or trucking towards a maritime terminal, and maritime repositioning. An empty container takes the same amount of space in a truck, railcar, or containership slot as a full container. Shipping companies spend, on average, $110 billion per year in the management of their container assets (purchase, maintenance, repairs), of which $16 billion is for the repositioning of empties. This means that repositioning accounts for 15% of the operational costs related to container assets. To cover these costs, shipping companies charge higher freight rates on the 'full' leg and lower rates on the backhaul. These freight rate practices are thus an important factor in the shipping costs towards developing countries in Africa, Asia, and the Caribbean. The outcome is higher costs for imported goods, which is economically damaging for low-income countries.

## 4 REPOSITIONING STRATEGIES

Within large commercial gateways, containerized distribution and empty repositioning are facing numerous challenges:

- Transport companies must cope with **access and storing charges** at terminals as well as wear and tear on equipment.
- Truck drivers are **losing hours waiting to access** terminal gates and distribution centers to return empty containers and chassis.
- Terminal operators **lose productivity** because of congestion and face pressures from localities to reduce the number of idle trucks at their gates.

The fundamental reason behind the repositioning of a container is the search for cargo to ensure the **continuity of paid movements**. A container is an asset whose usage level is linked with profit and it must continuously be in circulation. Its velocity involves higher turnover rates, and three main options are available to promote this velocity:

- If there are few opportunities to load empty containers on the backhaul trip, an **efficient repositioning system** must be in place to ensure the overall productivity of the distribution system. Transloading is part of such a strategy as it frees maritime containers by moving loads into domestic containers so that there are fewer risks that shipping companies will impose surcharges because of imbalanced containerized flows.
- Improve the **efficiency of existing cargo rotation** with a better link between import and export activities by synchronizing flows. Instead of returning directly to the rail or maritime terminal, an empty container can be brought immediately to an export location to be loaded. However, an asymmetry between import and export-based logistics makes this a difficult proposition.

- Develop an **export market** taking advantage of filling empty containers with new cargo, notably commodities. This can imply various strategies such as substitution from bulk to containers or the setting up of consolidation centers enabling the regrouping of small cargo batches into container loads. This particularly benefits small companies and enables them to access new global markets.

The case of the United States is particularly telling. For 100 containers entering the country, half will be repositioned empty to foreign markets. Of the 50 that remain, most return empty to port terminals awaiting for export cargo to become available. The empty container is picked up from the port terminal and taken to a distribution center to return to the terminal once loaded. Only five of the 50 containers will be loaded with export cargo shortly after being unloaded of import cargo without coming back empty first to the maritime terminal. Cargo rotation appears as a simple repositioning strategy but requires fairly complex coordination. It can take place if import and export activities are located nearby and thus enable a quick rotation. Otherwise, an intermediary stage implying the usage of an empty container depot is required. Thus, cargo rotation is an operational process for repositioning that can be supported by empty container depots, which are physical infrastructures (Box 8.5). Those two elements require a management system where actors involved in supply chains interact to combine mobility needs and the availability of containers.

## Box 8.5 Container repositioning using an empty container depot

*Among the variety of roles that an empty container depot can fulfill, the most prevalent include:*

- *A **neutral location** where empty containers owned by leasing companies and maritime shipping companies can be stored, waiting to be reused or*

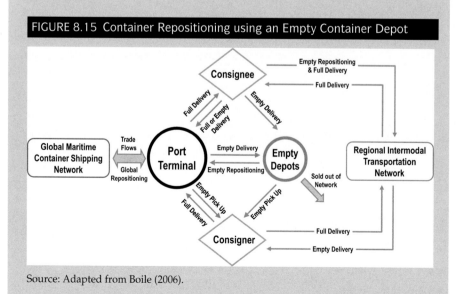

FIGURE 8.15 Container Repositioning using an Empty Container Depot

Source: Adapted from Boile (2006).

*repositioned. It supports an exchange market for container assets between different actors involved in supply chains (e.g. importers and exporters) (Figure 8.15).*

• *An **extension to a maritime (or rail) terminal**, often referred to as a satellite terminal (an extended gate), that can have greater flexibility in its access and opening hours. In particular, a maritime terminal may have access constraints due to local congestion at peak terminal hours. Empty containers can be stored at the empty depot and made available for export activities. Containers that need to be repositioned to the maritime terminal can be brought in outside peak hours (when more truck drivers are available). The depot can also act as a buffer to the maritime terminal capacity, notably because the storage of empty containers is a lower added value activity that can be perceived as a suboptimal usage of the maritime terminal's real estate assets.*

• *A **closer location** to logistics activities helps reduce movements, which is particularly beneficial for a metropolitan area where maritime (or rail) terminals are in high density and congested areas. The depot enables better response to the demands of freight distribution activities and can have multiplying effects if located within a logistics cluster. These effects include a more timely availability of empty containers and a better potential for cargo rotation between import and export-based firms within the cluster.*

## 5 THE DIGITALIZATION OF CONTAINERS

Like other elements of the transport sector, containers are being transformed by information technologies. The container is the object of digitalization and the diffusion of **smart containers** that allow for additional information to be made available to carriers, terminal operators, and cargo owners. This information is related to the identification of the container, its location, and its physical characteristics. In particular:

• The **locational coordinates** of the container can be used to calculate the estimated time of arrival along the transport chain.

• **Temperature, humidity, and air pressure** information are particularly relevant for reefers and cold chain logistics.

• **Geofencing** information can trigger notifications when a container has entered an area (e.g. a terminal) and to assess any locational security breach.

• **Shock detection** assesses if the container was subject to stress levels beyond a defined threshold, particularly if the cargo carried is fragile.

• Information about the container **doors and locks** may include details of whether doors were opened during transit.

The goal is to provide a better level of control over the transport chain, which leads to derived benefits for supply chains. It also enables a clearer identification of the liability if theft, damage, or a breach in the container integrity took place.

Concepts have been brought forward to help connect the various commercial needs (imports and exports) with the availability of containers, such as **freight platforms** and the **virtual container yard**. These systems imply an online market where information about container availability is displayed without the necessity for the container to be in a physical storage depot. The container can be in circulation or at a distribution center, but the important point is that its availability, both geographically and temporarily, for a new load is known. The main goals of a virtual container yard are:

- Display **status information** about containers, such as their characteristics, location, and availability.
- Improve **information exchange** between actors involved in supply chain management, such as trucking companies, shipping companies, distribution centers, and equipment leasing companies.
- **Transfer the container lease** and the related documentation without bringing the container back to the depot or the terminal.
- Assist the actors in supply chain management in their decision-making process concerning the **usage of container assets**, namely returns and exchanges.

Therefore, a virtual container yard is a clearinghouse where detailed information is made available to the involved actors. Small and medium-sized firms are the most likely to use a virtual container yard as they generally have less logistical expertise and available resource to manage containerized assets. Large logistics firms and maritime shipping companies are less likely to use such a system since they already have substantial expertise and their own management systems. An emerging strategy to involve all the actors in a platform enabling a market for the exchange of empties. Thus, repositioning strategies are important in managing containerized assets, but effectiveness is difficult to achieve.

# Chapter 8.5 Port cold chains

*Cold chain technology has allowed ports to play an active role within these supply chains, particularly with refrigerated containers (reefers).*

## 1 COLD CHAIN LOGISTICS

Developments in reefer transportation and logistics have facilitated the growth in the **global demand for cold chain products**. Although the reefer is a homogeneous transportation product, the markets it services are highly heterogeneous, ranging from agricultural goods, to pharmaceuticals and chemicals, and even fresh flowers.

*The **cold chain** involves the transportation of temperature-sensitive products along a supply chain through thermal and refrigerated packaging methods and logistical planning to protect the integrity of these shipments. There are several means by which cold chain products can be* *transported, including refrigerated trucks and railcars, refrigerated cargo ships, reefers, and air cargo.*

While global supply chains are relatively modern expansions in the transportation industry, the refrigerated movement of temperature-sensitive goods is a practice that dates back to 1797, when British fishermen used natural ice and salt to preserve their fish stockpiles while at sea. By the nineteenth century, an **ice trade** emerged and allowed for rudimentary forms of refrigeration. By the early twentieth century, the invention of refrigeration allowed for local, year-round production of ice. This marked the downfall of the conventional ice trade with the construction of the first refrigerated ships, where a section of the cargo hold was refrigerated, occurring in the 1880s. At that time, France was starting to receive large shipments of frozen meat and mutton carcasses from South America, while Great Britain imported frozen beef from Australia and pork and other meat from New Zealand. This process was stimulated by a shortage of meat production in Europe and substantial surpluses in developing countries. By 1910, 600,000 tons of frozen meat were being brought into Great Britain alone.

In addition to frozen meat and fish, refrigeration allowed for the setting up of tropical fruit trades that required specialized reefer ships designed for that sole purpose. The first reefer ship for the **banana trade** was introduced in 1902 by the United Food Company to carry tropical fruits from Central America to the United States. This enabled the banana to move from being an exotic fruit that had a small market because it arrived too ripe, to one of the world's most consumed fruit and the fifth most traded agricultural commodity. A whole range of handling procedures and equipment has been developed, making the banana a core driver of cold chain logistics (Box 8.6). Its impacts on the reefer industry were monumental and encouraged the construction of cold storage facilities near ports.

Banana trading multi-nationals were initially **fully vertically integrated** as they owned plantations, port terminals, reefer ships, ripening centers, and cold storage facilities. An important dimension of the banana trade concerns its containerization. In the past, tropical fruits were predominantly transported in specifically designed reefer ships. The last quarter of a century has seen rapid containerization of the banana trade, which now accounts for 20% of all maritime reefer usage. For instance, about 60% of all the bananas imported in the United States are carried in refrigerated containers. Accordingly, the specialized reefer ship is gradually being phased out to be replaced by specialized containerships, most with their own cranes, designed to carry refrigerated containers. Large fruit companies such as Dole, Chiquita, and Del Monte are transitioning towards reefer-only operations, which promote the creation of large reefer terminals able to handle such volumes. Additionally, conventional container shipping lines offer reefer capacity on their ships, capturing a growing share of the banana trade.

Globalization and more reliable cold chains can significantly impact supply chains by expanding available options in terms of locations and processes. This results in an increase in the quantity and quality of products available on markets as well as lower costs.

## Box 8.6 The transport and handling of bananas

*The banana is one of the most important perishable commodities in international trade. Cargoes of bananas are carried either in the holds of reefer (refrigerated) vessels or in refrigerated shipping containers. A voyage may take a few days or several weeks from the loading to the discharging port. Over the past decade, the banana trade has been fast-moving to almost full containerization. The international banana trade is based on the harvesting and transportation of hard, green, unripe fruit, which is later ripened in the country of consumption. The lowest temperature at which bananas may safely be shipped is in the region of 13.3°C, which is optimal for extending postharvest life. At temperatures below this critical value, there is a risk of chilling injury.*

*One of the major developments of banana handling techniques was the packing of bananas in cardboard boxes. Advances in refrigerating technologies are very important for the development of banana reefer transport and allow for bananas to reach the consuming centers faster and with better quality. The new methods for transporting perishable technologies better control the cold chain and allow for tracking the process through computerized systems. When transported by sea, bananas are said to be 'put to sleep', reducing the amount of oxygen in the storage area, to extend their shipping life. Some of the technologies used are controlled atmosphere, controlled humidity, remote access monitoring, enhanced airflow, better insulation materials and techniques, and internal monitoring controls.*

*Equipment typically used in the discharge process includes quayside cranes, forklifts, and pallet jacks. Some of the vessels that arrive at the terminal do have their own onboard cranes, but quayside cranes are faster and more efficient than on-board cranes:*

- *When* reefer **containers** *are transported by a mainline container vessel, the reefer container usually ends up at a full container terminal in the port. It is then brought to the banana facility by truck or barge (if available).*
- ***Reefer vessels*** *usually also have reefer containers on deck. These reefer vessels call at the banana terminal directly, where they first unload the reefer containers before engaging in below deck cargo handling operations of palletized banana boxes.*

*The equipment used to discharge bananas depends on the unit load used:*

- ***Discharge of reefer containers*** *is handled by mobile shore cranes or, when availably, by STS container cranes. Reefer containers are plugged in at the electrical outlets that are provided at the terminal and their cargo is stripped later on in a warehouse adjacent to the quay. The pallets that are inside the containers are transferred to the warehouse with forklifts and are processed in the same way as the rest of the pallets.*
- ***Discharge of pallets*** *occurs inside the vessel with pallet jacks and forklifts, the pallets are placed in a pallet cage or pallet tray where up to eight pallets can be accommodated depending on the equipment. The pallets are offloaded in the quayside and, again, forklifts waiting on the quayside collect them and move them inside the warehouse. Consequently, the pallets are exposed to the open air for a limited amount of time and only for*

*transportation from the quayside to the warehouse. A number of reefer ves-
sels have side-doors and the loading and discharging is done via the ships'
side-door and cargo elevators. But these operations are not as productive as
using the terminal's cranes.*

- **Discharge of loose boxes** *used often to occur in the hold of the ship. In
order to unload loose boxes, spiral unloaders were used that could reach any
required point in the ship's hold to take in the boxes. In the hold, the boxes
were manhandled onto the telescopic belt and traveled automatically into
the spiral. As soon as the loose boxes were discharged they were guided to
the warehouse using a conveyor belt. Palletizing robots were used to pallet-
ize the boxes before bringing these to the cold store.*

With the introduction of pallet cages and containerization, the number of banana
boxes handled per minute per crane increased from 50 when using a spiral
unloader to 385 for the pallet cage and 480 when pallets are containerized.

As soon as the pallets are offloaded from the vessel, they are transferred to
the warehouse. Depending on the type of warehouse (automated or not) different
processes apply:

- **Automated warehouse**. This type of facility uses an automated storage
and retrieval system (AS/RS), then the pallets enter the reception area of
the warehouse and are placed on the conveyor belt with a forklift. As the
pallets move along the conveyor belt, they pass a scanning device that scans
the barcode affixed to the carton. In this way, the warehouse management
system of the terminal is updated. Each pallet follows a pre-designed path
to the actual stacking area, and they are stored according to temperature.
- **Traditional warehouse**. Block stacking is typically used, and the pallets
are stacked on the aisles by temperature and depending on how they need to
be delivered (by vessel, container, etc.).

When the receiver/buyer requests their cargo, their pallets are collected from the
warehouse, moved to the shipping area, and loaded onto the dedicated truck. In
this process, the truck is parked against a docking space at the warehouse. The
pallets are loaded onto trucks using forklifts. There is little exposure to non-
controlled air. The trucks are refrigerated trailer trucks.

## 2  REFRIGERATED CONTAINERS

### 2.1  The reefer market

Refrigerated containers (**reefers**) account for a growing share of the refrigerated cargo transported around the world. While in 1980, 33% of the refrigerated transport capacity in maritime shipping was containerized, this share
rapidly climbed to 82% in 2017 (Figure 8.16). Two major factors account for the
growth in the transportation of refrigerated containers:

- The rise in **global incomes**, particularly in developing economies, is
accompanied by a nutritional transition. This drives the consumption of
imported fresh foods.

FIGURE 8.16 Share of Refrigerated Transport Capacity in Maritime Shipping, 1980–2017

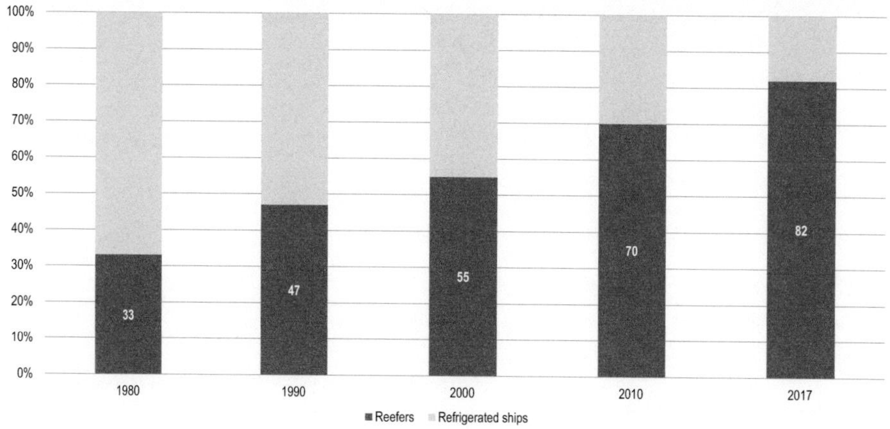

Source: Adapted from Drewry Shipping Consultants.

- The growing **availability of refrigerated containers and equipment and cold chain techniques** allow for the transport of temperature-sensitive goods in better conditions and over longer distances.

The structure of global maritime shipping is thus adapting to service the reefer trade, implying a **shift away from specialized ports**, or specialized terminals within ports, to standard container terminals. The reefer has become a common temperature-controlled transport unit used to ensure load integrity since it can accommodate a wide range of temperature settings and a wide range of temperature-sensitive products. It is also a versatile unit able to carry around 20 to 25 tons of refrigerated or temperature-sensitive cargo. It is fully compatible with the global intermodal transport system, which implies a high level of accessibility to markets worldwide. A wide variety of cargoes can be carried in reefers. On occasion, a reefer is used to carry a regular container cargo load if repositioned or if there is a shortage of standard containers.

About 2.9 million TEU of reefers were being used by 2018, representing about 5% of the global ISO container capacity. To compare, a regular 40-foot container costs around $5,000, while a reefer of the same size costs in the range of $30,000. The cost difference is attributed to insulation and the refrigeration unit that keeps the temperature constant. This implies that a reefer has less volume than a regular container of the same size. While a regular 40-foot high cube container can accommodate a volume of 76 cubic meters, a reefer of the same size handles 67 cubic meters (12% less). This shortcoming is compensated by the heavier loads that are usually carried in reefers. From a manufacturing standpoint, all the world's reefers are made in China. In 2015, MCI, a subsidiary of Maersk, began operation of a new reefer manufacturing plant in San Antonio, Chile. The main locational rationale was that manufacturing reefers next to major export areas of refrigerated cargoes (fruits such as oranges and grapes) would provide a free first move. However, the plant was closed in 2018, mostly due to high production costs.

The higher costs of the reefer and the additional equipment and monitoring required involve higher shipping rates. The rates vary according to the value of the temperature-sensitive cargo being carried as well as if it is frozen (lower rate) or fresh (higher rate). A reefer must be used four to six times per year as a revenue-generating movement to be profitable. Due to the specific trades they service, reefers are often repositioned empty or used as regular containers with their power supply turned off. As such, they are labeled as non-operating reefers. The reefer trade is a **full container load** (FCL) and **point-to-point** only. Unlike the regular container trade, there is no consolidation or deconsolidation function performed in reefer transportation since that would increase the risk of damaging what is being carried. Deconsolidation usually occurs either when the contents of reefers are transloaded into domestic reefers or at the distribution center when orders are assembled for customers (particularly for grocery). Under specific circumstances, reefers can even be used as refrigerated storage units.

## 2.2 Technical considerations

Reefer operations are subject to several crucial technical considerations. Proper **air circulation** must be ensured, meaning that reefers have gratings on the floor and that a clearance of about 15 cm must be kept between the cargo and the ceiling. Cold air coming out of the refrigeration unit flows through the bottom part of the reefer and as it warms up, it climbs towards the ceiling to flow back to the refrigeration unit, usually 0.5°C to 3°C warmer. The heat can be the outcome of ambient temperature permeating into the reefer (this is particularly the case when the ambient temperature is high) as well as the cooling of the cargo if it was loaded in at a warmer temperature than maintained in the reefer. All reefers are **painted white** to increase the albedo (share of the incident light being reflected; high albedo implies less solar energy absorbed by the surface). For instance, a low albedo container can have its internal temperature increase to 50°C when the external temperature reaches 25°C on a sunny day. In comparison, a high albedo container sees its internal temperature increase to only 38°C under the same conditions.

The refrigeration unit of a reefer requires an **electric power source** during transportation and at a container yard. For the road transport of a reefer, either a clip-on generator (called Genset; it attaches to the upper front end of a reefer) or an underslung generator (it attaches under a container chassis) are used. For modes such as maritime and rail that can carry multiple containers, the capacity of the power system determines the number of reefers that can be carried. Regular containerships have 10% to 20% of their slots adapted to carry reefers. Some ships have up to 25% of their slots dedicated to servicing routes with a higher intensity of refrigerated cargo (e.g. Latin American exports). The power is directly provided by the ship's generator. For rail movements, diesel generators are used to provide power to about eight reefer containers. These Genset units have the same dimensions as a 40-foot container and can use the same intermodal equipment as intermodal containers. A common loadout for unit trains is to have two stacked Genset units to power a group of 16 reefers. For smaller reefer loads or shorter distances, clip-on generators are commonly used. It is important to underline that the refrigeration units are designed to **maintain the temperature** within a prefixed range, not to cool it down. This means that the shipment must be brought to the required temperature before being loaded into a reefer, which requires specialized warehousing and loading/unloading facilities.

Another technical consideration concerns **monitoring the condition** of reefers and their cargoes. A variety of sensors are included in the new generation of smart reefers monitoring temperature and humidity conditions and using the cooling plant more efficiently. This enables improvement of the reliability of temperature control and extends the autonomy of the reefer. Still, vessel crews and terminal personnel need to physically monitor reefer conditions, which is time-consuming and subject to errors. An emerging trend and standard involve equipping reefers with remote management systems to monitor the temperature and humidity. These units are equipped with a GPS and a wireless communication device on the reefer controller unit to provide regular updates to a ship's onboard information systems to assess any issue that could occur along the cold chain. Thus, the reefer becomes a component of the Internet of Things (IoT), allowing it to be queried and monitored at any given time and location.

## 3 REEFER TERMINAL FACILITIES

The growth in cold chain logistics has increasingly required transport terminals such as ports to dedicate a part of their storage yards to reefers. This accounts for between **1% and 5% of the total terminal capacity** but can be higher for transshipment hubs or terminals in areas with an important reefer trade, such as the Philadelphia region and Antwerp. Around the world, large numbers of reefer slots are observed in three primary contexts (Box 8.7):

- **Commercial gateways** where the reefer trade involves the imports of food products for the domestic market. The level of reefer activity is usually related to market size and the level of economic development. This mainly characterizes European, Chinese, and North American ports with extensive and complex food distribution systems. This can lead to having concentrated levels of reefer activity, such as for the port of St. Petersburg since it acts as the main gateway for refrigerated goods for the whole Russian economy.
- **Transshipment hubs** connecting regional reefer trades such as Singapore, Dubai, Busan, and Algeciras. The purpose of these hubs is to transfer reefers between maritime shipping routes quickly. This takes place at transshipment hubs that have the best connectivity and level of performance.
- **Reefer export platforms** related to fruit and vegetable trades such as from South Africa, Brazil, Ecuador, Chile, and Costa Rica.

Because of the nature of their cargo, **reefers impose particular requirements on port infrastructure**, namely in terms of storage space, energy supply, and handling processes. Reefer storage requirements involve having an adjacent power outlet, known as a reefer plug. The task is labor-intensive, as each container must be manually plugged and unplugged. The temperature has to be regularly monitored as it is the responsibility of the terminal operator to ensure that reefers keep their temperature within preset ranges. With information technologies, monitoring reefers in a terminal is being automated, with essential information such as temperature and its fluctuation, humidity, and refrigeration unit power usage collected and stored. Any unusual event can be flagged for immediate intervention.

In a terminal, **reefer stacking areas** usually rely on three approaches:

- **Wheeled storage**. A conventional method where reefers are placed on chassis that are moved to a parking area where each parking slot has an electric reefer plug. This tends to be associated with lower operating expenses but consumes more space. Only regular trucks are required for terminal operations.
- **Stacked storage**. Using yard equipment such as reach stackers to stack reefers up to three in height. It allows for higher densities but requires more equipment and labor.
- **Rack storage**. An emerging method taking place at high throughput terminals where land can be scarce. The reefers are stored and stacked into rack systems that can hold between 20 and 30 reefers. Reefer racks have a common power supply and each reefer can be accessed and monitored through platforms. Such a storage system has higher capital costs but requires a reduced terminal footprint — four to six times less storage space than wheeled storage.

Even if reefers involve higher terminal costs, they are **very profitable** due to the high value of transported commodities. Depending on the intensity of reefer use, reefer activities can account for between 20% and 35% of the total energy consumption of a container terminal. Under specific circumstances, reefers can even be used as refrigerated storage units when there is not enough refrigerated warehousing capacity or when the reefer only stays for a short duration.

## Box 8.7 Reefer slots at container ports

*The majority of container terminals allocate some space for refrigerated containers (reefers) as they account for, on average, about 5% of all the TEU handled. This represents a separate and specialized port function that requires equipment such as reefer plugs (power outlets), power supply, and labor to monitor the reefers. At the same time, they are being handled at the terminal. Although handling reefers at ports involves additional costs, it also generates revenues due to the higher value of the cargo and its time sensitivity; it commands premium rates.*

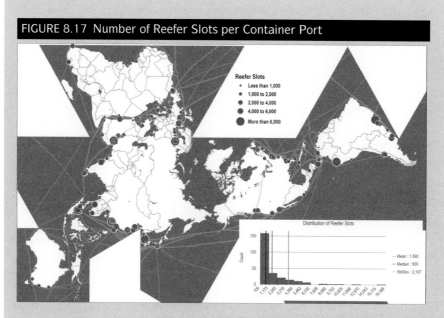

FIGURE 8.17 Number of Reefer Slots per Container Port

Source: Websites of port authorities and terminal operators.

*The following patterns in the geographical distribution of reefer storage capacity at container ports are observed:*

- *An inventory of the world's ports revealed a total refer storage capacity of more than 405,000 reefer slots. At the port level, the median number of reefer slots is 800, but with a very high standard deviation, underlining an* **outlier group of ports with very high numbers of reefer slots** *(Figure 8.17).*
- *Major* **transshipment hubs** *have a large number of reefer slots (3,000 and above) that are necessary to accommodate the connectivity between reefer shipping networks.*
- *Major* **commercial gateways** *that serve as distribution nodes for imported cold chain goods.*
- *Major* **cold chain export gateways** *supplying the global market with cold chain goods such as fruits, particularly in Central and South America and South Africa.*

# EPILOG

*The multidisciplinary, multisector, and worldwide analysis of the contemporary port industry and port governance and development reveals the dynamics, diversity, and continuous evolution of modern seaports and port-related activities. This epilog presents thoughts on emerging issues that will probably shape ports in the future and become central themes of port economics, management and policy.*

## 1 DEALING WITH VOLATILITY AND SHIFTS IN PORT DEMAND

Seaports act as **nodes in global supply chains** operating in an efficiency-oriented, competitive, and highly dynamic market environment. Economic globalization, based on the principles of free trade and open markets, have led to a growing demand for port services. Unlike any other point in history, the last half century propelled ports and maritime shipping into the global realm. However, **globalization is** under scrutiny. Changes in market opportunities and growing trade barriers can undermine the growth potential for ports. For example, Brexit, China–US trade frictions, and the difficulties surrounding existing and new bilateral and multilateral trade agreements add to the volatility and uncertainty in global trade flows. This challenges ports and port actors to show **higher flexibility and resilience** while inserting ports into global production and logistics networks.

Port resilience and adaptive capacity are also needed in the context of a whole range of potential disruptions. Economic shocks, health crises, and major trends such as nearshoring and reshoring, the energy transition, and automation are ongoing disruptions. The COVID-19 pandemic and its aftermath have underlined the importance of ports in global supply chains. Ports are intensifying their efforts to prepare for structural changes in port traffic levels, cargo mix, or the geographical distribution of foreland and hinterland flows. While the container business has attracted most of the attention in the past decades, it is expected that the future will bring a more balanced discussion focusing on other cargo segments and the passenger/cruise market. **Geographical considerations** will continue to play a fundamental role in the global structure of production, distribution, and consumption that ports and maritime shipping support.

## 2 INTERNATIONAL AND REGIONAL FUNCTIONS OF PORTS

The growth of international trade has given rise to **large hub ports**, which often combine intermediacy in the global shipping network with centrality towards specific hinterland markets. These developments have shown that ports are not only about fulfilling a derived demand. An integrated port cluster can serve as an economic engine for regional development and increase its attractiveness as a location for distribution, manufacturing and industrial activities, including the service sector. The locational and logistics capabilities of a port are forming an **integrated demand**.

Not all ports can and should aim for hub status. This leaves ports with the challenge of developing appropriate **functional and spatial strategies** that bring about a desirable mix of international and more regional functions. Each seaport has a specific footprint linked to its unique mix of cargo and passenger handling, logistics, and industrial functions. Major socio-economic conflicts are related to port development and operations. They can occur when community groups or other stakeholders perceive a clear imbalance between the benefits (added value, employment) and costs (congestion, environmental impacts) for the local community as ports develop a larger port footprint. Any potential erosion of public support for seaport activities should remain a key concern for port managers. Well-balanced **stakeholder relations management**, corporate social responsibility (CSR) programs, and effective city-port interactions are expected to play an ever more important role in decisions on the future of port footprints and the associated mix of port functions.

## 3 LEADING THE WAY IN ENVIRONMENTAL AND SOCIAL CHALLENGES

Port development and operations are not only guided by economic considerations. **Environmental and social issues** are having a growing impact on ports. Many ports are taking on a more enterprising role in dealing with the environmental, energy, and climate change challenges, partly because environmental aspects play an increasing role in attracting customers and potential investors. A port with a strong environmental record and a high level of community support is likely to be favored by market players.

The growing role of environmental and social considerations shapes the behavior and strategies of port-related actors. This includes a greater role being attributed to setting and achieving sustainability goals and rolling out initiatives in CSR, stakeholder relations management, and green supply chain management. Considering ports as only part of the problem is not constructive. Instead, they are an essential part of the solution to mounting environmental and social challenges. Ports are key nodes in vast transportation, logistics, industrial and information networks. Their **network position**, combined with observed **cluster effects**, makes ports ideal to lead the way in many domains such as energy transition, the greening of supply and transport chains, cargo bundling and optimization, modal shift in inland transport, the social dimension of automation, knowledge development and exchange, and transparency and visibility in global supply chains. Policymakers and stakeholders should provide ample room for port communities to take up and develop a leadership position.

## 4 AGILE PORTS THINKING

**Innovation and information technologies** are high on the agenda of many ports. Ports have come to understand that **coordination and integration** in supply chains are key to their future competitiveness. Port-related actors and port authorities are developing initiatives to strengthen the interconnectivity of ports concerning their physical, digital and operational networks. The number of initiatives in this area has proliferated in recent years, demonstrating that the evolution in how ports think has become a mainstream development. **Digitalization challenges** underline that this new way of thinking offers ports and their stakeholders a more efficient use of existing assets, which will continue to lead to new opportunities.

Still, many challenges remain. Cooperation between actors demands a conducive environment for innovation and data-sharing characterized by trust, mutual benefits, and sustainable business and revenue models. Conflicts on data ownership, competition for leadership, and regulatory challenges are expected to increase as data becomes a precious commodity. At the same time, port communities will have to address **cybersecurity** issues relating to data use and exchange.

## 5 THE CHANGING FACE OF PORT COMPETITION

Port competition is no longer restricted to attracting cargo volumes. The increasing importance of integrating ports and terminals in supply chains has increased the focus on creating added value linked to cargo passing through the port. Furthermore, port competitiveness can be better understood by following a supply chain approach. Ports compete not only as individual places that handle ships but as crucial links within global supply chains. Port choice becomes more a function of the overall network cost and performance.

While competition between adjacent ports remains important, port competition has expanded spatially due to advances in maritime and inland transport networks. Corridors, dry ports, and inland strategies of market players and port authorities have contributed to a highly dynamic and competitive landscape in serving local and more distant hinterland regions. Captive hinterlands and customers have made room for **shared hinterlands** and large **footloose port users**. The corporate strategies of these port users are having their impact on inter-port and intra-port competition.

To improve their operating margins, generate revenue, and offer a better service to their customers, market players in shipping, ports, and logistics simultaneously pursue two complementary strategies. The first is **cost control through horizontal integration**, and the second is **service differentiation through vertical integration** along the supply chain. Digital transformation and value capture along the chains play a key role in rolling out these strategies. Competitive issues to accommodate global supply chains have led to functional changes in seaports, as well as in the other nodes of the global transport and logistics network. Ports increasingly seek cooperation and coordination by bundling their transport flows with the hinterland. Nodal competition is supplemented by nodal cooperation.

Port competition is increasingly affected by **consolidation and scale increases** in shipping and logistics. The introduction of ever-larger container vessels was once seen as a clear benefit for global trade and maritime operations. Economies of scale at sea brought by mega-ships lowered the unit cost per container transported and brought about changes in the port hierarchy. In recent years, concerns were raised about the **distribution of costs and benefits** of these large ships among the actors involved. Issues related to the impact of mega-ships on supply chains, terminal operations, public spending on nautical accessibility, and society at large were brought to the fore. A limit may have been reached, or there may still be additional economies of scale to be realized. Debates about massification, concentration, and scale increases in the port and shipping industry will remain at the forefront, as the COVID-19 pandemic and incidents such as the Suez Canal blockage of 2021 have made policymakers, regulators, and the public much more aware of the crucial role of shipping and ports in facilitating global trade.

## 6 TOWARDS A MULTI-SCALAR APPROACH TO PORT PERFORMANCE

Port performance is often approached from a port competitiveness and competition angle. From this perspective, cargo throughput and vessel traffic remain important output measures. However, ports are challenged to develop a multi-scalar approach to port performance by **developing indicators** in supply chain performance, maritime and inland connectivity, financial performance, customer satisfaction, sustainability, socio-economic significance, port governance, and port resilience. There is also a focus on the effectiveness of CSR initiatives and stakeholder relations management or on achieving broad sustainability goals. The COVID-19 pandemic has underlined the importance of **risk management** and resilience in a seaport context characterized by uncertainty and volatility. Ports are expected to develop capabilities in port resilience planning and to enhance the **adaptive capacity of ports**, to cope with economic shocks and trends, and with the challenges imposed by climate change.

Still, many challenges remain. **Interdependencies**, or lack thereof, between various port performance measures remain relatively underexplored. Furthermore, many of the newer indicators are still rather experimental, with concerns expressed about their feasibility, acceptability, and relevance, particularly when comparing ports (benchmarking). Also, the identification and relevance of performance indicators might be influenced by the objectives and beliefs of relevant actors.

## 7 THE SEARCH FOR THE RIGHT PORT GOVERNANCE

Changes in the competitive environment, and environmental and social challenges, along with the changing functions of ports, have intensified the quest for a **suitable port governance model**. Innovative ideas and customized approaches to port governance have emerged in past decades. Port governance reforms have brought tensions and opportunities, not least because ports have to function in a global economic system while adapting and embedding in a regional or local political and economic context. Opportunities exist to advance the measurement of the effectiveness and efficiency of port governance solutions and provide tools that can help actors find the best governance fit.

One of the most remarkable trends in port governance is the shift from the management of individual ports to **managing multi-port groups or regions**. Port authority mergers and other far-reaching cooperation schemes are on the rise in response to mounting market and financial pressures and provide opportunities to avoid duplication of facilities and unnecessary competition. This could trigger regulatory responses as monopolistic and oligopolistic situations could emerge.

Port governance reforms have often resulted in a change towards more autonomy, more commercially oriented strategies, resilience, accountability, and a push for rational investment. They have also opened avenues to **new revenue and business models** for port authorities. While the pricing structures of port authorities differ worldwide, most ports hold on to their traditional revenue base and pricing system. Landlord port authorities remain heavily dependent on **port dues and land fees** as their financial backbone, yet these are often designed using simple and rather rigid pricing methods. Port pricing strategies and revenue models are expected to change over time, for example through exploring the possibility of designing more **dynamic, flexible, and differentiated pricing methods**. Moreover, port dues and land fees might complement other revenue streams from investments in digital transformation, energy transition, and the circular economy.

The **centrality of port authorities** will likely endure. Contrary to the skepticism that accompanied the rebalancing of the public-private interface in port governance in past decades, the search for and implementation of port governance models are expected to sustain the core role of port managing entities. The same is true for the role of **terminal operators**, especially given their multinational character, as well as the continuation of vertical integration trends. A different balance between port authorities and terminal operators might emerge, yet their interaction will be fundamental for the purpose of advancing ports.

## 8 SUSTAINING FUNCTIONAL DIVERSITY

Functional diversity has been a common denominator of the evolution of ports from simple critical infrastructures facilitating trade to nodes in sophisticated global supply chains and offering a functional and spatial clustering of port-related activities. A large number of dimensions, such as scale, geographical attributes, governance and institutional settings, port functions, specialization, and the diverse dynamics of the different port markets, have produced a uniqueness in the progression of each port. Irrespective of the critical and challenging issues that might prevail in the future, there is no reason to expect a homogenous reaction and adjustment of ports. The **diversity of ports** worldwide will undoubtedly endure, continuing to make ports an industry worth investigating.

\*\*\*

## 9 A NOTE FROM THE AUTHORS

This book offers a wealth of insights on port economics, management, and policy and covers multiple themes and issues. Even if it is the result of decades of observation and analysis, we are aware that the book might not may not cover all current issues in ports to the extent they may warrant. Still, we hope its content will sharpen your knowledge and understanding of ports and help assess current developments and future challenges in the port industry, which is an inspiring, exciting, and highly dynamic world. When dealing with ports, you might not be able to direct where the wind will take you. We hope this book can help you to adjust the sails. Thank you for having sailed with us on this seaport journey.

# REFERENCES AND SUGGESTED READINGS

## INTRODUCTION: A MULTIFACETED APPROACH TO SEAPORTS

Alderton, P. and Saieva, G. (2013). *Port Management and Operations*, London: Routledge.

Brooks, M.R. and Cullinane, K. (eds.) (2007). *Devolution, Port Governance and Performance*, London: Elsevier.

Brooks, M.R. and Pallis, A.A. (eds.) (2012). *Classics in Port Policy and Management*, Chelteham: Edward Elgar.

De Langen, P.W. (2020). *Towards a Better Port Industry: Port Development, Management and Policy*, Abingdon: Routledge.

Haralambides, H. (ed.) (2015). *Port Management*, London: Palgrave.

Pallis, A.A., Vitsounis, T.K., De Langen, P.W. and Notteboom, T.E. (2011). Port economics, policy and management: content classification and survey, *Transport Reviews*, 31(4), 445–471.

Talley, W.K. (2018). *Port Economics*, 2nd Edition, New York: Routledge.

van Klink, A. (2003). The Kempen nexus. The spatial-economic development of Rotterdam and Antwerp, in: Loyen, R. (ed.), *Struggling for Leadership: A Century and a Half of Antwerp-Rotterdam Port Competition (1870–2000)*, Physica-Verlag, Series Contributions to Economics, Heidelberg, pp. 143–159.

## PART I   PORTS AND MARITIME SHIPPING

Arvis, J.F., Mustra, M.A., Ojala, L., Shepherd, B. and Saslavsky, D. (2012). *Connecting to Compete 2012 Trade Logistics in the Global Economy*, Washington, DC: The World Bank.

Cariou, P., Parola, F. and Notteboom, T. (2019). Towards low carbon global supply chains: a multi-trade analysis of $CO_2$ emission reductions in container shipping, *International Journal of Production Economics*, 208, 17–28.

Chaos, S.R., Pallis, A.A., Marchán, S.S., Roca, D.P. and Conejo, A.S.A. (2020). Economies of scale in cruise shipping, *Maritime Economics & Logistics*, Online First.

Chen, L. and Notteboom, T. (2012). Determinants for assigning value-added logistics services to logistics centers within a supply chain configuration, *Journal of International Logistics and Trade*, 10(1), 3–41.

Chen, J., Notteboom, T., Liu, X., Yu, H., Nikitakos, N. and Yang, C. (2019). The Nicaragua Canal: potential impact on international shipping and its attendant challenges, *Maritime Economics and Logistics*, 21(1), 79–98.

Crotti, D., Ferrari, C. and Tei, A. (2019). Merger waves and alliance stability in container shipping, *Maritime Economics & Logistics*, 1–27.

Cruise Industry News (2021). *2021 Annual Report*, New York: Cruise Industry News.

Cruise Lines Industry Association (CLIA) (2019). *2020 State of the Industry*, Washington, DC: CLIA.

Cruise Lines Industry Association (CLIA) (2020). *2018 Global Passenger Report*, Washington, DC: CLIA.

Cruise Market Watch (2020). www.cruisemarketwatch.com.

Daniels, J.D., Radebaugh, L.H. and Sullivan, D. (2017). *International Business: Environments and Operations*, 16th Edition, New York: Prentice-Hall.

Dicken, P. (2015). *Global Shift: Mapping the Changing Contours of the World Economy*, 7th Edition, New York: The Guilford Press.

Dowling, R.K. and Weeden, C. (2017). *Cruise Ship Tourism*, 2nd Edition, Wallingford: Centre for Agriculture and Bioscience International (CABI).

Ducruet, C. and Notteboom, T. (2015). Developing liner service networks in container shipping, in: Song, D.W. and Panayides, P. (eds.), *Maritime Logistics: A Guide to Contemporary Shipping and Port Management*, London: Kogan Page, 125–146.

Fletcher, M.A. (1958). The Suez canal and world shipping, 1869–1914, *The Journal of Economic History*, 18(4), 556–573.

Fusillo, M. (2006). Some notes on structure and stability in liner shipping, *Maritime Policy and Management*, 33(5), 463–475.

Ge, J., Zhu, M., Sha, M., Notteboom, T., Shi, W. and Wang, X. (2020). Towards 25,000 TEU vessels? A comparative economic analysis of ultra-large containership sizes under different market and operational conditions, *Maritime Economics and Logistics*, Online First.

Haralambides, H.E. (2019). Gigantism in container shipping, ports and global logistics: a time-lapse into the future, *Maritime Economics & Logistics*, 21(1), 1–60.

International Transport Forum (2015). *The Impact of Mega-ships: Case-specific Policy Analysis*, Paris: ITF–OECD.

Jansson, J.O. and Schneerson, D. (1982). The optimal ship size, *Journal of Transport Economics & Policy*, 16(3), 217–238.

Karabell, Z. (2003). *Parting the Desert: The Creation of the Suez Canal*, New York: Vintage Books.

Kiiski, T. (2017). Commercial cargo shipping along the Northern Sea Route: Destination-oriented and globally marginal, *Baltic Transport Journal* 1, 34–36.

Levinson, M. (2006). *The Box: How the Shipping Container Made the World Smaller and the World Economy Bigger*, Princeton, NJ: Princeton University Press.

Mangan, J., Lalwani, C. and Calatayud, A. (2020). *Global Logistics and Supply Chain Management*, 4th Edition, New York: Wiley.

McCullough, D. (1977). *The Path Between the Seas: The Creation of the Panama Canal, 1870–1914*, New York: Simon & Schuster.

MedCruise (2020). *Cruise Activities in MedCruise Ports: Statistics 2019*, Teneriffe: MedCruise.

Monios, J., Notteboom, T., Wilmsmeier, G. and Rodrigue, J.-P. (2016). Competition and complementarity between seaports and hinterland locations for attracting distribution activities, *PortEconomics Report 5/2020*, www.porteconomics.eu.

Notteboom, T. (2004). Container shipping and ports: an overview, *The Review of Network Economics*, 3(2), 86–106.

Notteboom, T. (2006). The time factor in liner shipping services, *Maritime Economics and Logistics*, 8(1), 19–39.

Notteboom, T. (2012). Container shipping, in: Talley, W. (ed.), *The Blackwell Companion to Maritime Economics*, Oxford: Wiley-Blackwell Publishing, 230–262.

Notteboom, T. and Cariou, P. (2013). Slow steaming in container liner shipping: is there any impact on fuel surcharge practices? *The International Journal of Logistics Management*, 24(1), 73–86.

Notteboom, T. and Neyens, K. (2017). *The Future of Port Logistics: Meeting the Challenges of Supply Chain Integration*, Brussels: ING Bank.

Notteboom, T.E., Parola, F., Satta, G. and Pallis, A.A. (2017). The relationship between port choice and terminal involvement of alliance members in container shipping, *Journal of Transport Geography*, 64, 158–173.

Notteboom, T.E. and Rodrigue, J.-P. (2009). The future of containerization: perspectives from maritime and inland freight distribution, *Geojournal*, 74(1), 7–22.

Notteboom, T.E. and Rodrigue, J.-P. (2011). Challenges to and challengers of the Suez Canal, *Port Technology International*, 51, 14–17.

Notteboom, T.E., Satta, G. and Parola, F. (2020). Brand strategies of container shipping lines following mergers and acquisitions: carriers' visual identity options, *Maritime Economics & Logistics*, Online First.

Notteboom, T.E and Vernimmen, B. (2009). The effect of high fuel costs on liner service configuration in container shipping, *Journal of Transport Geography*, 17(5), 325–337.

Notteboom, T.E. and Winkelmans, W. (2001). Structural changes in logistics: how will port authorities face the challenge? *Maritime Policy and Management*, 28(1), 71–89.

Pallis, A.A. and Vaggelas, G.K. (2020). The changing geography of cruise shipping, in: Wilmsmeier, G., Monios, J., Browne, M. and Woxenius, J. (eds.), *Geographies of Waterborne Transport: Transitions from Transport to Mobilities*, Cheltenham: Edward Elgar, 170–191.

Robinson, R. (2002). Ports as elements in value-driven chain systems: the new paradigm, *Maritime Policy and Management*, 29(3), 241–255.

Rodrigue, J.-P. (2006). Challenging the derived transport demand thesis: issues in freight distribution, *Environment & Planning A*, 38(8), 1449–1462.

Rodrigue, J.-P. (2013). Transport and globalization, in: Rodrigue, J.-P., Notteboom, T. and Shaw, J. (eds.), *The Sage Handbook of Transport Studies*, London: Sage.

Rodrigue, J.-P. and Notteboom, T. (2009a). The future of containerization: perspectives from maritime and inland freight distribution, *Geojournal*, 74(1), 7–22.

Rodrigue, J.-P. and Notteboom, T. (2009b). The geography of containerization: half a century of revolution, adaptation and diffusion, *GeoJournal*, 74(1), 1–5.

Rodrigue, J.-P. and Notteboom, T. (2010). Comparative North American and European gateway logistics: the regionalism of freight distribution, *Journal of Transport Geography*, 18(4), 497–507.

Rodrigue, J.-P. and Notteboom, T. (2013). The geography of cruises: itineraries, not, *Destinations Applied Geography*, 38, 31–42.

Slack, B., Comtois, C. and McCalla, R. (2002). Strategic alliances in the container shipping industry: a global perspective, *Maritime Policy & Management*, 29(1), 65–76.

Stopford, M. (1997). *Maritime Economics*, 2nd Edition, London: Routledge.

UN World Tourism Organisation (UNWTO) (2020a). 100% of global destinations now have COVID-19 travel restrictions, *UNWTO Reports*, 28 April 2020.

UNWTO (2020b). International tourist numbers could fall 60–80% in 2020, *UNWTO Reports*, 7 May 2020.

US DOT – MARAD (2013). *Panama Canal Expansion Study, Phase I Report: Developments in Trade and National and Global Economies*, Washington, DC: MARAD.

Vonck, I. and Notteboom, T. (2012). Economic analysis of the warehousing and distribution market in Northwest Europe, Brussels: ING Bank.

World Bank (2014). *Connecting to Compete: Trade Logistics in the Global Economy*, Washington, DC: The World Bank.

Yip, T.L. and Wong, M.C. (2015). The Nicaragua canal: scenarios of its future roles, *Journal of Transport Geography*, 43, 1–13.

Yip, T.L., Lun, Y.H.V. and Lau, Y.Y. (2012). Scale diseconomies and efficiencies of liner shipping, *Maritime Policy & Management*, 39(7), 673–683.

Zumerchik, J. and Danver, S.L. (2009). *Seas and Waterways of the World: An Encyclopedia of History, Uses, and Issues*, Santa Barbara, CA: ABC-CLIO.

## PART II   CONTEMPORARY PORTS

Bui, M., Adjiman, C.S., Bardow, A., Anthony, E.J., Boston, A., Brown, S., Fennell, P.S., Fuss, S., Galindo, A., Hackett, L.A. and Hallett, J.P. (2018). Carbon capture and storage (CCS): the way forward, *Energy & Environmental Science*, 11(5), 1062–1176.

Darwin, J. (2020). Unlocking the world: port cities and globalization in the age of steam, 1830–1930, Milton Keynes: Allen Lane/Penguine.

De Langen, P. and Sornn-Friese, H. (2019). Ports and the circular economy, in: Bergqvist, R. and Monios, J., (eds.), *Green Ports Inland and Seaside Sustainable Transportation Strategies*, London: Elsevier, 85–108.

Diabat, A. and Govindan, K. (2011). An analysis of the drivers affecting the implementation of green supply chain management, *Resources, Conservation and Recycling*, 55(6), 659–667.

Doerr, O. (2001). Sustainable port policies, *Bull*, 299, FAL 2011, 1–8.

Ducruet, C. (ed.) (2016). *Maritime Networks: Spatial Structures and Time Dynamics*, London: Routledge.

Ducruet, C. and Lee, S.W. (2006). Frontline soldiers of globalization: port-city evolution and regional competition, *GeoJournal*, 67(2), 107–122.

Fox, C., Gailus, S., Liu, L. and Ni, L. (2018). *The Future of Automated Ports*, New York: Mckinsey & Company.

Fraser, D. and Notteboom, T. (2014). A strategic appraisal of the attractiveness of seaport-based transport corridors: the Southern African case, *Journal of Transport Geography*, 36, 53–68.

Geerts, M. and Dooms, M. (2017). Sustainability reporting by port authorities: a comparative analysis of leading world ports, *IAME 2017 Conference*, Kyoto, Japan.

International Energy Agency (IEA), (various issues). World Energy Outlook.

International Transportation Forum (2020). *Decarbonising Maritime Transport: Pathways to Zero-Carbon Shipping by 2035*, Paris: OECD.

Lavissière, A. and Rodrigue, J.-P. (2017). Free ports: towards a network of trade gateways, *Journal of Shipping and Trade*, 2(7), 1–17.

Lee, P.T.W and Cullinane, K. (eds.) (2016). *Dynamic Shipping and Port Development in the Globalized Economy*, London: Palgrave Macmillan.

Lind, M., Michaelides, M., Ward, R. and Watson, R.Th. (eds.) (2020). *Maritime Informatics*, Cham, Switzerland: Springer International Publishing.

Merk, O. and Notteboom, T. (2015). Port hinterland connectivity, International Transport Forum (ITF) – OECD, Discussion Paper 2015-13, May.

Ng, A.K.Y., Padilha, F. and Pallis, A.A. (2013). Institutions, bureaucratic and logistical roles of dry ports: the Brazilian experiences, *Journal of Transport Geography*, 27, 46–55.

Nguyen, L.C. and Notteboom, T. (2016). Dry ports as extensions of maritime deep-sea ports: a case study of Vietnam, *Journal of International Logistics and Trade*, 14(1), 65–88.

Notteboom, T. (2001). Spatial and functional integration of container port systems and hinterland networks in Europe, in: ECMT (ed.), *Land Access to Sea Ports*, Paris: Economic Research Centre ECMT-OECD, 5–55.

Notteboom, T. (2008). Bundling of freight flows and hinterland network development, in: Konings, R., Priemus, H. and Nijkamp, P. (eds.), *The Future of Intermodal Freight Transport, Operations, Technology, Design and Implementation*, Cheltenham: Edward Elgar, 66–88.

Notteboom, T. (2009). The relationship between seaports and the intermodal hinterland in light of global supply chains: European challenges, in: OECD/ITF (ed.), *Port Competition and Hinterland Connections*, Round Table No. 143, Paris: OECD – International Transport Forum (ITF).

Notteboom, T. (2010). Green concession agreements: how can port authorities integrate environmental issues in the terminal awarding process? *Port Technology International*, 47, 36–38.

Notteboom, T. (2016). The adaptive capacity of container ports in an era of mega vessels: the case of upstream seaports Antwerp and Hamburg, *Journal of Transport Geography*, 54, 295–309.

Notteboom, T., Parola, F., Satta, G. and Risitano, M. (2017). A taxonomy of logistics centres: overcoming conceptual ambiguity, *Transport Reviews*, 37(3), 276–299.

Notteboom, T. and Rodrigue, J.-P. (2005). Port regionalization: towards a new phase in port development, *Maritime Policy and Management*, 32(3), 297–313.

Notteboom, T. and Rodrigue, J.-P. (2007). Re-assessing port-hinterland relationships in the context of global supply chains, in Wang, J. et al. (eds.), *Inserting Port-Cities in Global Supply Chains*, London: Ashgate, 61–66.

Notteboom, T. and Rodrigue, J.-P. (2009). Inland terminals within North American and European supply chains, *Transport and Communications Bulletin for Asia and the Pacific, UNESCAP*, 78, 1–57.

Notteboom, T. and Rodrigue, J.-P. (2010). Foreland-based regionalization: integrating intermediate hubs with port hinterlands, *Research in Transportation Economics*, 27, 19–29.

Notteboom, T., Van der Lugt, L., Van Saase, N., Sel, S. and Neyens, K. (2020). The role of seaports in Green Supply Chain Management: initiatives, attitudes and perspectives in Rotterdam, Antwerp, North Sea Port and Zeebrugge, *Sustainability*, 12, 1688.

Notteboom, T., Yang, D. and Xu, H. (2020). Container Barge network development in inland rivers: a comparison between the Yangtze River and the Rhine River, *Transportation Research Part A*, 132, 587–605.

Puig, M., Wooldridge, C., Michail, A. and Darbra, R.M. (2015). Current status and trends of the environmental performance in European ports, *Environmental Science & Policy*, 48, 57–66.

Rodrigue, J.-P. (2020). The geography of maritime ranges: interfacing global maritime shipping networks with hinterlands, *GeoJournal*, online-first, 1–14.

Rodrigue, J.-P., Debrie, J., Fremont, A. and Gouvernal, E. (2010). Functions and actors of inland ports: European and North American dynamics, *Journal of Transport Geography*, 18(4), 519–529.

Rodrigue, J.-P. and Notteboom, T. (2009). The terminalization of supply chains: reassessing port-hinterland logistical relationships, *Maritime Policy and Management*, 36(2), 165–183.

Rodrigue, J.-P. and Notteboom, T. (2010). Comparative North American and European Gateway logistics: the regionalism of freight distribution, *Journal of Transport Geography*, 18(4), 497–507.

Rodrigue, J.-P. and Notteboom, T. (2011) Port regionalization: improving port competitiveness by reaching beyond the port perimeter, *Port Technology International*, 52, 11–17.

Rodrigue, J.-P. and Notteboom, T. (2012). Dry ports in European and North American intermodal rail systems: two of a kind? *Research in Transportation Business & Management*, 5, 4–15.

Roso, V., Woxenius, J. and Lumsden, K. (2009). The dry port concept: connecting container seaports with the hinterland, *Journal of Transport Geography*, 17(5), 338–345.

Sarkis, J. (2003). A strategic decision framework for green supply chain management, *Journal of Cleaner Production*, 11(4), 397–409.

Slack, B. and Wang, J.J. (2002). The challenge of peripheral ports: an Asian perspective, *GeoJournal*, 56(2), 159–166.

Slack, B. and Comtois, C. (2010) Identification des modeles de gouvernance d'un pole logistique en lien avec la realite quebecoise, Amenagement d'un pole logistique au Quebec: cadre d'analyse de l'etude de faisabilite, Etude 1.2.

Wilmsmeier, G., Monios, J. and Lambert, B. (2011). The directional development of intermodal freight corridors in relation to inland terminals, *Journal of Transport Geography*, 19, 1379–1386.

Witte, P., Wiegmans, B. and Rodrigue, J.-P. (2017). Competition or complementarity in European inland port development: a case of overproximity? *Journal of Transport Geography*, 60, 80–88.

Yang, D., Notteboom, T. and Zhou, X. (2021). Spatial, temporal and institutional characteristics of entry strategies in inland container terminals: a comparison between Yangtze River and Rhine River, *Journal of Transport Geography*, 90, 102928.

## PART III   PORT TERMINALS

Brooks, M.R., Pallis, A.A. and Perkins, S. (2014). Port Investment and Container Shipping Markets, OECD-ITF Discussion Paper 2014-3, Paris: OECD.

Center for Civil Engineering Research and Codes (CUR) (2002). Handbook Quay Walls, CUR-Publication 211E, September 2005, Gouda, the Netherlands.

Cheng, Z., Gong, L. and Li, C. (2020). *Design and Practice of Cruise Ports*, Singapore: Springer.

Davidson, N. (2018). Retrofit terminal automation measuring the market, *Port Technology International*, 77, 1–3.

Defilippi, E. (2004). Intra-port competition, regulatory challenges and the concession of Callao Port, *Maritime Economics and Logistics*, 6, 279–311.

Dempster, J. (2010). *The Rise and Fall of the UK Dock Labour Scheme*, London: Biteback Publishers.

Farrell, S. (2012). The ownership and management structure of container terminal concessions, *Maritime Policy & Management*, 39(1), 7–26.

Frey, C.B. and Osborne, M.A. (2017). The future of employment: how susceptible are jobs to computerisation? *Technological Forecasting and Social Change*,
114, 254–280.

Gordijn, R. (2017). Amsterdam port: building the largest sea-lock, *Port Technology International*, 75, 36–38.

Green, A. (2000). The work process, in: Davies, S. et al. (eds.), *Dock Workers:
International Explorations in Comparative Labour History, 1790–1970*, II, Aldershot: Ashgate.

Haezendonck, E. and Moeremans, B. (2019). Measuring value tonnes based
on direct value added: a new weighted analysis for the port of Antwerp,
*Maritime Economics & Logistics*, 22(4), 661–673.

Hammami, M., Ruhashyankiko, J.F. and Yehoue, E. (2006). Determinants of
public-private partnerships in infrastructure, IMF Working Paper, IMF
Institute.

Huybrechts, M., Meersman, H., Van De Voorde, E., Van Hooydonk, E., Verbeke, A. and Winkelmans, W. (2001). *Port Competitiveness: An Economic and
Legal Analysis of the Factors Determining the Competitiveness of Seaports*, Antwerp: Editions De Boeck.

Ioannou, P. and Jula, H. (2008). Automated container terminal concepts, in:
Ioannou, P. (eds.) *Intelligent Freight Transportation*, Boca Raton: CRC Press,
7–35.

Kon, W.K., Rahman, N.S.F.A., Hanafiah, R.M. and Hamid, S.A. (2020). The
global trends of automated container terminal: a systematic literature
review, *Maritime Business Review*, 6(3), doi:10.1108/MABR-03-2020-0016.

McBride, M., Boll, M. and Briggs, M. (2014). Harbour approach channels—
design guidelines, PIANC Report No. 121.

McKinsey (2017). Expert interviews; McKinsey Container Terminal Automation Survey.

Mitroussi, K. and Notteboom, T. (2015). Getting the work done: motivation
needs and processes for seafarers and dock workers, *WMU Journal of Maritime Affairs*, 14(2), 247–265.

Moody's Investor Service (2019). Automated terminals offer competitive
advantages, but implementation challenges may limit penetration, 24 June
2019.

Notteboom, T. (2007). Concession agreements as port governance tools, in:
Brooks, M.R. and Cullinane, K. (eds.), *Devolution, Port Governance and Performance*, London: Elsevier, 449–467.

Notteboom, T. (2010). *Dock labour and port-related employment in the Euro-
pean seaport system: key factors to port competitiveness and reform, report for
European Seaports Organization (ESPO)*, Antwerp: ITMMA - University of
Antwerp.

Notteboom, T. (2018). The impact of changing market requirements on dock
labour employment systems in northwest European seaports, *International
Journal of Shipping and Transport Logistics*, 10(4), 429–454.

Notteboom, T., Pallis, A.A. and Farrell, S. (2012). Terminal concessions in seaports revisited, *Maritime Policy and Management*, 39(1), 1–5.

Notteboom, T., Parola, F., Satta, G. and Torre, T. (2019). Skills and competences
in maritime logistics: managerial and organizational emerging issues for
human resources, *Impresa e Progetto Electronic Journal of Management*, 3,
doi:10.15167/1824-3576/IPEJM2019.3.1240.

Notteboom, T. and Rodrigue, J.-P. (2011). Emerging global networks in the container terminal operating industry, in Notteboom, T. (ed.), *Current Issues in Shipping, Ports and Logistics*, Brussels: Academic & Scientific Publishers, 243–270.

Notteboom, T. and Rodrigue, J.-P. (2012). The corporate geography of global container terminal operators, *Maritime Policy and Management*, 39(3), 249–279.

Notteboom, T. and Verhoeven, P. (2010). The awarding of seaport terminals to private operators: European practices and policy implications, *Trasporti Europei/European Transport*, 45, 83–101.

Notteboom, T. and Vitellaro, F. (2019). The impact of innovation on dock labour: evidence from European ports, *Impresa e Progetto Electronic Journal of Management*, 3, doi:10.15167/1824-3576/IPEJM2019.3.1230.

Notteboom, T., Verhoeven, P. and Fontanet, M. (2012). Current practices in European ports on the awarding of seaport terminals to private operators: towards an industry good practice guide, *Maritime Policy and Management*, 39(1), 107–123.

Pallis, A.A. (2014). Container terminals, in: Garrett, M. (ed.), *Encyclopedia of Transportation: Social Science and Policy*, Volume A, London: Sage.

Pallis, A.A., Notteboom, T. and de Langen, P.W. (2008). Concession agreements and market entry in the container terminal industry, *Maritime Economics and Logistics*, 10(3), 209–228.

Pallis, A.A., Parola, F., Satta, G. and Notteboom, T. (2018). Private entry and emerging partnerships in cruise terminal operations in the Mediterranean Sea, *Maritime Economics and Logistics*, 20(1), 1–28.

Parola, F., Notteboom, T., Satta, G. and Rodrigue, J.-P. (2015). The impact of multiple-site acquisitions on corporate growth patterns of international terminal operators, *International Journal of Shipping and Transport Logistics*, 7(5), 621–635.

PIANC-The World Association for Waterborne Transport Infrastructure (2016). Working Group 152 Guidelines for Cruise Terminals, Brussels: PIANC.

Port Technology International (2018). Navis survey: terminal automation 'critical' to survival. https://www.porttechnology.org/news/survey_terminal_automation_critical_to_short_term_survival.

Psaraftis, H.N. and Pallis, A.A. (2012). Concession of the Piraeus Container Terminal: turbulent times and the quest for competitiveness, *Maritime Policy and Management*, 39(1), 27–43.

Rodrigue, J.-P., Notteboom, T. and Pallis, A.A. (2011). The financialisation of the terminal and port industry: revisiting risk & embeddedness, *Maritime Policy and Management*, 38(2), 191–213.

Schröder-Hinrichs, J.U., Song, D-W., Fonseca, T., Lagdami, K., Shi, X. and Loer, K. (2018). *Transport 2040: Automation, Technology, Employment-The Future of Work*. Open Access Reports, Malmö: World Maritime University.

Scott, J. (2012). Trends in marine terminal automation, *Port Technology International*, 54, 82–85.

Theys, C., Notteboom, T., Pallis, A.A. and de Langen, P.W. (2010). The economics behind the awarding of terminals in seaports: towards a research agenda, *Research in Transportation Economics*, 27(1), 37–50.

Turnbull, P.J. and Wass, V.J. (2007). Defending dock workers—globalization and labor relations in the world's ports, *Industrial Relations: A Journal of Economy and Society*, 46(3), 582–612.

Van der Plas, R. (2013). Maasvlakte 2, providing ample space for the future, *Port Technology International*, 58, 20–22.

Van Hooydonk, E. (2013). Port labour in the EU: labour market qualifications & training health & safety-Volume I — The EU perspective, Study commissioned by the European Commission, Brussels.

Van Niekerk, H.C. (2005). Port reform and concessioning in developing countries, *Maritime Economics and Logistics*, 7, 141–155.

Vandamme, M., Bernaers, G. and Aerts, F. (2007). *Construction of the Deurganckdok in the Port of Antwerp, Belgium*, in: MTEC 2007: Proceedings of the 2nd International Maritime-Port Technology and Development Conference, 26–28 September 2007, Singapore, 43–48.

van't Hoff, J. and van der Kolff, A.N. (eds.) (2012). *Hydraulic Fill Manual: For Dredging and Reclamation Works*, Vol. 244, Boca Raton, FL: CRC Press.

Verhoeven, P. (2010). Dock labour schemes in the context of EU law and policy, in: Dempster, J. (ed.), *The Rise and Fall of the UK Dock Labour Scheme*, London: Biteback Publishers, 129–145.

Wang, G. and Pallis, A.A. (2014). Incentives approaches to overcome moral hazard in port concession agreements, *Transportation Research E: Logistics and Transportation Review*, 67, 162–174.

Wang, G., Pallis, A.A. and Notteboom, T. (2014). Incentives in cruise terminal concession contracts, *Research in Transportation Business and Management*, 13, 36–42.

## PART IV   PORT GOVERNANCE

Baltazar, R. and Brooks, M.R. (2006). Port governance, devolution and the matching framework: a configuration theory approach, *Research in Transportation Economics*, 17, 379–403.

Bergqvist, R. and Egels-Zandén, N. (2012). Green port dues—the case of hinterland transport, *Research in Transportation Business & Management*, 5, 85–91.

Brooks, M.R., Cullinane, K.P.B. and Pallis, A.A. (2017). Revisiting port governance and port reform: a multi-country examination, *Research in Transportation Business and Management*, 22, 1–10.

Brooks, M.R., McCalla, R., Pallis, A.A. and Van der Lugt, L. (2010). Cooperation and coordination in strategic port management: the case of Atlantic Canada's ports, *Canadian Journal of Transportation*, 4(1), 29–42.

Brooks, M.R. and Pallis, A.A. (2008). Assessing port governance models: process and performance components, *Maritime Policy and Management*, 35(4), 411–432.

Brooks, M.R. and Pallis, A.A. (2012). Port governance, in: Talley, W.K. (ed.), *The Blackwell Companion to Maritime Economics*, New York: Blackwell, 232–267.

De Langen, P.W. (2004). Governance in seaport clusters, *Maritime Economics & Logistics*, 6, 141–156.

De Langen, P.W. and Haezendonck, E. (2012). Ports as clusters of economic activity, in: Talley, W.K. (ed.), *The Blackwell Companion to Maritime Economics*, New York: Blackwell, 638–655.

Dooms, M. van der Lugt, L., Parola, F., Satta, G. and Song, D.-W. (2019). The internationalization of port managing bodies in concept and practice, *Maritime Policy & Management*, 46(5), 585–612.

European Sea Port Organisation (ESPO) (2016). *Trends in EU Port Governance*, Brussels: ESPO.

Fraser, D. and Notteboom, T. (2015). Institutional development paths in seaports: the Southern African case, *European Journal of Transport and Infrastructure Research*, 15(4), 506–535.

Huo, W., Zhang, W. and Chen, P.S.L. (2018). Recent development of Chinese port cooperation strategies, *Research in Transportation Business & Management*, 26, 67–75.

International Maritime Organization (IMO) (1992). International Convention for the Prevention of Pollution from Ships, 1973 and the Protocol of 1978 Relating to the International Convention for the Prevention of Pollution from Ships, 1973. MARPOL 73/78 Consolidated Edition, 1991. IMO, London.

Knatz, G. (2017). How competition is driving change in port governance, strategic decision-making and government policy in the United States, *Research in Transportation Business & Management*, 22, 67–77.

Lam, J.S.L. and Notteboom, T. (2014). The greening of ports: a comparison of port management tools used by leading ports in Asia and Europe, *Transport Reviews*, 34(2), 169–189.

Maritime Administration (MARAD) (2002). *Maritime Trade & Transportation 2002*, Washington, DC: United States Department of Transportation.

Musser, L. (2020). The right people at the right time, workforce initiatives that help align ports' needs with skilled candidates, *Seaports*, 57, 10–14.

Ng, K.Y.A. and Pallis, A.A. (2010). Port governance reforms in diversified institutional frameworks: generic solutions, implementation asymmetries, *Environment and Planning A*, 42(9) 2147 – 2167.

Notteboom, T. (2018). The regionalism of port cooperation schemes: an international comparison, *The Jean Monnet Symposium on the Future of the European Port Policy*, Chios, 28–29 June 2018.

Notteboom, T., de Langen, P.W. and Jacobs, W. (2013). Institutional plasticity and path dependence in seaports: interactions between institutions, port governance reform and port authority routines, *Journal of Transport Geography*, 27, 26–35.

Notteboom, T., Ducruet, C. and de Langen, P.W. (2009). *Ports in Proximity: Competition and Coordination among Adjacent Seaports*, Aldershot: Ashgate.

Notteboom, T. and Haralambides, H. (2020). Port management and governance in a post-COVID-19 era: quo vadis? *Maritime Economics & Logistics*, 22(3), 329–352.

Notteboom, T. and Lam, J. (2018). The greening of terminal concessions in seaports, *Sustainability*, 10(9), 3318.

Notteboom, T. and Yang, Z. (2017). Port governance in China since 2004: institutional layering and the growing impact of broader policies, *Research in Transportation Business and Management*, 22, 184–200.

Pallis, A.A. (2007). Whither port strategy? Theory and practice in conflict, *Research in Transportation Economics*, 21, 345–386.

Pallis, A.A., Arapi, K.P. and Papachristou, A.A. (2019). Models of cruise ports governance, *Maritime Policy and Management*, 46(5), 630–651.

Pallis, A.A. and Kladaki, P. (2019). Inter–organisational relationships of European port management entities, in: Panayides, P.M. (ed.), *Routledge Handbook in Maritime Management*, London: Routledge, 283–298.

Pallis, A.A., Papachristou, A.A. and Platias, C. (2017). Environmental policies and practices in cruise ports: waste reception facilities in the Med, *Spoudai Quarterly Economic Journal*, 67(1), 54–70.

Pallis, A.A. and Vaggelas, G.K. (2017). Port governance: a Greek prototype, *Research in Transportation Business and Management*, 22, 49–57.

Pallis, A.A. and Vaggelas, G.K. (2018). Cruise shipping and green ports: a strategic challenge, in: Bergqvist, R. and Monios, J. (eds.), *Green Ports: Inland and Seaside Sustainable Transportation Strategies*, Cheltenham: Edward Elgar, 255–273.

Pavlic, B., Cepak, F., Sucic, B., Peckaj, M. and Kandus, B. (2014). Sustainable port infrastructure, practical implementation of the green port concept, *Thermal Science*, 18(3), 935.

Puig, M., Wooldridge, C., Michail, A. and Darbra, R.M. (2015). Current status and trends of the environmental performance in European ports, *Environmental Science & Policy*, 48, 57–66.

Saragiotis, P. and de Langen, P. (2017). Achieving full and effective corporatization of port authorities, reform models from global experience. Trade and Competitiveness in Practice, World Bank Group.

UNESCAP (1992). *Assessment of the Environmental Impact of Port Development*, New York: United Nations.

Vaggelas, G.K. and Pallis, A.A. (2019). Configuration and Prospects of the Piraeus shipping cluster, *Spoudai Quarterly Economic Journal*, 69, 3–17.

Van der Horst, M.R. and de Langen, P.W. (2008). Coordination in hinterland transport chains: a major challenge for the seaport community, *Maritime Economics & Logistics*, 10(1–2), 108–129.

Verhoeven, P. (2010). A review of port authority functions: towards a renaissance? *Maritime Policy & Management*, 37(3), 247–270.

Wang, S. and Notteboom, T. (2015). The role of port authorities in the development of LNG bunkering facilities in North European ports, *WMU Journal of Maritime Affairs*, 14(1), 61–92.

## PART V   PORT COMPETITION

Berry, L.L. and Yadav, M.S. (1996). Capture and communicate value in the pricing of services, *Sloan Management Review*, 37(4), 41–51.

Cahoon, S. (2007). Marketing communications for seaports: a matter of survival and growth, *Maritime Policy & Management*, 34(2), 151–168.

Cahoon, S. and Notteboom, T. (2008). Port marketing tools in a logistics-restructured market environment: the quest for port loyalty, *Proceedings of IAMEAnnual Conference*, Dalian, China, 2–4 April.

Chlomoudis, C.I., Karalis, V.A. and Pallis, A.A. (2003). Port reorganisation and the worlds of production theory, *European Journal of Transport Infrastructure Research*, 3(1), 77–94.

De Langen, P.W. and Pallis, A.A. (2006). The effects of intra-port competition, *International Journal of Transport Economics*, 33(1), 69–86.

De Langen, P.W. and Pallis, A.A. (2007). Entry barriers in seaports, *Maritime Policy and Management*, 34(5), 427–440.

ESPO (2016). *Trends in EU Ports Governance 2016*, Brussels: ESPO.

Goss, R. (1990). Economic Policies and Seaports: 1. The economic functions of seaports, *Maritime Policy and Management*, 17(3), 207–219.

Haralambides, H.E., Verbeke, A., Musso, E. and Benacchio, M. (2001). Port financing and pricing in the European Union: theory, politics and reality, *International Journal of Maritime Economics*, 3, 368–386.

Heaver, T.D. (1995). The implications of increased competition among ports for port policy, *Maritime Policy and Management*, 22(2), 125–133.

Hughes, A.M. (2003). *The customer loyalty solution*, New York: MacGraw Hill.

Kaselimi, E.N., Notteboom, T.E., Pallis, A.A. and Farrell, S. (2011). Minimum Efficient Scale (MES) and preferred scale of container terminals, *Research in Transportation Economics*, 32(1), 71–80.

MedCruise (2016). *Ports Together*, Piraeus, Greece.

Notteboom, T.E. (2002). Consolidation and contestability in the European container handling industry, *Maritime Policy and Management*, 29(3), 257–269.

Parola, F., Pallis, A.A., Risitano, M. and Ferretti, M. (2018). Marketing strategies of port authorities: a multi-dimensional theorisation, *Transportation Research Policy and Practice Part A*, 111, 199–212.

Uyttendaele, P. (2012). Public private partnerships in ports: pitfalls and challenges, *ESPO Annual Conference*, Sopot, 10–11 May 2012.

Van Den Berg, R., De Langen, P.W. and Van Zuijlen, P.C. (2017). Revisiting port pricing; a proposal for seven port pricing principles, *WMU Journal of Maritime Affairs*, 16(3), 421–438.

## PART VI    PORT PERFORMANCE

Arvis, J.F., Vesin, V., Carruthers, R. and Ducruet, C. (2019). *Maritime Networks, Port Efficiency, and Hinterland Connectivity in the Mediterranean*, Washington, DC: World Bank Group.

Brooks, M.R. (2012). *The AAPA Customer Service Initiative Report*, Washington, DC: AAPA.

Brooks, M.R., Knatz, G., Pallis, A.A. and Wilmsmeier, G. (2020). Transparency in port governance: seaport practices, PortReport No 5. PortEconomics.eu.

Brooks, M.R., Knatz, G., Pallis, A.A. and Wilmsmeier, G. (2021). Visibility and verifiability in port governance transparency: exploring stakeholder expectations, *WMU Journal of Maritime Affairs*, online first, 1–21.

Brooks, M.R. and Pallis, A.A. (2013). Time to assess: port users perspectives are important, *Port Technology International*, 60, 27–28.

Brooks, M.R. and Schellinck, T. (2015). Measuring port effectiveness: what really determines cargo interests' evaluations of port service delivery? *Maritime Policy & Management*, 42(7), 699–711.

Brooks, M.R. Schellinck, T. and Pallis A.A. (2011). Port Effectiveness: Users perspectives in North America, *Transportation Research Record*, 2222, 34–42.

Chung, K.C. (1993). *Port performance indicators, Infrastructure notes, no. PS-6*, Washington, D.C.: World Bank Group.

Dooms, M. (2014). Port industry performance management, *Port Technology International*, 61, 16–17.

European Sea Ports Organisation (2020). *ESPO Environmental Report 2020*. Brussels: ESPO.

Ferrari, C., Merk, O., Bottasso, A., Conti, M. and Tei, A. (2012). Ports and regional development: a European perspective, OECD Regional Development Working Papers, 2012/07, Paris: OECD.

IAPH-WPSP (2020). *Guidance on Ports' Response to the Coronavirus Pandemic*, Antwerp: International Association of Ports & Harbors (IAPH).

Linkov, I. and Palma-Oliviera, J.M. (eds.) (2017). *Risk and Resilience*, Amsterdam: Springer.

Martin, R. (2012). Regional economic resilience, hysteresis and recessionary shocks, *Journal of Economic Geography*, 12(1), 1–32.

McKinsey Global Institute (2020). Risk, resilience, and rebalancing in global value chains, New York: McKinsey.

Merk, O. and Dang, T. (2012). Efficiency of world ports in container and bulk cargo (oil, coal, ores and grain), *OECD Regional Development Working Papers*, 2012/09. Paris: OECD.

Notteboom, T., Pallis, A.A. and Rodrigue, J.-P. (2021). Disruptions and resilience in container shipping, ports and supply chains: the COVID-19 pandemic vs. the 2008–2009, *Financial Crisis: Maritime Economics and Logistics*, 23(2), 179–210.

Pallis, A.A. and Syriopoulos, T. (2007). Port governance models: a financial evaluation of greek port restructuring, *Transport Policy*, 14(2), 232–246.

Pallis, A.A. and Vitsounis, T.K. (2010). Key interactions and value drivers towards port users satisfaction, in: Hall, P.V., McCalla, R. Slack, B. and Comtois, C. (eds.), *Integrating Seaports and Trade Corridors*, Aldershot: Ashgate, 119–136.

PORTOPIA (2017). Ports Observatory for Performance Indicators Analysis, Collaborative Research Project, 7th European Framework Programme.

PPRISM (2013). Port performance indicators selection and measurement indicators, Collaborative European Research Program.

Rodrigue, J.-P. and Wan, G.W.Y. (2020). Cruise shipping supply chains and the impacts of disruptions: the case of the Caribbean, *Research in Transportation Business and Management*, online first.

UNCTAD (2016). Port performance linking performance indicators to strategic objectives, Port Management Series, 4, Geneva: UNCTAD.UNCTAD (2020). COVID-19 and maritime transport: impact and responses. UNCATD/DTL/TLB/NF/2020/1, Geneva: UNCTAD.

UNCTAD (various issues). *Review of Maritime Transport*, Geneva: UNCTAD.

Vaggelas, G.K. and Pallis, A.A. (2018). Lessons learned from measuring shipping companies and other port users' perceptions of port performance, *IAME Annual Conference*, Mombasa, Kenya.

Vonck, I. and Notteboom, T. (2013). *Economic Analysis of Volatility and Uncertainty in Seaports: Tools and Strategies towards Greater Flexibility, Resilience and Agility of Port Authorities and Port Companies*, Bietlot: Gilly.

Vonck, I. and Notteboom, T. (2016). Panarchy within a port setting, *Journal of Transport Geography*, 51, 308–315.

## PART VII   PORT POLICIES AND DEVELOPMENT

Association Internationale des Villes et Ports (AIVP) (2018). Agenda 2030: 10 goals for sustainable port cities. www.aivp.org.

Chlomoudis, C.I. and Pallis, A.A. (2002). *European Port Policy: Towards a Long Term Strategy*, Cheltenham: Edward Elgar.

Coeck, C., Notteboom, T., Verbeke, A. and Winkelmans, W. (1996). A resource-based perspective on strategic port planning, *Proceedings of the 11th International Harbour Congress*, Antwerp, 29–40.

Container Alliance. https://www.containeralliance.com.

De Langen, P.W., Van Meijeren, J. and Tavasszy, L.A. (2012). Combining models and commodity chain research for making long-term projections of port throughput: an application to the Hamburg-Le Havre range, *European Journal of Transport and Infrastructure Research*, 12(3), 310–331.

Derudder, B. and Taylor, P.J (2016). Data Set 28, Globalization and World Cities (GaWC) Research Network.

Ducruet, C. (2003). The trans-scalar development of transportation hubs: a quantitative comparison of European and East Asian Container Port Cities in the 1990s, *Inha University Bulletin*, 1(2), 171–199.

Ducruet, C. (2007). A metageography of port-city relationships, in Wang, J.J., Olivier, D., Notteboom, T. and Slack, B. (eds.), *Ports, Cities, and Global Supply Chains*, Aldershot: Ashgate, 157–172.

Haralambides, H. and Acciaro, M. (2015). The new European port policy proposals: too much ado about nothing? *Maritime Economics and Logistics*, 17, 127–141.

Jacobs, W., Koster, H. and Hall, P. (2011). The location and global network structure of maritime advanced producer services, *Urban Studies*, 48(13), 2749–2769.

Menon Consulting (2017). The leading maritime capitals of the world. MENON Publication 28/2017, MENON Economics, DNV-GL.

Merckx, F., Notteboom, T. and Winkelmans, W. (2004). Waterfront redevelopment: re-establishing the link between city and port, in Misztal, K. and Zurek, J. (eds.), *Development of Maritime Trade, Transport and Tourism - XXI Century Vision*, Gdansk, 105–126.

Notteboom, T. and Winkelmans, W. (2003). Dealing with stakeholders in the port planning process, in Dullaert, W., Jourquin, B. and Polak, J. (eds.), *Across the Border: Building upon a Quarter of Century of Transport Research in the Benelux*, Antwerp: De Boeck, 249–265.

Notteboom, T., Parola, F., Satta, G. and Penco, L. (2015). Disclosure as a tool in stakeholder relations management: a longitudinal study on the port of Rotterdam, *International Journal of Logistics Research and Application (IJLRA)*, 18(3), 228–250.

Pallis, A.A. (2006a). EU Port policy developments: implications for port governance, *Research in Transportation Economics*, 17, 161–176.

Pallis, A.A. (2006b). Institutional dynamism in the EU policy-making: the evolution of the EU Maritime Safety Policy, *Journal of European Integration*, 28(2), 137–157.

Pallis, A.A. (2007). Maritime interests in the EU policy-making: structures, practices and governability of collective action, *WMU Journal of Maritime Affairs*, 6(1), 3–20.

Pallis, A.A. (2008). Lobbying EU institutions: strategies and governance of contending maritime interests, *Current Politics and Economics of Europe*, 19(3), 179–202.

Pallis, A.A. and Tsiotsis, S.G.P. (2008). Maritime Interests and the EU Port Services Directive, *European Transport*, 38, 17–31.

Pallis, A.A. and Vaggelas, G.K. (2008). EU port and shipping security, in: Talley, W.K. (ed.), *Maritime Safety, Security and Piracy*, London: Informa, 327–357.

Pallis, A.A. and Verhoeven, P. (2009). Does the EU port policy strategy encompass proximity?, in Notteboom, T., de Langen, P.W. and Ducruet, C.B. (eds.), *Ports in Proximity: Essaye on Competition and Coordination among Adjacent Seaports*, Aldershot: Ashgate, 99–112.

Parola, F., Satta, G., Notteboom, T. and Persico, L. (2020). Revisiting traffic forecasting by port authorities in the context of port planning and development, *Maritime Economics & Logistics*, online first.

Peng, W.Y. and Chu, C.W. (2009). A comparison of univariate methods for forecasting container throughput volumes, *Mathematical and Computer Modelling*, 50(7), 1045–1057.

Regulation (EU) 2017/352 of the European Parliament and of the Council of 15 February 2017.

Rodrigue, J.-P. (2016). The role of transport and communication infrastructure in realising development outcomes, in Grugel, J. and Hammett, D. (eds.), *The Palgrave Handbook of International Development*, London: Palgrave Macmillan, 595–614.

Rodrigue, J.-P. (2017). Transport and development, in Richardson, D., Castree, N., Goodchild, M.F., Kobayashi, A., Liu, W. and Marston, R.A. (eds.), *The International Encyclopedia of Geography*, New York: John Wiley & Sons.

Rugman, A. and Verbeke, A. (1990). *Global Corporate Strategy and Trade Policy*, London: Routledge.

Slack, B. and Gouvernal, E. (2015). Container transshipment and logistics in the context of urban economic development, *Growth and Change*, 47(3), 406–415.

Taneja, P. (2013). The flexible port, volumes 2013–2016 of TRAIL thesis series, ISSN 1566–0788.

Taneja, P., Walker, W.E., Ligteringen, H., Van Schuylenburg, M. and Van Der Plas, R. (2010). Implications of an uncertain future for port planning, *Maritime Policy & Management*, 37(3), 221–245.

United Nations (2018). *World Urbanization Prospects*, New York: UN.

Van Dooren, N. (2012). Port Vision 2030 shows the way for the port of Rotterdam, *Port Technology International*, 53, 36–40.

Van Dorsser, J.C.M., Wolters, M. and Van Wee, G.P. (2012). A very long term forecast of the port throughput in the Le Havre-Hamburg range up to 2100, *European Journal of Transport and Infrastructure Research*, 12(1), 88–110.

Winkelmans, W. and Notteboom, T. (2002). Dealing with uncertainty in port capacity planning, *Port Technology International*, 16, 187–189.

## PART VIII   PORT MARKETS

Arduino, G., Carrillo Murillo, D. and Parola, F. (2015). Refrigerated container versus bulk: evidence from the banana cold chain, *Maritime Policy and Management*, 42(3), 228–245.

Behdani, B., Fan, Y. and Bloemhof, J. (2019). Cool chain and temperature-controlled transport: an overview of concepts, challenges, and technologies, in Accorsi, R. and Manzini, R. (eds.), *Sustainable Food Supply Chains*, Cambridge, MA: Academic Press, 167–183.

Boile, M. (2006). Empty marine container management: addressing a global problem locally, *85th Transportation Research Board Annual Meeting*, Paper 06-2147.

Boile, M., Theofanis, S., Baveja, A. and Mittal, N. (2008). Regional repositioning of empty containers: a case for inland depots, *Transportation Research Record: Journal of the Transportation Research Board*, 2066(1), 31–40.

BP (2020). Statistical Review of World Energy. https://www.bp.com/en/global/corporate/energy-economics/statistical-review-of-world-energy.html

DNV-GL (2020). *Ports: Green Gateways to Europe*.

Drewry (2011). *Multipurpose Shipping, Market Review and Forecast*, London: Drewry.

Dynamar (2010). *Breakbulk Operators, Fleets, Markets*, Alkmaar: Dynamar.

Gui, L. and Russo, A.P. (2011). Cruise ports: a strategic nexus between regions and global lines, evidence from the Mediterranean, *Maritime Policy & Management*, 38(2), 129–150.

International Transportation Forum (2020). *Navigating towards Cleaner Maritime Shipping: Lessons From the Nordic Region*, Paris: OECD.

Lau, Y.Y., Tam, K.C., Ng, A.K.Y. and Pallis, A.A. (2014). Cruise terminals site selection process: An institutional analysis of the Kai Tak Cruise Terminal in Hong Kong. *Research in Transportation Business and Management*, 13, 16–23.

Lekakou, M.B., Pallis, A.A. and Vaggelas, G.K. (2009). Which homeport in Europe: the cruise industry's selection criteria, *Tourismos*, 4(4), 215–240.

Lujala, P., Ketil Rød, J. and Thieme, N. (2007). Fighting over oil: introducing a new dataset, *Conflict Management and Peace Science* 24(3), 239–256.

Meeuse, G.C. (1977). *Technologische aspecten van het geïntegreerd transport*, Rijswijk: Nederlands Vervoerswetenschappelijk Instituut.

Notteboom, T. and Pallis, A.A. (2020). *IAPH-WPSP Port Economic Impact Barometer One Year Report: A Survey-Based Analysis of the Impact of COVID-19 on World Ports in the Period April 2020 to April 2021*, IAPH: Antwerp.

Pallis, A.A. (2015). Cruise shipping and urban development state of the art of the industry and cruise ports, OECD-ITF Discussion Paper 2015-14, OECD: Paris.

Pallis, A.A. and Arapi, K.P. (2016). A multi-port cruise region: dynamics and hierarchies in the med, *Tourismos*, 11(2), 168–201.

Pallis, A.A. and Papachristou, A.A. (2021). European cruise ports: challenges since the pre-pandemic era, *Transport Reviews*, 41(3), 352–373.

Papachristou, A.A. Pallis, A.A. and Vaggelas, G.K. (2020). Cruise home-port selection criteria, *Research in Transportation Business and Management*, Online First.

Rodrigue, J.-P. and Notteboom, T. (2015). Looking inside the box: evidence from the containerization of commodities and the cold chain, *Maritime Policy & Management*, 42(3), 207–227.

Rodrigue, J.-P. and Wang, G.W.Y. (2020). Cruise shipping supply chains and the impacts of disruptions: the case of the Caribbean, *Research in Transportation Business and Management*, Online First.

UN/CEFACT (2019). Smart containers: real-time smart container data for supply chain excellence.

Vaggelas, G.K. and Pallis, A.A. (2010). Passenger ports: port services and their benefits, *Maritime Policy and Management*, 37(1), 73–89.

Vigarié, A. (1999). From break-bulk to containers: the transformation of general cargo handling and trade, *Geojournal*, 48, 3–7.

Vonck, I. and Notteboom, T. (2012). *An Economic Analysis of Break Bulk Flows and Activities in Belgian Ports*, JCBGAM: Wavre.

Wang, S. and Notteboom, T. (2014). Shipowners' structure and fleet distribution in the LNG shipping market, *International Journal of Shipping and Transport Logistics*, 6(5), 488–512.

# INDEX

Note: *Italic* page numbers refer to figures and page numbers followed by "n" denote endnotes.

# Taylor & Francis eBooks

### www.taylorfrancis.com

A single destination for eBooks from Taylor & Francis
with increased functionality and an improved user
experience to meet the needs of our customers.

90,000+ eBooks of award-winning academic content in
Humanities, Social Science, Science, Technology, Engineering,
and Medical written by a global network of editors and authors.

## TAYLOR & FRANCIS EBOOKS OFFERS:

A streamlined
experience for
our library
customers

A single point
of discovery
for all of our
eBook content

Improved
search and
discovery of
content at both
book and
chapter level

## REQUEST A FREE TRIAL
### support@taylorfrancis.com

 Routledge
Taylor & Francis Group

 CRC Press
Taylor & Francis Group